The publisher gratefu
of the Ahmanson Fou
of the University of California Press

THE ANTHROPOLOGY OF CHRISTIANITY

Edited by Joel Robbins

Converting Words

SACRA THEOLOGÍA from Diego de Valadés, *Rhetorica Christiana,*
1579, surrounded by directional glyphs from Copán. See page iv.

Converting Words

Maya in the Age of the Cross

———

William F. Hanks

UNIVERSITY OF CALIFORNIA PRESS

Berkeley   Los Angeles   London

University of California Press, one of the most distinguished university presses in the United States, enriches lives around the world by advancing scholarship in the humanities, social sciences, and natural sciences. Its activities are supported by the UC Press Foundation and by philanthropic contributions from individuals and institutions. For more information, visit www.ucpress.edu.

University of California Press
Berkeley and Los Angeles, California

University of California Press, Ltd.
London, England

Library of Congress Cataloging-in-Publication Data

Hanks, William F.
    Converting words : Maya in the age of the cross / William F. Hanks.
       p.   cm. — (The anthropology of Christianity ; 6)
    Includes bibliographical references and index.
    ISBN 978-0-520-25770-2 (cloth : alk. paper)
    ISBN 978-0-520-25771-9 (pbk. : alk. paper)
    1. Mayas—Religion.   2. Mayas—Colonization.   3. Christianity and other religions—Mexico—Yucatán (State).   4. Christianity and culture—Mexico—Yucatán (State).   5. Maya language—Mexico—Yucatán (State)—Influence on Spanish.   6. Spanish language—Mexico—Yucatán (State)—Influence on Maya.   7. Catechisms, Spanish—Mexico—Yucatán (State).   8. Catholic Church—Missions—Mexico—Yucatán (State).   9. Mexico—History—Spanish colony, 1540–1810.   10. Spain—Colonies—America—Administration.   I. Title.
    F1435.3.R3H36   2010
    299.7'84215—dc22
                                                       2009030688

Manufactured in the United States of America

19   18   17   16   15   14   13   12   11   10
10   9   8   7   6   5   4   3   2   1

The paper used in this publication meets the minimum requirements of ANSI/NISO Z39.48–1992 (R 1997) (*Permanence of Paper*).

FRONTISPIECE: *Sacra Theología* 'Holy Theology' from Diego de Valadés, *Rhetorica Christiana*, 1579, p. 14 (courtesy of The Bancroft Library, University of California, Berkeley). In the image, a Franciscan friar, inspired by the Trinity and surrounded by the protective flames of faith, preaches the mystery of the Trinity, "three and one," with three flames rising from his head. He stands atop seven books, whose titles indicate the three disciplines of the Trivium (rhetoric, logic, grammar) plus the four disciplines of the Quadrivium (geometry, arithmetic, music, astronomy), derived from Plato's *Republic* and taught in monasteries. Resting on this foundation, the preaching friar is portrayed as learned in the liberal arts, pointing with his right index finger toward heaven, where the Father, Son, and Holy Spirit emanate grace represented as descending lines. Himself a mestizo friar who mastered Nahuatl, Latin, and Spanish, Valadés compresses the dynamic of converting words, informed by knowledge and enflamed by faith, into a single image. The image of a surround of flames will recur four centuries later in Maya shamanic discourse, where it represents protection of the shaman against evil unleashed in exorcism. The four glyphs are the inscriptional variants of the Maya cardinal directions, from Copán. North (zenith) is at the top, South (nadir) at the bottom, East to the right, and West to the left (see Bricker 1983). Their placement in this image is intended to suggest the embedding of Christian conversion in the sweep of Maya space-time.

CONTENTS

ILLUSTRATIONS

FRONTISPIECE

Sacra Theología from Diego de Valadés, *Rhetorica Christiana*, 1579, p. 14

PLATES

FIGURES

MAPS

TABLES

My first exposure to the world explored in this book was in a 1976 graduate seminar in what was then called "classical Maya," taught by Norman McQuown at the University of Chicago. Mac introduced us to the colonial dictionaries and grammars and taught us to read the alphabetic Maya texts aloud, paying very close attention to the grammar. At the time I was preparing for doctoral research in linguistic anthropology, focused on the structure and use of modern Maya. Only some years later would I come to focus on the colonial language, as I now call it, but the first exposure had been formative. In the course of fieldwork in Yucatán, I became closely associated with a *hmèen* 'shaman (roughly)' named Sebastian Castillo Mo but best known as Don Chabo. We worked together continuously for sixteen years, until his death in 1996, and I learned and recorded most of the major rituals that he performed, many of which I witnessed or participated in multiple times. In his performance of rain ceremonies (known as *ch'áa chaák*), exorcisms *(pa' ik')*, land purifications *(hetz lú'um)*, and many spiritual cures (especially the *santiguar*, a therapeutic blessing), Don Chabo was what some would consider an idolater but I consider a mystic of great wisdom. From early on in our work, I became convinced that the cultural and spiritual premises of his practice could only be understood in the light of colonial history, especially the missionizing process. His ways of fusing apparently old forms of both Catholicism and Maya were simply too subtle and too deep to fit the models of syncretism or *mestizaje*. It was this conviction, echoing in the chambers of colonial grammar and discourse, that pushed me to the research on which this book is based.

The colonizing process was guided by a surprisingly systematic logic, even though it was implemented under sometimes chaotic circumstances. The terms of that logic are clearest in the project of *reducción*, which may be glossed 'pacification, conversion, ordering', according to context. Often compromised by circumstances and deeply equivocal in its results, *reducción* was nonetheless a powerful agent of change, with very far reaching consequences among the Maya. In Yucatán it was spearheaded by the forced relocations called *congregaciones*, under the guidance of the Franciscans, who dominated the missions in the early decades and remained a force long after the secular clergy took over the dominant role in the seventeenth century. Some of what I describe here was undoubtedly shaped by specifically Franciscan methods, although thorough comparison of the orders and the seculars is beyond the scope of this book. In historical terms, my argument is that *reducción* was far more central in the history of the Maya than has been recognized by scholars, notwithstanding excellent discussions by Nancy Farriss, Sergio Quezada, and John Chuchiak, whose works have been vital to my research. Louise Burkhart, Serge Gruzinski, and Robert Ricard are among those who have written important studies of the evangelization of indigenous peoples in New Spain, and there is an extensive literature on idolatry (Greenleaf, Alberro, Gruzinski), colonial religion and parish dynamics (Taylor), and the history of the Catholic Church in Mexico (Gómez Canedo, Schwaller, Taylor). Idolatry in Yucatán, with its exotic details and the inquisitional fervor with which the Franciscans and the secular Provisorato sought to extirpate it, has been a major topic in the literature (Chuchiak).[1] By contrast, this book deals only occasionally with questions of idolatry, focusing instead on the broader structures of thinking, speaking, and acting against which idolatry and other forms of insubordination were defined.

Reducción was a total project, aimed at coordinated transformations of space, conduct, and language. Of these, language was the most central, and the effects of *reducción* are nowhere as clear as in the transformation of meanings and usages in Maya. It turns out it was easier to forsake colonial space by fleeing across the southern frontier than it was to forsake *Maya reducido*, the language of the colony. Once caught up in the new version of Maya, there was, in a sense, no turning back the clock. Because of its extreme portability and its ubiquity in human affairs, the new language spread faster and penetrated deeper and more tenaciously into Maya culture than any other aspect of *reducción*. My first goal is to demonstrate the broader transformations in the three domains and to provide a sense of the principles by which they were guided. As Maya people adapted to changing circumstances, they came to appropriate and internalize the new forms of expression shaped by *reducción*. Neither the transformations nor their adoption were guided entirely by intentions, whether missionary or Maya, and the conversions they would effect spun far out of everyone's control. Indeed, one of the most striking features of the entire project of *reducción* is that it became self-replicating and iterative quite apart from anyone's beliefs or intentions. A world in *reducción* was one in which a limited number of schemas were repeated throughout the spheres of space, conduct, and language. Like the mental habits discussed by Panofsky (1976) and the civilizing process of Elias (1994), the mind-set of *reducción* was embodied in a whole constellation of social forms and ways of perceiving. The properties of iteration, self-replication, and dispersion were integral to *reducción*, as well as to its ultimate inability to contain the conversions it set in motion.

The act of "reducing" always implied an analysis of its object and the (attempted) imposition of a different regularity. Like conversion more generally, it always established a break between the present and the order to which it would be turned. Practically, it did this by establishing codes of conduct and space, such as radial spheres of administration (center + periphery) and the perimetric boundaries delimiting spaces of jurisdiction. The latter were, according to the ethnohistorian Tsubasa Okoshi, without precedent in preconquest Maya political organization. *Reducción* also introduced action schemas such as the *visita,* in which a higher authority moves from center to periphery; the *congregación,* in which peripheral actors are gathered in a center; and the considerable range of actions construed as "entering." In colonial Maya, the term for "enter" would become the root used to express conversion (*oc-sic ba ti* 'cause oneself to enter into'), belief (*ocol ol* 'enter heart'), translation (*oc-sic ti than* 'cause to enter language'), and transfiguration (*ocol ti uinicil* 'enter into humanity'), among other ideas. Such schemas of inspecting, gathering, and entering proliferated in the colony, recurring in built space, ordinary social actions, and ways of speaking. They also recur again and again in single domains, as illustrated by the translation of four distinct Spanish concepts with a single schema in Maya. These various transformations are coordinated because they all fall within the scope of a single set of mental habits.

The three main products of *reducción* were *pueblos reducidos* 'ordered towns', *indios reducidos* 'ordered Indians' acting in accordance with *policía cristiana* 'Christian civility', and *lengua reducida,* the new version of the native language attuned to proper civility and religion. In addition to a common background of mental habits, the three spheres were combined, or articulated, in the course of social action: the ordered landscape of towns and jurisdictions was the field in which colonial action and language were embedded, to which they responded, and which they partially defined. The plan was to inculcate a coherent set of mental habits and practices, to instill what in current social theory is called a "habitus." As much as any other factor, this self-replicating capacity in the very logic of *reducción* accounts for its impact, despite the relatively small number of missionaries who actually implemented the project and despite the fragmented and resistant circumstances by which their efforts were compromised. By coordinating changes in space, conduct, and language, *reducción* created a special sort of circularity, in which each of the three domains fed into and responded to the others, the whole creating a field of overdetermination in which new forms were dispersed.

What were the consequences of *reducción* for the Maya? How does a people or a culture even survive in the face of invasion, forced dislocation, disease, natural disaster, forced conversion, and linguistic reform? Farriss (1984) made this basic question the centerpiece of her classic history of the colony, and the question has remained central in more recent work as well. It leads one to focus on resistance, flight, insubordination, "spaces of autonomy" (Bracamonte y Sosa and Solís Robleda 1996), and, for some at least, the persistence of apparently precolonial forms and practices among the Maya. The issue of survival dovetails neatly with the long-standing interest in idolatry, since the idolater is just that, a survival of otherness surrounded by the Christian doxa that defines him as an "idolater." On this point also, the questions with which this book is concerned are slightly different, although both cultural survival and ritual difference are in the background. The Maya obviously did survive the long trauma of European colonialism, as evidenced by the more than two dozen Mayan languages spoken today by about three million people, of whom 900,000 speak Yucatec Maya. This is a testament to their creativity and resilience, which I have come to venerate. But here we must be careful, because the Yucatec spoken in the postcolony is a particular sort of Maya, and the people who speak it are Maya in a particular way.

Anyone who has spent time among contemporary Yucatec people will recognize the trickiness of language and identity in the peninsula, since the first thing most Mayas will tell you today is that the language they speak is not "legitimate Maya," nor are they themselves "Maya." Both statements are uttered as often in Maya language as in Spanish, and what they affirm is that both language and identity are *amestizado* 'mixed', or as contemporary Maya speakers say with a laugh, *xá'ak'á'an* 'mixed, spiced up'. There is an analogy here to Néstor Canclini's concept of hybrid cultures, except that, as I show, the historical roots are far deeper than contemporary popular culture and media would suggest. The same could be said of New World Spanish, French, Portuguese, and English or the complicated identities they index, although the question rarely seems to arise. From quite early in the colonial period in Yucatán, the indigenous language and the European language came to shape one another such that, in a broad contact zone, it became difficult or pointless to sort out the indigenous from the nonindigenous elements of what was becoming a single social world. At the extremes, of course, one recognizes the sheer Castilian of Crown or high-ranking authorities, as well as the more or less sheer Maya of texts like those in the Ritual of the Bacabs. But most of the action is in the middle between these extremes, and how we think of that middle will set the frame for how we think of the colony. The colonizers and the missionaries obviously tried valiantly to distinguish. They divided the world into Spaniards versus Indians (also called *naturales,* a term that implied both local and illegitimate birth; the Franciscans distinguished themselves from both), Christian versus heathen. Under *reducción* and the colonial administration, they made laws that attempted to ossify these and related distinctions. The basic model of syncretism as a European overlay atop an indigenous core came directly out of this way of thinking, and the missionary frenzy to identify and locate idolatry can be seen as a last-ditch effort to draw the line. In fact, this way of describing the conversion process fits well with the missionary idea that what was indigenous was hidden within. It is the mirror image of what occurred: superficially Maya forms of discourse came to stand for a semantic core of European ideas, something I examine in detail in Part II. But such dualism failed both historically and conceptually, because what emerged was a dynamic fusing of elements in a new social world, what Jane Hill and Kenneth Hill (1986) have called a set of "syncretic practices," not a composite of traits defined by their supposed origins (a point nicely spelled out by Warren [1998]). This dynamic fusion is the central theme of this book: how did it occur, what processes did it entail, and what were its consequences?

My answers to these questions unfold in three steps. First, an outline of the colonial field in which *reducción* was conducted. This includes an outline of the project as a whole (chapter 1) and the reorganization of the province into ordered towns and *guardianía* mission units, akin to parishes, as well as the persistent problems of population control and the frontier (chapter 2). The structures of governance, missionary pedagogy, and the embedding of *policía cristiana* in the towns are the focus of chapter 3. Taken together, the first three chapters sketch out the field of *reducción,* which is the social space in which colonial conduct and the colonial language were shaped, from semantics to discourse genres. Although I discuss some of the difficulties the missionaries encountered, and the fragmentation of their efforts, the main focus of this first part of the book is to take the measure of the project of *reducción.*

Part II explores the creation and codification of *Maya reducido,* the new version of Maya imbued with Christian thought. It comprises chapters 4 through 8, which make up the pivot point of my argument. It is through these processes that the ordering logic of *reducción* is converted into Maya—transposed and transformed from Latin and Spanish into Maya as best the missionaries could make out with their assistants. This translingual space of encounter was organized around two sets of practices. The first had to do with commensurating Maya and Spanish, aligning the two languages so that one could translate between them. This massive project was ongoing throughout the colonial period and sets up what I treat as the first conversion: European and Christian meanings were converted into Maya utterances. This conversion worked through the genres of the bilingual dictionary and the practical grammar. The second set of practices presupposes commensuration but goes on to codify the newly commensurated language in canonical texts. The genres that concern us here are doctrinal: the catechism, the confessional, and the sermon. Doctrinal Maya not only codified the language of the sacred; it was systematically inculcated in the obligatory doctrinal classes and repeated in many sacramental contexts such as mass, individual baptisms, confession, and matrimony.

Whereas language is mostly backgrounded in Part I, it becomes the central focus of Parts II and III. Here my engagement with linguistic anthropology becomes clear, and I draw on prior work by myself and many others. I have benefited from long engagement with the ideas and writings of Paul Friedrich, Richard Bauman, Dell Hymes, Jane Hill, Bambi Schieffelin, Charles Briggs, Greg Urban, Anthony Woodbury, Alan Rumsey, Asif Agha, Webb Keane, Aurore Becquelin Monod, Valentina Vapnarsky, and Victoria Bricker. In order to keep the exposition straightforward and nontechnical, however, I have tried to avoid theoretical discussion and let my description of the historical processes carry the ideas. The one exception is chapter 4, in which I try to spell out my approach to field, habitus, and genre, topics I have written on elsewhere. My goal here is a concise statement of the approach with clear examples. These concepts are subsequently refined and fleshed out with extended discussions of Spanish-to-Maya dictionaries (chapter 5), Maya-to-Spanish dictionaries (chapter 6), practical grammars of Maya (chapter 7), and the all-important doctrinal genres (chapter 8).

Part III follows the movement of *Maya reducido* from the missions into the field of governance in the *pueblos reducidos* and ultimately to the forbidden indigenous genre of the Books of Chilam Balam. My point is to show how and why the new, pervasively neologistic variety of Maya was dispersed through the fields of governance and mission set out in Part I. That it *did* spread will be demonstrated beyond any reasonable doubt, and the implication is that the overall colonial field, including the frontier zone and the so-called *despoblado* 'unpopulated zone', functioned as a single sweeping discourse formation across which modes of expression and communicative practice moved. At the same time, it gives pointed evidence that Maya speakers incorporated the new language instead of seeking to isolate themselves from it. As if rejecting the very dichotomies embedded in the discourses of idolatry and survival, they absorbed the new version of their language, using it for their own ends and ultimately making it their own. Chapter 9 examines land documents and the representation of space, and chapter 10 explores petitions—both of which were produced in the course of governance in the town councils. Chapter 11, the last substantive one in the book, follows the trail of Christianized Maya into the Books of Chilam Balam, demonstrating the profound impact it had on this native genre. Readers familiar with these books will recognize that my argument reverses a long scholarly tradition in which these works are read for their pre-Columbian content, not for their value as an index of colonial transformation and surely not as a testament to the spread of a new, Christianized version of Maya. The spread of the new language was the dispersal of a universe of meanings, typical uses, evaluative postures, and ways of referring. It was the most far-reaching legacy of *reducción* and is still very much with us today. In this sense, I hope that this book also contributes to the growing literature on the anthropology of religion, in which the transformative capacities of language are increasingly studied. In the end, colonial and specifically Christian Maya came to be written by Maya for Maya, not only in the fields of governance in the *pueblos reducidos,* but also in unauthorized and even forbidden genres, hidden from the intrusive surveillance of missionaries and colonial officials. The epilogue offers brief remarks on the Caste War of the mid-nineteenth century and the practice of Don Chabo, both of which are thoroughly embedded in *Maya reducido,* that is, Maya in the age of the cross.

A NOTE ON ORTHOGRAPHY

The primary sources cited in this book are mostly Maya and Spanish, produced in Yucatán, New Spain, or Spain, and dated between the fifteenth and nineteenth centuries. Over such a broad span of time and space, there are many orthographic variations and ad hoc spellings, particularly in the Maya texts. Moreover, many key texts have been published in multiple editions, which has introduced further variations. This has posed a formidable challenge to accurate rendering of original orthography and punctuation.

During the proofing and copyediting stages of the work, Mischa Park-Doob and I have tried to be as accurate to source as practical, without sacrificing legibility for the reader. The resulting compromise has led us to maximize accuracy to source when directly quoting but to revert to normalized spellings elsewhere. Spelling of Maya place-names is especially inconsistent in both Spanish and Maya language sources; for normalized spellings we generally followed Gerhard 1993. In all cases, readers interested in paleographic precision should consult the originals.

Areas especially prone to variation include (1) the use of accents in Spanish and the acute accent marking high tone in Maya; (2) the occasional use of [h] to mark initial glottal stop in Maya; and (3) the alternation between [u] and [v] for the bilabial glide, (4) between [ç], [z], and [s] for the voiceless sibilant, (5) between [x] and [h] for the pharyngeal continuant, (6) between [i] and [y] for the palatal glide, and (7) between [dz] and [ɔ] for the glottalized affricate /ts'/. Marking of glottalization, pitch, and vowel length is notoriously inconsistent in the Maya sources, as is the opposition between glottalized and plain stops. I have freely altered spacing and boundaries between morphemes and words in Maya for legibility and divided lines into manageable chunks to suit the purposes at hand. Chapters 5 through 8 are intended to be usable as reference material for further study of the missionary sources, and we have tried to be as accurate to source as possible. Where Maya texts are transliterated from handwritten archival sources, the author is responsible for the paleography.

ACKNOWLEDGMENTS

If a book like this can be said to have a beginning, it is in the contributions of others that it began. As a graduate student and then faculty member at the University of Chicago, Bernard Cohn, John Comaroff, Paul Friedrich, Nancy Munn, Michael Silverstein, Terry Turner, and especially Norman A. McQuown had a formative impact on my thinking about language and history. From 1980 to this day, Sebastian Castillo Mo, aka Don Chabo, has been a mentor and exemplar. Among scholars of colonial Latin America, Tom Cummins, the members of the Ethnohistory Workshop at the University of Pennsylvania, and especially Nancy Farriss led me into the intricacies of anthropological history and were invaluable interlocutors. Grant Jones, Sergio Quezada, and Matthew Restall shared their work generously and helped me wade further into the colonial materials (over my head, as it turned out). From the late 1980s to the mid-1990s, sustained engagements with Serge Gruzinski, Don Rice, Michael Warner, Gary Gossen, Greg Urban, Manuel Gutiérrez Estévez, and Aurore Becquelin Monod reshaped my thinking about Mexico, the Maya, and what it means to study a discourse formation. Richard Bauman has been a valued friend and teacher since the beginning of my career, and our engagement during this period helped shape my approach to genre, among other things. Tim Earle, Cynthia Robin, and Jack Sidnell at Northwestern University were fellow students of Latin America and the Caribbean from whom I learned a great deal and whose encouragement of this work was most helpful. At Berkeley, José Rabasa, Patricia Bacquedano López, Niklaus Largier, and William Taylor have made significant contributions to my understanding of Mexican and Church history. There are no adequate thanks for the contributions of George Foster and Mary Le Cron Foster as scholars and benefactors of anthropology and linguistic anthropology at Berkeley. Over the past decade, I have benefited from long and productive engagement with Aurore Becquelin Monod, Maurizio Gnerre, Flavia Cuturi, John Haviland, Alan Rumsey, Nick Enfield, and, in recent years, Philippe Descola, Carlo Severi, and Sachiko Ide. This is a formidable group of interlocutors from whom any linguistic anthropologist would learn, and I am grateful to each of them. Victoria Bricker shared her published and unpublished work on colonial Maya and has been willing to entertain my ideas even when they depart from her own views. In my view, Vicki exemplifies Mayanist scholarship at its very best. I owe a special word of thanks too to Araceli Poot and Patricia Martínez of the Centro de Apoyo para la Investigación de Yucatán, Mérida, Yucatán. They helped me greatly with the Colección Carrillo y Ancona and shared their unpublished transliterations of documents with me.

My doctoral advisees at the University of Chicago, Northwestern, and Berkeley have been among my closest interlocutors, and this book has benefited directly from the work of Robert Hamrick, Daniel Suslak, Cristiana Giordano, Tatyana Mamut, Beatriz Reyes Cortes, Saúl Mercado, and Ariana Mangual. Deanna Barenboim and Nancy Mann provided expert editing of the last two versions of the manuscript, and Deanna was invaluable as my research assistant in the penultimate phases of its preparation. Rob Hamrick, Alysoun Quinby, Christine Kovaks, and Mischa Park-Doob also provided invaluable work as paid assistants, organizing the near-chaos of computer files, archival materials, and more than two hundred hours of audio and video field data in Maya. They also helped coordinate the making of numerous handouts and maps of colonial Yucatán. Rob's knowledge of Mayan linguistics and the realities of contemporary Guatemala and Christie's abilities with film have been a valuable complement to my own passions and have helped make my office a place one can actually do some work. During the final phase of copy editing, Mischa was an exceptional assistant in everything from spell checking Spanish, Maya, and English to correcting citations, chasing down sources, improving translations, and suggesting valuable revisions in the prose. Vanessa Lyon provided critical assistance acquiring images and permissions on an unreasonably accelerated schedule, and Yuri Herrera helped proof the Spanish and caught several errors that Mischa and I had missed.

For written comments on the manuscript in its final stages, on substance as well as form, I am indebted to William Taylor, Richard Bauman, Jane Hill, Todd Ochoa, Joel Robbins, and Carlo Severi. Mario Humberto Ruz and John Lucy read and commented on the first three chapters. Were it not for the comments of this group, this book would surely be less clear and more prone to misstatement.

I gratefully acknowledge the National Endowment for the Humanities for their support through the research grant History and Discourse: The Colonial Roots of Maya Shamanism (Jan. 1, 1992–Dec. 31, 1994), of which Nancy Farriss and I were co-PIs. This project provided time and resources for a collaboration in which I learned a great deal about historical anthropology in general and colonial Yucatán in particular. Between 1996 and 1997 I received a John Simon Guggenheim Fellowship for the project, which allowed me to plunge into the history of the missions for the first time. Although I was unable to write the book I had optimistically projected for that year, the research I did was requisite to everything that followed. To these institutions I give my heartfelt thanks.

During this long gestation, I was an invited professor at Casa de América in Madrid (1993, 1999), the University of Paris X, Nanterre (1995), the École des Hautes Études en Sciences Sociales, Paris (1988, 1992, 2007), the University of Copenhagen (1996, 1999), the European School of Advanced Studies, Naples (2003), and the summer school of the International Center for Semiotic and Cognitive Studies, San Marino (1998). In each of these settings and at conferences in between, I presented seminars on this research and benefited greatly from dialogue with colleagues working on related topics.

To all of these individuals and institutions, I remain indebted. In their various ways, they set a high standard of excellence and fostered the kinds of international collaborations so acutely needed in the world today. I hope this book approximates that standard, despite any shortcomings of its author. Jennifer Johnson Hanks, my wife, has helped sharpen my thinking with her incisive questions and suggestions, her humor, her generosity of spirit, and her abiding patience with my work habits. Her love is the stuff of optimism fulfilled. Our infant son, Benjamin, graciously turned and descended to earth two days after the manuscript was completed, thereby demonstrating that not all great timing is learned. My daughter, Madeleine, has listened to talk of the project for many years, asked disarmingly pointed questions, and inspired me with her sheer smarts and zest for life. In 1997 Richard Bauman likened this project to standing beneath Niagara Falls trying to catch the water with a tin cup. After another decade by the falls, spent mostly in the rapids, I think he was right; this is what came of it. A final word of thanks to Stan Holwitz and Rose Vekony, my editors at the University of California Press. Stan moved this project along with a speed and simplicity rarely achieved in academic publishing. Rose brought the publication to completion with meticulous editorial work, an expert eye, and the ability to envision the finished book when it was still in draft form. To Stan, Rose, and their colleagues at the Press, my sincere thanks.

1

Introduction

The Field of Discourse Production

The Spanish conquest of Yucatán rested on two major columns, military sub-jugation and the so-called *conquista pacífica* 'peaceful conquest'. The military conquest was carried out by a relatively small number of soldiers, armed with swords, armor, muskets, horses, and dogs, and assisted by their indigenous allies. After decades of advances, setbacks, and regroupings, it came to an end, at least officially, in 1547. The peaceful conquest, by contrast, was carried out by an even smaller number of missionaries and their recruits, armed with monumental built spaces, the cross, religious vestments, the Bible and doctrine, the Host, wine and oil, and speech.

The objective of the *conquista pacífica* was to convert the natives from hea-thens into Christians living in accordance with *policía cristiana,* which we might gloss roughly 'Christian civility'. This conversion was necessary in order to incor-porate native peoples into the colonial society, for to be a member of society entailed being Christian. Etymologically linked to the Classical *polis,* the term *policía* in sixteenth-century Spanish designates honorable conduct befitting citizens. As Covarrubias (1995 [1611], 827) put it, it was a *"término ciudadano y cortesano"* 'term of citizenry and honor'. In a revealing example, Covarrubias cites the expression *"consejo de policía,"* which he glosses as *"el que gobierna las cosas menudas de la ciudad y el adorno della y limpieza"* 'that which governs the small things of the city and its decorum and cleanliness'. The sense of decorum found in tidy details and the tie to orderly living in towns and cities define the conceptual core of *policía* as it was brought to Yucatán. It involved at once built space, the care and presentation of the body, a code of conduct, and the orderly relation among the three.

1

In the evangelization of the Indios, *policía cristiana* had a special importance: it was a means to the end of conversion.[1] As Tomás López Medel expressed it in his historic *Ordenanzas* of 1552:

> ... *tanto más hábiles y dispuestos para la doctrina cristiana y para recibir la predicación de el santo evangelio, cuanto más están puestos en la policía espiritual y temporalmente.*
> (Cogolludo 1971 [1688], 391)

> ... (they will be) all the more apt and disposed towards Christian Doctrine and towards receiving preaching of the Holy Gospel, insofar as they are placed in proper civility (both) spiritually and temporally.

In this passage the spiritual and the temporal are at once distinguished and joined together, as López Medel nicely articulates the prevailing belief among missionaries and Crown representatives that in order to really persuade the Indios of Christianity, it was necessary to habituate them to a new way of being in the everyday social world. The appearance and neatness of collective life, the "small details," would help transform the Indios' disposition, bringing both the aptitude to receive Christianity and the inclination to do so. Much as in Elias's (1994) civilizing process, or Bourdieu's (1977) concept of habitus, the idea of *policía* was to instill ways of perceiving, experiencing, and behaving, rooted in the little details of the body in its social life and in the disposition to reproduce them.

In order to be placed in *policía cristiana,* the Indios had to be reorganized. This was to be achieved through a process called *reducción.* Although it is tempting to translate *reducción* as 'reduction', to do so is misleading, since the term implies no necessary decrease in size or number. It did imply pacification and subordination to the new rule of law and to the hierarchical relations of colonial society. The term derives from the verb *reducir(se),* which Covarrubias defines as *"convencer(se)"* '(become) convince(d)', or we might say "persuaded." The related term *reducido* is commonly found in Spanish documents of the period, with the meaning *"convencido y vuelto a mejor orden"* 'convinced and put in better order' (Covarrubias 1995 [1611], 854).

It is widely recognized that the colonial *reducción* had two focal objectives. The first was to relocate the Indios into centralized towns called *pueblos reducidos* 'ordered towns', some already existing and others newly created (Farriss 1984; Quezada 1992). This process is what is sometimes referred to as *congregación,* the policy whereby the Indios were congregated in order to facilitate missionary instruction and surveillance. The demographic concentration was accompanied by the establishment of the missions and of the well-known quadrilateral town layout found throughout the Spanish Americas.[2] Most towns were simultaneously defined by local government and by their position in the ecclesiastical structure of the province, implying a chain of jurisdictions from the local chapel and town council to the head town, the *guardianía,* the province of San Josef de Yucatán, New Spain, the Crown, and the pope. Hence an "ordered" town was one whose internal organization was orderly, and whose place in the larger colonial structure was well articulated.

The second sense of *reducción* bears not on the spatial distribution of Indios but on their dispositions and conduct: *Indios reducidos* were those who were "convinced, persuaded" and behaved in accordance with *policía cristiana.* In other words, the twin foci of *reducción* join together precisely the three aspects of *policía*—social space, the human body, and everyday social conduct. The process of *reducción* consisted of the introduction of *policía* into the indigenous population, with the added effect that Indios would practice civility not because they were forced to do so but because they were persuaded of its rightness.

As amply reflected in their writings from early on, the missionaries were well aware that the Maya were already living in *policía,* of a sort. Seeing the great architectural programs of Chichén Itzá, Izamal, Mayapán, and Uxmal, the obvious stratification of Post-Classic Maya society, the movement of trade goods over long distances, the *ah kin* priests, and hieroglyphic writing (which they called *carácteres* 'characters') and learning of the intricacies of the Mayan calendar, they were under no illusion that the society they came to order was not already orderly.[3] The Franciscan missionaries criticized the Spanish for the violence and havoc they wreaked in military conquest and the extractions of the colonial regime, both of which impeded the saving of souls. Their program, by contrast, would be an orderly ordering. They would take what was already there and purify it, refashion it, and make of it a new world in the sense of worldmaking described by Goodman (1978). On the landscape, they built nodal places such as the convents of Maní, Izamal, and Mérida, using the very stones taken from the temples they destroyed there, often building on the same sites.[4] In the sphere of human conduct, they recognized the civility of Maya social life and the religious sensibility of the people, even though they considered these capacities to have been debauched by the devil and the lies of indigenous leaders. Thus they would purge the falsehoods, the "vomit of idolatry," and the "false gods" around which so much seemed to revolve, and put truth, faith, and the trinity in their place. The indigenous capacity for order and religion would be a resource. In terms of language, they learned Maya as best they could, working with assistants, and had great respect for its expressive power. Seeking to cut away the inherently false words of idolatry and superstition, they reused the remaining language to build cathedrals of meaning around their triune god. The reorderings of *reducción* were based therefore at least partly on analysis and disassemblage of what was already there. The ideal was to reorder, prune down, supplement, and reorient what already existed. The challenge was to do so without fostering the persistence of the old world from which the parts had come. The result was pervasive ambiguity, ambivalence, and an almost morbid fear of the unseen and the insincere hiding beneath the appearance of truth. We might call this the missionaries' dilemma.

I argue that the *reducción* actually had a third object, equally important with space and conduct, and equally salient in the peaceful conquest. That third object is language. On the face of it, speech and communicative practices are inalienable parts of *policía* in everyday social life, just as they are the necessary medium in which to persuade would-be converts of the message of Christianity, and also the medium in which much prayer and religious practice takes place.[5] But the tie to language runs deeper still, since the indigenous languages were the objects, and not only the instruments, of *reducción*. The missionaries sought to *reducir* the Indian languages, including Yucatec Maya, by describing them in terms of rules and patterns. The result of this kind of *reducción* is a grammar, or a set of rules that specify the structure and regularity of the language. In the overall project, town layout, regional governance, civility of conduct, grammar, and proper speech are of a single cloth.

The linguistic sense of *reducción* is occasionally evident in the front matter of colonial grammatical descriptions, which include phrases like *"Arte de lengua Maya reducida a sus succintas reglas"* 'Practical grammar of Maya language ordered to its succinct rules' (Beltrán 2000 [1746]). Similarly, missionary accounts routinely state that the friars *"redujeron la lengua,"* meaning they produced grammatical manuals of it. The idea here is that a grammar consists in the analytic ordering of the language by rules, much as the behavioral *reducción* is an ordering of everyday conduct and the spatial *reducción* is an ordering of inhabited space. And just as the spatial and behavioral *reducción* intentionally transformed Indian lifeways, so too the linguistic *reducción* was wrapped up in the concerted attempt to transform the Indian languages.[6] Missionary grammars, manuals, and dictionaries occupy a gray zone of ambiguity, at once descriptive and prescriptive, analytic and regulatory. Working with the relevant materials on and in Maya, I have become convinced that analysis and translation were actually forms of *reducción* in the strong sense of systematically re-forming their object. This is one of the themes that runs throughout this book.

My first point, then, is that the peaceful conquest of the Maya of Yucatán was framed, in Spanish thought, in an encompassing conceptual framework whose key terms were *policía cristiana* and *reducción,* each of which had at least two distinguishable and interrelated senses. The *reducción* was the centerpiece of early missionary practice. I want to underscore that the term designates a bringing to order, and that it had three quite distinct objects: built space, everyday social practice, and language. Each of these three implied a different kind of intervention, but all were guided by the same telos: the conversion of the Indios into

Christians, living in *policía cristiana* and speaking a language apt as a medium of Catholic practice.[7] In this telos, language was pivotal, both as an object to be analyzed and altered and as an instrument with which to analyze and alter other aspects of Indian life.

The changes wrought by all three kinds of *reducción* contributed to the process of conversion. We tend to think of conversion in terms of a charismatic change in an individual's religious beliefs. In the colonial context, however, the concept is primarily collective, not individual; we are talking about the social and cultural conversion of entire ethnic groups as part of colonial domination. While it may be productive to distinguish religious conversion from other kinds of deep transformation, it is critical to view conversion as a social and cultural process whose scope is historically variable.[8] Not only is there no reason to assume religious conversion as a bounded category, but there is overwhelming evidence that religious beliefs and practices were pervasively woven into social life in both the Spanish and Maya sectors of the colony.

Perhaps most important, to describe conversion in the language of religious beliefs is to privilege the belief states of individual subjects, when what we should be concerned with is the dynamic practices of social groups. This error in turn leads to unanswerable questions such as whether or not the Maya became "authentic" converts who really believed just the right things. This question haunted many missionaries, but it is secondary in the history proposed here. Rather, what will occupy us is the emergence of the colonial field and the related conversion of social practices, lived space, and language. These changes are of a piece with spiritual conversion, but they go far beyond what anyone believed.[9]

For the missionaries in colonial Yucatán, the focal object of *conversión* clearly was Indian behavior and beliefs, as is evident from their actions and from the standard definition of *convertir(se)* as "convince, be convinced or repentant" (Covarrubias 1995 [1611], 350). Recall that one meaning of *reducir(se)* was also "to convince," a semantic joining consistent with the policy linkage between the *reducción* and *conversión* of Indian subjects. By combining conviction with repentance, *conversión* designates a voluntary turning away from past and current ways, to take on different, better ways. It must be kept in mind that while force was in fact liberally used in the *conquista pacífica*, its defining features were persuasion, habituation, and discipline. In reference to social space, *conversión* designates transformation from one state into another (a usage attested in early modern Spanish; see Covarrubias 1995 [1611], 350). In Yucatán this bore primarily on the northwestern region of the peninsula, where the resettlement was concentrated and most of the missions were established.

The linguistic *reducción* was aimed at what can be appropriately called the "linguistic conversion."[10] This consisted in the transformation of Maya language from the pagan, idolatrous code that (to Spanish ears) it had been into a revised

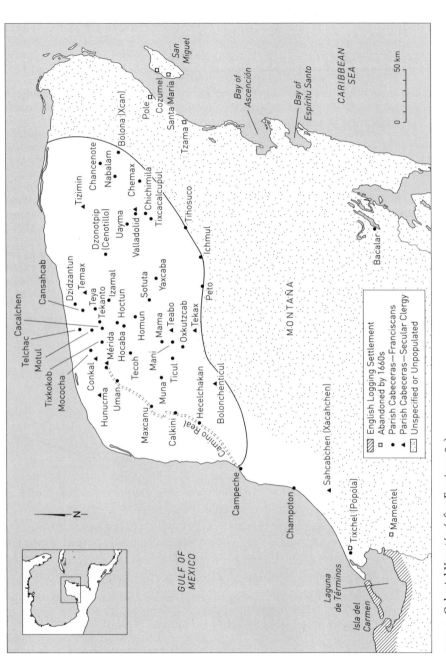

MAP 1. Colonial Yucatán (after Farriss 1984)

Legend:
- English Logging Settlement
- □ Abandoned by 1660s
- ● Parish Cabeceras—Franciscans
- ▲ Parish Cabeceras—Secular Clergy
- Unspecified or Unpopulated

Labels (clockwise / by region):

CARIBBEAN SEA

50 km

San Miguel
Santa María
Cozumel
Pole
Tzama
Bolona (Xcan)
Bay of Ascención
Bay of Espíritu Santo

Chancenote
Nabalam
Chemax
Chichimilá
Tixcacalcupul
Tihosuco
Tizimin
Dzonotpip (Cenotillo)
Uayma
Valladolid
Ichmul
Bacalar

Dzidzantun
Temax
Cansahcab
Teya
Tekanto
Izamal
Hoctun
Sotuta
Yaxcaba
Peto
MONTAÑA

Telchac
Cacalchen
Motul
Tixkokob
Mococha
Conkal
Uman
Mérida
Hocaba
Homun
Mama
Teabo
Oxkutzcab
Tekax

Hunucma
Tecoh
Mani
Ticul
Muna
Hecelchakan
Bolonchenticul

Maxcanu
Calkini
Camino Real
Sahcabchen (Xacachen)

Campeche
Champoton
Mamentel
Tixchel (Popola)

GULF OF MEXICO
Laguna de Términos
Isla del Carmen

—N—

and reordered language fitted to the discursive practices of an emerging community of Christian Indios. In concrete terms, this entailed creating in Maya very powerful discourse markers such as the cross, the quadrilateral spatial grid (oriented from east to west), dates, titles, signatures, and the naming of places and persons. It also entailed altering the semantic values of preexisting expressions by linking them to specific practices and selected experts. We might say that the *reducción* entailed what Putnam (1975) called a "division of linguistic labor," that is, a differentiated field of discourse practices. The semantic values (meanings) of verbal expressions were socially established by that same structured field. Hence there was a constant dynamic between changes in the field and changes in the universe of reference to which the language was fitted.

From the outset, then, we must take the measure of the missionary project of *conquista pacífica* and *conversión.* It was aimed at nothing short of a remaking of Indian life, from heart, soul, and mind to self-image, bodily practices, lived space, and everyday conduct, including speech. Clearly more than mere colonization, it was what we can call a total project simultaneously focused on multiple spheres of Indian life. For this, the missionaries had, as they put it in their letters, to know the Indios "inside and out," and their methods were as extensive and intensive as their goals. They would live among the Indios in *convivencia*, in monasteries placed in the centers of *pueblos reducidos,* where they would teach, discipline, and oversee. They would travel, mostly by foot, from monastic centers to the *pueblos de visita* 'visit towns', where they would preach and administer the sacraments. Many of the missionaries provided health care to the sick as well, at a time when cyclic droughts, epidemics, and pestilence wrought havoc on the indigenous population (Cook and Borah 1972). They also set about learning Maya language, producing the grammars, dictionaries, and other descriptions needed to "order" and teach it to others. This ordering made it possible to translate Christian doctrine, prayers, sermons, and parts of the sacraments into Maya language. In short, they set about to Christianize Maya language along with the universe to which it pointed.

In all of this, the *reducción,* with its threefold focus on social space, human conduct, and language, was central. To put it in distinctly modern terms, the *reducción* represents the systematic attempt to design and inculcate a new habitus in the Indian communities. To this habitus would correspond a new Indian subject: individuated, classified, governed, and fundamentally religious. While we can distinguish conceptually between the three main lines of this effort, there was a great deal of overlap in practice. For a pueblo to be genuinely *reducido,* its populace should be made up of *indios reducidos,* living in *policía cristiana.* The one could not be achieved without the other. Similarly, the point of ordering the towns was for more effective oversight, preaching, and *convivencia,* and these were inconceivable without being able to talk with the Indios. The Indios would continue to speak their own language, but it had to be a new version of that language, purged of the "vomit of idolatry" and the insubordinate genres of hieroglyphic reading and history telling: reduced by erasure, yet incremented with the means to speak to and of God and his designs.

Rather than think of three separate *reducciones,* then, it is more productive to see them as three faces of a single, very complex process. To be sure, the three faces were turned toward one another, so that each produced both the means to further the others and the index of their effectiveness. Whatever its actual outcomes, the scope and aim of the missionary project were set to maximally overdetermine the emergence of a new kind of Indio in a new kind of social and spiritual world. The results of missionization are often described as fragmentary, confused, or even superficial (Burkhart 1989, 184–93; Gibson 1966, 75), essentially a thin Christian overlay upon a predominant and deep indigenous core.[11] This is the classic model of syncretism in which indigenous people appear to be Christian but in fact continue to be non-Christian. This book points in a different direction. Christian practices done in Maya appear indigenous, whereas the meanings are in fact Christian—the opposite of the syncretism model. Moreover, Maya engagement with Christianity was anything but superficial or short-lived, even if it was partial, contradictory, and put to uses never envisioned by the friars. The position on intercultural processes in this book is much closer in spirit to Taylor (1996, 6), who cites Gramsci, E. P. Thompson, and James Scott on the mixing of resistance and deference, persistence and change and Ashis Nandy on the nature of postcolonial relations between colonizers and colonized.

The missionary project in Yucatán was shaped by a variety of factors, starting with the preponderant role of the Franciscans.[12] In 1544 the first eight friars arrived, four from Guatemala and four from Mexico. Among the first group were Villalpando and Bienvenida, who established the first Franciscan house in Oxkutzcab in 1547. Villalpando is said to have "reduced" Maya language to a grammar of sorts and established the first missionary school in Mérida, where some two thousand elite Maya children were taught to read and write alphabetic Maya. By 1547 nine more Franciscans were recruited from Toledo (where Landa and Ciudad Real, among others, had taken the habit). Over the following sixty years their numbers would grow modestly to staff twenty-eight parishes in 1606 and thirty-seven by 1656 (Clendinnen 1987, 51; Patch 1993, 38). Whereas the order monopolized the conversions until the 1570s, the secular clergy became more important thereafter, especially in the extirpation of idolatry (Chuchiak 2000b, 161).[13] Chuchiak (2000b) details the involvement of bishops (of whom a number were prominent Franciscans), the *cabildo eclesiástico* (advisory to the bishop), and secular vicars in the discovery and extirpation of idolatry through the first century and a half. Several of the individuals who figure prominently in subsequent chapters of this book played key roles in the extirpations, including Bishops Toral, Landa, Montalvo, Salazar, and Sánchez de Aguilar, the secular dean at the head of the *cabildo eclesiástico* and the author of a famous *informe* 'report' on Maya idolatry. Notwithstanding the centrality of the Franciscans in the missions, their numbers were always low relative to demand, which led to a sort of indirect missionization in which native assistants called *maestros* 'teachers' played a pivotal role in the actual indoctrinations.

The Franciscans brought to their project a particular orientation, which helped them distinguish themselves from secular clergy and nonclergy alike. The specificity of the order would make its own study, but here I can give a few brief indications.[14] At the heart of the order was the sanctity of poverty, the great value placed on humility, simplicity, and ecstatic experience over and above intellectual understanding. The embracing of poverty contrasted maximally with the Spanish extractors of wealth in labor, goods, and, increasingly with time, money (Patch 1993, 28–30). There was of course substantial extraction from Maya people in support of the missions, but the friars themselves lived poor. The ecstatic presence of God is perhaps nowhere more dramatically embodied than in the stigmata of Francis. The crucifixion is manifest in the body of the saint, in union with the passion and suffering of Jesus. The body will also become its own focus in the missions, not only for the regulation of sexuality (Burkhart 1989; Chuchiak 2007; Gruzinski 2000), but in the gestures, postures, silence and utterance, gaze, tears, and prohibitions and selective abstinences that the friars observed and inculcated in their flocks. This extended as well to the orderly arrangement of bodies in collective processions, seating arrangements, and the distribution of activities on the convent patios. Just as a *pueblo reducido* was both organized internally and articulated externally, so too the missionized body was ordered within and in relation to others.

The Franciscan premium on simplicity appears to have given rise to a preference for simple, transparent statement over elaborate metaphors in missionary Nahuatl (Burkhart 1989, 26–28). In relation to Maya, there is an analogous premium placed on transparency in translations of Christian concepts (see chapter 6 below). As a monastic order, the Franciscans also emphasized their separateness from the world (Clendinnen 1987, 45 ff.) and the observance of a strict rule, which included cycles of daily prayer and contemplation. It is difficult to gauge the degree to which these various values carried over into the indigenous parishioners, but the centrality of the cross, the body, speech, and daily practice are all salient in their teachings. Finally, the Franciscans saw themselves as exemplars, living in imitation of Christ and teaching by example, something clear in Lizana's (1988 [1633]) almost hagiographic descriptions of the early friars.[15]

THE MAKING OF A TRANSLANGUAGE

In New Spain and Peru there was debate as to whether the main vehicle of evangelization was to be indigenous languages or Spanish. In many places, a missionary would need to master three or more different native languages in order to communicate with local people, and Spanish was argued by some to be the more efficient choice (Gómez Canedo 1977, 154–64). In others, linguistic plurality was overcome by imposing a single indigenous language upon a landscape of many other languages, as Nahuatl was imposed in parts of New Spain. In Yucatán this was not the case. Maya was the only indigenous language native to the northern peninsula, and the Franciscans, who dominated the missions for the first century, were committed to learning it. For that, the language had first to be *reducido*.

In Yucatán and New Spain the ability to speak native languages was a point of contention between the monastics and the secular clergy, who vied with one another for authority over evangelization. Throughout the Church documents we find claims and counterclaims between bishops, Franciscan provincials, and others, as to who knew the language better. In their *memorias* to the Crown, laying out the state of the missions, both monastic and secular authors consistently distinguish between missionaries who are *lengua* and ones who are not. To be *lengua* was to have the following three characteristics: (i) to be a native speaker of a European language, (ii) to be capable of speaking the local indigenous language, and (iii) to be able to interpret between Spanish and that language.[16] Thus in Yucatán the *lengua* is always a European capable of interpreting between Maya and Spanish.

It is evident in the writings of Cogolludo (1971 [1688], 2:433 ff.), Lizana (1988 [1633]), and others that to be *lengua* was a sign of erudition, achievement, and practical ability.[17] Crown policy stipulated that the missions were to be staffed with clergy who could communicate in the native languages; so, in the *memorias,* there was no disagreement about the importance of being *lengua* but only about who was and who was not, to what degree, and at what cost of training.[18] The same valuation is evident in the staffing of the Yucatecan missions. In Yucatán, as in New Spain, there was an explicit hierarchy among the clergy: full *lenguas* could preach and hear confession, *medio lenguas* could hear confession but not preach, and missionaries who could not speak the language of the Indios could do neither.[19] In short, competence in Maya was a form of capital and a justification for claims to authority.

Accordingly, the religious did a variety of things to demonstrate their own expertise in Maya and to use it in their writings. Missionary *lenguas* wrote dictionaries, vocabularies, *artes* (practical grammars), grammars, lexicons, in short, a whole range of linguistic studies. All these works present asymmetrical metalinguistic analyses in which Spanish is the metalanguage (and the source language for most translations), while Maya is the object language. All rules and explanations are given in Spanish; it is self-evident, though still worth stating, that we find no grammars or lexicons of Spanish written in Maya. The primary objective of the missionary works was to lay down the points of interlingual transference, in the asymmetric movement of meaning from Spanish and Latin into Maya.

These materials were used in convents at Mérida, Izamal, and Maní to train incoming European missionaries who needed, in theory at least, to learn Maya before heading to the outlying *guardianías,* or mission units. That is, texts written by *lengua* authors were used by *lengua* teachers to produce a corps of *lengua* missionaries—another iteration of the kind of circularity we saw with the three spheres of *reducción.*

There is some indication that the same works were used in the training of at least some native Maya speakers in the *gramática* of their own language. While clearly secondary to the main aims of missionary texts, this practice raises fascinating questions. Sánchez de Aguilar notes that Gaspar Antonio Chi was moderately well trained in *gramática* but does not specify whether in Spanish or Maya. Beltrán de Santa Rosa María, writing in the mid-eighteenth century, says in no uncertain terms that his manual of *"Idioma Maya reducido a succintas reglas"* should be studied by native Maya speakers. Without knowledge of their own grammar, he says, "they might say what they know, but they don't know what they say" (cf. also Pagden 1982, 127 ff.). Insofar as missionary grammars and dictionaries were learned by native Maya speakers, they functioned as evangelical tracts in the most direct sense: "This is how we speak from now on."

The other side of missionary Maya was the various evangelical works the *lenguas* authored—the catechisms, sermons, manuals, dialogues, and scripts for speech while engaging in the sacraments. These define the moral and spiritual order to which the Indios were to be brought by *reducción.* They would be used mainly in two contexts, reflecting their dual status. First, they would be used to train missionaries, for whom the doctrinal content of the texts was already familiar, but the phrasing and exposition in Maya had to be learned. Second, they would be used in training Maya neophytes, who presumably knew the language but had to learn the doctrinal semantics and frame of reference. While evangelical texts in Maya have attracted scant attention in the scholarly literature, they are a singularly rich source of historical evidence and provide many piquant examples of the world to which the Indios were to be *reducidos.* One reason doctrinal discourse is important is that its influence reached far beyond the "religious" dimensions of conversion.

The doctrinal materials differ from the dictionaries and other metalinguistic works in genre, format, thematic content, and style, but there are strong ties between the two kinds of discourse. In addition to their common frame of religious reference, they also share many details of linguistic form, common authorship, consistent pedagogical aims, many cross-references, and other intertextual ties. For instance, many of the example sentences in the manuals and dictionaries overtly mention bits of doctrine, or presuppose the doctrine in order to be intelligible. This kind of crossover is one of the vectors along which colonial Maya language would come to change, and it extended far into the practices of Indian authors in the *repúblicas de indios* 'Indian republics'. By way of illustration, we turn to the translation of "almighty" in *Dios Omnipotente* 'Almighty God'.

THE BODY AS TOTALITY

The *Diccionario de Motul,* which is both the most extensive and the earliest extant Maya dictionary (ca. 1585), defines *tuzinil* as *"todo, cantidad concreta"* 'all, concrete quantity'. As an illustration, it gives the sentence *tuzinil yanil Dios* 'God is everywhere'. Precisely the same example sentence recurs in Beltrán's grammar of Yucatec (1742, 191), also illustrating *tuzinil* in an alphabetized list of "prepositions, adverbs and conjunctions." This work was written a century and a half later. After the Motul, the next most extensive and earliest dictionary is the mid-seventeenth-century *Diccionario de San Francisco* (probably about fifty years later). In this work, the entries under *tuzinil* make no doctrinal reference, curiously, but the term *uchuc* 'powerful' is illustrated with the expression *uchuc tumen ti zinil* 'powerful in everything', a minor variant of the *tuzinil* form cited in the Motul and Beltrán works. In the 1684 grammar of Fray Gabriel de San Buenaventura, there is no entry for the term *tuzinil,* but there is for *uchuc,* which is glossed as 'power, (that which is) possible'. It is illustrated with the by now familiar phrase *uchuc tumen tuçinil,* glossed 'all-powerful' (San Buenaventura 1888 [1684], 37). (The orthographic variation of *c* cedilla, *s,* and *z* does not affect the example.)

It is interesting to note that the San Francisco dictionary and the San Buenaventura grammar cite identical phrases, both under the heading *uchuc.* Neither work indicates whether the phrase has any doctrinal reference. After all, the kind of power designated by *uchuc* was not specifically divine, and one might imagine a worldly figure to whom "power in all things" was attributed. But the circle closes when we realize that this expression is precisely the one used by the missionaries in doctrinal texts to translate the omnipotence of God. The Credo, for instance, begins *Ocaan ti uol Dios yumbil uchuc tumen tuzinil* 'I believe in God the Father Almighty' (Coronel 1620b; Beltrán 1912 [1757]). Furthermore, to my knowledge the expression never occurs in any written document, either missionary or Maya authored, in reference to anything other than the Christian God. Whatever the potential uses of the term on the basis of its grammar and semantics, it was rigidly pegged to the omnipotence of God.

The intertextual recurrence of example phrases and idiosyncratic glosses runs like a red thread through the missionary corpus, marking a trail through time and space and indicating which authors read which others. The fact that so many of the examples are doctrinal indicates that the metalinguistic works and the evangelical ones were part of a single formation—an expectable corollary of the *reducción*.

This fact has consequences for historical research, of which two are worth underscoring here. First, the missionary linguistic works are far from mere descriptions; they are codifications of an ongoing process of linguistic conversion. Second, the evangelical works were far from innocent translations of doctrine. Rather, they embodied and helped propagate the emergent version of Maya that was to be the product of *reducción*. This new translingual Maya had a pervasive impact on written genres produced by Maya authors themselves. This includes prominently the Books of Chilam Balam, banned by the missionaries and usually considered the most "native" of the postconquest genres. Hence the entanglements of linguistic *reducción* reached far into the Maya sector of the colonial discourse field. Let's follow the thread of *tuzinil*.

In the entire corpus of nine extant Books of Chilam Balam (in excess of 230,000 words), there are only two tokens of the form *tuzinil*, one in the Book of Kaua and the other in the Códice Pérez.[20] In both cases, the referent is the Christian God. In the Kaua, there is a long and detailed dicussion, in Maya, of the significance of the sacrament of Mass, and of the gestures and vestments used in it. The passage begins:

> *Discursos sobre las Misas y significas;*
> *He tu yocol Padre ichil sachristia tu suhuy cilich homtanil ca cilich colel Santa Maria*
> *cu yocol Xpto cahlohil uch'ab ca bakel utial ulohic balcah tusinil*
>   (163, line 1)

> Discourse on masses and (their) meanings;
> When the Father enters the sacristy, the sacred holy sanctuary of our holy lady Blessed Mary, Christ our savior enters to take (the form of) our flesh, to save the things of the world *in their totality.*

Throughout this section of the Kaua manuscript, the text equates actions performed by the priest with biblical references, mainly to the incarnation and crucifixion of Christ. In the portion cited, the term *tusinil* refers to the all-embracing totality of the world within the scope of divine power, much like the sentence *tuzinil yanil Dios* in the Motul and Beltrán works. The difference, of course, is that the Kaua book was written by and for Maya speakers.[21] The theological interpretations found in the Books of Chilam Balam are often exotic and possibly subversive in intent. Yet the linguistic forms are identical to those of the missionaries. It is the *lengua reducida* that is being voiced by the Indian authors.

In the Códice Pérez (1949 [n.d.]), the term occurs in a passage that ventrilo-quizes the teachings of the friars in both phrasing and doctrinal meaning:

> Haili bin ocsabac ti ol Dios tuhunale
> uchuc tumen u sinil yetel yalmat'anil
> (Miram and Miram 1988, 165, line 12)

> The only thing that shall be committed to faith (is) God alone
> Almighty and his words

Here we find the precise epithet for God that was formulated by the translators of the Credo and that appears in the *Doctrinas* of both Coronel (1620) and Beltrán (2000 [1746]). What is most striking about this and the previous example is that they are the only instances in the entire corpus of the Books of Chilam Balam in which the lexical form *(t)uzinil* occurs. If the form were merely a standard way of expressing totality, as the dictionaries represent it to be, why would it be so rare, and why would it refer exclusively to the Christian God?

The answer is that the term was not a common Maya expression at all, at least not by the evidence of the documents that exist today. Rather, it is a gram-matically plausible neologism, evidently created by the missionary translators to render divine omnipotence in Maya. The grammatical analysis of the expression follows the well-established morphosyntactic pattern for making what linguists call relational nouns: [t(i)–u–STEM], where the stem consists of a noun or verb with or without a suffix. Hence it is formally parallel to *tulacal* 'all' (lit. 'in its totality'), *tumen* 'by, because' (lit. 'by its doing'), *tutsel* 'alongside' (lit. 'at its side'), *tuyuchucil* 'by the power of', and so forth. For *tuzinil*, the stem element is *zinil*, which is further analyzable as *zin-il*, a verb root plus *-il* suffix.

At this point the plot thickens, and we can appreciate the frame of reference of the missionaries, for the root *sin* is a "positional verb" meaning "extended," as in a thread or other flexible object stretched out, or as in the limbs of the body when fully extended. In this meaning, as a verb, it was perfectly ordinary and clearly in use throughout the colonial period, as indeed it is in modern Maya (Barrera Vásquez 1980, insert on 729; Bricker, Pó'ot Yah, and Dzul de Pó'ot 1998, 246). Furthermore, within the rich morphology of the language, the derived form *sin-il* is readily construable as meaning something like "(fully) extended, (full) extension." It is therefore relatively easy to read the collocation *tusinil* as "in its full extension," and the expression would have been transparent, if somewhat odd, to any native speaker in the sixteenth century.

What is distinctive about colonial missionary usage is that this otherwise ordinary gesture was linked to the crucifixion and Passion of Christ, which in turn points to the Resurrection, which was the sign of God's omnipotence over life and death.[22] This is not just any "full extension," but one linked first to the crucified body and then to its triumphal resurrection. The standard translations of the term "crucified" show the same pattern of usage: Christ was *sinan ti cruz* 'stretched out on (the) cross', a phrasing that recurs in both missionary works and the Books of Chilam Balam (see Miram and Miram 1988, Book of Kaua, 165, line 5; Book of Chumayel, 48, line 3). Moreover, for reasons that would take too long to spell out here, the full phrase *uchuc tumen tuzinil* is grammatically ill formed, or at least odd, and I have found nothing parallel to it in Maya sources. Nothing, that is, except minor variants of the phrase, any one of which could be replaced by "Dios omnipotente," *salva veritae*. In sum, we might say, stretched out + resurrected = Almighty.

I have spelled out the story of this little word in some detail because it illustrates a number of critical features of the discursive field in which *reducción* and *conversión* unfolded. First, the missionaries learned Maya very well, or they had excellent collaborators, or both. A similar subtlety of translation recurs throughout the corpus of their writings. Second, it is impossible to detect the presence of European elements in Maya language by looking only for borrowed terms. The missionary is present in the Maya itself. Third, the doctrinal works and the linguistic works can be understood only by reading them against one another. This does not mean that the grammars and dictionaries are descriptively inaccurate, or that the *doctrina* was written in gibberish intelligible only to a missionary. On the contrary, both classes of works are masterful, and we learn a great deal about the ordinary language of Maya speakers by studying them. But the Maya of the missionaries was a conversion from ordinary Maya, refracted through the lens of *reducción,* buttressed and overdetermined by the reordering of the social world in which the language was to circulate. Words that would be used to convert were themselves the product of this, the first conversion. Hence the making and use of *Maya reducido* was a "syncretic practice" in the sense developed by Hill and Hill (1986) and Hill (2001). Starting from the opposition between European languages and Maya, it involved creating and redefining Maya terms according to the meanings of their European counterparts. This redefinition involved suppressing the division between the languages and obscuring thereby the European history of the meanings. The resulting fusion of languages played on the kinds of bivalency and simultaneity described by Woolard (1998).

A similar logic applies to so-called Spanish borrowings, such as *missa, sacramento, christianoil,* and *beyntisyon*. In using these expressions in otherwise Maya discourse, the religious were producing a version of Maya in which selected Spanish elements were simply part of the vocabulary.[23] Many of them function as proper names, and their presence in Maya is neither accidental nor haphazard. It is the result of a decision not to translate. In the case of neologisms like the one discussed above, the semantics of the terms are indexed to Christian doctrine, and the expressions become specialized and indexically bonded to the religious frame in which they were first produced.

This new *lengua reducida* made its way into the deepest corners of the Indian communities—even, I will argue, those that were unsubjugated. The fact that the Books of Chilam Balam are saturated with cross-talk and evidence of the missionaries is surprising only if one assumes a hermetic boundary between the two sectors, Indio and Español. But the circulation of discourse over that boundary was robust and consequential. Over time, and across the main genres of colonial discourse, the doctrinal roots of *Maya reducido,* and the indexical grounding of many erstwhile native expressions in Catholic doctrine, would contribute to a process of semantic and grammatical reanalysis of Maya. It is this process that I refer to as the linguistic conversion, and the language through which it played out was what I call a translanguage.[24] It was neither European nor Maya in any simple sense but a language produced of the joining of two languages already turned toward one another, adapted to the task of producing the semantic universe of *conquista pacífica.*

A SHIFTING VOICE FOR INDIAN AUTHORS

It was in the mission towns and *repúblicas de indios* that the elaborate program of conversion was implemented.[25] The evangelization was undertaken through *convivencia* with the Indios, a "shared living" embodied in the placement of *conventos* in the centers of Indian towns. Just as the monastery building program created economically and politically important places, so too the lived spaces of church and monastery defined large fields of social engagement. Indios occupied an array of positions in the convents, including domestic help, labor in construction and groundskeeping, and a range of liaison posts through which the friars sought to extend their control. Indios, particularly the children of the elite, were the beginning and advancing students in the schools on monastic grounds, where obligatory *doctrina* was administered.

The high end of Indian participation in the mission were the *maestros cantores* 'choir masters', who oversaw a good deal of the indoctrination of children. In certain cases, privileged relations developed between individual missionaries and individual students, such as Gaspar Antonio Chi, the student and later collaborator of Fray Diego de Landa, the first Franciscan provincial. Indios in the pueblos who collaborated well with the friars and became their trusted helpers were described in church documents as *indios de confianza.* These were the people called upon to watch over chapels and churches and to work with the friars. At the low end of Indian engagement, Indios who confessed their faith were described as *almas de confesión* 'souls of confession', who would require periodic administration of the sacraments. Thus:

Maestros cantores	Literate, teachers, choir masters, with maximal access to the church
Indios de confianza	Provisorily trusted *indios reducidos* in the towns
Almas de confesión	*Indios reducidos*

Pueblos reducidos were governed by a *cabildo* 'town council', the form of governance imposed by the Spanish *reducción* and which defined the *república de indios* (Farriss 1984, 234). The Indian *cabildo* consisted of one *gobernador*, sometimes called *batab* 'chief'; one scribe; two *alcaldes;* four *regidores;* one *escribano;* plus a series of lesser positions. Adjunct to the *cabildo* was the group of local elders called *principales* (one *principal* for every fifty residents), who are frequently referred to in notarial documents as witnesses to the proceedings that the documents record.[26]

The interaction between this introduced form of government and the preexisting Maya forms is complex and has been studied by a variety of scholars, including Roys (1943, 1957), Farriss (1984), and Quezada (1992). For present purposes, what is most interesting about the *cabildo* is that it marks important points of contact between missions and local governments. The positions of *escribano* and *maestro cantor* were vital ones in the towns, and served as stepping-stones to even higher office. Their occupants were former students in the missionary schools. The *gobernador* was at least in principle responsible to the priest to assure the attendance of town members at Mass and *doctrina*. The *principales* were also enlisted by the missionaries. And clearly, engagement in the orderly functioning of *cabildo* and church was part of *policía cristiana*. These were the sites at which the *reducción* and *conversión* took place.

Different varieties of language corresponded to different spheres of everyday life in the Indian towns, in both missionary and nonmissionary contexts. Insofar as they interacted directly with the church, Maya speakers would have been exposed more or less systematically to the translanguage of missionary Maya. At the same time, they would have been exposed to varieties of Maya language spoken among native speakers in a wide range of contexts. Although there is no direct evidence of the ordinary Maya spoken at this time, there is ample evidence in the existing documents that the language varied significantly between the native histories of the Books of Chilam Balam, the incantations of the Ritual of the Bacabs, and the *cabildo* Maya of the notarial documents. There is every reason to believe that the missionary translanguage interacted with a repertoire of stylistically distinct Maya varieties typical of different discourse genres.

Contact with missionary education and genres produced a wide range of interlingual abilities on the part of Indian agents.[27] At the high end of language performance were what Spanish authors in Yucatán called *indios ladinos,* those rare individuals who mastered Spanish expression. The term *ladino* was used in

FIGURE 1. Reciprocal speakers: *lengua* and *ladino*

Yucatán to describe a very few highly educated Indios, such as Gaspar Antonio Chi, who could cross over the discourse boundary and speak Spanish with near-native ability—much as the *gran lengua* could cross over the inverse boundary from Spanish into Maya. Unlike the *lenguas, indios ladinos* are not described as a group. I use the term here to define the high end of a spectrum of language abilities, perhaps rarely achieved but nonetheless real as a conceptual and linguistic category. It indicates more than mere knowledge of Spanish, suggesting the adeptness and sophistication to use it like a Spaniard. Covarrubias (1995 [1611], 697) derives the term from *latino,* designating in Spain those individuals among the *"bárbaros"* who had learned the *"lengua romana."* These were taken to be *"discretos y hombres de mucha razón y cuenta, ... diestros y solertes en cualquier negocio"* 'discreet men of reason and account, ... adept and astute in any business'. From this perspective, *ladino* and *lengua* were reciprocal terms, each designating an interlingual ability but from inverse vantage points (fig. 1).[28]

But the two terms also had further entailments in which they differed decisively. The term *ladino* does not focus on the act of interpreting, the way *lengua* does, nor does it have the residual theological reference of *lengua*. To say that someone is *ladino* is to say he operates effectively in Spanish and is also astute. Given that most of the instruction provided by the missionaries was in Maya language, whether via interpreters or directly, for an Indio to acquire the ability of a *ladino* meant that he had gained a different kind of access to the Spanish world, with a hint of privilege and political effectiveness. Being foreign, the *ladino* did not have the same credibility with the Spanish enjoyed by the European *lengua*. As Sánchez de Aguilar (1996 [1639], 97) observed, *indios ladinos* were not universally appreciated by Spaniards. If the *lengua* was erudite and trustworthy, the *ladino* was slick and ambiguous.

In terms of linguistic ability, *lengua* was a matter of degree, there being many priests who were described as *medio lengua* 'half lengua', whereas *ladino* was more of a logical extreme, and no Indios were described as *"medio ladino,"* even though knowledge of Spanish was certainly gradient among Maya people. The different overtones of the expressions derive in large measure from the broader constructs to which they corresponded: the Spanish image of the Indios and the

TABLE 1 Partial Summary of Genres Produced by Maya Authors

NOTARIAL GENRES	FORBIDDEN GENRES
Carta, letter	Books of Chilam Balam (9 extant)
Deslinde, land survey	Ritual of the Bacabs
Título, land titles	
Acuerdo, accord	
Testamento, will	
Petición, petition	
Election records	

Spanish image of themselves. Neither expression occurs, to my knowledge, in any of the genres produced by Maya authors, and neither has any precise equivalent in Maya. The absence is noteworthy, since works by Indios display or overtly comment on the same interlingual abilities covered by the *lengua/ladino* dimension but use different terms.[29]

Most of the discourse production in the pueblos was in Maya and, when written, was transcribed in the Spanish-based orthography developed by the missionaries. But what kind of discourse and what kind of Maya? The kinds of works produced by native authors were distinct from those of the missionaries. To my knowledge, no Indian authors produced grammars, dictionaries, or other such metalinguistic instruments. What they did write was a substantial corpus of land surveys, accords, chronicles, letters, wills, petitions, and other records of local events, much of it from the pens of local scribes in the pueblos (table 1). Such documents were the required concomitants of the business of government. At least in the early years, the scribes were trained by the friars in the *escuelas* and *doctrina* sessions. Like the other *cabildo* representatives, they would be former students of the church.[30] Hence the path from school and church to local government and writing was one of the vectors along which *Maya reducido* moved into the spheres of pueblo life, wrapped in the mantle of *policía* 'civility'. When Indian authors wrote using the orthography and interlanguage of their missionary teachers, they appropriated some of the means of their own conversion. But if the aim was cultural autonomy, it was a dangerous game. To the extent that those means were shaped by Spaniards, the Indian authors were helping to achieve the Spanish aim of implanting their discourse within that of their native subjects.

To the obligatory bureaucratic genres must be added the forbidden native genres such as the Books of Chilam Balam and the Ritual of the Bacabs. Together these make up what is widely considered a native corpus, and there is broad agreement among Mayanists that at least parts of these texts derive from preconquest Maya discourse, probably transliterated from lost hieroglyphic tracts. From my perspective, what is most important is not that they speak a pure native voice, which they do not, but that they were forbidden, authored by, and directed to Indios. Whatever the status of this claim, there is ample evidence that the Maya appropriated Spanish-based writing for their own purposes. Within the bureaucratic corpus this is already evident, but it is flagrant in the case of the so-called native genres. Group readings of these texts were explicitly forbidden, under pain of considerable punishment, and yet clearly the Books of Chilam Balam continued to be recopied and to grow in content. These texts display the ongoing use of Spanish-based writing as a means of reproducing an explicitly and self-consciously Maya perspective. This ideological framing of the texts is in sharp contrast, however, to the ample evidence that what they voice in many passages is the translanguage of *Maya reducido,* the product of missionary authors and their native collaborators.

Just as the missionary grammars and *doctrinas* formed part of a single discourse, the notarial documents produced in the *pueblos reducidos* and the so-called native genres also form a single discourse, with many intertextual ties. There is a relationship between the two pairs in terms of the positions they occupy in the overall field: the *doctrina* (maximally obligatory) and the native genres (maximally forbidden) are in a sense opposites, each embodying a rhetoric of sociocultural identity, defined partly in opposition to the other. The metalinguistic works of the missionaries and the notarial documents of the native elites form the midrange, where the practical tasks of translation and governance were at stake. This corresponds to a significant parallel between the positions of the key agents in their respective sectors of the field: among Europeans, it was the missionaries who had access to, claimed knowledge of, and interpreted the Maya. Among the Maya, it was the educated elites who had access to, claimed knowledge of, and interpreted the world of Spanish and Catholicism. It is unsurprising that the two groups collaborated, since their positions were mutually dependent and in many contexts reciprocal (as in the case of the *lengua-ladino* reciprocity). The collaboration of the native elites was what made it possible for missionaries to become *lengua* (in the broad sense of knowing the language and the world it stood for). Conversely, the training and legitimization conferred on Indian collaborators by the missionaries brought with it access to writing, public office, and the privileges of monastic support.

Even as we recognize the homologies and reciprocities of these social groups and the discourses they produced, we must bear in mind that the relations between them were deeply ambivalent and always asymmetric. The friars brought the *doctrina* into the Indian republics in order to convert them. There was no such effort on the part of the Maya elites to convert the missionaries, and the native genres were hidden, not thrust forth as tools in a counterevangelization. Apart from sporadic acts of violence, there was no reciprocal effort on the part of the Maya to punish missionaries or destroy their paraphernalia. In the logic of *reducción,* the missionary goals were multiply overdetermined, as we have seen, whereas no such self-reinforcing campaign was launched by Maya groups.

These several facts become fully consequent not because they sever the bonds of reciprocity and homology, reducing the relation of missionary to Indio to simple domination. Rather, they combine with those bonds, blending collaboration with domination in a volatile and sometimes baleful mix. The unstable combination of love, hate, respect, and contempt that marks missionary writings about the Indios, and vice versa, is not reducible to simple domination or resistance.[31] The discourse processes that mediated the ongoing *reducción* make sense and take effect only because of the way they articulated with the intercultural field of the colony. The dynamic ambiguity of the one finds its reflex in the equally dynamic ambivalence of the other.

Looking across written genres authored by native Maya speakers, one can see a variety of links between erstwhile native Maya, notarial Maya, missionary Maya, and Spanish discourse. These intertextual links, and their embedding in Indio discourse, provide compelling evidence of how Maya discursive practices articulated with the broader ecclesiastical and institutional field of the colony. More important, they illustrate the degree to which the Spanish and the Indio make up a single field, despite the jural, administrative, and spatial separation of the *repúblicas de indios* and the *repúblicas de españoles* 'Spanish republics'.[32] Linguistic and discursive elements moved between the far extremes of the field by way of the *lenguas*, the *ladinos*, the missionary teachers and indigenous collaborators, the scribes and other elites in the *cabildo*, and even the insubordinate Indios who sought to refuse Spanish ways, or co-opt them for their own purposes. Genres that were strictly colonial provided the means of creating texts in which many Indians saw their own interests furthered. In the act of pursuing their interests, though, they participated in their own conversion. Just as the missionary *lengua* courted subversion by transposing *doctrina* into Maya, the *indio ladino* and Indian elites more generally ran the risk of undercutting themselves even as they sought to defend their own interests.

In both cases, I think, the irony is that successful acts achieved unwanted effects, in some cases the exact opposite of wanted effects. It would be wrong to think of this as merely a flaw in the execution of the act—as if a missionary translator could have avoided the vulnerability to subversion if only he could have gotten the translation just right, or as if the *indio batab* 'chief' who enlisted support for a project could have avoided being co-opted if only he had been as adept as a *ladino*. The ironies of intercultural communication in a situation like colonial Yucatán are not reducible to mistakes. They are intrinsic to the structure of the field, in which discourse agents are systematically Janus-faced, and their works systematically ambiguous. Theirs was discourse in the breach between sectors of the colony that were linguistically, culturally, socially, and legally distinct.

Quite apart from what anyone believed or intended, the discursive field, with its translanguage and interlocking positions, provided the pathways along which the basic conversion could proceed. That conversion lay in the habituation to new practices and modes of self-construction, embedded in the colonial field. It was from the combination of *reducción, policía cristiana,* and the linguistic practices they entailed that colonial Maya emerged, and it is there that we must look for the nature and consequences of conquest.

PART I

The Scope of *Reducción*

2

Perpetual *Reducción*
in a Land of Frontiers

The Maya were highly organized before the arrival of the Spanish—especially prior to but also after the demise of the Mayapán confederacy in the mid-thirteenth century. Given the accumulated experience of the Spanish and the missionaries in New Spain and elsewhere and given what they found in Yucatán, there is no question that they recognized that the Maya were already living in a complex society. There was a single language across the peninsula, a dense expanse of Maya "towns," clear status distinctions among social groups, and rule of law, not to mention the tangible if diabolical achievements of the temples and monumental building programs. Perhaps most important for our purposes, the missionaries knew these things. Landa, Lizana, and Cogolludo all discuss Maya history or society, and the *probanzas* 'certification' made by indigenous elites to defend their privileges are replete with information about Maya history. Whether or not they saw the Maya accurately, their starting point was not a tabula rasa but an already developed order.[1]

But the kind of order that interested the Spaniards was different, and it required both simplification and recasting of the indigenous political geography. This chapter spells out the main lines of spatial transformation entailed by the *reducción*. To be *reducido* was above all to live in a stable place, in which things were done in their proper settings and people behaved in ways appropriate to those settings. The concept of propriety here derives from *policía*, itself derived linguistically from *polis* 'town'. Thus it is unsurprising that the order imposed by *reducción* revolved around the *pueblo* 'town' (see here what Farriss [1984, 160 ff.] calls the "urban bias" of the Spanish).[2]

We begin with a brief sketch of the political geography of Yucatán at the Spanish arrival.

NOTES ON THE POLITICAL GEOGRAPHY
OF POST-MAYAPÁN YUCATÁN

The pre-Columbian Maya were literate and sophisticated in mathematics, astronomy, calendrics, monumental architecture, arts, and crafts. They were engaged in long-distance trade networks linking them to the rest of Mesoamerica. They were urban and urbane long before the Spanish made their appearance. To properly contextualize the social world into which *reducción* inserted itself would require a separate monograph or more. There is a rapidly growing literature on Post-Classic Mayan history, which in Yucatán begins with the fall of Chichén Itzá and the emergence of Mayapán as a major capital around 1200 C.E.[3] Here I want only to highlight a few features of Maya society that were relevant to the formation of the colony in the sixteenth century.

When Cortés made landfall on the northern Caribbean coast of Yucatán in 1519, the Maya he encountered were speakers of the language now known as Yucatec Maya. They were residents of semi-independent territories called *cuchcabal* 'territory, jurisdiction'.[4] Looking across the peninsula from the Caribbean to the Gulf of Mexico and south to about present-day Chetumal, there were approximately sixteen such geopolitical units. They varied in size, regional significance, and degree of organization, but they all consisted of a central town plus a variable number of smaller dependencies. Among the central places were Maní, Izamal, and T'ho (Mérida), which were already important urban centers that would be transformed in the *reducción* under the Spanish. Other places either grew or, more often, withered under colonial rule (Cook and Borah 1972, 55–75).

In the previous century, Yucatán had witnessed the breakup of the Mayapán confederacy. This occurred around 1441 and was followed by about seventy years of turmoil, including waves of pestilence and civil wars, followed by the arrival of the Spanish, their diseases, and the havoc that ensued. Mayapán proper was a defensively walled city about sixty miles west of Chichén Itzá. Measuring three by two kilometers, it had a population of approximately fifteen thousand within the walls and an extensive population outside the walls to the east, west, and south. For two and a half centuries, Mayapán was the main ruling center of Yucatán. Having displaced Chichén Itzá in about 1200 C.E., it was itself sacked and mostly abandoned around 1441. It was the last major Maya center before the coming of the Spanish, and its emergence defines the onset of Post-Classic Yucatán (Sharer 2005, 592). Landa, Lizana, and Cogolludo are among the early authors who comment on Mayapán, and it figures prominently in the Books of Chilam Balam. This is indicative of the salience of Post-Classic history in the colonial discourse. Even those Spaniards who belittled the Maya in certain contexts were well aware that they had a long and complicated history. Most of the leading missionary

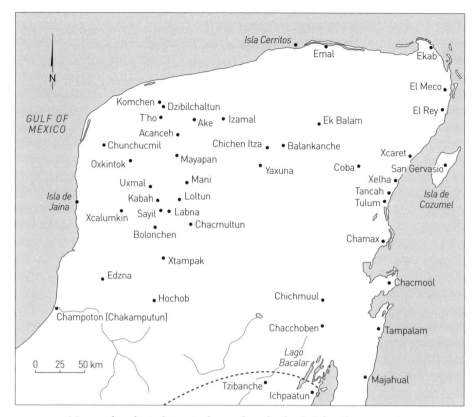

MAP 2. Maya archaeological sites in the northern lowlands (after Sharer 2006)

authors delved into the history, both as a way to display their own expertise and as a way to better understand the challenge they faced.

There is today a growing body of archaeological, faunal, and artifactual evidence that Mayapán was exceedingly densely populated. The intramural space was occupied by some four thousand structures, including the monumental central area. The center was defined by a roughly rectangular plaza surrounded on all four sides by temples, of which the largest was the nine-tiered *castillo* on the south face, modeled on the *castillo* at Chichén Itzá (Sharer 2006, 594 ff.). Among the remains found within the walls are a great quantity of marine shells, obsidian from Ixtepeque (in the southern highlands, some 700 km as the crow flies), and abundant traces of turkey, dog, and deer, apparently consumed as young adults (Masson, Peraza Lope, and Hare 2002). There are many internal walls, some of which appear to mark the boundaries of compounds and single homesteads and others of which evidently define enclosures or alleys (Masson, Peraza Lope, and Hare 2002). Masson and colleagues (2002) note a sharp difference between the faunal remains within the walls, especially the monumental center where dog, white-tailed deer, and turkey dominate, and remains outside the walls, where these animals are very scarce. That faunal remains comprise mostly young adults suggests the animals were raised rather than procured by hunting. The cumulative implication is that the people within the walls were elite, specialized in certain crafts, producers and consumers of meat, and engaged in trade relations with the coast and other parts of Mesoamerica.

The extreme density of social life in Mayapán is a powerful reminder that Maya people had ample precedent for congregated living in urban centers at the heart of which were monumental buildings where ritual offerings were conducted. The nucleation entailed in the Spanish policies of *congregación* and *reducción* was nothing new to the Maya. Moreover, the Maya priests who would have officiated ceremonies in the central area were in all likelihood among the small proportion of people who were literate. Through iconography, codices, and inscriptions, elite centers such as Mayapán were also centers of discourse production, in which priests played a key role in writing and maintaining books. All these patterns would be reproduced, in altered form, under the colonial *reducción*.

Mayapán was governed by what is called *multepal* 'group rule' in the Books of Chilam Balam. The idea is that there were representatives of numerous leading lineages residing within the walls who spoke for or embodied different regions of the peninsula. There is debate in the literature regarding the precise list of lineages represented in the *multepal,* with Sharer (2006, 598) citing the Books of Chilam Balam as evidence that they included the Chel and the Cocom, both of whom were also present at Chichén Itzá; the Xiu, who probably descended from lords at Uxmal; and the Canul, who were evidently warriors brought to Mayapán from the gulf coast of Tabasco to enforce the will of the Cocom. Quezada (1993, 30) suggests a longer list with representatives of nine lineages, including the ones just mentioned, and Quezada and Okoshi (2001) provide fine-grained analysis and a wealth of documents pertaining to the Xiu lineage around Maní. In either case, the participating lineage leaders formed a sort of joint rule in which the Cocom appear to have been dominant, particularly after 1283 when Mayapán became a major commercial center, exporting salt, rare clay used in making "Maya blue" pigment, cotton, honey, and pottery. The Cocom and the Xiu were enemies from this time forward, as the Spanish would later learn. At the turn of the fifteenth century, the Cocom expelled the Xiu from Mayapán, and in 1441 it was the Xiu who in turn staged the overthrow of the Cocom, the killing of all but a single member of the lineage, and the sacking of the city. With the city destroyed, the remaining inhabitants separated. The Chel moved nearby to the town of Tecoh, where the Franciscans would later establish a parish. The Cocom reestablished themselves in Sotuta. The Xiu went south to Maní.

It was this state of affairs that the Spanish stepped into. The Xiu were among their first allies, and Landa's main informant, Gaspar Antonio Xiu, was of this lineage. Maní, their capital, would become an early *cabecera de guardianía* 'head town of parish' in which a convent was built. The Pech, the ruling lineage in the "province" of Ceh Pech, also became early allies of the Spanish. The Cocom remained implacable enemies of both the Spanish and the Xiu. In 1536 Xiu leaders went from Maní to Chichén Itzá on pilgrimage, for which they had to traverse Cocom territory. Granted safe passage by the Cocom, they were instead ambushed and massacred by them. Against this backdrop of interregional conflict and vendettas, the Spanish faced a mixture of allies and enemies. Even though they all spoke the same language, there was never a single Maya voice that could represent the interests of all Maya people on the peninsula. Had the Spanish encountered Mayapán at its peak of power, the military resistance would have been more coordinated, but the centralization may have made the conquest easier. As it was, the armed resistance to Spanish conquest persisted until the official military subjugation in 1547, about twenty-eight years after first contact. As is well known, Maya groups in the southern peninsula and south to the Petén held out quite effectively for another century and a half.

According to Roys, the sixteen *cuchcabalob* 'provinces' fell under three broad types of territorial organization in Yucatán at the time of the Spanish conquest: (1) highly organized areas under the rule of a single individual, (2) those lacking a single ruler but where the leading families in individual towns tended to come from the same patriline, and (3) loosely affiliated areas that Roys hesitates to call organizational units at all. Territories of the first kind included Maní, Sotuta, Ceh Pech, Hocabá, Cochuah, Champotón, Cozumel, and possibly Ah Kin Chel (Roys 1943, 59).[5] These account for many, although not all, of the Maya language documents that have survived from the sixteenth century—in particular, the Chilam Balam of Chumayel (Maní), the Yaxkukul Chronicle (Ceh Pech), the letters to the Crown (Maní, Ceh Pech, Ah Kin Chel, Champotón), and the papers of the Xiu of Yaxhá (Quezada and Okoshi 2001).

Farriss (1984, 148 ff.) argues that the three-way typology proposed by Roys distorts what was in all likelihood a more fluid situation, in which "a continuum of finer gradations between centralized rule and casual, temporary aggregations" was typical. In any case, she observes that provinces (even the most loosely affiliated) were united by ties "for the most part hierarchical in nature, with a rank ordering of towns at the subprovincial level," and demarcated by boundaries.

The most highly organized provinces (including Roys's first type) were ruled by an individual who bore the title *halach uinic* 'True Man'. Citing Landa's *Relación*, Roys states that the office of the *halach uinic* was accessible only to individuals of

MAP 3. Maya provinces of Yucatán at time of contact (after Roys 1957)

a certain family, passing from father to son (or temporarily to younger brother until the son came of age; cf. Quezada 1993, 19–59; Okoshi 2006b). In at least some cases, the *halach uinic* evidently had judicial, military, political, and religious functions that included ruling the capital town of his territory, formulating foreign (probably interterritorial) policy, and serving as the superior judge, governor, provincial, or inspector of religious order. Farriss (1984, 148) maintains that different *halach uinics* exercised different degrees of control over their territories, a fact of obvious significance to the contextual semantics of the terms referring to rulers. It is unclear from the sources consulted here whether the *halach uinic* had anything resembling a territorial council from which he received advice, although it is reasonable to assume that he was advised on at least certain matters from the local level. In view of the well-known bellicose relations among certain "provinces" (such as Maní and Sotuta), it is reasonable to assume that frontier towns would have been loci of dispute on which the *halach uinic* would have received local intelligence and advice. In any case, the *halach uinic* was evidently assisted by a *hol pop* 'head of the mat', with a *nacom* 'war chief' in charge of coordinating military activities. The latter was in turn assisted by an unspecified number of *hol can* 'warriors' (lit. 'head of sky' or 'head of serpent').

The sources of income of the *halach uinic* included (1) the agricultural produce produced by his own slaves, (2) gifts presented by litigants in the court in which he presided, and (3) tribute from the towns over which he had control (including maize, beans, chile, honey, cloth, game, and, where appropriate, salt, fish, and slaves) (Roys 1943, 61). One of the functions of the *halach uinic* was to appoint chiefs at the level of the towns over which he ruled. These local chiefs, who carried out the policies of the *halach uinic*, bore the title *batab* and likely served as advisors to the territorial ruler. There appears to have been significant regional variation in the authority of these town-level chiefs. Roys suggests that the *batabil* 'chiefship' was also hereditary in the patriline, but he also notes cases in which it was not. In areas lacking a *halach uinic*, the *batab* gained office according to rules of accession by patrilineal descent and evidently served as the ultimate individual authority in matters military, judicial, and administrative. *Batabs* presided over town councils whose collective decisions could limit their actions. The main members of these councils were *ah cuch cab* 'counselors' (lit. 'earth bearers'), acting as ward representatives, and *ah kulels* 'deputies' (or assistants) beneath them.

The sources of income for *batabs* varied as did their authority. According to Roys (1943, 62), in territories headed by a *halach uinic*, the *batab* did not receive tribute, although town residents supplied him with agricultural and domestic labor, and litigants offered him gifts in his capacity as local magistrate. In other cases (including Sihunchén [northern Ah Canul] and the Cupul area), considerable tribute was extracted. Like the *halach uinics*, *batabs* appear to have been the objects of honorific address and treatment by their subject populace. Both *halach uinics* and *batabs* belonged to what Farriss (1984, 234) has called the "first-tier elite" in pre-Hispanic and early colonial political organization. Beneath them were the "second-tier" authorities, which included the *ah cuch cabs*, the *ah kulels*, and possibly the *ah kin* 'high priest' and *ah cambesah* 'chief teacher'. In a less official capacity, local elders and notables, called *nohxib* 'great men' or *nucteil* 'great trees' in Maya and *principales* in Spanish, wielded influence and were collectively consulted by the *batab*.

Elements of this system would persist well into the colonial period—especially the *batabil* and some of the minor town-level functions. The documents of Sahcabchén are signed by *batabs* as late as the 1670s. Moreover, the Sahcabchén documents indicate that *batabs* in some cases had authority over as few as ten families—that is, that the structure was numerically flexible.

LÓPEZ MEDEL AND THE SPIRIT OF THE LAWS

The *reducción* was to alter the kinds of political and economic relations both within and between Maya towns. The town units themselves were consolidated, resulting in a decrease in number, from what Farriss (1984, 162) estimates to be 400 or more Maya towns in 1549 to a total of only 177 in 1582.[6] In the process, many places that had been separate towns in the past were joined together as the *parcialidades* 'subdivisions' of a single one. In many cases, this meant uprooting a local population and moving it into a central place, leaving behind an abandoned town. The relocations were backed by force and legitimated by the 1552 *Ordenanzas* of López Medel. According to reports by some *encomenderos* in the *Relaciones de Yucatán*, the Spanish went on to destroy the abandoned towns and orchards in order to discourage Indios from fleeing the newly formed *pueblos reducidos*. Writing in February 1579, Giraldo Díaz Alpuche, *encomendero* of Dzonot in the jurisdiction of Mérida, described the process like this:

> *Dicen también estos indios viejos que fue mucha parte, para morirse tanta gente, despoblarse los pueblos donde estaban poblados en sus asientos viejos para allegarlos cerca de los monasterios, y que el instrumento de despoblarlos fue un Tomás López, Oidor de Su Majestad, . . . [quien] mandó despoblar los dichos pueblos para allegarlos junto a los monasterios como tengo dicho, y los pueblos que no querían despoblarse de sus asientos les mandaba poner fuego a las casas.*
> (Relaciones de Yucatán 1983, 2:85–86)

> These old Indios also say that many left, for there having died so many people, to abandon the towns where they lived in their old residences, in order to bring them in around the monasteries, and that the instrument to depopulate them was one Tomás López, Auditor of His Majesty, . . . [who] ordered that the said towns be abandoned to bring them in around the monasteries as I've said, and those towns that did not want to abandon their homes, he ordered the houses to be burned.

Díaz Alpuche goes on to say that the Franciscans were left in charge of enforcing the relocations, that they did in fact leave a trail of devastation behind them, and that many Indios died as a result. He attributes the deaths to the forced movement, as well as to the great sorrow the Indios felt at leaving their homes behind. Himself a *conquistador* who had been in Yucatán for forty years at this point, Díaz Alpuche states that for every ten Indios at the time of the conquest, eight or more had by now perished. As Patch (1993, 26) has pointed out, the concentration of people under *reducción* almost surely exacerbated the disease contagion. It is noteworthy that Díaz Alpuche does not mention illness as a cause of depopulation, evidently preferring to place the burden on the Franciscan enforcement of López Medel's *Ordenanzas*. This anti-Franciscan posture is of course what we would expect of Díaz Alpuche, an *encomendero* whose interests lay in weakening monastic power over the Indios. (The constant tension between the Franciscan missionaries and the *encomenderos* is well known in the historical literature and amply reflected in the documents of the period.) In an ironic twist of the typically laudatory use of *"policía"* by Spanish authors, he notes that it was exactly the enforced *policía* of the missionaries that gave the Indios broken hearts and led them to die, for lack of the will to live (*Relaciones de Yucatán* 1983, 2:85).

In 1552 Yucatán fell within the jurisdiction of Guatemala, and the *oidor* Tomás López Medel was sent there to make a *visita,* to set tribute levels and establish a basic template for the governance of the province. López Medel's *Ordenanzas* were directed specifically at the organization, behavior, and governance of the *repúblicas de indios,* and they say little directly about the analogous aspects of the Spanish sector of the population, or about the *encomenderos.* According to both Landa (Rivera ed. 1985, 69) and Cogolludo (1971 [1688], 1:390), López Medel was sent to Yucatán at the insistence of the missionary friars, to establish order so that the spiritual conversion could proceed. The Franciscans in Yucatán had sent a representative to Guatemala to seek remedy from the excesses and calumnies of the *encomenderos,* so they said, and López Medel's *visita* and *Ordenanzas* were that remedy. Cogolludo introduces his discussion of the process with the heading *"Fué necesario hacer leyes con autoridad real, para evitar en los indios algunos ritos de su gentilidad"* 'It was necessary to make laws with royal authority in order to avoid among the Indios certain of their gentile rites'. From the Franciscan perspective, it is surely true that such laws were necessary for the purging of idolatry and the conversion of the Indios into Catholics. But there is more to López Medel than the missionization, and his laws go far beyond the realm of "gentile rites," about which they say relatively little.

As will become clear, the *Ordenanzas* did contribute greatly to the *reducción,* and so to the evangelization. But the perspective of Landa and Cogolludo is weighted toward the Franciscan order, to which both belonged, and leaves out critical aspects of the context in which López Medel was writing. That context includes the passing of the New Laws in 1542, their subsequent modification in 1549, and the widespread difficulty encountered by the Spanish in trying to implement them. These difficulties were especially acute in Yucatán, because of its relatively peripheral and isolated status compared to Guatemala and New Spain. López Medel was one of a group of *visitadores* 'inspectors' selected by the Council of the Indies to execute the laws in the Audiencia of Guatemala (Pereña et al. 1992, 11). On January 9, 1552, López Medel was issued a series of Royal Provisions giving him sweeping powers, to reside in and personally inspect Yucatán, Cozumel, and Tabasco; to distribute lands; to set up and select members of local governments; and to regulate the actions of Indios and Spaniards alike. During his residence, his authority was to supersede all others and was backed by the punishments spelled out in the New Laws for all who would resist. These were read aloud on June 13, 1552, by the scribe in the *cabildo* of Mérida, whose members dutifully acquiesced, kissing the document and placing it upon their heads as a sign (Rubio Mañé 1942, 115–42).

Among the royal instructions to López Medel were ones instructing him explicitly to enforce the tribute assessment clause of the New Laws and to set the amounts and kinds of tribute to be assessed in a large area, including Yucatán. He was also to terminate the practice of extracting personal service by Indios to *encomenderos,* replacing it with appropriately defined levels of tribute (document reproduced in Ares Queija 1993, 581–84), to be paid in cash according to the 1549 royal *cédula.*[7] By February 5, 1552, he had issued tribute levels for the town of Motul, which fell within the *encomienda* of Francisco de Bracamonte, himself a member of the Mérida *cabildo.* López Medel's jurisdiction extended from Santiago de los Caballeros to Mérida and included Yucatán, Campeche, Petén, Tabasco, Chiapas, Verapaz, and Huehuetenango (Pérez-Prendes et al. 1992). Hence while his instructions contained clauses regarding the establishment of proper order for the missionization and his activities in Yucatán were pivotal to the *reducción,* these things were embedded in a much broader frame.

In his writings, López Medel, like others, took a critical stance regarding the New Laws, arguing forcefully *against* their immediate application, in favor, for instance, of a gradual phasing out of slavery instead of immediate abolition (Pérez-Prendes 1992). He justified this plan on the grounds that Indios needed guidance, supervision, and a means of gainful employment. In the process of spelling out his elaborate view of the Indios, he affirmed the justness of their subordination and sought to defend the rights of the *encomenderos,* with certain exceptions. Significantly, López Medel traced much of the disorder and destitution of the area to the fact that worthy Spaniards were leaving in droves, because of the chaos and the strictures placed on them by Crown laws. The flight of the Spanish, as he saw it, left the New World in the hands of the least capable and deprived the area of the impetus and competence it needed to develop into a productive and orderly society. If good Spaniards were overly burdened, he judged, then they would simply leave. Hence for him the twin goals of stabilizing the Spanish residents and reforming the Indios were of a piece: both presupposed the subjugation of the Indio, and both were needed for the advancement of society. Among his many writings, it is the 1552 *Ordenanzas* that are the most often cited in historical works treating Yucatán. These ordinances are addressed to Indian leaders and communities and are entirely centered on order in Indian towns.[8]

In his preamble to the *Ordenanzas,* López Medel indicates the special necessity of such laws for the region in question. He says, *"En esta dicha provincia se vé mas claro esta necessidad, por ser los naturales de ella tan fuera de conservacion é traza, é órden de vivir"* 'In this said province one sees most clearly this necessity, for its natives are so outside of conservation and plan and orderly living' (Cogolludo 1971 [1688], 1:391).[9] The three reasons he states echo the dimensions of *reducción: conservacion* 'maintenance' of order; *traza* 'plan' (in both senses of blueprint, as drawing and the conceptual schema it portrays); and *órden de vivir,* a virtual gloss of *policía.*

In accord with his judgment that the Indios needed the guidance and protection of their Spanish colonizers, including the missionaries, López Medel proposed a broad-based vision of how the Indian republics should function. In subsequent chapters, I examine in detail the behavioral and linguistic dimensions of his vision and how it was amplified by the spiritual *reducción.* For now, it is enough to say that, like the missionaries, like the *encomenderos* (see Acuña 1982, 2:85), and like the Crown itself, López Medel considered *"policía y orden de vivir"* as a precondition for the spiritual and temporal well-being of the Indios. To live in *policía,* they had to reside and circulate within properly laid out spaces. This included everything from the proper treatment of the individual body to residence, the definition of the town, and conditions on travel between towns (see plate 1).

López Medel's concern with Spanish flight is echoed in a theme that runs through the entire length of his *Ordenanzas,* namely, the idea that people, objects, and events belong in their proper places. Reading his text, one senses that all forms of motion were dangerous, whether the movement of Spaniards out of Yucatán, the circulation of Indios (leaders or commoners) outside their towns (Cogolludo 1971 [1688], 1:391–92), the traversings of Indian hunters in the forest (1:403), the hiding of Indios from the missionaries (1:396), the voluntary relocations of Indios from their "natural" towns to others (1:392), or the scattering of Indian houses in the forest (1:392). The very first *ordenanza* states:

> Primeramente, que todos los caciques y gobernadores, principales y alguaciles . . . residan y estén en sus propios pueblos. . . . No se ausenten de ellos con largas ausencias.
> (Cogolludo 1971 [1688], 1:391)

> First, let all the chiefs and governors, notable men and councillors . . . reside and remain in their own towns. . . . They are not to remove themselves for long absences.

López Medel goes on to clarify that a *larga ausencia* is any period longer than forty days but that for shorter periods, of about eight days, the Indian leaders were free to be away from home. Commoners are placed under analogous strictures and forbidden to be absent from their hometowns for more than thirty to forty days maximum, for any reason (Cogolludo 1971 [1688], 1:394).

López Medel's care to quantify the duration of absences from the hometown is part of a broader rhetoric of proper proportion that he states in terms of numbers.

At the outset of the second ordinance, he observes that there is a proliferation of Indian leaders and that *"la muchedumbre causa confusion y discordia"* 'multitude causes confusion and discord'. This then justifies the rule that there shall be one and only one *principal* 'respected elder' to work with the cacique for towns with fifty or fewer residents *(vecinos),* two for those between 50 and 100, three for 101 to 150, and so forth, up to a maximum of six *principales* for towns whose population exceeds 400 *vecinos* (Cogolludo 1971 [1688], 1:392). Similarly, every town is to have one and only one church (1:394) and one and only one market (1:402). An Indian man is to have one and only one wife (1:397), with whom he is to reside in a separate house. All bows and arrows held by men of the town are to be confiscated and burned, but "two or three dozen" sets are to be maintained in the house of the cacique, in case of emergency (1:403). Indios are to cease throwing parties for more than a dozen people (1:401). López Medel's insistence on enumerating people and things is echoed in his enumerations of tribute levels, which he rendered in Mérida, on December 28, 1552, in partial fulfillment of his instructions from the Crown (see López Medel, in Ares Queija 1993, 584–85).

Another broad theme that runs the length of the *Ordenanzas* is what we might call the surveillance of the public. A variety of collective activities evidently practiced by Indios are to be henceforth prohibited. As López Medel puts it:

> *No menos sospechosas, y ocasionadas á males y delitos, y otras liviandades son las juntas, que los caciques y principales de esta dicha provincia, cada cual en su pueblo acostumbran hacer, donde ociosamente traban pláticas indebidas.*
> (Cogolludo 1971 [1688], 1:393)

> No less suspicious, and occasioned by evil and transgression, and other improprieties, are the meetings that the chiefs and notables of this said province, each in his own turn, are accustomed to holding, where they lazily engage in improper discourse.

Nocturnal meetings were strictly banned, to be effectively replaced by the daytime meetings of the *cabildo,* presided over by the same caciques, *gobernadores,* and *principales* but with the priest(s) in attendance.[10] There are three factors involved here: the proper place and time for collective discussion, the proper forms of that discussion, and the surveillance of which the priestly presence is a metonym. That same desire to surveil is behind the frequent references to secret activities of the Indios, all of which are prohibited. Hence the meetings referred to just above were understood by López Medel in the context that *"[algunos caciques y principales] . . . hacen juntas y llamamientos á los naturales en lugares apartados y escondidos por señas y coyóles* [sic], *que les envian"* '[some chiefs and notables] . . . hold meetings and assemblies of natives in out-of-the-way and hidden places by signals and messengers they send them' (Cogolludo 1971 [1688], 1:393).[11] This observation nicely joins the themes of improper placement of meetings with secrecy, the one going hand in hand with the other. It also implies the mediation of native go-betweens, equally outside of surveillance and probably circulating at night, or in any case unnoticed. Alongside these were the Indios who hid their children to prevent them from being baptized (1:396) and the ones who clandestinely got married without proper examination by the priest (1:397), both behaviors to be prevented. Just as mobility was to be replaced by proper placement, then, and excessive numbers were to be made proportional, so too all forms of secrecy were dangerous and to be replaced by publicly witnessable events.

López Medel envisioned various forms of public spectacle. For those who secretly married more than once, the punishment was to be severe and meted out in public (the perpetrator being branded with the number "4" on his or her forehead and dispossessed of half of his or her goods) (1:397). In a more positive sense of spectacle, each town was to maintain one cross with proper vestment, which an appointed Indio was to carry before all the people of the *congregación,* with them following him or her to and from *doctrina* classes, in a public procession (1:395). The examinations of consanguine and affinal relations that were to precede marriage were to be done in public, and López Medel mentions explicitly that anyone who failed to speak in public, thereby bearing false witness, would be whipped (1:397).

In these various usages, we see a range of ideas associated with "publicness." First, for an event to be public, it had to be accessible to, and usually directly witnessable by, the collective residents of the town. The strategic display of veneration in missionary processions and theatrics was a means of convincing the collectivity of the Christian message. The punishment carried out in public was that much more humiliating than the one carried out away from the public eye. The prenuptial examination of the couple was a public event in which silence, failure to speak the truth when called upon, was deception. If forbidden activities were dark, disorderly, and hidden, activities proper to *policía* were done by day, in the open light of common knowledge and colonial surveillance, in order to foster order in the town. In this world, the opposite of the "public" is not the "private," a concept absent from López Medel's view of Indio life, but rather the "hidden, clandestine."

López Medel's idea of the public as a sphere of common knowledge extended to the general display of the *Ordenanzas* themselves. Albeit in simplified form, the *Ordenanzas* were to be announced in the center of all towns, so that Indios and local Spaniards alike would know the rules to which they were accountable. Similarly, when tribute levels were appropriately set, the Indios were to be clearly informed of them by their caciques, who were also responsible for collecting the tribute and delivering it to the *encomendero.* In letters written to the Crown in 1550 and 1551, López Medel advised the Crown to order the printing and posting of the Ten Commandments, the sacraments, and other Christian things, as well as the rules of daily conduct in all towns.[12] In both written and oral modes, publication would simultaneously inform people of the state of the laws and constitute them as a receiving public.

The individuals addressed in public examinations or proclamations were socially "interpellated." They were called out and engaged in a collective, collectively witnessed action, in which they occupied specific positions requiring certain ways of acting. Thus the ones examined under pain of punishment, the ones informed of the publicly proclaimed law and thereby made "knowingly" subject to it, and the ones forcibly congregated were all drawn forcibly into the field of *reducción*. In this process, the center of the town and the church would have a privileged role. It was there that written postings would be placed, doctrinal schools would be conducted, and the congregation would gather in procession.

Although López Medel explicitly mentions the *traza* 'plan' as something lacking among Indios, and he clearly had a strong model in mind, still he does not actually spell out the spatial or political organization of the *pueblos reducidos*. There are no street plans or other diagrams, although such devices were widely used at the time. What can be established on the basis of the *Ordenanzas* is that the newly created town was to have the following elements. First, a church was to be built of stone and maintained clean and locked, free of animals and loiterers. Second, doctrinal schools were to be built according to the dictates of the missionaries, and *vecinos* were to build stone houses in the center, each in an allotted place. Third, a hospital was to be built, where the sick would be cared for, and a hostel where travelers could stay temporarily. A large cross with appropriate vestment was to be erected and carried in public processions. A single market was to replace all other forms of scattered or itinerant commerce. There should be a repository for the storage of surplus grains, for provisioning during times of drought. There were to be no agricultural fields within the town, or a cemetery, or extensive stands of trees, all of which would henceforth be kept outside the town. The town was therefore a bounded, richly ordered space in which activities, interactions, and discourse production were to occur in their proper places.

López Medel does not draw out the quadrilateral street plan and central plaza, so well known from the *reducciones* throughout Spanish America. Yet he clearly has this in mind, and the concentration of activities in rectilinear central spaces is consistent with it. Of course, the well-known *reducción* plans did not actually correspond to Spanish towns, a fact pointed out by Foster (1960) and further evident in Kagan (1989). Rather, what we have here is an ideal template to which people would be gradually brought. When the *Ordenanzas* stipulate that Indios were to remain in their towns and that activities were to be conducted in specific places and times, it is to this ideal template that they refer.

It is of course impossible to know precisely the degree to which López Medel's plan was implemented. Here as elsewhere in the historical records, it is hard to relate policies and plans to patterns of action and actuality. Still, there is reason to think that both the *Ordenanzas* and the *doctrina* were applied with quite dramatic effect. This is so partly because of the way these things fit into a series of other events. In 1562 the Crown appointed the first *alcalde mayor* of the province, don Diego de Quijada. Quijada instigated the construction of many roads among the pueblos, of just the sort López Medel had called for, and he also collaborated actively with Landa, then provincial of the Franciscan order in Yucatán. When Francisco Toral was appointed first bishop of the province, he stepped into a field in which Landa and Quijada were prosecuting the *reducción* at full force in the form of an inquisition complete with testimony under torture and the infamous auto-da-fe held in Maní in 1562.[13] Oidor García Jufre de Loaysa had visited the province in 1560 (for the first time since López Medel) and supported the *reducción*, in addition to pushing for the installation of the *cabildo* government. Recall that López Medel had not recommended the *cabildo* eight years earlier but saw his *reducción* as preparatory to it. Hence in pushing for the new government form, García Jufre de Loaysa in a sense fulfilled López Medel's plan, pushing it to another level of specificity. These several factors lent support to the *reducción* as part of the overall transformation of social space.

REDUCCIÓN IN A REGIONAL PERSPECTIVE

In the years between the mid-1550s and the mid-1580s, there was what can be described as the first wave of mass *reducción*.[14] The number of Indian towns in the province was cut roughly in half (Farriss 1984; Quezada 1993), suggesting that numerical reduction was at least a corollary of the reorganization process. At the same time, new places were created by *congregación*, and persisting ones were redefined by their subjection to secular and evangelical rule. According to church records, by 1580 there were 176 *pueblos de visita* associated with twenty-two convents, and Quezada (1993, 101) estimates that by the mid-1560s approximately 200 *pueblos reducidos* had already been created.[15]

The evidence suggests that this massive reorganization was backed by effective force. Populations that fled rather than submit saw their towns and lands burned and their foodstores stolen. With the spread of the *encomienda* (García Bernal 1972), the Spanish *capitanes a guerra* 'war captains' were in place around the peninsula, and they made up the majority of members in the *cabildo* of Mérida. The missionaries are often said to have led the *reducciones*, but it was these captains who enforced initial compliance on a large scale and who remained a present threat to any subsequent resistance. In at least some of the *reducciones*, there were also armed *indios reducidos* who assisted in the enforcement.

In this context as elsewhere, there are examples of Indio caciques who collabo-

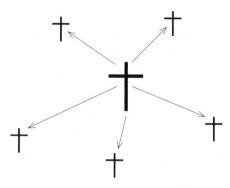

FIGURE 2. The radial structure of the *guardianía*

rated actively with the *reducción*. Some, like Pablo Paxbolon, cacique of Tixchel, led the search for *sublevados* 'fugitives, rebels' who had fled into the bush, with the aim of bringing them into the *reducción* themselves (Solís Robleda and Peniche 1996, 3–7). In a description of his services, Paxbolon is praised by a Spanish official as *"muy cristiano"* and *"de mucha autoridad."* Although Paxbolon was one of a doubtless small number of exemplary Indios, many indigenous leaders engaged with the *reducción*. Caciques were the go-betweens for labor conscription in the building program. They occupied the position of central authority in coordinating the extraction of tribute and other forms of service. Finally, in the written documentation produced in the pueblos (both *reducidos* and not), they are typically the first named principals or signatories (providing they knew how to sign). These facts point to the combination of force and Indian collaboration without which the landscape could not have been reorganized.[16]

The evangelical aims of *reducción* were embodied in the radial distribution of the Indian towns. The operative unit was the *guardianía,* made up of a mission center plus a series of dependent towns. The head town was staffed by clergy, under the leadership of a *guardián,* plus a substantial workforce of Maya helpers. The central place in the *guardianía* was where the friars resided, the *cabecera* 'head town', as contrasted with the dependencies, the *pueblos de visita,* to which the friars traveled periodically to offer the sacraments and doctrinal instruction. The convents and massive architectural programs were built in *cabeceras;* lesser churches or chapels were erected in the *pueblos de visita.* Some of the towns so configured were newly created; others represented a population expansion or contraction of an already existing Maya place (on these transformations, see Farriss 1984; Quezada 1993; Cook and Borah 1974, vol. 2).

The spatial organization of the *guardianía* conformed to the schema in figure 2, in which the large cross in the center is the *convento* and the smaller ones around it are *pueblos de visita*.[17] To inhabit any part of the *guardianía* was to be "*bajo campana*" 'under (church) bell'. The radial movement of priests and *indios reducidos* between the center and the outliers was combined with the circuitous movement of priests going from *visita* to *visita*. The figure does not display spatial orientation, relative distance, or relative size of the *visitas,* all of which in fact varied. What it does capture is the center-satellite organization and the movement of people, ideas, and language between multiple satellites and the center.[18]

The population ratios of Indios to missionaries were extraordinary. According to a 1586 *memorial* authored by the Franciscan provincial fray Pedro Cardete and sent to the Crown, the average ratio of priests to Indios was about 1:1,600. The range was from a low of 1:685 in Tixchel to a high of 1:2,960 in Xecelchakán. Such ratios infuriated several bishops, among them some Franciscans with experience elsewhere, doubtless because they were threefold higher than comparable ratios in other parts of Spanish America. In Guatemala, for instance, the policy, if not the practice, was to maintain ratios no greater than 1:500 (Scholes et al. 1938, 95). Of the twenty-two *guardianías* described in the 1586 *memorial,* six exceeded 1:2,000.

When we compare the number of clergy to *pueblos de visita,* the numbers are similarly bleak. A total of forty-eight *sacerdotes* led the evangelization of 168 towns (including the *cabeceras* and the *visitas*). In Mérida and Campeche, there were 6 towns per *sacerdote.* In seven of the twenty-one *guardianías,* each *sacerdote* had to administer to 4 or more towns. This spatial dispersion entailed arduous travel, the intermittent presence of the priests, and a relatively larger role for local helpers, *indios de confianza* 'trustworthy Indios'. Furthermore, each pueblo had its own local government, and relations between clergy and local caciques were on occasion adversarial. This factor complicates the political and social functioning of the *doctrina.* Whatever population problems the Spanish faced as a whole, the clergy were much worse off.

Between 1580 and 1610 there were five major reports on the state of the missions in the province of Yucatán:[19]

Fray Fernando de Sopuerta, Provincial, to His Majesty (1580)

Gobernador Don Guillén de las Casas, to His Majesty (1582)

Bishop fray Gregorio de Montalvo, to His Majesty (1582)

Fray Pedro de Cardete, Provincial, to the Council of Indies (1586)

Provincial and Difinidores of the Province of San Joseph de Yucatán, to His Majesty (1610).[20]

Along with other letters, these reports give a detailed picture of the development of the ecclesiastical field and some of the major processes that guided the *reduc-*

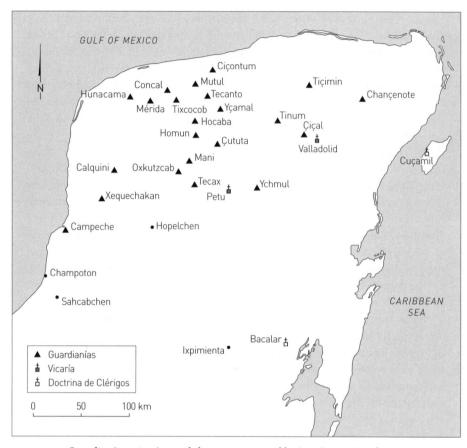

MAP 4. *Guardianías, vicarías,* and *doctrinas* reported by Las Casas, March 25, 1582. Spellings unaltered.

ciones.[21] All five include inventories of the *guardianías,* accompanied by numbers or names of the dependent *visita* towns attached to them, the distances between *visitas* and the center, and a wealth of other information.

The first trend that emerges from comparing the five reports is the growth in the number of *guardianías,* from 19 (1580) to 22 (1582) to a high of 28 (1610). This is consistent with the progressive expansion and greater inclusiveness of the *guardianía* system as it encompassed new units or redefined existing ones. Over the same period, the number of *visitas* belonging to single *guardianías* decreased consistently. For example, Mérida had 12 *visitas* in 1582 but only 5 in 1610. Cumkal had 11 *visitas* in 1580 but only 6 in 1582 and 4 in 1610. Izamal and Valladolid (also called Sací) both went from 18 *visitas* in 1580 to 7 in 1610; Maní,

MAP 5. *Cabeceras de doctrina* reported by Franciscan *provincial* and *difinidores*, June 8, 1610. (© William F. Hanks 2007)

from 10 in 1582 to 3 in 1610. This decline was certainly by design, as the missionaries were continually attempting to improve the ratio of Indios to religious in the *guardianías*.

The *memorias* also reflect the dynamic by which *visita* towns grew into centers and were redubbed *guardianías* with their own satellites. This accounts for the nine new *guardianías* named between 1586 and 1610. The 1610 *guardianías* of Mocochá, Telchac, Cansahcab, Temax, Cacalchén, Chichimilá, Teabo, Ticul, and Muna had all been *visitas* in 1586. Evidently, *visita* towns varied significantly in size and importance; as dependent towns grew in population, number, or local significance, they were redefined as *guardianías,* to be the residence of a designated *guardián* and the central site of a convent.

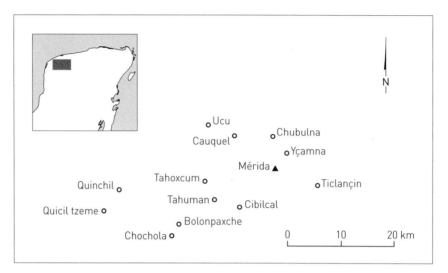

MAP 6. Mérida and its *visitas* reported by Las Casas, March 25, 1582
(© William F. Hanks 2007)

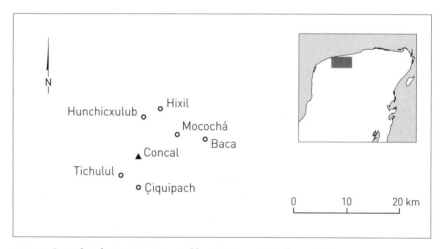

MAP 7. Concal and its *visitas* reported by Las Casas, March 25, 1582
(© William F. Hanks 2007)

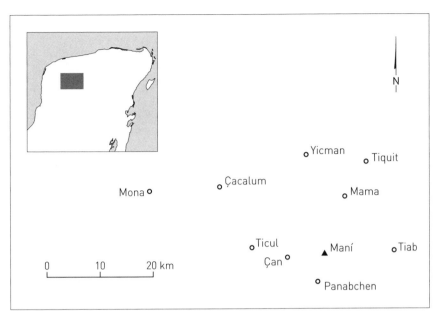

MAP 8. Maní and its *visitas* reported by Las Casas, March 25, 1582
(© William F. Hanks 2007)

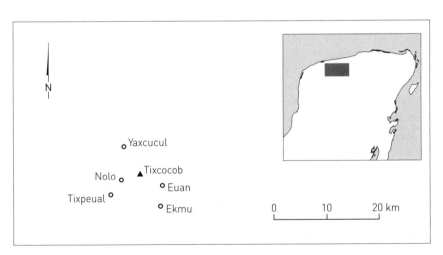

MAP 9. Tixcocob and its *visitas* reported by Las Casas, March 25, 1582
(© William F. Hanks 2007)

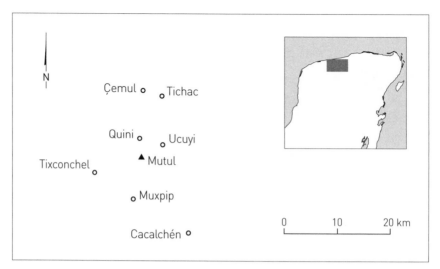

MAP 10. Motul and its *visitas* reported by Las Casas, March 25, 1582 (© William F. Hanks 2007)

Three of the five reports specify the distance in leagues (approximately 4 km) between the head town of the *guardianía* and the *visita* towns. Given travel on foot, the *guardianía* was a form of organization best suited to a certain scale. The more distant or numerous the population of a pueblo, the more difficult it would be to indoctrinate the people. Hence the *reducción* was fragile, incomplete, and subject to resistance and flight. This is a constant problem throughout the early to middle colonial period, cited by friars, bishops, and provincial governors alike. It is also an essential part of the background for the ongoing conflict between the Franciscan friars and the secular clergy as they competed for authority over *doctrinas*.

The proper balance, not often achieved, combined lines of authority (*guardián* to priest to parishioner), demography (ratios of priests to people, number of *tributarios* for the tax base and labor force), and distance. In 1582 the *guardianía* of Campeche had *visitas* as far away as 30 leagues (Çapotitlan), 22 leagues by land and sea (Tixchel), and 12 leagues (Champotón) (Scholes et al. 1938, 62). By 1610 Campeche had no visitas over 8 leagues distant, and Champotón and Tixchel had become separate *guardianías* (Cogolludo 1971 [1688], 2:52; Scholes et al. 1938, 162).

Reports like the ones sketched here were produced within a broader framework in which the local missions were governed from Mérida, México, and ultimately Europe.[22] On this broader context, Cogolludo's monumental *Historia de Yucatán* (1688) provides a wealth of information pertinent to the ecclesiastical field. The redefinition of *visita* towns as *guardianías* with their own *visitas*, the naming of the *guardianías,* and the designating of the *guardianes,* as well as the election of the provincial and the *difinidores* who worked with him, were all accomplished at meetings that took place every three years. These meetings, called *capítulos* 'chapters', were convened under the leadership of officials from México or the *comisario general,* an official with authority over all Franciscans in the Americas. They brought together the leaders of the order in the province, the provincial governor, and officials from outside the province (usually from New Spain) (García Añoveros 1990, 92–111). They were held in Mérida, typically between March and July, and their purpose was to evaluate and elect superiors and to oversee the governance of the order in the province. *Capítulos* were held in 1579 and thereafter every third year into the seventeenth century.

The precise functions of the *difinidores* are difficult to determine. According to Cogolludo (1971 [1688], 2:21), these friars, of whom four were named at each *capítulo,* had the task of reviewing *memorias* written by *guardianes* in the missions, which gave accounts of local activities and contributions from *encomendero* landholders. All those elected to the position of *difinidor* were already *guardianes,* and in several cases cited by Cogolludo, newly elected provincials were promoted from the rank of *difinidor.* Cogolludo refers at several points to the "R. *Difinitorio*" 'reverend *difinitorio*', which evidently included the four *difinidores* plus the provincial (e.g., 2:52). Hence the *difinidores* appear to be a select council of sorts, elected in tandem with the provincial and working with him during his three-year term of office. Former provincials could also be reappointed as *difinidores,* as was the case with Sopuerta, who was provincial from 1579 to 1582 but *difinidor* from 1585 to 1588. The governance structure of the province was a field through which both friars and discourse moved, and Cogolludo's summary of these meetings is replete with information relevant to the developments that concern us here.

On May 27, 1579, fray Fernando de Sopuerta was elected provincial at the age of thirty. Born in Yucatán, he had been trained in the *doctrina* of Landa, Torre, and the early wave of missionaries. Over the next twenty-seven years, he would be elected provincial three more times, each for the standard three-year term. He was also the author of the 1580 report cited above. At the same 1579 *capítulo,* Hecelchakán was named a *guardianía,* and Gaspar de Paz (*guardián* of Campeche), Pedro Cardete (*guardián* of Calkiní, also author of the 1586 report), Gaspar de Najera (*guardián* of Mérida), and Pedro de Pañalver (*guardián* of Maní) were named *difinidores.*

Six years later, in 1585, Cardete was elected provincial and Tixchel and Umán were newly named *guardianías.* In 1586, one year into Cardete's term as provincial, don fray Juan de Izquierdo was named bishop by the Crown, a post he would take up only in 1590 because of his responsibilities in Guatemala. Izquierdo would go on to write recommendations to the Crown that some of the missions be removed from Franciscan authority and assigned to the secular clergy (Cogolludo 1971 [1688], 2:79). At the 1603 *capítulo,* fray Antonio de Ciudad Real, widely considered the main author of the Motul dictionary, was named provincial. His three-year term was marked by ongoing conflict with then-bishop Diego Vásquez de Mercado, a secular priest to whom Pedro Sánchez de Aguilar was *provisor.*[23] Sánchez de Aguilar, as we will see, wrote a highly influential study of Mayan "idolatry" based on experiences gained during his time in the *guardianías.*

The five major reports under discussion here, like Ciudad Real's linguistic work and Sánchez de Aguilar's report on idolatry, are all part of the cycle of governance in the missions. They give pointed evidence of the collaborative relations between individuals such as Sopuerta and Cardete, as well as their career paths through the hierarchy. This hierarchy embodied the dynamic connections tying *visita* towns into *guardianías, guardianías* into *difinitorios, difinitorios* into the provincial, who was the apex of the order in Yucatán, and the province into New Spain and beyond. It may be, as Farriss (1984) argues convincingly, that Yucatán was a "backwater" compared to places like México and Lima; but the structure of the global Church was designed to integrate units at different levels. In so doing, it provided extremely flexible pathways through which knowledge and practices moved.[24]

Between the *capítulos* there was another kind of meeting, typically held in the second year of the cycle, often convened in *guardianías* outside Mérida. This second kind of meeting, the *congregación,* was celebrated under the supervision of the provincial and *difinidores,* with the occasional presence of higher officials from beyond the province. At the *congregaciones,* places were designated as central: in 1581 Oxkutzcab, Hunucmá, Tixkokob, and Tinum were made *guardianías;* in 1591 fray Juan de Padilla was elected *guardián* of the convent in La Habana (Cogolludo 1971 [1688], 2:83–85); and in 1602 Maxcanú and Telchac were named *vicarías.* Cacalchén, Mocochá, Chichimilá, Teabo, and Tecoh were named *vicarías* in 1607 and elevated to *guardianías* at the *capítulo* of 1609 (2:178).

There are differences among the sources regarding the number of towns created during this period, but there is no disagreement as to the trend. A social landscape on which approximately four hundred towns and settlements existed before the *reducción* was forcibly transformed into a colonial province with roughly half as many pueblos. Equally important, of course, is the concentration of people in those towns. According to Quezada (1993, 98–100), nearly all the Indios residing within the province were congregated into the *cabecera* towns, where caciques were also forced to reside. The abandonment of original settlements, and their destruction at the hands of the Spanish, would account for the drop in total number of towns. The gathering into a single place of people from many different ones gave rise, again according to Quezada (1993, 99), to barrios within the towns. In other words, as Farriss (1984, 162) also observed, the newly created *pueblos reducidos,* both *visitas* and *cabeceras,* often reproduced at the barrio level relations that had previously obtained between distinct named places.

Among the regional implications of these trends, Quezada (1993, 98) points out that the northern coast of the peninsula was largely depopulated during these years, as people were gathered into the more central places under Spanish control. Furthermore, as Farriss (1978) demonstrates, there was also a great deal of population movement across the southern and eastern frontier, as Indios fled the oppressions of the *reducción.* The image one gets of the period is that of a massive reordering of the province from a political geography based on *batabs* and *halach uinics* into a lesser number of more highly concentrated places articulated into spheres of authority, with barrios answering to *pueblos reducidos, visitas* to *cabeceras, guardianías* to the province as a whole, and Yucatán to New Spain and beyond.

The *reducción* also involved a building program for convents, churches, and roads, with labor and materials extracted from Indian populations. The monasteries and churches were major collective projects that took literally thousands of Indian laborers and years to finish. The materials involved—stone, wood, mortar—were all available locally but of course required gathering and preparation; so the building program contributed further to the development of markets. In many places, such as Mérida, Izamal, and Maní, the Franciscans chose to erect their buildings upon the platforms of pre-Columbian sites, reusing the very materials of the structures they destroyed. According to Quezada (1993, 73 ff.), they chose the sites for these massive projects according to several broad criteria: centrality for the purpose of political administration, religious prominence for the Indios (e.g., Izamal had been an important pilgrimage site even before Diego de Landa oversaw the erecting of the massive convent and church of Nuestra Señora de Izamal), population density, and proximity to major roads.

In its role as an extractor of tribute, goods, and labor, the Church interacted with common Maya people in several ways. Among the *semaneros* 'weekers' who performed personal service, a goodly number found themselves under the direction of the clergy: Farriss (1984, 53) estimates that twelve to seventeen *semaneros* were customarily engaged at any time to look after the three or four friars who occupied the *conventos* in the *cabeceras de doctrina.* Taking into account the other caretakers of the church plus the female helpers, a given *convento* would maintain a conscripted workforce of about one hundred Indios. The delivery of all this labor was mediated by Maya elites, as was local governance in the pueblos. But it is likely that many ordinary Indios labored in close contact with the friars and their world.

Indios in the *pueblos reducidos* were also a source from which value was extracted. Individual Indios in the colony were subject to no fewer than seven taxes and levies: (1) the standard tribute paid to the *encomienda* (which persisted in Yucatán until the late eighteenth century); (2) the *limosnas* and *obvenciones* extracted by the clergy; (3) the *holpatan* tax levied to support the Indian court; (4) the community taxes used to underwrite local projects; (5) the charges routinely levied by clergy for performing baptisms, marriages, and burials; (6) the obligatory tuition paid for required classes in Christian doctrine; and (7) the fees paid to bishops on the occasion of confirmation.[25] Goods including maize, cotton cloth, and beeswax were extracted through the *repartimiento,* which in Yucatán took the form of forced loans to Indios, to be repaid with goods whose payment value was much lower than market prices. The resulting tax burden was a source of great friction and a topic of complaints in Maya discourse.

The pattern is similar in the case of labor. Individuals residing in the Indian pueblos were subject to the *tequios* (one day of labor per week on community projects), were conscripted to unpaid labor for the church and on state construction projects, and were required to perform *servicio personal,* with each community having to meet a weekly quota of *semaneros* assigned to Spaniards by official permits—nominally one week per year per tributary, but in practice more than triple this level (Farriss 1984, 50).[26]

These forms of extraction were largely mediated by native elites, and while they achieved an undeniable material domination, they evidently failed to transform the core frameworks of Maya culture (a point on which Farriss [1984] and Bracamonte y Sosa and Solís Robleda [1996] agree). Their lack of cultural consequence was reinforced by the often-cited demographic imbalance of the colony: in 1586 Spaniards accounted for only 0.8 percent of the population, a figure that grew to an underwhelming 7.9 percent in 1790. No incentive was offered to induce Maya people to assimilate to Spanish culture, since there was no place for them to occupy in the *república de españoles,* save their subordinate position as *indios naturales.* Moreover, Maya language was used in the missions and *pueblos reducidos,* which relied to a great degree on Indian instructors and were entirely governed by Indian leaders (elected, to be sure, under the watchful eyes of the missionaries).

A LAND OF FRONTIERS

There is abundant evidence that Maya people resisted the *reducción,* to such an extent that in the mid-seventeenth century some missionaries spoke of *reducción perpetua* 'perpetual reduction'. The resistance took a variety of forms, spelled out by Farriss (1984), Jones (1989), Chuchiak (2000b), and Bracamonte y Sosa (2001), among others. These ran the gamut from armed rebellion and flight to litigation and simple refusal.[27] Looking back at map 4, one can see the rough line at which the densely subdivided northwest drops off to the apparently empty eastern and southern zones. This rough demarcation is what historians of the area call the "frontier" and what the Spanish often called the *despoblado* 'uninhabited land' or *montaña* 'high forest'. In fact, as has been amply demonstrated by the afore-mentioned authors, the frontier zone was populated and known in detail by Maya people. It was a sphere through which many people and a great deal of commerce crossed, moving commodities such as wax, salt, and metal tools. It was a zone of enormous and continual activity at the threshold between the urban north and west and the wooded expanse to the eastern and southern regions.

In her early work on Mayan population dynamics in the colony, Farriss (1978) distinguishes two kinds of movement, both of which played key roles in the province. "Flight" describes the movement of large groups of people who migrated from one or more *pueblos reducidos* across the frontier, beyond the sphere of Spanish governance. From this perspective, the frontier zone was a refuge for those multitudes of Maya who sought to escape the oppression and taxation that came with being *reducidos*. The second kind of movement, "drift," occurred when groups moved between communities within the sphere of *reducción*. This could also be driven by the will to escape, but it would mean reintegration into another community, at least potentially. It is perhaps unsurprising in view of the demographic and spatial circumstances of the missions that such population movement took place. But Farriss and those who followed her in the study of migration and resistance have demonstrated that they were dominant factors in the colony, not a sideshow. They resulted in lost tribute revenues, armed conflict, protracted attempts to re-*reducir* (by force or persuasion) people who had fled, the need for armed garrisons in strategic sites, and the persistence of forbidden ritual practices that the Europeans called idolatry.[28]

While we can give an initial outline of the frontier in spatial terms, the idea and the historical phenomenon go far beyond space. Farriss (1984, 16) observes that the frontier was an economic and social reality for everyone in the colony, implying that even in areas well within the core *reducciones*, the consequences of flight were felt. In his important study of Maya resistance during the first century and a half (1540s–1690s), Jones (1989) expands the concept of the frontier into a series of boundaries or dichotomies, which he calls "frontier oppositions." Already in the Post-Classic and persisting into the colonial period, there was what scholars have taken to be a division between the northern zone and the southern zone. The former was dynamic, economically vital with traders and entrepreneurs, urban, sophisticated, and multiethnic. By contrast, the south was depicted as static, relatively isolated, unsophisticated, rural, and "supremely traditional" (Jones 1989, 4). Jones sets about to fundamentally alter this picture of the south by reanalyzing the region in terms of the "frontier processes" he identifies in places such as Tipu, Bacalar, and the area controlled by the Itzá. He shows among other things that the frontier zone was anything but static and empty and sets about to understand it from the perspective of Maya political geography.

In an important series of studies, Pedro Bracamonte y Sosa, Gabriela Solís

Robleda, and Paola Peniche have moved the concept of the frontier to a new level while also exploring the history of the southern *montaña* in considerable detail (Bracamonte y Sosa and Solís Robleda 1996; Bracamonte y Sosa 2001; Solís Robleda and Peniche 1996). These works advance a productive thesis based on what Bracamonte y Sosa and Solís Robleda call "Maya spaces of autonomy," by which they mean the freedom to practice traditional Maya forms of life, ritual, kinship, and belief—ultimately, the space in which to persist as a culturally distinct society on the margins of the colony. According to their thesis, this partial autonomy was consciously pursued by Maya people and was "paid for" at the cost of rendering demanded forms of tribute and labor and supporting the missions. In other words, in what they call a "colonial pact," the Maya traded partial autonomy (the sine qua non of persistence) for selective subjugation. Note that in this formulation the space of autonomy would lie beyond the "frontier," yet need not be spatially outside the colony. The idea is that the autonomy represented by the geopolitically defined frontier could be achieved, at least in part, within the sphere of *reducción*. The key was to partition off spheres of social life, enriched by contact with *sublevados* over the geographic frontier, but ultimately driven by the will to reproduce social and cultural difference in the very midst of the colony.

However we conceive of the boundaries that make up the frontier complex, they were porous. Farriss (1984, 104) points out that the distinctions between city and country were permeable and that the labor demands resulted in a great deal of population movement. This is certainly clear in instances such as the Mirones expedition of 1621, in which workers from the Sierra towns of Oxkutzcab, Ticul, Maní, and Tekax were to open up a road from the Sierra region all the way to Guatemala (Jones 1989, 160). The building program of the churches and convents required many thousands of laborers, who came from all parts of the colony. At the same time, there was so much flight, especially to the south and east of Campeche, that one imagines not so much a boundary between the *reducción* and the rest as a great, shifting contact zone in which Mayas and Spaniards crossed in both directions. Cogolludo (1971 [1688], 2:142–43) says as much when he observes:

> *Tiénese por cierto, por muchas experiencias que en esta tierra se han visto, que no se trata materia alguna tocante los indios, y en especial de reduccion, que luego no corra la voz entre ellos, y llegue la noticia á los infieles vecinos. Y no hay que admirar, cuando se tiene por cierto que los de estas provincias se comunican con ellos muy de ordinario, llevando machetes, hachas, sal y otras cosas.*

> It is held for certain, based on much experience seen in this land, that [there is] no matter touching on Indians, and especially [about] *reducción*, that the word does not pass among them, and the news reaches the neighboring infidels. And there is no cause for admiration when it is known that those [people] from these provinces communicate with them very often, bringing machetes, axes, salt and other things.

Cogolludo goes on to state that living among the infidels were a great number of baptized fugitives, many of whom knew how to read and write and had served as sacristans or cantors in their pueblos inside the province. In other words, flight gave rise to contact between the linguistic and ritual knowledge that sacristans had acquired as agents of *reducción* and the indigenous systems that *reducción* sought to replace. The refuge zone was a contact zone in which the two systems were neighbors and commingled. The position of the fugitive former sacristan was especially ambiguous because at least some of them went on to convince "infidel" Maya to render themselves to the friars, as occurred in early-seventeenth-century Campeche (2:143).

If the *montaña* was a contact zone, so was the interior *reducción,* and many of the *pueblos reducidos* that it included. Perhaps the most dramatic evidence of this is the widespread persistence of Maya ritual practices throughout the colonial period, as revealed in the testimony taken during the inquisition and episcopal campaigns to extirpate idolatry. According to Chuchiak (2000b, 393), the clergy apprehended twenty-eight *ah kin* priests within the *reducción* zone in the sixteenth century alone. Bishop Gonzalo de Salazar in 1612 wrote to the pope that there were over four hundred *ah kin* priests incarcerated in Mérida at that time, and he had twelve thousand confiscated ritual objects in the episcopal palace alone (Chuchiak 2000b, 389). Between the 1560s and 1640, nine hieroglyphic codices were confiscated, and over the first two centuries of *reducción,* more than two dozen public Maya temples or "idol houses" were discovered (Chuchiak 2000b, 422), many of them inside the *reducción* zone and all apparently still in use. The upshot of these brief remarks is that the orderly landscape of *pueblos reducidos* and *guardianías,* with their neat radial structure, existed alongside and commingled with its opposite, a landscape of hieroglyphic discourse and "idolatrous," that is, non-Christian, ritual. The landscape of *reducción* was doubled in this sense, not reduced. A parallel doubling is evident in the translations between languages, which multiply the means of expression, and in forms of spatial organization corresponding to Post-Classic ritual hierarchy that continued to operate inside *pueblos reducidos* (see chapter 3). Given the apparent quantity of *ah kin* priests compared to the paucity of Franciscans and given the pull of the frontier, it is fair to say that *reducción* met with stiff competition and that knowledge and practices moved widely around the peninsula. To get a sense of this movement, consider the case of Sahcabchén.

The pueblo of Sahcabchén was established as a *congregación* in 1615, a place to which fugitive Maya from the *montaña* region were reduced. In the early years of the seventeenth century, Franciscan friars had undertaken a major series of *reducciones* in the area south of Campeche, in what they called the missions of the *montaña* (see Chuchiak 2000b; Bracamonte y Sosa 2001, 101 ff.). There were alarming reports at the time of idolatries committed in this area and elsewhere in the province, and many Indios were scattered or beyond the control of the colony. By establishing *guardianías* and the governance framework they entail, the friars aimed to stabilize and convert the population to *policía cristiana*. By the time Sahcabchén was established in 1615, this effort had been ongoing for over a decade. In 1604 Dr. Pedro Sánchez de Aguilar was granted the right to seek out and reduce "idolaters" in three outlying settlements in the area of Chancenote, on which he rendered his report in 1608. In the same year, then-provincial Ciudad Real ordered two Franciscan friars to participate in the *reducciones* at Tixchel and Champotón (Chuchiak 2007, 9). In a familiar pattern, Sánchez de Aguilar had congregated some one hundred people into Chancenote, confiscated and subsequently destroyed their idols and three hieroglyphic books, and converted them by baptism, catechism, and instruction in the faith (Solís Robleda and Peniche 1996, 29, 40).[29] Sánchez de Aguilar's (1613) major work on idolatry comes out of this context and illustrates the urgency felt by the religious in the face of apostate idolaters and the apparent persistence of idolatrous practices. Worse still, the documents are replete with references to idolatrous Maya *ah kin* 'priests' and *bobat* 'prophets', many of whom were former teachers or specialists in the Catholic missions from which they had fled. Sahcabchén, a Franciscan *guardianía*, would become the center of reconversion of fugitives who would be brought in from the outlying forests. According to Bracamonte y Sosa (2001, 140), nearly one thousand Mayas were *reducidos* in the *montaña* region in 1615. Further, there are a number of petitions from Maya people in the bush, requesting permission or expressing willingness to move into Sahcabchén of their own accord. For example, a 1624 petition criticizes secular clerics but expresses great reverence for friars and the provincial—who, in return, expresses love and reassurance, permits the petitioners to move to Sahcabchén, and issues instructions to the *guardián* and friars in the area to give them free choice over where they would reside (Solís Robleda and Peniche 1996, 53). The implication of this is that flight, like *reducción* itself, was reversible: over time, people moved their residences in both directions.

In the decades between the 1620s and 1670 there were continual problems with Indian flight, raids on *pueblos reducidos* by unsubjugated Maya, insurrection, and repeated attempts at (re-)*reducción*. In 1622–23 fray Juan Delgado, *guardián* of Hecelchakán (just south of Calkiní) took part in a recongregation of people who had fled to the extreme southern town of Ixpimienta (Jones 1989, 157–58). Fugitives from Hecelchakán passed through the town of Hopelchén on their way south, and it was there that they were re-reduced. Among the people from whom testimony was taken was one Andrés Cob, who stated that in Ixpimienta there was a temple with four *ah kin* priests who oversaw ritual practice (Jones 1989, 164–65). The priests were originally from the towns of Homún,

Maní, Pocboc, and Tekax and almost certainly had been themselves taught in Christian doctrine.

Twenty years after its founding as a *pueblo reducido,* Sahcabchén was the site of a rebellion in which Spaniards were put to death, apparently in response to repeated abuses of the Indios. The rebel Maya once again became fugitives in the *montaña,* only to be subsequently pardoned and re-reduced by the *guardián,* fray Juan Gutierrez (Bracamonte y Sosa 2001, 227). In a span of some three months in 1644, approximately 9,225 Indios were reduced in both the southern and northern sectors of the colony, 2,444 in the area of Campeche and Tixchel alone (Bracamonte y Sosa 2001, 206). Some persons swept up in *reducciones* in the frontier zone were sent back to their towns of origin rather than forced to remain in the new pueblos to which they were congregated. Thus in 1663 a large number of Maya returned from Ixpimienta to their original town of Oxkutzcab (Jones 1989, 157).[30]

By the mid-1660s the growing stream of Maya fugitives abandoning the colony for the *montaña* was alarming, and Sahcabchén was one of several southern missions that provided ready access to the refuge of the frontier (Bracamonte y Sosa 2001, 232 ff.). Decrying the endless abuses and extractions of money, goods, and services, a large number of Maya fled from Sahcabchén into the bush in the final years of the decade. By February 28, 1670, Franciscan missionaries were addressing letters to the fugitive caciques, attempting to induce them to return to the *guardianía,* where they would be held without fault and treated with love. The caciques responded that they loved the Crown and the friars also but refused to return out of distrust for the Spanish, resentment of the *repartimiento,* and unwillingness to pay *limosnas* (Solís Robleda and Peniche 1996, 124–27).[31] During spring and early summer 1670, a remarkable series of exchanges took place in which groups of rebel Maya caciques from Ychtok, Tanlum, Kukvuitz, and Canactún received and responded to letters from the friars and Governor Frutos Delgado, all regarding their flight into the *montaña,* their reasons for fleeing Sahcabchén, and their reluctance to return (a selection of documents is reproduced by Solís Robleda and Peniche 1996).

A proper description of these documents and the events they describe is beyond the aim of this book. A concise description is given by Bracamonte y Sosa (2001), a thorough treatment by Chuchiak (2000a, 2000b); for present purposes I pull out selected bits of evidence as they bear on *reducción* as a process. On May 4, 1670, the *cabildo* of Mérida met to discuss the *reducción* of *indios huidos* 'Indios (who have) fled' from the town of Sahcabchén. Present at the meeting were *"el ilustrísimo reverendísimo señor maestro don fray Luis de Cifuentes Sotomayor"* of the Council of His Majesty and bishop of the provinces; Dr. don Frutos Delgado, governor; the *alcaldes ordinarios;* the *alguacil mayor;* the captain of the city; *regidores; sargentos mayores;* and *alfarezes,* most or all of whom were both *encomenderos* and captains. The *escribano mayor,* don Pedro Díaz del Valle, was also present and wrote the minutes. The names listed at the end of the document total thirty-one, with the bishop first, the governor second, and the rest thereafter. At the meeting the *encomenderos* and members of the *cabildo* voted unanimously to undertake a *reducción* by force, preferably in the coming month of January, when the cool, dry weather would be advantageous. The operation would be underwritten by the *encomenderos.* After the vote, the bishop spoke and presented a different plan, namely, to establish a military presence in Sahcabchén but not to undertake *reducción* in the surrounding countryside. The goal was not to attack the Indios but to frighten them. He observed that the Indios responded more favorably to the threat of force than to force itself.

In this case the bishop was a Franciscan, and his suggestion that the Maya responded better to fear than to force is emblematic of the Franciscan claim to know the Indios better than the *encomenderos* did. In fact, the *encomenderos* and the Franciscans were rivals in the colony: both laid claim to the time and production of the Indios, and each group accused the other of incompetence and immorality. The distinction between the two groups reemerged in the complaints of the Indios themselves: they resented the "Spanish," who included saliently the *encomenderos* and military forces as well as the seculars who were by now so active in the idolatry extirpations. By contrast, they loved the friars, who, as it happened, belonged to the same order as the bishop. The Franciscan friars in the *guardianía* of Sahcabchén addressed the fugitive Indios lovingly and reassured them of forgiveness, whereas Governor Frutos Delgado extolled their desire to live in *"vida sociable"* (a near-gloss of *policía*) but warned them of the bloodbath that would ensue if they did not submit (May 28, 1670).[32] Here we see the well-known fault lines between the missionaries and the "Spanish" both in discourse about the Indios and in discourse addressed to them.

Whereas the missionary program was designed to lead inexorably to *indios reducidos* living in *policía cristiana* and speaking *lenguas reducidas,* the documents directed to and from the Sahcabchén region indicate that the facts worked out differently. An individual could be *reducido* at one time, then flee to become a fugitive or an apostate idolater, then subsequently return to the *reducción.*[33] *Reducción* was serial in practice, and the *indio reducido* of today might well be yesterday's apostate, or tomorrow's idolater; hence the "perpetual *reducción.*"

One of the results of this kind of movement was a robust circulation of knowledge between the *pueblos reducidos* and the frontier. The Maya caciques who wrote to the governor and church officials displayed a keen awareness of the different factions among the colonizers. In clear and simple language, they reject the abuses of the "Spanish," who they condemn and refuse to engage. At the same time, they reaffirm their willingness to pay tribute at specified levels and their love of Crown and God. The fugitive Maya thus present themselves as civil, reasonable interlocutors who in effect negotiate their position in the colony. Whether by experience or by Franciscan coaching, they take a stand in the field of competition between friars, *encomenderos,* the bishop and the governor, and ultimately the Crown.

Among the documents gathered by Solís Robleda and Peniche (1996) are the testimonies of three Maya caciques, taken in Mérida in June 1670. The testimony was taken through an interpreter, and none of the three signed because none knew how to write. All three had reentered the sphere of *reducción* in the town of Cauich, returning from a place they called Zayab, in the *montaña* south of Sahcabchén. Two of the three were originally from Hopelchén, about twenty leagues (80 km) southeast of Calkiní. The third was from Chiná, just outside Campeche. All three had left their hometowns for Zayab fifteen years earlier (i.e., ca. 1655). Although their testimony is recorded in Mérida, it was to Cauich, south of Campeche, that all three "returned," and there they and their children were baptized by the *guardián* of Campeche. This illustrates the movements of flight-and-return *reducción,* and it also suggests that the patterns of flight led to new relationships between Maya who ended up in the same place, having come from unrelated and sometimes distant ones.

This documentation gives invaluable evidence that flight and return were more than movements of people. They were movements of knowledge and discourse practices. That fugitive caciques would write letters to Spanish or missionary officials, complete with opening and closing formulas, is itself a remarkable fact. It is even more remarkable that their letters were so subtly engaged in the politics of the colony. In effect, they negotiated their own subjection in the letter of January 24, 1671, saying what they were willing to do and what they would not do. To be sure, this critical document was put to paper by a Franciscan, giving evidence that here, as in so many other politically charged exchanges between Indios and the Spanish government, the friars were right at their side, coaching them. But this very coaching is a kind of indoctrination, because it engages the rebel Indios in a form of mediated communication specific to the colony. They may well have resisted *reducción,* but their resistance was expressed in discourse that conformed to its expectations.

We may presume that these indigenous letters were actually produced orally and *"trasuntados"* 'gathered and translated' by colonial interpreters or *lengua* friars.[34] Yet unless the letters specifically misrepresent what their principals said, they give compelling evidence that these Maya were comfortable and familiar with the genre of letter writing and that, in the case of the three men from Cauich, they knew how to give testimony under oath, a knowledge extensively displayed, and perhaps in a degree learned, in the idolatry trials. They even record the practice by the *indios huidos* of holding written directives from the colonial authorities to their foreheads as a sign of allegiance.[35] These facts indicate that the discourse forms of the colonial field were carried over the frontier like so many seeds waiting to take root among the fugitives.

The irony of perpetual *reducción* is that, however frustrating it was for the friars, it involved the massive and ongoing exportation of knowledge and discourse from the core colony to its peripheries, and back again. Of course, the missionaries were mostly convinced that the Indios had learned the outer forms of proper conduct but remained inner idolaters, rarely to be trusted. A similar vision of Spanish overlay on an indigenous core has persisted in the historiography as well. Yet flight exported the forms of *reducción* even as it undercut the surveillance and religious purposes of *reducción*. Flight and return in effect integrated what Cogolludo (1971 [1688], 2:219), writing in Oxkutzcab, called *"acá dentro en la provincia"* 'here inside in the province' with the much-feared outer frontier, embedding each in the sphere of the other.

3

To Make Themselves New Men

This chapter moves from the politico-religious landscape of the province to the *pueblos reducidos,* where the conversions of conduct and language were actually played out. Whatever impact doctrinal language and practice would have on the Indios, it would arise in the local fields of daily life. What were the structures of governance and fields of engagement that ordered towns and the conduct of their inhabitants? How were the *guardianías* staffed, and what roles were accessible to Maya? How did the missions interact with the *cabildo* government in *pueblos reducidos*? How did they interact with the town as a public space, transforming it into a field of signs? These questions must be answered before we can ask how language in the pueblos embodied the strategies and consequences of *reducción.*

The answers reveal *reducción* at the local level as a universe of ordering practices, engaged by actors in particular social positions. This orderliness in part lay in repeating patterns of representation and authority. Certain relations were repeated at different levels, such as the center-periphery model with movement into and away from the center. The repetition of core patterns had the effect of creating the kind of homologies that Bourdieu judged as basic to habitus and field.[1] But this systematic character of the *reducción* was only part of the story. The designed order was pervasively vulnerable to the actual actions of Indios. Contravening the stability of canonical *reducción* was persistent population movement. Against conversion of belief were apostasy and the persistence of practices considered idolatrous.[2] Against the use of reading and writing for doctrinal purposes was the appropriation of specifically colonial forms of discourse as the means for acting outside the colony, or making counterclaims to those of the colonizers. A careful understanding of how these tensions were played out provides critical context for understanding linguistic practices.

GOVERNANCE OF THE *GUARDIANÍA*

Pueblos reducidos ran the gamut from distant *visita* towns, where the religious presence was tenuous or intermittent, to head towns, where the religious resided and in many of which there were monumental convents and churches. Both kinds of town were vulnerable to population movement. The events of the seventeenth century laid bare the problems of flight and dispersal. Maya people moved into and out of *pueblos reducidos* in ways neither the missionaries nor the secular authorities could control. Moreover, according to Cogolludo (1971 [1688], 1:291–92), by the 1640s the *pueblos reducidos* became sufficiently populous that it was difficult to administer them effectively. He observes that though attendance at Mass was monitored, 50 percent absenteeism was common.

Upon this difficult background, the radial spaces of the *guardianía* laid down a skeleton for governance, linking multiple *visitas* to a single *cabecera*. Monasteries, located in the head towns, were the primary residences of the friars, from which they traveled periodically to inspect and minister to the *visitas*. The monasteries were adjoined to the church complexes, comprising outdoor chapels, walled gardens, patios, and instructional spaces for the schools. In these complexes many of the friars' activities took place, including instruction of Indios in *doctrina;* instruction of newly arrived missionaries in Maya language, evidently by missionary teachers; analysis and redaction of metalinguistic works such as dictionaries and grammars; translation of doctrinal texts from Spanish or Latin into Maya; redaction of sermons; and celebration of the sacraments and feast days. Unlike the monasteries of Europe, the ones in Yucatán were located in, and helped define, the centers of the towns. From here the friars moved outward to the *visitas,* while people of the *visitas* came into the head town for sacraments and feast days. That is, just as officials from New Spain came to Yucatán on *visitas* and bishops in Mérida made *visitas* of the province as part of their term in office, so too the friars in the head towns made *visitas* to their dependencies. In each case the practice of *visita* meant traveling to the target place to see with one's own eyes and to make present the authority of the center. Inversely, just as the religious from around the province were gathered in *congregación* every few years, so too the indigenous people were "congregated" in the head towns for fiestas, as they had been initially "congregated" in the *pueblos reducidos* for residence.

Whereas *visita* implies movement of authorities from a hierarchically superior center to the outer spaces it governed, *congregación* implies the inverse: movement from an outlying space into a central one by persons subject to authority from the center. The attention paid in the *memorias* to distance between the center and the satellites indicates the importance to the missionaries of the symmetry of *visita* and *congregación*. And this symmetry illustrates a much broader pattern in colonial governance: basic relations, such as *cabecera* to *visita, congregación, provincia* 'province' (a term inherently relational in that it applied equally to Yucatán and to any of its major areas), and *reducción* itself recur again and again at different levels. The result is a repeating pattern of relations that creates a hierarchical array of homologous units, like the modular joining of individual *guardianías* in the encompassing province.

One of the interesting features of the center-satellite model is that it creates no perimeter. Whereas relations surely existed between *visita* towns, there is no evidence (to my knowledge) that the *guardianía* was delimited by any border or boundary. Indeed, in the densely concentrated northwest, the distribution of towns was such that *guardianías* were in effect interdigitated, with neighboring towns belonging to different mission centers.[3] On such a landscape, the movement of people and discourse between centers and satellites was controlled, whereas the "lateral" movement among satellites was more aleatory. Cogolludo (1971 [1688], 1:293, 296) notes that the calendar of feasts was more regularly observed in the head towns than in the *visita* towns, just as the head towns housed the monumental spaces of the convents. Similarly, the convents had organs and various musical instruments for sacred music, whereas the *visitas* got by with flutes and less elaborate instruments. These are all indicators of the centrality and hierarchical superiority of the head towns relative to their dependencies.

In a real sense, head towns were "exemplary centers."[4] The churches and monasteries found there were exemplars of God's presence; the elaborate combination of sight, sound, smell, sacred objects, gestures, and collective copresence of Catholic practice embodied the new world toward which *reducción* was directed. The Franciscans saw themselves as exemplars of a holy life lived in imitation of Christ, in poverty and hard work. The *policía cristiana* they tried to instill in those they reached would also exemplify the new actor, the *indio reducido*. This would be true especially in the centers, where interactions between missionaries and Mayas were more intense and easier to surveil.

Towns, evidently on both levels, were subdivided into *parcialidades*, or barrio sections, to improve governance.[5] Cogolludo notes that *patrones* 'patrons' and *principales* 'respected elders' were named for every barrio, the former being responsible to inform the priests of all those in need of sacraments and the latter playing multiple roles in local governance (spelled out below). In addition, each section of a town had appointed *alguaciles* and *tupiles* who together enforced Christian practice (Cogolludo 1971 [1688], 1:294). Like the province and the towns themselves, the barrios were given saints' names, as a means to avoid confusion (1:291) and mark their status as reduced places. Thus the subdividing of space corresponded to a proliferation of place-names and positions to which individuals were named. The functions of these positions included surveillance, enforcement, and administration of *reducción*. As the anonymous report in the *Códice Franciscano* observes, the indigenous people "in the time of their infidelity" had been governed by "centurions and tribunes." This would be the model for their guidance in Christian doctrine as well. The native leaders would take attendance, enforce participation in the sacraments, and report any men who separated from their wives or who cohabited outside matrimony. They would also give notice of all those in their pueblos who had fled from other pueblos and report all who held parties or got drunk. Finally, they were to denounce all who posed as doctors but were actually *hechiceros* 'witches' performing superstitious rites rooted in the ancient infidelity (*Códice Franciscano* 1941, 71–72).

In the same passage of the *Códice Franciscano,* it is noted that in the *visita* towns, the friars selected pairs of trusted men, *indios de confianza.* The relations among these, the *patrones,* and the *principales* are somewhat obscure but appear to be a matter of emphasis: the primary function of the *indios de confianza* was to oversee the cleanliness and protection of the church and sacred objects, to maintain written records of *limosnas* 'donations', to teach doctrine, to perform the sacrament of baptism for infants in extremis, and to bury the dead (*Códice Franciscano* 1941, 72). These multiple positions in the missionary field served as the capillaries through which the *reducción* flowed outward into the local neighborhoods of the towns.

Beyond the overall strategy of spatial *reducción,* as described in chapter 2, the Franciscans had a well-developed plan for how the program would be implemented on the ground. Parts of this plan will be familiar from López Medel's ordinances, which call for *policía cristiana* in everyday life, along with detailed specification of which spheres of activity were to be nurtured and which ones suppressed. It is unsurprising that López Medel's plan resembled Franciscan practices, given that he himself was a member of the order. A document of unknown authorship included in the *Códice Franciscano* (1941, 55–72) makes some key points regarding the Franciscan approach to conversion, which amplify López Medel's reasoning.[6] Drawing on half a century's experience with the missions in New Spain, the document starts from the need to teach people according to their abilities, making a sharp division between *plebeyos* 'plebeians, commoners' and *principales.* The former, called *macehuales* in Yucatec, would receive one kind of indoctrination and the latter another.[7]

The term *principal* is ambiguous: under one reading it designates members of the hereditary elite, people who had been or still were leaders in the indigenous community. In this sense, it is glossed in Nahuatl as *tepixtles* or *tequitlatos* and in Yucatec Maya as *chunthan* 'first word'. This is the sense foregrounded by Bracamonte y Sosa and Solís Robleda (1996), for whom the *principal-chunthan* represents the trace of traditional governance within the colonial order. In other cases, though, the Spanish term designates an appointee who has been selected by the priests for his capacity of leadership in the specific business of *reducción* (cf. discussion of López Medel in chapter 2 above). Spanish laws stipulated that there be *principales* who were to play a leadership and surveillance role in the *pueblos reducidos*. So long as the missionaries looked to the hereditary elites for leadership in the *doctrinas,* the two senses would converge. Hence when an author distinguishes the children of the *principales* from the others, there are two possible dimensions in play: the fact that their fathers are of the hereditary elites and the fact that their fathers are implicated in fostering the *reducción*.

I underscore this difference because it is explicit in the Franciscan plan that the sons of the *principales* were to be groomed for leadership in the Christian colony. It was a delicate balance: the missionaries aimed to produce forward-looking elite male converts who would play leadership roles in the *reducción,* yet they recruited from an elite whose legitimacy was grounded outside the *reducción*. The plan was to train them rigorously, far beyond the basic four prayers taught to everyone. According to fray Francisco de Toral, first bishop of Yucatán, the prayers were to be mastered in order: the Our Father, followed by the Ave Maria, then the Credo, and then the Salve. Only after mastery of these four would those students who wished be given the opportunity to learn reading and writing (Scholes et al. 1938, 28).

The division between elite and commoners was played out explicitly in the different spaces in which they were taught. The elite boys were taught in the *escuela,* a dedicated structure on the north side of the church, whereas *plebeyos* were gathered for instruction on the outside patios and were forbidden to enter the school space (*Códice Franciscano* 1941, 56). In this context, *plebeyo* includes both *macehuales* and the daughters of the elite. This categorization at once demotes elite females and feminizes the lower position.[8] *Plebeyos* were to be gathered from their homes onto the church patio at sunrise before Mass, as well as after Mass, when they were separated into groups according to which prayer they were learning. During these sessions, they were instructed, induced to study, and examined.

DISCIPLINING THE SENSES

Missionary pedagogy was aimed at thorough conversion of the indigenous peoples. The *Códice Franciscano* (60) observes that they were to be induced to *"hacerse nuevos hombres"* 'make themselves (into) new men', a task that would require daily practice and repetition of the doctrine. The idea was that through repeated performance of the collectively recited prayers and catechism within the regular rhythms of a daily round, doctrine would enter the memory: *"Estos niños que se crían en las escuelas, cada día entran puestos en orden, como en procesión, á la iglesia, á oir misa y Vísperas, y antes que los despidan de la escuela dicen á voces la doctrina, una vez antes de comer y otra á la tarde"* These children who are raised in the schools, every day they enter in order, as in a procession, to the church to hear Mass and the vespers, and before being dismissed from school, they say the doctrine aloud, once before eating and again in the evening' (57). Likewise, the indigenous instructors known as *cantores* 'cantors' and *menestriles* 'music instructors' needed daily practice in the schools in order to truly learn the divine offices. Indeed, this emphasis on the formative power of repeated practice is present in the rule of the Franciscan order itself, and was part of the practice of the friars, as well as their students. In the case of the students, the bulk of this repeating practice involves oral performance of sacred language in the collective settings of *doctrina* (see plate 2).

The use of punishment was an integral part of missionary teaching, justified on the grounds that the Indios were like children: *"porque ellos son como niños, y para bien regirse hanse de haber con ellos como con los niños los maestros de las escuelas, que en faltando ó en no dando la lección, ó en haciendo la travesura, luego los escarmientan con media docena de azotes"* 'For they are like children and in order to be governed they have to have with them, as with children, the schoolteachers who, should they fail or not know the lesson or commit transgression, punish them with a half dozen lashes' (59). The use of corporal punishment to enforce attendance and attention to the *doctrina* was evidently general in the missions and extended to children of the elite and the commoners, as well as to adults.

The pain of corporal punishment was one of a series of bodily experiences that the missionaries sought to induce in their students. It obviously had the aims of sanctioning misbehavior, enforcing rules regarding proper language and conduct, and compelling Indios to engage with the *doctrina*. But no amount of pain could assure proper memory of sacred texts or turn the Indian soul toward God. For this, a subtler phenomenology came into play. The oral performance of *doctrina* in collective settings gives a clue, because the student engaged in such a practice was both producing sound and experiencing the collective surround of other voices sounding the same text. The coordination of body postures and the separation of the sexes, mentioned by numerous sources, would further reinforce the collective concert and the inscription of *reducción* on the body. And then there is music—the singing of *canto llano* 'plainsong', the wind instruments, the sonorous filling up of the spaces themselves. The built space, with its interior acoustics, light, mass, volume, and density of signs, would greatly amplify the sense of collective copresence with the "mystery of God." The *Códice Franciscano* observes:

y toda esta armonía es de grandísimo provecho entre ellos para su cristianidad, y muy necesario el ornato y aparato de las iglesias para levantarles el espíritu y moverlos á las cosas de Dios, porque su natural que es tibio y olvidadizo de las cosas interiores, ha menester ser ayudado con la aparencia exterior; y á esta causa los que los gobernaban en tiempo de su infidelidad los ocupaban lo más del tiempo en edificación de sumptuosos templos, y en adornarlos mucho de rosas y flores, demás del oro y plata que tenían, y en muchos sacrificios y cerimonias, más duras y recias que las de la ley de Moisén. (58)

and all of this harmony is of great benefit among them for their Christianity, and the ornament and splendor of church is essential to lift up their spirits and move them to the things of God, for their nature is tepid and forgetful of interior things, and it is necessary to help them with exterior appearance, and for this reason those who governed them in the time of infidelity occupied them most of the time with edification of sumptuous temples and with much adornment of roses and flowers, in addition to the gold and silver they had, and in many sacrifices and ceremonies, harder and harsher than those of the law of Moses.

In this passage, the author(s) reinvoke the interaction between interiority and exteriority, a distinction that was fundamental to Franciscan thought and that we have already encountered under several guises. López Medel's premise that *policía* in conduct was requisite to, and would actively foster, conversion is a case in point. The various exclusions from pueblo space (no cemeteries, no large stands of trees, one and only one market, etc.) as outlined in the *Ordenanzas* create a normative division between inside and outside, by mapping activities and objects onto the one or the other. The care and ornamentation of the churches created spaces of synesthesia in which practitioners would experience the interiority of the sacred space as opposed to the world outside it. This same space, already interior, would in turn operate on the memory and beliefs, moving the spirit and soul toward God. The passage just cited offers the justification for such a plan: the Indios are forgetful and not attuned to interior things; we must therefore induce them to remember by engaging their bodies and appealing to their senses. Moreover, the indigenous leaders, already in the time of infidelity, had understood this, and the missionizing church would continue in kind.

It is clear throughout the Franciscan writings on *doctrina* that the aesthetic experience of ritual practice was recognized as formative for the "new men" of conversion. Beyond *compelling* engagement, the friars sought to *induce* the desire to engage and *induce* retention by memory. The senses played a key role, and just as Pascal and others would later observe, sumptuous spectacle both occupied the idle and turned their souls toward majesty. Performance combined with repetition in the morning observance: After being counted, students were seated. They performed the entire *doctrina* two or three times out loud and were then given a sermon in their own language. After the sermon, Mass was sung, and by about 9:00 A.M. it was over and they were sent back to their houses (*Códice Franciscano* 1941).

Vision is also a powerful modality for conversion, and the missionary attention to it is evident in the adornment of the church, the candles and their light, the images, the vestments, and the visible gestures performed. For the purpose of committing to memory, the use of pictures was favored: *"pues es cosa natural imprimirse en la memoria lo que en aquel tiempo se percibe; y para percibirlo ya presuponemos, como es así, que para los indios el mejor medio es la pintura"* 'it is a natural thing for something perceived to inscribe itself in memory; and to perceive it we presuppose, and it is so, that for the Indio the best means is by painting' (60). This statement reflects the missionary appreciation of the skill of Nahua and other scribes at producing hieroglyphic and pictographic books. It also reflects the remarkable ability with which Indian craftsmen developed the mastery required to paint canvases and built spaces.[9] The concern with exciting the senses through music and art extended also to language. The language of indoctrination was to be beautiful. Translations of doctrinal material, including sermons, prayers, and catechisms, were to be made aesthetically pleasing, to draw the Indio into the text and move the soul toward the things of God. In sum, neophytes were to be induced to turn toward God by sensory and aesthetic experiences, which were in turn coordinated in the teaching, the celebration of rituals, and the routine sequences of practices, like the morning cycle sketched above.

There is of course much more to the pedagogy of the missionaries, but the basic telos is the same: in order to move the soul toward God and induce the memory to retain holy words, the church should create corporeal and aesthetic experiences, presenting to the senses objects that evoke pain and pleasure. The making of new men entailed making new bodies and a new *prise de conscience* to go with them. To be sure, the conceptualization and the enactment of pedagogy were most elaborate in the training of the elite, but the system was aimed at all. The formative practices used in the missions express a social ontology of the desired subject (see plate 3).

BISHOP TORAL'S VISION

The vision of spiritual conquest set forth in the anonymous Franciscan document is fine-tuned in a set of *Avisos* authored by fray Francisco de Toral, first bishop of Yucatán. Toral's *Avisos* are contained in a letter by him, reproduced as document 12 in the *Documentos para la Historia de Yucatán* (Scholes et al. 1938, 25–34). Born in Ubeda and ordained a Franciscan in Andalucía, Spain, Toral came to New Spain around 1542. He spent nearly twenty years as a missionary among Popoluca speakers in the Valley of Mexico and was himself a *gran lengua* of the language. He wrote an *arte* and a *vocabulario* and translated the *doctrina* into Popoluca. He was deeply familiar with the *guardianía* system and had himself been a *guardián*. In 1562 he was appointed bishop of Yucatán by the king, at a time when the province was rife with conflict. Under the zealous leadership of Provincial fray Diego de Landa, the Franciscans had discovered evidence of widespread idolatry among apostate Maya and had undertaken an inquisition.[10] The traumatic consequences included testimony extracted under torture, public humiliations, fines and incarcerations, and the infamous auto-da-fe held in Maní in 1562, at which Maya books and artifacts were burned and many members of the elite shorn of their hair and stripped of their status.[11] In the same year, 1562, Toral assumed the position of bishop. His job would be to rein in Landa and the other zealots of his order, to reassess the claims of idolatry, and to restore some stability to a province in apparent chaos. His outsider status and lack of knowledge of Maya surely hampered his abilities, and given his linguistic sophistication, he was well aware of the importance of the knowledge he lacked. By 1566 he had failed obviously, requested of the Crown permission to retire, was denied his request, and ultimately witnessed Landa's appointment as bishop—his archrival replacing him in the highest position of authority in the provincial Church. During the same years, Landa produced the *Relación de las cosas de Yucatán*, as part of his defense before the Council of Indies against charges stemming from the persecution of idolaters.

Toral's *Avisos* were likely produced in conjunction with his episcopal *visita*, which he conducted over ten months in 1563, the year following his appointment as bishop (Scholes et al. 1938, xxi; *Códice Franciscano* 1941, 12:25–33).[12] This would suggest that they were based in large measure on his previous experience, probably augmented by what he was able to observe during the *visita* and what he was told by the guardians in the missions. Despite the context of his appointment, there is no mention of idolatry or the excessive force it provoked, although these factors were ever present in the background. Rather, Toral's purpose was to instruct those engaged in the missions, priests and natives alike: "*para que sepan los naguatlatos y ahcambecahes lo que han de hacer en cosas de los sacramentos y en orden de iglesias . . . y en otras cosas para el bien espiritual y remedio de los naturales en ausencia del padre sacerdote, y para el mismo sacerdote*" 'so that the interpreters and teachers know what they have to do in matters of the sacraments and in [the] order of [the] churches . . . and in other things for the spiritual good and remedy of the natives in the absence of the sacerdotal priest, and for the sacerdote himself' (Scholes et al. 1938, 25). The plan is consistent with other Franciscan statements of the evangelical mission and adds further detail to the depiction of Franciscan pedagogy.

Toral's approach was analytic. The first step was to teach the Indios what was true and what was false. If they could assent to the true and dissent from the false, they could be baptized even if they were too old to memorize the *doctrina*. According to Toral, this distinction between true and false lies at the base of idolatry, apostasy, and heresy, all of which entail turning to the false. It is also the first and most basic measure of the believer, who is in the right by assenting to truth and dissenting from falsity. In the practice of *doctrina*, assenting and dissenting are speech acts performed in response to questions or statements that are, in turn, true or false. The exercise is called *dialogos* in the Yucatecan catechisms (see chapter 8), and Toral gives some illustrative examples. In a more abstract sense, the assenting that marks the proper stance in relation to truth is also a basic feature of believing. The *Catechism of the Catholic Church* (2000, 42) cites Aquinas: "Believing is an act of the intellect assenting to the divine truth by command of the will moved by God through grace." Thus, in starting with the minimal prerequisite of conversion, Toral made not only a rhetorical move but a logical one as well (Scholes et al. 1938, 25–26).

When the catechism is taught, to the young and those capable, it is done in a specific way, and we can also see Toral's plan for doctrinal practice (Scholes et al. 1938, 28–31). All children are to matriculate and meet daily for one hour on the patio of the church (recall that only the elite children meet inside the school, and the patio is the general gathering place). As noted above, the order in which prayers are learned is fixed: the Pater Noster, the Ave Maria, the Credo, and then the Salve. Each must be mastered before the next is attempted. Toral insists that the teachers are to see that students do not mix up the prayers. Thus the curriculum was designed to discipline the memory, shaping it to texts that are all interrelated but must be kept separate. If we assume the *Códice Franciscano* text as backdrop to this one, then we might expect Toral's students to be singing, using pictures, and being affected by the beauty of the doctrinal language. Whereas the *Códice Franciscano* text specifies the morning cycle, Toral makes pointed remarks on prayers in the evening, at bedtime, and when waking in the morning. The *muchachos de la escuela* (i.e., the elite boys) would recite the *primas de noche* from their front doors or in the streets daily, so as never to lose it from memory or leave off reciting it. At bedtime they were to make a sign of the cross and a *santiguar* 'blessing' and then say (*decir*) the four prayers and the general confession. All this was to be done with *sentimiento interior* 'inner feeling'— specifically *dolor* 'sadness'—and *arrepentimiento de sus pecados* 'repentance for their sins'. The outward gesture of prayer and contrition would correspond to the subject's interior state of contrition. The same expiatory discipline was to be followed upon rising in the morning.

In this program, examinations played a pivotal role. Clearly, they served as discursive instruments for surveilling the state of learning of the neophyte. They also asserted the authority of the examiner and the value of the knowledge being tested. The old as well as the young were to be examined in doctrine. If they did not know it, the teacher was to designate for them a three-month period during which they must learn it. If they still did not learn, they were to be made to come to church every day for an hour in the morning, and it was to be taught them in their own *pueblos*. Once they knew the four prayers, they were no longer to be compelled to return to church for special instruction, except on Sundays and holy days. Toral emphasizes that all students should be tested every six months. He was certainly aware of the danger of backsliding and forgetting, and the cyclic examination served to reactivate and maintain proper memory.

Given all that we have seen of the *reducción,* it is unsurprising that Toral devotes some attention to the proper care of space. Crosses are to be erected at the entrances and exits of the towns and at the entrance to the church and the patio. *"Y en llegando a la cruz se hinquen de rodillas y adoren en ella a Nuestro Señor Jesucristo alegando los ojos del alma a la contemplación de este misterio"* 'And upon arriving at the cross they are to kneel and adore in it Our Lord Jesus Christ, drawing the eyes of the soul to contemplation of this mystery' (Scholes et al. 1938, 28). Note that the cross is both a sign marking a threshold and a sacred symbol that calls for a bodily expression of devotion. In this act of kneeling adoration, the "eyes of the soul" are turned to the mystery of Jesus Christ. We see here an elegant merger of body and soul, both aligned to the built space of *reducción,* each of the three elements reinforcing the other two. The adoring kneeler simultaneously turns to the divine and sanctifies the symbol and its placement. Just as exclusion was a key operator in the pedagogical spaces of school and patio, so too it helped define spaces. Churches, cemeteries, and patios were *"de arte que no pueden entrar bestias"* 'of design so that beasts may not enter them'. Ornaments were to be kept clean and safely stored in their cases, under lock and key (29). In one of the few points that betray Toral's awareness of the unauthorized movement of Indios into and out of *pueblos reducidos,* he stipulates that no Indio is to be married in a vicarship or *guardianía* other than his or her official one (33). In this chain of rules we can see the interweaving of *doctrina* and subject formation with space. This foreshadows the more fine-grained mutual adjustments and reinforcements that lay behind the language of conversion.

Toral gives interesting clues to the roles played by native assistants in the missions, especially at the level of *pueblos de visita,* where no priest was resident. In every town there was a native leader who cared for the church (implementing the aforementioned rules) and taught the boys. This individual was a *sacristán mayor* 'senior sacristan', and his role was to propagate the knowledge needed to live with the church and care for its spaces. He was to *"enseñe ayudar a misa a los muchachos para que sepan servir bien en la iglesia y altar y vacían la iglesia cada día"* 'teach the boys to assist with Mass so that they know how to serve well in the church and they empty the church every day' (Scholes et al. 1938, 29). Note in this passage that proper care of the space entails cleaning it out every day, so that it remains isolated for certain purposes. We can see in this chain of reasoning that Toral's *reducción* would be accomplished in large part by the training of trainers who would in turn train others. The self-replicating quality of this cycle fit into what we might call the "indirect rule" of the missions. In extreme cases in which an infant was ill and no priest available, the native helper could baptize the dying child. First, he had to verify that the child had not already been baptized, since this sacrament was to be performed once only, in contrast to the other sacraments and doctrinal activities, which were repeated. Then he was to say the words correctly, handle the water in the manner required, and have the requisite intention (27).

The special case of the native administration of baptism leads Toral into a discussion of how death is to be handled in the absence of the priest (Scholes et al. 1938, 29–30). The sick person was to be brought to the priest for confession, if possible; if no priest was available, the *ah cambesah* 'teacher, maestro' was to go to the sick person's house and instruct him to make peace with the God who made him. This was to be achieved in a process in which the sick person had to work to recall each and every sin and offense since last confession, feeling the required sorrow for having broken the commandments. This act of examination and contrition was even more crucial if the person, after being baptized, had *"tornó a idolatrar invocando al demonio, quemándole copal u ofreciendo alguna cosa, que se acuerde bien de todo y le pese grandemente de ello. Y si tiene alguna cosa dedicado al demonio que la dé luego, o diga adonde está, y declare si hay algún idólatra en su casa o en otro alguno"* 'turned to idolatry invoking the devil, burning copal incense to him or making some offering, he is to recall everything well and give great weight to it. And if he has some thing dedicated to the devil, he is to give it over, or say where it is and declare if there is any idolatry in his home or in some others' (29). The examination and the revelation of hidden idolatry—the truth about a falsehood—would cleanse the person in preparation for death. At the same time, the progressive application of this procedure would weed out the idols and paraphernalia of idolatry with the successive deaths of those who worshiped them. As part of the same process, the *ah cambesah* was to help the dying person remember every one of his or her mortal sins, memory here being the way to be rid of the remembered act. Toral then quotes the speech to be uttered by the dying person and the native assistant who was leading him or her to a "good death."[13] The crucifix and holy water were to be put on the person's head, so that he or she could kiss it, and he or she was to be reminded of Christ's passion (30).

Toral further specifies a range of points that I will not examine in detail here. These include the necessity of written records of baptism and of the worldly goods the dying bequeath to their survivors, an extended description of proper marriage, the salary to be given translators *(naguatlatos)*, the proscription against nocturnal parties and especially dancing to native texts, the proscription against working on holy days, the fasting days, and finally the injunction to wear clean fine clothing to Mass (Scholes et al. 1938, 30–33). This range of topics is reminiscent of López Medel's ordinances and reflects the standard practice, or at least the standard theory, of the missions.

COGOLLUDO'S LANDSCAPE

In the mid-seventeenth century fray Diego López de Cogolludo, one of the most distinguished historians of Yucatán, wrote a massive two-volume history that described the *"gobierno espiritual y temporal"* 'spiritual and temporal governance' of the Indios in Yucatán (Cogolludo 1971 [1688], 1:290–96). Whereas Toral's *Avisos* were just that, instructions, Cogolludo was a historian writing in retrospect about what actually had transpired (at least as he saw it). There is no question that Cogolludo's perspective, like that of López Medel, Landa, Toral, and so many other major figures, was shaped by his being a Franciscan. Yet his *Historia* is recognizable to modern eyes as a work of history, not a polemic driven by dogma or an ecstatic devotional text like that of Lizana. At a minimum, Cogolludo is as precise as Landa was in the justly famous *Relación,* and much less politically motivated. His account adds a perspective from the mid-seventeenth century, and he gives more clues to the problems of absenteeism and the unauthorized mobility of Indios (see plate 4).

Cogolludo shares with other Franciscan authors the idea that spiritual conversion would be achieved in significant measure through carefully orchestrated sensory experiences. The distinction between an inner life given over to God in prayer and an outer life of worldly engagements is also evident. One aim of missionary work was to regulate the relations between the two, so that the soul of the Indio would be cultivated for devotion (Cogolludo 1971 [1688], 1:295). The care of the spaces of worship and the use of music were ongoing parts of ordinary practice. Thus Cogolludo (1:295) observes that in all pueblos, *visita* and *cabecera* alike, sacristans and *cantores* were named who cared for the church and its ornaments and served at the altar. Being readily available, cut flowers were kept in the church. In every *pueblo,* he says, however small, the divine offices were solemnly performed *canto de órgano y capilla formada,* as the music required. In the *visita* towns where funds were insufficient to acquire an organ, the *cantores* used a kind of flute with low tone, *contre altos* 'contraltos', *tenores* 'tenors', and *tiples* 'sopranos'. By contrast, in the convents there were many musical instruments, starting with organs, usually brought from Spain with donations *(limosnas).* Other instruments included *bajoncillos, chirimías, bajones,* and *trompetas.* As usual, the objective was to move the Indios and induce love of the divine majesty. On Saturday afternoons, the *Salve Regina* was sung to the mother of God with solemnity and the attendance of the pueblo, especially the women. In the head towns, *cofradías* 'brotherhoods' were formed for the worship of Our Lady, and their members periodically performed sung Mass (1:295–96).

Cogolludo (1:291–92) also brings much finer detail to the question of how the Franciscans monitored and enforced the practice of *doctrina.* General attendance was taken after Mass, by the *doctrinero* 'doctrine teacher' (who would likely be a Maya). All the *vecinos* of the pueblos were arranged by *parcialidad* (by barrio or other division), with their names written on *tablas* 'tables'. In the past attendance had been taken on the patio of the church, but by the mid-seventeenth century the populations had grown too large, and it was in the central plaza of the *pueblo* that people were gathered to be counted. If an absence was noted, the *principal* of the corresponding section was expected to give account to the *doctrinero*. Cogolludo notes that these *principales* were called *chunthan* in Maya and observes that common reasons for absence included sickness, temporary absence from town, or the fact that the individual had fled. He adds that flight was very common, and absenteeism often exceeded 50 percent.

If a local individual was absent without account, there was a method of discovering him or her. Each section had at least one *alguacil*, who was a local Maya man, and the first step was for the *alguacil* to find the missing person and bring him or her back to the *doctrinero*. If this failed, then all those attending Mass were given a knotted rope that they were to return at the next feast day. Anyone lacking a rope would then be recognized as having missed the Mass. The absentees were brought before the *doctrinero* and could receive a flogging, if the town *gobernador* so ruled. According to Cogolludo, Mass during the week was usually attended by a couple of women from each *parcialidad,* and the *gobernadores* rarely missed it (1:293). Note that it was trusted and elite Maya men who carried out the surveillance and sentencing of other Maya people. Their engagement would further the purposes of *reducción* by spreading its codes of conduct and forms of authority.

Maya children were like young plants in need of assiduous care (Cogolludo 1971 [1688], 1:293–94). Boys under fourteen and girls under twelve were considered children and were expected to attend Mass and catechism classes daily. They were gathered by the *alguaciles* and led to church in procession, the boys on one side and the girls on the other, led by the *tupil* 'constable' holding a cross raised high. As they processed to church, they sang in loud voice, *séptimo tono*. Once in church, kneeling and separated by gender, they continued to sing. The *tupiles* then counted them by their *cuerdecitas* 'little ropes', which bore names, and recorded the count on *tablas*. Those absent were sought out and given a few lashes. Again a pattern is repeated at a different level: for the adults the enforcers were *principales, alguaciles,* and the *gobernador;* for children, they were *tupiles* working with *alguaciles;* for both, the knotted ropes were the instrument of monitoring attendance. In an echo of Sánchez de Aguilar's *Informe* on Maya idolatry, Cogolludo (1:295) notes that, with all this pedagogical care, failure to learn the doctrine must be an indicator of maliciousness, bad nature, or distraction. Examinations of doctrine were also held at marriage and at annual confession.

The rigorous routine that Cogolludo spells out was even more intense on the numerous feast days, at which collective celebration was both required by doctrine and embraced by the pueblos. The main bells were rung at prime, calling the faithful to the church. Upon entering the church, they were separated, the men on the side of the gospel and the women on the side of the epistoler. Having done the prayer to the blessed sacrament, all sat on the ground, with officials on benches. The sacristans then sang the four prayers (Our Father, Ave Maria, Credo, and Salve) in *séptimo tono,* with the pueblo repeating. The rest of the Christian doctrine was then sung in *tono llano* 'plain song', and then terce was sung, leading into Mass. The morning observance was done earlier than in Spain, owing to the excessive heat. At the onset of singing of doctrine, two *tupiles* or *alguaciles* took up position at the doors, giving public lashes to latecomers. There were also afternoon services, where attendance was less rigorously monitored and local officials usually gathered. In addition to the major feast days, there were great public festivals on Monday and Friday of holy week, on the feast of the institution of the blessed sacrament. On the feast day of each pueblo's patron saint, there was a great collective feast at which copious amounts of turkey were consumed (and for which the turkeys were raised throughout the year). People from throughout the *comarca* 'district' came to the feasting town and were received by its residents, with chiefs receiving chiefs, councillors receiving councillors, and so forth (Cogolludo 1971 [1688], 1:296). Thus the festivals were sites for collective interaction that reinforced the Catholic calendar, the religious definition of the feast, and the rituals it called for. By bringing together leaders from different pueblo governments, feast days also provided a framework for politically significant interpueblo dialogues.

GUARDIANÍA AND COFRADÍA

All the practices sketched in the foregoing presuppose a field of positions that brought to their elected or appointed agents titles, forms of authority, and responsibility. For instance, catechism classes imply the co-engagement of a *doctrinero* (whether cleric or indigenous *maestro*) and his students, whereas the sacraments engage competent ministers and those receiving, and the surveillance of adults and children implies different classes of functionaries collaborating to identify and apprehend truant Indios. Similarly, fiestas imply participating groups and ritual observances, engaging the *cofradías,* church representatives of various sorts, and members of the governing councils of adjacent towns. The *concilios* and *congregaciones,* held on a four-year cycle, brought together church officials from all the *guardianías* and embodied the pinnacle of the Franciscan order in the province. The interactions between the provincials, the bishop, and the *alcalde* and *cabildo* of Mérida were dense, frequent, and of great consequence for all parties, as we saw in the case of Sahcabchén. Within the *guardianía,* the religious staffing was separate from the *cabildos* and *gobernadores,* but the two coordinated on numerous matters.

Still, the religious were most directly involved in implementing the pedagogy sketched above. The sources use various terms to refer to the missionaries.[14] The most general term, *religioso,* was used for regular and secular religious alike, including ordained priests *(sacerdotes),* lay brothers *(legos),* choir leaders *(coristas),* deacons and subdeacons *(diáconos, subdiáconos),* and (evidently) *novicios.* Although a number of positions in the missions were filled by Maya individuals, no Maya were *religiosos,* a category reserved for men of European or creole descent. The secular clergy were ordained priests and served as *curas* 'parish priests'. The secular analogue of the Franciscan *guardianía* was the *vicaría,* its leader being the *vicar.* Secular clergy were frequently creole men, that is, locally born but of European descent, whereas the Franciscans drew their friars almost exclusively from Europe. A *frayle profeso* was a friar (for present purposes a Franciscan) who had taken vows, and the category therefore excludes *novicios* but includes *sacerdotes,* lay brothers, deacons, subdeacons, and choir leaders. As we have seen, the *guardianías* also had one leading priest, the *guardián. Guardianes* were always ordained priests, as were the *difinidores* and other province-level leaders in the order.

The occupants of these different positions played distinct roles in the missions. Ordained priests were authorized to administer the sacraments, most notably baptism, confession, communion, and marriage. Lay brothers and deacons assisted and did some preaching but did not confess, say Mass, or give the homily at Mass. Under extreme circumstances, as we have seen, nonpriests could baptize and bless the dying, but only if no priest was available, and always with the intention to do as the priest would normally do.[15] While the *guardián* was responsible for the orderly and proper functioning of the *guardianía* as a whole, it is virtually certain that oversight of the teaching and ongoing practice of *doctrina* was shared with the other priests and *frayles profesos.*

One of the striking features of the *memorias* and other Franciscan writings is the way ecclesiastical competence intersects with linguistic competence. There was an explicit hierarchy of language abilities, codified in terms of which functions individual priests were capable of performing in the native language. The practical importance of this distinction is obvious, and it was a key element of Franciscan rhetoric in defending the order's power in the province. Thus most documents treating the staffing of the missions specify how many priests in each place could preach in the language, how many could hear confession in the language, and how many were linguistically unable to minister to Indios at all. Any priest capable of preaching in Maya could also hear confession in the language, but the inverse did not hold: a priest with partial competence could hear confession but not preach. In this case, he was described as *media lengua.* While the friars frequently underscored their intimate knowledge of Maya language, it is clear from the records that priests who did not know it could nonetheless ascend the ranks from *sacerdote* to *guardián* to *provincial*. Hence the hierarchy of linguistic competences did not correspond precisely to the hierarchy of official positions but was consequential for the staffing and functioning of the *guardianías*.

It is well known that the Yucatecan missions drew heavily on the labor and engagement of Maya people, without which they would have collapsed. Much of the organizing, teaching, monitoring, and enforcing of the *doctrina* was actually carried out by Maya adults whom the religious considered *indios de confianza*. The presumption is that the *indios de confianza* were supervised by the religious, but the demographic and geographic realities of the province suggest that the degree of supervision varied widely. Moreover, effective oversight would require that the *frayle* supervisor be able to communicate clearly with his Maya helpers. This further complicates the task, since relatively few religious were truly *lengua,* and there is no evidence that their Maya helpers spoke much Spanish, aside from the high-ranking and exceptional ones. Thus the actual functioning of the missions was to a certain extent beyond the control of the missionaries, and they knew it.

The most general terms used by European authors in reference to Maya people were *indios* and *indios naturales,* terms widely used in New Spain and elsewhere in the Spanish Americas. Of all the souls so designated, it was the *almas de confesión* 'souls of confession' who were most in need of ministering. In his 1586 letter to the Crown, Bishop Pedro de Cardete counts the *almas de confesión* in Yucatán, to support his argument that more friars were desperately needed to minister to so large a flock. He notes that three thousand to four thousand tribute payers (i.e., adult men) corresponded to about eight thousand *almas de confesión,* excluding unmarried persons, children, and the elderly (and ignoring the distinction between members of the elite and plebeians). This ratio is approximate and is proffered as a rough demographic indicator of demand for religious. It assumes that all adult men, and most adult women, are married; the excess women are presumably widows. By excluding children and the elderly, Cardete also manages to exclude much of the young population in need of doctrinal classes and the elders who were preferred helpers around the church and monastery. The reason for this exclusion may be that the teaching and maintenance functions of missions lay largely in the hands of nonreligious Indios anyway, and what the *almas de confesión* most needed was the sacraments, which only the priests could administer. Since the *confesión* in question is the confessing of faith, an *alma de confesión* was *reducido* and had already crossed the first threshold on the road to conversion. It is obvious that children close to marriageable age and elderly persons who had undergone religious training were in this sense *"de confesión."* The vast majority of these people spoke Maya but not Spanish, especially as the Franciscan schools ceased to function and Spanish and Latin therefore ceased to be taught to the children of the elite.

Among the *almas de confesión* were a much smaller number of Indios who demonstrated their understanding of and loyalty to the missionary project. These were the *indios de confianza* 'trustworthy Indios'. The term typically designates men or women who had been baptized and converted and who maintained regular relations with the religious. While it does not imply any particular language ability beyond the requirements of the faith, it does imply familiarity and a show of adherence to the doxa of the missions. Some of these individuals had been extensively trained and had achieved *ladino* abilities in Spanish or, in truly exceptional cases, Latin. Others were less deeply trained but had built up *confianza* with the religious through their deeds and displays of proper intention. It is obvious in the record that some *indios de confianza* subsequently fled or engaged in apostasy; this status was just as reversible as was *reducción*. Still, at any given time, it was from the trustworthy that individuals were recruited to the important roles in the missions: *confianza* was the first requisite for access to other positions.

A number of minor positions were occupied by *indios de confianza*. The sacristans maintained the church and its ornaments, keeping it safely locked and protected from animals. Occasionally called in Maya *ah canan* 'guardians, watchmen', sacristans played a particularly important role in *pueblos de visita,* where the religious were absent for extended periods. According to Cogolludo (1971 [1688], 1:293), the sacristans also led the faithful in singing the four basic prayers before Mass. In addition, in every pueblo or *parcialidad* there were *fiscales* whose responsibility was to gather the children for catechism classes. The *sacristanes* and the *fiscales* are both mentioned explicitly in the 1681 *Recopilación de las leyes de los reynos de las Indias,* where it is stipulated that in every *reducción* there was to be one sacristan to maintain the church, who would be held free of all taxes and personal service (*Recopilación* Libro VI, Título III, Ley vi). There was to be one *fiscal* for towns of about one hundred inhabitants and up to two *fiscales* if size dictated, these individuals to be men of good standing between fifty and sixty years of age (*Recopilación* Libro VI, Título III, Ley vii).

Cogolludo is among several Franciscans to mention these positions and adds a few others to them. The latter include the *tupil,* who was to lead the children heading into doctrine classes, himself carrying a cross raised on a staff at the head of the procession (Cogolludo 1971 [1688], 1:293; and see above). Like the sacristan, the *tupil* was salaried. In the same section, Cogolludo also mentions the *alguacil,* who appears to have the same function; *tupil* and *alguacil* may even be different terms for the same position. Finally, Cogolludo (1:292) mentions *patrones,* who were also given a staff with a cross or divine image atop it and who were to notify the *doctrinero* of anyone in the community in need of sacraments. Cogolludo's description suggests that there may have been two *patrones* per *parcialidad,* the two alternating weeks in order to maintain their agricultural work. The *alguaciles, tupiles, fiscales,* and *patrones* were all appointed or elected on January 1 of each year, at the same time that officers were elected to the town *cabildos*. This suggests an overlap between the spheres of mission and town governance, a point to which I return at the end of this chapter.

The line between the religious and their Maya assistants was most direct in the major positions involving the teaching of reading, writing, *doctrina*, and religious music. The best known of these were the *maestros cantores* 'cantor masters', sometimes referred to as *maestros de capilla* 'chapel masters', as *maestros de escuela* 'school masters', or as *ah cambesah* 'teachers'. The relationship between these different titles is uncertain, and Collins (1977, 242–43) convincingly argues that they designate overlapping or identical positions. Toral's *Avisos* (1563) and Maya documents tend to use the Maya expression, whereas Cogolludo (1971 [1688], 1:296) appears to favor *maestro de capilla,* and references to the *(maestros) cantores* are scattered throughout the historical record. What is clear and agreed upon is that there was at least one position in the missions in which the functions of teaching and indoctrinating were concentrated. This position was always occupied by an *indio de confianza* and obviously presupposed advanced training in literacy and doctrine, as well as assiduous practice of the religion. The *maestro* would have been trained either directly by the religious or by other *maestros* working under the tutelage of the religious. The position was a pivotal one in the plan of *reducción,* since the *maestro* trained and selected the *escribano* 'notary', who would play a key role in the *cabildo* government. Moreover, as we saw with Toral's *Avisos,* the *maestro* was empowered to perform baptism in the absence of the priest and to prepare the dying for a "good death." According to Farriss (1984, 335–38), the *maestros cantores* had the authority to appoint the organists, musicians, and singers of the liturgy; the sacristans; the *fiscales de doctrina;* and a host of *patrones* involved in marriage and burial. Given the sheer scope of the verbal and ritual practices that *maestros* engaged in, taught, and supervised, they were in effect *doctrineros* and the closest of all Indian collaborators with the religious. Farriss suggests that the position had antecedents in the pre-Columbian positions *ah kin* '(high) priest' and *ah cambesah* 'teacher'. The *maestros* also interacted with the *cabildo* government, and the position of *maestro* was a stepping-stone to government office.

There is no evidence to my knowledge as to how many *maestros* were active in any given *guardianía* at a single time, but the suggestion of the sources is that there was at least one per pueblo. This would be the most conservative guess, assuming that all the different terms in the previous paragraph are alternative ways to denote the same position. It is also evident that there was great variation between *guardianías* and over time in the province, just as there was in the shape of *cabildo* councils.

At the same time, we should register the magnitude of the indigenous role in actually conducting the evangelization. Whether by policy or by demographic necessity, the religious relied upon a cadre of Maya coworkers, without whom there would have been no *reducción*. These Maya listened and watched for friars, they gathered students and apprehended the wayward, they spoke for the religious in the schools and doctrine classes, and they were pivotal in producing the scribes who would serve in the councils. They taught and led divine song and musical accompaniment. They were authorized to baptize in the absence of the priest and had constant access to the church, which they tended. When we turn to the Maya-language discourse through which this elaborate program was realized, these same Maya people are the ones who voiced the prayers and catechism, who sang the hours, who assisted in the translation of everything from prayers to petitions, dictionary entries to verb paradigms. It was also they who fled, bringing knowledge and practices over the frontiers that crisscrossed provincial life, assuring that in rebel settlements too technologies of expression from the *reducción* would be practiced, even when the goal was to repudiate the oppression. In chapter 11, I will argue that key passages of the Books of Chilam Balam were likely written by maestros, and Chuchiak (2000b) documents many cases in which maestros were discovered to be practicing *ah kin*. This doubling in the valence of the *maestro* echoes the doubling of the landscape under the spatial *reducción* and the doubling of the linguistic space as a result of translation. Even if their understanding or faith fell short of the *confianza* invested in them, *maestros* were vital generative agents in propagating the new language of *reducción*.

Overlapping with the missions, but largely beyond the missionaries' control, were the community structures called *cofradías*. These were introduced in the late sixteenth century and were originally lay brotherhoods to which pious individuals would belong and pay dues, devoted primarily to the care and cult of the church and *santos*. Recall Cogolludo's (1971 [1688], 1:295–96) mention of the *cofradías* formed in the head towns. As Farriss (1984, 154ff., 265–72, 321–50) explains at length, the *cofradías* came to be powerful financial institutions, owning cattle ranches, engaging in trade, and gathering and expending enormous wealth. Indeed, they played a pivotal role in what Farriss calls the strategies for collective survival of the Maya under Spanish rule, since they operated mostly outside the pale of colonial taxation and according to the mandates of their Maya communities. Central to the activities of the *cofradías* were the care and processional display of the local saints to which they were devoted, the care of the church and its ornaments, and the underwriting of great celebrations during the *fiestas. Fiesta* activities apparently included copious displays of fireworks, bullfights, dances, solemn processions of the *santo* surrounded by leaders from both the *cofradía* and the town council, the burning of large numbers of candles, and enormous collective feasts. Cogolludo speaks of the *fiestas* as events at which leaders from various towns came together. Hence the *cofradías* were powerful organizations at the edges of the missions and the towns.

Farriss (1984, 234) summarizes the leadership positions in the *cofradías*. These included an upper tier of *patrones* 'patrons' and *escribanos de cofradía* 'brotherhood scribes', a middle tier of two *priostes* 'stewards' and four *mayordomos* 'stewards', and a lower tier of laborers on the *cofradía* ranches. The upper- and middle-tier positions were occupied by members of the elite and were subject to yearly elections. According to Farriss, the scribes maintained superb financial records of the ranches and the expenditures of the association. She also notes that *cofradía* members were called upon to care for the sick and elderly and to assist the dying to *morir bien* 'die well' with the help of part-time *fiscales* who would give notice of all who needed the sacraments. These tasks are identical to the ones that Cogolludo (1791 [1688], 1:292) assigned to the *fiscales de doctrina* and barrio-level *patrones* and also overlap with the tasks that Toral in his *Avisos* assigned to the *maestros*. That Farriss describes these functions and positions in terms of the *cofradías*, whereas Toral and Cogolludo do so in the context of the missions, suggests a significant overlap and interaction between the two. This is consistent with the fact that the *cofradías* made the processions of the saints in the *fiestas* and that their members (*mayordomos* in particular) dressed and cared for the saints during the year. It would appear that the *cofradías* took on the role of caring for the spaces and ornaments of ritual worship, the *santos* whose names were given to *parcialidades,* and many of the great collective festivities of the feast calendar. They even paid the salary of the *maestro cantor* (Farriss 1984, 326).

CABILDOS IN THE MISSION TOWNS

Corresponding to the major role played by Maya people in the spiritual *reducción* of the *guardianías* is their even more preponderant role in local governance in their pueblos. Governance was to *policía* what the pueblo was to spatial *reducción*. In his early master plan, López Medel already set out a minimal structure of town governance but did not install *cabildo*-style councils. About thirty years later, in 1583, don Diego García de Palacio, Oidor de la Real Audiencia de Nueva España, did install the *cabildo* system. In the highest position, the system had a *gobernador* who was designated by colonial authorities. In the early years, the preference would have been for a member of the Maya elite, whereas in the mid-seventeenth century heredity gave way to ability, and the position was given to the most competent *indio de confianza,* even if he was not a member of the elite (Cogolludo 1971 [1688], 1:290). Beneath the *gobernador* were the officers of the *cabildo,* which included two *alcaldes,* four *regidores,* the *mayordomo,* and the various *alguaciles*. All these were elected annually, on January 1. This system spread around Yucatán during the latter part of the sixteenth century, and its functioning in the seventeenth century is described by Cogolludo (1:290–96). It has also been studied with care by several recent historians, including Farriss

(1984), Quezada (1993; 2001, 52–54), Restall (1997), Bracamonte y Sosa and Solís Robleda (1996), and Thompson (1978).

It is challenging to determine the actual functioning and boundaries of the councils in the Maya *repúblicas de indios*. One reason is that there was significant variation over time and space in the form *cabildos* took, as Restall (1997) demonstrates with witness lists and election records from numerous towns. This makes it difficult to construct a single chart of the positions and the rules governing their occupancy. Second, the governance of the pueblos involved at least four semi-independent organizations: the preexisting *batabil* system (see chapter 2), the *cabildo* proper, the *cofradía* organizations, and the Indian positions in the missionary field. Each of these defined a hierarchy of positions, with titles and distributions of authority. It is sometimes hard to tell which title or sphere of action goes with which position. Moreover, not all the lesser positions were regulated by the Spanish, and they varied widely. There were also several cases in which positions in two or more sectors (e.g., *cabildo* and *cofradía*) had a single title (e.g., *mayordomo*), though they were different offices (see Farriss 1984, 234). In other cases, for instance, *tupil* and *fiscal*, it is unclear whether we should treat a position as part of the *cabildo* or part of the mission, since the officeholder seems to have had responsibilities in both sectors, and the terms are inconsistently used in the sources. Restall also notes that some of these titles "floated," being applied in ways that suggest an almost honorific and nonliteral usage.

The *cabildo* itself was engaged in a wide range of activities (Restall 1997, 51–83). Acting as a group, it had the authority to apply the law, and its members were sometimes called *justicias* 'magistrates'. It was also a center for discourse production in the form of documentation and archival maintenance of town records. It was the *cabildo* that notarized documents, and the local *escribanos* were high-ranking, paid members. Document production entailed a number of formalizing practices such as meetings, processions (especially for land documents), inspections, and witnessings. Votes were taken, and the texts of various genres produced by the *escribanos* were collectively ratified. Thus governance in the *pueblos reducidos* defines a field with multiple spheres of activity, at least four distinct but overlapping systems of authority, a formidable lexicon of titles, and the capacity to produce significant discourse genres. The field of governance is pivotal for our purposes, since Maya was the language used and so much of the existing Maya documentation was produced in the towns. In effect, the interaction between missions and town governance greatly amplified the discursive effects of *reducción*.

At the pinnacle of the towns were elite officials variously titled *gobernador* or *batab* 'chief' and often referred to as "cacique," or chief. There is significant debate among historians as to the relation between the Maya position, which was hereditary among the elite, and the Spanish position, filled through appointment by colonial authorities. There is agreement that in the early stages of the colony, the Spanish recognized the *batabs* and drew from the elite for appointment to office. Farriss (1984) argues that the *batab* eventually merged with the *gobernador* and that the *cabildo* system was established by the early 1580s. By contrast, Quezada (1993, 105), focusing on the first thirty years of the colony, emphasizes that the indigenous system persisted and the *cabildo* was slow to become established. Restall (1997, 62 ff.) opts to treat *batab* and *gobernador* as two separate positions, partly on the grounds that *batabs* held office for as long as twenty years, whereas the *gobernadores* held office for much shorter periods. These contrasting interpretations might be due in part to variations in the governance of different towns, but they also bear on many of the same places, suggesting that the sources are ambiguous. The cause of ambiguity seems to be the fact that *batab* and *gobernador* are sometimes equivalent or merged as designations of the head of the *cabildo,* but at other times or places, they are distinct, since *batab* indexes the indigenous system of governance, whereas *gobernador* indexes the Spanish. Such are the pitfalls of the doubling of language under *reducción*. Whatever the correct solution, all three terms appear often in the documents produced by the towns. What is known is that the pre-Hispanic system of government and the *cabildo* system were different, that they intersected and came to overlap in the *pueblos reducidos,* and that both Spanish and Maya terms were used in reference to positions in both structures.

Among the critical positions in town governance was that of the *escribano.* In Yucatecan towns, the *escribano* was a member of the elite, whose training included *doctrina* and whose signature was the graphic sign of colonial authority. Like the notary, the *escribano* maintained records, but unlike an average notary, his position was a stepping-stone to higher office. *Escribanos* were sometimes called *ah dzib hun* 'book (paper) writers', a position likely present in the pre-Spanish *batab* system.[16] According to Cogolludo (1971 [1688], 1:296), the classes led by *maestros de capilla* on the patios and schools taught writing and reading and helped produce scribes. Restall also reports that *cabildo* members selected the apprentices to the *maestros* each year, a report that I have been unable to confirm in the sources. If true, this would mean that the town council selected the students of the *maestro,* even though the *maestro* was first and foremost an agent of the missions. Restall (1997) seems to include the *maestro* and the *tupil* as part of the *cabildo* but also points out that they were both civil and religious in function. I think a safer interpretation is that both were agents of the mission, and the *maestro,* not the *cabildo,* selected those students whom he would train for the position of *escribano.*[17] This is also consistent with Restall's observation that in some cases an individual called a *tupil doctrina* had teaching duties normally associated with a *maestro,* and in Tekantó a *tupil doctrina* subsequently became an *escribano.* In other words, the *escribano* occupied a position in town governance, but candidates were selected and trained within the sphere of the missions. Hence this pivotal position in governance and discourse production straddled the line between mission and town council. Cogolludo notes that the attendance of council members at *doctrina* and the sacraments was closely monitored, another indicator of the close relation between the two spheres.

There is agreement that most of the *cabildo* members were elected or named on the first day of each year. According to Cogolludo (1971 [1688], 1:292), this would include two *alcaldes*, four *regidores*, and one *procurador*. These three were high-ranking positions, occupied by members of the elite and subject to ratification by the *gobernador* acting in the name of the Crown. The *alcaldes* and *regidores* in particular assumed a central role in town governance and were typical signatories to notarial documents. Cogolludo also mentions four officers whose primary functions appear to be in the missions (see previous section of this chapter), though they seem to have been named along with the *cabildo* officers on the first of the year. These were the *fiscal*, one *alguacil* or *tupil* per *parcialidad*, and the *patrones*, who were to know every sick person in the barrios and give notice to the *doctrinero* of all who needed sacraments (1:294).[18] *Patrones* were given a *vara* 'staff' with a cross or an image atop it, and they seem to have worked in pairs, alternating weeks, so as to be able to maintain their agricultural labor.[19] He also makes vague reference to the election (or appointment) of "other ministers" to assure that the "naturally lazy" Indios worked their fields properly.

Cogolludo is consistent with the other sources in citing the importance of the *principales*, elder men of good reputation, drawn from the elite in each barrio, who would encourage participation in the missions and speak on behalf of the barrio in the sphere of governance. He notes that the caciques convened the *principales* for significant acts and that they gathered punctually, which suggests a regular role in town governance, even though they were not members per se of the *cabildo*, nor were they subject to yearly appointment. Also called the *chunthan* or *noh xib* 'elder males' in Maya, *principales* embody the intersection of the *batabil* with the *cabildo* and the *cabildo* with the missions. In a field marked by ambiguous agents, the *principal* was among the more ambiguous.

There are several other titles mentioned by Cogolludo, Restall (1997), Farriss (1984), and Quezada (1993) that recur in the documents I discuss. These include the *ah cuchcab* 'earth bearers', a term that originally designated counselors to the *batab*. As with the *ah kulel*, they were leaders associated with sections of the town. There is agreement in the literature that the *ah kulel* position rapidly fell away with the establishment of the *pueblos reducidos*, whereas *ah cuchcab* continued to appear in the documents. The use of the latter term was sufficiently ambiguous that Farriss (1984, 234 ff.) suggests that the position merged with that of *regidor* in the *cabildo*, although Restall (1997, 68) questions the association. Restall (1997, 70) also mentions three other terms, *teniente* 'lieutenant', *justicia*, and *belnal*. The latter two were apparently general terms for town officials.[20] Outside the *cabildo* and the accepted structures of the colony, residents of the *pueblos reducidos* were simply called *ah cahnal* 'resident', a term blind to gender or status.

Alongside these numerous ambiguous positions was another organizational system in the Maya pueblos. This one was organized by the Maya priesthood and centered on the indigenous religion that *reducción* sought to replace. Chuchiak (2000b, 411–16) describes the system as it was revealed in inquisitional testimony. Maya pueblos, including *pueblos reducidos,* were divided into four sectors called *cuchteel,* or in Spanish 'barrios'. Each sector had a directional coefficient (ENWS), the corresponding color according to long-standing Maya symbolism (red, white, black, yellow, respectively), and an *ah cuchcab* 'earth bearer'. Each was also presided over by an *ah kin,* trained and appointed by an *ah kin may,* a higher priest. Thus, in any major pueblo, there could be a single *ah kin may* plus four *ah kin.* In addition to this structure, each of the four sectors had what Landa described as a religious brotherhood, headed by the *ah kin.* The *ah kin* were structurally opposed and violently repressed by the missionaries. Whereas the Spanish authorities explicitly recognized the elite and drew on the leadership pool of the *batabil,* at least in the early decades, there was no such accommodation with the *ah kin* priests. The Franciscans considered them arch idolaters and sought to destroy them, along with the "pots," images, and books with which they worshiped false gods. Like those of the lesser *ah men,* whom the Spanish outlawed as *hechiceros* posing as doctors, their activities were intrinsically false and of great concern to the colonial authorities. Chuchiak (2000b, 412) cites the case of Calotmul, which was revealed to have this entire structure in 1595, almost fifty years into the colonial period. Documents from the seventeenth century indicate elements of this alternate system of religious governance persisted, and Chuchiak suggests that it was to be found in nearly all major pueblos. Thus even within the sphere of *reducción,* the internal governance of the pueblo defined a field in which *reducción* coexisted with its opposite. It is unclear how much influence this parallel universe had on colonial governance, but it provides elegant evidence that the counterforce embodied by the frontier was strong inside the colony as well.

. . .

Some of the difficulty sorting out the missions, the *cofradías,* the *cabildos,* and the indigenous background of town governance comes from the language used in the documents. As we would expect on linguistic grounds, not all expressions are equally specific. Some of the usages appear inconsistent—hardly surprising given the historical, social, cultural, and political scope of the processes we are describing. On other points, it appears that the different structures were designed with common features, such as the elite/nonelite division, the hierarchical organization of positions, and the recurrence of positions such as *cantor, sacristán, fiscal,* and *alguacil* at different levels. But a careful reading of these four spheres of life in the *pueblos reducidos* also suggests that some of the ambiguities and overlaps were by design and may ultimately have abetted the *reducción*. After all, these were among the pathways through which the *reducción*, the practices of *policía*, and the *lengua reducida* would move out from the missions into the towns and beyond. By the same token, they defined some of the lines along which the *reducción* was itself shaped by the province and the people in which it was embedded. Restall (1997, 73–74) observes that individuals rarely held the same offices in the *cabildo* two years in a row; this turnover would amplify the effect by increasing the flow of people who would directly engage with the business of prayer and *policía*. Participation in the *cabildo* would further the conversions.

The ongoing processes of adjustment and variation among *pueblos reducidos* (vividly shown by Restall [1997, 70–74]) would reflect the push and pull of social realities in the Yucatecan towns. The missionary master plans were altered in the course of their execution. In his 1586 letter to the Council of Indies, Bishop Cardete comments at length on the conflicts that had become endemic between *guardianes* in the missions and *batabs* in the towns (by which he almost certainly means *gobernadores*). As we know, the friars considered corporal punishment a critical part of their loving pedagogy, but the native officials evidently undercut them by telling townspeople that they had no authority to punish. When asked to mete out punishment, the *batabs* and others insolently refused, suggesting that the seamless cooperation projected in some of the Franciscan writings was overly optimistic. Like flight and idolatry inside the *pueblos reducidos,* the interactions between governance structures also multiplied the sites at which a frontier between Indio and colonizer could be asserted.

Through the multiple spheres of the *reducción* and the coexisting anti-*reducción* of flight and frontier, forms of knowledge and practice proliferated, including categories of persons and objects, the production of public and private signs, and ultimately an entire field of genres, each corresponding to certain positions in the field of the *guardianías* and *pueblos reducidos*. The missionary orchestration aimed at inducing the Indios to make themselves new men, as the Franciscans put it. The body would play its role, occupant of spaces built and natural, site of experiences pleasurable and painful. The realities were obviously more complicated and shifting than the plans, but the outcomes indicate that what transpired over the course of these processes was basic and history-making. Each new distinction, with its articulated hierarchy and sphere of action, was a virtual frontier. The former or future apostate might engage in the forms of *reducción* without the anticipated beliefs or entailments. In effect, when we look within the pueblos we see a profusion of boundaries, every one of which is a site of potential, partial, or ephemeral autonomy. The clearest evidence of the consequences of this elaborate program lies in the discourse its participants produced. That of the actors in the pueblos demonstrates *reducción* at a much finer level than any of the sources discussed so far.

PART II

Converting Words

I HAVE CONCENTRATED SO FAR on the establishment and organization of the Provincia de San Josef de Yucatán, including the regional configuration, the *guardianías,* and the main forms of governance at the level of the *pueblo reducido.* At this point I begin to shift attention toward the role of language in this overall process. Each of the organizational forms described functioned simultaneously as a field of communicative practices. The mission was the site of doctrinal instruction, and of the church where children were taught and religious practice took place. From the missions came linguistic studies composed or brought together by missionary *lenguas,* including the dictionaries, grammars, and such doctrinal works as Coronel's *Doctrina Cristiana en Lengua Maya* (1620). The *cabildo* was in turn the site in which a large corpus of "official" or "notarial" documentation was produced, of which approximately two thousand Maya texts are currently extant (Restall 1997). Beyond the frontier of normative *policía,* the forbidden genres of the Books of Chilam Balam and the Ritual of the Bacabs were recopied and evidently reproduced in readings or performances. Thus the structures of the evangelical Catholic Church and of governance in the pueblos provide a sort of social map on which to plot the movements of discourse. While I have drawn so far mostly from Spanish-language sources, I will shift progressively to Maya ones, which will be the focus for the remainder of the book.

There are good reasons to think that discourse production was a central aspect of the *reducción.* Speech is utterly central in the religious practices of prayer, doctrine class, and the sacraments, not to mention in reading or listening to the Bible itself. The relation between the Word, the Christian God, and creation is emphasized in both *doctrina* and liturgy. The *cabildos,* in turn, did not merely govern. They were obliged to keep records, and the ones they kept were susceptible to being adduced in litigation, such as disputes over land rights (Restall 1997). The *cofradías* also kept records of funds and expenses. Even *indios sublevados* communicated with missionaries by means of written letters. There is no question that linguistic practice was a modality for a wide range of significant religious and social acts. Linguistic practice here includes situated speech and interaction, alphabetic writing, reading, and the mostly tacit ideas that language users have about their own and others' language. Insofar as these ideas are linked to the positions of speakers in the society, and especially when they evaluate or justify certain ways of speaking (writing, reading, etc.), they are what linguistic anthropologists have come to call language ideologies. When we say that *reducción* spread by way of linguistic practices, we mean that it replicated itself through speech and gesture, writing, reading, and different genres of discourse. Intersecting with actual uses of language, and structuring speakers' expectations about usage, linguistic common sense or ideology played a significant role in shaping *Maya reducido.* This is nowhere more obvious than in the metalinguistic works of the missionaries.

The writings of the religious in Yucatán and New Spain show unambiguously that they valued and sought mastery of the native languages. The *Relación* from New Spain (also known as *Códice Franciscano* [1941]), produced in New Spain circa 1571, makes it perfectly clear that in many *doctrinas* in the province, the *guardián* is *lengua* and that he teaches the language to others under his authority. This was the case for Nahuatl and Otomi, and also evidently for Maya in Yucatán, at least in theory. A royal *cédula* in 1573 instructed the bishop of Yucatán to use ministers who know *la lengua* in the *encomienda* towns of the Royal Crown. The *cédula* points out that since so many ministers do not know the language, people are dying without confessing, and they cannot understand the *doctrina* or the preaching. Thus knowledge of the native language is a prerequisite to the ministry of the faith. As we saw, Bishop Gregorio de Montalvo (Scholes et al. 1938) used the term *"media lengua"* for *sacerdotes* who could confess but not preach in the language. That Montalvo would comment on language ability is entirely typical of the memorial genre, but that he would distinguish degrees of ability is interesting. It provides evidence that *reducción* relied on a differentiated range of language abilities, with the preaching *lengua* at the top of the scale.

Bishop fray Juan Izquierdo's 1601 letter to the Crown is almost entirely devoted to the importance of the native language and the abysmal state of knowledge of the Franciscans in Yucatán (Scholes et al. 1938, 129–32). Izquierdo argues that the *"hijos de la tierra, clérigos beneméritos"* 'sons of this land, worthy clerics' should be given authority over six *guardianías,* thus staking out a pro-secular position in the ongoing disputes between Franciscans and seculars over control of the missions. He reasons that they speak the language better than the Franciscans ever will, because they "drank the language with their mother's milk." The pastor must know his flock, he continues, but it is costly to train friars in Maya, all of whom come from Castilla. It takes years, and half of them never learn. Izquierdo, who spoke no Maya himself and had only recently come to Yucatán after thirty years in Peru, proposed to examine the language abilities of all the friars who had been here for a long time, with the aid of an interpreter. He expresses dismay that the friars confess using a booklet and asking simple questions, a complaint that would apparently fit Montalvo's *"media lengua"* confessor. This is surely a sin, he says, and Your Majesty should save yourself from it by assigning *guardianías* to clerics.

In an interesting twist on the theme of language ability in Maya, Sánchez de Aguilar reports in his *Informe* that Maya speakers are extraordinary raconteurs who speak with eloquence, humor, and great specificity. Given the display of linguistic virtuosity that they are capable of, it is clear that they are capable of learning the *doctrina*. Thus, he reasons, if they do not learn and convert, it is because they have ill will, not because they lack the ability.

Lizana's 1633 *Historia* extols the great precision of Maya and leans heavily on the *lengua* capacities of those he profiles in his ecstatic *devocionario,* commenting at length on their language abilities and the written works they produced. Cogolludo (1971 [1688], 1:292, 433) reiterates that the evangelization of Maya people was conducted in their "natural language," in order that they understand it better (see also Farriss 1984, 111). The missionaries of the previous century had translated the catechism, and more recently it had been "perfected" and printed so that it could be read by the Indios. Writing in the mid-seventeenth century, Cogolludo is almost certainly referring to the *doctrina* and sermons of fray Juan Coronel, published in 1620. Cogolludo is consistent with all the other major sources that the distinction between *lengua* and non-*lengua* priests was pervasively relevant and that much of the evangelization was carried out by native Maya speakers in their own language. This nexus and the training and employing of native teachers will play a pivotal role in furthering the transformation of Yucatec Maya into a *lengua reducida.*

It is noteworthy that much of the commentary on Maya language in the missionary writings takes the form of claims and counterclaims about who has such mastery. The 1681 *Recopilación* implicitly recognizes the problem, when it specifies that *doctrina* should be taught by *lenguas,* at least on its *encomiendas* of the Crown. Sixty-one years later, Beltrán de Santa Rosa (1757) points out the woeful errors that result from improper translation of the *doctrina,* based on imperfect knowledge of Maya. To translate the "body of Christ" as *"ucucutil cristo,"* as Coronel had done, was to equate the host with the sexual organ of the redeemer. To translate "the Lord is with thee" in the Ave Maria as *"Yumbil yan auokol"* was to say in Maya, "the Father is on top of you," with all the shockingly inappropriate sexual connotations such a statement would suggest. In short, there was no debate whatsoever as to the need to know the Maya language, but there were constant debates and accusations regarding who met the need and who did not.

The use of Maya in the missions relies first and foremost on translation, the accuracy of which was required if the Indios were to learn truths instead of falsehoods. Beltrán's point was not a new one, even if his examples were howlers. The 1571 *Códice Franciscano* calls for the gospels and epistles to be printed in translation in the native languages, because at that time they were recopied by hand with errors introduced due to lack of understanding. When priests then go about preaching and teaching with defective hand-copied translations, they fall into error and *"hartas gazafatones, y aún plega a Dios que no digan algunas herejías"* 'tired nonsense, and they even hope to God they do not speak heresies' out of their ignorance (*Códice Franciscano* 1941, 61).

It is noteworthy that no missionary, to my knowledge, ever suggested that his native-language helpers, who were *indios de confianza,* had misled him purposely on a matter of translation. The problem was accuracy to the sacred texts, and if they were mistranslated, even the *doctrineros* might simply assume it was a proper rendition. But if Beltrán was right in his criticisms of earlier *doctrinas,* then it is hard to imagine that such errors would go unnoticed by *indios ladinos* or *maestros cantores.* Both of these groups would have access to both the Maya and the Spanish (or Latin) versions of discourse and could compare them. In the absence of any evidence that such errors were actually picked up by native Maya speakers, it is reasonable to assume that either the offending translations were actually ambiguous, and a proper reading could be derived from them (even if a highly improper reading were also possible), or, alternatively, Maya language changed over the course of the first two hundred years of the colony. Such a change would have to explain the association of *cucutil* with the male body part as a metonym of the entire body, and the gloss of *tawokol* as 'on top of you' instead of an earlier meaning that covered 'above you' as well. In any case, the translation process was an experimentation and a dynamic process of revision. It was also an arena in which competing claims to legitimate knowledge and ability were made as individuals and missionary groups struggled to see who would carry out the *reducción* and subsequent maintenance of Christian communities.

The inquisition and extirpations in Yucatán revealed idolatrous language along with the practices it helped define. According to Landa, Sánchez de Aguilar, and the records of the idolatry trials in Yucatán, Maya ritual practice included ritual offerings of human blood and sacrificial lives, the copious use of incense, altars, ceramic embodiments of deities, and ritual speech. It was usually described in terms that focalize its verbal dimensions. It was *falsedad* 'falsehood', *vómito* 'vomit', and consisted in words so permeated by evil and evacuated of truth that Sánchez de Aguilar refuses to reproduce them, even though he claims to know the incantation he is condemning. As early as Toral's *Avisos* (n.d., ca. 1563), nocturnal reading of native texts was forbidden, and the burning of native books at the 1562 auto-da-fe in Maní is too well known to need rehearsing here. The upshot of these facts is that language was also the object of sustained censorship, and native books in particular were seen as dangerous idolatrous objects to be burned or confiscated. The *reducción* proceeded by way of erasure through the attempted extirpation of a whole sector of Maya discourse, in both its written and oral phases.

It was not only the missionaries who placed a premium on language abilities and the advantages of bilingualism. Given the frequency with which Franciscan friars collaborated with Maya people in writing letters and other notarial documents, it is unsurprising that they too comment on language, albeit less often than the missionaries themselves. The series of letters sent to the Crown from *pueblos reducidos* in northwestern Yucatán during the first half of 1567 comment explicitly on the Franciscan knowledge of Maya. They contrast the Franciscans, who speak to them lovingly in the language of "here," to the seculars, who speak to them only through interpreters and who do not know them or their language. By contrast, the Yaxkukul land surveys focus on language through extended quotation and commentary on speech. The Books of Chilam Balam, though forbidden, nonetheless continued to be recopied and are replete with representations of language, both quoted and commented on. The sheer quantity of documentation produced by Maya authors in the Indian republics indicates that although many of the colonial genres would be new, the act of writing and its multiple relations to governance and ritual practice were well known and rapidly transposable onto the new genres. It is self-evident from the hieroglyphic corpus that Maya were literate long before the Spanish arrived, but this literacy appeared to transfer over to alphabetic textuality as well.

The next chapters pursue the thesis that we cannot understand *reducción* or the conversions it furthered without understanding the language through which it operated. Part of that language is Spanish and part is Maya, and neither can be properly interpreted without reference to the other. Conversely, we cannot properly construe the language of this far-flung formation without understanding the fields of *reducción*. We will proceed stepwise, starting with an introduction to the main genres and the three-way relation among genre, field, and habitus. If discourse provided vectors for *reducción*, it did so in several different ways, subject to different constraints and with different consequences. Chapters 5 and 6 form a pair whose focus is the bilingual dictionaries, the Spanish-to-Maya works and then the Maya-to-Spanish ones. Chapter 7 treats the three major *artes* produced by colonial missionaries. Together the dictionaries and *artes* make up the metalinguistic works of the missionaries. The doctrinal works, discussed in chapter 8, implement the version of Maya developed by the missionary linguists. Whereas the linguistic works were all bilingual, the doctrinal ones are almost entirely monolingual Maya (the Spanish and Latin master texts being presupposed). We will see that the missionary discourse is substantial and deeply coherent, suggesting a single sphere of discourse. This is what we would expect given the coherence and systematic design of the missionary field, but its discursive consequences have yet to be examined. The robust interpenetration of metalinguistic works and doctrinal ones casts doubt on the proper reading of the colonial grammars: are they descriptive works, prescriptive ones, or fragmentary primers for rendering the holy word in an unholy language? At the same time, the doctrinal works, which might at first appear insignificant curiosities, turn out to be in fact a sort of Rosetta stone for the interpretation of metalinguistic works. We turn now to the metalinguistic works and the world of practice they project.

4

From Field to Genre and Habitus

The *reducción* was implemented in a complex field where several systems of governance interacted and where all these different spheres and the positions they entailed for individual people and groups corresponded with particular spaces and places. To describe the social context of *reducción* as a "field" is to underscore certain of its features. In each of the three spheres of space, conduct, and language, there were highly organized schemas that defined actor positions such as *provincial, guardián, frayle, maestro cantor, alcalde, batab,* and *sublevado.* Similarly, places were defined, such as the *pueblos de visita,* the *cabeceras,* the *convento* grounds, the rectilinear center of the *pueblos,* the four quadrants of the *ah kin* priests, and the province as a whole, bounded by the *montaña* to the east and south. Interwoven with these multiple divisions and positions were the varieties of language that circulated through them. This includes such varieties as the catechism, the example usages in the dictionaries, the singing of prayer and doctrine, the notarial genres produced in the *cabildos,* and even the forbidden writings of the Books of Chilam Balam. In a slightly abstract sense, language varieties and genres can themselves be thought of as positions in a field of discourse. Thus when we speak of the colonial field it is actually an abbreviation, since this field is made up of several interacting subfields. The long-term consequences of *reducción* are the result of the way it coordinated these subfields into an overarching project.

There is a large literature on the concept of field in social theory, and it plays a central role in the approach that I take to colonial practice in this book.[1] A couple of elements deserve mention here. First, a field is defined as a space of positions and position taking, that is, a space in which social actors engage with one another in their capacities as occupants of certain positions: the priest and the sinner in the confessional, the *gobernador* and the *alcaldes* in the *cabildo,* the *ah kin* and the members of the "brotherhood" of the quadrant in the pueblos. By "position taking," sociologists mean the historically specific act of actually occupying the position, as opposed to an abstract definition of it. Hence what is important is not only the position of *guardián* but also how Coronel, Ciudad Real, or Lizana discharged that position, perhaps changing it in the process. The field is therefore both a schematic structure and a historical actuality. Second, any field is a space of engagement in which certain values are at stake and in play. For the Spanish colonists, those values included saliently the labor, goods, and money extracted from the indigenous people; and for the missionized Maya, part of the value that circulated in the ecclesiastical spheres of church and mission was the grace, support, and legitimacy to which those "in the right" had access. For the missionary, a major part of the value that moved through the missions was the souls of the Maya whom they sought to turn toward their God. However one ultimately defined it, conversion was clearly a value both in itself and as a resource for gaining privileges.

A third element of field that is pointedly relevant to the history described here is the boundary. To describe a social context as a field is to say it is partly defined by boundary mechanisms and the conflicts to which they nearly always give rise. All the positions mentioned above were limited in terms of who could occupy them. Recall that the Franciscans recruited almost exclusively from Spain, especially in the early years, that no indigenous people in Yucatán were ordained, that the *maestros, sacristanes,* and other helpers were recruited exclusively from *indios de confianza,* that one gained access to the position of scribe in the *cabildo* by undergoing doctrinal training with a *maestro,* and so forth. In all these ways, the positions are bounded by prerequisites and exclusions. Similarly in physical space, boundaries were critical and embodied perhaps most dramatically by the frontier zone separating the *provincia* of the *reducido* from the *despoblado* of the fugitives, insurgents, and idolaters. The code of *policía cristiana* acted as a normative boundary, inside of which the actor was in the right and outside of which he was in the wrong. In effect, when we expanded the concept of the frontier from the spatial zone to what Jones (1989, 1998) called "frontier processes," we treated it as a boundary in the theoretical sense.[2] The same problem of boundary lies at the heart of syncretism, since to divide an indigenous inside from a Hispanicized exterior, as the classic description does, amounts to sundering the person into two parts, each of which belongs to a different field. Without the boundary between the two fields, the idea of syncretism collapses in on itself.

A fourth element of any field is what Bourdieu (1985, 20–21) called, following Wittgenstein, a "language game," that is, a set of ways in which language was used, along with a set of beliefs and assumptions that undergird usage, and specific stakes at play in language. The discourses produced in the fields of *reducción* were many and highly differentiated and corresponded to a coherent system of genres. Among the relevant beliefs were the ideas that Spanish and Maya could be intertranslated; that certain forms of language were inherently true and others inherently false; that notarial documents were authentic when properly produced, dated, signed, and attested by witnesses (even if what they allege turns out to be untrue); and that making the sign of the cross (saying the words and doing the gesture with the proper intention) would protect the subject from evil. These are among the mostly tacit assumptions that I revisit in the coming chapters.

There is one last idea that the term "field" invokes and that played a pivotal role in the *reducción*. This has to do with the way that engagement in a field shapes the actor. I have noted at several points that the Franciscan missionaries saw the repeated, regular practice of *doctrina* as an integral part of the effort to convert indigenous people to Christianity. A century later, Pascal, among others, notes this effect, that prayer can induce belief; the more general idea that action can shape the actor is a tenet of much contemporary social thought. The Franciscans were keen to incite the memory via the senses precisely for the purpose of shaping the remembering subject. In practice theory, also called "reflexive sociology" (Bourdieu and Wacquant 1992), there is a principled relation between the positions an actor occupies in the field and his own developed dispositions, such that the field inscribes itself on the actor in the form of positionally reinforced perspectives, ways of evaluating, and habitual actions. In short, one becomes what one does.

In the colonial context, the routines of practice codified under *reducción*, in the form of *policía cristiana* and proper religious observance, would be a critical part of the "civilizing process." This is not to say that any actor is reducible to a homunculus merely repeating what is demanded by the fields of interaction in which he engages. No such imperial fantasy would find a referent in colonial Yucatán. Rather, repeated or highly valued practices *tend toward* routinization and memorization and can become automatic for the actor. Eventually, the categories (identifications and exclusions) that imbue these routinized dispositions come to have the status of ways of seeing the world and oneself. In the colonial context, the perspectives and values that were inculcated by practices attuned to *policía* and *reducción* come to filter the subject's own view of himself (or itself, if the subject stands for a collectivity, as it does in the mass conversions under discussion). This gives rise to "hegemony," the internalization of a system of domination such that an actor's own interests appear to be reflected in the very system that dominates him.[3] To be concrete, the field of *reducción* tended to produce certain dispositions and evaluative perspectives among those who occupied it, missionaries and Mayas alike. The reproduction of field positions in actors' dispositions was neither automatic nor exhaustive, obviously. Yet it was a design feature of the missionary project, one that would help propagate the schemas of *reducción* at the level of indigenous actors. This process of inscription, formation, and disposition I will call the habitus. The basic idea is that we are dealing with the social production of a new, specifically colonial subject and that among the causal elements that shaped this subject was the field in its relational form. Rather than treat conversion as a change in belief or intention, apparently subjective and "private," this book treats it as a social product of the interplay of field and habitus.

As discussed in chapters 2 and 3, then, the multiple boundaries of *reducción* were dynamic and the project was sometimes fragmentary, reversible, or compromised by circumstances and determined resistance. The division between inside and outside was embodied in the extremely porous frontier between the reduction zone and the *despoblado*. It also was embodied within the pueblos, where the constraints of *policía cristiana*, the strictures of orthodoxy, the obligation to engage in religious ritual and training, and the surveillance of the friars all contributed to normative definitions of acceptability. The limits of acceptability defined a boundary beyond which conduct was punishable, idolatrous, false, secret, or disordered. In general, we can say that every action was a potential site for the boundary between interiority and exteriority, *reducción* and the partial autonomy that came with being out of bounds. Daily practice in the *pueblos reducidos* produced indefinitely many such boundaries. In other words, *reducción* was generative.

A critical part of its generativity lay in its relation to language. For it was through the forms of discourse produced in the missions and towns that *reducción* was put into practice, and forms of language traveled just as surely as did people and objects. The *lengua reducida* was an objectification produced by the translingual practices of missionaries and Mayas, but it was at the same time a practical instrument used to form new missionaries and new Christians. Proper speech and writing fostered *reducción* among the Indios who would be induced to practice it. For this it had to be transformed into a language of *policía cristiana* and governance, and it had to be used across the several spheres of pueblo life. The articulations between *doctrina*, catechism classes, *cofradías* and fiestas, *cabildo* and *batabil*, all provided pathways for the new language to move into the pervasively interpenetrating spheres of pueblo life. Franciscans were known to participate frequently in official acts taken by the *cabildo*, and they were clearly involved in coauthoring numerous letters sent to province-level officials or above. Linguistic practice was a primary vector of *reducción*, and the missionaries were keenly aware of this.[4]

Many of the positions spelled out over the previous two chapters entailed, as part of their ordinary functions, that their occupants produce or work with specialized genres. Missionary discourse included the *memorias* we have already seen, as well as the evangelical works, dictionaries and grammars, sermons, and doctrinal scripts to which I turn in the next four chapters. The *cabildo* produced land surveys, *cartas*, petitions, and records of agreements; other groups produced bills of sale of land, testaments, chronicles, and so forth. It is not entirely clear to what degree writing entered into the pre-Columbian *batabil*, but the Books of Chilam Balam are replete with descriptions of actions taken by rulers of various sorts, as are the hieroglyphic inscriptions. This suggests strongly that written records were kept, in genres whose properties we can only infer or guess at today.

Genre distinctions in colonial Maya discourse are organized by six main parameters: (1) *metalinguistic classification* as displayed in the texts themselves, including the ways in which language is represented; (2) the *production and reception format* of the work, distinguishing principal, author, scribe, witness, authority addressed, and authority invoked; (3) the *deictic centering* of the work in the here-now of its production via signatures, dates, and places of production (including those attached to the front matter of published works) and in appeals to firsthand evidence; (4) *variation in style,* including opening and closing formulas, persuasion, claims to authenticity, verse parallelism, and rhetorically charged tropes; (5) *multimodality* in performance dimensions involving the interaction of bodies, objects, built space, gesture, and perception; and (6) *iteration* in transdiscursive series, through multiple copies or performances and intertextual repetitions.[5]

METALINGUISTIC LABELING

For now, I use the term "genre" heuristically to designate kinds of discourse. In many cases, these kinds are named by terms in Spanish or Maya or both: *kahlay* 'history'; *carta* 'letter'; *deslinde* and *tzol pictun* 'survey'; *petición* 'petition'; *Padre Nuestro* 'Our Father'; *Discursos Predicables* 'preachable discourses (sermons)'; *testamento* and *takyahthan* 'will and testament'. In other cases, there may be varieties of language use that we wish to treat as specific genres, though they are not named as such in the discourse itself. For example, there is a stylistically marked genre of discourse used to report the *tzol pictun* 'order of the boundary markers', which is the core of the *deslinde*. This recurs in land surveys and in the Books of Chilam Balam, always reporting the actual survey or visitation of places. Cyclic in poetic form and highly constrained in content, the discourse of *tzol* ordering is highly distinctive.[6] In any event there is a considerable vocabulary for kinds of discourse and the works that instantiate them, and this is heuristically useful in making a first approximation of the genres. This vocabulary of types is what linguistic anthropologists call metalinguistic, because it refers to kinds of language or linguistic practice. Such vocabularies are well known in the literature and give us precious clues as to how speakers of the language categorized linguistic works and language itself.

There are three main ways that colonial Maya texts are labeled as instances of genres. First, the work may be described or referred to as such and such a genre in the body of the text itself. For example, the March 9, 1567, letter sent by a group of Maya leaders to the Crown contains a great deal of metalinguistic self-description, including the following statement toward the end of the text:

131.1	*he ca okot batech lae*	here we beg you
131.2	*caix yeteh ti gouernador*	and to the Governor also
131.3	*cautzac unatic*	that he might understand it
132.1	*caix utzac uhach anticoon*	that he [governor] might truly help us
132.2	*cautuchite cadzib hun tech*	that he might send our written paper to you

The expression "written paper" in line 132.2 refers to the letter itself and is in this context a rough gloss on the Spanish *carta*. The first favor requested of the governor was evidently that he actually send the "written paper" to the Crown rather than ignore it. The performative expression "here we beg you" in line 131.1 frames the letter more precisely as a petition. Another example of text-internal genre identification is provided by the Yaxkukul land document, which describes itself as an *ynformasionil derecho* 'report of rights' (Barrera Vásquez 1984, 16) and later as a *forma derecho de froceso [sic]* 'certificate of rights of process'.

Second, the genre label may occur as a title before the start of the work. This is the case, for instance, with Coronel's (1620) catechism, in which the genre label "Doctrina Cristiana" occurs on the title page, along with Coronel's full name and title, the place of production (Tekax, where Coronel was *guardián* at the time), the bishop to whom the work is directed, the seal of approval from the superiors of the order, and the name of the printing house. Third, a label may be placed on the document by a subsequent scribe or reader. Thus in the case of the March 9, 1567, letter, there is a notation at the top of the document, presumably put there by the royal scribe who drafted the document but possibly at the governor's request as he sent it along to the Crown.[7] Written with notarial abbreviations, the notation was designed to facilitate the handling of the document by the Crown or the Council of Indies. It says unceremoniously *"cta delos indios a su mag. Estatraduzida"* 'Letter from the indios to his majesty. It is translated' (meaning that it is accompanied by a Spanish translation). In all three varieties of genre identification, the text itself bears the label, either in the body or at the margins. The varieties may also be combined in a single text, as they are commonly in notarial works.

Metalinguistic expressions may also be used inside one text in reference to another one. That is, the genre attribution comes in the form of reported speech or commentary. Thus Landa and many others refer to the *libros* 'books' and *profesías* 'prophecies' of the Maya, just as Sánchez de Aguilar (1639) refers to the incantations of witches:

> *Tambien vsan llamar a ciertos Indios viejos hechizeros que ensalmen con palabras*
> *de su gentilidad . . .*
>> (Sánchez de Aguilar 1996, 84)
>
> They are also accustomed to call on certain old Indian witches who treat illness
> with words from their gentile (culture) . . .

Sánchez de Aguilar's text is replete with discussions of language itself and the language abilities of the missionaries and of the Maya they were missionizing. In a similar way, when the Yaxkukul land documents mention Tomás López Medel's order that *uppislahal luumob* 'the lands were to be measured' (see chapter 2), the order itself is referred to as *el gran Autto* 'the great Edict' (Barrera Vásquez 1984, 18–19). All of these display the author's metalinguistic assessment of someone else's speech or writing, an assessment from outside, as opposed to the performative self-identification of the text-internal examples.

The classification of a document, utterance, or practice as such and such a genre expresses a metalinguistic judgment or an act of recognition. The use of genre labels is actually the tip of an iceberg made up of various sorts of reported speech and commentary on language and communicative practices. It is noteworthy, for instance, that letters, Maya and Spanish, typically contain little reported speech, whereas land surveys, the Books of Chilam Balam, the Ritual of the Bacabs, and the *doctrinas* all contain reported speech, and sometimes direct quotation with attribution. One of the dimensions on which genres differ is precisely how they objectify discourse. Clearly, native genre labels in ordinary language are not analytic categories but rather practical ones, and they provide only partial, secondary evidence of the actual kinds and features of discourse. What they do provide primary evidence of are the metalinguistic judgments of their authors. Metalinguistic discourse provides primary evidence of how actors construe language, speech, and writing. When a speaker or author describes a missionary practice as *tzec* 'preaching (correcting, scolding)', or a manual as a *confesionario* 'confessional manual', a piece of writing as a *carta,* and so forth, the metalinguistic label frames its object, organizing a whole set of beliefs and expectations about the object.

Any genre schematizes practice and implies a configuration of features and positions. So, quite apart from native or analytic categories of language use, we can distinguish genres according to the participation frameworks in which they arise or are received. Is there a named author or addressee? Are there witnesses or others in whose name the work is produced? Who are all these people, and what positions did they occupy in the fields of the missions and the pueblos?

PRODUCTION FORMAT AND AUTHOR POSITION

One noteworthy feature of colonial Yucatecan writings is the salience of the author position. As Foucault (1971, 28–32, 979) observed, only some kinds of discourse are endowed with an author, and while authorship may appear at first to be a natural property of any discourse, in fact it is the product of a complex set of operations. In colonial Yucatán, these operations involved elaborate sequences of approvals, as well as deictic centering. Moreover, whenever we find a named author on a work, there are numerous other features that are present, including rhetorical devices that authenticate and reinforce the veracity of the text. Thus with the emergence of the colonial author comes the emergence of an array of other discourse effects. In the Spanish sector, the *lengua* and especially the *gran lengua* were the authors of various kinds of writings, from doctrine to metalinguistic works, reports, and book-length historical descriptions. The *difinidor,* the provincial, and the bishop were all authors of reports and *memorias de visita.* These texts are presented as true statements of their authors' assessments and knowledge; hence the author is a named principal in Goffman's (1974) sense.[8] Similarly, in the Maya sector *cartas* and petitions have named authors who are the principals and who vouch for the truth of their representations. Among works with authors, some (but not all) bear actual signatures as well as precise dates of composition. All the notarial works, for instance, are autographic and signed, whereas none of the doctrinal works has an actual signature, even if the author is named. The autographic works have an original individual text token on which the signature is placed at a specific time and place. By contrast, non-autographic ones have no such initial original object on which the author's signature appears. For printed works, of course, such as Beltrán's *Arte* or Coronel's *Discursos Predicables,* there is front matter that contains unique statements by named authors, but even here, it is a printed spelling of the name and not a signature that nominates the author; once the work is set to print, copy number 1 and copy number 200 are equivalent.

Alongside the authors there were other persons involved in the production of legitimate discourse. These include, for instance, the scribes, who were not authors but who did the writing and vouched for the fidelity of the written text to the words and sentiments of the principals. In some cases, the scribe named himself with title and attested to having read the text back to its principals to assure fidelity. When such attestation occurs, it comes in a statement after the signatures, at the bottom of the page (e.g., March 9, 1567, letter). There are also the witnesses "in front of whom" the text was produced and declaimed as a check on its accuracy and truth. The witnesses are named prominently in *cartas,* land surveys, accords, chronicles, *cabildo* records, and virtually all the discourse produced as part of town governance. They are named in the third person, set apart from the principals, but they sometimes affixed their signatures, and they were part of the legitimating apparatus of the document. In this sense, they partook of the responsibility of principals, though they were neither principals nor authors.

There are evangelical genres for which the author position is either suspended or greatly reduced. When Coronel wrote the *Doctrina Cristiana* in Maya, the prayer texts were of course universal and governed by the Church; he was merely the translator, responsible for the accuracy and aptness of the Maya. On the other hand, the sermons he composed (entirely in Maya without Spanish gloss) embedded points of liturgy and doctrine in texts of which he was the composer—and subsequent authors, such as Cogolludo, attributed them to him. Similarly, the Books of Chilam Balam were certainly created by writers whose function was authorlike insofar as they chose the themes, words, and sentiments expressed; yet these writers are not named, and the texts are not attributed to them. The same can be said of the dictionaries produced in the *guardianías,* since they are self-evidently the fruits of labor by individuals, yet they represent the missionaries' accumulated knowledge of the semantics of the language, not the individual proposals of so and so. A dictionary like the Motul was not "authored" but rather *trasuntado,* gathered together from notes and other papers. It is usually described not as a work of "writing" but as a work of *reducción.* If by "author" we designate the starting point in the production of a text—its source—then few of the major works have neatly defined authors. Rather, they are the product of recopying and reworking over long periods. The text-external point of reference that would have been provided by a fixed author is in fact provided by a historical series. Thus Coronel in the early sixteenth century explicitly says that his grammar and *doctrina* are based on earlier texts, probably by Villalpando and Landa, among others.

To the author, the principal, the scribe, and the witnesses, we must add one more position, namely, that of the individuals or power *in whose name* or *by whose authority* the work is produced. Major missionary works such as Coronel's *doctrina* and grammar are preceded by a complex apparatus of approvals and licenses to publish. In lesser genres, such as letters, authors may speak in the name of "our lord and majesty" (the Crown), or of other authorities. This was of course a common feature of Spanish discourse at the time, and it is echoed in the sign of the cross, which was used to introduce or end prayer, "in the name of the father and of the son and of the Holy Spirit." The same sign of the cross occurs frequently in Maya notarial documentation as an officializing device, or as a marker between sections of longer texts (see Hanks 1996). For certain works by missionaries, in addition to the named authorizing agent, there is a dedication, implying another position in the participation framework of the text. Thus Lizana's impassioned history of Yucatán is actually a devotional text dedicated to the Virgen de Izamal, whose image had been the source of numerous miracles and pilgrimages to the great church in that town.

Alongside the framework for producing the document was the framework of its reception. Many of the missionary writings, particularly major works, are addressed to individual bishops or church officials. Others explicitly address the *lector* 'reader', projecting an open-ended readership. Letters were typically addressed to individuals whose names or titles are stated in the beginning or ending of the text. In the case of the *doctrina* and of substantial portions of the Ritual of the Bacabs, the written work is actually a script intended for infinitely many performances by indefinitely many persons. Thus when the Credo begins, *"ocaan tinuol . . . "* 'I believe in . . . ', the first-person singular pronoun is a place holder for whoever recites the prayer. The *confesionario* is similarly a script the priest would follow, with a second-person place holder for the confessee, as in, *"Yan xin a çipil ti hunpay chhupal?"* 'Have you ever perchance had dishonest relations with your brother's wife?' (Coronel 1620a, quoted in Acuña 1998, 195). Missionaries read or worked from the script in asking the questions designed to elicit confessions. Often, particularly for works addressed to high-ranking officials of church or government, there are several intermediary addressees, such as the governor through whom Maya nobles addressed the Crown in their letters. Lizana explicitly addresses his history to "Padre Fray Francisco de Ocaña Padre de la Orden: Confesor de la Reina nuestra Señora y comisario General de todas las Provincias de las Indias," yet the actual readers whose approval precedes the text are fray Pedro de Mata, Provincial, fray Rodrigo de Segura, and fray Luis de Bivar, all in Mérida. Without their approval the work would not go to its addressee. Land surveys and *cabildo* documents may or may not have named addressees, but their maintenance in the local archives anticipates that they will be read by subsequent readers. The reception of the work is a history of encounters between it and the various readers, audiences, or performers who receive it. And, of course, individual works followed different actual trajectories.[9]

To recapitulate, the production and reception of colonial Yucatecan discourse entailed various agent positions, including principals, authors, signatories, witnesses, authorities, scribes, addressees, and intermediaries. Different genres correspond to different configurations of positions. This is a key factor, for instance, in the contrast between notarial genres and nonnotarial ones. Notarial works imply agent positions defined by the *cabildo,* whereas a doctrinal work like Coronel's implies at least three different fields: the officials who granted the licenses and approvals reproduced in the front matter of the completed work, the pedagogical context in which a *frayle lengua* used the work to teach the language to other religious, and the pedagogical context in which a Maya *maestro cantor* or *doctrinero* used it to instruct indigenous children in doctrine.

INDEXICAL CENTERING IN THE DEICTIC FIELD

But participant positions are only the first step toward adequately situating the genres. We must look more broadly at the indexical field in which a work arises, that is, the "here" and "now" from which it speaks. In the notarial works, texts bear names of places at which they were produced, along with the date of signing, the former usually encoded as "Here (at . . .)" and the latter as "Today, the . . . " By contrast, a *doctrina menor* such as Coronel's or Beltrán's situates itself historically in the front matter; but in the main text, there is no indication of indexical grounding to time or place, just as there is no identification of the "speaker." This absence of deictic grounding is precisely one of the design features of doctrinal literature, because it is intended to be repeated indefinitely many times in indefinitely many places.

The best way to get a sense of how different genres bind to different deictic fields is with a couple of examples.[10] For contrast, let us look briefly at two works: Sánchez de Aguilar's well-known *Informe Contra Idolorum Cultores* (1639), a major work in Spanish based on observations of Maya people and knowledge of their language; and Coronel's *Discursos Predicables* (1620), a major collection of sermons written in *gran lengua* Maya. A proper description of either of these would require far more detail; the following summary remarks are intended merely to illustrate the coherence of the deictic field as a significant dimension of contrast among genres of discourse practice. We will return to these and other works in greater detail in the following chapters.

Sánchez de Aguilar's well-known *Informe* was published in Madrid in 1639 but was written between 1613 and 1615, when he held the position of dean of the cathedral in Mérida, Yucatán. He wrote the work in response to the Real Cédula of April 24, 1604, in which the Crown requested of Bishop fray Juan de Izquierdo (see chapter 2 and introduction to part 2) a report on the state of idolatry in the province of Yucatán. By the time it was published, Sánchez de Aguilar had been appointed Canónigo de la Santa Iglesia Metropolitana de la Plata in the province of Los Charcos (Peru). Thus if we equate the "now" of the text with the date at which the composition of the body was completed, then the date for this work is 1615. But this initial equation focuses solely on the body of the work and does not shed light on the front matter (see table 2), including the author's addressing it to King Felipe IV and the official approvals to publish (see plates 5, 6).

Between January 1, 1636, and the actual publication in mid-1639, there was a cascade of discourse acts, all of which took place in Madrid. Each act leaves a documentary trace in the front matter of the work, and each helps frame the work and bind it to time and space. These other acts and other agents finalize and authorize Sánchez de Aguilar's text, so that what had been a draft or set of papers becomes a recognized and publishable work.

TABLE 2 Front Matter of Sánchez de Aguilar's *Informe* (in order of appearance)

OBJECT	DATE	PLACE	AUTHOR/PRINCIPAL
Title page			
Suma de Privilegio	June 12, 1638	Madrid	Crown
Suma de Tasa	April 12, 1639	Madrid	Señores del Consejo
Fee de Erratas	April 7, 1639	No place given	Licenciado Murcia de la Llana
To King Felipe IV	January 1, 1636	La Plata, Peru	Sánchez de Aguilar
Aprovación	February 6, 1638	Convento de La Vitoria, Madrid	Padre Alonso de Herrera
Licencia del ordinario	February 4, 1638	Madrid	Licenciado Lorenço de Iturriçarra
Aprovación	February 27, 1638	Convento de la Santísima Trinidad, Madrid	Padre Fray Damián López de Haro
Eighty-line epic-style poem	n.d.	—	Anonymous "religious devotee of the author"

What should we make of the twenty-one-year delay between composition and submission for publication? In his dedication to the Crown and *Prólogo al lector,* Sánchez de Aguilar cites five reasons for the delay: his fear that the work would embitter too many people, his poor health, the time commitments entailed by his changes of job, his lack of money to pay for publication, and the depression caused by his loss of an even larger *Doctrina Cristiana* manuscript during a ship-wreck. Of these, the first is the most interesting for our purposes, for it points to the here-now of the work and the reception its author anticipated. To understand this, we must reach further back to the turn of the seventeenth century, where the effective beginnings and sources of the work lie.

In 1602 then-Bishop Juan de Izquierdo communicated to Sánchez de Aguilar that idolatry was to be a topic of deliberation in the Council of Indies. The early idolatry trials conducted by Landa in the 1560s had set off what was to remain the central, agonizing problem for the evangelical church in Yucatán, namely, the persistence of apostate and heretical idolatry among Maya people who had already been converted to Christianity. Among the many conflicts engendered by idolatry and attempts to curb it was a root conflict between the Church and the secular government of the province. The Church claimed the right to pun-ish idolaters without the prior approval of the state governor, whereas the state asserted its sole authority over legitimate punishment. In the forty years between Landa's hearings and the turn of the century, the Church had been barred from physically punishing Indios, and many of the clergy (secular and regular) blamed this for what was considered a resurgence in idolatry. Sánchez de Aguilar's work is a tightly constructed polemic arguing that the Church does have authority to punish, that punishment is absolutely essential and called for, but that the governor should be consulted.

In 1603 Sánchez de Aguilar, as *vicario general,* wrote a letter to the Crown on the matter of idolatry, reinforcing the belief that it was a significant and destructive problem in Yucatán. On April 24 of the following year, the Crown issued its *cédula* to Bishop Izquierdo, and this set the ball rolling in earnest. Six and one-half months later, Sánchez de Aguilar was granted the authority to round up apostate Indios from three settlements to which they had fled (Solís Robleda and Peniche 1996, 29). Between 1606 and 1608 he served as *cura vicario* in Chancenote on the northeastern frontier of the *reducción* zone. In a written statement by then-Bishop Vásquez de Mercado dated January 11, 1606, it is certified that Sánchez de Aguilar had indeed carried out the *reducción* of thirty *montaraces* 'mountain people', that is, men, women, and children who had been living in idolatry on the far side of the frontier but who were now practicing Christians (39). On December 4, 1608, Sánchez de Aguilar told Bishop Vásquez de Mercado that he had by then reduced one hundred people, whose idols and three books he had carefully inspected, shown to other authorities, and burned in public. He had also preached in Maya on the event in the preceding days (41).

This sequence of events preceding the drafting of the *Informe* is palpably relevant to the work. Sánchez de Aguilar's experiences as a *cura* on the frontier are referred to many times in the work itself and are the obvious basis for many of his statements about the behavior and proclivities of Maya people. At various points throughout the work, he refers to things he witnessed and knows from past experience, and he mentions the town of Chancenote and the people around it. He also mentions Izquierdo among many historical actors during the year before the writing, as well as citing numerous laws and documents dated during this period or earlier. In a real sense, then, the 1615 date of the text was merely a heuristic, a moment in a cumulative process. If we do not attend to that process we cannot understand why Sánchez de Aguilar was so certain that his work would embitter people and remind them of things they wished to forget. For he was laying bare not only depravity among the converts but also de facto failure among the missionaries and was reopening the wounds of church-state conflict over authority to punish.

What we see from this reading of the front matter, then, is a historical process whose roots lie at least as far back as the acrimonious events of 1562, in which the bishop and the Franciscan order were locked in conflict, and that moves forward through the persistent concern with apostasy and idolatry in the early seventeenth century. When Sánchez de Aguilar decided to publish the work he set off a second cascade of events involving its authorization for print and actual production. Yet from within the text, we see the author as an eyewitness who writes from co-present experience of the matter at hand, asking rhetorical questions and answering them in the first-person singular, claiming evidentiary superiority over all other authorities in the peninsula on the grounds that he is the witness with longest experience, for he alone was born in Yucatán, unlike the European monastics (Sánchez de Aguilar 1996 [1639], 75). This explicit appeal to longevity and firsthand experience is echoed throughout the text when Sánchez de Aguilar refers to practices, idols, and individuals he saw during his *niñez* 'youth'. For a work like this one, the temporal centering in the deictic field is best thought of not as a moment but as a historical process in which past experiences and events shape any present. This process was cumulative between about 1602 and 1615, as well as between 1636 and 1639, but it was discontinuous or interrupted between 1615 and 1636. I have found only indirect evidence that the text circulated during this hiatus.[11]

Similar dynamics apply to the centering of the work in deictic space. During the time of composition, Sánchez de Aguilar was in Yucatán, evidently in Mérida, where he was dean. Yet the evidentiary basis of his statements comes mostly from his travel around Yucatán and especially along the frontier, where he brought *sublevados* to *reducción*. The regional "map" of the province and its limits is a necessary frame of reference in order for readers to follow his arguments, and while the authorial voice remains centered squarely in the writing space, it adduces knowledge gained from firsthand experience outside of it. The exchanges between him and the bishops imply the space of Mérida, where they all worked, whereas exchanges with the Crown implied Spain. By 1636 Sánchez de Aguilar was in an entirely new setting in Peru, and he wrote from there in his address to the Crown and his prologue to the reader. By contrast, it was in Madrid that the work received its official approvals and was ultimately published. To my knowledge, the first publication in México was the 1892 edition from the Museo Nacional. Thus the spatial situatedness of the work, like its temporal emergence, is marked by interruptions. Sánchez de Aguilar within the text is firmly grounded in local events in Yucatán, within the *reducción* and outside it, but Sánchez de Aguilar the author of the dedication and prologue is implicated also in Peru and Spain. This spatial field is in sharp contrast to the one for Coronel's *Discursos Predicables* and those for the notarial documents.

The appeal to eyewitness testimony and the use of actual observations as a basis for legitimating Sánchez de Aguilar's claims is also in effect "deictic" because it indicates the copresence of the author with the persons and events he is describing. I have already mentioned that he emphasized his long experience in Yucatán (Sánchez de Aguilar 1996 [1639], 24, 75) and his many firsthand discoveries of Maya practices (36, 83), even going so far as to cite things he learned as a confessor of Indios (66). The rhetoric of immediate sensory-based knowledge extends to his argument that the only effective way to deal with idolatry is to discover idolaters *in flagrante* (37).

In 1620 Coronel's *Arte en lengua de Maya* was published in México along with his *Doctrina Cristiana* and *Discursos Predicables*. This three-part work makes a revealing contrast with Sánchez de Aguilar's *Informe*. The two men were contemporaries, Sánchez de Aguilar a native Yucatecan and high-ranking member of the secular clergy and Coronel a *guardián* and *difinidor* of the Franciscan order in Yucatán. They were both active in the province during the first two decades of the seventeenth century, and Coronel was *guardián* in Tekax or Mama during the very years when Sánchez de Aguilar composed the *Informe*. When he decided to publish it in 1636, Coronel had just been appointed *guardián* of the convent of the Recolección de la Mejorada in Mérida—a position he declined in favor of retiring to his cell, where he prayed in solitude until his death in 1651 (Cogolludo 1971 [1688], 2:670). The two men's works fit squarely within the discourse of *reducción*, and each represents its author's best understanding of Maya language and practice. Both were intended for use among members of the missionary Church: whereas Sánchez de Aguilar's *Informe* argued for specific policies regarding idolatry and the separation of authority between Church and state, Coronel's work was pedagogical in design. It was used both to train missionaries in Maya language and to train Maya speakers in Christian religion in the missions. Both works were published with elaborate front matter in which we can trace the approval and licensing process and glean a great deal of information regarding the spatial and temporal circumstances in which they were finalized. For present purposes, I concentrate on the front matter of Coronel's work. The textual content of the *Arte* is examined in chapter 7; the doctrine and sermons are treated in chapter 8, alongside other works of these genres.

In the introduction to his edition of Coronel's *Arte* (1998), René Acuña notes that the exact chronological sequence of Coronel's life is unclear, or as he puts it, a *rompecabezas* 'puzzle'. There is consensus that Coronel was born in about 1569 in the villa of Torrija de la Alcaria, Spain, and studied at the University of Alcalá de Henares. He appears to have taken the Franciscan habit in 1584 and come to Yucatán either that year or nine years later (Cogolludo 1971 [1688], 2:669). According to Cogolludo, he died in Mérida on January 14, 1651, having spent approximately sixty years in Yucatán, about forty-eight of them teaching Christianity to Maya people. He served many times as *guardián*, in the *conventos* of Mama, Tekax, and the Recolección de la Mejorada, Mérida (2:669). The *Memoria* of Bishop Juan de Izquierdo places Coronel as *guardián* of Tekax in 1610, during the same period in which Izquierdo had asked Sánchez de Aguilar to report on his experiences, and the title page of the *Arte* itself places him there in 1620, suggesting a long tenure. He was elected *difinidor* in 1621 following the publication of his opus and was Cogolludo's Maya teacher when the latter first came from Spain. According to Cogolludo (2:135), Coronel's work was widely used for learning Maya by both Franciscan and secular ministers, and Coronel was himself a renowned *maestro* of the language who preached with elegance. In his

TABLE 3 Curriculum Vitae of Juan Coronel

1569	Coronel is born in Spain
1584	Coronel takes the habit
1593	Coronel enters Yucatán
1603	Sánchez de Aguilar is *vicario general* in Yucatán
1606	Sánchez de Aguilar is *cura vicario* of Chancenote
1610	Coronel is *guardián* of Tekax
1615	Sánchez de Aguilar completes his *Informe* (does not publish)
1620	Sánchez de Aguilar's *Doctrina* is lost at sea (intended to publish)
1620	Coronel is *guardián* of Tekax
1620	Coronel's opus is published in México: *Discursos, Arte, Doctrina, Bocabulario*
1621	Coronel is elected *difinidor*, Yucatán
1634	Coronel is *guardián* of Mama
1636	Coronel is *guardián* of Recolección de la Mejorada, Mérida
1636	Sánchez de Aguilar dedicates his *Informe* and submits for publication
1639	Sánchez de Aguilar's *Informe* is published in Madrid; he is in La Plata, Peru
1651	Coronel dies, Mérida

dedication to Bishop Salazar in the front of the *Arte*, Coronel notes that by 1620 he had been teaching the language to newly arrived fathers from Spain for twelve years. Hence while Sánchez de Aguilar was serving as *cura vicario* in Chancenote in 1608, establishing himself as an agent of *reducción* on the frontier, Coronel was already serving in the *guardianías* and establishing himself as a *lengua* teacher of missionaries and *naturales*. Table 3 provides a synopsis of Coronel's career, with several entries from Sánchez de Aguilar for comparison.

The proximal circumstances of the 1620 publication of Coronel's opus are embedded in a larger history. Of particular relevance is the period from 1610 (and perhaps earlier), when Coronel was *guardián* of Tekax, until 1621, when he was elected *difinidor* of his order in Yucatán. It is likely that the publication and wide use of his opus contributed to his advancement, and Cogolludo (1971 [1688], 2:696) suggests that he would have been a likely provincial, had he been less rigid and demanding. The work itself would have drawn on his growing knowledge of Maya from the region of Tekax. When we look at the front matter of the 1620 publication, we enter a more fine-grained phase in the life of Coronel's work (table 4). The first feature that stands out is the compactness of the deictic field. The time between Coronel's dedication (January 16) and the license to publish (April 30) was a mere three and a half months, compared to the three years required to finalize Sánchez de Aguilar's *Informe*. Moreover, whereas the *Informe* spanned Yucatán, Peru, México, and Madrid, Coronel's work was composed, dedicated, approved, and licensed between the *guardianías* of Tahuman and

TABLE 4 Front Matter of Coronel's Opus (in order of appearance)

OBJECT	DATE	PLACE	AUTHOR/PRINCIPAL
Title page			
Licencia	April 30, 1620	México	El Márquez de Guadalcaçar
Parecer 'opinion'	April 29, 1620	México	Fray Fernando Durán
*Dedicatoria**	January 16, 1620	Mérida	Fray Ioan Coronel
Bishop acknowledges	January 17, 1620	Mérida	Fray Gondiçalus, Bishop of Yucatán
Evaluation	January 25, 1620	San Francisco Tahuman, Yucatán	Fray Francisco Torralva
Concurring opinion	January 27, 1620	Mérida	Ioan Gómez Pacheco
Licencia	February 29, 1620	Mérida	Fray Gonçalus, Bishop of Yucatán
Opinion	March 9, 1620	Mérida	Fray Ivan de Azebedo, Provincial
Al Lector	n.d.	—	Fray Ioan Coronel

*Al Maestro Don Fray Gonçalo de Salazar, Bishop of Yucatán

Tixkokob, the provincial capital (Mérida), and México. It is likely that the delay in Sánchez de Aguilar's case was at least partly due to the distances involved, or what Means (1932) called the "space time lag" between the New World and Spain.

The contrast between Sánchez de Aguilar's and Coronel's works in spatial and temporal fields squares with the contrast in the level of institutional structure they engaged. Whereas the former dedicated his work to the Spanish king himself, the latter dedicated his to the bishop of the province. The bishop in turn passed Coronel's work to two locally recognized *maestros de lengua maya* for their opinions, one a Franciscan *difinidor* (Torralva) and one a secular (Gómez Pacheco), both in the missions. The approval of the Franciscan provincial was also provided, further anchoring the work to both monastic and secular hierarchies in the province. By contrast, there is no Yucatecan representation whatsoever in the front matter of Sánchez de Aguilar's *Informe,* and all the key approvals and licenses are sited in Madrid, though the author wrote his dedication from Peru. Cogolludo prominently cites Sánchez de Aguilar, suggesting that the latter's work was read in Yucatán. In short, we get the sense that his work was both more cosmopolitan than Coronel's and more time-consuming to produce. Coronel's election to *difinidor* just after publication suggests that it helped establish him as a leading authority. By contrast, Sánchez de Aguilar's 1939 publication does not appear to have had a similar positive impact on his career.

When we look to the content of the nine items in Coronel's front matter (see table 4), we move still closer into the deictic field in which it arose. Durán's *parecer* 'opinion' was signed in México, but his authority lay in his prior experience in the missions. Coronel's dedication to Bishop Salazar implies that the two had interacted during an earlier *visita* in which the bishop came to the town where Coronel was *guardián* and encouraged him to publish the work. Salazar's first move, within a day, was to recommend two expert readers, whose approval he subsequently cited in issuing the license. By the time the Franciscan provincial gave his approval, the work had been vetted and approved by the bishop.

It is a common feature of authorized discourse in the colony that its authority was grounded in space, time, and institutional positions, but the grounding process varied with genre. Whereas both Sánchez de Aguilar's and Coronel's works accomplished this grounding in their front matter, notarial genres did so with signatures, titles, and dates and places of signing—all parts of the text itself. Moreover, whereas the signatories to a notarial document were themselves its authors and witnesses, it is precisely not the author of a published work who authorizes. The latter kind of authority obligatorily comes from outside the work.

The front matter of published works always indexes a relatively extended sequence of acts, whereas the signing to finalize a notarial document, a letter, or a *memoria* is a punctual act. Even if it in fact took days or weeks to accomplish, the signing is inscribed in the text as a single event. The sequence of acts documented in the front matter of published works can be partly determined by the dates the documents bear. Thus Coronel's dedication preceded the bishop's recommendation, which in turn preceded the opinions rendered by Torralva and Gómez Pacheco, and so forth. But this chronology raises at least two questions. First, Gómez Pacheco's opinion is dated eight days before Torralva's, yet what Gómez Pacheco states is that he agrees with Torralva's opinion. If we take the dates at face value, then the two likely discussed the work before formulating their individual opinions. Second, the very speed of the process makes one wonder how Coronel, a *guardián* in Tekax, enjoyed such access to the bishop that his request would be acted upon immediately. Had the bishop already made arrangements for Torralva and Gómez Pacheco to serve as readers? Was Coronel's manuscript already circulating locally so that the readers were prepared in advance? Such questions have no obvious answers, and they serve as reminders that our ability to reconstruct the deictic framework of any work is limited by both the paucity of documents and the selectivity of what was documented.

STYLISTIC DIFFERENTIATION OF GENRES

When we move from the authorizing deictic framework of these works to the language of the text itself, another whole plane of genre contrasts emerges. The *Informe* is organized as a relentlessly rational argument with subarguments, counterarguments, supporting evidence, and conclusions. Coronel's sermons, aimed at an audience of *indios reducidos,* are rich in rhetorical devices and biblical images. Here, as in the prayers and dialogues of *doctrina,* the rendering in Maya suggests that Coronel (like other Franciscan *gran lengua* authors) sought to craft language that was beautiful and moving, as well as accurate. Coronel's *Arte* follows broadly the model of Nebrija and the grammars of Latin he would have studied as part of his training in *latinidad:* it describes the language in a certain order, using many tables and listing exceptions to proposed rules. The *artes* of Coronel (1620), San Buenaventura (1684), and Beltrán (1746) all speak in two voices: the analytic metalanguage of a grammarian describing a linguistic system and the supposedly ordinary Maya usage in the example sentences. The same is true of dictionaries, where the headwords may be Maya or Spanish, the glosses are in the other language, and the examples are all in erstwhile ordinary Maya. Consequently all the metalinguistic genres are stylistically regular, yet each one combines at least two stylistically contrasting voices. Depending upon the genre, notarial documents display highly distinctive phrasings and formats, including opening and closing formulas and ways of referring to persons. The coming chapters explore in some detail stylistic differentiation in works by both missionaries and Mayas. On the one hand, the movement of stylistic elements between genres, and the resulting blending of genres, was among the most powerful vectors for the formation and spread of the new *lengua reducida.* On the other hand, the deliberate regimentation of style was a key part of the "civilizing" work of *reducción.* In effect, to be *reducido* and to display *policía cristiana* was to speak correctly, that is, to take up an appropriate position in the field of normative styles.

An important cluster of discourse effects is organized around what we might call persuasion and credibility: the use of evidence (as in the *Informe*), the citation of authoritative texts, the naming of witnesses to the signing of a text, the assertions of long-term firsthand experience with the matter at hand, the claim of rights based on descent or habitation. The concern in these cases is not primarily to *authorize* the statement but to make it convincing to a reader. Obviously, the need to persuade is paramount in texts like Sánchez de Aguilar's *Informe,* the exhortations of a preacher, or a petition requesting a favor or service. But persuasion and credibility are also key in the *doctrina.* Although the doctrinal text encodes the power of the Church-sanctioned original on which it is modeled, and needs no other evidence of its truth, the missionary must persuade. Hence we find in the *doctrinas* traces of how the missionaries understood the linguistic sensibilities of their subjects. There is a great deal of grammatical parallelism that would appear familiar to any student of Maya literature. There are images and recurrent couplets that accord well with what is known of Maya canons of style.

MULTIMODALITY:
SPEECH, ANIMATION, INSCRIPTION

Nearly all the genres treated here are what contemporary linguistic anthropologists call multimodal. Behind the apparently silent and austere abstractions of writing lay oral exchanges, performances, and interactions that involved bodies, gestures, objects, and built spaces. Powerful root symbols such as the cross were realized in multiple modalities, from spoken words to hand gestures and body postures, to the wooden cross in front of the home or the one worn around the neck, to the written and graphic crosses used to divide sections of manuscripts, to the ones used as boundary markers on the landscape (Hanks 1996). Just as it is key to understand *reducción* as a single logic played out in space, conduct, and language, so too the discourse genres of *reducción* are multimodal. Consider the interplay of orality and writing.

There is no evidence that Sánchez de Aguilar's *Informe* or the Motul dictionary was crafted for oral performance. By contrast, all of the *doctrina*, the confessional manual, and the sermons are scripts designed to be performed aloud—in some cases involving extended groups of speakers in unison, and in others, a single individual or pair. The *artes* give no direct indication of oral performance, yet we know they were used in classroom settings that were oral as well as visual. Notarial documents are written and archived, but they display many oral features, including rhyme and metrical regularities that would be perceived only in oral performance. Though it may seem at first counterintuitive, the most productive way to work with notarial texts is to read them aloud. In some cases, where an official scribe wrote the document, there is a scribal attestation to the effect that the text once copied out clean was read aloud to its principals and they assented to its accuracy. In all these cases, what comes to us as a text on paper is indissociably entangled with orality, most of which is erased in Spanish glosses or translations.

Writing is already plural in the sense that we have at least the following variants:

1. Typeset printing (contemporaneous ≠ subsequent)
2. Scribal handwriting (official ≠ unofficial, regional or above ≠ local)
3. Recopying, *trasuntar*
4. Loose leaf versus bound
5. Unauthorized (with scribe identified ≠ not identified)

The works of Coronel (1620a, 1620b), Sánchez de Aguilar (1996 [1639]), San Buenaventura (1888 [1684]), and Beltrán (1912 [1757, 1740]) were all published during the active lifetimes of their authors. Print publication required the authorization and deictic grounding of dated approvals and licenses. The sphere of distribution can be difficult to ascertain, but Coronel explicitly states that one reason to print the work is so that it can be produced in small bound volumes that can be carried by the priests, who could hardly circulate carrying stacks of manuscripts between hard covers. By contrast, the Motul and San Francisco dictionaries were printed long after the lifetimes of those who composed them. They are finalized by scholarly prefaces written much later that set out the provenance of the work and grounds for considering it authentic. Such works are not authorized. They are *authenticated*.

With handwritten texts such as notarial documents and local archives, different distinctions apply. Duplication implied rewriting and raised the question of accuracy. Colonial Maya documents display a wide range of graphic ability on the part of their composers, from the pristine orthography of a sixteenth-century royal scribe to the uncertain and inconsistent spellings of a local record keeper. The use of abbreviations and autographic emblems also varies across the corpus. The copyist is rarely named, as is the case with the forbidden Maya works of the Books of Chilam Balam and the so-called Ritual of the Bacabs. In cases like these, the handwriting is critical to dating the document but leaves open the dating of its source texts. Thus hand copying usually muddles both the work's content and its context. There is much evidence in the writings of the missionaries that they were aware of this problem and concerned about its implication for the *reducción*. How could the Indios learn proper *doctrina* if the versions of the *doctrina* they were taught were marred by errors and inconsistencies?

In the title and dedication to his *arte*, Coronel states that he had *recogido* 'gathered', *recopilado* 'recopied', and *enmendado* 'emended' papers written by the older priests. In his writing practice, which I believe to have been typical of *gran lengua* authors, he gathered together the writings of his predecessors and organized them into a coherent work in the genre, revising where necessary. The product gains legitimacy from its sources but makes no claim to replicate them. The revisions rarely indicate the original forms they replace, a point rightly lamented by Acuña (1998). Thus what it meant to write was to recopy, revise, and reorganize. Although I have seen no evidence indicating that this process was called a *reducción* of the work, it falls squarely within the conceptual scope of *reducción* understood as ordering and rendering coherent.

Within the sphere of orality there are important differences between individual speaking, individual performance of a script, group reading and reception, and singing. The paradigm context in which sermons were delivered was the church or classroom, where the missionary (or the *maestro*) declaims the sermon to an audience consisting of *indios reducidos* separated by gender. Landa, Cogolludo, and others tell us that the *doctrina* was performed in *canto llano*, which the *Diccionario de Autoridades* (1726, 2:125) defines as follows: *"Es aquel cuyas notas ò puntos procéden con igual y uniforme figúra y medida de tiempo. Llámase tambien música Eclesiastica, por ser la que comunmente se usa en la Iglésia"* 'It is that (singing) whose notes or points proceed with equal and uniform figure and measure. Also called Ecclesiastical music, for being commonly used in the Church'. The effect of singing the prayers in unison and regular measure, sometimes accompanied by organ or other instruments, would surely be more intensive and memorable than that of solitary recitation without melody. Indeed the use of singing in religious practice implies a considerable transformation of the doctrinal text from its script status into the somatic and densely aesthetic experience of group intoning. The missionaries were well aware of this, of course, and used singing as a way to move the soul and imprint on the mind of the practitioner. By contrast, the same doctrinal scripts were used in a very different oral context when individuals were tested on their knowledge before receiving the sacraments.

The repeated performance of doctrinal scripts was an intrinsic part of *reducción* and conversion, in which both habits and a habitus were instilled in the practitioners. We can think of this inscribing as another modality of discourse—without the material object of a written text, but with the commitment to memory and accurate reproduction. The child who repeats the Credo or the Our Father daily effectively entextualizes the script on his or her body and mind. The accompanying signs of the cross, postures, and gestures reinforce this inscription by engaging further senses and kinds of attention. In a real sense, the written script, the built space, and the entire gestural realization of prayer function as scaffolding for the reforming of the individual's mind and evaluative posture. That so many of the prayers are spoken in the first-person singular further engages the praying self. The missionaries in Yucatán would almost certainly have agreed with Pascal that people do not come to pray because they believe but come to believe because they pray. Any supporting elements such as music, regulated bodily engagement, group performance, images of *santos,* and ritual care of sacred spaces would reinforce this transformative effect, even if the outcome proved unpredictable.

In sum, multimodality was pervasively relevant to the means and ends of writing in the colony, and it varied across genres. The different modes are best thought of as different vectors along which the discourse of the *reducción* proliferated into embodied practices of Yucatecan people. Obviously for the missionaries, the objective was to control the accuracy and correctness of this proliferation, something they were ultimately unable to do. But beyond the missionary dilemma, scripted and other forms of discourse circulated between writing, repetition, and enactment, from word to image and back. This circulation was integral to the plan and actual functioning of *reducción*.

ITERATION

Printing and recopying, with or without intentional revision, like translation itself, served to repeat, that is, iterated texts. The intended usage of a *doctrina* script is also iterative, in that it is designed to be reperformed on indefinitely many occasions by indefinitely many individuals. As Foucault (1971, 44) observed, doctrinal discourse tends to disperse itself. In each iteration, the persons occupying the roles of *I* or *you* shift and the language of the script becomes the language of the performer. In this transposition, the various deictic elements provide the nodes at which the script is recontextualized over and over again, the words and sentiments grounded in a new actuality each time. Thus the linguistic structure of doctrinal language is designed to be dispersed across indefinitely many repetitions, each one singular in reference.

In contrast, notarial texts are onetime productions whose deictics are rigidly tied to an original context. The *I, we,* and *you* denote named authors or participants on a specific occasion, and even if the text is recopied, the references remain by design constant. The same holds for the approvals and licenses that finalize published works. With grammars and dictionaries, the presumptive object of reference is the language as it should be spoken at the time and region of composition and does not shift with each new reading of the work. Doctrinal texts and large parts of the Ritual of the Bacabs are distinctive because they are both scripts, which project *virtual* deictic fields. It is only when the participant positions are occupied that they become *actual*.

Nevertheless, notarial documents and authorizing licenses are still subject to iteration. It is a striking feature of works produced in the *cabildos* that they often come in series of nearly identical exemplars. Thus the Yaxkukul land documents (Barrera Vásquez and Rendón 1974 [1948]) comprise two surveys of the same town, dated just days apart and with significant overlap. The 1562 *cartas* sent to the Crown and reproduced in Zimmermann (1970) form a series of thirteen texts, with two main variants, each of which appears in multiple copies. In the cases of serial *cabildo* documents, the different text tokens typically have different signatories, which may indicate that serial production had the strategic advantage of providing groups of Maya nobles with the opportunity to display their consent as coprincipals to the same token text. From outside the *cabildo*, the Books of Chilam Balam display so much repeated material that Barrera Vásquez (1984) proposed that they all derived from a single Ur-text with variants by town. These texts are at least partly defined by the iteration of certain fragments of text and certain themes, a fact that emerges clearly in the concordance of Miram and Miram (1988). One motivation for iterative production of discourse was doubtless the need to ensure that a text was not lost in transit or lost to the punishing heat and humidity. But this is an insufficient explanation of the cases cited here.

Iteration and the kinds of series texts enter into contribute to genre distinctions and should be considered systematic features of the discourse formation.

More subtle is the play of iteration resulting from the unannounced use in one text of language that comes from another. The example sentences and glosses found in *artes* and dictionaries give striking evidence that their authors read one another and recycled many of the very same forms. Many fragments of *doctrina* are transposed into notarial documents: the sign of the cross, religiously freighted self-description, epithets for God, and depictions of Christian religion as well as idolatry. It is not only that these various genres all refer to the same social and spiritual world, although this is true. More, they iterate the same words, phrases, and tropes. They presuppose overlapping universes of reference and encode the same or similar perspectives on the things they describe. From a sheerly textual perspective, the result is a proliferation of intertextuality across genres. Offsetting the many divisions of production format, style, and deictic centering, these intergeneric commonalities run like red threads through the discourse. They provide clear evidence that the field of *reducción* was indeed a field of discourse production. Though some of the best evidence of this is intertextual series, what most concern us here are not the texts but the practices of which they are residua. These practices relied on iteration, voicing speech from elsewhere, engaging the field by taking up a position relative to those whose words are revoiced. Iteration is the discursive reflex of repetition, a vital element in the formation of the colonial habitus.

· · ·

This chapter has shifted focus from the socially defined fields of *reducción,* Part I, to the discourse practices of *reducción* that are the focus of the remainder of this book. The six parameters introduced above—metalinguistic classification, production and reception format, deictic centering, stylistic variation, multimodality, and iteration—are by no means exhaustive and will be refined over the coming chapters. They imply a way of reading that will be unfamiliar to many historians and anthropologists and that has never to my knowledge been applied to any of this corpus. Not only can we not read texts in isolation, because of iteration, but we must read even banal notarial documents aloud because of multimodality, and we must attend precisely to deictic centering, without which we can never understand the actuality of discourse practice. We must recognize that the concept of the author in the colony was basically different from ours and that stylistic variation is not only a feature of "literature." There is no language without style, and *reducción* gave rise to a veritable florescence of aesthetically worked language, much of which arose in unlikely settings, such as the catechism class and the town council.

The next four chapters deal with works produced by the *gran lenguas,* namely,

the grammars, dictionaries, and doctrinal materials that established the apparatus of conversion. These are all works of conversion. The linguistic works may
be thought of as mappings of the semantic space of Maya language from the perspective of Spanish language and thought. Without at least a preliminary survey,
the language could not be taught, nor could the translations of *doctrina* proceed.
The task was fraught with danger, since the entire evangelization was to be conducted in Maya: false equivalents would yield false beliefs. The translations had
to preserve the original in spirit and letter, yet make sense to Maya speakers. For
this reason, I start with the metalinguistic works in chapters 5, 6, and 7, before
moving on to the doctrinal ones in chapter 8. However, it will become clear that
the two classes of genre presuppose one another. The *doctrina* uses the language
as it is described in the grammars and dictionaries, and the latter describe and
presuppose the language as used in the *doctrina*. The first step in the history of
this discourse is to establish that circularity.

The union of linguistic and doctrinal genres embodies the first conversion,
when God and *policía cristiana* were made Maya. In this moment and those
works, the friars' choices of translation and their claims to knowledge depended
maximally upon their grasp of Maya practices and the help of their Maya-
speaking assistants. It is tempting to assume that the *maestros cantores* provided
helpful feedback on the texts they taught, but there is no direct evidence of this to
my knowledge. There is evidence that the friars checked their texts with assistants
who would have been *indios de confianza,* possibly *maestros,* and in some cases
indios ladinos. As we will see, some of the translations were elegant, some failed
or were perniciously ambiguous, and others were so novel or fraught with danger
that the Spanish term was simply retained. Sahagún's sermons clearly crossed
a line in adopting Nahuatl metaphors for Christian concepts, and they were
repressed by the Church.[12] The *gran lenguas* were agents of a conversion from
Latin and Spanish practices in which they had been trained into Maya practices
in which they would form others; and their own career paths, as they underwent
training in the new language, in a sense replicated this conversion. In mapping
into the semantic space of Maya, the *gran lenguas* trod on ground as uncertain as
the caves in the southern forests by night. And they knew it.

First Words

From Spanish into Maya

Thus far I have drawn freely from the written works of religious authors, including Landa, López Medel, Toral, the Franciscan provincials, the bishops, Sánchez de Aguilar, Lizana, and Cogolludo. The works in question were all written in Spanish and directed to a Spanish-speaking audience, with only occasional and selective words or phrases cited in Maya. They were of several genres, including the official *ordenanza;* the episcopal or provincial *memoria;* the *historia* and *relación,* which share a wide temporal and thematic scope; the *informe,* with its narrow thematic focus; and the *carta* (letter). All these genres have well-defined authors, named in the signature, on the title page of the work, or within the text. These authors are also principals responsible for what their texts say and how they say it. In most cases, the authors write not merely as individuals, but as the occupants of offices in the system of governance, whether bishop, provincial, or, in the case of Sánchez de Aguilar, the person designated to respond to a Crown directive. The combination of positional authority, responsibility, and personal name gives authorship a special salience in these genres.

There is no evidence, to my knowledge, that these genres had any significant impact on Maya language or on the communicative practices of Maya speakers. Although some of the works were produced in the *guardianías* or on the basis of intimate experience there, none was translated into Maya, nor were any used as pedagogical texts. We can see more or less impact of Maya on the texts in these genres, in the form of citations from the language, descriptions of the people, and so forth. But these traces of Maya are firmly subordinated to the Spanish design and direction of the texts. The authorial voice is unambiguously Spanish, as is the audience. In such texts, Maya plays the role of the object written about, not the audience to whom the writing is addressed. Moreover, these are unequivocally *written* works, which circulated as such and did not obligatorily involve reading aloud, declaiming in public, or memorization (with the exception of the *Ordenanzas* of López Medel, which were to be declaimed publicly throughout the province).

In the colony's division of linguistic and discursive labor, these Spanish works played a key role: they embodied the background of descriptive and explanatory knowledge according to which the missionaries aimed and adjusted their efforts. They are part of the sense-making process through which the Europeans developed an understanding of the Maya by objectifying them in words and images. Part of this background was shaped by emerging stereotypes of Maya people, their practices, and their language. Such stereotypes included, for instance, the virtuosity of Maya speakers as storytellers (Sánchez de Aguilar), the elegance and subtlety of the language (Landa, Sánchez de Aguilar, Lizana, Cogolludo), the resistance of Indios to indoctrination and their lack of resistance to idolatry, and the stereotype of proper Christian practice against which most Maya people were found lacking. In all cases, such stereotypes are formed first by the positional perspective of the Spanish within the project of *reducción* and often within the more exacting perspective of Franciscan missionary practice. Only secondarily and occasionally are they sheer descriptions based on evidence. Landa learned a great deal about Maya culture, but his main work, the *Relación de las Cosas de Yucatán,* was written as part of his own legal defense before the Council of the Indies and is profoundly marked by his convictions about God and proper religion. Similarly, Sánchez de Aguilar evidently spoke Maya fluently, but his glowing remarks on the subtlety of the language are little more than a setup for his devastating critique of those who fail to learn Christian doctrine: these people are intellectually and verbally capable, and failure to learn is therefore a sign of malice or ill will. Punish them for it.

But there is another level of discourse about and in Maya that was to play a different role in the overall scheme of *reducción.* Some of the same missionaries, and many others, wrote works designed to have a direct impact on Maya practice. These are truly instruments of *reducción,* and they bite into the language more precisely and more consequentially than any of the aforementioned works. Although they are written in Spanish genres, these instruments are either bilingual or (rarely) entirely in Maya. The dictionaries are all bilingual, as are the *artes.* The extant catechisms are predominantly in Maya, but they are translated from Spanish or Latin master texts, and they are organized according to the demands of the *doctrina menor* as a genre.[1] With the sermons we come face-to-face with missionary texts entirely in Maya without Spanish gloss or master text. These works were automatically consequential for missionary Maya because they embodied a version of the language directly: they were *in Maya reducido* and not only *about* it. Even more important, they were used in pedagogical settings where Maya was being spoken, such as the classroom, the confessional, and the training sessions in which newly arrived missionaries were taught the language of Yucatán.[2] Target speakers were induced to recite, memorize, and perform dialogue in the Maya language *as formulated by missionaries.* By way of the catechisms, sermons, and sacraments, the language as represented in the dictionaries and *artes* made its way out of the convent and into the pueblo. This movement of discourse is foundational in the project of *reducción* and is a condition of possibility for the new world that would result.

DICTIONARIES AND THE PROBLEM OF AUTHORSHIP

The instruments of *reducción* were produced by missionaries working with native Maya speakers (who are rarely acknowledged). Some of them were authored, in the full sense of having named creators who were the principals of record. This is the case for all three of the *artes* I examine in chapter 7, as well as the catechisms and sermons discussed in chapter 8. All the *artes* were published and have the entire deictic framing that I set forth in chapter 4, including record of submission, approvals, and dedication. We know who produced Coronel's *Doctrina Cristiana,* something of his life and times, where it was approved and published, when it was submitted, and which year it appeared in print form. The same can be said of the other catechisms and the *artes.* This is in sharp contrast to the situation with the five major dictionaries. Notwithstanding the inferences of successive generations of historians, not one of the major dictionaries associates itself with a named author. None is dated. None is associated with any particular place apart from what can be reconstructed of its provenance. None except the Vienna *Bocabulario* even has a title. There is ample evidence in Lizana and Cogolludo that the *lenguas* involved in preparing major written works were known as such by their contemporaries in the order, yet there is no evidence whatsoever that these *lenguas* laid claim to authorship over their dictionaries. I argue that in Yucatán at least, these absences are not accidental. They are systematic features of the genre. Dictionaries, or *bocabularios* as they were more commonly called at the time, simply lack deictic centering.

It bears underscoring that the absence of author, place, and date for the dictionaries is, by all evidence, part of the genre and not a circumstantial deficit due to the accidents of history. The temptation for modern historians to infer authors, dates, and places has proven irresistible, but it is ultimately misleading. The San Francisco dictionary was found in the *librería* of the *gran convento de los franciscanos,* Mérida, by Pío Pérez in the nineteenth century. The Vienna *Bocabulario* is so called only because the manuscript was rediscovered in Vienna, through a process that Acuña nicely spells out. Acuña (1984, xxiv) observes that the place-name Motul was given to the "Motul" dictionary by Berendt, and it was later retained by Ralph Roys. Berendt's inference was apparently based on the dubious evidence that one example sentence in the work mentioned a natural event known to have occurred in the area of Motul. Acuña himself suggests that the Maya represented in the work indicates excellent knowledge of the variety spoken in the Cumkal-Motul area. But neither rationale is convincing, in part because the regional variations suggested by Acuña have never been worked out. I do not believe we know enough to make that judgment.

What is known is that the friars traveled on a regular basis from their convents to others, to *visitas,* and into the capital for *concilios* and *congregaciones.* Insofar as dictionary makers are known or inferred, they would have traveled around the province. Antonio de Ciudad Real, Juan Coronel, and Gabriel de San Buenaventura all occupied posts at the level of *difinidor* or higher in Franciscan provincial governance. This suggests that they were called upon to make *visitas* or reports involving broad regions if not the entire province. Beyond this, Ciudad Real acquired exceptionally broad and detailed knowledge during the four years that he accompanied fray Alonso Ponce de León on his *visita* of New Spain. Between fall 1584 and September 1588, the two made *visitas* of hundreds of places throughout New Spain, Guatemala, Nicaragua, Honduras, and Yucatán. Between July and September 1588, they made *visitas* in Yucatán, going to twenty-two *cabeceras* and passing through many *pueblos de visita* along the way. The account of what they learned is written in the *Tratado Curioso y Docto de las Grandezas de la Nueva España,* an unpublished, undated manuscript attributed to Ciudad Real and likely composed around 1590, when Ciudad Real was in Alcalá de Henares. Any provincial would have exposure to Maya language and practices from around the region, and Ciudad Real is merely an extreme case. Lacking any author, the San Francisco dictionary was found in the library of the main Franciscan convent in Mérida, where it was probably consulted and annotated by friars with ties to various *guardianías.* A similar situation would have obtained for the other dictionaries as well. In my estimation, it is misleading to suggest that these works were "from" any specific place narrower than the northern peninsula, including the reduction zone and what was learned of the outside through the campaigns of extirpation and *reducción.*

Similarly, the attempt to designate dates for these dictionaries runs afoul of the recopying known to have been practiced widely in the colony. The material object of the text came into being at a certain time, but the discourse inscribed in it came from other times and places. There is abundant textual evidence in the dictionaries that they all involved recopying from other sources, although this is not mentioned in the works themselves and citation to source is all but nonexistent. This is actually typical; even the *artes* and *doctrinas,* with named authors, are known to have been gathered together, recopied, and emended from previously existing papers. Those source texts would have been from different places, just as the Maya heard by a *lengua* provincial on *visita* would be from throughout the province. The inquisitional trials yielded a mountain of testimony taken from Maya speakers, and the very process of translating it into Spanish would have expanded missionary awareness of the range of Maya language as spoken by its native speakers. Similarly, the source texts for linguistic and doctrinal works would have been earlier by various amounts of time than the work into which they were inserted. As a result, there are many striking overlaps among the dictionaries. These overlaps run the gamut from repetition of (near-)identical example sentences to idiosyncratic definitions, parallels in the sequential ordering of subentries, and a common presence of doctrinal language. They all presuppose the existence of one or more *artes,* from which they draw the grammatical notes and part-of-speech labels they use.[3] None of them explains the orthography or gives any indication of pronunciation, facts the competent reader would have found in the *arte.*

That none of the dictionaries was published is consistent with their being, effectively, open-ended. It is also possible that the encyclopedic knowledge embodied in such works was purposely guarded by the order as the capital that underwrote their claim to special knowledge of the Maya. If so, the dictionaries are analogous to the Books of Chilam Balam: closely guarded textual emblems of an esoteric knowledge. The Motul may have remained intact as Antonio de Ciudad Real left it, so to speak, but it was left in manuscript form throughout the colonial period, during which many other genres were brought to print. It never became a master text duplicated verbatim in print. This implies that access to the work was very restricted, likely within the Franciscan order. To put it in Bakhtinian terms, the dictionaries are not finalized: they were never brought to closure except in the retrospective inferences of scholars and scholarly editions.[4] Such finalizing in retrospect hides an intriguing fact: the only other genres of colonial Maya that display a comparably low degree of indexical resolution and a similar lack of finalization are the forbidden Maya genres. The dictionaries are more similar on this dimension to the Books of Chilam Balam than they are to the catechisms or *artes.*

Where, then, do dictionaries fit into the broader discursive formation, and how did the language they represent take shape and have consequences? To address these questions, we must look closely at the works themselves. In this and the next chapter I concentrate on the dictionaries, which create what we might call the lexicon of conversion. In the dictionaries the points of partial equivalence between Spanish and Maya were defined, and it is through those correspondences that the first conversion was induced, from Spanish and Latin *into* Maya. In table 5 the first two dictionaries have Spanish headwords with Maya glosses, and the second two are inverse, Maya headwords with Spanish glosses. All four are relatively rich in example sentences in Maya. The present chapter concentrates on

TABLE 5 Missionary Lexicons (Extant)

Dictionaries

SPANISH TO MAYA

Bocabulario de maya than por su abecedario (Anon., n.d., ca. 1670, also known as Vienna
  Dictionary)
Diccionario de San Francisco, Part 2 (No title, Anon., n.d., ca. early 1700s)
Diccionario de Motul, Part 2 (No title, Anon., n.d., ca. 1600)

MAYA TO SPANISH

Diccionario de Motul (No title, Anon., n.d., ca. 1600, attributed to fray Antonio de Ciudad Real)
Diccionario de San Francisco, Part 1 (No title, Anon., n.d., ca. 1690)

Shorter vocabularies (included in these authors' *artes*)

Coronel (1620), *NOMBRES de los miembros y partes del cuerpo humano*
Coronel (1620), *Declaración de las partículas*
San Buenaventura (1684), *Particulas mas notables que varian los verbos, dispuestas por el abecedario*
Beltrán (1746), *Semilexicón yucateco*

---

the first two works, from Spanish into Maya, with only occasional notes from the
Maya-to-Spanish dictionaries.[5]

The names given the works are more or less arbitrary, but they are well established in the scholarly literature and are retained here for ease of reference. I use
the shortened names commonly used by Mayanist scholars: "the Motul," "the
San Francisco," and "the Vienna." The San Francisco is actually two separate
dictionaries; Part 1 is Maya to Spanish, and Part 2 is Spanish to Maya. Part 2
evidently was written later and overlaps only partially with Part 1. Thus the
Motul and the San Francisco Part 1 are directly comparable Maya-to-Spanish
works, whereas the San Francisco Part 2 and the Vienna are comparably Spanish
to Maya. The Motul and the Vienna are available in facsimile, thanks to the
exemplary scholarship of René Acuña, and I cite them to folia, whereas the two
parts of the San Francisco were published in continuous pagination without folio
numbers and are cited to page of the Michelon (1976) edition. In examples and
citations, I abbreviate the four as M(otul), SF1 (San Francisco Part 1), SF2 (San
Francisco Part 2), and V(ienna), as in "M:222v" (Motul dictionary, folio 222 verso)
and "SF2:681" (*Diccionario de San Francisco* Part 2, page 681). As a general term of
reference, I call these works "dictionaries," distinguishing them from the lesser
"vocabularies" included in the *artes*.[6]

According to Arzápalo Marín's analytic edition (1995, iii), the Motul consists
of 15,975 lexical entries, with 19,259 different words and a total of 87,155 word

tokens.[7] In his facsimile edition, Acuña (1984) notes that the manuscript consists of two bound sets of two hundred folia each. The San Francisco has not been as thoroughly analyzed, but Berendt (preface to *Diccionario de San Francisco*, 1976, xii) notes that Part 1 contains approximately 2,500 *artículos* (which I take to be main entries, not counting many derivatives), whereas the Spanish-Maya Part 2 contains about 8,000 *artículos*. Acuña (1993, 15–16) notes that the Vienna consists of 209 "usable" folia (others being damaged or illegible), with approximately 14,000 Spanish headword entries, associated with about 40,000 Maya usages (including multiple tokens of the same forms). Although it is difficult to compare these counts precisely, the Motul is by far the largest of the four dictionaries, followed by the Vienna, the San Francisco Part 2, and then the San Francisco Part 1. The Motul is mostly in a single hand, with a limited number of pages apparently interpolated in a second hand, and the San Francisco Parts 1 and 2 as currently available was recopied by D. Juan Pío Pérez in the nineteenth century, leaving open whether the originals were done by a single copyist or several (Michelon ed. 1976). The Vienna, by contrast, shows no fewer than seven different hands, according to Acuña (1993, 17–18), with arabic page numbers added later in an eighth hand. All four dictionaries were brought to print long after the deaths of their supposed makers, suggesting that they were never really intended for print publication.

Nevertheless, the dictionaries share several features of format that indicate a relatively stable genre. They all distinguish headwords from glosses in the form of a two-column list with the following four features.

1. Headwords are set off in the left column, followed by glosses in the right column, plus examples illustrating usage of the headword or its equivalent, with or without modulation. This simple format distinguishes the source or "matrix" language (left column) from the target language (right). For the Motul and the San Francisco Part 1, the matrix language is Maya and the target, into which it is translated, is Spanish. The San Francisco Part 2 and the Vienna have the inverse arrangement. Every gloss represents an equivalence between the matrix language, which is the focal object, and the target language, which expresses a metalinguistic comment on the object.
2. Entries are organized alphabetically by headword in the matrix language. Many entries display multiple derivatives or examples of the headword, and when they do, the sequence of these elements tends to be thematic, not alphabetic. Thus there is an inversion between alphabetic (not thematic) entries and thematic (not alphabetic) subentries.[8]
3. Orthographies are grossly equivalent in all four dictionaries, with some variation in the handling of glottalized affricates (ch' vs. chh vs. C for glottalized [tʃ']; dz vs. ɔ for [ts']), the representation of vowel *i* or *y*, the use of

h, the sequential order of first letters in headwords, and the use of doubled vowels to mark length, glottalization, or pitch). The Motul is unique in the care with which it uses doubled vowels. The Vienna and the San Francisco Parts 1 and 2 are much less consistent, and in this regard resemble Coronel (1620a, 1620b) and San Buenaventura (1888 [1684]). Except for the variable features noted, the four dictionaries overwhelmingly agree on the spelling of comparable expressions.

4. New letters start in midpage rather than on a new folio or side. This precludes simple adding on of new entries at the end of a letter. The regularity with which pages are filled and the alphabet unfolds suggests that the Motul and the Vienna were each a single, internally complete copy. It is unknown whether the San Francisco dictionaries displayed the same feature.

The preceding four features are heuristically useful for readers, because they organize a great deal of information in graphic form. More important, for us they give a first indication of the relative stability of the genre and the amount of agreement among *lenguas* as to how Maya language was to be represented.[9] The problems of pitch, length, and glottalization in the vowels were never solved, but the Motul indicates clearly that they were an issue. For the most part, there was a surprising amount of agreement regarding the graphic representation and meaning of Maya expressions. The commonalities across the dictionaries reflect a trend toward standardization in missionary Maya. Whatever the actual practices of native Maya speakers, the missionaries had achieved a very high degree of consensus on their understanding of the language. The fact that this understanding is also embodied in *artes,* catechisms, the confessional manual, and sermons means that it was rooted in a broader spectrum of genres and works. More than any supposed author, the field and the archives of the Franciscan order in Yucatán are the source of the text.

The shorter vocabulary lists of Coronel, San Buenaventura, and Beltrán are obviously related to the stand-alone dictionaries but contrast sharply with them. The shorter lists are included as part of an *arte* and therefore are indexically grounded to authors, reviewers, and places and dates of publication. They are relatively short and are mostly ordered by semantic themes or fields (body parts, kinship terms, etc.), as opposed to the arbitrary sequence of an alphabet. All three contain substantial subsections listing particles and other form-function classes that would have been quite unfamiliar to speakers of European languages and that are semantically very diverse. Within these subsections, particles are ordered alphabetically. Thus the main sections are thematically defined, but when semantic coherence breaks down, as it does with the "particles," the arbitrary principle of alphabetic order is applied (the opposite of the hierarchy described above for dictionaries). In comparison to the dictionaries, the minor vocabularies have few example sentences. Whereas the dictionaries (except for the Vienna *Bocabulario*) lack titles, the vocabularies embedded in the *artes* do have titles. Both Coronel and San Buenaventura titled their semantically focused lists *"bocabulario,"* whereas Beltrán a century later called his a *"semilexicón."* On the evidence of usage, all these works belonged to the genre *bocabulario,* a term that was also used in reference to the dictionaries; thus it would appear that this genre was very flexible. But the lesser scope and embedded, subordinate status of the vocabulary list make it a secondary exemplar of the genre; therefore, for the remainder of this and the next chapter, I concentrate on the dictionaries.

THE THEMATIC SCOPE OF THE DICTIONARIES

The dictionaries represent an impressively broad knowledge of Maya language and practices. There is of course an enormous amount of doctrinal language in the examples, and there is no question that the dictionaries and the evangelical works are part of the same *reducción.* In discussing the term *calepino* that has been applied to the Motul (to my knowledge, first by Lizana), Acuña notes that it was used at this time in reference to compendious dictionaries that drew heavily on literature in the matrix language, citing examples from actual texts in the manner of the eighteenth-century Spanish *Diccionario de Autoridades,* the *Oxford English Dictionary,* or the French *Robert.* In the case of the Motul, the texts cited were not literary, since there was no acceptable corpus of Maya literature, but rather doctrinal (Acuña 1984).[10] Acuña goes so far as to suggest that the lost *artes* of Villalpando and Landa are partially reproduced in the grammatical commentaries.

Yet it is critical to recognize from the outset that the works are broader than this, and they embody a more varied knowledge of Maya, as Acuña also notes. The Motul truly does reflect extraordinarily broad and subtle knowledge of the language, although the other works also have unique strengths. The example sentences refer to many aspects of ordinary Maya-language usage. They also show utterances that would be spoken by a range of speakers, including friars in the course of the sacraments, friars outside the ritual context, Maya men, and Maya women. Indeed, the language here is so varied and rich in voices that one imagines the maker(s) taking notes in the manner of a fieldworking linguist: transcribing utterances heard and then integrating them into the dictionary. Lizana claimed to have seen the rough draft of Ciudad Real's *calepino* (aka the Motul), along with two sacks of draft notes. Were we to find those two sacks, I wager they would include not just recopyings from earlier missionary works but also many utterances heard and noted on the fly. The Motul is also very rich in metalanguage, of the sort that one would have to know in order to ask informants the meaning of expressions. The San Francisco 1 is more limited and mechanical, but it is still diverse in its entries, especially in the subclassification of domains such as food, agricultural practice, kinds of writing, and affective states.

It is subtler to judge the scope of the San Francisco Part 2 and the Vienna, because the matrix language is Spanish, the native language of all the missionaries, *lengua* or not. Therefore, the question for these two works is not how much the makers knew about the matrix language but which parts they felt it necessary to render in Maya, and, of course, how they did it. The Vienna and the San Francisco Part 2 suggest that they attempted to construct a broad universe of Maya talk about doctrine, governance, idolatry, translation, language itself, and all manner of objects, persons, and practices in the pueblos as well. By juxtaposing related entries, we can see where they agree, where they complement one another, and where they appear to disagree.

FROM SPANISH INTO MAYA

For our purposes, the two Spanish-to-Maya works, the San Francisco Part 2 and the Vienna, provide a good point of entry into the realm of converting words occupied by the dictionary makers. Since Spanish is the matrix language, the entries will be immediately more familiar for English readers than were we to start with the Maya-to-Spanish works. Moreover, assuming that the makers of these dictionaries were Franciscans, which seems beyond question, then Spanish was their native language as well. Which parts of their native language did they translate into Maya, which words did they leave in Spanish, and what can their works tell us about the emergence of *Maya reducido*?

A careful comparison of any two of the four dictionaries would be monographic in length. In this chapter and the next, I focus selectively on certain entries, which I have chosen for their relevance to *reducción* and the forms of evangelization, governance, and daily practice that it entailed. We want to see how the dictionary makers commensurated between the Maya, which they had to discover or generate, and the Spanish terms, which often had multiple uses and always had background associations.

In table 6 the English headings have been added to indicate the themes around which the Spanish entries are clustered. The classification is heuristic, and there are surely other Spanish headwords in the Vienna and the San Francisco Part 2 that could have been selected. The aim of the selection is to spell out a core of vocabulary pertinent to the main spheres of *reducción* and to examine the translation decisions and strategies that the dictionary makers pursued. I show that they were both systematic and creative in the way they went about translating Spanish to Maya. By juxtaposing the Vienna and the San Francisco Part 2 on each of these terms, we can also take the measure of the relatedness between the two works: do they provide similar glosses, similar examples, congruent understandings? I

TABLE 6   A Lexicon for *Reducción*

FIRST PRINCIPLES		GOVERNANCE	
1. Bautizmo	'baptism'	18. Regidor	'municipal official'
2. Convertir	'convert'	19. Regimiento	'reign'
3. Creer	'believe'	20. Región	'region'
4. Dios	'God'	21. Elegir	'to elect'
5. Crucificar	'crucify'	22. Elección	'election'
		23. Congregación	'congregation'
SACRAMENTS		24. Pueblo	'town'
6. Missa	'mass'	25. Visita(r)	'inspect(tion)'
7. Comunión	'communion'	26. Guarda(r)	'to keep, guard'
8. Confesar	'confess'		
		MARGINAL PRACTICES	
PEDAGOGY		27. Huir	'flee'
9. Disciplina	'discipline'	28. Idolatra(r)	'idolater, idolize'
10. Doctrinado	'indoctrinated'	29. Ídolos	'idols'
11. Maestro	'master'	30. Ídolo	'idol'
12. Cantor	'cantor'	31. Named idols cited in the Vienna (419–20)	
LANGUAGE AND SIGNS			
13. Arte	'practical grammar'		
14. Escribir	'to write'		
15. Ladino	'ladino'		
16. Testigo	'witness'		
17. Señal	'sign'		

show that they do, and this indexes the process of standardization in which the dictionaries were caught up. I also revisit several of these semantic fields in the next chapter, which works from Maya headwords back to Spanish glosses.

Much of the Maya that occurs in the Spanish-Maya works also occurs in the Maya-Spanish ones. The explanation for this consistency cannot be simply that the missionaries correctly chose the Maya forms with the desired meanings, because before the Spanish arrived there were no Maya forms for concepts like baptism, religious conversion, crucifixion, communion, Mass, confession, and idolatry, even if there were occasional arguable analogues. Just as there were no Indios in the New World before the Europeans mistakenly dubbed the people of the Americas "Indians," there were no terms for key aspects of Catholic practice or *reducción*. The language of the missions was a new sign system, in which Maya forms were joined to Spanish meanings, a process that would inevitably alter both. When a translation or way of phrasing a Spanish concept recurs across the dictionaries, therefore, it reflects an incipient stabilization of the translanguage of the missions.

It is noteworthy that the San Francisco Part 2 has no entries for *conversión, reducir, reducción, sacramento, bocabulario, copilar, recopilar, cruz, crucificar.* The Vienna lacks the first six of these and also lacks *doctrina* and *comunión* but does have "crucifixion" and "crucifix." Neither dictionary mentions *lengua* in the sense of the bilingual missionary, the inverse of the *indio ladino*. The San Francisco Part 2 glosses *missa* as shown below, but the Vienna does not list this term at all. We can only speculate on the rationale for these absences. Perhaps *reducción* and *bocabulario* were needed only for discussions among the missionaries in Spanish; perhaps *doctrina* and *comunión* were so thoroughly presupposed that they were rarely mentioned. When the missionaries did refer to these concepts, they apparently retained the Spanish, as we will see in the example sentences. Both works devote attention to idols and idolatry, but the Vienna adds a list of fifteen named Maya "idols" that indicates significant exposure to Maya beliefs. Each of the dictionaries is especially strong in some areas, presenting elaborate lists of forms absent from the other works. Although they are not copied wholesale from one another, the complementarities reinforce the impression that they presuppose one another.

FIRST PRINCIPLES

Baptism, conversion, and communion are threshold events in which the Christian subject is made and remade. The Maya forms used to express these concepts were established early on and do not appear to have changed significantly during the colonial period. We find the same expressions with minor variations in the Motul and the San Francisco Part 1, as well as in the *artes* and evangelical texts.[11]

As will become clear in the next chapter, the Maya verb *oc* 'to enter' was used for a family of Christian ideas including baptism, *oc haa* ['enter' + 'water'], belief, *ocol ol* ['enter' + suffix + 'heart'], and conversion, *ocçah ba* ['enter' + causative + reflexive] (lit. 'cause oneself to enter'). The collocation of these three basic Christian concepts in derivatives of the same Maya root is indicative of the missionary translation strategy. The apparent aim was to use a limited number of Maya expressions to convey the maximum number of Spanish or Christian concepts. Notice that there is no *linguistic* relation between the words "baptism," "belief," and "conversion" in Spanish, but there is a deep *doctrinal* relation between the concepts they stand for. The Maya renderings make this doctrinal relation transparent. Obviously, this was heuristically useful both to missionaries, who could learn Maya more quickly by relying on their theological knowledge, and to their Maya students, who would more rapidly grasp the arcane interconnections among aspects of the new religion.

These entries illustrate a recurrent question in missionary dictionaries. Are the Maya expressions translations of the Spanish words, or alternative descrip-

EXAMPLE 5.1

Bautismo (SF2:518)	'baptism'	*caput zihil*
Baptismo (V:141)	'baptism'	*caa put çihil*
el sacramento del baptismo	'the sacrament of baptism'	*u sacramentoil oc haa*
bapti[ç]ar*	'to baptize'	*ocçah haa ti pol,*
		caa put çihçah
ps⁰	'passive'	*ocçabal haa ti pol*

*Spanish material in square brackets was interpolated by Acuña 1993 and does not appear in the original Vienna from which Acuña transliterated his edition.

EXAMPLE 5.2

Convertir (SF2:550)	'to convert'	
convertir (una cosa en otra)	'convert one thing to another'	*oczah ti uinicil*
convertirse (una cosa en otra)	'convert one thing to another [to become chief]'	*ocol ti uinicil, ocol ti ba[b]alil*
convertirse o reconciliarse con el que agravió	'convert or reconcile oneself with the person whom one aggrieved'	*ualkezah ba ti, oczah ba ti, ualkezah ba*
Conbertirse (V:203)	'to convert (oneself)'	
conbertirse a Dios, y la tal conuersión	'convert to God, and such conversion'	*ocçah ba ti Dios, ualkeçah ba ti Dios*
conbertirse una cosa en otra	'one thing convert(s) to another'	*ocol ti*
—	'convert to wine'	*oc ti binoyl*
—	'convert to human form our lord in God'	*oci ti ui[ni]cil ca yumil ti Dios*
conbertirse la sal en agua	'convert salt to water'	*haahal taab*
no tardó en conbertirse en agua la sal	'the salt immediately converted to water'	*mai tac xan hi u haa hal taab*

tions of the prototypical objects to which the Spanish words refer? The expression *caput zihil* is literally ['two' + 'times' + 'born']; that is, it designates rebirth. It is the phrase used to denote the resurrection of Christ as well as the baptism of a new Christian. Rather than translate the term "baptism" per se, it describes the doctrinal meaning of baptism, the original threshold event in which the "new man" is born and given a new name, in likeness with the resurrection of Christ. The standard rendering of "baptize" is *oc ha* ['enter' + 'water'], which describes the manner of executing the sacrament rather than its essence or consequence.

The Vienna offers the periphrastic phrase "the sacrament of baptism," with "sacrament" left untranslated (though given a Maya ending) and the manner of the practice rendered as 'enter-water'. For pedagogical purposes, this phrase would render transparent the tie between the Maya and the sacrament name. Although *caput zihil* occurs in descriptive contexts throughout the missionary writings, it is *oc ha* that names the sacrament.

The entries for "convert" and "conversion" raise slightly different questions. The San Francisco Part 2 makes no mention of religious conversion in the sense of a revision of beliefs. Rather, it takes "convert" in the miraculous sense of changing one thing into another, such as water into wine or salt into water. The frame of reference here is the miracle of transformation, including the incarnation of God as man. Thus *oczah ti uinicil* ['enter' + causative + 'to humanity'] designates not just any material conversion, as San Francisco Part 2 (550) suggests, but specifically the entering of God into human form. Stripped of its religious framing, conversion of attitude is rendered as 'reconciliation among aggrieved parties', a concept that recurs in association with conversion in all of the dictionaries. In the Vienna, the first entry is religious conversion to the Christian God, and the example sentences spell out the incarnation as *Oci ti ui[ni]cil ca yumil ti Dios* [enter + past + 'to humanity our lord God'] 'Our Lord God became human'. The verb *ualkeçah* is literally 'to cause to turn, revolve', a near-equivalent to *reducir*. As we will see in the next chapter, it is a standard way to refer to conversion with an emphasis on redirecting the subject or inducing him or her to turn back toward God.

This key term is translated by stems derived from the root *oc* 'enter', just as we will see in the Motul and San Francisco Part 1 dictionaries. The first point to note is that there is no attempt to render in Maya the mundane sense of *creer* 'believe (that)', as in 'I don't believe (that) it will rain today'.[12] Instead, what is rendered is the monumental 'believe (in), to hold a conviction, to have faith'. Among the nine entries in the Vienna, there are two example sentences that merit special attention. The first is *Creer en sueños* 'to believe in dreams'. This expression also recurs in the Maya-Spanish dictionaries, reinforcing the impression that the Franciscans were abidingly worried about this practice. It is glossed in Maya as *occah ti ol uayak; nay u than uayak*. The former is the straightforward translation of 'believe dreams' ['enter' + 'cause' + 'to' + 'heart']. The second phrase is more opaque and appears to derive from *nay* meaning 'doze, dream', or perhaps from the homophone *nay* 'to incline, lean, tip over'. In either case, it is semantically impossible to derive 'believe in dream(s)' from this phrase, which is either an error or perhaps something the missionaries might have said *about* believing in dreams.

The second provocative example is *Creo en Dios Padre* 'I believe in God the Father', which is rendered *ocan t[i] uol Dios Cit bil* ['entered' + 'to' + 'my

EXAMPLE 5.3

Creer (V:211)	'to believe'	
creer generalm[en]te	'believe in general'	*ocçah ti ol,*
		ocol ti ol
cree en Dios	'believe in God'	*ocez t au ol Dios*
creer, tener creído	'to believe, hold as belief'	*ocan ti ol*
creo en Dios Padre	'I believe in God the Father'	*ocan t[i] uol Dios Cit bil*
creer, tener ffee	'to believe, have faith'	*oc olal*
Ju[an] tiene ffee o cre[e]	'Juan has faith or believes'	*oc olal u cah Ju[an]*
creyente o fiel que cree	'believer or faithful who believes'	*ah oc olal [.l.] ocan ti ol*
creíble cosa	'believable thing'	*ocçaben ti ol*
creer en sueños	'to believe in dreams'	*ocçah ti ol uayak [.l.]*
		nay u than uayak
Creer (SF2:557)	'to believe'	
creencia y fé	'belief and faith'	*ocolal*
creer	'to believe'	*ocol ti ol,*
		oczah ti ol
no lo creo	'I don't believe it'	*he hoi*
creible	'believable'	*oczaben ti ol*

heart' + 'god' + 'infinite']. This example sentence is identical to the first line of the Credo as translated by Coronel (1620b): *Ocaan ti uol Dios Citbil* 'I believe in God Almighty' (Acuña ed. 1998, 149). It is worth noting that *citbil* is not used in this context by either San Buenaventura (1888 [1684]) or Beltrán (1859 [1746]). Beltrán in particular singles it out as a term used by the Maya for one of their own divinities and therefore rejects it, substituting the more widely attested *yumbil* 'revered Father'. I have not been able to find *citbil* in either of the San Francisco dictionaries, either as headword or as part of any of the associated expressions. According to Arzápalo Marín's (1995) monumental edition of the Motul, complete with index, the term never occurs in that source either. Thus its occurrence in the Vienna is potentially an index of relatedness to Coronel's *Doctrina* or to the Chilam Balam texts. As we will see in the discussion of the forbidden Books of Chilam Balam, the term does occur in several of these works, and every token is associated with the Christian God—thus looping back to the *doctrina* and dictionary. The implication, I believe, is that this term is a neologism created by early-seventeenth-century missionaries but not widely used. While the *-bil* element is obviously the familiar reverential suffix, the source of *cit* is unclear to me.

The ideas of God and the cross are so basic to Christianity that they occur all over the missionary writings, often in the Spanish forms *dios, cruz*. The Maya translations for *dios* were all based on the root *ku,* which was also used to translate

EXAMPLE 5.4

Diós (SF2:585)	God	*ku*
diós vivo	'living god'	*cuxul diós,*
		cuxul ku
diós único	'sole god'	*hunab ku*
dioses de gentiles	'gods of gentiles'	*u kuul ah ma ocolalob*
Dios (V:278)	'God'	*Ku*
Dios os guarde	'God watch over you'	*u canan tech Ku*
Dios de paz	'God of peace'	*u Diosil hun olal,*
		u Kuil hun olal

"church" (*ku nah* ['god' + 'house'], *otoch ku* ['house' + 'god']) and certain forms of worship. The missionaries were quite aware that in using a preexisting Maya term for "god," they ran the risk of encouraging syncretism and confusion between the Christian God and the diabolical idols they were seeking to extirpate. Thus although both dictionaries cite the bare root *ku* for *dios,* this root usually occurs with qualifiers meant to disambiguate. The living God, the God of peace, the God who watches over individuals are all aspects of the specifically Christian concept. By contrast, *u kuul ah ma ocolalob,* another periphrastic description, translates 'the god of those who do not believe', that is, any non-Christian divinity (cf. ex. 5.29). This negative definition classifies all non-Christian gods as beyond the sphere of belief, where belief is already identified with Dios. The use of *hunab ku* ['one' + suffix + 'god'] for the singularity of God is linguistically transparent to the oneness of the Father, Son, and Holy Spirit and occurs widely in the missionary writings.[13]

Whereas there is no entry in the San Francisco Part 2 for either "cross" or "crucifixion," the Vienna presents a range of expressions. Observe that the Spanish term *cruz* occurs in every one of these Maya phrases, except for the last translation of "crucifix." The occurrence of the Spanish term in many otherwise Maya phrases once again indexes that the cross in question is specifically the one on which Christ died. The Maya descriptive phrases are thereby bound to the Christian referent. *Uin bail Xpo* translates 'likeness of Christ' and has nothing to do with the cruciform per se, except that the prototypical image of Christ is on the cross. The expressions based on *çin* 'stretched out' focus on the disposition of the crucified body and recall the language of omnipotence discussed in chapter 1 of this book. The root *bah* actually means 'to nail' and focuses on the specific method of attaching Christ to the cross, simultaneously implying that the cross in question is made of wood, not some other material. The implication of 'wood'

EXAMPLE 5.5

Cruçificar y enclauar en cruz (V:213)	'crucify and nail to cross'	bah ti cruz
cruçificado así	'thus crucified'	bahan ti cruz
pasº	'passive'	bahal ti cruz
cruçificar y estender en la cruz	'crucify and extend on cross'	çin ti cruz,
		çin che ti cruz
cruçificado ser así	'to be crucified thus'	çin ex ti cruz
crucifixo	'crucifix'	çijnil ti cruz,
		çin che tabal ti cruz
cruçifixo	'crucifix'	uin bail Xpo

is then made explicit in the compound *çin che* used for "crucifix" and "crucify," where *çin* is the positional root and *che* is 'wood', hence 'stretch out (on) wood'. The Vienna makes excellent use of the verbal morphology by deriving this stem into the transitive verb *[çin-che-t]* 'stretch it/him out on wood', which is then passivized *[çin-che-t-ab]* '(he) has been stretched out on wood' and cited in the incompletive stem shape *[çin-che-t-ab-al]* 'he has been stretched out on wood, crucified'. There can be no question that the dictionary relied on an already highly developed knowledge of Maya grammar, without which forms like this one would be impossible to generate or understand.

Thus in general we see that the rendering of key Spanish terms into Maya embodied an analysis of the theological concepts as well as an attempt to build into the Maya phrasing transparent clues to the relations among Spanish concepts. In this process, the lines between translation, explanation, and alternative description of objects were blurred. Similarly, the lines between the two languages were blurred insofar as the Maya glosses often include Spanish terms in grammatical collocation with Maya ones. The language being formed was a hybrid at all levels.

RELIGIOUS PRACTICES

The case of "Mass" is similar in that the Maya explains the concept associated with the Spanish term. A glance at the terms in ex. 5.6 indicates that the Spanish term was not translated but that various qualifiers were added to it to yield a typology of masses (spoken, sung, minor, major, dedicated to the deceased or to "Our Lady"). The Vienna describes Mass as "the lowering of God by the priest," and this phrasing picks up on the pervasive verticality of the sacrament. Once again, this is not a translation of the term "Mass" but rather a pedagogically useful explanation of one of its aspects. Note that Mass said for an individual (whether alive or deceased) is said *yokol* 'over' him/her, another bit of verticality. In these translations, the theological background is subtly embedded in the Maya

EXAMPLE 5.6

Misa rezada (SF2:670)	'spoken mass'	*thanbil misa*
misa cantada	'sung mass'	*kaybil misa*
misa decir	'say mass'	*utzcinah misa*
misa decir para alguno	'say mass for someone'	*manzah misa yokol*
misa oir	'hear mass'	*chan misa*

Missa (V:474)	'Mass'	
respecto de la consagración se puede deçir emçah Ku, que es "bajar a Dios" el sacerdote	'of consecration one can say lower God, which is the priest "lowers God"'	*emçah Ku*
misa se dice o se está diciendo missa	'mass is said or being said'	*ualak,* *lic yuchul missa*
missa cantada	'sung mass'	*kaybil misa*
[missa] resada	'spoken mass'	*than bil misa*
[missa] mayor	'high mass'	*noh missa*
missa de nuestra Señora	'mass of Our Lady'	*u missail ca Coolel*
[missa de difuntos]	'mass for deceased'	*u missail cimenob*
missa por un difunto	'mass for a dead person'	*missa yokol hun tul cimen*
misa decir [por] alguno	'say mass for someone'	*mançah misa okol*

EXAMPLE 5.7

Comunión (SF2:545)	communion	
comunión	'the body of our lord is received'	*ukamal u cucutil yumil bil*

phrasing: the Christian God is high in the heavens but is made present among men down on earth in the sacrament of Mass as celebrated by a priest. In Spanish, those who attend this celebration are said to "hear Mass," but in Maya they *chan* 'watch' it as a spectacle. Here the gaze directed toward the altar stands for the deeper attentiveness to the Mass that was expected of the well-reduced Indio.

The sacrament of communion was simply not translated and does not occur in the Vienna headwords. The long phrase *ukamal u cucutil yumil bil* actually translates as 'the body of (the) lord is received' and is an explanation of the taking of communion, not a translation of the sacrament name.[14] It is worth noting that the Spanish *comunión* also meant any participation or communication among members of a group, but this generic sense was never even considered in the Maya dictionaries.

The practicing Christian subject was enjoined to reconcile himself with God through the sacrament of confession. In this sacrament, the properly attentive

EXAMPLE 5.8

Confesar (SF2:547)	'to confess'	
confesar con tormento	'to confess with torment'	*ppaa chi*
confesar o decir verdad	'to confess or say truth'	*tohcinah than,*
		toh pultah
confesarse, confesión	'to confess, confession'	*choch keban,*
		toh pul keban,
		tohcabtah,
		tohpultah
confesión sin paréntesis	'confession without omissions'	*tao tohcabil chi*
confesión general	'general confession'	*yuk confesión*
no te alarde de ser pecador	'be not a proud sinner'	*ten cen ah zipile*

Confesar (V:196)	'to confess'	
confesarse de todos sus pecados sin dexar ninguno	'to confess all of one's sins without omitting any'	*xup toh cab tah keban*
confesar sin orden ni conçierto, ni del todo	'confess without order or reason, nor completely'	*tomen tom,* *tomin tom*
no te confieses así, dexando de deçir algún pecado	'do not confess thus, omitting some sin(s)'	*ma a tomen tom haalic tzolic a keban,* *baci a tomen tom hal te a tzolob a keban*
confesarse diçiendo los pecados a bulto y sin orden	'confess saying sins lumped together without order'	*çopp toh cab tah keban,* *çopp halmah keban,* *çipil*
no te confieses así	'do not confess that way'	*ma a çopp toh cab tic a çipil*
confesar [a] otro	'confess to another'	*choch çipil,* *choch keban*
confesóme el Padre	'the Father confessed me'	*u chochah in çipil Padre*
confesar admitiendo a otro a la confesion	'to confess, admitting another to confession'	*occah ti confesar*
no me quiso admitir	'he did not want to admit me'	*ma yoltah Padre yoceç en ti confesar*
confesor que confiesa al penitente	'confessor who confesses the penitent'	*ah choch keban*

confessee has examined himself to determine his sins and told these sins truthfully to a confessor priest, who then absolves the individual and imposes a penance, which the penitent then performs as an expiation (see plate 7). Given the
complexity of the sacrament, it is unsurprising that there are several Maya expressions, used according to which aspect of confession they focus on. Across all the
dictionaries, the most standard terms are *tohpultah* ['straight'+'cast'], *tohcinah
than* ['straight'+causative+'speech'], *tohcabtah* ['straight'+'earth'] (from which

toh cabil chi ['straight' + 'earth' + suffix + 'mouth']), and *choch keban* ['untie' + 'sin'].
Of these, the first three designate the speech act in which the confessee engages,
with 'straight' being a standard image for 'true'. The reference to untying focuses
on the priest's role in unbinding the burden of sin by absolution. Judging by the
examples in ex. 5.8, the missionaries were concerned with the torment people felt
in confessing and with the relative disorder and incompleteness of Indian confessions. The Vienna cites two examples that suggest that priests judged the readiness
of individuals for confession before admitting them to the sacrament.

These example sentences also establish the equivalence between the two Maya
terms selected for "sin," namely, *keban* and *çipil*. Whatever the relation between
these two terms in the semantics of Maya outside the *reducción,* within it, they
became synonyms. The phrase *ten cen ah zipile,* cited in the San Francisco, is
presented as an interlingual equivalent of the imperative *no te alarde de ser
pecador,* which evidently means 'don't show off that you are a sinner'. However,
the Maya says simply 'I who am a sinner'. Here the relation between the Spanish
and the Maya is a matter of sheer speech practice and not semantics: the Maya
form is not a translation of the Spanish injunction but a speech act in response
to it. In fact, this exact phrase is the first utterance in the prayer for confession
in Coronel's and Beltrán's catechisms, which is derived from the Latin *Confiteor*
(Acuña 1998, 150).[15] That is, just as "I believe in God the father" is the first line of
the Credo, "I who am a sinner" is the first line of the prayer known in Spanish
as *Yo pecador* 'I, a sinner'. The two speech acts are basic to the formation of the
practicing Catholic subject.

PEDAGOGY

All the Maya entries in exs. 5.9–5.12 are based on verb roots that designate actions
associated with the Spanish headwords: *hadz* 'strike', *cambez* 'teach (cause to
learn)', *kay* 'sing', *men* 'do', and *kam* 'receive'. The roles of teacher and student,
master and disciple are then derived as 'he who causes learning' and 'he who
is caused to learn' respectively. The morphology of the Maya renders the reciprocity of the roles transparent. Complex forms like *[cam-bez-ab-il]* 'has been
caused to learn' and *[cam-bez-ah-aan]* 'having been caused to learn' once again
make powerful use of grammatical rules deriving causatives, passives, adjectives,
and statives. Both the San Francisco Part 2 and the Vienna cite the form *ah
men* [Agent + 'do'] as translating 'master' (of a mechanical skill)—an interesting
choice, given that this same term was widely used in reference to Maya shaman
curers whom the missionaries sought to repress. This term was never used in
reference to the doctrinal teachers known as "maestros cantores" in Spanish,
who were designated as *ah cambezah* 'teachers' or *ah kay* [Agent + 'sing'] 'singers'.

EXAMPLE 5.9

Disciplina, enseñanza (SF2:585)	'discipline, teaching'	*cambezah*
disciplina, azote	'discipline, blow'	*hadzab kaan*
disciplinar en costumbres	'to discipline in habits'	*chich tzec**
disciplinarse	'to discipline oneself'	*hadzba*
discípulo	'disciple'	*cambezabil uinic, cambezabil uinicil*
discípulo (el que aprende)	'disciple, who learns'	*ah cambal*
Diçiplina para açotar (V:276)	'discipline by blows'	*kaan, hadzab kaan*
diçípulo que aprende de la doctrina	'disciple who learns doctrine'	*ah kamal than*
diçípulo haçerse de otro	'(to) become disciple of another'	*ocol ti cam beçah uinicilil*

*The term in the San Francisco is *cich tzem*, which I take to be a typo or scribal error for *chich tzec*, a well-known expression meaning 'castigate harshly'. The term *tzem* occurs in the dictionaries with the meaning 'thin, emaciated', which makes no sense in this context. The reference to "costumbres" is not reflected in the Maya gloss.

EXAMPLE 5.10

Doctrinado (SF2:587)	'indoctrinated'	*cambezahan*

EXAMPLE 5.11

Maestro u oficial (SF2:659)	'master or official'	*ah men*
Maestro de escuela o de algún arte que enseña (V:457)	'school master or of a skill he teaches'	*ah cambezah*
maestro de arte mecánica o oficial ansí	'master of mechanical art or official'	*ah men*
Maestre de escuela (SF2:658)	'school master'	*ah canbezah*

EXAMPLE 5.12

Cantor de la escuela y coro (V:169)	'cantor of school or choir'	*ah kay*
cantores maiores, que señalan los indios en la escuela	'major cantors who signal the Indians in school'	*kayom*

LANGUAGE AND SIGNS

The gloss of *arte* is highly suggestive because it translates both the written genre of grammatical description and the scientific knowledge or ability that this work is intended to capture. The Vienna links this to the tradition of *grammatica* in Latin, suggesting that while there may have been *artes* of Maya, there was no *gramática* of Maya, perhaps since it falls outside the scope of the classical languages of Europe. One imagines that in teaching an *arte* like Coronel's the instructor might have referred to it with the term *idzatil,* yet this term never occurs in the titles of such works and is in fact rare in the missionary writings. The Motul entries for this term make no mention of language but rather gloss it as *idzat, idzatil, idzattah* 'astuto, hábil, ingenioso, entendimiento (etc.) para bien y para mal' (astute, skilled, ingenious, understanding [etc.] for good and for evil) (M:222r).

The dictionaries are rich in terms for writing, most based on the Maya root *dzib* 'write', *dzibtah* 'write it'. There was another term used in Maya for written language, namely, *uooh, uoohtah* 'write, write it', but this appears to have been associated with hieroglyphic writing and was seldom used by the missionaries in reference to European alphabetic writing. An in-depth exploration in chapter 6, using the Maya headwords as our point of departure, will shed light on further associations of *dzib* in Maya as well as additional vocabulary for qualities of graphic form (large, small, ill formed, flowing) and kinds of written text, particularly letters, books, and contracts. Note in ex. 5.14 that the San Francisco Part 2 translates the reciprocal exchange of writing, evidently in the form of letters, and that it also gives some evidence that the writing of scribes was typified as flowing or rapid. I have been unable to find the Maya term *lalach* in the other dictionaries, which may indicate scribal error in the San Francisco Part 2. If the target form were *halach* 'true, excellent', then the Maya gloss would suggest that the scribe was the truest or best of writers, just as the pre-Columbian "governor" was a *halach uinic* 'true person'. The translation of "contract" is based on the verb *kax* 'to bind, tie' and *moc* 'to tie with a knot'. In both cases, the contract is construed as a verbal act that binds its maker by oath or commitment. The Vienna dictionary has nineteen entries for *escribir,* which agree for the most part with the other three dictionaries and are not reproduced here.

The position of *ladino,* like that of *lengua,* was a key element of the conceptual threshold between Maya and Spanish cultures. Whereas the San Francisco Part 2 has no entry for this term, the Vienna glosses it as in ex. 5.15. The Maya *ah ohel* [Agent + 'know'] means simply 'one who knows', and *nonoh ti than* ['great' + 'great' + 'at' + 'language'] means 'great at language'. Whereas the Spanish term unambiguously entails that the *ladino* is a non-native Spanish speaker who has mastered Spanish, the Maya glosses make no reference to which languages

EXAMPLE 5.13

Arte (SF2:507)	'art, skill'	idzat
arte o çiençia, astuçia, maña (V:117)	'art or science, skill, ability'	ydzatil
gramática (V:371)	'grammar'	ydzatil latín than

EXAMPLE 5.14

Escribir (SF2:605)	'to write'	dzib, dzibtah, uooh, uoohtah
escritura, lo que se escribe	'writing (what is written)'	dzib, udzibal
escribirse en retorno	'to write one another back'	paclam dzib
escribir letra corrida como escribano	'to write fluidly like a scribe'	lalach dzib
escritura de contrato	'writing of contract'	udzibal kaxthan, mocthan

EXAMPLE 5.15

Ladino (V:437)	'Indio fluent in Spanish'	ah ohel, nonoh ti than

are in play or which one is native for the "knower." The two Maya expressions in ex. 5.15 could be applied equally well to *lenguas* and *ladinos,* and also to anyone particularly gifted in his or her own native language. Neither the Vienna nor the San Francisco Part 2 has any entry for *lengua* in the sense of a person who masters language. Thus the neat inversion and semantic richness of the two concepts in Spanish is collapsed into a single generic notion in the Maya.

The telling of truth was a critical part of both Christian practice and the functioning of the *cabildo,* where witnesses were a regular part of document production. In ex. 5.16 we see the two aspects, to be a witness and to testify, where the latter is a speech act and the former is a state of knowledge. In both dictionaries, the language of testifying overlaps that of confession, with straightness and truth being the core attributes. Just as the missionaries developed language in which to evaluate confessions, they also watched for false witness. Consider the related expressions in the Motul (M:214v), where the term *yamab* is translated as 'the bad that is told of someone, without knowing its truth, false witness', and is illustrated with another question from the confessional manual: *yaan ua a yamab yokol hunpay?* 'have you told lies about another (person)?' By contrast, the

EXAMPLE 5.16

Testigo (SF2:748)	'witness'	*yah ohelil be*
testimoniar	'testify'	*tohcinah than,* *hah cunah*
testimonio	'testimony'	*tohahcunah thanil*
testimonio falso	'false testimony'	*pakpach,* *yamaab,* *yamaab yokol,* *pah,* *pak yamab*
testimonio dar	'give testimony'	*hahcunah than*
Testigo (V:609)	'witness'	*ah ohel,* *yah ohelil be*

witness whose knowledge is called upon to verify facts is *ah ohel* [Agent + 'know'] 'knower' or *yah ohelil be* [possessive + agentive + 'know' + suffix + 'deed'] 'the knower of deed(s)'.

The missionaries lived in a world of infinitely many signs, in which perceptible forms were taken to stand for objects and events apart from themselves. They also judged the Maya to live in a world of signs, in which many objects and events, while perceptible in themselves, were also portents, images, or traces of things beyond themselves. This universe of counterparts was critically important to the missionaries, who sought to bring the beliefs and practices of the Maya into alignment with their own. They recognized natural events such as clouds and lightning as signs of coming rain, physical symptoms as signs of disease, scars as signs of prior injuries, footprints as signs of an animal. Some signs were produced by humans as intentional indicators, such as the gestures of merchants, *coyoltah* [signal + transitive]; hand signals like *u beel kab* ['its' + action + 'hand'] 'palm signal' or *tuchhub* 'finger pointing'; and markings like *chuh ich* ['burn' + 'face'] 'branding (of cattle or slaves)'. Other signs were mnemonic devices made to remind the bearer of some item, and still others were portents of the future.

The Maya term *uayaz ba* is actually part of a rich family of terms glossed in the Motul (439v–440r) as 'signal, figure or opinion, visions seen in dreams, dreams, prognostications'. The stem *uayaz* is likely also related to *uaay* 'animal familiar of witch or necromancer'. Like the image of a person or place (*u uayazba uinic* 'the image of a man'), the *uaay* familiar figure is the image or manifestation of the witch, with which (s)he is identified (M:439v). When the Holy Spirit descends upon humans in the form of fire, it does so *tu uayazba kaak* ['in' + 'its' + 'image' + 'fire'] 'in the form (image) of fire'. The Motul points out that the visions seen in dreams are usually transgressive, and it illustrates this form with the example *yan ua a*

EXAMPLE 5.17

Señal (V:590)	'sign, signal'	*chicul*
señal de llober	'sign of rain'	*u chicul u tal haa,* *u kin haa*
señal dar quando se compra algo	'give sign to purchase something'	*coyol tah,* *coyol cinah*
señal de la palma de la mano	'sign with palm of the hand'	*u beel kab*
señales de biruelas	'signs of smallpox'	*u chec echil kak,* *u chhomol kak*
señal que dan [a] alguno o [que] él lleba para acordarse	'sign that they give one or that one brings as a reminder'	*u chicul kahçah*
señal, por conjetura de lo que a de benir	'sign to guess what is to come'	*uayaz ba*
señal de la herida	'sign of an injury'	*chec,* *chec ech*
señalar gmte	'to sign in general'	*chicil beçah,* *dza chicul*
señalar con el dedo índice mostrando	'to indicate, showing with index finger'	*tuchhub,* *tuchh ba*
señálame así tu caballo	'point out your horse to me'	*tuchhub te a tzimin ten*
señalar con yerro o errar esclabos o ganado	'to mark with branding slaves or cattle'	*chuh ich,* *hotz ich*
señalar rayando	'to signal by a line'	*ppel,* *hoth*
señalar día, tiempo, plaço	'to signal day, time, place'	*xot kin,* *ppel kin*

uayazcabtic xiblal 'Have you dreamt visions of a male?' The Spanish gloss offered for this Maya sentence goes far beyond the Maya and is cast in the language of the confessional: *¿has por ventura soñado a algún hombre, vístole entre sueños como que pecaba contigo?* 'have you by chance dreamt of some man in dreams as he sinned with you (i.e., had sex with you)?' (M:439v).

Obviously, the Maya forms in ex. 5.17 used to translate the different senses of *señal* are themselves heterogeneous. The sign in general, the natural sign, and the reminder sign are all based on the root *chicul, chicil,* which is derived from the root *chic* 'to appear, be perceptible' (cf. *chicaan* 'visible', *chicpahal* 'to appear'). Signs made with or on the body are described in terms of specialized verbs, body parts, or the manner of marking the body. The signal by drawn line and the signal for day, time, and place get still other terms. To these the San Francisco Part 2 (SF2:736) adds yet others: 'sign, footprint of dog', *mool;* 'signal for hunters', *hoch haban tah;* and 'signal with grass', *hochh xiu tah*. While there are relations among some of these expressions within the grammar of Maya, we must recognize that what unifies the forms in ex. 5.17 is not the semantics of Maya. It is the Spanish understanding of signs and the use of the term *señal* that motivate the list. As we have seen several times before, the act of translating this range of usages into Maya effectively creates a family-likeness relation among the Maya forms where none had existed before, because of their new ties to related Spanish words.

GOVERNANCE

The *reducción* entailed installing the *cabildo* form of government in the Maya towns (see chapter 3). The *regidores* are often signatory to *cabildo*-produced texts, in which case the title was cited either in the Spanish or with one of the terms displayed in exs. 5.18–5.20. The expression *yahau cab* ['its' + 'ruler' + 'region'] is rarely used in my experience and never figures as the official title of an officer. By contrast, *cuchcabal* and *ah cuch cab* are frequently encountered in the documents (and see chapter 2 above). The root *cuch* is 'to bear (a load)' and *cab* is 'region, earth', so that the term for *regidor* in the *cabildo* is identical to the Maya term 'earth bearer', a well-known class of Maya divinities from long before the Spanish arrival in Yucatán. A major place such as Maní had a broader region of authority comprising many towns and known collectively as *u cuchcabal Maní* 'the region/ province of Maní' (Quezada 1993). An alternative phrasing of the relation of the central place to its satellites is *mektan cah* 'dependent town', a term that focuses on the subordination of the satellite places to the central one rather than on their being part of the same spatial region. By using these terms to translate *regidor*, the San Francisco Part 2 and the Vienna analyze the *regidor* position as one with jurisdiction in both spatial and executive dimensions.

The language of elections as shown in exs. 5.21–5.22 is based on a schema in which the individual elected to an official position is stood up or seated in that position. The verbs *uaa* 'to stand up, be erect' and *cul* 'to be seated' are what Mayanists call positional verbs, meaning that they designate physical positions of bodies and other objects. Like all positionals, they form the transitive by causativizing the stem, which yields *uacunah* 'to cause to stand' and *culcinah* 'to cause to be seated', as in the examples above.[16] This causative stem is then passivized in the form *uacunabil* as in *uacunabil ah xot than* ['stand' + causative + passive + Agentive + 'judgment'] 'official judge'. The positions to which one is stood or seated are coded with the prepositional *ti* 'to' and include *belancil* 'actor', *batab* 'chief' (*gobernador* of *cabildo*), *alcalde* 'mayor', *testigo* 'witness', *padre* 'priest', and even *obispo* 'bishop'. The first of these terms appears to be the generic one for officials of the government.[17]

As we know, the towns in which *cabildo* governments were installed were mostly the product of the policy of *congregación* whereby disparate groups were forcibly united into the new towns. While the Vienna has no entry for *congregación* at all, the other three dictionaries do. Note in ex. 5.23 that I have cited

EXAMPLE 5.18

Regidor (SF2:719)	'alderman'	*ah cuch cab, yahau cab*
Rejidor (V:564)	'alderman'	*ah cuch cab, ah beel nal, ah mektan cah*

EXAMPLE 5.19

Regimiento, parcialidad (SF2:719)	'precinct'	*cuchcabal*

EXAMPLE 5.20

Región (SF2:719)	'region'	*cab*
Rejión o prouinçia (V:564)	'region or province'	*cuchcabal, peten*

EXAMPLE 5.21*

Elegir (SF2:590)	'to elect'	
electo	'elected'	*uaan tibelancil, culan ti belancil*
elegir para oficio de república	'to elect to government office'	*uacunah ti belancil, culcinah ti belancil*
***uacunabil** ah xot than* (SF1:375)	'arbitrate (as judge)'	arbitrar (como juez)
ualhi ti batabil *uacunah, uacuntah*	'they made him chief' 'bring (guiding)'	hicieronle cacique llevar (guiando)
uacun Pedro ti testigoil *uacunah ti belancil,* *culcinah ti belancil,* *ti beelnalil*	'present Pedro as witness' 'elect (to government office)'	presenta a Pedro por testigo elegir (para oficio de república)
***uaacunah** tii alcaldeil, tii padreil* (M:438r)	'make one alcalde, priest, etc.'	hacer a uno alcalde, fraile, etc.
uaacunah tii testigoil	'present as witness'	presentar por testigo

*Entries from the Maya matrix dictionaries are included in order to fill out the relatively terse glosses provided in the Spanish matrix ones. Note that when Maya is the matrix language, it appears in the left column, with the Spanish gloss in the right column.

EXAMPLE 5.22

Elecsión (V:291)	'election'	*ua cunah*
elector	'elector'	*ah ua cunah*
elegir para offiçio o dignidad	'to elect to office or honor'	*ua cunah ti beel ancil*
elegióme por obispo	'(it) elected me bishop'	*ua cunahen ti obispoil*

EXAMPLE 5.23*

Congregación (SF2:547)	'congregation'	*molay*
Molay (M:307v)	'assembly, congregation, college and council'	junta, congregación, colegio y ayuntamiento
u molay uinicoob	'assembled people'	junta así de gente
u molay ah ocolaloob	'the assembly of the faithful'	———
u molay alab oltzil cristianoob	'the Catholic Church'	iglesia católica
Molay, *ah tancab kunail* (SF1:241)	'cabildo, council'	cabildo, consejo
molay	'college, congregation'	colegio, congregación
molay (u__) uinic, u molol uinic	'council of people'	ayuntamiento de gente

*Entries from the Maya matrix dictionaries are included in order to fill out the relatively terse glosses provided in the Spanish matrix ones. Note that when Maya is the matrix language, it appears in the left column, with the Spanish gloss in the right column.

examples from the Maya-Spanish works, to fill out the concept of *"congregación."* In all cases, the verb root used for the gathering is *mol* 'to gather, pile together, amass'. The noun form is derived by adding to this root the suffix *[ay]*, whose semantic import is obscure. The Motul and the San Francisco Part 1 both gloss *molay* as 'congregation' or 'college'. The Motul further associates it with the Catholic Church, construed as *u molay alab oltzil cristianoob* 'the gathering of the Christians of faith'.

The towns in which *cabildos* functioned were known generically as *cah* 'town', with several other terms used to qualify the kind. The *chinam* is a fortified town, prototypically one taken by force and fortified for protection. The term *kiliz* is glossed by the Motul as roughly 'an old or wealthy person with a large family and long residence of a place'. *Tocoy* means 'old, former, abandoned', and *lab* means 'rotted, falling down'; both were used in reference to the towns abandoned in the course of *congregación*. The root *piz* combines with certain nouns to yield 'only, mere' or 'common, vulgar,' the apparent sense of *piz cah* in the Vienna.

According to the San Francisco Part 2, the subordinate *visita* towns in the

```

## EXAMPLE 5.24

| Pueblo (SF2:710) | 'town' | cah, chinam, cacab, cahal |
|---|---|---|
| pueblo tomar (por suyo) | 'take town (for oneself)' | chinamtah |
| pueblo antiguo o gran | 'old or large town' | kiliz cah |
| pueblo despoblado | 'abandoned town' | tocoy cah, lab cah |
| pueblo (de__) en pueblo llevar | 'bring from town to town' | cahal cah |
| **Pueblo** (V:543) | 'town' | cah |
| pueblo bulgo o jente menuda | 'small or unpopulous town' | piz cah |
| pueblos de diferentes jentes | 'towns of various peoples' | lotay cah |

## EXAMPLE 5.25

| Visita, sujeta al convento (SF2:766) | 'visita, subject to a convento' | cuch cabal |
|---|---|---|
| visitar | 'to inspect' | thibah, xoytah, zut, thib |
| visitar templos | 'to inspect temples' (*xoy* = 'to do something [while] circulating') | xoy (*xoy* = hacer algo rodeando)* |
| visitar pueblos | 'to inspect towns' | zut cah |

*The San Francisco Part 2 uses the symbol for "equals" in this gloss, making explicit the interlingual equivalence relation on which the entire dictionary is based.

*guardianías* were designated by the same term used for political jurisdictions, as shown in ex. 5.25. That the identical term *cuchcabal* is used for both underscores yet again the merger of the two systems of governance. Unfortunately, the Vienna has no entry for *visita*. The act of making a *visita*, which entailed traveling to places for on-site inspection, was construed as circular movement, with the verbs *xoy* 'to walk about, circle, visit (temples or persons)' (see also SF1:404; M:461r–461v) and *zut* 'return, turn around'. The focus of these expressions is the physical displacement required to make the *visita* more than the information gathering for which the *visita* is performed. Given the glosses of the Maya forms, these expressions suggest that the *visitas* consisted of sequences of towns visited seriatim, in the manner of walking a circuit from place to place. Such walking processions appear prominently in the land survey documents produced in the towns and also in the Books of Chilam Balam, suggesting a deep relation between
```

EXAMPLE 5.26

Guarda(r) (V:374–75)*	'to protect and keep'	
guarda	'guardian'	*ah canan, ah taacun*
entregóse a Pº por guarda	'it was given to Pedro for safekeeping'	*kubi ti Pº u canan te, ti canantabal*
guarda de milpas	'guardian of fields'	*ah canan col*
guardar de comer a alguno, y guardar algo	'prevent someone from eating, and save something'	*likçah hanal, ya[c]un tah hanal*
guardad los mandamientos de Dios	'keep the commandments of God'	*taacuntex yama thanil Dios*
guarda las sobras de la comida, que mañana las pidiré	'save the leftovers of food, that I will ask for tomorrow'	*kin te yala hanal, çamal in katic*
¡guardaos!	'look out!'	*tex ika!*
guardaos, no caigáis en el pozo	'careful, don't fall in the well'	*hik lubuc ex ti chhen*
guardaos de pecar	'keep away from sin'	*bal a ba ex ti keban*
Guarda, guardar (SF2:624)	'guard, to guard'	
guardado (la fruta bajo algo para madurarla)	'stored (fruit under something to ripen it)'	*kilbil*
guardar las espaldas	'protect your back'	*mac pach*
guardar entre ceniza o cal para que no se dañe	'keep in ash or lime to preserve'	*taanbezah*
guardia del campo	'rural guard'	*u balamil katun*

*Because of the length and semantic variety of entries under the Spanish *guarda*, I have reproduced only selected entries from the Vienna and the San Francisco Part 2.

governance and rituals of perambulation. There are many other expressions for travel and mobility scattered throughout the dictionaries, including *helep ucah padreoob* 'múdanse los padres de un lugar a otro' (the priests move from one place to another) (M:182v).

The term *guarda* and its derivatives have a remarkable thirty entries in the Vienna, of which the forms in ex. 5.26 are a selection. There is no entry in either dictionary for the position of *guardián* to which friars were elected, nor for *guardianía*. The Spanish word *guardar* and its cognates had a range of distinct usages, including to watch over or protect (people, animals, a place), to save or preserve (leftover food), to hold to a rule or norm (*guardar los mandamientos de Dios* 'keep the commandments of God'), to abstain from a behavior (*guardar de comer* 'abstain from eating'), to prevent. It is also the root of "guard" in the sense of a military force, provocatively glossed by the San Francisco Part 2 as *u balamil katun* 'the jaguars of war'. In the imperative form, *guarda* conveys the illocutionary force of a warning or admonition (*¡guardaos!* 'Look out!'; cf. French *en garde!).* What is most striking about the Maya forms associated with the word by way of these several uses is that they are a grab bag, virtually unrelated to one another by anything other than the translation process. Thus the stem for 'protect' is *canan(tah)*, from which we get *ah canan* 'guard', whereas 'conserve' is *yacun tah* or *dzac cun*, the observance of a law is *taacuntah*, and 'abstain' is based on the Maya *likezah* 'to put up (away)' and *bal ba* 'to hide oneself (from)'. The admonitive is conveyed in Maya with the particles *ika* and *hik*, as in *tex ika!* 'Look out, you!' and *hik aualab ti Padre* 'Look out, don't tell it to the priest'.

This illustrates one of the general features of Spanish-to-Maya dictionaries, as opposed to Maya-to-Spanish ones. In the latter case, the dictionary maker starts from observed facts of Maya usage and attempts to gloss them in Spanish. The result is that a single Maya root is associated with various Spanish expressions, as we will see in detail in chapter 6. By contrast, the Spanish-to-Maya dictionaries start from the *lenguas'* own native and everyday language. Given a familiar Spanish usage, the question was whether and how to render it in Maya. It is important to see that the answer to this question was rarely based on a literal translation of the Spanish words or phrases. Rather, the equivalence between the two was sheerly pragmatic, based more on situational factors than on linguistic ones. Consider the following example, where I have separately glossed both the Spanish head phrase and its Maya "translation":

> *Guarda las sobras de la comida, que mañana las pidiré*
> Save the leftovers from the meal, which I will request tomorrow

> *kin te yala hanal, çamal in katic*
> heat (the) remains of food, tomorrow I ask for it

On purely linguistic grounds, there is no relation between the Maya and the Spanish verbs in the first clause—*guarda* 'save' and *kinteh* 'heat (up)'. What ties the two together is not language at all but the practice of heating food to boiling point before setting it aside for later consumption. In the tropical heat of Yucatán before the age of ice and refrigeration, this was the only way to prevent food from spoiling overnight (a practice still used by rural Maya people). Thus in order to make sense of the dictionary, the reader must already know something about the social worlds in which the languages were used. If we fail to distinguish what is said in the headword and gloss from what is conveyed when they are used in typical contexts, many glosses make no sense.

MARGINAL PRACTICES

Because flight was a real and constant concern over the first two centuries of the colony, we would expect the *lenguas* to have developed a language for talking about it in Maya, if only for intelligence gathering. The Vienna vindicates this

EXAMPLE 5.27

Huir (V:408)	'to flee'	
huir comoquiera, y huida	'to flee however, and flight'	*pudzul*
no sabe huirse	'he does not know how to flee'	*ma yohel pudzul*
huid a otra ciudad	'flee to another city'	*pudzen ex ca xic ex tu yanal cah*
huir huiendo	'to leave fleeing'	*pudzu benel*
huída cosa	'fled thing'	*pudzan*
huir de otro	'to flee from another'	*pudzul,*
		pudz lah,
		pudz le
huir azer a otro	'to cause something to flee'	*pudzçah,*
		pudzeçah
huir de peligro	'to flee danger'	*lukçah ba*
huidor, que se huie	'one who flees'	*ah pudzul*
huirse muchos o escaparse	'many flee or escape'	*pudz lahal*
huir lejos, y la tal huída	'to flee far away, and such flight'	*nach pudzul*
huirse para no bolber	'to flee to not return'	*hun kul pudzul*
huir de otro y apartarse dél	'to flee another and separate from him'	*cuz ba ti*
fue huiendo a tie[rr]a de Egipto	'he was fleeing to the land of Egypt'	*bini ti pudzul tu luumil Egipto*
huid del Demonio y del pecado	'flee the Devil and sin'	*pudz lex Cizin,*
		pudzlex keban
huigo de ti por tus maldades	'I flee from you because of your evil ways'	*lic in cuzic in ba tech tumen a lob il*

expectation, with sixteen subentries under the heading *huir* 'to flee'. The basic root in Maya is *pudz* 'to flee, escape', with intransitive *pudzul* 'to flee, flight' and causative *pudz(e)çah* 'make another flee'. Note that this concept also had biblical and Christian references, in which flight is a form of liberation from oppression or sin. In reference to Indian flight in Yucatán, we find flight from places and persons by individuals and groups, far away and forever. The imperative form 'flee to another city' is a provocative example. Were it illustrative of something a missionary might say, it would suggest that the missionaries colluded in the very flight they nominally abhorred, although this is little more than speculation. Group escapes to distant places were known to have occurred along the frontier, as discussed in Part I of this book.

Idolatry was a constant concern for the missionaries, and the dictionaries give clear evidence that they developed a language in which to describe and classify it. The preferred term for the spirit agency materialized in the idol was *cizin* 'devil', the same term used for the evil principal of the Christian hell. In idolatry, the

EXAMPLE 5.28

Idólatra (SF2:640)	'idolater'	*ah pay ciz,* *ah cizinil than*
idolatrar e idolatría	'idolize and idolatry'	*pay cizin,* *tooc pom ti cizin*
idolatría (una especia de __ o conjuros) al viento o espíritu y al sol	'idolatry (a kind of __ or conjurings) of the wind or spirit and of the sun'	*tzac ik,* *tzac kin*
idolo, estatua de barro	'idol, clay statue'	*pat bil kat*
idolo de palo	'idol of wood'	*culche*
idolo hacer	'(to) make (an) idol'	*pat cizin,* *pat culche*

idolater invokes or conjures the devil by burning *pom* 'copal incense' or performing the action *pay* 'to pull, draw in, call forth'. This verb root is also used in the standard translation of *rezar* 'prayer', which is *payal chi* ['pulling' + 'mouth']. It focuses on the verbal action of addressing spirits in order to make them present, drawing them to the place of prayer. Missionaries were acutely aware that the Maya used material "idols" that they made of clay and wood, an awareness evident in both the San Francisco Part 2 and the Vienna.

The verb *pat* has a range of uses and is frequent in the dictionaries. The usage cited in ex. 5.28 is consistent with the Motul, which glosses it as *"hacer ollas, cántaros y otras vasijas de barro, de cera o masa"* 'to make pots, pitchers, and other vessels of clay, wax or corn paste' (M:367r). The difference is that the Motul never associates this activity with the making of idols but treats it instead as an everyday occupation. A second sense of *pat* is to 'form' or 'give form to' something, as in *tu patahoon Dios tii uinicil* 'God formed us as humans' (M:367r–v). The same root occurs in *pat cunah* ['form' + causative] and *pat cantah* ['form' + 'narrate'] 'to declare, narrate at length, to clarify a matter'.

The Vienna includes most of what is in the San Francisco Part 2 plus more vocabulary and a list of fifteen named Maya "idols" with notes on their features. For ease of exposition, I present this information not in the dictionary's original order, but under three rubrics: the act of worshiping the devil, the idol as a material form in the image of the devil, and the names of fifteen known idols, with notes on their provenance and purpose.

The entries in exs. 5.29–5.30 reflect some of the missionary understanding of idolatry.[18] They effectively analyze the practice into the material forms of the idol, the postures of adoration and obedience, the verbal acts of conjuring, the act of burning incense, and the activities performed in producing idols, with different verbs for working clay and wood *(pat)* as opposed to stone *(thoh)*. By relatively simple grammatical formations (compounds, derived adjectives, transi-

EXAMPLE 5.29

Ydolatrar (V:418)	'idolize'	
ydolatrar*	'to worship idols'	*kul Cizin*
ydolatrar	'to treat them all as god(s)'	*kuulilan tah*
ydolatrar	'to devil worship'	*tan lah Cizin*
ydolatrar llamando	'to conjure'	*pay Cizin*
ydolatrar quemando incienso al ídolo o Demonio	'to idolize, burning incense to the idol or Devil'	*toc pom ti Cizin*
ydolatrar	'to speak (the) devil'	*Cizinil than*
su oficio es ydolatrar	'his occupation is to idolize'	*pay Çiçin u beel*

*English glosses the Maya, which gives various senses of 'idolatrar'.

EXAMPLE 5.30

Ydolo, generalmente (V:418–19)	'idol, in general'	*patbil Cizin*
ydolo de varro	'clay idol'	*pat bil kat*
— de madera	'wooden idol'	*pat bil che*
—	'stone idol'	*thoh bil tunich*
ydolo de barro	'idol of clay'	*lac*
ydolo o imagen, figura del Demonio	'idol or devil's image'	*u uinbal Cizin*
ydolo, estatua que se adora	'idol, statue one adores'	*cul che, u uich Ku*
ydolos y dioses de los gentiles	'idols and gods of the gentiles'	*kuulob*
dos ídolos tiene	'he has two idols'	*ca tul u Çiçin*

tive verb phrases with direct and indirect objects, possessive phrases), the Maya glosses provide a great deal of detail about the objects and practices to which the Spanish entries refer. The missionaries would have gathered all this background knowledge in the course of the *reducciones* and the ongoing attempt to extirpate the practices under discussion. Sánchez de Aguilar's famous *Informe contra Idolorum Cultores* followed on his extensive experience on the frontier, just as any *guardián* in the *doctrinas* would have been constantly on the lookout for idolatry. The idols described as pots and vessels were exactly of the kind the missionaries confiscated, studied, and destroyed. It is possible that they discussed them with their close Maya assistants or with one another. At the same time, the language shown here is highly improvised. Every time the term "devil" is inserted into a Maya gloss, it is the vision of the missionary that guides the so-called translation. Whether the erstwhile Maya idolater would call his clay brazier the *uinbal* 'likeness' of a god is unclear, but in *Maya reducido* this word is mobilized for the idol just as it is mobilized for the cross (*u uinbal Christo* 'the likeness of Christ').

EXAMPLE 5.31 Named idols cited in the Vienna (419–20)

Of place and provenance

Ydolo de Cosumel, que pintaban con una flecha en la mano	'Idol of Cozumel, painted with arrow in hand'	Ah Hula Ne, Ah Hul Nab
Ydolo q[ue] tenían los antiguos en el asiento de Mérida	'Idol of Mérida in past'	Uac Lom Chaan
Ydolo, otro de los indios de Mérida, y [por él] llamóse ansí el ku o çerro grande que está detrás de San Fran[cis]co, al oriente	'Idol of Mérida (the large mound east of San Francisco)'	Ah Chun Caan
Ydolo de las crueldades, a quien los de Campeche sacrificaban sangre humana	'Idol of Campeche (for blood sacrifice)'	Kin Cha Haban, Kin Ich Ahau Haban
Ydolo, [otro] de los de Campeche	'Idol of Campeche'	Mo Co

Of purpose

Ydolo maior que tenían estos indios de esta tierra, del qual decían p[ro]ceder todas las cosas y ser [él] incorpóreo, y por esto no l[e] hacían ymagen	'Greatest idol the Indios had, which they said to have created all things, and which was incorporeal'	Colop u Uich Kin
Ydolo[s] q[ue] decían ser de éste	'Idol said to be from that one'	Hun Ytza[m] Na, Yax Coc Ah Mut
Ydolo, otro q[ue] adoraron, que fue hombre, por aber allado el arte de las letras desta tie[rr]a	'Idol formerly the human who introduced the art of writing in the language of this land'	Ytzam Na Kin [I]ch Ahau
Ydolo del agua, de los panes, de los truenos y relámpagos	'Idol of water, rain, thunder and lightning'	Chac
Ydolos de la caza	'Idols of the hunt'	Acan [Ç]um, Ah Tabay, Ku Bolay, Ceh La[c]

Others (unclassified)

Ydolos, otros	'Other idols'	Ah Bolon Ahau, Ah Bolonil

There is another striking parallel between the language of idolatry and the language of Christian practice. The Maya root *ku* 'god, precious' designates the demon worshiped by the idolater, and the same root is the only accepted translation for the Christian God (see ex. 5.4 above). To worship false gods is rendered *kuulilantah,* which is actually a rather complex form: the root *ku* is derived into *kuul* '(its) god', which is then derived into *[kuul-ilan],* 'god-revered' and finally into *[kuul-ilan-tah],* a transitive verb. The result is roughly 'to god-revere it'. The Spanish entry adds that the gods in question are false, although the San Francisco Part 1 associated parallel expressions with proper worship of the Christian God. The phrases *u uich ku* 'the face of God' and *kuulob* '(its) gods' are based on the same root. The former could as easily apply to a portrait of Christ, and the latter could as readily designate divine things of Christianity, although the plural marker is inconsistent with monotheism. These ambiguities and lexical relations imply that the dictionary was treading a very fine semantic line between designating the true God and designating the false. It was economical to use the same set of forms in the two cases, but it risked muddling them as well. A speaker of *Maya reducido* would make tacit relations between the two opposing systems, implicitly granting divinity to 'gods' nonetheless equated with the Devil.

The verb *tan lah* 'worship-obey' projects another range of associations in the Maya. This stem was also used to describe the posture of obedient subjection of royal subjects before the Crown. It occurs in letters by Maya authors directed to the Crown in the 1560s and is glossed in the San Francisco Part 1 (331) as 'servant, to serve, to watch over something, to care for the sick'. The precise form *tan lah* is also glossed 'to administer sacraments', meaning that the priest giving the sacraments is described in the same way as the idolater in flagrante delicto, thus potentially confounding the two. In the Maya letters to the Crown, the term expresses the servile posture of the proper subject, which is an aspect of *policía* imbued with royal subjecthood. Thus behind these translations lay sometimes extensive associations and correspondences in the semantics of *Maya reducido.* Whether the missionaries could control the resulting proliferation of potential meanings in the Maya is doubtful. Indeed, I will argue they could not.

The Vienna also provides a list of named "idols" in Maya. Some of these recur in other missionary writings and in the forbidden Maya works, including the Ritual of the Bacabs and the Books of Chilam Balam (Arzápalo Marín 1987; cf. Chuchiak 2000b, chapter 7). In ex. 5.31 I have reordered the Vienna list to make it more accessible.

Combined with the preceding examples, the list in ex. 5.31 reflects a detailed knowledge of at least some Maya divinities and the likely practices in which they were worshiped. It would be interesting to compare it to the divinities mentioned by Landa and Sánchez de Aguilar and in the inquisitional testimony, although that is beyond the scope of this chapter. Given the centrality and recurrence of idolatry as a problem in the province, it is likely that the main Franciscan convent housed cumulative, annotated lists of items confiscated and idolatrous practices observed or described by informants and that this dictionary draws on the cumulative knowledge derived from the idolatry trials, the successive *reducciones,* and the investigations of individual *lengua* priests. The reference to "idols" from Cozumel, Mérida, and Campeche is consistent with such a centralized database and reflects further the broad regional sources of the dictionary.

· · ·

This chapter began with the problem of origins as it applies to the instruments of linguistic *reducción.* Who wrote the Motul, the Vienna, or the San Francisco dictionaries? Where and when were they produced? It is tempting to try to identify author, place, or date on the basis of subtle clues and erudite inferences. But the result distorts the history of dictionary making in Yucatán. The works themselves are systematically silent on provenance, and the individuation of author, place, and date is simply not part of this genre as it was practiced in the first two centuries of the Yucatecan colony. Moreover, there are good reasons to believe that these three elements of dictionary production were *in principle* vague, not sharply defined and singular. We do not know who wrote any of these works because there was no single author. The recopying of old texts, the citations from catechisms, the traveling of friars among the *guardianías,* and the exposure of the *lenguas* to Maya from multiple places inevitably pluralized the voices and the sources of the works. The continuities in scribal hand and the fixed order of entries written continuously on folia both suggest that at least portions of the dictionaries were done by individuals in sustained projects of writing. But the work of composition and the source of much of the dictionary came not from the writers but from the discourse formation to which they belonged. From the viewpoint of content, the origins of these dictionaries were not individuals in discrete places and times. Rather, they are the works of the Franciscan missions as a textual community spread over time, place, and waves of *lenguas* in sustained dialogue with Maya people.

The dictionaries are clearly related to one another and to the broader discourse of missionary Maya that includes the *artes,* the catechisms, and the sermons. Moreover, their broad thematic scope ties them into speech practices under many different circumstances. The Maya they codify was not invented out of whole cloth by the friars but was already marked by and in dialogue with Maya as spoken by its native speakers, including men, women, officials, commoners, the faithful, and the incorrigible. The importance of the *bocabulario* as a historical document lies in the knowledge it codifies, knowledge that ramifies into all of the other genres in Maya, including ones produced by Maya people themselves. The question of historical provenance ultimately turns on practices and the emerging variety of Maya developed within the scope of *reducción*. One effect of dictionary writing was the ongoing codification of this new variety. Strictly speaking, it was a whole new sign system in which Maya speech forms were backed by Spanish correspondences, a hybrid improvisation from top to bottom. When we detect common ways of translating key concepts in different works, we have evidence of the incipient stabilization of the new language through iteration, citation, and codification.

The interlingual glosses of the *bocabulario* are intrinsically metalinguistic. They fix the modes of commensuration between the two languages, the correspondences that pair terms from one language with descriptive backing from the other. Thus although the column and row layout of the written text invites us to conceive a direct relation between the matrix language (headwords) and the target language (glosses), in reality there are hidden factors. Both the headword and the gloss stand for utterances in their respective languages, and there are therefore at least four elements in play: the headword, its typical usage, the gloss, and its typical usage. If we fail to distinguish the semantics of the headword and gloss from their potential uses, the resulting muddle misrepresents both languages. Sometimes the headword is pragmatically unequivocal, and the correspondence to Maya appears straightforward. In other cases, the Spanish headword has multiple uses in the matrix language, and the result is a dispersion of Maya phrases to render the different uses of the Spanish. This produces, in the language of the dictionary, a family effect among Maya forms otherwise grammatically unrelated to one another. For example, the Spanish words *guarda* and *señal* have so many different uses and varieties in Spanish that they project whole constellations of Maya glosses whose only connection to one another is through the Spanish terms they gloss. Consistency among the *bocabularios* is historically important precisely because common glossing organizes common series of Maya terms into families clustered around Spanish concepts. This is the ordering work of *reducción* within the fine structure of the language.

Anyone who has spent time with a colonial dictionary knows that these dictionaries are virtually unlimited resources for historical study. This is so not because a language is a collection of words (it is not) or because the dictionaries are pristine records of the state of the language (they are not). Rather, the bilingual dictionary is a metalinguistic map that allows commensuration between the languages and the movement of meaning between them. It is an instrument for converting words. It embodies the understanding and perspective of its makers. The Spanish-to-Maya *bocabularios* embody the history of commensuration without which *reducción* would have been impossible. But this same richness makes our task difficult, and I have been very selective in sampling from the San Francisco Part 2 and the Vienna, as I will necessarily be in the next chapter, which examines the Motul and the San Francisco Part 1.

The guiding principle in the present chapter has been to concentrate on terms pertinent to the *reducción,* most of which are already familiar. I hope that these terms for religious conversion and practice, teaching, language and writing, governance, and other basic concepts will help the reader convert from the Spanish-based background of Part I into the new world of Maya that I explore for the remainder of this book. This was the first conversion for the missionaries as well, from their European idioms into the world of Maya, a task as fraught spiritually as it was semantically. For it is in the actual translanguage of intercultural commensuration that we must seek out the conceptual and behavioral transformations that defined *reducción* as a project. It should come as no surprise that this translanguage commingles church with town governance, belief with conversion, and dreams with signs.

Commensuration

Maya as a Matrix Language

In the previous chapter, I showed that the process of translating Spanish into Maya was a matter of commensuration: (1) the Spanish form and (2) its standard meaning were brought into alignment with (3) a Maya form and (4) its standard meaning. The two-column format of the dictionary abbreviates this four-part construct, with the matrix language (L1) on the left and the target language (L2) on the right. The resulting apparently simple couplet aligns the forms as a way to align the meanings. When I call the two orders of signification "standard," I mean that the headword and the L2 gloss are to be understood in their most normal or typical way. For the Spanish language, the sense of the standard would be based on a long tradition of *latinidad, gramática, doctrina,* and other intellectual pursuits, as well as the native speech habits of the missionaries themselves. For Maya language, the sense of what was standard was more problematic for the dictionary makers. Not being native speakers and not having access to any tradition of linguistic description or prescription in Maya (if such a tradition existed), they were at the mercy of their observations of the usage around them, their discussions with native-speaker collaborators, and their field studies in the *guardianías* and pueblos.

COMMENSURATION AND TRANSLINGUAL MEANING

If we look closely at the Maya glosses of Spanish terms, it becomes clear that the Maya is no mere restatement of the Spanish. Obviously the differences between the languages make it impossible to convey precisely the same meanings, but the divergence between headword and translation is more dramatic than this impossibility would dictate. In most of the language of *reducción*, the Maya actually spells out by means of compounding and derivation relations that are only implicit in the Spanish: baptism as *oc ha* 'enter water', confession as *pul keban* 'cast off sin', and prayer *(resar)* as *payal chi* 'pulling mouth'. In such cases, the Maya encodes an alternative analysis of the concept for which the Spanish stands. To make sense of this process, we must distinguish the Spanish expression (the linguistic form), its standard meaning (its signification in the Saussurian sense), and the object to which it refers (its denotation). For example, the Spanish verb *convertirse* 'to convert (intransitive)' was commonly used for the transformation of one thing into another, for religious conversion, and for reconciliation with the other party in a grievance. The San Francisco Part 2 glosses *'convertirse'* as *ocol ti uinicil,* which actually means 'convert to human'. The referent of the Maya form is unambiguously the "conversion" of God into man, whereas the Spanish is vague as to which kind of conversion is in play. The Spanish-to-Maya dictionaries therefore convey a whole universe of commensurate meanings, and the translation process renders explicit in Maya what is implicit or ambiguous in the Spanish. In understanding the Maya expressions, a speaker would simultaneously internalize the theological backing of the Spanish to which they correspond.

But the translation of Spanish into Maya is only part of the story. The Motul and the San Francisco Part 1 perform the inverse translation, with Maya as the matrix language and Spanish as the target language. These reverse bilingual dictionaries were powerful tools for discourse production. They made it possible not only to cross-check translations from Spanish into Maya by reversing the translation but also to understand discourse in spheres of action in which Maya was the instrumental language. Under *reducción,* this included the pueblos with their *cabildos,* the fields of the *guardianía* (head towns and *visitas*), the frontier towns, and the abundance of idolatry testimony. In any situation in which a missionary sought to understand speech or writing in Maya, or in which he collaborated with Maya speakers in producing a text, access to Maya *as a matrix language* was required.

It is important to distinguish between actually consulting one of these dictionaries, which was almost certainly a specialized activity subject to limited access, and drawing on the knowledge that the dictionaries bring together. A work of the scale of the Motul was certainly not circulated for broad consultation in the *guardianías.* We may assume that it was kept in one place and made available to relatively few individuals. The San Francisco, found in the library of the central convent in Mérida, would have been available for consultation by those with access to that library—minimally the *guardianes,* the *definidores,* the provincial, and the friars in training who studied Maya language in Mérida. But those writing or seeking to understand sermons would also draw on the *lengua* knowledge that the dictionaries embodied. This knowledge of cross-language correspondences emerges in most of the other genres in which Maya language figures prominently.

There is a tension in all four of the colonial dictionaries between the need for accurate descriptions of Maya usage, on the one hand, and the will to alter the language to fit the needs of the missions, on the other. The two works examined in this chapter display an impressively broad exposure to Maya language, both to expressions and to their standard meanings: they delve into such domains as kinship, food production, agricultural practice, the human body, emotions, and ways of speaking. In the range of uses represented and the sheer scope of Maya language reproduced, it is clear that the missionaries aimed at a high degree of fidelity to Maya usage. They wanted to get the description right, and they almost certainly did research, including fieldwork. At the same time, for reasons by now obvious, these works are also very rich in language needed to explain and implement the *reducción*. For this, they had to improvise. The result of this improvisation can be seen in the various neologisms created in Maya to designate key concepts pertinent to religious conversion and Christian orthodoxy. They also created an array of specialized usages of otherwise apparently ordinary Maya expressions. Indeed, the tension between fidelity to Maya usage and improvisation to create new usages is evident in both the inventory of Maya forms in the dictionaries and the kinds of meanings with which they are associated.

This tension leads to a special sort of reflexivity in all four of the bilingual dictionaries. These works represent Maya language as the *lengua* missionaries came to know it, as it was used in the missions and the pueblos. In this sense, they are descriptions of Maya language and how at least some Maya speakers spoke. At the same time, they are self-descriptions insofar as the version of Maya they depict is already shaped by the categories of the missionaries' civilizing project. The dictionary is at once a lens through which the mission looked at the Indio and a mirror in which it looked at itself. Knowing what he already knew of doctrine, the novice missionary student of Maya would immediately experience recognition in the Maya neologisms for doctrinal concepts. This self-representative quality in the works is pedagogically useful, since recognition fosters understanding. It is also a form of violence, since it contributes to remaking the Maya in the image of the European.

Cross-language commensuration is bidirectional, at least in principle—if L1 = L2, then L2 = L1—but in point of fact this reversibility is more a logical possibility than a historical actuality. The two languages were asymmetric. It went without saying that it was the Maya that was to be reformed according to the meaning patterns of Spanish, not the other way around: the Maya matrix dictionaries (Motul, SF1) both include neologisms such as the previously cited expressions for baptism, confession, and prayer, whereas neither of the Spanish matrix works (Vienna, SF2) calls upon neologisms in Spanish to express concepts valued in Maya. Similarly, although provincial Spanish usage would undergo significant shifts as it absorbed the local spheres of reference, there is no *systematic* torquing of the Spanish semantics to redefine it in terms of the semantics of Maya glosses. The Spanish glosses of Maya headwords are rendered in standard Spanish.

Judging by the texts themselves, dictionary making was guided by a few basic principles. Although never codified, to my knowledge, these principles are evident in the way the cross-language correspondences between Maya and Spanish were selected and formulated. They included what I will call *interpretance, economy, transparency,* and *indexical binding*.

Interpretance

Commensuration is the general process of bringing the two languages into alignment, so that meaning can move from one to the other. It is the basis of what we commonly call "translation": in translating between Spanish and Maya, one necessarily assumes that "the same thing" can be said in both languages, however approximate the sameness. In the dictionaries, matrix word and gloss are cited not as the utterances of so and so but as anonymous linguistic types, and the matrix language headword is put forth as an object for metalinguistic comment by the target language. A parallel relationship is readily attested in monolingual discourse. It happens any time a speaker defines his or her words, as in "a 'busdriver' is someone who drives a bus" or "when I say 'inside' I mean inside the yard." What is special in the bilingual dictionaries is that the matrix object and the metalingual comment are in different languages.

The two are commensurated by the glossing process itself. This pairing is a case of what Peirce called interpretance: the L2 gloss is another sign to which the L1 headword gives rise. The principle of interpretance states that the gloss is a valid interpretant of the headword. The metalingual gloss conveys, in effect, "Expression X (L1) is the counterpart of Expression Z (L2)." Although what Expression Z designates may be only one of a range of meanings of X, the principle says that there is at least one valid interpretant in L2 for Expression X in L1.[1] Simple as it is, this founding principle is necessary for the work of translation. Without it, there would exist no bilingual dictionaries.

There is a striking similarity between the missionary dictionaries and the well-known couplet structures of Maya and Nahuatl poetic style (Garibay 1953; Edmonson 1982; Edmonson and Bricker 1985; Tedlock 1983; Hanks 1986, 1987, 1990). In the couplet there are two parts, a first line and a second. The two are bound by phonological, syntactic, or semantic parallelism. In clear cases, there is end rhyme or salient alliteration, although grammatical parallelism is also common without rhyme, as is semantic parallelism. Whatever the formal basis of the parallelism, the second part is an interpretant of the first, just as the L2 gloss is an interpretant of the L1 headword in a dictionary. In a poetic variant dubbed *difrasismo* 'disguise' by Garibay (1953), the two parts of the couplet together stand for some third concept, unstated but inferable. Thus, *tupop, tutzam* 'at the mat, at the throne' together stand for the ruler's office, 'your footprints, your mud' stand for 'your arrival' at a place, and so forth. The inventory of such couplets is sufficiently rich and conventionalized in Maya that Edmonson (1986) proposed to use the couplet as the basis of his translations of the Books of Chilam Balam (cf. Hanks 1988). For our purposes, what is most provocative is that the bilingual dictionaries of the missionaries performed an operation quite similar to that of a widely attested indigenous literary style. The headword and the gloss are in effect a semantic couplet.[2]

Economy

The principle of economy guided dictionary makers to take maximum advantage of derivation, inflection, and compounding to convey the greatest number of concepts in the smallest number of roots in the foreign language. Recall, from chapter 5, all the various stems derived from *oc* 'enter' to gloss baptism, conversion, and transformation; the variety of qualifications added to *misa* 'Mass' to yield a typology; the typologies of 'writing' derived from *dzib;* and the derivatives of *cuch cab* 'rule' used in the language of pueblo governance. What these have in common is that they show the missionary strategy of learning a small number of polyvalent roots in Maya, whose derivatives were proposed as the Maya equivalents of Spanish concepts.[3] For language learners, such as the missionaries, and students of doctrine, such as the Maya parishioners, the principle of economy was heuristically useful. The repetition of a given root or stem in numerous derived forms in effect makes the learning easier. By manipulating even simple grammatical rules, one can call upon a single Maya root to translate multiple expressions in Spanish. This involves a good deal of improvisation: even if the Maya grammatical forms were standard native usage, pairing them with Spanish concepts re-forms them into new signs. This is effectively a process of neologizing the Maya, whose consequences I examine in Part III of this book.

In order to put the principle of economy into practice, dictionary makers had to have access to grammatical knowledge of Maya. They had to know, or find out, how one forms verb-noun compounds according to the patterns of the language, how to form transitive stems from polyvalent roots, how to express possessive relations, how to mark person on verbs of different categories, and so forth. All this knowledge points to the *arte,* the genre in which grammatical formation is the focal object of description. The dictionaries and the *artes* are complementary parts of commensuration, the one focused on lexical meaning and the other focused on regularities of grammatical form. Each presupposes the other. However creative the improvisations of the dictionary makers, they were at least partly constrained by the norms of Maya grammar and usage. For if they strayed too far from the native grammar—for instance, if they decided to omit person marking on the verbs, or to simply ignore ordinary word order, or to redefine words wholesale, without regard to their native meanings—then the result would be gibberish. Moreover, even within the set of phrases generated by Maya grammar, the missionaries appear to have preferred some over others. This is where the next principle, transparency, comes into play.

Transparency

Relative transparency is the degree to which the target language gloss analyzes in its semantics the concept associated with the matrix language headword. A gloss that is highly transparent is compositional in the linguistic sense: the meaning of the whole is derived from the meaning of the parts and the grammatical relations between them. A grammatical composition is transparent if the parts are readily segmentable and each one can be associated with an aspect of meaning. The principle says that transparent glosses are better than nontransparent ones. For example, the Maya renditions of baptism and confession are both highly transparent: *oc* 'enter' + *ha* 'water' is a composition in which the verb + noun corresponds directly to two salient parts of the act designated by the Spanish term; *pul* 'cast, tell' + *k'eban* 'sin' corresponds to two salient aspects of the sacrament of confession. Notice further that in both instances, the rule of composition places the verbal element first, followed by a noun designating the place or object on which the action is performed. The regularity of the syntactic formation is part of its transparency; the highly familiar construction verb + noun makes it easy to segment the parts of any new example. Given the complexity of the sacramental rituals designated by these terms, the Maya glosses can make transparent only selected features of the whole. Hence it is unsurprising that these and other sacraments received multiple glosses, focalizing different aspects or phases of the sacraments ('enter water' vs. 'second birth' for baptism, 'tell sins' vs. 'untie sins' for confession, etc.). As a rough approximation, any time the Maya form provides a description or "analysis" of the Spanish concept, the gloss is relatively transparent.[4] If individual parts of the Maya gloss are easily mappable onto individual parts of the Spanish signified, all the better.

The twin principles of economy and transparency can be thought of as aspects of a single, more general principle of optimal glossing. According to economy, the semantic and derivational potential of the foreign language (Maya) is put to maximal use so that the smallest number of roots can translate the largest number of distinct concepts. According to transparency, the grammatical composition of Maya glosses encodes an easily grasped analysis of the Spanish concept into discrete parts. Both principles guide the labor of translation and word formation in *Maya reducido,* in which the optimal phrasing was the one that best captured the Spanish-Christian concepts while rendering them easiest to grasp in their Maya forms. One necessary consequence of optimality so construed is that there is a great deal of grammar in the bilingual dictionaries, not only in the example sentences, but in the headwords and primary glosses as well. The difference between the dictionary and the *arte*, in this light, is more a matter of proportion than of kind: in the former, lexical meaning is focal and grammar is presupposed, whereas in the latter, grammar is focal and lexical meaning is presupposed.

Indexical Binding

Whereas economy and transparency focus on the properties of Maya words and phrases relative to the Spanish *concepts* they translated, there is another principle that bears on the relation between the Maya forms and the *typical objects* to which their Spanish counterparts referred. So while Spanish *confesar, convertir, guarda,* and *visita* all had multiple uses in Spanish, the Maya glosses to which they are associated are overwhelmingly focused on objects relevant to *reducción*: the confession of sins in the context of the sacrament, as opposed to merely stating what is true regardless of context; the conversion of God into man, salt into water, and stones into bread, as opposed to other kinds of conversion. Among the many examples of *guarda,* there are individual Maya translations for the senses 'abstention, to abstain' and 'observant, to keep to the commandments or to the law'. These are prototypical things that one "keeps." Although the Spanish term *visita* had multiple uses as well, the first one singled out in the Spanish-Maya dictionaries was the *visita* of a convent, that is, the peripheral "village" unit within the *guardianía.* In such cases, the Maya glosses pick out typical objects from the universe of *reducción.* It is not that they could be used *only* for the objects in question. Rather, the glosses are exemplary of the most salient or typical use(s) of the Spanish headword, at least in the minds of the missionaries.

In some cases, the resulting association between Maya form and Spanish referent became a more stable and selective bond, so that the Maya expression came to be used mostly or even exclusively for reference to the object to which it is associated. For example, the terms *ahau* 'ruler' and *noh* 'great' had multiple uses in Maya (including uses in hieroglyphic inscriptions), and the phrase *noh ahau* 'great ruler' could in theory be used for different kinds of 'ruler'. However, it came in fact to be used exclusively for reference to the Spanish king. Similarly, *ah tepal* 'ruler' could be used for various kinds of ruler in Maya, but it happened to be the preferred translation for 'majesty' in *Rey de su Magestad* 'King His Majesty'. Consequently, *ah tepal* came to be used almost exclusively in reference to the Spanish king. Through this kind of association, Maya expressions became bound to certain kinds of object within the colonial universe of *reducción.* This is a species of language change whose roots are in the compositional practice of dictionary making, where the indigenous expression is indexically bound to the colonial object.

These four principles obviously overlapped and interacted. They were rough guidelines or maxims, not rules that were followed mechanically, and there is much lexical material in the dictionaries that falls outside one or another of them. Interpretance is purposely vague, and it is the one among them that appears unavoidable and intrinsic to the act of translation. The remaining three were closely adapted to the aims of *reducción*. Economy gave rise to a great deal of grammatical composition and semantic extension in both headwords and glosses, and it was tempered by transparency. The combination of economy and transparency yielded glosses that would be optimal from the perspective of learning, readily construable and descriptive. Indexical binding went a step further by tying the Maya form to an exemplary object or type associated with the corresponding Spanish term. This effectively turned the Maya expressions toward the universe of colonial reference, just as transparency turned the semantics of Maya toward the meanings of Spanish words and phrases. It is possible that these four principles could be further reduced and almost certain that there are others as yet unmentioned. For our purposes at this point, they indicate that dictionary composition was systematically oriented to the aims and needs of *reducción*. The resulting commonalities among the dictionaries, as well as the detailed correspondences in their choice of words and glosses, were part of the process of standardizing *Maya reducido*.[5]

FRAY ANTONIO DE CIUDAD REAL, EXEMPLARY *LENGUA*

As we have seen, none of the major Yucatec Maya dictionaries has a named author, just as none has a date and only one (the Vienna *Bocabulario*) has a title. In a sense they are the works of the nameless Franciscan *lenguas* who recopied earlier sources and observed usage in various places around the province. The Motul dictionary is unique because it is usually attributed to fray Antonio de Ciudad Real, mostly on the basis of Lizana's description of him. Although he was not an "author" of that text, he appears to have played a central role in producing a work of similar scale. Lizana (1988 [1633], 241) dubs Ciudad Real "the Antonio de Lebrija of Maya" and asserts that he was famous among the *lenguas*. Lizana also claims to have seen the work he calls a *calepino,* or compendious dictionary, and says that it comprised six volumes, of which two volumes of two hundred folia each were in clean copy, plus a large quantity of draft notes. Of the notes, he says, *"los borradores llenaba* [sic] *dos costales"* 'the rough drafts filled two [large] sacks'. Lizana continues that the work *"dar luz y claridad a todos los que la (lengua) aprendiesen y allí hallasen cuantas frases"* 'shed(s) light and clarity for all those who might learn (the language) and might find in it so many phrases'. Cogolludo (1971 [1688], 2:268–69) later recapitulates Lizana's account but adds that Ciudad

Real also produced *"bocabularios,"* one from Maya to Spanish and the other from Spanish to Maya.[6] According to both historians, Ciudad Real labored some forty years on his masterwork, producing along the way a series of sermons (which have been lost) and a treatise on New Spain (cf. Carrillo 1872, 164). The received assumption in the field is that the dictionary he was working on was the one we call the Motul, and Ciudad Real is therefore its author.[7]

There can be no question that Ciudad Real was an exemplary *gran lengua*, perhaps the most exemplary of all the *lenguas*. Many *lenguas* are said to have worked on vocabularies and dictionaries, but he is the only one to whom an existing stand-alone dictionary is commonly attributed (whether or not he is actually its "author"). His career is marked by a great diversity of experience and exposure to Maya. Born in Ciudad Real, Spain, in 1551, he entered the Franciscan order in 1565 at the age of fourteen and took the habit in the *convento de San Juan de los Reyes de Toledo* (Carrillo 1872, 163). He first came to Yucatán in 1572 with fray Diego de Landa, following Landa's exoneration in Spain of charges that he had exceeded his authority as provincial during the idolatry trials of the 1560s in Yucatán. In his 1580 *memoria* to the Crown, fray Sopuerta places Ciudad Real in Tekax, where he was *guardián,* with three *pueblos de visita* and approximately one thousand *"casados"* (married [male] adults). According to Lizana (1988, 241), Ciudad Real was made secretary to fray Francisco de Noriega when the latter served as provincial, and in this capacity, he twice accompanied Noriega on *visitas* throughout the province.

Cogolludo (1971 [1688], 2:269–70) and Lizana concur that fray Antonio was gifted at governance as well as language, and he was named by the provincials in 1584 to serve as assistant to fray Alonso Ponce de León of the Holy Province of Castille, Commissary General of New Spain. After about a decade in Yucatán, this appointment took him away from the province until 1588, when he and Ponce made their three-month *visita* in Yucatán. Lizana (1988 [1633], 241) states that Ciudad Real accompanied Ponce on *visitas* to all the provinces of New Spain and beyond, a fact amply attested in the *relación* of Ponce's travels (including New Spain, Guatemala, El Salvador, Honduras, and Yucatán). During his travels, Ciudad Real evidently continued to work on his *calepino,* and, when the two had returned to Spain, he composed the work now known as *Tratado Curioso y Docto de las Grandezas de Nueva España.*[8] Lizana goes on to say that the two men returned to Havana from Spain and subsequently returned to Spain again, where Ponce was elected *guardián* of a convent in Alcalá de Henares. Ponce later moved to Guadalajara, where he died, and Ciudad Real was brought back to Yucatán by fray Maldonado in 1592.

Thus for about eight years, Ciudad Real was living and traveling outside the province, honing his observational and organizational skills, learning about other cultures and the missions in other areas. Between July and September

1588, the two visited all the major convents and many of the *pueblos de visita,* further expanding Ciudad Real's already considerable knowledge of the region. In Alcalá de Henares, he would have been exposed to one of the most vital centers of intellectual activity in Spain. It is unclear where Ciudad Real was posted upon his return to Yucatán, but on August 20, 1600, he was elected as one of four *difinidores* in the province, and on January 5, 1603, he was elected provincial (Cogolludo 1971 [1688], 2:104). Cogolludo (2:159–60) notes that during his tenure as provincial, Ciudad Real became embroiled in a dispute between an *indio principal* and a member of the secular clergy at the convent in Tizimín. In the continual conflicts between the religious and the secular clergy, Ciudad Real's tenure as provincial appears to have been especially difficult. On July 5, 1617, at the age of sixty-six, having spent fifty-one years as a Franciscan, fray Antonio died in the convent in Mérida.

If we assume provisorily that fray Antonio was the prime mover in the production of the Motul dictionary, what does his biography tell us about the work or other comparable works? First, the association between his work and the place named Motul is nowhere confirmed. I have found no evidence that Ciudad Real ever served in Motul.[9] He traveled widely throughout his career, within the province of Yucatán, around New Spain, and in Spain itself. Travel was common among the *lenguas,* many of whom served as *guardián, difinidor,* or *provincial* in the provincial order, as he did. There is little reason to believe that the scholarly work of most individual *lenguas* would embody a strictly local variant of Maya, and even less reason to think that collective *lengua* works such as dictionaries would be local to any single place.

Ciudad Real's life and works epitomize the *gran lengua.* He was a *gran latino* schooled in *latinidad* at the same convent in Toledo from which Landa had come. He wrote works in Spanish, Spanish to Maya, and Maya to Spanish. He was a teacher of Maya, suggesting that many missionaries were exposed to his work. If we take at face value Lizana's claim that Ciudad Real worked for "forty years" on the *calepino,* then he would have worked on it up until his last years, since he did not arrive in Yucatán until 1573. Finally, as *difinidor, provincial,* and renowned master of Maya, he would have been aware of other scholarship on the language by both his predecessors and his contemporaries. Among these contemporaries was fray Juan Coronel, whose 1620 opus was prepared in the first two decades of the 1600s, in the same convent of Tekax where Ciudad Real had been *guardián* a few decades earlier. Ciudad Real's life and career are interesting not because they confirm the tie between the man and the work called the Motul, which they do not. Rather, they are interesting because they illustrate the diversity of the *lenguas'* linguistic knowledge, whose sources included training in grammar and *latinidad,* the practice of recopying preexisting papers in the convents, and the practice of composing linguistic or doctrinal works and the various reports they produced in their administrative capacities. Moreover, because they traveled, *lenguas* such as Sánchez de Aguilar, Ciudad Real, San Buenaventura, and Beltrán were exposed to Maya usage in many different places. Through their work and that of other *gran lenguas,* the collective missionary knowledge of Maya verbal practices and the commensuration of Maya with Spanish were codified.

A Note on Orthography in the Motul and the San Francisco Part 1

Peculiarities of spelling in Maya, like idiosyncratic phrasing, can provide compelling evidence of intertextual connections. Tozzer (1977 [1921]) gives the false impression that the Motul and the San Francisco Part 1 were orthographically identical, but they in fact differ on a number of details. None of the dictionaries contains an explanation of the letters of the alphabet, their order, or their phonetic values. These factors would have been handled in an *arte* (although phonology is conspicuously absent from Coronel 1620). The Motul uses the following alphabet (Arzápalo Marín 1995, xxvii):

> *a, á, aa, b, c, ç, z, tz, ɔ (written dz here), ch, ch (written chh here), e, é, ee, h, y, i, í, ii, ij, k, l, m, n, o, ó, oo, p, pp, t, th, u, ú, uu, v, x*

Most of these segments are used with their Spanish values, with the exception of letters created for certain consonants: tz for the affricate /ts/, ɔ for the glottalized affricate /ts'/, ch for the glottalized affricate /ch'/, pp for glottalized /p'/, and th for glottalized /t'/. The Motul is unique in attempting to distinguish length and pitch (or glottalization) in the vowels by doubling and the acute accent, and it also shows hard /h/ *(recia)* and [ij].

The alphabet in the San Francisco Part 1 overlaps with the Motul but shows some variation. Glottalized /ch'/ is realized as capital C, and the letters ç, ij are missing. The acute accent is not used, and doubled vowels occur only with aa, oo, and occasionally ee. Thus 'i, u' occur only in simple form. Whereas alternative graphemes for /ts'/ are merely different ways to represent the same distinction, the difference in vowel representation implies that the San Francisco fails to make distinctions that the Motul does make.[10] The alphabetic order of the letters also differs, since the San Francisco Part 1 has < . . . p, pp, t, th, tz, u, x, y, z, dz>, whereas in the Motul we find < . . . z, tz, dz, ch, chh, . . . >. Minute as these details may be, they indicate that the two works differ in how they represent the sounds and alphabetic order of words in the language. In short, the details of orthography were far from uniform, even though there is strong evidence that they are both works within a single emergent standard.

Pronouns and Deictic Elements

The Motul and the San Francisco Part 1 are similar in their handling of pronouns; neither makes any attempt to include pronouns among the entries, except for reflexives (myself, yourself, etc.) and possessives (mine, yours, etc.), both of which are formed by prefixing the possessive pronoun to a noun stem (*ba* for reflexive, *tial* for possessive). Lexical (*ten, tech,* etc.), bound prefixal (*in-, a-,* etc.), and suffixal forms (*-en, -ech,* etc.) are all missing from the headwords in both dictionaries. The Motul cites the predicative forms *cen* 'I who am' and *cech* 'you who are' (M:69v) but fails to cite the corresponding plural forms *coon* and *ceex*. The San Francisco omits the entire series. These omissions do not reflect ignorance of the language. The forms in question were used repeatedly in the example sentences. Rather, the pronouns were a core topic in the *artes*, and their absence in the dictionaries is a matter of division of labor. This further reinforces the claim that the genres were well defined and complementary. [11]

KEY TERMS IN *REDUCCIÓN* AND THEIR STRATEGIC AMBIGUITIES

The scope of these dictionaries precludes systematic comparision here on anything more than a small set of terms. Table 7 displays the terms I have selected, according to relevance to the main themes of *reducción*. Note that all ten forms in the table have several meanings, at least one of which is metalinguistic. For the first four terms, the metalinguistic sense is evidently the primary meaning, whereas the remaining six show nonlinguistic meanings in first position, with apparent extensions to linguistic practices. Although there are only ten roots listed here, compounding, derivation, and semantic extension combine to yield scores of expressions and an array of distinctions. Thus the Maya-Spanish dictionaries show a proliferation of headwords and subheadings due to the principle of economy as it applies to the matrix language. To convey the workings of *reducción* at this level, I will examine the entries to which these roots gave rise.

Many of the semantic extensions adumbrated in table 7 map precisely onto the lines of relatedness among aspects of *reducción*. They display a tremendous economy, expressing diverse interrelated senses with compositions derived from single roots. Thus, for instance, crying and weeping are bundled together with contrition, penance, and supplication, just as sin is associated with heaviness of heart, remorse, compunction, and repentance. We see in such families of associations the affective modalities of early modern Christian practice and *policía cristiana*. The association between putting people in order and interpreting from one language to another, or between reading and obeying, could not be more true to *reducción* as a project. In examining these forms, we get a privileged inside view of the working of *reducción* as a semantic project aimed at forming a habitus.

The Motul and the San Francisco Part 1 dictionaries display different combinations of economy, transparency, and indexical binding. The Motul is stronger on the semantic extensions of the roots, relating such senses as counting, reading, obeying *(xoc)*, entering, meaning, admission, and the start date of some practice

TABLE 7 Key Words in *Maya reducido*

1. *Than*	'speak', 'language', 'govern(ance)', 'carnal know(ledge)'
2. *Dzib*	'write', 'writing', 'paint(ing)', 'bless', 'desire (carnal)', 'imagine'
3. *Xoc*	'count', 'read', 'obey', 'jealous(y)'
4. *Tzeec*	'preach', 'punish', 'correct'
5. *Tzic*	'obey', 'respect', 'attend to', 'converse'
6. *Tzol*	'arrange in order', 'recount in order', 'interpret'
7. *Ualak*	'return', 'reconcile', 'convert', 'interpret'
8. *Oc*	'enter', 'believe', 'baptize', 'convert (belief)', 'transform', 'signify', 'translate'
9. *Ok*	'cry', 'repent', 'be contrite', 'be clement', 'supplicate'
10. *Keban*	'sin', 'sadness', 'betrayal', 'repent', 'confess'

or law *(oc)*. By contrast, the San Francisco presents grammatically constructed typologies of over forty ways of speaking, eight kinds of writing (penmanship), and nine sins—most or all of which are lacking in the Motul. Both extension and grammatical collocation fulfill the principle of economy by drawing on the grammatical and semantic resources of language, but grammatical constructions are the more transparent insofar as they are compositional. Whereas the semantic extensions would have been discernible only by persons who spoke Maya very well, since they turn mostly on subtle distinctions of usage, the typologies are derived by productive application of simple syntactic rules. Below, I examine the entries in the order in which they are listed in table 7, starting with the verbs of linguistic practice (speak, write, count, preach).

Than (ex. 6.1)

The Motul has relatively few entries for the verb root *than* 'to speak, language', and it offers no typology of kinds of speaking. What it does present is evidence that this verb had at least four other senses, probably derived by extensions, but distinguished in the entries. These senses are '(to) govern', 'cause and reason', 'power and duration', and 'to have carnal knowledge of the other sex'. The entries are listed in the first part of ex. 6.1.[12]

Contrast the Motul with the list of entries from the San Francisco Part 1 (SF1). Note first that SF1 makes no mention of the extensions that are laid out in the Motul. The entire series of entries designates different ways or kinds of speaking, distinguishing no fewer than forty Maya expressions where the Motul lists a mere few. This contrast is typical of the two works: whereas the Motul makes pragmatically and semantically subtle distinctions in the different uses of a single expression, the San Francisco uses basic grammar to elaborate transparent typologies. In the present case, all the types of speaking in SF1 are compounds formed in the same way: the root *than* 'speak, speech' is preceded immediately by a qualifying

EXAMPLE 6.1

Than (M:431v–431r)

		'word, language, talk'
than	palabra y plática, lengua o lenguaje	'word and talk, language or kind of speech'
latinthan	lengua latina	'Latin language'
thanah, thanab	decir, hablar y platicar; conocer mujer el varón, o varón la mujer; es vocablo honesto	'say, speak and converse, to know women (of a man), to know men (of a woman), it is a proper word'
than	causa o razón	'cause or reason'
than	fuerza, poder y duración	'force, power and duration'
hunkul uthan yahaulil Dios	perpetua o eterna es la duración del reino de Dios	'perpetual, or eternal, is the duration of the kingdom of God'
than	bien es	'it is good'
than ca xiicech	bien es y acertado que te vayas	'it is good that you go'
thanalthan, thananthan	diálogo o disputa de palabra	'dialogue or verbal dispute'
thanalthaneneex	hablad en diálogo	'talk in dialogue'
thanalthanbil	en diálogo	'in dialogue'
thanancil	gobernar, mandar, regir; tener gobierno	'govern, order, rule, have government'
thanben	afable	'affable'

Than (SF1:357–58)

		'word, speak, language'
than, can, cantah, tah	palabra, hablar, parlar, lengua	'word, speak, speak, language'
thanen	habla!	'Speak!'
payan uthan, bekech uthan	habla delgada como de mujer	'thin speech like a woman's'
pochach than tah	palabras de menosprecio	'words of deprecation'
cici than	palabras blandas	'mild words'
chacan than	palabras airadas	'airy words'
ppaz than	palabras de escarnio	'derisive words'
dzidzic than, dzic ach than	palabras siniestras	'sinister words'
tzuctzuc than	palabras torpes, hablar de cosas torpes	'indecent words, speak of indecent things'
coco than, baxal than, coppen than, hoyan than	palabras de burla	'words of joking, jeering, jibing'
bibic than	palabras de pocos momento, de a poco más o menos	'words of little import, of more or less'
zauinal than	palabras preñadas y decirlas	'fraught words, and to speak them'

ah zacach than	palabrero, hablador, que habla mucho	'big talker, he who talks a lot'
thanal than	hablar en diálogo	'to speak in dialogue'
tohol than	hablar derecho, franco	'speak directly, frankly'
xoy than, xoy pach thantah, chhapach thantah	hablar por rodeos	'to talk in circles'
chunchun thantah	hablar con cautela	'to speak with caution'
et hun thantah, et ppizan than	hablar por semejanzas	'to speak in similes'
tzicbal, choom thantah, coothantah	hablar de burla	'speak in jest'
chhubchhub chi	hablar meneando los labios como rezando	'speak moving the lips as (when) praying'
zahal than	hablar con miedo	'to speak with fear'
halmah ti xicin	hablar a la oreja	'to talk into the ear'
hubthantah	hablar mucho en confusas	'to speak a lot and in confusion'
nuchpolthan	hablar a la cabezas juntas	'to talk with heads together'
nach bach than, zuucab than	hablar con ironía	'to speak with irony'
holta holta than	hablar cuatro	'to speak as four'
lol ach than	hablar prolijo y descometidamente	'to talk with prolixity and disregard'
bith bil than	hablar por las narices	'to speak through the nose'
ha ach chhin thantah	hablar a uno queriendo entender a otro	'to speak to one, wanting another to overhear'
chico than, nonol okthan, nunupp chi, chhub chi than, chub chi tah	hablar entre dientes	'to speak between the teeth'
chiic chiic hool bil than	hablar con meneos de cabeza y no con lengua	'to speak with nods of the head and not with language'
yol than	hablar amorosamente	'to speak lovingly'
chunlic than, chunlic can	hablar con fundamento	'to speak with a basis'
tich kab than	hablar de mano	'to speak with the hands'
zipkalac than	hablar lo que se viene a la boca, sin órden, sin concierto	'to say whatever comes to the mouth, without order'
ppech kal chi, ppechi ach, co chi	parlero	'big talker'
baihi ciac u than	como se dijera	'however it is said'
thanal than, calacal, buhulbuh, ppitlimthan	arguir, porfiar, contender, disputar, competir	'argue, insist, contend, dispute'

expression, thus [x-*than*], where x may be any one of about forty terms. It is argu-able that in providing this list, the San Francisco conflates words with readily derivable phrases, but by presenting them in a single list, it treats them explicitly as associated kinds. It also implicitly encourages the missionary to create similar compounds ad libidum. The Motul may well list many of these kinds, and others, but they are alphabetized separately under the qualifiers and not unified into a typology. The entries are listed in SF1 in the order of their appearance, which is not alphabetic but evidently by association.

Although it is grammatically simple, the list in SF1 deploys at least seven underlying categories, each with multiple subcategorizations: voice quality, pro-lixity of speech, tropes, dialogic interactions, communicative gestures, affectively charged speech, and evaluations of speech. Most of these varieties of speech would have been encountered or practiced outside the sphere of doctrinal teach-ing and liturgical practice; the friars were obviously aware of how the language was used in various different settings, only some of which they would have par-ticipated in directly. That nearly all the expressions are simple compounds, where *than* is the main verb or noun, implies that the parts of the phrase are readily segmentable and each contributes to the meaning of the whole. In other words, the forms in SF1 are highly transparent as well as grammatically economical. The profusion of distinctions in the Maya headwords nicely illustrates the strength of interpretance as a generative principle: the commensuration of the two languages is basically an open-ended process, and there is no suggestion that the forms in SF1 were an exhaustive list of kinds of speech.

Dzib (ex. 6.2)

Writing was as important as speaking in the *reducción,* and the transformative effect of missionary practice on writing was even more immediate than that on speech. At least some elites were already literate, and had been for about fifteen hundred years before the arrival of the Europeans. But there appear to have been restrictions on who produced and understood writing and what range of uses it was put to. The codices, artworks, and inscriptions all indicate that historical accounts, auguries, dates, and ritual texts were maintained, and if the Books of Chilam Balam are indicative, various other themes were expressed in writ-ing. Under *reducción,* writing became alphabetic as opposed to glyphic, and the varieties and genres of writing changed in a basic way. Since glyphic writing was closely associated with idolatry in the minds of the friars, it was eradicated. Many of the written genres were forbidden, any glyphic works found by the religious were likely to be destroyed, and new kinds of writing were introduced. The root *dzib,* which had been used for glyphic writing, was enlisted to translate a range of previously nonexistent kinds of writing, including the personal autograph, correspondence by letter, documents used in bringing suit against someone, and

EXAMPLE 6.2

Dzib (M:129v–130r)		'write'
dzibtah, -te	escribir	'to write'
dzibnen, dzibmeneex	escribe tú, vosotros	'write'
maa bahun indzibte huun tech	nunca te he escrito una carta	'I have never written you a letter'
dzib	es también pintar y dibujar	'it is also to paint and draw'
dzibte u uimbail San Juan		'draw the likeness of Saint John'
dzibal	escrito o escritura y la pintura	'written or writing, and painting'
dzibal	firma o nombre de alguno, escrito	'signature or name of someone, written'
dzibtah, -te, bee	hacer proceso contra alguno	'to bring suit against someone'
dzibteex ubeel Juan		'bring suit against Juan'
dzib ich	santiguarse	'to bless onself'
dzibte a ich tii cruz	santiguate	'bless yourself by the cross'
dzibnaattah, -te	imaginar o pensar con la fantasía	'imagine or think with fantasy'
dzib ool	lo mismo	'the same'
lay udzib auool be, maaix uil la cachie	imaginabas que era éste y no fué así	'you thought it was that, but it was not so'
baal cudzibtic auool?	¿qué estás imaginando?	'what are you imagining?'
dzib ool	ganoso y deseoso, que tiene deseo carnal	'aroused and desirous, he who has carnal desire'
dzib oolech ua tii chhuplal/xiblal?		'are you desirous of a woman/man?'
dzibooltah, -te	desear así	'to desire thus'
dzibooltah, -te	también desear en buena parte, con afecto	'also to desire in a good sense, with feeling'
dziboolteex benel tii caan	desead ir al cielo	'desire to go to heaven'
dziboolach	deseoso de mujeres, con deseo carnal	'desirous of women'
dziboolachil	aquel deseo	'that desire'
dzib olal	deseo carnal y tenerle	'carnal desire and to have it'
dzibolaan	cosa que es deseada	'a thing desired'
dzib oolil	el deseo carnal	'carnal desire'
udzib oolil xiblal tii chhuplal	el deseo carnal que el hombre tiene de mujeres	'the desire of man for woman'
dzibooltabal	ser deseado en buena y en mala parte	'desired, in a good and a bad way'
dzib puczikal	imaginar, lo mismo que *dzib ool*	'imagine, the same as *dzib ool*'

(continued)

EXAMPLE 6.2 *(continued)*

Dzib (SF1:462–63)		'write'
dzib, dzibtah, uooh, uoohtah	escribir	'write'
dzib, udzibal	escritura (lo que se escribe)	'writing (what is written)'
choon u dzibal	escritura borrada	'erased writing'
mehen dzib	escritura delgada	'fine writing'
chichip dzib, xixip dzib	escritura sin órden	'write without order'
xach dzib, xaxach udzibal	escritura rara	'strange writing'
utzul dzib	escritura buena	'good writing'
nucuch dzib	escritura de letra gruesa	'writing with thick letters'
udzibal kaxthan, mocthan	escritura de contrato	'writing of (a) contract'
thunil dzib, boomil dzib	punta de escritura	'writing point'
dzibal	escritura, la pintura	'writing, painting'
dzibilah, ziil, zii kabtah	presente que se ofrece y darlo, don, ofrenda, ofrecer	'present offered as gift, and to give it, gift, offering'
dzibil lec	jícara pintada	'painted gourd'
dzib kah lay	matricular	'matriculate'
dzib ol, yan ol	apetecer	'to appeal (to)'
dzib ol, dziboltaben	deseable (con mucho afecto)	'desirable'
dzib ol,	imaginación, fantasía,	'imagination, fantasy'
tucul	antojarse lo que no es	'envision what does not exist'
tudzib uol, tudzib auol	a mi parecer	'it appears to me'
dzib ol	deseoso (de cosa torpe o mala, casi siempre de lujuria, codicioso)	'desirous (of an indecent or bad thing, almost always lust, greed)'
dzibolen ti chhuplal	deseo una muchacha	'I desire a girl'
dzibolen ti benel ti caan	deseo ir al cielo	'I desire to go to heaven'
ma bahun dzibnacen tech	nunca te escribí	'I have never written to you'
dzibtah huun tu batanba,	cartearse,	'to exchange letters'
paclam dzib tu batanba	corresponderse por cartas	'correspond by letter'
balx ku dzibtic a uol?	¿como te imaginas a Dios?	'how do you imagine God?'
dzib uinbail	pintar, dibujar	'paint, draw'
macx dzibte uinbail la	¿quién pintó esta imágen?	'who painted this image?'

registration *(matrícula)*. Although both the Motul and the San Francisco Part 1 note that the verb *uooh-tah* was also used for writing, it appears likely from the Motul (F451r) that *uooh* was more closely associated with glyphic writing, since it is translated as "caracter, letra," and it is rarely used by the friars in their writings. Whatever the semantic distinction between *dzib* and *uooh* before the arrival of the Spanish, it appears clear that specifically alphabetical writing came to be designated with the former term, and the latter was marginalized as hieroglyphic writing was suppressed; the Motul does not mention *uooh-tah* under the heading *dzib*.[13]

What is most striking in the Motul entries for *dzib* is the semantic range of the form, which was also used for drawing and painting (portrait or likeness). Via derivation or compounding, it also designated 'to bless (oneself)', 'to imagine what is not actual', and 'to fantasize or desire (especially carnal desire)'. The use of *dzib ich* for blessing illustrates both the economy of grammatical formation and the indexical binding of the form to the specifically Christian act of blessing oneself with the sign of the cross. With the exception of blessing *(dzib ich)*, which appears to be a missionary neologism, the remaining uses are all attested in the Books of Chilam Balam. The disproportionate emphasis placed in the Motul on ways of referring to sexual desire is a frank indication of the missionary obsession with regulating sexuality, a major theme in the confessional manual and in the language of sin.

There is broad agreement between the San Francisco Part 1 and the Motul on the core meaning of *dzib* 'writing' and on the use of this same form for imagination, fantasy, and lust. The 'blessing' usage of the Motul is missing in the San Francisco Part 1, and the elaborate focus on carnal desire is greatly diminished. By contrast, the San Francisco pursues its classificatory aims, supplying a typology of six kinds of penmanship (thin, thick, disordered, erased, odd, good) reminiscent of the typology of voice quality under *than* 'to speak'. Notice that all these types are derived in exactly the same fashion as the kinds of speaking: the root is preceded by a qualifier [x-*dzib*]. These expressions would have been used in evaluating the writing of students and novice missionaries. They are all highly transparent. Both dictionaries note the meaning 'paint/draw (a likeness)' and they share the sense that *dzib ool* 'desire' is especially carnal but may also be used for the Christian desire for union with God. This otherwise discomforting pairing of two rather different desires in a single term likely echoes the theological idea that Christ is to the Church as a husband is to his wife.

Beyond the typology of penmanship, the San Francisco Part 1 distinguishes the writing of contract, register *(matrícula)*, and letter exchange, as well as the painting of gourds versus the painting of likenesses.[14] Where the two works overlap, there is strong evidence that they come from the same sources. Notice the following example sentences in ex. 6.2:

M	*maa bahun indzibte huun tech*	nunca te he escrito una carta	'I have never written you a letter'
SF1	*ma bahun dzibnacen tech*	nunca te escribí	'I never wrote you'
M, SF1	*dzibolen ti chhuplal*	deseo una muchacha	'I desire a girl'
M	*baal cudzibtic auool?*	¿qué estás imaginando?	'what are you imagining?'
SF1	*balx ku dzibtic a uol?*	¿cómo te imaginas a Dios?	'how do you imagine God?'

The difference between the two versions of "I have never written (a letter) to you" is linguistically regular. The gloss from SF1 makes it clear that even without specification of "a letter," that is the intended meaning. The change in verb form is due to the absence of a direct object in the SF1 version, which is well formed and precise. Indeed, the verb form *dzib-n-ac-en* displays impressive knowledge of the derivational patterns of Maya transitive verbs; it is what modern linguists call an antipassive, in which the underlying object (what is written) has been omitted. Moreover, the stem is correctly in the perfective shape rather than the simple past *(dzib-n-ah-en)*, an alternation governed by the negative element *ma bahun* 'never'. 'I desire a girl' is identical in both cases and would have been encountered or suggested in the context of confession. The last example, "what are you imagining?" is even more telling. The presence of the /-x/ suffix on *balx* in the San Francisco Part 1 is a regular alternation of *baal* 'thing, what'. The remainder of the example appears very different in the glosses, but in the Maya, the only difference is the substitution of glottalized /k/ for plain /c/ in the expression *cudzibtic ≠ ku dzibtic*.

I consider *ku dzibtic* a recopying error. Given the glosses and alphabetic placement of the form, the form would have been in the original handwritten text. It is not attested in any other context to my knowledge and is simply ungrammatical. Both the syntax and the morphology are wrong. The copyist of the San Francisco Part 1 has mistakenly transliterated /k/ instead of /c/ and then attempted to make sense of the erroneous form by referring to God *(ku)*. Once we correct the error, the example is well formed and identical to the one in the Motul.

We might assume that sexual desire and the imagination of God were themes that missionaries would deal with in the normal course of tending to their flocks. Sex was a hot topic in the confessional, and *dzib ol* occurs in the manual. That the two dictionaries have nearly identical expressions and glosses strongly suggests that they are related to one another and to other doctrinal genres. But the example "I never wrote (a letter) to you" is more idiosyncratic, and its occurrence in both works is even stronger evidence of their relatedness. The only context in which I am aware of written correspondence between missionaries and Maya people was when the Maya were outside the province, in the *despoblado,* and the missionaries were trying to convince them to come back in and accept Franciscans peacefully in their midst. Recall from chapter 3 that the Sahcabchén negotiations took place through letters exchanged between groups of Franciscans, groups of Maya chiefs, and the church in Mérida. In the example sentence, the addressee is a single individual, however, not a group, suggesting that individuals, not just groups, exchanged letters in Maya. Whatever the case may be, the sentence is sufficiently idiosyncratic that its recurrence in the two dictionaries must be the product of recopying from common or overlapping sources.

Xoc (ex. 6.3)

The verb root *xoc* has four principal senses, all of them recognized by both dictionaries: count, read, obey, and be jealous. The Motul suggests that the root is ambiguous between count and obey, citing the 'reading' sense only in collocation with the direct object *huun* 'letter'. The apparently exotic meaning 'jealousy' is actually easily derived in Maya by combining *xoc,* not with *huun,* but with the noun *ool* 'heart, intention, feeling', yielding something like 'an accounting heart, an accounting of the heart'. Although the forms cited and most of the examples are different in the San Francisco Part 1, it displays the same four senses, in the same order. Indeed, the order of senses is precisely identical, even where it is irregular: count, obey, count, read, be jealous. The second instance of 'count' should have preceded the 'obey' sense, were the list semantically consistent. Yet in both works, it follows it, in the same form: *xocaan* 'cosa que está contada' in the Motul; *xocan* 'sumar (en cuenta)' in the San Francisco Part 1. Of all the stem shapes of this root, it is unclear why these works would choose this participle and no others, were they not derived from a common schema or text.

Beyond the schema of four senses and the order of their presentation, the two works are once again complementary in the small details. They cite the following expressions:

M, SF1	*xoc huun*	'read (book) and reading'	leer (libro) y lección
M	*xoc ool*	'jealous'	celoso
	xocoolen	'I am jealous'	
SF1	*xocol, ah xoc olal*	'jealous, be jealous'	celoso, tener celos, celar
M	*ah xocoolen tin chhuplil*	'I am jealous of my wife'	
SF1	*xocolnen ti chhuplal*	'I am jealous of my wife'	tengo celos de mi mujer

The two cite identical expressions for 'read', although the San Francisco Part 1 claims that this is book reading in particular, whereas the Motul says letter reading (it could in fact mean either). They agree on jealousy, but the Motul illustrates it in the first-person singular, whereas the San Francisco Part 1 shows the agent nominalization *ah xoc olal* 'he who is jealous'. By contrast, the change is reversed in the next example, where Motul has the *ah* nominalization *ah xocoolen tin chhuplil* 'I am (habitually) jealous of my wife', but the San Francisco Part 1 does

EXAMPLE 6.3

Xoc (M:46ov)*		'count, obey'
xocah, -ob	contar	'count'
xocah, -ob	obedecer, respetar o tener respeto	'obey, respect'
xocaan	cosa que está contada	'something counted'
xoc huun	leer y lección	'to read, and reading'
xocaan huun	carta que está leida	'letter that is read'
xoc cuentas	rezar por cuentas	'pray in counts'
xoocol	acento en la primera silaba, ser contado, leido, obedecido	'accent on the first syllable, to be counted, read, obeyed'
xoc ool	celoso	'jealous'
xocoolen, ah xocoolen tin chhuplil		'I am jealous, I am jealous of my wife'
xoc oolil	hombre celoso	'jealous man'
xoctzil	cosa respetada y tenido en mucho	'something respected and highly valued'
xoctzil u than Dios	_____	'the word of God is highly valued'

Xoc (SF1:401)		'count, obey'
xoc, haycunah	contar, numerar	'count, enumerate'
kal xoc	contar de 20 en 20	'count twenty by twenty'
ppeppel xoc	contar de uno en uno	'count one by one'
xoc, tzic	obedecer, obediencia	'to obey, obedience'
ma axocic uthan cizin	no obedezcas o cuentas palabras del demonio	'do not obey or recount the words of the Devil'
uxocan yulel uaye udzahc in pach ti keban	cada vez que viene aquí, me fuerza a pecar	'every time (s)he comes here, (s)he forces me to sin'
xocan, bak xoc, hun molcinah	sumar (en cuenta)	'to total (by count)'
xoc huun	leer (libro) y lección	'to read (book) and reading'
huntadz xoc huun	leer a hecho	'read well'
ppeppel xoc huun	leer deletreando	'read letter by letter'
caput xoc huun, caa xoc huun, xoc huun tucaten	leer otra vez	'read again'
xocol, ah xoc olal	celoso, tener celos, celar	'jealous, be jealous'
xocolnen ti chhuplal	tengo celos de mi mujer	'I am jealous of my wife'
xocol, zauin	mujer celosa	'(a) jealous woman'

*Spanish contar is ambiguous between counting (enumeration) and recounting (narration). The Motul retains the ambiguity, whereas the San Francisco Part 1 cites only the enumeration sense.

not. The glosses are essentially identical. The San Francisco Part 1 apparently has an error in that *xocolnen ti chhuplal* has no first-person possessive pronoun, and a more careful translation would be 'I was jealous of (a) woman', as in 'I tend to be jealous of women'. The orthographic difference is minuscule: omitting the /n/ in *tin chhuplal* 'of my wife' results in *ti chhuplal* 'of woman', and inserting [n] in *xocol-n-en* yields a past tense. These tiny errors suggest that as the friars recopied, certain utterances were replicated over and over, so that even if the Maya was altered, the glosses were iterated. We might also note that the expression in question occurs in exactly the same position in the two texts, penultimate, after a list of other uses.

The most significant difference between the two treatments of *xoc* is that the San Francisco Part 1 once again displays a taste for typology. Using compounds formed according to the template [x-*xoc*], it distinguishes counting 'one by one' and 'twenty by twenty' and reading 'fluently', 'letter by letter', and 'for a second time'. The evaluative focus on voice quality in speaking, graphic quality in writing, and quality of execution in reading would all figure in the schools. Indeed, there is an almost didactic quality to the economy of both dictionaries, especially in the pursuit of transparency evident in the San Francisco Part 1.

Tzeec (ex. 6.4)

Both dictionaries gloss *tzeec* with two related senses, to mete out punishment/ correction and to preach (a sermon). They agree that verbal punishment is so designated, but neither clarifies whether corporal punishment would get the same term. The Motul adds the specification that punishment under the law is included, which could have been physical as well as nonphysical. The second sense of *tzeec* focuses on the missionary genre of the sermon, although the San Francisco Part 1 suggests that 'to pursue a discussion or line of reasoning' also fits the term. Note that when it is glossed 'preach' in the San Francisco Part 1, the verb is intransitive, whereas when it is transitive, the object codes the person 'castigated, punished': 'who is the priest who preached?' has the intransitive past *tzeecni*, whereas the transitive *tzeectah* is glossed 'castigate, correct (someone)'. The two dictionaries appear to disagree on which of the meanings is the first, punishment for the Motul or preaching for the San Francisco Part 1. Whereas the former gives no indication of how the intransitive stem is formed, which is highly significant to the entire derivational paradigm, the San Francisco systematically distinguishes intransitive *(tzeec, tzeecni)* from the transitive *(tzeectah, tzeecte)*. Moreover, in its example sentences, the San Francisco displays both the sermon reading (*¿quién es el padre que ha predicado?* 'who is the priest who preached?') and the ordinary punishment reading (*castigas a tu hijo por que no pagues sus pecados* 'punish your son so you don't pay for his sins'). For this term, the San Francisco Part 1 claims greater transparency in the distinction between transitive ('punish') and intransitive ('preach').

EXAMPLE 6.4

Tzeec (M:117r)		'punishment, preach'
tzeec	castigo y corrección, penitencia por justicia; predicar	'punishment and correction, penalty under law; preach'

Tzeec (SF1:367)		'sermon, preach, punish'
tzeec	sermón, predicar	'sermon, preach'
mac padreil ti tzeecni	¿quién es el padre que ha predicado?	'who is the priest who preached?'
tzeec; binzah than	proseguir plática o razonamiento	'pursue a discourse or reasoning'
tzeec, chichol	castigo	'punishment'
ma chaan tzeec ti Pedro	no basta o aprovecha castigo a Pedro	'punishment does not benefit or suffice for Pedro'
tzeecben, tzeeclem	corregible	'corrigible'
tzeectah	castigar, corregir	'punish, correct'
tzeecte a mehen ca achac a kochin u keban	castigas a tu hijo por que no pagues sus pecados	'punish your child so you don't pay for his sins'

The two senses of *tzeec* differ primarily by the modality of the correction, the one being a religious genre and the other being a punishment meted out by authority (priest to parishioner, legal system to subject, father to son). Both, of course, are indexed to *reducción*. That sermons are thought of in this light provides an interesting window on missionary thinking: to preach was to correct error. The less specific term *plática* 'speech, talk' was also used for priestly sermonizing; hence even the gloss *proseguir plática o razonamiento* could have applied to preaching. This is what we would expect under *reducción,* especially the initial phases, where the aim was to re-form the habits of indigenous people, to correct them rather than to maintain them. Moreover, the friars were insistent on the necessity of punishment in transformative pedagogy. The idea that an individual (Pedro in the example) would not benefit from punishment is contrasted with the forms glossed as 'corrigible'. Like punishment, corrigibility was at the heart of *reducción* and was carefully monitored by the missionaries.

Tzic (ex. 6.5)

In order to be corrigible, as opposed to merely punished, one had to attend to the meaning of the punishment and be able and willing to follow its rationale. The next expression focuses squarely on this proper state of receptivity. *Tzic* is associated with three obviously related senses, to obey, to pay attention to, and to converse. On this root, the two dictionaries offer about the same degree of detail, although there is only partial overlap in the forms they cite. The Motul cites the passive stem in initial position and is clearly more concerned with the pitch and length contrast between the passive (*tziicil*, high tone and glottalization on the first syllable, neutral on the second) and the nominalization (*tziciil* high tone on the second syllable, neutral on the first) than with the niceties of their meanings. From the first sense based on obey, the entries shift to '*hacer caso*', which I have glossed 'to pay attention to', in the sense of taking something or someone seriously. The 'respect, honor' meaning is then easily construable as an extension from 'pay attention to'.

The example sentence 'do not pay attention to the songs of birds' expresses a concern present throughout the Franciscans' writings. The Maya, they felt, placed great interpretive weight on signs and auguries, including dreams and the calls of certain birds, which are mentioned by Sánchez de Aguilar, Landa, and others. In the example, the stem is transitive (*atziciceex*) and the bird's call is the direct object (*yauat chhichhoob*). The thrust of *tzicic* here is to notice the birdcall, treat it as meaningful, and derive its consequences. The San Francisco Part 1 lacks this example, but it too illustrates the transitive in its first example sentence, *yalah Dios catzicic u chun thanob* 'Dios dijo que obedezcamos a nuestros prelados'. In this sentence, the verb stem is identical to the one in the Motul, hence transitive, and the direct object is *nuestros prelados* 'our prelates'. The gloss is slightly peculiar, because the phrase *chun thanob* was ordinarily used in reference not to the prelates but to the town-level groups of senior Maya nobles usually called *principales* in Spanish (see chapter 3 above). There is a neat contrast between the injunctions 'don't attend to auguries' and 'do attend to God's word', another instance of indexical binding to the moral order of *reducción*.

The Motul is quite systematic in combining the stem *tzic* with different objects, using the grammar to extend the semantic range of the Maya in transparent constructions. The reflexive *tzic bail* yields self-importance or arrogance (excessive reverence paid oneself). The reciprocal *tzic batan ba* yields mutual honor and respect, and the derived transitive form *tzicilte* designates the object or person to which or whom respect is given. Skipping ahead to the last entry in the Motul, we find three expressions that are applied to a person for whom one has love and reverence, 'my beloved and revered father'. The suffixes -*tzil* and -*ben* are widely attested in reverential expressions, and the forms cited actually recur in the openings to letters and other writing to higher authorities. The San Francisco cites *tzic-ben-tzil*, combining the two, although this is not shown in the Motul.

The conversational genre *tzicbal* is widely attested and readily derivable from the root *tzic* plus the suffix -*bal*, which ordinarily derives a noun or intransitive verb from a verb (hence *xim-bal* 'walk', *hok-bal* 'go out', *bin-bal* 'go', etc.). The glosses in the two dictionaries are both verbal: (M) '*parlar o estar en conversación*', (SF1) '*conversar*'. The San Francisco Part 1 fails to display the transitive form of this stem, thus inviting the false assumption that the conversational sense is limited to the intransitive. The Motul clarifies, citing the transitive *tzicbaltah, -te* 'to

EXAMPLE 6.5

Tzic (M:118r–118v) — 'to obey, respect, converse'

tziicil	ser obedecido, el acento en la primera sílaba	'to be obeyed, accent on the first syllable'
tzicil	en la última sílaba, la obediencia	'on the last syllable, obedience'
tzic	hacer caso	'pay attention to'
maa a tziciceex yauat chhichhoob	no hagáis caso de los cantares de los pájaros	'do not pay attention to the songs of birds'
tzicbail	soberbia, presunción, vanagloria	'arrogance, presumption, vaingloriousness'
tzic batan ba	honrarse y respetarse unos a otros	'honor and respect one another'
tzicilte	honrado, venerable	'honored, venerable'
tzicil than	palabras bien criadas y corteses	'courteous and well-reared words'
tzic than	la obediencia y reverencia que se debe a Dios y a los hombres	'the obedience and reverence due to God and to persons'
tzicbaltah, -te	tratar en conversación alguna cosa	'treat something in conversation'
yan ua a tzicbaltic yetel a laakoob a mucul pak keban a zipcie?	¿has por ventura tratado en conversación que fornicaste?	'by chance, have you conversed about having fornicated?'
tzicbal	parlar o estar en conversación	'talk or be in conversation'
tzictzil, tzicben, tin yatzictzil yumil	a mi amado y reverenciado padre	'to my beloved and revered father'

Tzic (SF1:368–69) — 'to obey'

tzic, tzic than, xoc, chha than	crianza, obediencia, obedecer	'upbringing, obedience, to obey'
yalah Dios ca tzicic u chun thanob	Dios dijo que obedezcamos a nuestros prelados	'God said we are to obey our prelates'
ixma tzic; ixma tii	incorregible	'incorrigible'
tzic (ix ma ___)	rebelde	'rebel' (n)
tzicbal, huhub can, huhub than, kukutz can	decir cuentos o gracias (en las conversaciones)	'tell stories or witticisms (in conversation)'
tzicbal, can, canancil	conversar	'to converse'
tzicben, tzicbentzil, tzic tzil	obedecible, celebrar	'worthy of obedience, to celebrate'
tzic than, chha than	obediencia, obedecer	'obedience, to obey'

treat something in conversation', or as we might say in English, to discuss or tell something. The example once again brings us face-to-face with confession. The gloss *¿has por ventura tratado en conversación que fornicaste?* is in the exact form of probing questions in the confessional manual, as we will see, and the concern with fornication is by now familiar.[15]

The postures and conduct joined in *tzic* map nicely into the proper *policía* associated with *reducción*. To be obedient and respectful is integral to proper conduct within the scope of higher authority. It is this same frame that motivates the San Francisco Part 1 to include the negative form *ix ma tzic* 'one who (habitually) does not obey', meaning 'rebel'. Given what we already know about the prevalence of flight and Maya rebelliousness during the seventeenth century, there is little question that disobedience was a primary concern for the friars.

Tzol (ex. 6.6)

A slightly different perspective on *reducción* is provided by the verb root *tzol*, which is glossed in two ways, 'to arrange (objects in space)' and 'to recount (words or events in language)'. The verbal sense appears to be primary for the simple transitive stem *tzol(ic)*, whereas the spatial arrangement sense emerges in derived forms *tzol cul* [*tzol* + 'sit'] 'sit in order', *tzolaan* [*tzol* + stative] 'be in order', *tzoltal* [*tzol* + intrans suffix] 'place oneself in order', *tzol ol* [*tzol* + 'heart'] 'place oneself in order (esp. morally)', and *tzolanil* [*tzol* + stative + *il*] 'be ordered (in a manner)'. All of these are highly transparent grammatical constructions in which the parts are readily segmented and associated with distinct meanings. The two senses clearly have in common the concept of putting objects, words or bodies, in proper order. From the verbal meaning of 'tell in order', there is a minor extension to *(ah) tzol than* [(Agent) + *tzol* + 'language'] 'interpret(er)'. The latter applies to interlingual interpretation and intralingual explanation, both of which are defined by the production of metalinguistic speech that recapitulates other speech.

There are further refinements in each of the works. The Motul nicely adds the expressions *tzolaan bee* [*tzol* + stative actions] and *tzolaan cuxtal* [*tzol* + stative + 'life'], both with the meaning 'order of life, story of life', or what we might call 'curriculum vitae'. We might wonder what sort of life would be so described, and the San Francisco gives an intriguing hint in the example *yab in zipil ma tzolben* 'muchos son mis pecados no se pueden decir ni contar por orden'. The gloss suggests that sins in multitude are not sufficiently orderly to be 'recounted in order'. The suffix *-ben* attached to the root derives an adjective roughly glossable as 'worthy of, able to be', much like English *-able* in 'respectable' (cf. *tzicben* 'respectworthy,' glossed as 'worthy of obedience' in the previous example). Thus, although the gloss makes clear that disorder is the problem with the sins, the Maya form could as well be interpreted as 'many of my sins are

EXAMPLE 6.6

Tzol (M:119v)		'to put in order, recount'
tzolah, -ob	poner orden y ordenar así	'place in order'
tzolcantah, -te	contar por orden	'recount in (proper) order'
tzolaan bee	orden y modo de vida, crónica o historia, vida de alguno	'order and mode of life, chronicle or history, life of someone'
tzolaan cuxtal	modo y orden de vida	'mode and order of life'
tzol cultal	sentaos por orden	'sit down in order'
tzol culcinah	asentar o poner por orden	'to seat or put in order'
tzol culeneex	sentados por orden	'seated in order'
tzoltal	ponerse en orden o estar así puesto	'to get in order'
maa yoolah tzoltal	no quiere estar puesto por orden	'he does not want to be put in order'
tzolthan	intérprete, interpretar de una lengua a otra, relatar y hacer algún razonamiento y decir por orden lo que otro nos dice	'interpreter, to interpret from one language to another, to relate and pursue some reasoning and to say in order that which another has said to us'

Tzol (SF1:370–71)		'recount, put in order'
tzol, tzol tzol	contar	'(re)count'
lay bin tzolic teex tulacal lo	este os lo contará por orden	'that one will recount it to you in order'
catzol u benelob	en dos renglones marcharon	'they walked double file'
tzol, tzolcinah, tholcinah	poner en órden o renglera	'to put in order or rows'
tzolex a ba	poneos por órden	'get in order'
tzolan	ordenado, coro, cosa en órden	'ordered, choir, something in order'
ma utz tzolanil	no está bien ordenado	'it is not well ordered'
ma ti tzecni ti maya than chambel tzolbil uthan	no predicó en la lengua sino por intérprete	'he did not preach in the language but instead through an interpreter'
yab in zipil ma tzolben	muchos son mis pecados no se pueden decir ni contar por órden	'my sins are so many they cannot be said or recounted in order'
tzolantah dzib	dictar (al que escribe)	'to dictate (to him who writes)'
tzol cultal	asentarse por órden	'to sit in order'
tzol ol	ponerse en órden	'to get in order'
tzol than	interpretar, naguatear, relatar, contar por órden	'to interpret, to interpret, to relate, recount in order'
tzol (Ah___) than, chilam	interprete	'interpreter'

unworthy of recounting (so bad are they)'. The speech act of *tzol* is further derived in the San Francisco Part 1 into dictation, where one speaker says words to be written down in the same order by a scribe: *tzolantah dzib* [*tzol* + stative + transitive + 'write'] 'to tell in order to (one who) writes'. Whether or not any such expression was used by Maya speakers outside the sphere of colonial governance, it is crystal clear that the production of notarial genres depended on dictation, and it was likely a form of pedagogical exercise in the schools. Through the economy of grammar, the San Francisco Part 1 spells out a great deal of specifically colonial knowledge rooted in the forms of governance under *reducción*.

The background frame of *reducción* is powerfully present in ex. 6.6. The arrangement of people in space is one of the first foci of the project, and the examples designate practices of ordering that we know the friars engaged in. Recall that in the *doctrina*, religious services, and processions, Maya people, especially children, were ordered in lines and separated by sex. In the church and school they would have been seated *(tzol cul)*, and in the processions filing two by two *(ca tzol ubenelob* ['two' + *tzol* + 'they go']). The command to get in line or proper place would have been routine, and there would be those who resisted: *maa yoolah tzoltal* 'no quiere estar puesto por orden', 'he does not want to be put in order'. Whereas *tzic* focuses on respect and obedience, *tzol* focuses on orderliness. Both forms extend to ways of speaking, as we would expect from the *reducción*, one respectful and the other orderly. This placing in verbal order extends easily to both cross-language interpretation and intralingual explanation, but the San Francisco Part 1 suggests that the compound [*tzol* + *than* 'speech'] was primarily associated with interlingual translation, at least in the missionary version of Maya. Thus we have virtual glosses of *reducir* in its spatial sense and in its linguistic sense. By including the examples for 'order and way of life', the Motul completes the picture with the behavioral *reducción*. A life *tzolaan* is a life in *policía*.

Ualak (ex. 6.7)

Part of *reducción* is a turning from one way of life toward another. This act of turning was equated with the Maya verb form *ualak* 'volver o tornar', as shown in ex. 6.7. In addition to the physical sense of turning around an object (including one's body), both dictionaries gloss the reflexive form *ual kezah ba* as 'convert'. This is actually a causative with the reflexive pronoun as its direct object: [*ual* + *kezah*] [*a* + *ba*] 'cause to turn your + self', or 'cause yourself to turn'. Thus it does not translate *"convertir"* in the meaning of 'bring about the conversion of another', as in "the friar converted the boy." Rather, *ualkezah ba* designates the inner movement of the one who converts. The Motul indexically binds this kind of conversion to the Christian God, even though on sheerly grammatical grounds, the same expression could be applied equally well to other self-transformative

EXAMPLE 6.7

Ualak (M:441r–441v)	to return, convert, interpret
ualak	volver o tornar	'revolve or turn'
ualkezah ba tii Dios	volverse o convertirse a Dios	'revolve or convert oneself to God'
ualkezah tii	interpretar, volver de una lengua a otra	'to interpret, turn from one language to another'
tu ualkezah tii Castillathan	volviólo o tradújolo al castellano	'(he) turned or translated it into Castilian'

Ualak (SF1:377–78)	to return, convert, interpret
ualak	vuelta, volver	'(a) turn, to revolve'
ualak than, kex than	vuelta de palabras	'exchange of words'
ualkac uthan, zut pac	mudable (en lo que dice)	'changeable (in speech)'
ualak yol	mudable (en el propósito)	'changeable (in meaning)'
ualkac zutpac a thanex	ya direis uno, ya direis otro	'now you say the one, now you say the other'
ualkahal tu ba, ualkahal ti ol	volver en si el errado	'to return to himself, the errant'
ualkalac yol	inquieto	'unquiet, unsettled'
ualkezah ba ti, oczah ba ti	reconciliarse con el enemigo, convertirse	'to reconcile with the enemy, to convert'
ualkezah ti maya than	traducir en lengua maya	'to translate into Maya language'
ualkezah ti thanil	interpretar, volver en otra lengua	'to interpret, to turn (it) into another language'

conversions, including apostasy. The San Francisco Part 1 gives the more ambivalent gloss 'to reconcile with the enemy, to convert'. When the object or direction to which one converts is stated, it is coded with the preposition *tii*, meaning 'to'.[16] Thus to 'convert to God' is to 'cause yourself to turn to God'. This act of turning is reminiscent of the etymological source of the Spanish *"reducir"* 'to lead back'.

Both dictionaries indicate that the causative stem was also used for interpretation, construed as causing one language to turn to another, or turning what is said in one language into another. Language 1, or a statement in language 1, is the object turned, and language 2 is the target to which it is turned. This is precisely the action effected by the bilingual dictionary itself, turning from the headword to the gloss. Recall that while *tzol* is used for interlingual interpretation, it is also used for intralingual explanation. *Ualkezah* appears to be limited to interlingual interpretation: it is the canonical act of both *indios ladinos* (Maya into Spanish) and *frayles lenguas* (Spanish into Maya). That this is coded as a turning once again echoes the turning of *reducción* in the physical, behavioral, and linguistic sense.

The San Francisco Part 1 provides several additional examples of direct relevance to the making of *indios reducidos*. The form *ualkahal* is a derived intransitive that retains the turning away and toward that we have seen but apparently carries an added overtone. *Ualkahal tuba* 'to turn to himself' and *ualkahal ti ol* 'to turn to heart' both mean to backslide, to return to one's old, erroneous ways. It is not clear from the examples whether the same Maya expressions would be usable if the turning in question were from error to rightness, instead of the other way around. That interpretation can move in either direction, Spanish to Maya or Maya to Spanish, suggests that it could be used that way, but this dictionary focuses on backsliding into error rather than recovery from it. The same negativity is evident in the form *ualkalac,* an adjective probably best glossed as 'vacillating, turning on itself'. Applied to *yol* 'his/her heart', this yields the affective state of turmoil that comes with inconstancy in the Franciscan imagination. Applied to speech, it is the talk of one who goes back on his word, is inconsistent, or talks in circles.

There is an emerging theme in the San Francisco Part 1 dictionary. In the entries examined above, it is more consistently focused on evaluation than is the Motul. This includes the quality of voice, speech, graphemes in writing, fluency in reading, obedience and incorrigibility, and now the lack of constancy. Some of these qualitative distinctions would have been put to work in the pedagogical settings of school and sermon; others seem more suited to the confessional. Along with the metalanguage of linguistic practice came the language of order and disorder, goodness, badness, and the states of the heart and soul. A work of synthesis par excellence, the dictionary unifies all these spheres of thought and practice in the act of articulating one language to the other. The terms under discussion are core nodes in this basic articulation. Many of the Maya forms essentially redescribe the concepts or referents of corresponding Spanish expressions, thereby laying bare an entire universe of associations that may be absent or only implicit in the Spanish.

Oc (ex. 6.8)

The target toward which one converts is not only a point of orientation but also a space into which the convert enters. For the convert, the world is new and will call forth a new subject. 'To cause yourself to turn to God' is more than a reorientation. It is an entering into a new reality, a critical part of the process by which the Indios would "make themselves new men." It is thus appropriate that the verb root *oc* 'enter' figures widely in the missionary discourse about conversion. It is one of the most productive in the dictionaries (see plate 8).

These two sets of entries are extraordinarily detailed catalogs of forms based on *oc*, nearly thirty in all. They show an exuberant range of interpretance by way of grammatical constructions, semantic economy, transparency of meaning, and indexical binding to certain objects of reference. The Motul and the San Francisco Part 1 agree that *oc ha* (or *ocaa*) is the term for baptism, literally 'enter + water', that the reflexive form *oczah ba* 'cause oneself to enter' is the expression for religious conversion, that *ocol(al)* ['enter' + 'heart' + suffix] was used for believe (belief), and that in being elected or named to a position of authority, one 'entered it' *oc(ol) ti* ['enter' (intrans) + 'to'] or was 'caused to enter it' *oczah ti* ['enter' + causative + 'to']. The Motul focuses on metalinguistic uses of the term and provides a set of examples in which it translates as 'meaning, import'. These are precisely the kinds of expressions one would need to do systematic fieldwork on the language. The causative with 'language' as direct object, *oczah than,* is glossed as 'admit' or accept the speech or authority of another, that is, adopt its import. Curiously, the Motul never even mentions the simple spatial meaning of the root, 'to enter' (intrans) and 'to put in' (causative), as in *ocol ich nah* 'to enter (the) house', although the San Francisco Part 1 does cite this usage, and it is well attested in the other sources. Looking across these entries, the Maya draws together in a single root the concepts stood for by Spanish *creer* 'believe', *bautizar* 'baptize', *convertirse* 'convert', *convertir* 'transform', *admitir* 'admit (be moved by)', and *elegir* 'elect'. This is typical of core Maya expressions, which are the central nodes in sometimes far-flung sets of semantically associated expressions.

The compound *ocaa* [*oc* + 'water'] is the canonical translation for baptism, which occurs throughout the dictionaries, grammars, doctrinal literature, and even Maya-authored genres. In Christian thought, entering water is the intended image, where water would be the space into which the subject enters, or which is poured over the subject. The Maya is slightly different, however. The full phrase for baptism is *oc(ol) ha ti hool* or *ti pol*, which means literally 'water enters to/on (the) head', not the other way around. The phrasing is undoubtedly motivated by the practice of pouring water over the head of the person being baptized, yet the grammar is muddled. The first gloss given to simple *oc ha* by the San Francisco Part 1 is 'leaky (as in a roof that allows rain to pass)', suggesting that the phrase had nonsacramental uses as well as the more common sacramental one. As with the translation of 'omnipotent' as *uchuc tumen tuzinil,* though the grammar is peculiar, the expression became relatively fixed. Suspended between near-literality and a figurative image, it functioned virtually as a name for the sacrament.

The Motul takes advantage of the paradigm-building potential of compounds and verb-object phrases, using the familiar schema 'verb + x' to produce *oc(ol) keban* ['enter' + 'sin'] 'fall into sin', *oc(ol) keban ti ol/pucsikal* ['enter' + 'sin' + 'heart'] 'to become angry', and *oc(ol) patan* ['enter' + 'tribute'] 'tribute is introduced'. Both dictionaries gloss *ocol ku* ['enter' + 'divinity'] as 'abstinence, continence (sexual)', and San Francisco Part 1 adds the expression *ocaan ik ti* ['entered' + 'wind' + 'to (him)'] 'be flatulent', a rather different semantic domain. In all these cases, the noun following the verb is construed as the subject that enters. When no subject is indicated, resulting in *oc(ol) ti* 'enter into it', the gloss may be 'convert (change into)', as in *oci ti uinicil* 'convert (one thing into another)'. This sense of conversion is illustrated with the conversion of God into man, wine into water, and stones into loaves—clearly reflecting the biblical frame of reference.

The transitive forms of *oc* are derived as causative, where the causer of the entering is coded as agent (subject of transitive), and the object made to enter is coded as grammatical object. The minimal causative is *oczah* [root + *zah*], which the Motul glosses as 'admit', with the example *maa a uoczic u dza dzib olal baalcah* 'no admitas los deseos que te da el mundo', more or less 'do not give in to the lurid fantasies of the material world'. The San Francisco Part 1 also cites the plain causative stem, glossing it as 'to sow (seeds)'. As I have already mentioned, the causative plus reflexive *(oczah ba)* is glossed as 'to reconcile (oneself) with another, make peace or convert'. The San Francisco Part 1 cites the same usage, with similar examples, both of which echo one of Coronel's sermons, as will be discussed in chapter 8.[17]

The causative followed by *than* 'speech' *(oczah than)* is a more transparent phrasing for 'admit words, agree' (SF1:270). Interestingly, the nominalized form of the latter, *ah oczah than* 'he who admits speech' is glossed as 'middleman, go-between', a participant role that the friars would have both relied upon and engaged in themselves. The same causative stem followed by *ol* 'heart' is glossed as 'believe' by the Motul *(oczah ol),* whereas the San Francisco Part 1 cites the fuller form *oczah ti ol* ['put in' + 'to' + 'heart'] 'to believe and give credit'. The illustration is *uoczah tii uool in uayak* 'I believed in my dreams', a likely statement of contrition in the confessional context, since dreams were an indigenous form of augury discouraged by the friars. If we substitute *ya* 'pain' for *than* 'language',

EXAMPLE 6.8

Oc (M:340v–343v)*		'to enter'
oc		'to enter'
	significa, quiere decir y esto es, cuando se vuelve un vocablo de una lengua a otra	'means, intends and that is it, when an expression is turned from one language to another'
hal ten hi baal oci	dime, ¿qué quiere decir esto?	'tell me, what does this mean?'
lay oc telo	esto quiere decir	'that is what it means, that means'
baal oc ta uayil thaneex loie?	¿qué quiere decir esto en vuestra lengua de aquí?	'what does that mean in your language of here?'
lay oc laye, he oc laye	esto quiere decir	'that's what that means'
baal oc tathaneex, baal oceex ta than	¿qué queréis decir?	'what do you mean?'
ocaa	bautizar y bautismo	'to baptize and baptism'
ocaa ucah padre	está el padre bautizando	'the father is baptizing'
ocaan haa tii hool	el que está bautizado	'the one who is baptized'
ocaan keban tin puczikal	enojado estoy y en pecado	'I am angry'
ocaan patan	introducido se ha el tributo	'tribute was introduced'
oczah	admitir	'to admit'
maa a uoczic u dza dzib olal baalcah	no admitas los deseos que te da el mundo	'do not admit the desires that the world gives you'
oczah ba	reconciliarse con otro, hacer las paces o convertirse	'reconcile with another, make peace or convert'
ocezeex a ba tii Dios	convertíos a Dios, reconciliaos con él	'reconcile yourself, convert to God'
ukinil oczah ba hele lae	ahora son días de convertirse el hombre	'now are the days for man to convert'
oczah ool	creer	'to believe'
oczah tii	convertir una cosa en otra	'convert one thing into another'
yoczah tunich tii uahil	convirtió las piedras en pan	'he converted stones into loaves'
oczah tii almehenil	ennoblecer a uno	'to make someone a noble'
oczah tii alcaldeil, batabil, tupilil, testigoil	hacer a alguno alcalde, cacique, tupil, testigo	'to make (someone) *alcalde*, chief, officer, witness'
oczah tii castillathan, tii mayathan	volver o traducir en la lengua de Castilla o en la de Yucatán	'to turn or translate into the language of Castilla or Yucatán'

oczah tii confesar	confesar a alguno	'to confess someone'
maa bin u kati yocezen tii confesar	dice que no me quiere confesar	'he says he does not want to hear my confession'
oczah tii nohxibil	poner a uno por principal de otros	'to make one the leader of others'
oczah tii ool	creer y dar crédito	'believe and give credit to'
uoczah tii uool in uayak	creí en mis sueños	'I believed in my dreams'
oczah than	admitir la razón o lo que otro dice	'to recognize the reason or (import of) what another says'
ocol keban	caer en pecado	'to fall into sin'
ocol kuu	castidad, continencia y religión	'chastity, continence, and religion'
ocol patan	introducirse el tributo	'tribute (be) introduced'
ocol tii	convertirse	'to convert (oneself)'
ocol tii ool	creer	'believe'
ocaan ua Dios tauool?	¿por ventura crees en Dios?	'do you believe in God?'

Oc (SFi:268–70)

ocaan haa tu hool /o/ pol; caput zihan	bautizado	'baptized'
ocaan ik ti	tener ventosidad	'to have flatulence'
ocan ti padreil	ordenado de padre	'ordained as priest'
oc haa	cosa que se llueve	'something that leaks'
hach oc haa uotoch	mucho se llueva mi casa	'my house leaks'
ocol	entrar, entrado	'enter, entered'
ocol tu batabil ti uinicil	hacerse batab	'to become chief'
ocolal**	creencia, fé	'belief, faith'
ocolalil (ix ma ___)	infidelidad, infiel (no cristiano)	'infidelity, infidel (not Christian)'
ocol haa ti pol /o/ hool	bautizarse	'to be baptized'
ocol ku, numocol ku, num coycab	castidad, abstinencia	'chastity, abstinence'

(continued)

EXAMPLE 6.8 (continued)

Oc (SF1:268–70) (continued)		'enter' (continued)
ocol kutah, coycabtah	hacer abstinencia	'to be abstinent'
ocol ti uinicil	convertirse (una cosa en otra)	'to convert (one thing to another)'
ocol ti ol	creer	'to believe'
oczah ti ol	meter en el corazón algo haciendo mucho caso de ello	'to put in one's heart something, making much of it'
matan yocol ti uol	no lo creo, no hago caso de ello	'I do not believe it, I make nothing of it'
oki u keyah tiuol	enojéme	'I became angry'
oczaben ti ol	creible	'credible'
oczah	sembrar, sembrado	'to sow, sown'
oczah ba ti, ualkezah ba ti	reconciliarse (con el enemigo), convertirse	'reconcile (with the enemy), convert'
ma a nachcunic u kinil a uoc dzic a ba ti Dios	no alargues el tiempo de reconciliarte con Dios	'do not put off the time when you reconcile with God'
yoczahon tu yum cahlohil	reconciliónos con su padre nuestro redentor	'we were reconciled with his father, Our Redeemer'
oczah ti padreil	ordenar de misa	'to ordain for Mass'
oczah ti testigoil, uacunah ti testigoil	presentar por testigo	'to present as witness'
oczah ti uinicil	convertir (una cosa en otra)	'convert (one thing to another)'
oczah than, oczah okot ba	admitir palabras o ruegos	'to admit words or entreaties'
oczah (ah ___) than, ah kulel, ah chumuc cabal than	medianero	'go-between'
oczah (ah ___) ya	revoltoso	'rebellious'
oczah (ah ___) ya tu lakob	malsín	'(a) malicious gossip'

*The Motul never glosses oc as 'to enter', but I have added it for clarity.

**SF1 fails to distinguish length and pitch in the vowels, and consequently its orthography conflates some distinctions. The form ocol is ambiguous between oc-ol 'to enter, enters' and oc 'ool 'enter+heart' or 'believe'. The difference is phonologically and otherwise clear in the spoken Maya.

the resulting expression is *oczah ya (tu lakob)* ['put in' + 'pain' + 'to his fellows'] 'malicious gossip (troublemaker)'.

Both dictionaries cite the causative stem followed directly by *ti* plus a complement: *oczah ti alcaldeil* (unglossed in the Motul) 'elect him as alcalde', *oczah ti nohxibil* 'put one as the principal of the others', and *oczah ti almehenil* 'to induct into nobility'. The San Francisco Part 1 cites *oczah ti padreil* 'ordenar de misa' 'ordain for (celebrating) Mass' and *oczah ti testigoil* 'to present as witness'.[18] The priest who confesses someone may be said to *oczah ti confesion* 'induce him in confession' and *yoczah(on) tu yum cahlohil* 'reconcile (us) with the father of our redeemer'. If the object of 'to' is the name of any language, then the sense of the phrase is 'to translate', as in *oczah tii castillathan, maya than* 'translate (it) into Castilian, Maya', a usage cited in the Motul but absent from the San Francisco Part 1. Finally, there are a few more derived forms in the entries that are cited in the San Francisco but missing from the Motul. We have already seen the -*ben* suffix attaching to verb stems and meaning roughly '-ible/able'. The San Francisco Part 1 (270) cites *oczaben ti ol* with the meaning 'credible', *ocolal* 'belief', and *ocolalil (ix ma__)* 'infidel, infidelity (not Christian)'.

In sum, the entries derived from *oc* 'to enter, to mean' cover the sense or import of a sign, the act of accepting or acceding to another's word or purport, the sacrament of baptism, the taking up of a position, conversion and reconciliation, belief and the infidel. One is struck by the sheer economy of this semantic field, which spans *reducción* as a project designed to change the belief states, intentionality, and existential posture of the convert. So concentrated are the meanings built up on this form that any speaker who learned these entries would be well on the way to understanding the relations between these various aspects of *reducción*. For the friar, to whom the theological and semantic background of the Spanish terms was already familiar, the Maya would be mnemonically effective in its transparency and indexical binding to the religion. It would also be new in that the Maya creates associations that are missing or only latent in Spanish, for example, that believing and translating are both kinds of 'entry'. For the Indian neophyte, to whom the Maya forms would presumably be familiar or readily construable, the pairing of grammatically transparent constructions with Spanish meanings would essentially explicate the Spanish, making the otherwise daunting pedagogical task a bit easier.

Reducción and conversion had affective dimensions, as well as conceptual and behavioral ones. The convert living in *policía cristiana* would experience certain complex emotions, associated with prototypical objects and parts of the body, expressive of different states of the heart, and subject to different evaluations, as good or bad. The last two lexical items I want to examine are *ok* 'cry' and *keban* 'sadness, betrayal, sin'. Between them, these two forms are the basis of a wide range of derived expressions used to translate 'to cry, to be sad, to take pity, to be contrite, to have compunction or compassion, to repent, to be pious, to feel heavy, anxious, or remorseful, to betray'. Tears in particular have a long and deep history in Christian thought: they manifest the affective state of compunction and the spiritual state of contrition (Nagy 2000, 25), as well as mark the moment at which the believer is overcome with the presence of God and thus ready to receive him (Nagy 2000). They are an embodied metonym for piety. Before confession, the shedding of tears prepares the believer for the act of contrition, the sine qua non of reconciliation with God. In the habitus of the Christian, the shedding of tears is the corporeal manifestation of states of the heart and spirit, states that were to be aligned, ordered, and set in motion in the missionary project. Looking closely at the semantic universe of crying, we see a major part of the fine structure of this field, at once physical, emotional, and spiritual (see plate 9).

Ok (ex. 6.9): Happy Are Those Who Cry

An initial glance at ex. 6.9 indicates that the San Francisco is once again richer than the Motul, and the two differ on some key definitions. The Motul does not cite the transitive forms (causative *okzah* 'to cause to cry' and reflexive *okot ba* 'to cry [about] oneself'), concentrating instead on the intransitive stems *ookol* 'to cry' and *okom (olal)* 'pain, contrition'. By contrast, the San Francisco Part 1 cites both transitive constructions but not the simple intransitive *ookol*, nor does it gloss any of the forms as 'cry', surely the most basic sense of the root. The two are nearly complementary in this respect. At the same time, both cite *okom olal* ['cry' + 'heart' + nominal suffix] for 'contrition' and *okom ich* ['cry' + 'eye'] for 'compassion, pity'. These two compounds are morphosyntactically identical, with the verb stem in *[-om]* followed immediately by a term designating the corporeal site at which the sadness is manifest: the heart for contrition and the eyes for compassion. The *[-om]* suffix is glossed in the grammars as 'that which has to occur', a sort of obligative that in this case conveys 'he who has to cry (in the heart, in the eye)'.

Looking at the two entries as a single whole, there are four distinct stems: *ook-ol* and *ok-om*, both of which are intransitive, and *ok(e)zah* and *oko-tic, te*, both of which are transitive. The intransitive forms may both be followed by either *ol* 'heart' or *ich* 'eye', as noted just above. In this case, the body part designates the part of the person engaged in the crying or sadness of the verb root. Both dictionaries cite the form *oko ol tah* 'to repent (something), be sad (about something)'. Given its derivational pattern, this form illustrates the incorporation of the body part noun *ol* 'heart' into the verb to form a complex stem, which is then derived in *[-tah]*, just as we would expect of such noun incorporations.[19] The abstract

EXAMPLE 6.9

Okol (M:347v–348v)		'to cry'
ookol	llorar	'to cry'
ookol ich	compasión	'compassion'
ookol ool, puczikal	compunción	'compunction'
okom olal	fatiga, pena, dolor, angustia	'fatigue, pain, hurt, anxiety'
okom olal tumen keban	contrición	'contrition'
yokom olalil keban	contrición	'contrition'
okom ooltah, -te a keban	——	'repent your sins'
okomoolte unumyaa Cah Lohil	——	'repent the suffering of Our Redeemer'

Ok (SF1:271–73)		'to pity'
ok(e)zah ich, okol ich, otzilhal	tener piedad	'to have pity'
okom olal tumen keban, u yata olal puczikal	contrición	'contrition'
okom oltah, okomcunah ol, yayah ti ol	entristecerse, dolerse	'to become sad, to be in pain'
okom taben	cosa de ser dignamente llorada	'thing worthy of crying over'
ma okom taben u cimil cucut	no merece ser llorada la muerte del cuerpo	'the death of the body does not merit being cried over'
okot ba	ruego, rogar, abogar	'entreaty, request, pleading'
lay uchun uoktic in ba tech loe	por eso te ruego	'that is why I beg of you'
bin uokte in ba ti Dios ca u zatez in zipilil	vine a rogar Dios para que me perdone de mis pecados	'I have come to beg of God that he forgive me my sins'
okzah ich, okol ich, oyolal	clemencia, piedad, tener piedad	'clemency, pity, take pity (on)'
hibahun lic yokzah ich teex	no hay muchos de vosotros piadosos	'not many of you are pious'
okzah (ah __) ich	piadoso	'pious (__ person)'

noun *okom ol-al* 'pain, suffering' is consistent with the analysis of the incorporated stem *[okom ol]* as nominal, meaning roughly 'heart cry'. The two transitive forms introduce a direct object on which the act of crying is directed. With the causative stem, the object is the eye(s), just as in the parallel intransitive, and the gloss is to 'cause oneself to cry, to take pity (on)'. The agentive nominalization from this stem, *ah okzah ich*, is glossed 'pious (one who is __)'. Whereas neither dictionary specifies it, the object or person on whom one takes pity is coded with the all-purpose preposition *ti __* 'to, of__'. The final transitive stem is derived not by causativization but by an "applicative" transitive, for which the derivational suffix is *[-tah, -te]* rather than *[-zah]*. This yields *ok(o)-te* 'cry (it)', which in the examples cited is always followed by the reflexive pronoun, with the meaning 'to cry oneself, to beg'. The cause for which one cries (sin) or the recipient of the expression (God or another person) is coded as *ti__* 'to__', as in *bin uokte in ba ti Dios* 'I shall cry myself to God, beg mercy of God'.

There are further derivatives of these stems cited in the San Francisco Part 1. From *okom ol* ['cry' intrans + 'heart'] is derived *okom ol-al* 'heart cry(-inghood), pain' and *y-okom ol-al-il keban* 'its heart cry(-inghood) sin, sin's pain, contrition'. Finally, the San Francisco Part 1 also cites the derived adjective *okomtaben [okom-t-ab-(b)en]* 'cry-aspect-trans-passive-able' 'worthy of being cried over'. This form reflects a subtle and accurate understanding of an important feature of the derivational morphology of the Maya verb: an intransitive root can be transitivized, the resulting stem can be passivized, and the passive can be derived into an adjective. The cyclic application of morphological rules altering transitivity is unlike anything in Spanish but is central in the grammar of the Maya verb. Similarly, the multiple examples of noun incorporation in the entries display a solid grasp of this typically Maya grammatical pattern. The pursuit of economy and transparency demanded an impressive mastery of the Maya while at the same time embedding the affective modalities of Christian piety in the very semantics of the language.

Keban (ex. 6.10): The Sadness of the Sinner

All this crying and sadness is intimately related to sin and suffering, which are themselves construed as parts of the human condition. As the Motul (243v) puts it in the examples, *kebanchahal u beel zanzamal* 'cada día comete pecados' 'he commits sins every day' and *maax yax iliceex kebanchahal yokolcab* 'no es la primera vez que veis pecar en el mundo' 'this is not the first time you have seen (people) sin in the world'. The implication is that sin is all around us in ordinary life, as indeed it was after Eden. In the sphere of sin, the Maya is called upon to distinguish numerous types (of body, speech, intention; venial, mortal; of betrayal, debt, witchcraft). It formulates the ways to be rid of sin (to cast off, untie, wash away, repay), as well as the different affective states associated with them (remorse, sadness, suspicion, restlessness, worry). The genius of the Maya is that all these concepts are expressed in forms derived from the root *keban* 'sin'. It is derived as a verb, transitive and intransitive, as an adjective, and as an element in compounds joining it to other words. This one form therefore traces out a whole space of distinctions among interrelated meanings whose corresponding Spanish forms are mostly unrelated. The oppositions and combinations of forms are made transparent by grammatical regularity and the easy segmentability of the Maya constructions. The Maya is, literally, a systematic analysis of sin and the experience of sin, guided by the principles of transparency and indexical binding to the Christianizing project. The resulting list is extraordinarily detailed (see plate 10).

The easiest way to bring order to the mass of information displayed in ex. 6.10 from the Motul and the San Francisco Part 1 is to work from the morphosyntactic structure of the Maya forms. When preceded immediately by a verb root, the noun *keban* 'sin' functions as an underlying object: *choch keban* ['untie' + 'sin'] 'confess, absolve', *tohpul keban* ['straight throw' + 'sin'] 'confess', *pul keban* ['cast' + 'sin'] 'betray by consorting with the enemy', *poc keban* ['wash' + 'sin'] 'confess', *bool keban* ['pay' + 'sin'] 'perform penance', *pak keban* ['plant' + 'sin'] 'fornicate'. When the noun is followed by *ol* 'heart', the resulting compound *keban ol(al)* designates 'bad conscience, suspicion, remorse'. Followed by *than* 'speech' in *kebanthan* ['sin' + 'speech'], it designates 'betrayal, plans made to do evil, calumny'. Followed by the intransitive verb *cuxtal* 'live', it yields *kebancuxtal* ['sin' + 'live'] 'to live in misery and travail'. These compound noun forms are then further derivable, as in *kebanooltzil* ['sin' + 'heart' + adj. suffix] 'something worthy of being sad about, something done against the will'.

The simple noun may be modified by preceding adjectives, a grammatical resource used productively by the San Francisco Part 1 (187–88): *ahaubil keban* ['ultimate' + 'sin'] 'mortal sin', *uchacil keban* ['reddest' + 'sin'] 'grave sin', *zal keban* ['light' + 'sin'] and *mehen keban* ['young' + 'sin'] 'venial sin', *zihnal keban* ['birth' + 'sin'] 'original sin'. The Motul achieves a similar typological effect using the possessive phrase in *u keban aakab* ['its sin' + 'night'] 'sins of the night' (as in orgiastic parties), *ukebanil ocol* ['its sin' + 'theft'] 'the sin of theft', *ukebanil tzicbail* ['its sin' + 'pride'] 'the sin of pride', *ukebanil ueyuncil* ['its sin' + 'cohabitation'] 'the sin of cohabitation (without marriage)'. Between the use of prenominal adjectives and possessive structures, it is possible to construct a nearly limitless typology of sins, which the missionaries certainly would have used in the course of teaching and taking confessions.

There are three morphological patterns for deriving *keban* into a verb, two intransitive and one transitive. The first of the intransitive forms is *kebanchahal* ['sin' + *chah* + *al*] 'to become sinful, sad', as in *kebanchahal beel* ['become sin' + 'deeds'] 'commit sins' and *kebanchahal pukzikal* ['become sin' + 'heart'] 'become sad, heartsick'. These are all cited in the Motul. The second intransitive formation

EXAMPLE 6.10

Keban (M:243r–243v)

keban	pecado en general	'sin in general'
u keban aakab	pecados que se hacen de noche como convites	'sins committed at night as guests'
ukebanil ocol	pecado de hurto	'sin of theft'
ukebanil tzicbail	pecado de soberbia	'sin of pride'
ukebanil ueyuncil	pecado de amancebamientos	'sin of cohabitation'
kebantah, -te	pecar, hacer pecado	'to sin, to commit a sin'
tzicbail ukebantah cizinoob	soberbia fue el pecado de los demonios	'pride was the sin of the devils'
cooil u kebantah Juan	vicio de carne fueron los pecados de Juan	'vices of the flesh were the sins of Juan'
yan in kebantic xiblal	he pecado con un hombre	'I have sinned with a man'
keban	con desasosiego, inquietud	'with restlessness, disquiet'
keban u chictahal ixim ten	con inquietud hallo el maíz pensando que lo tengo que pagar	'with unease I find the corn, thinking I will have to pay for it'
kebanal ool, kebanal olah	inquieto de conciencia, sospechoso, receloso	'of restless conscience, suspicious, distrustful'
kebanal yolah tzucachiloob	así tiene remordimiento el lujurioso	'thus the lustful have remorse'
kebanal olal	aquella inquietud y congoja, remordimiento o escrúpulo de conciencia	'that disquiet and anguish, remorse or scruples of the conscience'
licil u choobaol tii keban olal	con lo que se limpia la (mala) conciencia	'with which the bad conscience is cleansed'
tukamah u cucutil yumilbil tii yan keban olal tu puczikal	recibió el cuerpo del señor con mala conciencia	'he received the body of the lord with a bad conscience'
kebanooltzil	cosa lastimosa y digna de sentirse	'a pitiable thing, worthy of sadness'
kebanooltzil yilabal u beel ah cizinil thanoob	lastimosa cosa es ver lo que hacen los idólatras	'it is pitiful to see what the idolaters do'
kebanooltzil u cocintabal ix maayum ix maanaa	lastimosa cosa es, cargo de conciencia es ser injuriados o maltratados los huérfanos	'it is pitiful, a burden to the conscience for orphans to be cursed or ill treated'

kebanooltzil in bootic in ppax	de mala gana y contra mi voluntad pago mis deudas	'with ill will and against my will I pay my debts'
kebancuxtal	vivir con miserias y trabajos	'to live in misery and travail'
kebancuxaan	el que vive así con miserias	'he who lives so, in misery'
kebanchahal u beel zanzamal	cada día comete pecados	'every day he commits sins'
maax yax iliceex kebanchahal yokolcab	no es la primera vez que veis pecar en el mundo	'it's not the first time you've seen sinning in the world'
kebanchahal puczikal		'be very sad or receive great sin'
kebanchahal ucah in puczikal cimci inyum	mucho siento la muerte de mi padre	'I am very sad over the death of my father'
bacacix zanzamal kebanil yoloob maaix chalan keban tucul yoloob tumen maail utz u beeloobe, etc.	aunque cada día les remuerde la conciencia y no tienen quietud por sus malas obras, etc.	'even though every day their conscience is unsettled and they have no peace because of their bad deeds, etc.'
keban uool tumen in ppax maa in boote	estoy inquieto y con escrúpulo de conciencia por las deudas que no he pagado	'I am restless and with pangs of conscience for the debts I have not paid'
in kati ualab in than u kebanmaa uool, u kebanmaa in tucul, tin hanal, tin uenel uaix tin ximbal	quiero decir lo que me trae inquieto y desasosegado, comiendo, durmiendo y andando	'I mean what leaves me restless and anxious, eating, sleeping, and walking about'
keban ool	el que tiene sospecha de otro	'he who is suspicious of another'
keban uool tech	sospecha y recelo tengo de ti	'I am suspicious and wary of you'
kebanthan	concertar para hacer algún mal y el tal concierto	'to agree to do some evil and such agreement'
yan ua a kebanthan tii chhuplal binil a uutzcinic la uac tii kebanil?	¿por ventura haste concertado con alguna mujer para cometer algún pecado?	'by chance, have you conspired with some woman to commit some sin?'
yutzcinah u kebanthan ca u conah cah lohil	hizo o cometió traición y vendió a Nuestro Redentor. De aquí sale:	'he committed betrayal and sold Our Redeemer. From this we get:'
kebanthanil	traición	'betrayal'
kebanthanil cimzah	matar a traición	'kill by betrayal'
kebanthan	calumniar	'to calumniate'

(continued)

EXAMPLE 6.10 (continued)

Keban (M:243r–243v) (continued)

		'sin, sadness, anxiety, anger, betrayal' (continued)
kebanthan ucah ten	ándame calumniando	'he goes around calumniating me'
pul keban (M:385r)	cometer traición yendose secretamente a los enemigos	'commit betrayal going secretly among the enemies'
boolkeban (M:055r)	penitencia	'penitence'
choch keban (M:145r)	confesar los pecados, absolverlos, y la tal confesión y absolución	'confess sins, absolve them, and that confession and absolution'
benel incah tii choch keban	voy a confesarme	'I am going to confess'
tu chochah in keban padre	———	'Father absolved my sins'
tu chochahen padre tin keban	———	'Father absolved me of my sins'
ah choch keban, ah choch tukeban	el que se confiesa	'he who confesses'
chochaan inzipil, in keban	ya estoy confesado o absuelto de mis pecados	'I am already confessed or absolved of my sins'
chochaan	cosa que está desatada	'something that is untied'
chochaan u beeloob tu men obispo	están descasados por el obispo	'they are unmarried (annulled) by the bishop'
chochaan u cunyah Juan	deshecho está el encantamiento de Juan o el hechizo que había hecho	'the enchantment or the spell that Juan had cast is undone'
choch beel	descasar, deshacer el casamiento	'to unmarry, to undo marriage'
choch can, choch numyaa, choch than	contar quejas, miserias y trabajos	'to tell complaints, miseries, and travails'
choch cuntah, -te, choch cunyah	desencantar lo encantado o deshechizar	'to disenchant the enchanted or to lift a spell'
choch kaxthan, choch mocthan, choch nuchthan	deshacer el concierto hecho	'to undo a previous agreement'
chochobil, u chochobil keban	absolución del pecador	'absolution of the sinner'

Keban (SF1:187–88)

keban, tanal, zipil	pecado	'sin'
maa kebantic a numya	no tomes los trabajos por ocasión de pecar	'don't take work as an opportunity to sin'
keban uol tumen in ppax	estoy triste por mis deudas	'I am sad because of my debts'

pak keban	pecado de fornicación	'sin of fornication'
ixppen	pecador sodomita	'sodomizer'
paklam hay	pecado entre mujer y mujer	'sin between women'
ahaubil keban	pecado mortal	'mortal sin'
uyail keban, u chacil keban	pecado grave	'grave sin'
zal keban, mehen keban	pecado venial	'venial sin'
zihnal keban	pecado original	'original sin'
ah tam keban	grande pecador	'(a) great sinner'
toplom it, toplom chun	pecado de sodomia *ad invicem*	'sin of sodomizing one another'
keban (ah ___)	pecador	'sinner'
keban (ixma ___)	inocente	'innocent'
keban chahal	pecar	'to sin'
kebanhal yol	tener pesar o inquietud de conciencia	'to have heaviness or disquiet of conscience'
keban olal, tuclac tumen zipil, mumudznac puczikal, xot kin lobil naat	inquieto, remordimiento de conciencia, conciencia mala	'disquiet, remorse of conscience, bad conscience'
keban than	traición	'betrayal'
tohpultah, tohcabtah, tohpul keban, choch keban (SF1:343)	confesarse, confesión	'to confess, confession'
tohpulte a keban, chocho a keban, utzcin a keban pulyah, uay (SF1:307) ...*	confiésate	'confess'
	emponzoñar, hechizar	'to poison, bewitch'
	...	—
bool keban, poc keban, pocancil keban yokol, poc tanal (SF1:34)	pagar pecados (pasados)	'to pay for (past) sins'
bool keban, utzcinah uyaal tulul keban (SF1:35)	hacer penitencia	'to do penance'
bool (ah ___) keban	penitenciado	'penitent'

*Several types are omitted here.

is cited only in the San Francisco Part 1. It is *kebanhal ol* ['sin'+ *hal* + 'heart']
'to be heavy with bad conscience'. Finally, the transitive form *keban-tah, tic*
['sin' + trans] is cited in both works with the gloss 'to sin'.

It is unclear to me whether the form *keban* existed in Maya outside the *reducción*, and if so, what semantic range it had. Occurrences in the Books of Chilam
Balam suggest that the compound *kebanthan* may have been used for something
like 'betrayal', but it is certain that most of the forms cited above were generated from the joining of Christian belief with Maya language. The specifically
Christian categories of sin, remorse, heaviness of heart, and bad conscience
echo the attention paid to crying and its relation to piety in the earlier example
of *ok* 'to cry'. Moreover, the betrayal sense—if it existed independently in un-
Christianized Maya—is swept up in the same network of associations. Note in
the examples that the Motul (243v) illustrates *kebanthan* 'betrayal' with 'the
selling of Our Savior', presumably referring to Judas's betrayal of Christ. This
demonstrates one of the common patterns of change that Maya underwent in
the *reducción*: preexisting expressions were redefined and integrated into a range
of relatively fixed phrases indexically bound to Christian referents. The expressions designating confession are especially suggestive in this regard. *Tohpultah* is
glossed as 'confession' in the San Francisco Part 1, whereas it literally means only
'to cast straight, speak truthfully', without any mention of 'sin'. The reference to
the Catholic sacrament and sin is implicit but can be made transparent in the
compounded form *tohpul keban* 'truthfully tell sin', which is epitomized in the
sinner's declaration in the confessional. *Chochkeban*, on the other hand, designates what the priest does; he 'unties sin' through absolution. In other words,
these collocations are derived according to standard Maya morphosyntax, using
preexistent elements but producing new, semantically specialized expressions.
The emotions of anxiety, sadness, and heaviness of heart would of course be
associated with sin only if the sinner had the Christian disposition to regret the
sinful action. The subject projected by this lexical field is not a happily sinning
bon vivant but a guilt-ridden, remorseful betrayer of God's promise.

. . .

The Motul and the San Francisco Part 1 display an acute metalinguistic awareness of Maya on the part of the missionary *lenguas*. They clearly understood
such exotic grammatical patterns as noun incorporation and the cyclic application of rules deriving transitives, causatives, passive stems, and adjectives. By
manipulating these processes, they were able to create compound and complex
forms that both expressed key concepts and displayed their relatedness. In this
sense, the Maya forms that are the matrix headwords in these dictionaries are
more transparent to the relations between baptism, belief, conversion, and so
forth, than were the corresponding Spanish terms. It is the conceptual back-

ing of the Spanish terms, more than their grammatical composition, that the Maya conveyed. Commensuration proceeds by way of conceptual analysis. There is little question that some of the resulting hybrids were neologisms, whereas others appear to have been serendipitous parallels between word formation in Maya and concept formation in the *reducción*. The tension between improvisation and fidelity to the Maya is in play throughout all four of the dictionaries. The language is being remade in the process, into a bilingual hybrid in which grammatical forms in Maya are associated with concepts from Spanish. Notice that this is the opposite of what the received model of syncretism suggests: rather than a European overlay on an indigenous core meaning, the *lengua reducida* paired indigenous signifiers with European concepts. Ultimately, even if they achieved a high degree of fidelity to Maya grammar, this interpretance required improvisation, and the resulting signs were neologisms.

Comparison of these two dictionaries provides strong evidence that they were related to one another and to the Vienna and the San Francisco Part 2. Taken as a set, the four works demonstrate that by the time of their writing, the lexical semantics of *Maya reducido* had stabilized to a high degree. Just as we would expect from the recopying, traveling, and collective labor of analysis by *lenguas* and their Maya assistants, the language of these dictionaries is the product of an already rich history. In the universe of *Maya reducido,* each of the contributing languages was already turned toward the other. The resulting hybridity was therefore not the product of combining two entirely separate languages but of fusing languages already adjusting to one another. Although Maya is the matrix language for the Motul and the San Francisco Part 1, it is a Maya already aligned to the conceptual background of the *reducción.* By creating the phrase *oc ha* 'enter water' to designate baptism, for instance, the friars inserted this sacrament into a semantic field that also generated the means of designating conversion *(oczah ba),* belief *(ocol ol),* and election to status or office *(ocçic ti).* The process became rapidly circular because the Maya forms aligned with Spanish concepts changed in meaning as a result, just as the Spanish concepts were effectively interpreted and given new semantic associations by their Maya renderings. Once this process of coarticulation was set in motion, the languages were never again entirely distinct.

The Grammar of *Reducción*
and the Art of Speaking

Although dictionaries were initially related to *artes,* the two genres present many contrasts. The colonial Maya *arte* is a published work by a named author, endorsed in a series of approvals and licenses by named individuals at stated dates and places, and appearing under a title page stating the year and place it was made final by the press. An unpublished work may remain open-ended, whereas one that has been vetted and printed is complete. The kind of information in the two genres is also different. The dictionary aligns the semantics of expressions in the two languages, creating a relation of partial equivalence. By contrast, the *arte* states the regularities immanent in a single language. The bilingual dictionary is reversible, and either language can serve as matrix. In a grammatical description, the relation between the matrix language and the object language is irreversible. The *artes* of Coronel (1998 [1620]), San Buenaventura (1888 [1684]), and Beltrán (2002 [1746]) are all written in Spanish (matrix language) about Maya (object language). One cannot reverse the parts and come up with *artes* in Maya about Spanish. The grammar is focused on the principles of form and construction that either are immanent in the object language or should be normatively followed in speaking it. Since the project of *reducción* was to produce a new version of Maya, not a new version of Spanish, Maya is always the normativized object language of grammar. The *artes* were also pedagogical tools used in the classroom, whereas there is no evidence the dictionaries were so used. Finally, the *artes* fit Maya into categories derived directly from Latin, whereas the dictionaries are immediately focused on the relation between Maya and Spanish. For these several reasons, the *arte* genre is distinctive, and individual *arte* works are relatively autonomous in relation to dictionaries and other aspects of missionary linguistics.

This relative autonomy is offset by the fact that the *arte* presupposes and is partly shaped by the lexical and semantic knowledge embodied in the dictionary. The two are mutually necessary. One cannot understand any of the dictionaries without sufficient knowledge of grammar to parse the entries. The objectives of economy and transparency could be approximated only if one put grammatical processes to good use in formulating Maya constructions. Similarly, one cannot make sense of the *arte* without some understanding of the Maya expressions that its rules describe. That understanding is what the dictionary codifies. Moreover, both the dictionaries and the *artes* are oriented to the *doctrina*. They draw many of their examples from the catechism and confessional, which in turn put both kinds of linguistic knowledge to use in the service of religious instruction. Knowledge of grammar, however imperfect, was dispersed through the other genres. The autonomy of the *arte* is therefore in tension with its opposite: to a significant degree, works in the genre are shaped by knowledge and language derived from other genres. In short, the colonial *arte* is a discrete genre, but one deeply embedded in the broader field of missionary discourse production and hybridized as a result.

The historical sources suggest that at least one *arte* was produced during the first wave of *reducciones* in the mid-sixteenth century. Landa described Villalpando as the first to reduce Maya to *"alguna manera de arte . . . que se estudiava como la Latina"* 'a sort of *arte* . . . which was studied like the Latin' (cited by Acuña 1996, 18). Cogolludo also reports that Villalpando *"en breuissimo tiempo reduxo el idioma de estos Indios à reglas ciertissimas, y ordenò un Arte para aprenderle, hablando con gran propriedad"* 'in little time reduced the idiom of these Indios to certain rules, and ordered an *Arte* for learning it, speaking with great propriety' (also cited by Acuña 1996, 18). Villalpando's work was never published and has been lost, but it is likely that Coronel had access to it in the early seventeenth century as he wrote his own *arte*. Over the first two hundred years of the colony, three *artes* of Maya were published, of which Coronel's was the first:

Arte en lengua de maya, fray Juan Coronel (1620)

Arte de la lengua maya, fray Gabriel de San Buenaventura (1684)

Arte de el Idioma Maya reducido a succintas reglas, y Semilexicón yucateco, fray Pedro Beltrán de Santa Rosa María (1746)

These three works come at intervals of about sixty years; even Coronel's work was composed about sixty years after the first major wave of alphabetic writing of Maya in the mid-sixteenth century. It is entirely likely that in the intervening years fragments of grammars were developed by gifted *lenguas,* but the published works provided the uniformity of master texts for use in the language classes in the convents. That they appear at such regular intervals might indicate the missionaries considered this the appropriate life span of such texts.

WHAT IS AN *ARTE*?

The *Diccionario de Autoridades* has nine separate headings for the term *arte,* the first four of which have to do not with language but with skill more generally. The first entry defines it as *"La facultad que prescribe reglas y preceptos para hacer rectamente las cosas"* 'The faculty that prescribes rules and precepts for doing things correctly' (*Dic. Autor.* 1:422). The fifth entry states, *"Se llama tambien el mismo libro en que están escritas las reglas y preceptos del arte. Por antonomásia se llama assi el de Nebrixa, en que se contienen las reglas de la Grammática. Lat."* 'The very book in which the rules and precepts of the *arte* are written is also called *[arte].* By antonomasia, the one of Nebrija is called thus *[arte],* in which are contained the rules of Latin grammar'. The subsequent entries shift back from language to artful or skillful knowledge and the manner in which actions are executed. Interestingly, the *Diccionario* cites the term *Arte de las artes,* which was applied to *"política y razón del estádo, ò sea el arte de reinar"* 'policies and reason of the state, that is, the *arte* of rule' (*Dic. Autor.* 1:423). The *arte* as it was used by missionary *lenguas* in Yucatán descends directly from this broader European background. The link to Nebrija is especially direct, since his *Introducciones latinas* (ca. 1488) sets out much of the template that recurs in the Maya *artes.* The relation between skillfulness and the rule of the state recalls the duality of *reducción* as a process of governance and a process of analysis.

When we look to the term *Gramática* in the *Diccionario de Autoridades,* the affinity between this genre and the business of *reducción* is even more evident.

> *GRAMATICA. f.f, El arte de bien hablar y escribir. Es comun à todas las Lénguas, y particular à cada una, y principio y fundamento de todas las ciencias. Enseña la pronunciacion de las letras, la declinacion de los nombres, la conjugacion de los verbos, la construccion de las partes de la oración, el sonido y accento diverso de las palabras, la distincion de las vocales y consonantes, y la orden de hablar con propriedad, pureza y policía.*
>
> (Dic. Autor. 4:71)

> Grammar, feminine. The art of speaking and writing well. It is common to all languages and particular to each one, the principle and basis of all sciences. It teaches pronunciation of the letters, the declension of the nouns, the conjugation of the verbs, the construction of the parts of the utterance, the diverse sound and accent of words, the distinction between vowels and consonants, and the order of speaking with propriety, purity, and *policía.*

The first point to note here is that grammar is defined as an *arte* in the sense of speaking and writing *well.* Early modern and classic grammars were prescriptive rather than descriptive. Like the contemporary linguist, the grammarian posited by the *Diccionario de Autoridades* takes "grammar" to be universal because all languages have it, yet particular because each language has its own version. The missionaries met Maya on this same footing, drawing on both their knowledge of grammar as universal, that is, Latin, and their knowledge of Maya as particular. The parts of the *Gramática* listed above will also recur in both Nebrija's Latin grammar and the missionary studies of Maya. The final reference to orderly speech is a near-gloss of correct speech under *reducción:* proper, pure, and with *policía.* The term *Gramática* was also used to designate the study of Latin (*Dic. Autor.* 4:71), a connection with obvious historical roots in the classical tradition.[1] The related term *Gramático* is glossed as 'he who studies or knows or has studied *Gramática*', of whom Nebrija is cited as exemplary.

THE SHADOW OF NEBRIJA

In order to write an *arte,* one needs a metalanguage of grammatical terms and a schema in which to present the regularities of the object language. For these things, the missionaries looked to their training in Latin *grammatica.* Antonio de Nebrija's *Introducciones latinas contrapuesto el romance al latin* (ca. 1488) provides an authoritative statement of the primary model. In this work, Nebrija defines the parts of speech according to the classical model: *nombre, pronombre, verbo, participio, preposición, adverbio, interjección, conjuncción* (Esparza and Calvo 1996, 35). In the Maya *artes,* the nouns are largely ignored and the pronouns presented first, followed by verbs and participles, adverbs, and long lists of particles. Thus the overall division and order of parts is similar.[2]

Nebrija's work is organized into five books, of which the third is entirely in the form of pedagogical dialogue, strongly reminiscent of the doctrinal dialogues of the Maya catechisms (see chapter 8). It defines the basic grammatical terminology that is also used in the Maya *artes.* Consider the following:

NEBRIJA'S METALINGUISTIC DIALOGUE

Quantos son les generos de los uerbos?
Cinco: actiuo, passiuo, neutro, deponente, comun

Qual es el uerbo activo?
El que acaba en '-o' y tiene passiuo en '-or', como yo amo, yo so amado

Qual es el passiuo?
El que acaba en '-or' y tiene actiuo en '-o' como yo so amado, de amo

[. . .]

Quantos son los modos de los uerbos?
Cinco: indicatiuo, imperatiuo, optatiuo, subiunctiuo, infinitiuo
      (Esparza and Calvo 1996: 110)

How many are the types of verbs?
Five: active, passive, neutral, dependent, common

Which is the active verb?
The one that ends in '-o' and has a passive in '-or', like I love, I am loved

Which is the passive?
The one that ends in '-or' and has an active in '-o', like I am loved, from I love

[...]

How many are the modes of the verbs?
Five: Indicative, imperative, optative, subjunctive, infinitive

The terms "active," "passive," and "neutral" are common in the Maya *artes*, with meanings similar to those given by Nebrija. They designate verb classes according to what a modern linguist would call transitivity: active means transitive; passive is derived from the transitive; and neutral verbs, being intransitive, have no passive form. The difficulty for the missionaries was that in Maya there are other values for transitivity.[3] In particular, there are what linguists call middle voice forms (as in English "the sale items sold well"), objectless forms ("the pool player broke"), and noun-incorporated forms ("to sandblast," "to wallpaper"). All of these have distinct paradigms in Maya, with no obvious analogues in Latin. To their credit, the missionaries noted several of the patterns involved with these exotic facts, but the Latin template nonetheless obfuscates the Maya regularities.

Nebrija presents Latin verbs in terms of four verb conjugations (plus the irregulars), and the Maya *artes* distinguish four conjugations. The problem is that the Latin ones make linguistic sense, whereas the Maya do not. The Latin conjugations are as follows.

NEBRIJA'S FOUR CONJUGATIONS OF LATIN

Conjugation 1   *amo, amas, amar* 'to love'
Conjugation 2   *doceo, doces, docere* 'to teach'
Conjugation 3   *lego, legis, legere* 'to rule'
Conjugation 4   *audio, audis, audire* 'to hear'

The corresponding Maya conjugations are based on the verbs (1) *nacal* 'to ascend', (2) *cambeçah* 'to teach', (3) *tzic* 'to obey', and (4) *canan* 'to guard'. By a curious transposition, the second and third conjugations in Maya are thematically related to their Latin analogues, but the grammatical basis of the classes is entirely different. As we will see, the proposed Maya verb classes are only partly coherent, and the missionaries' assumption of four conjugations led them to overlook important facts or give them short shrift. The Maya form for 'teach' in conjugation 2 is a derived causative (< *can* 'learn' + *zah* 'cause'), whereas the others are root forms, which makes the comparison difficult. In Maya, there are also special classes of stems left out of this schema, including positional verbs (*cul-uc-bal* 'to be seated') and deverbal adjectives (*dzan-dzan-cil* 'spongy', *ku-kup kil* 'stuffy'). And because some of the categories are ill defined, the *artes* make false generalizations. For example, Coronel states rules applying to verbs ending in -*tal,* but his rules apply only to some verbs ending in -*tal;* others follow entirely different principles, because this presumed suffix is not actually an accurate indicator of class membership.

The five modes (indicative, imperative, subjunctive, optative, infinitive) all appear in the *artes,* mostly in the order cited by Nebrija. They apply awkwardly to Maya, however, since the supposed subjunctive and optative stem shapes are not distinguished in Maya, the imperative also overlaps with them, and there is no obvious analogue of the Latin infinitive form. Because the categories did not translate well to the indigenous language, the missionaries rendered them with phrases comprising a verb stem plus a preverbal particle. This strategy permitted the *lengua* missionary to work through a series of verb modes from Latin—a familiar metalinguistic template—in the decidedly unfamiliar terrain of Maya. This produced a transparency effect, since the Maya was compositional, apparently regular, and nicely fitted to the Latin template. At the same time, however, it sacrificed fidelity to the Maya, since so much of the verbal morphosyntax is left out of those categories or distorted when represented through them.

FRAY JUAN CORONEL, *ARTE EN LENGUA DE MAYA* (1620)

The earliest extant *arte* of Maya was Coronel's, which was published along with his *doctrina* and sermons in 1620. Having examined the front matter of this published opus and known details of Coronel's life in chapter 4, here I want to focus on how Coronel codifies the language and what this tells us about *Maya reducido.* I start with a brief summary of ways his work misrepresents the languages by imposing the Latin template or simply by overlooking facts of Maya. As it is the first *arte,* I will examine it more closely than the other two.

Among the features of Maya that are left out or misanalyzed in Coronel's *arte* are the following. (1) The sequential ordering of person suffixes in Maya follows the hierarchy first person < second person < third person (where '<' indicates 'precedes'), although this is never mentioned.[4] (2) The combination of first-person plural and second-person plural pronouns yields inclusive first person (-*on-ex* 'we', meaning 'you all plus me') but is never mentioned. (3) Derived possessive pronouns (*intial, atial,* 'mine, yours', etc.) and lexical pronouns (*ten, tech* 'I, you', etc.) are both transparently derived from the relational particle *ti* 'to, for, from, in', but this relation is missed by Coronel. (4) Coronel's attempt to translate the present indicative into Maya with the periphrastic schema [verb pronoun -*cah*] as in *nacal in cah* 'I ascend' causes severe confusion. For one thing, this formation is a progressive (as in "I am ascending"), not a simple present. There is no simple present in the language. For another, this progressive is a marked structure that occurs only with intransitive verbs. Since the four conjugations include transitives as well as intransitives, the paradigms are muddled. Finally, because the person marking in *cah* clauses attaches to the *cah* element and not to the main lexical verb (hence *nacal in cah,* not **in nacal cah*), Coronel erroneously concludes that the pronoun follows the main verb. In fact, it is actually prefixal to the auxiliary. This is a very basic misconstrual of the Maya. (5) Coronel's attachment to the Latin template leads him to miss the enormous class of positional verbs in Maya.[5] These verbs, which designate the positions and dispositions of bodies, have highly distinctive paradigms and ought to be a conjugation class. Instead, they are mixed in with the other conjugations.[6]

This list could be extended and surely refined. The essential point is not to criticize Coronel for the infelicities of his *arte* but to highlight some consequences of using the Latin template. Despite the distortion that this inevitably produced, Coronel's work manages to describe a great deal of the grammar of Maya. Moreover, the use of example sentences gives evidence that many of the phenomena left out of the explanatory portions of the work were nonetheless familiar to the *lenguas.* Coronel accurately describes at least two ways to derive transitives (via causativization and simple transitives), noun incorporation, passive formation, several forms of complementation, and numerous particles. All these were used in the dictionaries. It is also important to recognize that the *arte* is not a proxy for missionary knowledge of Maya. The analytic work of formulating the rules of a grammar is different from the interactive work of producing and understanding utterances in the language. The two kinds of knowledge are distinct, and two equally competent speakers of Maya could produce *artes* with widely differing degrees of accuracy. It is therefore understandable that both the dictionaries and the *artes* contain examples whose form is not explained by the rules proposed in the *arte.* It is also plausible to assume that some of the inconsistencies in the *artes* are the result of copying from multiple sources. Even Coronel, whose 1620 *arte* was the first to be published, states that he has copied from the work of the earlier *lenguas.*

The Pronoun System

Coronel describes the Maya pronoun system in terms of three series, which he labels first, second, and third. All three distinguish three persons (I, you, he) and two numbers (singular, plural). The series are readily distinguished from one another by their forms as well as by their functions. The first is prefixal, and when attached to a verb, these forms mark subject as in *in-bin* 'I go', *in-tzicbal*

'I converse'.[7] When affixed to a noun, the same forms mark the possessor, as in *in-yum* 'my father', *in-keban* 'my sin'. The series is displayed in table 8. In both functions, the plural markers *ex, ob* for second and third person follow the element to which they attach, resulting in the discontinuous person marking as in *a-bin-ex* 'you (pl) go'. Coronel notes correctly that the first series pronouns have special alternates when they prefix to a noun or verb that begins in a vowel, as in *v-auat* 'my voice', *u-ol* 'my heart', *y-ol Juan* 'Juan's heart', *v-ohel, au-ohel, y-ohel padre* 'I know, you know, father knows'.

TABLE 8 *Primeros pronombres* 'first pronouns'

in	'I'	*ca*	'we'
a	'you'	*a . . . ex*	'you (pl)'
v	'he, she, it'	*v . . . ob*	'they'

SOURCE: Acuña 1998, 49.

The reflexive pronouns, which Coronel calls "reciprocals," are formed by prefixing series 1 pronouns to the root *bah* 'self', as in *in-cimçah in-ba* 'I killed myself', *u-cimçah u-ba* 'he killed himself', and *a-cimçah a-ba-ex* 'you (pl) killed yourselves'. Rather than devote a separate series to the reflexives or the prevocalic forms, Coronel groups them both under the first series. This captures the appropriate generalization that they are all based on the same prefixal series and that the supposed reflexive pronoun in Maya is actually a possessed noun.

The second series are suffixed to verbs and nouns to mark either (1) the subject of neutral verbs (intransitives) in the preterite perfect and all nonindicative verb stems, as in *bin-en* 'I went', *nac-ex* 'you (pl) ascended', or (2) the patient, where Spanish (or English) would use accusative case morphology/spelling changes. Thus a suffixed *-ex* may be either a subject or an object, depending on the verb, as in *a-cimçah-ex-ob* 'you (pl) killed them', *u-canantah-ex-ob* 'they guarded you (pl)'. The forms are set out in table 9. Note that there is no third-person singular (he, she, it), which is simply null.

TABLE 9 *Secundos pronombres* 'second pronouns'

en	'I'	*on*	'we'
ech	'you'	*ex*	'you (pl)'
—	'he, she, it'	*ob*	'they'

SOURCE: Acuña 1998, 50.

Coronel's third series are neither prefixes nor suffixes but rather independent words. These are used in reference to the subject or the object, preposed to the verb as in *ten tu hadzah* 'I (am the one whom) he struck', *tech cin payic* 'to you I call out'. Although Coronel does not say so, the examples just cited are special focus forms, to which the corresponding plain forms are *tu-hadzah-en* 'he struck me' and *cin-payic-ech* 'I call you'. He also fails to mention an important asymmetry between the first and second persons and the third: the former can also be used for dative, *cindzaic tech* 'I give it to you', whereas the third person cannot: **cin dzaic lay* 'I give it to him' is ungrammatical.[8]

TABLE 10 *Terceros pronombres* 'third pronouns'

ten	'I'	*toon*	'we'
tech	'you'	*teex*	'you (pl)'
lay	'he, she, it'	*loob*	'they'

SOURCE: Acuña 1998, 50.

Coronel does not remark on the fact that the first- and second-person forms in this series are obviously derived by attaching the suffixal pronouns (series 2) to the prepositional particle *t(i)-* 'to, for, at, from'. This same preposition marks dative case, and that is why the first and second person can be used in that function, but the third not. The third-person forms are actually demonstratives, recruited to fill in the hole left by the absence of third-person pronouns based on *ti.* Coronel also omits what is arguably a fourth series based on the particle *c-,* as in *c-en* 'I who am', *c-ech* 'you who are', and so on. These forms are common in the first and second person in the colonial corpus, and they come up in Coronel's example sentences, indicating that he clearly knew them. Like the possessive forms for 'mine, yours, his, ours, theirs', they are listed in the dictionaries and used in the examples, but none of the colonial grammars treats them as a stand-alone series. This complementarity between the dictionaries and the *artes* is striking: the dictionaries list the *c-en, c-ech* series and the nominalized possessives, whereas the grammars do not; inversely, the grammars present the main series of pronouns, whereas the dictionaries do not mention them. The San Francisco Part 1 has no entry for *ba,* meaning 'self', but the Motul lists it and defines it as the reciprocal pronoun, clearly taking it to be the noun on which the series is based. The Motul analysis is consistent with Coronel, and we can see the degree to which the dictionary and the *arte* presupposed one another.

In general, Coronel gives an accurate, although incomplete description of person marking in Maya. By collapsing the preconsonantal and prevocalic variants of the prefixal forms into a single series (first) and then deriving the reciprocals from this via possession of the root -*ba* 'self', he nicely captures the correct generalization. On these points, Coronel moves beyond the Latin template and characterizes the Maya with impressive economy. Perhaps because the *arte* is a pedagogical instrument and the chapters on pronouns come at the very beginning of the work, he does not delve into more advanced features of the Maya system. For instance, the third series actually has one more form that Coronel omitted: *t-on-ex* 'us (me and you pl)'. This form is used when the speaker explicitly includes himself or herself along with two or more addressees, as when addressing a group. Furthermore, because suffixal pronouns are used to mark both the plurality of the subject and the direct object of the transitive verb, there is a whole class of forms with two suffixal pronouns, as in *a bisic-ex-ob* 'you (pl) bring them' and *a cambeçah-on-ex* 'you (pl) taught us'. In effect, any time a transitive verb has a plural subject and an overt object, we expect two suffixes. By simply not mentioning these, Coronel also ducks the question of what order to put them in. Note in the two examples just cited that the first person precedes the second and the second precedes the third. In the modern language this is a clear rule governing suffixal pronouns, and it is consistent with usage in Maya texts in the colonial period (for the modern system, see Hanks 1990). It is unclear whether Coronel knew the full facts about suffixal pronouns but omitted them for simplicity or whether he omitted them because he did not know them. Either way, what he does cover of the pronouns, he does very well. As we will see, San Buenaventura provides a different, less effective classification, which Beltrán will in turn follow.

The Verb System

Coronel's treatment of the verb is complicated, and I can touch only on selected aspects of it here. In what follows, I sketch out the main lines of his approach and argue that the Latin template from which he was working led him to overlook critical features of the verb system in Maya. As we have seen repeatedly, the example sentences of the *arte* and the dictionaries suggest that the missionaries knew or had access to more Maya than they could explain.

Nebrija's four-way division among Latin conjugations was apparently the model for Coronel's four-way division of the Maya. For the most part, a Latin verb's conjugation can be determined by the shape of the infinitive form and the way it conjugates in the present and perfect, as any student of a romance language knows. Evidently inspired by this model, Coronel proposed four conjugations for Maya, holding aside irregular verbs. These are displayed in table 11.[9]

Each of the columns (I–IV) in table 11 corresponds to a verb class, and the verbs shown (ascend, teach, obey, guard) are the ones Coronel uses to exemplify the conjugations. The rows display only some of the paradigmatic forms that Coronel lays out, sticking closely to the Latin verb paradigm as his model

TABLE 11 Coronel's Four Verb Conjugations

TENSE	I *NACAL* 'ASCEND'	II *CAMBEÇAH* 'TEACH'	III *TZIC* 'OBEY'	IV *CANAN* 'GUARD'
Present	*nacal a cah*	*cambezah a cah*	*tzic a cah*	*canan a cah*
Imperfect	*nacen*	*cambez*	*tzici*	*canante*
Preterite perfect	*nacech*	*a cambezah*	*a tzicah*	*a canantah*
Future	*nacacech*	*a cambez*	*a tzicib*	*a canante*
lic___*	*a nacal*	*a cambezic*	*a tzicic*	*a canantic*
		a cambezah	*a tzic*	*a canan*

SOURCE: Acuña 1998, 53–85.

*This stem shape is not included in Coronel's paradigms, although once again it is well attested in the colonial corpus. It is what modern grammarians call the "incompletive," used for reference to actions not completed at the time of speaking. Alternate forms in II–IV reflect transitive patterns (ending in *-ic*) vs. intransitive ones (ending in *ah, ø*).

(present, imperative, preterite perfect, future). Basically, conjugation I consists of simple intransitive verbs, conjugation II causative verbs, conjugation III simple transitives, and conjugation IV transitive verbs derived from nounlike stems. Coronel presents the paradigm for each conjugation in semitabular form, listing the present, preterite imperfect, preterite perfect, past perfect, future imperfect, future perfect, imperative, future imperative, optative mode, subjunctive, and infinitive (with breakdowns for tense in the last three). This organization and the grammatical labels are identical to Nebrija's paradigms in the *Introducciones latinas*. After all four paradigms are presented, Coronel goes through what he calls *excepciones* 'exceptions'.[10] These consist of lists of stems that fit the conjugations, as well as notes on apparent subclasses and some irregularities. Much of what Coronel knows of the verbs is in these notes, including subclasses of verbs that fail to fit his paradigm.[11] For instance, he illustrates the all-important incorporating verb forms, in which a noun or other element from the clause is actually incorporated into the verb, yielding a new verb stem. Among the examples already seen from the dictionaries are *chan misa* 'to mass-attend', *oc ha* 'baptism (water-enter)', *pul keban* 'confess (sin-cast off)', *dzib ol* 'desire (heart-write)', and many others. Unfortunately, he includes the incorporated forms as a subset of conjugation I, whereas this is certainly wrong (of Coronel's four conjugations, they are most similar to the fourth).

Transitivity is pervasively important in Maya and has consequences for person marking, stem formation, and voice formation, including passive ('I was seen by you' vs. 'you saw me') and objectless forms ('I sew' vs. 'I sew the shirt'). Incorporated forms are objectless, unless further derived, and they therefore interact with transitivity in a fundamental way. The forms in the bottom row were added by me and are not mentioned by Coronel, who knew of them but judged them to fall outside his paradigm. The auxiliary element *lic* marks a present/future, whose precise meaning is unclear. What is important is that in this row we see the contrast between transitive forms (ending in *-ic*) and nontransitive ones (ending in *-al, -ah,* or Ø)—thus *lic a cambezic* 'you teach him' versus *lic a cambezah* 'you teach', *lic acanantic* 'you guard it' versus *lic a canan* 'you guard'.

Coronel's conjugations begin to break down when we look at his handling of the so-called present. He faced a dilemma here, because the present tense is a basic part of the Latin paradigm, whereas there really is none in Maya. He therefore selected the periphrastic construction verb + *cah* to approximate the Latinate present. Unfortunately, the auxiliary *cah* is a highly marked progressive aspect that occurs only with intransitives, predicate adjectives, and nouns. It normally excludes transitive verbs. This then confounds Coronel's conjugations, since the transitive ones cannot occur in the supposed present. The forms Coronel cites are actually objectless (i.e., not transitive): *cambezah a cah* means 'you're teaching', not 'you're teaching him'; *tzic a cah* is 'you're obeying (being obedient)', not 'you're obeying him'. The problem is made still worse by the fact that Coronel, again following the classical model, does not mark any of his transitive forms with suffixal pronouns indexing the object. This is because, even in the clearly transitive imperatives *(cambez, tzici, canante),* he is assuming a third-person singular object, which is unmarked because the form is null (see pronoun series 2 above). It is therefore impossible to tell from the morphology whether a stem like *a cambezah* is fully transitive (you teach him/it) or objectless (you teach), because either way there is no suffix marking the object. In example sentences elsewhere in the *arte,* Coronel cites the form *cambezah a cah ti palalob* 'you are teaching to children'. Note that the preposition *ti* has been inserted, because the children are not the direct object; they are the indirect object (dative). There is no direct object in this sentence. Therefore, when Coronel works his way down the rows in conjugations II–IV, he shifts willy-nilly between transitive and intransitive verb forms.

These seemingly arcane facts of grammar and analysis fit into a more general and basic pattern. Coronel and the other *gran lenguas* knew much more Maya than they were able to explain in their linguistic works. They knew the difference between transitive (which they called active) and intransitive (which they called neutral or absolute). They were already familiar with transitivity from the Latin case declensions, where accusative marks direct object and dative marks indirect object. What they evidently failed to recognize was that the parameter is intrinsic to the verb stem classes in Maya.

A similar, less complicated example is provided by his treatment of the subjunctive and optative moods, which he dutifully distinguishes in Maya in order to fill out the paradigm from Latin. The minor problem is that in Maya the stem shapes for these two are identical in all conjugations, and economy would dictate that Coronel collapse them into a single category representing both contrary-to-fact conditions and hopes. That he does not do so is perhaps understandable because the *arte* is a teaching instrument, and missionary students brought up on Latin grammar would expect a distinction.[12] By starting from four conjugations whose first paradigmatic form is the so-called present, he makes the same attempt at transparency to Latin but with worse consequences.

The dictionaries and example sentences in the *artes* abound in passive verbs and various kinds of adjectives and nouns derived from them. As discussed in chapter 6, stems like *dzibooltabal* 'to be desired', *ocsaben ti ol* 'worthy of being believed', *xoocol* 'accent on the first syllable, to be counted, read, obeyed' (from the Motul) all demonstrate that the missionary *lenguas* understood the rules for forming passives. Coronel does a relatively good job of describing the forms, although once again his rules for formation are off base. Under the heading 'participles in -*bil*', he notes that transitive verbs *(activos)* may be derived by affixing -*bil* to the preterite stem, to yield a form meaning 'thing which is or can be X-ed', where X is a transitive verb. His illustration is given in table 12.[13] The forms listed there are correct and the glosses appropriate, at least to some uses. This pattern helps explain the analogous forms of the dictionaries, including *cambezabil uinic* 'disciple'. Coronel follows them immediately with stems in -*ben* 'worthy of being', as in *yacunaben Dios* 'God is worthy of being loved', from *yacunah* 'love'. Thus *cambezaben* 'worthy of being taught', *tzicben* 'worthy of being respected', *okomtaben* 'worthy of being lamented', all of which occur in the dictionaries.

In general, passive stems are derived from active ones in two primary ways.[14] The first is what we can call "external," where the passive morphology follows the main stem. Thus we find *cambezabal* 'is taught', *miztabal* 'is swept', *okomtabal* 'is lamented', *yacunabal* 'is loved', *canantabal* 'is guarded', and so forth. In the second pattern, the bare root is suffixed by -*Vl* (a vowel that harmonizes with the root vowel). According to this rule, we find *molol* 'is gathered', *tzicil* 'is respected', and many others. This pattern can be called "internal" insofar as the root vowel actually shifts to mark the passive, although Coronel never says as much. This shift consists in changing the root vowel from short neutral tone to high tone with glottalization. Thus, for example, from *molah* 'gather it' we derive *molbil* 'gathered' and *mó'olol* 'is gathered'. Unfortunately, Coronel makes no attempt to describe or even consistently mark tone, length, or glottalization in the vowels. Thus, although he cites the right forms, his orthography is inadequate to capture the generalization that motivates them. By contrast, the Motul correctly expresses exactly this when it distinguishes *xoc ool* 'jealousy' from *xooc ol* 'is read'.[15]

We can see in Coronel's *arte* the first major codification of Maya grammar as the missionaries understand it. That it has so much in common with both Latin and Maya as represented in the dictionaries indicates that it occupies the

TABLE 12 Coronel's Participles in *-bil**

cambeçabil	< *cambeç + abil*	'thing that is or can be taught'
miztabil	< *mizt + abil*	'thing that is or can be swept'
molbil	< *mol + bil*	'thing that is or can be gathered'
tzicbil	< *tzic + bil*	'thing that is or can be respected'
chhabil	< *chha + bil*	'thing that is or can be got'

SOURCE: Acuña 1998, 76.

*Coronel observes that the top three stems show *-abil,* whereas the bottom two show *-bil.* The *-abil* forms he attempts to derive from the past stem *(cambezah, mistah, chhah),* by deleting the *-h* and adding *-bil.* The key difference, which he essentially states, is that the forms that take *-abil* form their passives externally, whereas the ones that take *-bil* form the passive by altering the root verb.

same translingual space as the other missionary genres. That the *arte* is only partly accurate is perhaps unsurprising but still consequential, because the work was used to train missionaries in the language and because it partly guided the doctrinal translations.

Example Sentences

Coronel's example sentences provide a wealth of additional information about the *arte* genre and about the grammar of Maya. Unsurprisingly for an *arte* that was published along with a confessional manual and a catechism, there is a great deal of doctrinal language in Coronel's example sentences, especially pertaining to confession and the teachings in the schools.[16] There is also an abundance of examples in which relations with missionaries and teachers are thematized. These illustrate some of the language of social relations in the fields of the mission. There is a conspicuous lack of language from or about governance in the *pueblos reducidos,* just as there is little about agriculture and not a word about idolatry. The immediate field of routine missionary practice is foremost, as befits an instrument whose primary use was to prepare priests for ministry in the Maya-speaking *doctrinas.*

As discussed in chapters 5 and 6, confession generated a great deal of linguistic production by the *lenguas.* First, it is a complex sacrament requiring the appropriate state of mind and ways of speaking, as well as preparatory work to recall all sins and follow-through to perform the penance given by the priest. It is dialogic in that the priest asks questions and the confessee provides answers, ideally in a coherent fashion. The confessee "straight casts" his sins and the priest "unties them" through absolution. All these aspects of confession are represented in Coronel's examples, as illustrated in the following five examples (Acuña 1998, 217, 258, 217, 269, 226).

kuchan v kin a ppatic a keban
The time is arrived (for) you (to) leave behind your sin(s).

in keban lic voktic
My sin(s) (are what) I lament.

haytenhi a çipil?
How many times did you sin?

ma bahun in chochob in çipil
I have never confessed (untied) my sin(s).

bax ma avutzcinah yalah padre tech?
What have you not fulfilled (that) father told you (to)?

Alongside religious practices such as confession, mass, and communion, the missions were centers of learning. We have already seen that the verb 'teach' based on *cambez* ('cause to learn') is prominent in the dictionaries and is the prototype for Coronel's conjugation II in the verbs. The three examples that follow (Acuña 1998, 227, 217, 219) illustrate the item. Whereas the first could have been uttered by anyone, the second would be uttered only by a Maya person and the third only by a missionary.[17] The third example also showcases the great economy of the Maya verb, since both *cambalte* 'to learn it' and *ah cambezahul* 'teacher (one who causes learning)' are derived from the same root *can* 'learn' according to two patterns of transitivization: *cambalte* is in the fourth conjugation, while *ah cambezahul* is the nominalized form of the familiar causative *cambezah* in conjugation II.

mac cambeçicech?
Who is teaching it to you?

in kati a cambeçic in mehen
I want you to teach my son.

hij in cambalte maya than ca yanac vah cambeçahul cuchi
I would have learned Maya language had I had a teacher.

The teachings of the missionaries included the *arte* itself, which was used in language instruction, and the catechism, which was used to instruct Indios in Catholic practice. The three following examples (Acuña 1998, 217, 229, 240) illustrate a few ways of phrasing the basic moral that those who serve God and are good shall be rewarded ("repaid") by going to heaven.

tanle Dios vchebal a benel ti caan
Serve God in order that you (may) go to heaven.

he yutzil vinicobe bin xijcob ti caan, hex vlobil vinicobe ah çatalobilo
The good people will go to heaven, while the bad people are lost alas.

he lic vtanlic Diose, lay bin botabac loe
He who serves God, he shall be (re)paid.

The middle example above uses several formation rules explained in the *arte,* including the irregular future *bin xic* 'will go' and the nominalized passive *ah satal (sá'at-al < sat* 'to lose [something]' via internal passivization). The syntactic parallelism of the two phrases in this example is also indicative of missionary poetics in *Maya reducido.* Schematically:

he y-utzil uinicob e	the people of good
bin xijcob ti caan,	shall go to heaven
he-x v-lobil vinicob e	as the people of bad
ah çatalobil o	are lost unfortunately

In the Maya here, the first and third lines are grammatically identical except for the addition of the suffix -*x,* which merely connects the two sentences. The phonetic form *lobil* occurs in the third and fourth lines, a repetition that adds to the poetic density. This is actually something of a pun since *v-lobil* 'of bad' is a possessed noun form (just as is *y-utzil* 'of good'), whereas *lobil* is a discourse particle that indicates adversity in general.[18] The cumulative effect of these coordinated parallelisms is a statement that is catchy enough to be memorable and aesthetically pleasing in its balance and clarity of contrast. These are just the qualities for which the Church officials called when they pointed out that beautiful expression would more effectively move the Indio spirit.

The next example gives a full statement of the expression *ocol ti vinicil,* which we encountered in the dictionaries. Recall that it was glossed there simply as '*convertirse*', although I argued that the presumed reference was to the "conversion" of God in the incarnation. This example sentence gives the full rendering (Acuña 1998, 231):

he ca yoltah ca yumil ti Dios ocol ti vinicile, ca tu tuxchitah yángel san Gabriel yicnal ca Colel ti Sancta María
When our lord in God wanted to enter humanity he sent the angel saint Gabriel to our lady Holy Mary.

The verb *tuxchitah* illustrates noun incorporation, where the root verb is *tux* 'send', the incorporated noun is *chi* 'mouth', the transitive derivation follows conjugation IV, adding -*tah,* and the whole means 'to order or command'.[19]

The example below (Acuña 1998, 216) is one of many in which writing is thematized, recalling the proliferation of terminology for writing in the dictionaries.

çuçu bin a dzibtic hun ten
Frequently you will write letters to me.

The following example (Acuña 1998, 219) is another sentence whose likely speaker would be a Maya person, in this case one whose father is on loving terms with the *guardián*. This was surely a position of privilege, and the father would have been at least an *indio de confianza,* if not an active collaborator with the missionaries.

yacunabi in yum tumen padre guardián
Beloved is my father by (the) priest guardian.

The next two examples (both Acuña 1998, 218) illustrate a theme that recurs in many of Coronel's citations. The first is an interrogative that would ordinarily suggest that the priest be informed of something, whereas the second is more conspiratorial and would be uttered by someone trying to keep something from the priest. I take the recurrent concern with telling things to be part of the surveillance of Indios by the missionaries, and these examples suggest some of the otherwise unrecorded utterances spoken in the pueblos.

cunx ca aualab ti padre?
What if you told it to father?

chan aualab ti padre
Do not tell it to father.

The last set of examples treats the theme of flight discussed in chapters 3 and 4. The first (Acuña 1998, 221) could be uttered only by a woman reporting on her husband's bad behavior. Wife beating is a recurrent topic in Coronel's examples and in the dictionaries, but here it is linked to flight. The cumulative effect of all four examples is to suggest that flight was not only a sociological reality but also a frequent topic of talk between missionaries and Mayas. The second and fourth (229, 270) would be uttered by a fugitive or suspected fugitive, while the third (235) incorporates an accusation that its addressee had fled.

v keyahen vicham caix v hadzahen, ca tun pudzi tun
My husband scolded me, then he beat me, then he ran away.

lay v chun bin in pudzebal loe
That is the reason I shall run away.

vohel a pudzci
I know you have run away (are a fugitive).

ma çamac pudzucen
I have never run away.

Coronel's *arte* makes a strong linkage between the dictionaries, with their grammatically rich lexicon, and the catechisms, with their lexically rich texts. Its roots are in the Latin-based *grammatica,* from which it draws much of its organization and metalanguage, and in the practical realities of missionizing in Maya, from which it draws many of its examples. It is at once a work of analysis in the project of commensuration and a pedagogical text that would be used to reproduce *lengua* knowledge of Maya. In the space of discourse genres, it is marked by transpositions from these distinct spheres of missionary knowledge. It is closer to an oral text than is any dictionary, because of its pedagogical uses, yet it is analytic the way the dictionary is, elaborating a universe of expressions from the intrinsic systematicity of the language. The importance of the errors is not only that they indicate the limits of missionary understandings; they also establish a baseline for the other *artes.* San Buenaventura never acknowledges the existence of Coronel, but he obviously copied a great deal from him, complete with errors.

GABRIEL DE SAN BUENAVENTURA, *ARTE DE LA LENGUA MAYA* (1684)

According to Carrillo (1872, 169), Gabriel de San Buenaventura was born in France and came to Yucatán from Spain, where he took the Franciscan habit. In Yucatán, he became very proficient in Maya and rose to the positions of *difinidor habitual, guardián* of the main Franciscan convent in Mérida, and *lector* of Maya language. According to the combined evidence of the title page and front matter of his *arte* (Acuña ed. 1996), he occupied all these positions simultaneously or in close sequence during the nine years that elapsed between his completing the *arte* (1674 or 1675) and its printing (1684). San Buenaventura's linguistic production was evidently considerable. Carrillo says that he wrote a massive three-volume trilingual dictionary (Maya, Spanish, French), reported to have been kept in the library of the convent in Mérida but likely burned during the war for independence (1821).

The front matter of San Buenaventura's *arte* includes several ad hominem endorsements of the work on the basis of the author's reputation or sheer brilliance. In his July 19, 1675, Mérida *censura,* fray Pedro de Arqueta, Predicador y Difinidor habitual, calls him *"Maestro de dicha Lengua"* 'teacher of this language' and speaks of his erudition and of the "truly prodigious" order and artfulness of his work. Br. Iuan Gómez Brizeño, himself Canónigo de la Santa Iglesia Cathedral de la Ciudad de Mérida de Yucatán and Examinador Sinodal en Lengua Yucatheca 'synodal examiner in Yucatec language', goes even further. In his April 15, 1676, *aprobacion,* he speaks of the joy of reading the work and the "revealing clarity of the author in reducing to rules and precepts the diffuseness of (Maya) language." On March 10, 1684, the Jesuit father Francisco Díaz

Pimienta disavows knowledge of Maya, presumably necessary to pass judgment on the *arte,* but nonetheless endorses printing the work on the basis of the author's "public fame." The most euphoric endorsement of San Buenaventura comes from the pen of D. Alfonso de Mondragon in his address to the Comissario General de las Provincias de la Nueva-España of the Franciscans (May 8, 1684, México). Mondragon says that San Buenaventura

> *à llegado à ser tan perfecto, y aventajado Maestro el Autor, que con la gloria de Inventor es el primero, que lo à reduzido à claras, breves, y generales reglas para todos utilissimas.*

> has come to be so perfect and advantageous a teacher, that with the glory of the Inventor, he is the first who has reduced (the language) to clear, short, and general rules very useful for everyone.

Mondragon's cover letter is the first document in the front matter of the printed work. He is of course misled or misleading when he describes San Buenaventura as the inventor of the Maya *arte,* understood as a terse reduction of the language. Either he did not know of Coronel's 1620 *arte,* or he is indirectly saying it was flawed. In either case, Mondragon makes no claim to knowing Maya, and the basis of his endorsement appears to be fray Gabriel's fame as a teacher. It is clear in the front matter that San Buenaventura was teaching Maya in the years after 1675, if not before, and that the fame he had accrued before the printing of the *arte* came in part from his performance in the classroom. Like those of Coronel and Beltrán, then, San Buenaventura's *arte* arose from experience in teaching missionaries the language.[20]

The full title of San Buenaventura's *arte,* along with the date, place, and publisher, is thus indicated on the title page (see plate 11):

> *ARTE DE LA LENGVA MAYA, Compuesto por el R.P.Fr. Gabriel de San Buenaventura Predicador, y difinidor habitual de la Provincia de San JOSEPH de YUCATHAN del Orden de N.P.S. FRANCISCO. Año de 1684. CON LICENCIA: En Mexico, por la Viuda de Bernardo Calderon.*[21]

The publication process for San Buenaventura's arte was spread out over nearly nine years, with the earliest document being an aprobación 'approval' dated May 19, 1675, and the latest the May 11, 1684, *licencia* 'license (to publish)' of the *señor provisor* and *vicario general* of the Archdiocese of México. This makes an immediate contrast with the speedy publication of Coronel's work, a mere four months from his dedication in January until the April 30, 1620, *licencia* (see chapter 4 above). Between these two documents from San Buenaventura are arrayed seven more, four from Mérida and three from México. What is striking is that there was a lapse of seven years and five months between the July 31,

1676, *aprobación* of Br. Alonso Gomez Briceño in Mérida and the March 1684 *censura* of fray Francisco Díaz Pimienta, also in Mérida. Immediately thereafter, the manuscript reached México and moved quickly through the channels to final *licencia* and printing. In other words, San Buenaventura's masterwork was waylaid in Mérida for more than seven years. What happened? Acuña (1996, 26) observes that the Dominican bishop of Yucatán, fray Luis de Cifuentes y Sotomayor, had supported publication and it was he who passed the manuscript to the synodal Maya instructor Gomez Briceño before April 1676. Unfortunately, fray Luis died the same year and was succeeded as bishop by two consecutive members of the secular clergy. Acuña plausibly suggests that the seculars were less disposed to publish the work of a Franciscan, and it is interesting to note that the next individual to whom the work was given for evaluation was a Jesuit. Here I think we see the tensions between the branches of the Church in Yucatán being played out in the publication process.

The *censura* by fray Pedro de Arqueta, dated July 19, 1675, may shed additional light on the reasons that San Buenaventura's *arte* was delayed for so long. Arqueta examined the work at the request of fray Alfonso Maldonado, the Franciscan provincial. He notes that San Buenaventura was currently *"Lengua y Guardian"* of the main Franciscan convent in Mérida. Praising the clarity of the rules in the grammar, he goes on to remark:

> Pues la dispocission, artificio, y traza, con que la dispone, es verdaderamente prodi-
> giosa, y si á esta tan conocida verdad se opusiere la malicia del tiempo, . . . diziendo
> que ya estaba escrito el Arte de la Lengua Maya, y que para que sirve haverlo
> reducido á este moderno estilo . . . (nunca juzga por demaciado lo que siempre puede
> ser provechoso).

> The disposition, artfulness and plan with which he displays (the grammar) is truly
> prodigious and if to this widely known truth, the malice of our times would object,
> (saying) that the *Arte de la Lengua Maya* was already written and why would we
> need to have it reduced to this modern style, . . . (never judge as excessive that
> which can be profitable).

Arqueta then observes that some religious have written the *arte* of the language as best they could, but the work of San Buenaventura overcomes confusion and obscurity. Knowing that Coronel's *arte* had been published about sixty years earlier and was widely used and knowing of no other published *arte* during this period, I assume that Coronel's work is at least one of the earlier ones to which Arqueta refers. This impression is reinforced by the extremely detailed correspondences between the two *artes,* from overall organization all the way down to shared example sentences. Yet, despite the blatant presence of Coronel's *arte* within San Buenaventura's, San Buenaventura never mentions or otherwise acknowledges Coronel. His work was sent to México with the disinformation that it was the first *arte* of its kind. Could it be that Coronel's *arte* had undergone recopying during which his authorship was submerged in the broader, anonymous corpus of linguistic studies of *Maya reducido*? At a minimum, this set of circumstances indicates that there were political tensions surrounding the act of publishing the new *arte*. Some of these were between the branches of the provincial Church, and some were generational.

Table 13 lists the documents that record this intriguing process, in the order of their appearance in the front of the 1684 publication. This order is disconnected from the chronological order of the individual documents, and I can figure out no principle that guides the sequence.

The front matter provides a wealth of additional information about the deictic grounding of the *arte*, the circulation of the manuscript, and the circumstances of its publication. We learn, for example, that one of the functions of the *difinidor* (see chapter 2) was to review and pass judgment on works like this one, at the request of the provincial. Thus fray Juan de Torres, difinidor habitual of the Franciscans in Yucatán, reports having read the work twice and found it worthy of publication (May 19, 1675, Mérida). Just two months later, Fr. Pedro de Arqueta, predicador y difinidor habitual, issues a judgment, also as instructed by fray Alfonso Maldonado, provincial (July 19, 1675, Mérida). Thus the upper hierarchy of the provincial order, the *difinidores* and the provincial himself, are directly involved in control over what gets printed and what does not. It also becomes clear in these documents that the pedagogical function of the *arte* was central to its existence. Not only did the author develop his analysis in the course of teaching the grammar, but the *arte* is itself judged as a pedagogical tool. Juan Gomez Briceño, the synodal examiner in Maya, makes it a point to say that San Buenaventura's *arte* can benefit both those from other places who hope to learn Maya and the *naturales* of Yucatán, who can correct barbarisms in their own speech. The normative force of the *arte* is nicely expressed in the fact that it is the master text for teaching and its rules divide the barbarous from the civilized. Once again we hear the echo of *policía*.

There are two interesting statements in these texts that bear on the Spanish conception of Maya language. In his *sentir*, fray Augustin de Vetancurt argues for the importance of teaching the word of God in the native languages. He starts from the analogy of Europe, where God's word is taught in Castilian in Spain, in French in France, and in each land in the mother tongue of its inhabitants. This he suggests is required for full comprehension of the mysteries of the faith and in any case is much more efficient. Mondragon's opening letter to Luzuriaga, commissary general of the Franciscans in New Spain, likens Maya to the word of God itself. Maya, he says, is *"tan proprio, que aun sus vozes explican la naturaleza, y propriedades de sus objetos, que parece fue el mas semejante al que en los labios de*

22222222222222222

TABLE 13 Front Matter of San Buenaventura's *Arte* (editions listed in order of appearance)*

May 8, 1684, Mexico. To N.R.^mo M. Fr. IVAN de LVZVRIAGA, Comissario General de las Provincias de la Nueva-España de la Serafica Orden de N.P.S. Francisco. Etc. Signed by B.L.P. de V.R.^ma Su m.^r y mas afecto Capellan D. Alonso de Mondragon.

May 19, 1675, Mérida (convento de N. Señora de la Asumpcion). APROBACION del R.P.Fr. Juan de Torres Difinidor habitual de la Santa Provincia de S. JOSEPH de Yucatan del Orden de N.P.S. FRANCISCO.

March 20, 1684, Mexico. SENTIR del R.P.Fr. Augustin de Vetancurt, Exlector de Theologia, Predicador jubilado, Chronista Appostolico de la Provincia del Santo Evangelio, Vicario, Cura Ministro de la Iglesia Parrochial del Sr. S. Joseph de los Naturales de Mexico.

March 16, 1684 [n.p.]. El Exmo Señor Virrey desta Nueva-España, vista la aprobacion concedio su licencia por su decreto de 16 de Março de 1684.

March 10, 1684, Mérida. Casa Profesa de N. Compañia de Jesus. CENSURA del R.P. Francisco Diaz Pimienta de la Compañia de JESUS.

May 11, 1684 [n.p.]. El Señor Provisor, Governador y Vicario General deste Arçobispado, vista la aprobacion concedio su licencia por auto de 11 de mayo de 1684 ante *Bernardino de Amezaga* Notario Publico.

April 15, 1676, Mérida. APROBACION del Br. Juan Gomez Brizeño, Canonigo de la Santa Iglesia Cathedral de la Ciudad de Merida de Yucatan Examinador Sinodal en Lengua Yucatheca.

July 31, 1676, Mérida. APROBACION del Br. Alonso Gomez Brizeño Cura Beneficiado por el Real Patronato del Partido de S. Tiago de Yucatá.

July 19, 1675, Mérida. CENSVRA del R.P.Fr. Pedro de Arqueta Predicador, y Difinidor habitual desta Santa Provincia.

*These nine documents are printed on paper without page or folio numbers. See Acuña 1996 for facsimile and critical transcription. The two documents marked [n.p.] were almost surely produced in México.

nuestro primero Padre diò a cada cosa su esencial, y nativo nombre" 'so basic that even its words explain the nature and properties of their objects; that it seems to be similar to (the language) that, in the lips of our first Father, gave every thing its essential and native name'. Although he likely knew no Maya at all, Mondragon has nicely expressed the idea of transparency that we saw in the dictionaries: the friars saw Maya as compositional and economical, and their translations sought to take full advantage of these features.

Before Acuña's (1996) critical edition of the San Buenaventura *arte,* the only accessible copy was the 1888 reprint (a run of seventy-six copies) edited by Joaquín García Icazbalceta. García Icazbalceta, in collaboration with Crescencio Carrillo, adds a list of errors at the end of the text but otherwise does not annotate it. The original 1684 text is reproduced in facsimile by Acuña (1996) and richly annotated in Acuña's transliteration. The original printed text is marked by copious errors in spelling and punctuation. Moreover, the pagination is inconsistent. The front matter folia are unnumbered. The *arte* itself, which follows, starts on page 1. Each of the first nine pages is assigned a number, but after page 9, there are five unnumbered pages, evidently inserted, after which comes page 10. However, the numbers from 10 through 41 actually designate folia and not pages. The combination of printing errors and incoherent pagination suggests that the production house for the original publication was less than well equipped for such a project. It is difficult to imagine that the text was proofed by anyone who knew Maya. In what follows I therefore cite Acuña's (1996) edition of the work, using his page numbers.

San Buenaventura's *arte* is profoundly similar to Coronel's, so similar that it is difficult to believe he did not copy from Coronel, whether knowingly or not. The overall organization of the two is nearly identical, although San Buenaventura adds a brief note on the sounds of Maya, lacking in Coronel, and he has reorganized some of the paradigms and provided a longer inventory of particles. Whatever the praises of San Buenaventura's *arte* coming from its endorsers, this work makes small incremental changes to Coronel's basic text and carries with it the Latin and Castilian background we saw with Coronel. The example sentences are not identical, but there is significant overlap, especially in the Maya forms chosen to exemplify conjugations, form types, and *"excepciones."* The presence of doctrinal practice as a frame of reference for examples is equally strong, and indeed San Buenaventura's *arte* concludes with a brief sketch of language used in administering the sacraments, including scripts in Latin and Maya, neither of which is glossed into Spanish. In general, the Latin floats closer to the surface of San Buenaventura's *arte* than it does in Coronel's. San Buenaventura uses the Latin declension to distinguish cases in Maya, even though, as he notes, Maya nouns do not have case endings (Acuña 1996, 58). Occasionally, he states a grammatical rule in Latin. For instance, when discussing the possessive pronouns, he notes that the first-person plural form reduces from *ca* to *c* when prefixed to a vowel-initial word. He treats this as a case of *sinefala* 'syncopation (of vowels)' that follows the Latin rule, which he states as *"vocalem rapuere alia subuente latini"* 'the Latins suppressed the vowel, when another followed' (61). When discussing a case of variation in the use of orthographic [y] and [i], he dismisses it as not rule governed, saying, *"Et de contingentibus non datur regula"* 'and of contingent things one gives no rule' (62). In the section devoted to the particle *ti* 'to, for, from, at, etc.', he offers the Latin example *"Domine, doce nos orare,"* glossing it as *Yumile, cambeç on ti payal chi* 'Lord, teach us to pray' (136).

The Pronoun System

San Buenaventura's treatment of the pronouns covers much the same ground as Coronel's, also omitting the *c-en, c-ech* 'I who am, you who are . . .' series as well as the possessives *in-tial, a-tial* 'mine, yours . . .'. Whereas Coronel's account reduces all the remaining pronouns to three series, San Buenaventura has five:

(1) the lexical series *ten, tech,* etc. (Coronel's 3); (2) the suffixal series *-en, -ech,* etc. (Coronel's 2); (3) the prefixal series before a consonant *in-, a-,* etc. (Coronel's 1); (4) the prefixal series before a vowel *u-, au-,* etc. (Coronel's 1); and an unnumbered fifth series of "reciprocal" pronouns *in ba, a ba,* etc., which Coronel lists as a subset of series 1 on the grounds that it is formed by prefixing series 1 possessives to the root *-ba* 'self' as in *in ba* 'myself'. Essentially, San Buenaventura's schema trivially reorganizes Coronel's by inverting the first and third series and splitting the preconsonantal, prevocalic, and reflexive pronouns into separate series. From the viewpoint of Maya grammar, this is no improvement and in fact obscures Coronel's insight that the three are variants of one and the same pronoun series. It is almost as if San Buenaventura wanted his work to appear different, even if the difference was trivial.

San Buenaventura erroneously fills in the third-person singular suffixal pronoun, which is actually null, as Coronel correctly observed. Instead of leaving the form blank, he cites the form *laylo* in the series *-en, -ech, laylo* 'me, you, that one'. The problem is that *laylo* is neither a suffix nor a pronoun but instead a bimorphemic demonstrative *(lay + lo)*. To insert this form in series 2 is no more than an ad hoc attempt to make the paradigm appear complete.

On the plus side, San Buenaventura cites a set of examples overlooked by Coronel in which a noun is both possessed and inflected for the equational relation, as in *in mehen ech* 'you are my son', *a mehen en* 'I am your son', and *a mehen ex on* 'we are your (pl) sons'. Note that in the last cited form two suffixal pronouns co-occur, marking plural possessor *(ex)* and plural subject *(on)*. Such doubled forms are fully grammatical and predicted by the paradigms but are unmentioned by Coronel.[22]

San Buenaventura's treatment of the verbs makes very minor advances on Coronel's. Incorporated verb forms, briefly mentioned in Coronel, are assigned their own section (Acuña 1996, 65), followed immediately by stems ending in *-ancil,* exactly as in Coronel. Causative verb forms are more fully treated (74–75), as are complement constructions. Occasionally, San Buenaventura marks pitch, as in *chan ≠ chaan* (115–16) and *matan ≠ matán* (132), although this is the exception to his otherwise simplified spelling of vowels. He also notes that on certain points, older Maya speakers use the language differently than do younger ones, an intriguing hint at variation (132).

Among the weaker features of the work is San Buenaventura's failure to make sense of passive formation: he never even notes the distinction between internal passives (with tone shift of the root vowel plus *-Vl* suffix) and external ones (with *-ab, -b* suffixed to transitive stem) (Acuña 1996, 73, 85). He repeats Coronel's erroneous use of *-cah* as the auxiliary for the present, which muddles conjugations II, III, and IV, just as it did in Coronel. Consequently, although the so-called present in conjugation IV is *canan in cah* 'I am guarding (intransitive)', the perfect is *in cananta* 'I guarded it (transitive)' (82).

Example Sentences

In his example sentences, San Buenaventura carries forward the thematic foci of Coronel. The relations between missionaries and Indios are evident in examples such as the following (Acuña 1996, 114, 128), both of which approximate ones cited by Coronel.

> *cunx ca avalab ti padre?*
> How about you tell it to father?

> *lay v chun in dzibtici huun tech lae*
> That is the reason I write letter(s) to you.

The doctrinal background is echoed throughout the *arte,* as the next four examples illustrate (Acuña 1996, 111, 112, 115, 131). In the first we are back to the moral principle that good conduct is rewarded with heaven. The other three revolve around remorse, confession, and absolution, respectively.

> *tohcin a beel ca utzac a binel ti caan*
> Straighten your ways in order to go to heaven.

> *in keban ci invoktic*
> My sin(s) (are what) I am weeping about.

> *ma a çopp halic a keban*
> Don't blurt out your sins (in disorder).

> *achocha a keban? Ma bahun in chochob*
> Have you confessed your sin(s)? I have never confessed (them).

The final two examples (Acuña 1996, 130, 124) focus on the performance of prayer and nicely capture the pedagogical practice of inducing students to perform the basic prayers aloud, from memory (the Our Father, Hail Mary, Credo, and Salve). The Maya in the second example is actually ambiguous, since *vohel Ocaan ti vol* could be glossed 'I know (the) Credo (the prayer)' or 'I know I believe'. In context it is clearly the former that is intended.

> *avalah va tucanppel oracionob?*
> Did you say the four prayers?

> *v ohel Ca Yum, v ohelix Ocaan ti vol xan.*
> I know Our Father and I also know I believe.

We see between Coronel and San Buenaventura a historical accretion of missionary knowledge, as well as the development of the *arte* as a hybrid genre in which Latin, Spanish, ordinary Maya, and the specialized language of doctrinal *Maya reducido* are embedded. Judging from his work, San Buenaventura appears to have known the language fairly well, but he did not make any major analytic advances over Coronel's *arte* of sixty years earlier (except perhaps for the inclusion of more particles, which are mostly unanalyzed). We find with fray Gabriel the same tension as in Coronel between what he knew and what he could explain given his Latinate schema.

FRAY PEDRO BELTRÁN DE SANTA ROSA MARÍA, *ARTE DE EL IDIOMA MAYA* (1746)

By contrast, the 1746 *arte* of fray Pedro Beltrán de Santa Rosa María appears to cross a threshold over which missionary knowledge of Maya expands to that of a native speaker. There is a question whether Beltrán's mother was a Maya woman, but there is no debate that he was born and raised somewhere on the Yucatán peninsula, and he states in writing that he spent so long speaking Maya that he nearly forgot Spanish. This is doubtless hyperbole on his part, given what is known of his history, but his work indisputably marks a new level of depth and subtlety. San Buenaventura's brief forays into the phonology become with Beltrán extended discussions of how the language is pronounced, including accurate analyses of fast speech phonology in which many sounds are elided.[23] The inventory of particles is expanded again, and the order of the sections of the grammar is rearranged. The four conjugations reappear, corrected, with the same exemplary Maya terms. But instead of placing the paradigms first, to be followed by statement of the rules, as his predecessors did, Beltrán reverses the order. Over the course of eighty numbered paragraphs (Third Article), he states the general rules of the verbs. This is then followed by the Fourth Article on *sinefala* and syncope (sound reductions involving the loss of one sound in the presence of another). Only in the Fifth Article does he state the paradigms for each of the four conjugations. There are ten more sections, or "articles," in the *arte*, including an extensive list of particles (Tenth Article, Copy of Prepositions, Adverbs and Conjunctions) and four more sections devoted to vocabulary organized by theme. These make up the "semilexicon" referred to in the full title of the *arte*, and they display the degree to which Beltrán had access to ordinary Maya vocabulary for such things as kinship, animals, and common household items.

Curiously, even as these changes bring Beltrán's *arte* much closer to actual Maya than any of its predecessors, the Latin background remains strong. In fact, Latin is much more evident in Beltrán's *arte* than it was in San Buenaventura's, and the contrast with Coronel is even more striking. All three rely on Latin as the background model, and Beltrán repeats most of the Latinate features of Coronel's and San Buenaventura's *artes*. But Beltrán cites whole phrases in Latin and makes comments to the reader in Latin in a way that Coronel does not. Coronel never uses more than an isolated grammatical term from Latin; San Buenaventura uses Latin at several points; with Beltrán, Latin is common. It is as if the presence of Latin in the work of missionary grammarians increased, rather than decreased, with time, even as their knowledge of Maya grammar improved.

Beltrán's *arte* owes much to Coronel, from whom he inherited the general framework and many examples. Yet he does not mention Coronel or any published *arte* other than San Buenaventura's. It is San Buenaventura whom he mentions often throughout the work. At the end of his 188-page *arte*, Beltrán states that he has just learned that Coronel had published an *arte* before San Buenaventura. Evidently he was under the false impression that San Buenaventura was the first to publish and the "protomaster" of Maya—an impression that was surely reinforced by some of the endorsements in San Buenaventura's front matter and his own failure to mention Coronel. In this process, Coronel the author was erased even as Coronel the text was reproduced.

According to Carrillo (1872), Pedro Beltrán was born and educated in Yucatán. His origins are obscure, but Acuña (2002, 16) infers that his mother was Maya, from statements made by Beltrán in the dedication of the *arte*. Beltrán lived in *"una montaña yerma"* 'a wilderness', preaching, giving sacraments *"y con ellos de continuo en su idioma confabulando"* 'and confabulating with them continuously in their language'. So submersed was he in Maya, he says, that he forgot many words in Spanish. Acuña infers that his training in the *arte gramático latino* 'Latin grammar' took place at the Jesuit Colegio in Mérida, where there was a chair in *gramática* (Latin grammar). Beltrán subsequently entered the Franciscan convent in Mérida around 1705, and entered the order around 1713. He was later sent to minister the faith in Teabo, a town in the south near the Puuc hills (Acuña 2002, 17).[24] Between 1720 and 1740, Beltrán ascended the provincial hierarchy of the Franciscans, eventually becoming the custodian of the order in Yucatán. He was also named *lector* of philosophy and of theology and *maestro* of Maya language, in addition to being the Revisor de Libros for the Holy Office. In 1742 he taught the Maya course in the Franciscan convent in Mérida, and in that year his *arte* was "composed and dictated." As a native speaker of Maya, Beltrán was never described as a *lengua*, but his published works would otherwise qualify him for the epithet. He published in 1740 a collection of prayers with the novena, in 1746 the *arte*, and in 1757 his *Declaración de la Doctrina Christiana en el Idioma yucateco*, all in México. His *doctrina* was reprinted many times, and as late as 1870, when Carrillo wrote his dissertation on the history of Maya language, it was still in use (Carrillo 1872, 171).

The title page of Beltrán's *arte,* reformatted for ease of presentation, reads as follows (see plate 12):

ARTE DE EL IDIOMA MAYA REDUCIDO A SUCCINTAS REGLAS, Y SEMILEXICON *YUCATECO*

POR EL R.P.F. PEDRO BELTRAN *de Santa Rosa Maria, Ex-Custodio, Lector, que fue de Philosophia, y Theologia, Revisor del Sto. Oficio, è hijo de esta Sta. Recoleccion Franciscana de Merida.*

FORMÓLO, Y DICTÓLO, *siendo Maestro de Lengua Maya en el Convento Capitular de N.S.P.S. Francisco, de dicha Ciudad. Año de 1742.*

Y LO DEDICA A LA GLORIOSA INDIANA SANTA ROSA MARIA DE LIMA.

CON LICENCIA: EN MEXICO, POR LA *Viuda de D. Joseph Bernardo de Hogal. Año de 1746.*

ARTE of the Maya idiom reduced to succinct rules, and Yucatec semilexicon

By the Reverend Father fray Pedro Beltrán de Santa Rosa María, Ex-Custodian, Lector of Philosophy and Theology, Revisor of the Holy Office, and son of this Holy Franciscan Recollection of Mérida.

He formulated and dictated it (while) being Master of Maya Language in the capitular convent of Our Revered Father Saint Francis in said city. The year 1742.

And he dedicates it to the glorious Indian Saint Rosa María of Lima.

With License: in México by the Widow of Don Joseph Bernardo de Hogal. The year 1746.

Beltrán's statement of his title as former custodian and *lector* implies that by 1746 he had already occupied and vacated those positions. It is interesting to note the contrast between these positions and the kind of trajectory Ciudad Real, Coronel, and other *lenguas* followed. There is apparently no evidence that Beltrán served as *guardián, difinidor,* or provincial of the order. The linkage between the *arte* and Beltrán's teaching in Mérida is made explicit in the next lines, where he "formulates and dictates" the work while teaching. One imagines the *arte* as a sequence of lectures. The dedication to the "glorious Indian Saint Rosa María de Lima" and the fervor with which he follows this theme in his dedication suggested to Acuña (2002) that Beltrán was actually paying homage to his own "Indian" mother.

Beltrán's dedication pursues an elaborate parallel between the beauty of the rose amid the thorns and the glory of Saint Rosa amid the thorns of Maya language. The thorns he finds in the "harsh" sounds of the language, which are so difficult as to hurt the tongue and force one into silence. This silence in turn means that even if one tries to pronounce the language, one's idea remains a secret (because unintelligible). And even though this *arte* is about a silence, let it not be silent. At this point Beltrán's delight in chiasmus takes over and he writes the following lines, which are formatted for ease of reading (punctuation is from Acuña) (see plate 13).

> *Aunque paresca silencio, el silencio no paresca y,*
> *aunque se aparesca la espina, la espina se desvanesca,*
> *haciéndose lenguas del Arte*
> *con este Arte de Lengua*
> *los que juzgan que es la Lengua un Arte de espinas lleno.*
>   (Acuña 2002, 31)

> Even though it might appear silence, silence does not appear and
> even though it might appear to be a thorn, the thorn disappears,
> becoming *lenguas* of the *arte*
> with this *arte* of the *lengua*
> those who judge that the *lengua* is an *arte* full of thorns.

Simplified, the verse structure is A, A', B, B', C, where each of A and B is internally composed of two parts in a relation of chiasmus. Beltrán takes evident pleasure in inversions and reversals, punning conspicuously on the silence of thoughts ill expressed in Maya and the silence of his *arte* (if it is not published). He places the saintly Rose, his patron, amid the auditory thorns of the language, with its "broken" (glottalized) sounds. In verselike blocks of text, the line-to-line parallelisms accumulate into full-blown poetic constructions. The first two lines are almost perfectly balanced, though in the first the verbs are simple, whereas in the second they are reflexive. The inversion between the third and fourth lines is another pun, since Beltrán knows that training in the *arte* is how one becomes a *lengua* (expert) and that what the *arte* is about is the *lengua* (language). The last line brings the whole to a conclusion, punning again on the term *arte*, as grammatical system and as pedagogical work, and returning to the thorns. What is perhaps most striking in Beltrán's use of poetic language is that it emerges out of otherwise stylistically simple text. We will see this same pattern, in which grammatical parallelism is interspersed in and emerges out of nonpoetic texts, again and again in both Spanish and Maya discourse.

In addition to the dedication, Beltrán wrote a substantial "Prologue to the Reader," a five-page apologia for the work, complete with Latin poetry showing the same features we just saw in the Spanish. The prologue begins with the following statement:

> *Es el Yucateco Idioma garboso en sus dicciones, elegante en sus períodos, y en ambas cosas conciso, pues, con pocas palabras y breves sylabas, explica a vezes profundas sentencias.*
>   (Acuña 2002, 41)

The Yucatec idiom is graceful in its diction, elegant in its periods, and in both things concise: with few words and brief syllables (it) explains sometimes profound judgments.

Shortly after this, Beltrán explains that he has studied San Buenaventura's *arte*, describing him as the "Proto-Maestro" and as yet (1746) the only one to have given his arte to be printed. The reason for his writing a new *arte* is explained in these lines:

> *Ofrezco en esta obra un Arte para que con facilidad aprenda este Idioma por reglas el que quisiere, porque, si es forastero, como se aplique diligente y con voluntad, lo comprehenderá en poco tiempo por la claridad de sus reglas, . . . y, si es Criollo, se perfeccionará muy mucho.*
>
> (Acuña 2002, 42)

I offer in this work an *arte*, so that with ease whoever wants to can learn this idiom by rules: for if he is a foreigner, as he applies himself diligently and with will, he will understand it in short order because of the clarity of its rules; . . . and if he is creole, he will greatly improve.

> *Y no se me diga que es superfluo mi trabajo por averse ya dado a luz otro Arte de este Idioma, porque responderé que ni su Author pudo decir todo lo conducente ni podía vivir en todos los tiempos, en cuyo transcurso o se muda mucho un Idioma o se adulteran las vozes, o se ofrecen nuevas cosas que advertir y yerros, que es forzoso enmendar perfeccionando y reduciendo a lo más corriente del tiempo.*
>
> (Acuña 2002, 42)

And let it not be said that my work is superfluous because there is already an *arte* of this idiom. For I will respond that neither could its author [San Buenaventura] say everything nor could he live in all times, in course of which either the idiom changes greatly, or the words become adulterated, or new things arise to give notice, and lacunae that need to be emended, perfecting it and reducing it to the most fluent (usage) of the time.

As someone evidently raised in the peninsular region in the late seventeenth and early eighteenth century, Beltrán is far more attuned to the social realities of spoken Maya than were his predecessors. In its frequent use of the term *Yucateco*, in the title and the prologue as well as elsewhere, his work contrasts with the writings of Coronel and San Buenaventura and likely reflects a growing sense of regional identity as the ranks of the creoles grew during the colonial period. He is also concerned with the "mixing" of Spanish with Maya, another predictable effect of the years over which the languages were part of the same colonial society. Thus at the end of the grammar (Acuña 2002, 319) Beltrán notes that he has derived the material from old and modern papers and has made up forms when need be. He laments the way Spanish is mixed with Maya and calls for the recovery of Maya terms of which many speakers are unaware. In all these ways, Beltrán displays an acute consciousness of the changing face of the language.

As was common in the colonial Church rhetoric, Beltrán states possible objections to his project, in order to defeat them one by one. In the lines that follow we see this rhetorical style combined with his flair for poetic inversions. "But" stands for the anticipated objections of those who will say his *arte* is of no use since the language is widely spoken.

> *Ya me pongo en que no faltará a esta obra su muy repetido pero que la tache. Uno será: pero, ¿para qué es este Arte, si ya casi todos hablan o saben hablar esta Lengua? A que respondo . . . que no todos la saben hablar; [y] que no es lo mismo hablar la Lengua que saberla hablar bien. Y assí, vice versa, diría yo sin temeridad que son muy pocos los que la saben hablar, pues, aunque la hablan, como no saben las reglas, no saben cómo la hablan; porque o se turban y yerran al hablarla, de que se sigue que no la saben bien hablar, porque, aunque hablan lo que saben, no saben lo que hablan por no saber lo que hablan.*
>
> (Acuña 2002, 43)

Now I address the repeated "but" that will not be lacking to criticize this work. One will be, But for what is this arte, if almost everyone speaks or knows how to speak this language? To which I respond . . . that not everyone knows how to speak it. [And] that it is not the same thing to speak a language and know how to speak it well; and vice versa, I would say without temerity that there are very few who know how to speak it; for even though they speak it, since they do not know the rules, they do not know how they speak it, or they make errors in speaking it, from which it follows that they do not speak it well; because even though they speak what they know, they do not know what they speak since they know not what they speak.

Beneath Beltrán's verbal pirouettes lies a kind of linguistic awareness that was less evident in the work of his predecessors. His definition of speaking well is not only to say what one knows but also to know what one says, that is, to know the rules governing it. This second-order knowing is metalinguistic; it is the province of the *arte*.

The body of Beltrán's work is preceded by the expected approvals and licenses (see plate 14). There are eight documents in the series, the first six of which were signed in Mérida and the last two in México. Of those from Mérida, the first three are signed by Franciscans, two friars and the provincial. The two friars both state that they examined the work upon the orders of the provincial. One of them is the provincial secretary and the other is a former *difinidor* who writes from the town of Teabo, where he was then vicar of the convent where Beltrán had served. The fourth and fifth *censuras* are by secular clergy, one the *clérigo domiciliario* of Mérida, Bachiller don Phelipe Santiago María de la Madera, and the other a parish priest who emphasizes the need for this work to further the spiritual nurturance of the Indios. Santiago María states that he is a native speaker of Maya, probably the only Maya speaker in the series aside from the Franciscan vicar of Teabo. After leaving the bishop's offices, the work went to México, where it received the *licencia del superior gobierno* from the viceroy of New Spain, don Pedro Cebrían y Augustín, and the *licencia del ordinario* from the vicar general of the Arzobispado of Mexico, don Francisco Xavier Gómez de Cervantes. The documents are in chronological order, and the entire process took under eleven months, starting on July 19, 1743, and concluding on June 12, 1744. The production process appears to have taken about eighteen to twenty-four months thereafter, and the work bears a publication date of 1746.

At 188 pages, Beltrán's *arte* is longer, more detailed, and more thoroughly explained than either of its predecessors. Whatever the uncertainties of his own life, he clearly knew Maya fluently, as is evidenced in his detailed and insightful discussion of sound change in ordinary speech and in such features as vocabulary for objects found around the ordinary household. His generalizations are more careful and precise as well. After discussing the sounds of the Maya and the perils of mispronunciation, Beltrán introduces the eight parts of utterance, lifted from Latin (sec. 17), and the cases, also based on Latin (secs. 18–23).[25] In what follows I concentrate selectively on those elements that help situate his work in relation to the other missionary discourse, including the earlier *artes*, the dictionaries, and the *doctrina*. I start with the pronouns, a point on which Coronel and San Buenaventura took different approaches.

The Pronoun System

Beltrán's treatment of the pronouns closely follows that of San Buenaventura, his partner in dialogue throughout the *arte* (Acuña 2002, 59–63). Like him, Beltrán has five pronoun series, in the same order: series 1, lexical *ten, tech, . . .* ; series 2, suffixal *-en, -ech, . . .* ; series 3, prefixal preceding a consonant *in-, a-, . . .* ; series 4, prefixal preceding a vowel *u-, au-, y-, . . .* ; and series 5, "reciprocals" (reflexives) *inba, abah, ubah, . . .* The overall schema and all but a couple of the examples are inherited nearly verbatim from San Buenaventura, and Beltrán's description suffers the same shortcomings. In series 2, the third-person form is null, but Beltrán follows San Buenaventura's dubious example and cites the lexical demonstrative *laylo* in the expected position. Beltrán makes an important correction to San Buenaventura when he notes that *yacunah incah ech* 'I am loving you' should actually be *yacunah incah tech,* changing the pronoun in final position from *-ech* (series 2, direct object) to *tech* (series 1, indirect object). This small change is consistent with my argument that the *cah* auxiliary is actually marked as nontransitive and therefore cannot be inflected for a direct object. As we will see just below, Beltrán had a much better understanding of transitivity than either of his predecessors. His series 3 and 4 are what he calls "mixed"; that is, they combine prefixal pronouns with suffixal markers of plurality. By splitting these two into separate series, Beltrán misses the generalization that it is one and the same pronoun series with a predictable alternation between preconsonantal and prevocalic forms. Moreover, in describing these as "mixed," he fails to distinguish between three grammatically distinct cases: (1) simple pluralization of the subject (as in *u binel ob* 'they go'), where the two pronouns are part of a single reference; (2) dual marking in which the prefixal form encodes the subject or possessor and the suffixal form encodes the object or possessum, as in *in cimsic ob* 'I kill them' and *u tzicic ech* 'he obeys you'; and (3) dual marking in which two suffixal pronouns co-occur, one of which pluralizes the subject or possessor and the other marks the object or possessum, as in *y ilic ob on* 'they see us' and *a yum ob ex* 'they are your fathers'. The only functionally "mixed" cases are (2) and (3). Beltrán's description of the reflexives (series 5) is identical to that of San Buenaventura.

The Verb System

Beltrán's analysis of the Maya verb makes substantial improvements on those of his predecessors, despite adopting the same schema of four conjugations, illustrated by the same Maya verbs. His fourth general rule for verb formation nicely captures the distinction between external passives (*cambezabal [cambez-ab-al]* 'to be taught') and internal passives (*tzicil [tzí'ic-il]* 'to be obeyed'), although he fails to note that in the internal case, the root vowel is glottalized in the passive (Acuña 2002, 67). His fifth general rule governs the formation of incorporated verbs, such as *chhahaa [chha + haa]* 'get water', *chucchho [chuc + chho]* 'hunt rat, (to) rat hunt', and *bechhkab [bechh + kab]* 'call + hand', '(to) call with the hand'. Beltrán accurately observes that as incorporated verbs, these form the past by suffixing *-nahi* as in *chhahaanahi* 'he got water', *chucchhonahi* 'he rat hunted', and *bechhkabnahi* 'he hand called'.[26] Moreover, he nicely observes that incorporated forms, which are nontransitive, can be transitivized and marked with an overt object: *u bechhkab tah u mehen* 'he hand-called his son' and *u bechhkab tah en* 'he hand-called me'. Thus Beltrán has accurately understood that the root verbs in these constructions are transitive, the noun incorporation produces a nontransitive stem, and this nontransitive can in turn be retransitivized by suffixing *-tah, -tic*. We can illustrate this: *u chuc-ic chho* 'he hunts (a) rat' (simple transitive), *u chuc chho* 'he rat hunts' (object incorporated, nontransitive), and *uchucchho tah ob* 'he rat-hunted them' (hunted them like rats). This cyclic derivation of intransitive from transitive and vice versa is at the heart of the Maya verb, and Beltrán, with his sensibility for formal inversion, has grasped it far better in his grammar than any of the earlier ones.

Beltrán's overall understanding of transitivity is an enormous improvement over that of earlier missionary grammarians. It leads him to make several improvements on the four verb paradigms, which were previously muddled on just this point. First, he notes that San Buenaventura's glosses in the second conjugation are wrong because he has omitted the 'it' pronoun for the direct object. Thus, *u cambezah* is glossed 'that one taught', whereas it should be 'that one taught him' (Acuña 2002, 99, sec. 155). Beltrán scrupulously follows his own rule in stating the conjugations, in which all transitive stems are glossed with transitive phrases in Spanish. Second, he notes in section 156 that *tzic* 'obey', the exemplar of conjugation III, is actually ambiguous. On one reading, it is *absoluto* 'intransitive' (*tzic* 'obey', *tzicnahi* 'he obeyed'), but on the other reading, it is *no-absoluto* 'nonintransitive' (i.e., transitive: *tzic* 'obey', *u tzicah* 'he obeyed him'). Finally, Beltrán has the insight to remove the auxiliary -*cah* (the so-called present) from all of the transitive stems (conjugations II, III, IV). Recall that this auxiliary is marked intransitive and caused confusion in the paradigms of both Coronel and San Buenaventura. Beltrán resolves this by citing proper transitive stems for the corresponding verbs in the 'present': *in cambezic* 'I teach him' (not *cambezah in cah*), *in tzicic* 'I obey him' (not *tzic in cah*), and *in canantic* 'I guard it' (not *canan in cah*). These are only three of the improvements Beltrán makes in the analysis of transitivity, which he addresses repeatedly throughout the *arte*. The cumulative result is that his *arte* is the first to be consistent and accurate on this key parameter. When we add to this the extensive list of verb stems that follows the conjugations (Acuña 2002, 171–223) we have a more economical analysis with a higher degree of fidelity to the facts of Maya than had ever been achieved by the missionaries.

Example Sentences

Beltrán's knowledge of the language is also amply demonstrated by his example sentences, many of which make subtle distinctions pertaining to numerous spheres of ordinary life in the *pueblos reducidos,* though his work remains grounded in the same missionary project to which the catechism, sermons, confessional, earlier *artes,* and dictionaries all belong. The following examples illustrate the transposition of language among these different genres of missionary discourse under *reducción.* They are taken from Beltrán's grammatical discussions and from the examples of particles listed in the "Yucatecan semilexicon." The first two (secs. 91, 221) show that the early colonial translation of God as Maya *ku* was still in use in Beltrán's time but was not the preferred term in the phrase "God Almighty," for which the Spanish *Dios* was retained (see chapter 1 above). As I discuss in the next chapter, Beltrán's *doctrina* explicitly rejects the use of Coronel's *ku citbil* for 'God Almighty', on the grounds that this term actually denotes an Indio god and will therefore cause confusion.

ku 'Dios'
kuyencunah 'hacer que sea Dios lo que no lo es, consagrar'
God
to make into God what is not, to consecrate

todo lo puede Dios *'tuzinil uchac tumen Dios'*, cuyo romance construido es así: todo es podido por Dios. Y de aquí quedó *uchuc tumen tuzinil* por 'el Omnipotente'.[27]

God can do everything 'Almighty is God', whose connotation is 'everything is possible for God'. And from this comes *uchuc tumen tuzinil* for 'Omnipotent'.

In the two examples below (secs. 94–95, 109), two precepts of Christian practice are stated in sentences illustrating the rules of verb formation. One noteworthy feature of the two sentences in the second example is the awkward Spanish glosses that Beltrán provides for them, with the subject nouns in sentence-final position. What motivates the odd syntax of the Spanish glosses, which I have tried to convey in the English, is that Beltrán attempts to retain the Maya word order in the Spanish gloss. This raises a question as to whether there emerged a variety of Yucatecan Spanish in which the order of elements is partially calqued from the Maya, a development we might expect as more speakers were native bilingual and Yucatán developed a regional identity. If so, this would be the reciprocal of the shift in Maya semantics to meet the demands of Spanish glosses in the dictionaries.

u dzabilah Dios cuxlic pixan 'la gracia de Dios es con lo que vive el alma'[28]
the grace of God is what enlivens the soul

he Domingo e ú kin u tilizcunic Dios christianoob 'el domingo es el día de venerar á Dios los cristianos'
kintunyaabil e u kinic u tocic úcol uinic 'el Verano es tiempo de quemar su milpa el hombre'
Sunday is the day to venerate God the Christians
Summer is the time to burn his field the man

Confession remains a common theme in Beltrán's examples, as it was for his predecessors. The next three examples (secs. 165, 192, 238) revisit lexical and grammatical elements we have seen repeatedly over the previous three chapters: the untying of sin, the confession that one is a sinner, and the question of missionary to Indio, Have you confessed? along with its stubborn response.

ú kintzil a chochic á keban 'hora es de confessar tu culpa'
Time it is to confess your sin

ten cen ah batab 'yo que soy cazique', al modo que se dice en el principio del Confiteor Deo *ten cen ah zipil* 'yo que soy pecador'

'I who am cacique', in the manner in which it says in the beginning of the Confiteor Dios 'I who am sinner'

quando se usa para lo interrogativo, lleva el verbo a pretérito sin mudarlo; como si se pregunta 'no te has confessado'? *ma ua á chocha á kebani,* y si con ella se responde ... que la cosa ni se ha hecho ni se hará, como *ma in chochahí* 'no me he confessado, ni pienso confesarme'.[29]

when used in the interrogative, it takes the verb in the preterite without changing it; as if one asks 'haven't you confessed'? and if the other responds with it ... the thing has neither been done nor will it be, as in 'I have not confessed and don't think I will confess'.

The following two examples (Acuña 2002, 240, 229) shift to other aspects of Christian practice, but they also exemplify simple dialogic exchanges in which the missionary asks or tells the Indio about himself. The first exchange occurs verbatim in the dialogic portion of the *doctrina,* and the second returns to the resistant Indio who may engage but against his will.

Ika: En respuesta, es afirmativa y quiere decir "sí, por cierto," v.g., *ocan ua Dios tauol?* "¿crees en Dios?" *ocan ika* "sí, creo"

Ika: In response it is affirmative, and it means "yes, for sure," for example "do you believe in God?" "Yes I believe"

Cayuile: Avrá de ser assí, bien está, assí se hará, pero denota que la cosa se haze o se hará de mala gana, como si diciendo a alguno que vaya a missa, *bin xicech ti missa* "irás a misa," responde *cayuile,* "está bien, lo haré pero de mala gana"

Cayuile: It will have to be, it is fine, it will be so, but it denotes that the thing is or will be done against the will, as if telling someone to go to mass, "you will go to mass," he responds *cayuile,* "it's fine, I will do it, but against my will"

The last two examples arise in Beltrán's discussion of relative clauses (secs. 260, 261) and illustrate the ambiguity of *tzeec* 'punish, preach'.

"Pedro, que pecó contra Dios, será castigado" *Pedro, heklay zipi ti Dios, bin tzectabac.*
Pedro, who sinned against God, will be punished.

"Predicando yo, cayó el templo" *Tan in tzeec, ca lub kuna.*[30]
While I was preaching, the temple collapsed.

MISSIONARY LINGUISTICS AS A HYBRID SYSTEM

In his excellent introduction to San Buenaventura's *arte,* Acuña (1996, 20) observed that the missionaries assumed that the principles of Latin were universal and the Maya would be reducible to them. I think Acuña is partly right and partly wrong. Latin grammar is only one of several frames of reference for

Maya linguistics. It is demonstrably significant but only one part of a larger space of genres. For all three grammarians, the first source of their respective *artes* is the work of their *lengua* predecessors. All state that they worked from older papers. For Coronel (1620), this would have included the work of Villalpando and perhaps Landa, among others. For San Buenaventura (1684), it was Coronel, and for Beltrán (1746), it was San Buenaventura. As early as Coronel, the Latin is embedded in the *arte* and virtually determines its core structure. But Coronel, or his missing sources, did the work of commensuration required to fit the structure to Maya. This is the moment at which the basic hybrid is constructed as grammatical system. It is this hybrid, not the Latin directly, that is inherited by San Buenaventura.

In the process of commensurating Latin and Spanish grammar to Maya *arte*, Maya language did not lose its distinctiveness. The fit was awkward, and the friars knew more Maya than could be accommodated by their Latinate framework. They added lists of particles, cited examples whose structures were unexplained, and made ad hoc adjustments to the Maya in order to make it fit. With time and talent, Beltrán would correct the more egregious errors in the verbs, and he would capture the rules of incorporation that are only adumbrated by Coronel. He also described the two passive formations more carefully, effectively inventing his analysis, since it was missing from San Buenaventura, his source. One goal of these works was to achieve a measure of fidelity to the facts of Maya. They would do this by accurate citation and increasingly accurate analysis. Alongside Latin as a model was therefore Maya usage, ordinary and ritual, as an object.

The *artes* were pedagogical instruments designed to foster the reproduction of *lenguas* and *lengua* knowledge. The classroom is another critical source, for these works were taught, or as Beltrán put it, "dictated." All three authors taught in Mérida. This linkage of the *arte* to the classroom curriculum of the missionaries may explain why the *artes* were published, whereas the dictionaries, not designed as teaching scripts, were not. The grammars were oriented to the needs of students who would go on to work in the missions. The numerous ties to catechism that we have seen are simultaneously ties to the classroom curriculum in which catechism was taught. Like transparency in the dictionaries, they strove to render the Maya clearly for a European student. Since the *arte* is a manual for speaking well, the three Maya *artes* are normative as well as descriptive. They state what should be, with an eye to what is.

Rather than reduce Maya to Latin, therefore, the missionaries attempted to reduce it to its own rules for speaking *well*. The first tension arises here, for the Maya in question was ambivalent between Maya as its speakers spoke and *Maya reducido* as its speakers *should* speak. The tension between normative and descriptive runs throughout the entire space of missionary linguistics. It mediates between Latin, Castilian, and Maya, on the one hand, and the grammars of all three, on the other. The second tension lies in the relative autonomy of the *arte* as a genre. On the one hand, the tradition of *gramática* provided templates for dictionaries and *artes*. There was a relatively clear division of linguistic labor between them in which the dictionary foregrounded semantics and the *arte* morphosyntax. But each presupposed the other, and neither was truly autonomous. They were embedded in and shaped by the same field of *reducción*.

The third tension is between citational reproduction of earlier sources and emerging discontinuities. San Buenaventura apparently breaks the historical sequence: not only does his work, together with the documents that authorize it, erase Coronel from the record, but Beltrán assumes that San Buenaventura's was the first published *arte*. Beltrán corrects the error at the end of his work, but he evidently had no idea just how much of San Buenaventura came from Coronel. At the same time, the gap between Beltrán and San Buenaventura is much greater than the one between San Buenaventura and Coronel; Beltrán was the innovator, and his work is substantially different from the others. Not only is it far longer and more detailed, but it is much more analytic as well. It is, in a word, the first modern grammar that pays careful attention to actual usage. It is noteworthy that one of Beltrán's innovations was his return to Latin, of which there is much more in his grammar than in those of his predecessors. Contrary to what one might expect, the work in which ordinary Maya is best described is also the one in which Latin is most present as a metalanguage and frame of reference. We must not imagine, therefore, that the history of Maya linguistics is either continuous or marked by a movement away from the Latin background. It was multidirectional, as well as multilingual.

The combined evidence of the previous three chapters indicates that the two primary genres of missionary linguistics, the dictionary and the *arte*, fashioned a *Maya reducido* that was hybrid at all levels. The tensions between normativity and description, autonomy and embedding, citation and innovation are intrinsic to the project. In view of the shortcomings of the first two *artes*, we might conclude, with Acuña (1996, 21), that Maya was *"reducida"* in an imprecise and merely superficial way. Similar observations were made in regard to Nahuatl by Burkhart (1989). But the Maya grammars and translations are better than this assessment suggests. Moreover, the relevant depth is not only analytic; it is historical, and it lies in the consequences of the project of *reducción*. However flawed or improvised, the missionary version of Maya was a social fact with repercussions. In the coming chapters I trace the dispersion of this new language into the space of colonial genres, starting with the *doctrina* in which Maya-speaking students would be inculcated.

The Canonical Word

. . . para confirmarse en la ley de Cristo,
y para hacerse nuevos hombres,
y capaces de muchos bienes espirituales
que ahora no alcanzan . . .

CÓDICE FRANCISCANO, SIGLO XVI

. . . to confirm themselves in the law of Christ,
and to make themselves new men,
and capable of many spiritual goods
that they do not now achieve . . .

The doctrinal works of the missionary *lenguas*—catechisms, a confessional manual, a manual for ministry to the sick, and sermons—constitute a substantial body of literature that has remained virtually unstudied beyond the scholarly introductions and notes of René Acuña (1996, 1998). To my knowledge, no scholars have attempted to compare the published doctrinal texts or to determine their relation to other colonial Maya texts. There are several likely reasons for this. For one thing, the scholars most engaged in analyzing Maya texts have pursued other topics. These include especially governance at the levels of region and town (see works by Barrera Vásquez, Okoshi, Quezada, Restall, and Roys in references) and the forbidden Maya literature, which has been mined for evidence of a uniquely Maya voice (see Barrera Vásquez, Edmonson, and Roys).[1] Farriss (1984) stands out for emphasizing the centrality of evangelization in changing Maya culture, but it was not her goal to analyze the Maya documentation in its linguistic specificity. If one assumes that attendance at church was spotty, as Cogolludo complained, and that the conversions were superficial, this lack of attention may seem justified, especially since the language of catechisms in Maya is marked by errors in spelling, neologisms, and other oddities. Based squarely on missionary templates grounded in European Christianity and written in an odd sort of Maya, the catechisms may seem little more than relics of an ineffectual project.

I argue that such a reading of the history is in important ways wrong. As we have seen, Acuña (1984) suggested that what made the Motul dictionary a *calepino* (see page 164) was its relation to doctrinal literature, that is, a body of literature in which the language encoded in the dictionary was actually used. I think Acuña is right in this. But there are other reasons to see this set of genres as pivotal in colonial discourse formation. First, the doctrinal discourse embodied the new form of Maya directly; catechisms were *in* Maya, not only *about* Maya. Second, the doctrine was authoritative, subject to official approval, enforcement, and sanction: the measure of truth in an economy of belief in which untruth was cause for punishment. Third, the translations of critical prayers and liturgical texts were repeated indefinitely many times throughout the reduced parts of the colony and beyond.

Fourth, the doctrinal texts are scripts that were spoken not only *to* Indio neophytes, but *by* them—morning and night on ordinary days and especially on holy days. Were it not for such texts, we would have no grounds to think that the linguistic works had any direct impact on Maya language itself. They would be isolated exercises in description, perhaps foisted on other non-Maya-speaking missionaries but surely of little consequence for the practices of native Maya speakers. By means of induced recitation, doctrinal practice both canonized the translation decisions of the linguists and provided a means of propagating their version of the language.

Fifth, the *guardianía* overlapped with the *cabildo* as a form of governance. The line among *guardián, maestro,* and *escribano* was direct. The various kinds of *fiscal* 'deputy' enforced doctrinal attendance, and missionaries are among the signatories or named witnesses to many of the important actions undertaken in the towns. The practice of prayer and religious observance therefore would have accrued significant social capital in the towns.

Finally, the population of Indios exposed to doctrine was large, because it was normative that neophytes learn the basic precepts and prayer *before* being baptized, assuming they were of appropriate age (Toral, *Avisos* 1563, 26).[2] For those too old to memorize the doctrine, it was enough that they knew how to agree and disagree correctly with statements pertaining to faith. For all others, children and adults, learning the doctrine was a prerequisite to the threshold sacrament of baptism and thus to all other sacraments. (Despite the well-known practice of mass baptisms, at least early in the evangelization, *proper* baptism always required that the neophyte abandon his or her idols voluntarily, in a state of profound contrition; see chapters 5 and 6 above.) For all these reasons, doctrinal discourse was central to the entire missionary project, and it lies at the very heart of the discourse formation in which colonial Maya was shaped.

There are two features of doctrinal language that merit special emphasis here. The first is that these texts are virtually all scripts designed to be repeated again and again. And nearly all of them contain first-person pronouns (I, we) and other indexicals (today, here) whose reference would be fixed only in the recitation of the prayer by an actual individual. Every time the Credo is repeated, the phrase "I believe" denotes a different individual. As I pointed out in chapter 4, this is the inverse of notarial genres such as letters and land surveys, in which all the indexical elements are specific, designed to maintain a constant reference regardless of who reads the document when or where. A notarial text may be subsequently referred to but never reperformed. In contrast, prayer projects an infinite series of experientially dense performances in which it schematically organizes the participant positions, intentions, and feelings of those who engage in it. Prayer does not describe the world, but makes it, and takes up a position or posture in it. Through prayer, semantic fields like those set forth in chapters 5 and 6 are mobilized in the actuality of the praying subject.

The second feature of prayers is that they are, by design, modular. They are easily fragmented into parts that can then be transposed into other genres. Not only was the phrasing of basic prayers ramified in the dialogic portions of the catechism, in the confessional, and in the sermons but, as we will see in coming chapters, fragments of prayer occur in other genres outside the missions as well. And the affective stance of contrition, begging for mercy and forgiveness, recurs not only across the discourse of prayer but also in notarial works. In short, a large part of the discursive power of doctrinal discourse lay precisely in its capacity to disperse; and the dispersion of the language brought with it a correlative dispersion of the meaning structures.[3] The canon of proper prayer was a resource for reframing discourse far beyond the church or monastery.

THE MAYA *DOCTRINAS*

The main published doctrinal texts in Maya during the period under discussion are set out in table 14. Of these, the most significant are the ones by Coronel (1620) and Beltrán (1757), which are the primary focus of the following discussion. The *doctrina* genre was complex in that it contained other genres: monological prayers addressed to God, precepts that were to be learned but were not recited as prayers or addressed to God, dialogic scripts for sacraments (especially confession and communion), and strictly pedagogical dialogues repeated in the classroom setting and at doctrinal exams. Among these different genres there were many cross-references, transpositions of key words and phrases. The relation between prayers and the pedagogical dialogues was metalinguistic: the dialogues explain and give the theological backing of the prayers. In a general sense, the *doctrina* was to religious practice what the *arte* was to linguistic practice. Both are complex genres in which other genres are embedded, and both were aimed mainly at guiding and instructing rather than merely explaining or

TABLE 14 Published Doctrinal Texts (Extant)*

DOCTRINAS

Coronel, Juan (1620), *Discursos Predicables con otras diversas materias.*
Beltrán de Santa Rosa María, Pedro (1757), *Declaración de la Doctrina Christiana en el Idioma Yucateco.*

SACRAMENTAL SCRIPTS

San Buenaventura, Gabriel (1684), *Forma Administrandi infirmis Sacramentum Eucharistae,* published with *Arte.*
Beltrán de Santa Rosa María, Pedro (1740), *Novena de Christo Crucificado, con otras oraciones en Lengua Maya.*

SERMONS AND OTHER TEXTS

Coronel (1620), *Discursos Predicables.*
Domínguez y Argáiz (1758), *Pláticas de los principales mysterios.***

*There is at least one additional *doctrina,* unpublished, of uncertain authorship. This work is part of the Colección Cresencio Carillo y Ancona, held in the Centro de Apoyo para Investigación de Yucatán (I-1700–002 2/3). It is written in a crude hand with many spelling errors and inconsistencies, and is titled *Catechismo para la enseñansa de yndios inpheles e varvaros [. . .]* 'Catechism for the teaching of infidel Indios and barbarians [. . .]'. It mentions fray Juan de Ererra (or Herrera), fray de Landa, and Hernando Cortés and appears to be dated 1620 or thereabouts, although the document is badly damaged and the reading difficult. The doctrinal portion is accompanied by a word list in columns and a calendar of 18 Maya months with their names, a dot and bar number, and the corresponding date in the European calendar. It also includes Maya words for numbers and groups of years (e.g., *tun* = 360 days, *katun* = 20 *tun*) and some notes on local history. I thank Patricia Martínez and Araceli Poot of the Centro for bringing this to my attention and providing me with a photocopy of the original. Because it is unpublished and poses many fascinating problems of interpretation, I do not examine it here.

**Although it is virtually contemporaneous with Beltrán's *Doctrina,* I do not examine the work by Domínguez y Argáiz (1758) here. Doctor don Francisco Eugenio Domínguez y Argáiz was *cura* of the Parish of the Holy Name of Jesus *intramuros* in Mérida and synodal examiner of the Bishopric of Yucatán. His collection of *pláticas* is in the sermon style, explaining the major elements of the faith and practice. Given that he was a highly placed secular priest, this work would make a fascinating counterpoint to the Franciscan works that dominated the missions, but it is beyond the scope of this book. The work is MS. 1967 in the Ayer Collection, Newberry Library, Chicago.

modeling. But, of course, whereas the *arte* and the dictionary were used primarily by missionaries, the *doctrina* was designed and used to shape the practice of Indio neophytes.[4]

Coronel's *Doctrina* in the *Discursos Predicables*

In the dedication of his work, Coronel lauds Bishop Salazar for having expended great effort to promote the spiritual welfare of the Indios. Over the course of three episcopal *visitas* that he conducted as of 1620, Salazar had urged all *naturales* to display the cross in their homes and around their necks. He had lent zealous support to the teaching of doctrine, learning it himself in Maya and singing it in the churches of Yucatán, thereby setting an example for all ministers to emulate. Salazar had encountered Coronel in the convent of Tekax, where he was *guardián,* and had encouraged him to publish his writings, which included the *arte,* the *doctrina,* a confessional manual, and an extensive collection of sermons—all in Maya.

In the dedication to Salazar and in the prologue to the reader, Coronel states that he has *"recogido y recopilado [algunos papeles] de los que los padres antiguos auían escrito, enmendando algunas cosas que en este tiempo ya no se vsan y co-rrigiendo lo que no estaba verdadero"* 'gathered and recopied [some papers] from those that the old priests had written, emending some things that in this time are no longer used and correcting what was not true' (Acuña 1998, 38). In the prologue, Coronel says that he has undertaken this task of recopying and revising because the ancient manuscripts contained *mentiras* 'lies', with wrong letters that prevented proper understanding and pronunciation. For the priest learning Maya, his work would provide a first set of texts to be memorized as practice in the language. For the Indios, it would provide something beneficial printed in their own language. By the time of this publication, Coronel had already been teaching the language to priests newly arrived from Spain for twelve years (i.e., since 1608), and he would continue to do so for many years thereafter. Beltrán suggests that in 1757 Coronel's *doctrina* was still the standard.

San Buenaventura's *Forma Administrandi*

In his published *arte* (1684), San Buenaventura concludes with a fragment of doctrine titled "Form of Administering the Sacrament of the Eucharist to the Ill." This differs from the published doctrines of Coronel and Beltrán in its thematic focus on a single kind of performance. It is also different because it is the script for the priest; the entire first part is in Latin, and it contains instructions on gestures the priest is to perform. A major part of the sacrament is dialogic, scripted in a series of statement-response pairs in Maya without gloss. Following this administering of the sacrament, San Buenaventura has five short *pláticas* 'talks' of about a sentence each, for exhorting Indios before and after confession, after baptism, after matrimony, and before extreme unction. The organization of the work is determined not by the norms of the *doctrina menor* genre but by the parts of the act named in the title. The short *pláticas* seem like add-ons. Unsurprisingly, the resulting text is much shorter than the *doctrinas* and lacks much of the material to be found in them.

Whereas Beltrán addresses Coronel's *doctrina* directly and evidently takes it to be the canon, he does not mention San Buenaventura's doctrinal text. This is noteworthy as he would almost certainly have read it. In his *arte,* Beltrán cites San Buenaventura's *arte* repeatedly. It seems clear that he did not consider the doctrinal part of that work to be of sufficient importance to address it directly in his own writings. I consider San Buenaventura's *Forma Administrandi* to represent a secondary doctrinal genre embedded in the *arte,* just as selective vocabulary lists are also embedded in the *artes.* The vocabulary list is to the stand-alone dictionary what the *Forma Administrandi* is to the stand-alone *doctrina.* Moreover, San Buenaventura's versions of certain basic prayers and his lexical choices for aspects of practice agree with Coronel's usage, with which he was demonstrably familiar. In what follows, therefore, I examine parts of San Buenaventura's text only for contrast, keeping the main focus on Coronel and Beltrán, whose works were clearly more significant to the history of the missions and the Maya people who engaged with them.

Beltrán's *Declaración de la Doctrina Christiana*

Beltrán's *Declaración* is a very short work, filling barely eleven three-by-five-inch pages in the 1912 edition. By contrast, it is preceded by twenty pages of *Advertencias* in which Beltrán addresses the work of Juan Coronel and justifies all the major changes he has introduced. The prefatory text reinforces the impression that Beltrán writes from a different conceptual position than the earlier missionaries. He points out that language change is inevitable, even though in the matter of prayer and liturgy, Pius V had issued a bull proscribing any additions to or subtractions from the holy texts. In the case of Yucatán, Beltrán is acutely concerned with what he considers the adulteration of Maya by its contact with Spanish and with the changes in the meanings of key expressions over the 137 years between Coronel's work and his own. He also notes that among experts, including translators, it is to be expected that there are differences of opinion to which the parties cling tenaciously. Next he observes that apparently trivial changes in spelling, punctuation, or pronunciation can have great consequences for meaning. This observation sets up an impressive list of errors in the *doctrina* as inherited from Coronel (whether because of Coronel's misunderstanding or because language change had altered the meaning of words that were accurate when first chosen).

Among the list of infelicities that he corrects, Beltrán mentions several that are directly relevant to the meaning of doctrine as it was imparted to Maya speakers. These errors, he says, give rise to dissonance and pernicious confusion, even leading priests to unwittingly speak nonsense or, worse, falsehoods. His first example turns on the apparently trivial mistake of substituting /dz/ for /tz/ in transcribing the word *tzic* 'to obey', as in the commandment *Dziceex a yum* 'Obey your father'. The problem is that *dzic* is a different verb and what the Maya actually commands is "Shave your father" (Beltrán 1912 [1757], 7). He later notes that in a passage from the prophet Hosea, God says he is to be henceforth called Baali. Beltrán observes with consternation that Baali happens to be identical to a term used in Maya for idols (8). In the same vein, Coronel (1620) had used the expression *Dios Citbil* for "God the Father" in the Credo and the Eucharistic prayer, but Beltrán rejects the phrase on the grounds that it is used in contemporary (mid-eighteenth-century) Maya for a native god. Beltrán goes so far as to say that he had recently discovered an idol so called, which had been buried alongside the wall around a house compound (solar). He reports unearthing and smashing the idol, and he advocates avoiding use of that term by substituting the unambiguous Dios Yumbil 'God Father' (9). Later in the Advertencias, he returns to this example, suggesting that the Indios are given to practicing idolatry and that this ambiguity encourages them to pray to their own idols while ostensibly voicing prayer to the true God. The likelihood of this ruse is made credible for Beltrán by the example of a small Maya idol that another missionary reportedly found hidden inside a hollow part of a likeness of God the Father; the semantic ambiguity of the name is like the material ambiguity of the holy image with an idol hidden within it. Beltrán argues that no amount of indoctrination will alter the Indio propensity to think of the idol when speaking the epithet for God. Thus the change in terminology is critical for him.

The term *cucutil* is used by Coronel for the body of Christ, and it appears in the Eucharist, the Credo, and the dialogues, as well as the colonial dictionaries. (See, e.g., SF2:545, which offers the example *ukamal ucucutil yumilbil* 'the body of the lord is received', a description of taking communion.) This word occasions one of Beltrán's most dramatic examples of unwitting confusion in the doctrine. He agrees that the term means 'body' in the physical sense but challenges the reader to ask "any Indio which part of the body is the *cucutil*," and he will learn that it is the sexual organs. As Beltrán puts it delicately in Latin, it is that part of the body that distinguishes males from females. What, he asks, would an Indio think he or she was doing in receiving communion? The probability of confusion would be all the greater because the Indios are feeble-minded. The body part meaning of *cucutil* is its "natural" meaning. Just as a cat trained to eat only on command will nonetheless revert to his nature if offered young rats, says Beltrán, so too the Indio trained in doctrine will nonetheless revert to the natural meanings of the terms in his language when presented with them. It is better all around to simply say *uinicil*, which is the daily term for 'body'.[5]

Beltrán subsequently takes aim at the relational noun *okol* 'above, atop, for' (Spanish *por*), which Coronel had used in several key passages. Coronel's Hail Mary uses *yumbil yan auokol* to translate 'the father is with you'. The problem according to Beltrán is that the Maya actually means 'the father is on top of you', which Beltrán considered vulgar and entirely inappropriate. He revised it to *yumbil yan auicnal* 'the father is with you'. In the same prayer, Mary is said to be blessed "among women," which Coronel had misglossed as 'above [*yokol*] women'. Citing the "Calepino or Vocabulary" on the uses of *okol*, he revises this one to 'blessed *ichil* [within, among] women'. In his third example of *okol* in the Hail Mary, Beltrán argues that the phrase *payalchinen cokol* 'pray for us' is proper and should be retained, despite calls for revision. Again citing the Vocabulario, Beltrán (1912 [1757], 15) notes that this usage of *yokol* to mark the beneficiary of a ritual act is proper Maya. As discussed in chapter 6, to say *missa yokol* someone is to say Mass on his or her behalf (see SF2:670, V:474).

In respect of the commandments of the Church and the sacraments, Beltrán makes changes that clearly reflect the current realities of his day. To the rule that believers should attend Mass, he adds that it should say *tuliz missa* 'entire Mass', because the Indios had the habit of leaving before Mass was finished. The sacrament of holy matrimony Coronel had translated as *kamnicte,* which means literally 'receive flower', evidently an older image of romantic love (found also in the Motul). Beltrán points to the literal meaning and says it baffles the Indios, who do not understand it to mean matrimony but only the exchange of flowers. Apparently, an image once potentially transparent to Maya speakers had become opaque and irrecoverable for them; conventional metaphor was lost and literality remained.[6] Beltrán offers the same kind of correction here as elsewhere: translate "marriage" with the ordinary Maya of the day, which is *dzocol-bel* (lit. 'finish-path') (Beltrán 1912 [1757], 23).

WHAT IS A *DOCTRINA MENOR*?

There was a relatively stable template for the organization of the missionary catechisms, just as there was for the *artes.* The Maya *doctrinas* are both of the kind called *doctrina menor* 'minor doctrines'. Such works are relatively short and designed for teaching children and neophytes, not for in-depth exploration of the faith.[7] According to the *Códice Franciscano,* the *doctrina menor* had four main parts: prayers, precepts, sacraments, and dialogues. The organization of Coronel's doctrine conforms closely to this normative template (table 15).

Beltrán adds some material to what Coronel already had and reorders the parts somewhat (table 16). Although Beltrán compares his work to Coronel's on a long list of points, he never addresses this difference in organization, which was evidently trivial from his perspective—suggesting that the order of parts in the genre template is flexible. Note that the first five elements do not vary. This is because these are the core prayers that had to be learned, in the order listed, before the neophyte could move on to more advanced material.

Despite the variation between Coronel's and Beltrán's works, a glance at tables 15 and 16 indicates that they overlapped to a great extent. Similar organization is found in the missionary catechisms produced in Nahuatl, such as that of Molina, with which Coronel was evidently familiar (he cites the Nahuatl works to justify his use of the grapheme /tz/ instead of /tʒ/ in the preface to his own work). Even as early as Pedro de Gante's pictographic version of the *doctrina,* the same basic parts are in evidence, mostly in the same order.[8]

TABLE 15 The Parts of the *Doctrina*, Coronel (1620)

El Persignarse	The sign of the cross
El Padre Nvestro	The Our Father
El Ave María	The Hail Mary
El Credo	The Credo
La Salve	The Salve
La Confession	The Confiteor Deo
Los Artícvlos de la fe	The articles of the faith
Los Mandamentos de Dios	The commandments of God
Los Mandamentos de la Sancta madre Yglesia	The commandments of the Church
Los sacramentos de la Sancta Madre Yglesia	The sacraments of the Church
Los pecados mortales	The mortal sins
Las obras de misericordia	The works of charity
Exposición de Doctrina Christiana (dialogic)	Exposition of Christian doctrine

TABLE 16 The Parts of the *Doctrina*, Beltrán (1757)

Persignarse	The sign of the cross
El Padre Nuestro	The Our Father
El Ave María	The Hail Mary
El Credo	The Credo
La Salve Regina	The Salve
Los Mandamentos de Dios	The commandments of God
Los Mandamentos de la Iglesia	The commandments of the Church
Los Sacramentos	The sacraments
El Confiteor Deo	The Confiteor Deo
Señor mio Jesuchristo	Lord Jesus Christ
Los Artículos de la fe	The articles of the faith
Las Obras de Misericordia	The works of charity
Los Pecados capitales que llaman mortales	The capital sins called mortal
Diálogo sobre el Credo y los Artículos	Dialogue about the Credo and articles
De el nombre y señal de el Christiano	Of the name and sign of the Christian
Diálogo de lo que debe saber el que es Christiano	Dialogue on what a Christian should know

Praying in Maya

The first order of business in the *doctrina* was teaching the sign of the cross and the four basic prayers. Much of the dialogue that occurs later in the works is designed to explain and fix the meaning of these core elements. As noted above, the individual prayers are distinct primary works in the genre *payalchi* 'rezar' 'prayer'. They are designed to be repeated by the faithful daily and before receiving the sacraments. They also would have been central in missionary pedagogy in the classrooms, and this helps explain why they spread into other writings in Maya.

THE SIGN OF THE CROSS
~CORONEL (1620)

EL PERSIGNARSE

Tumen uchicil, cilich cruz,
    tocon ti cahualob,
        yumile, caDiose,
tu Kaba Dios citbil
    yetel Dios mehenbil,
        yetel Dios Spiritusancto
Amen Jesus.

THE PERSIGNUM

By the sign of the beautiful cross,
    protect us from our enemies,
        lord, our God
in the Name of God almighty
    and God the son
        and God the Holy Spirit
Amen Jesus.

The first element in the doctrine, the sign of the cross, would also be the most frequently recited prayer, both because it was the first thing students had to master and because it was to be recited frequently in ordinary life. In its multiple manifestations, the cross was the root symbol of the Christian era, the protector, the opening gesture of major activities, including prayer and all rituals.[9] According to the *Catholic Encyclopedia,* the sign of the cross was originally a means of exorcism, to free the one signed from evil and protect against subsequent contagion.[10] This primary function is stated in the first three lines above. The enemies referred to are explained elsewhere in the doctrine: the devil, the material world, and the flesh. These opening lines are typical of missionary signs of the cross but are not part of the Latin persignum, which consists of the last four lines in the passage. The fourth line shows Coronel's use of the expression *Dios Citbil,* discussed above. Here we can see that it forms a minor verse couplet with the next line, based on the repetition of "Dios" and the reverential suffix -*bil* (also found elsewhere in *cole-bil* 'holy lady'). Coronel maintains the Latin *Spiritu Sancto,* as he does throughout his *doctrina.*[11]

In nomine Patris, et Filij, et Spiritus Sancti. Amen.

San Buenaventura's transcription of the prayers for the sick, the *Forma Administrandi infirmis Sacramentum Eucharistae,* begins with the sign of the cross in Latin. Note the absence of reference to protection or the enemies of faith. This is the version of the cross to be spoken by the priest, whereas the version in Coronel and Beltrán is to be spoken by the Indio faithful. Presumably the priest is fully aware of the tie between this root symbol and gestural sign, on the one hand, and protection, on the other, whereas the translation for Indios spells out the connection.

⌐BELTRÁN (1912 [1757], 25)

PERSIGNARSE

TUMEN u chicul cilich cruz
tocen ti kanalob yumbil hahal Dios,
tukabá Dios yumbil
yetel Dios mehenbil
yetel Dios Espiritu Santo.
Amen

PERSIGNUM

BY the sign of the blessed cross
protect me from enemies Lord true God,
in the name of God the father
and God the Son
and God the Holy Spirit.
Amen

Beltrán's version is nearly identical to Coronel's, with a few minor changes. The Latin *Spiritusancto* is translated into the Spanish *Espiritu Santo,* and there is no mention of Jesus at the final *amen.* In the first line of the recited text, *chicil* has been changed to *chicul,* apparently because of historical change in ordinary Maya (the *chicul* form is the one used today; see chapter 5 above). The phrase "protect us from our enemies" has been changed to "protect me from enemies."[12] As we would expect given Beltrán's introduction, the term *citbil* has been changed to *yumbil* in *Dios yumbil* 'God the Father'. Note also in the third line that Beltrán has changed *caDios* 'our God' to *hahal Dios* 'true God'. The latter form positions the Christian God in the sphere of truth in opposition to the falsehood of idols and is the epithet most often used today.

THE OUR FATHER
~CORONEL (1620) (ACUÑA 1998, 149)[13]

EL PADRE NVESTRO

Ca yum yanech ti caane,
  sancto cinabac a kaba;
    tac au ahaulil c okol,
utzcinabac au olah ti luum ba te ti caane;
    dza ca çamal kin uah toon hele lae,
      çateç ix ca çipil bay ca çaatçic v çipil ah çipilob toone,
ma ix au ilic ca lubul tac tum tabale,
      heuac lukezon ychil lobil.
        Amén Jesús.

THE OUR FATHER

Our father, you are in heaven,
  sanctified be your name:
    your kingdom come upon us,
    your will be done, on earth, and there in heaven;
      give us our daily bread today,
        and forgive our trespasses, as we forgive the trespasses of those who
          trespass against us,
  and do not see us fall into temptation,
    but separate us from evil.
      Amen Jesus.

As the first full prayer that neophytes would learn on their way to becoming Christians, the Our Father elaborates the first line of the *persignum* (in the name of the father) and sets the stage for what comes later. The paternal relation, the sanctity of the name, the idea that God has a kingdom and a will for the world, the providing of food, and the forgiveness of wrongs committed are all ramified throughout the *doctrina*. They jointly place the Christian subject in a relation of kinship with God (*yum* is the ordinary term for 'father'), subjection to God (*ahau-lil* is the ordinary word for 'political ruler' and 'rule', and the vertical reference in "upon us" reflects the same power relation), and receipt of divine munificence (the giving of food, the granting of forgiveness, and the protection from temptation). This God, moreover, has a will and intention (*auolah* is the ordinary term for 'your will, intention'; see the array of concepts translated by *ol* in chapter 6 above) much as a human ruler would. It is likely that for Maya subjects in the early colony, this way of configuring the relation to God would have echoed the long-standing practice of revering ancestors, and the commingling of divine rule and temporal rule was well established in Maya history. At the same time, the Christian subject can speak directly to God and stands before him as one of a community of believers, whereas these elements may contrast with pre-Columbian practice. The references to will and temptation hint at the cognitive complexity of the God-subject relation, which is elaborated in other prayers and especially in the practice of confession.

⌒BELTRÁN (1912 [1757], 25)

EL PADRE NUESTRO

CAYUM, yanech ti Caanob,
  cilich cunabac á Kaba:
    tac á uahaulil c okol,
utzcinabac á uolah, ti luum, baix te ti caane;
  Dza ca zamal Kin uah toon helelae;
    zatez ix ca zipil, bay ca zatzic ú zipil ah ziplob toone:
maix á uilic calubul ti tumtabale;
  heuac lukezon ichil lobil.
    Amen Jesús.

THE OUR FATHER

OUR FATHER, you are in the heavens,
  beautified be your name:
    your kingdom come upon us,
your will be done, on earth, and there in heaven;
  Give us our daily bread today;
    and forgive our trespasses, as we forgive the trespasses of those who
      trespass against us:
and do not see us fall into temptation;
  but separate us from evil.
    Amen Jesus.

The basic form of the Our Father, at least as defined by the Franciscans, was not changed over the colonial period. Beltrán makes several minor but suggestive revisions to Coronel's version. He pluralizes "heaven" in line 1 (Beltrán 1912 [1757], 12) and renders *sanctocinabac* as *cilichcunabac* in line 2. The term *cilich* occurs elsewhere in doctrinal language, as in the name Holy Mary *(Cilich Maria)*, and Beltrán shows a distinct preference for using Maya expressions rather than Spanish or Latin. Coronel's form *sancto-cin-ab-ac* is derived by causativizing the adjective ('cause to be holy'), passivizing the resulting stem ('caused to be holy') and then marking the form optative or subjunctive ('let it be caused to be holy'). This derivation pattern was explained in the *arte* (see chapter 7 above) and is one standard way to form a "third-person imperative." It is identical to the structure of *utz-cin-ab-ac* in line 4, where *utz* means 'good' and the resulting derived form means 'be it caused to make good, fulfilled'. This identical verb (*utzcinic* 'to fulfill') occurs in letters by members of the Maya elite addressed to the Spanish Crown, in reference to royal will (see chapter 9). Beltrán makes three more minor revisions. He rejects *tac tumtabale* in favor of *ti tumtabale* for 'into temptation', observing (correctly) that the latter is simply more accurate than the former (Beltrán 1912 [1757], 12). He rejects the use of the letter /ç/ in favor of /z/, an alternation we have already encountered in the dictionaries, and the form *ah zipilob* 'trespassers' is rendered *ah ziplob,* with syncope of the medial vowel. This syncope follows the rules for vowel elision that Beltrán laid out in his *arte,* and it makes the script that much closer to oral production.

THE CREDO

The Credo crystallizes the core of Catholic belief in a series of declarative state-ments in the first-person singular. It is a confession in the sense of expressing the subject's conviction of the mystery of the incarnation, crucifixion, and resurrec-tion. It formulates the basic ontology of God and the world into which his son was born, from which he was resurrected and to which he will return in judgment. Whereas the Our Father positions the praying subject as part of a "we," the Credo focuses almost intimately on the singular subject and performs his or her conviction. Recall from the dictionaries that *ocol ol* and its derivatives were used to translate 'believe', not in the mundane sense of thinking or "believing that," but in the monumental sense of "believing in."

~CORONEL (1620) (ACUÑA 1998, 149)

EL CREDO

Ocan ti uol Dios Citbil
 uchuc tumen tu çinile,
  y ah menul caan yetel luum,
Ocaanix ti u ol ca yumil ti Iesu Christo
 U ppelel Mehenile,
  lay hichhnabi ti Spíritu sancto,
  çihi ix ti çuhuy sancta Maria;
tali tu chi Poncio Pilato numci ti ya
  çijnci ix ti Cruz, cimi tun, ca muci ca ix emi tu kaçal Mitnal,
   Limbo u kabae.
Tu yox kin ca put cux lahi ychil cimenob, ca naaci ti caan;
 tij cuman tu nooh Dios Citbil
  vchuc tumen tuçinil;
Tij tun lukul ca bin tac v xotob v kin cuxanob
 yetel cimenob.
Ocanix ti uol Spíritu sancto

yetel Sancta Yglesia Católicae,
  v molay sanctoobe,
 v çatal ix keban xan
  v ca put cuxtal ix ca bakel
   yetelix hun kul cuxtale.
Amén Jesus.

I believe in God the Father
  almighty,
    the maker of heaven and earth.
I believe in our Lord Jesus Christ,
  the only Son
    conceived of the Holy Spirit,
      born of the Blessed Virgin Mary.
He was judged by Pontius Pilate,
  suffered, was crucified,
    died and was buried.
Then he descended into the evil hell;
  Limbo it is called.
On the third day he was resurrected among the dead and ascended into heaven;
  there he is seated on the right of God the Father
    almighty.
From there he will come to judge the living
  and the dead.
And I believe in the Holy Spirit
  and the Holy Catholic Church
    and the communion of saints
and the forgiveness of sins,
  the resurrection of our flesh
    and life everlasting.
Amen Jesus.

Ocan ti uol 'it has entered to my heart' and ocol ol 'enter heart, belief' are both highly transparent. Ocol ol consists of two parts, ocol 'to enter' (intransitive) + ol 'heart, intention, desire' (noun). Alongside other body part terms (cf. chi 'mouth', puksikal 'heart', kab 'hand', pol 'head'), it is often incorporated, as it is here. When the ol is possessed, by the one who "believes," it cannot be incorporated, and we find ocol ti uol 'it enters to my heart'. Thus ocan ti uol literally means 'it has entered to my heart'. The sense of ol is actually broader than English 'heart'. It encompasses the sprouting 'heart' of palm, along with the part of the self that feels happy, sad, hot, cold, relaxed, intentionally directed, committed or lustful—

all of which are designated in Maya with constructions of the form *x-ol*, where *x* may be an adjective or a verb. To say 'I am happy', one said (and says today) *cimac inuol* 'happy (is) my heart'. The derived form *ocol olal* translates 'faith', not merely mundane 'belief'. Thus the first line of the Credo expresses a monumental belief. It is doubtful whether all those who performed the prayer took on its full import, but the missionaries wanted them to. By inducing students to repeat and memorize it, by reinforcing its meaning in the dialogues and sermons, they sought to inscribe it on the hearts of their Indio subjects.

After the first two stanzas of the prayer, there are three that essentially present the narrative of Jesus' judgment, crucifixion, passion, death, resurrection, ascent to heaven, and ultimate return in judgment. These are all within the scope of what the praying subject believes in. Recall from the grammars that *nacal* 'to ascend' was the verb used to exemplify the first conjugation in all three *artes*. This part of the prayer lays out a sacred geography, opposing *emi* 'he descended' (into hell) to *naci* 'he ascended' (into heaven), with earth in the middle. The equation of 'the most bad hell' with Limbo is a missionary innovation without basis in the Latin Credo.[14] The formulation of 'seated at the right (hand) of God almighty' uses the neologism *uchuc tumen tuzinil*, explored in chapter 1. In the next to last stanza, the phrase *ocanix tiuol* is repeated a last time, with the Holy Spirit as its subject. Thus this verb occurs just three times in the prayer, once for the father, once for the son, and once for the holy spirit, resulting in a poetic icon of the trinity.

∽BELTRÁN (1912 [1757], 25–26)

EL CREDO

Ocan ti uol Dios Yumbil,
  uchuc tumen tu zinile,
    yah menul Caan yetel luum.
Ocanix ti uol ca Yumil ti Jesu-Christo,
  ppelel Mehenile,
    lay hichhnabi ti Espiritu Santo
      zihi ix ti Zuhui ixcilich Maria;
Tali tu chi Poncio Pilato:
  numci ti ya, zini ix ti Cruz;
    cimitun, ca ix muci,
Ca ix emi tu Kazal metnal limbo ú Kabae:
  Tu yoxkin caput cuxlahi ichi cimenob
    Ca naci ti Caan.
Ti ix culan tu noh Dios Yumbil uchuc tumen tu zinil.
  Ti tun likul cabin tac, ú xotob ú Kin cuxanob
    Yetel cimenob
Ocanix ti uol Espiritu Santo;

Yetel Santa Iglesia Catholica,
  Baix ú mul etmal Santoob.
Uzatalix Kebanxan.
  U caput cuxtalix ca bakel
  Yetelix hunkul cuxtal.
Amen Jesús.

THE CREDO

I believe in God the Father
  Almighty,
    the maker of heaven and earth.
I believe in our Lord Jesus Christ,
  the only Son
    conceived of the Holy Spirit,
      born of the Blessed Virgin Mary.
He was judged by Pontius Pilate,
  suffered, was crucified,
    died and was buried.
Then he descended into the evil hell; limbo it is called.
  On the third day he was resurrected among the dead
    and ascended into heaven.
There he is seated on the right of God the Father almighty.
  From there he will come to judge the living
    and the dead.
And I believe in the Holy Spirit
  and the Holy Catholic Church
    and the communion of saints
And the forgiveness of sins,
  The resurrection of our flesh
    And life everlasting.
Amen Jesus.

Among the changes Beltrán makes to Coronel's version of the Credo are the substitutions of *yumbil* 'revered father' for *citbil* 'infinite', *ixcilich Maria* for *sancta María* 'holy Mary', and *Santa Iglesia Catholica* for *Sancta Yglesia Católicae* 'holy Catholic Church'. These changes fit with Beltrán's overall strategy of bringing the language of prayer closer to the language actually spoken by Indios, in which Spanish, not Latin, was an integral part. Whereas the early missionaries translated 'communion of saints' using *molay* 'congregation', Beltrán alters it to *mul etmal*, which better captures the coparticipation implied in the Spanish (Beltrán 1912 [1757], 17).

THE AVE MARIA

∽CORONEL (1620) (ACUÑA 1998, 149)

EL AVE MARÍA

Cici ol ne(n) sancta María, chup ech ti gracia,
   Yumilbil yan auokol,
   pay num a cici thanbilil yokol chhuplal tu çinile
      pay num ix cici thanbilil au al ti Iesus.
   Sancta María çuhuye v naa Diose payal chinen c okol
      hele tu kintzil ix ca cimil
         coon ah kebane.
      Amén Iesús.

THE HAIL MARY

Hail Mary full of grace:
   Father is above you.
   Blessed are you among all women,
      Blessed is your son Jesus.
   Holy Mary blessed mother of God pray for us
      today and on the day of our death,
         we who are sinners.
      Amen Jesus.

∽BELTRÁN (1912 [1757], 25)

EL AVE MARÍA

Ciciolnen ix cilich Maria, chupech ti grazia:
   Yumilbil yan á uicnal:
   painum á cici thanbilil ichil chhupal tu zinile;
      painum ix cici thanbilil á ual ti Jesus.
   Yx cilich Maria ú naa Diose payalchinen c okol
      toon ah keban hele,
   tu Kin tzil ix ca cimil.
      Amen Jesús.

THE HAIL MARY

Hail Mary full of grace:
   Father is with you:
   Blessed are you among all women;
      blessed is your son Jesus.
   Holy Mary blessed mother of God pray for us
      we who are sinners today,
   and on the day of our death.
      Amen Jesus.

The Hail Mary is the basic prayer addressed to the mother of the incarnate God, Jesus. She is mentioned in passing in the Credo, but it is in this prayer that she is beseeched to pray for 'us sinners' on earth. *Cici ol nen* 'hail' is made up of the following parts: *cici + ol + nen* 'sweetly + heart + imperative', which means roughly 'have a sweet heart'. The form *cici thanbilil* 'hallowed' in the third and fourth lines builds on the same prefix *cici* but combines it with *than + bil + il* 'speech-passive-possessed', to yield 'blessedness' in 'greater is your blessedness than [that of] all women'. Coronel uses *okol* in the second and third lines, where Beltrán corrects the text to *-icnal* 'place' and *ichil* 'among', respectively. Whereas the Credo speaks in the first-person singular, this prayer is in first-person plural, and whereas the Credo is an individual confession of faith, the Hail Mary is a collective plea for intercession.

THE CONFESSION

⁓CORONEL (1620) (FOLIOS 222–224)

LA CONFESSION.

Ten cen Ahçipile tohcab incah tikeban-
    ti Dios, ti sancta María ixan yetel ti Sanctoob tulacal,
      techix cech Padre
çipen ti Dios, yetel tiyalmahtanil,
    tin tucul, tin than, tin beelixan,
lay okomiluol, tulalcalloe
    kalchijx incah, çatebal ti Dios, okotbaix incah.
      Tac cilich coolel. Ti çuhuy Sancta María. Yetelti sanctoob tulacal,
    cayoktubaob, tutan Dios uokol,
      cau çatez inçipil,
        caix adzab, uyaaltulul ten cech Padre.

THE CONFESSION

I who am a sinner declare (my) sin(s)-
    to God, to holy Mary also and to all (the) Saints,
      to you too Father
I have sinned against God and against the commandments,
    in my thought, in my words, and in my deeds,
All this saddens me
    I am contrite,[15] lost to God, and I am begging
      to our holy lady, to virgin Blessed Mary, and to all the saints,
    that they beg before God on my behalf,
      that he might take away my sin,
        and that you might give absolution to me Father.

The sacrament of confession is uniquely powerful as an instrument for shaping the Christian subject as one who reflects upon his own actions, feels remorse, declares his fault, and begs for forgiveness. Recall from the dictionaries that the missionaries developed an elaborate lexicon of terms to designate the various aspects of this key sacrament. In the first line, the speech act of confession is formulated as "*tohcab in cah ti keban*" 'I am truthfully (straight) telling sins', with God and the saints coded as third persons and the priest coded as the addressee.[16] The reference to thought, word, and deed subdivides the dimensions along which sins are committed, while the following stanzas lay out the affective space of remorse, contrition, the sense of loss, and the tearful entreaty for forgiveness. This range of affect is a critical part of confession, without which it would not be effective, and chapter 6 shows how elaborate and interconnected the vocabulary is for the range of negative feelings associated with sin. Moreover, in this prayer we see very clearly the mediating role that Mary and the saints play as intercessors on behalf of the human sinner before God.[17]

San Buenaventura (1684) (Acuña 1996, 148) includes a version of the Confiteor nearly identical to this, with a couple of minor revisions, whereas Beltrán makes substantial changes, as can be seen below.

⌖BELTRÁN (1912 [1757], 28)

EL CONFITEOR DEO

Ten cen ahçipile tohcabincah tin keban
  ti Dios uchuctumen tu çinil;
    ti ix cilich Zuhui Maria, ti San Miguel Archangel, San Juan Baptista,
      San Joseph, ti ix Apostolob San Pedro yetel San Pablo,
  yetel ti Santoob tulacal:
    techix cech Padre
chac zipen ti Dios, tin tucul, tin than, tin beelixan:
  tumen in zipil, tumen in zipil, tumen in noh zipil:
laix tah oklal okotbaincah ti cilich colel zuhui Maria,
    ti San Miguel Archangel, San Juan Baptista, ti San Joseph,
      ti ix Apostoloob San Pedro, yetel San Pablo,
      yetel ti Santoob tulacal,
      tech ix cech Padre,
ca á uokteaba tutan Dios uoklal.
  Amen Jésus.

THE CONFITEOR DEO

I who am a sinner declare my sin(s)
  to God almighty,

to holy Virgin Mary, to Saint Michael Archangel, Saint John the Baptist,
   Saint Joseph, and to the Apostles Saint Peter and Saint Paul,
and also to all (the) Saints;
   to you too Father.
I have sinned gravely against God in my thought, in my words and in my deeds,
   by my faults, by my faults, by my great faults.
For this reason I am begging to our holy lady virgin Mary,
   to Saint Michael Archangel, Saint John the Baptist, to San Joseph
      and to all the Apostles,
      and to you father,
   that you beg before God on my behalf.
      Amen Jesus.

Beltrán (1912 [1757], 23) considers Coronel's version of the Confiteor abbreviated, and he restores the names of the saints to whom the prayer appeals. He also restores the well-known *mea culpa, mea culpa, mea maxima culpa* in the line immediately following the reference to thought, words, and deeds. This prayer is noteworthy in that although God, Mary, and the saints are all coded in the third person, they are obviously the ultimate addressees to whom appeal is made (as is reflected in the name of the prayer, Confiteor Deo). The prayer is spoken to the priest, who is the overt addressee. Whereas Coronel ends with a request that the priest give absolution, Beltrán makes no reference to absolution but only to intercession. Like the Credo, this prayer is entirely in the first-person singular, and the opening statement *ten cen ah zipil toh cab in cah* 'I who am a sinner am declaring truth' is parallel to *ocan ti uol* 'I believe'. Both utterances perform the subject as one with the right belief and desire.

⤳CORONEL (1620) (ACUÑA 1998, 194 FF.)

CONFESSIONARIO BREUE PARA CONFESSAR LOS INDIOS

PÓNENSE LAS PREGUNTAS ORDINARIAS, EN LA LENGUA Y CASTILLA, SEGÚN LAS CULPAS QUE SE ACOSTUMBRAN COMETER, Y EN QUE ORDINARIAMENTE PECCAN Y SE LES PREGUNTA.

LO QUE SE LE HA DE PREGUNTAR AL PENITENTE ANTES QUE DIGA SUS PECADOS, ACABADO DE PERSINARSE Y DICHA LA CONFESSIÓN, ES LO SIGUIENTE:

1. *Bikini a chochah a keban . . . l . . . a tohpultah a keban?*
2. *Aualah ua a çipil tulacal ti padre?*
3. *Yan xin a çipil a muclah ti padre ca confessarnech?*
4. *Yan xin a çipil tubi tech ca confessarnech?*
5. *A dzoclukçah va yalah padre tech?*
6. *Ya va tavol a çipci ti Dios ah tepale?*
7. *Lic va a dzaic tauol mail bikin a çipil ti Dios tu caten?*
8. *Hala a çipil tulacal, ti ma tan a mucle hun ppeli*

*DÉXENLE DEZIR SUS CULPAS Y, CONFORME LO QUE DIXERE, SE LE PREGUNTEN LAS
CIRCUNSTANCIAS DE ELLAS Y, SI NO LAS DIZE, SE LE PREGUNTE LO QUE SE SIGUE:*

SOBRE LOS MANDAMENTOS DE LA LEY DE DIOS

[...]

9. *Yan xin auocçic tauol auayak bax yauat chhichhob?*
10. *Yan xin aualic hach than tukaba Dios bax 'yohel Ku', ichil a tuz?*

[...]

11. *Yan xin a çipil ti hunpay chhuplal (si es varón; y, si es muger) ti hun pay xiblal?*
12. *Hay tulx tu baob?*
13. *Hay tenhi ti hun tuli, cunx ti hun tuli?*

[...]

14. *Yan xin a pakic v pach hunpay bax a lobcinic v pectzil a lak?*

[...]

LOS MANDAMENTOS DE LA SANCTA MADRE YGLESIA

15. *Yan xin auukic balche?*

BRIEF MANUAL FOR CONFESSING INDIANS

ASK THE ORDINARY QUESTIONS, IN THE LANGUAGE AND IN SPANISH, ACCORDING TO THE FAULTS THEY CUSTOMARILY COMMIT, AND IN WHICH THEY ORDINARILY SIN AND IT IS ASKED OF THEM.

WHAT HAS TO BE ASKED OF THE PENITENT BEFORE (S)HE SAYS HIS (HER) SINS, AFTER MAKING THE SIGN OF THE CROSS, AND SAYING THE CONFESSION (CONFITEOR DEO), IS THE FOLLOWING:

1. When did you (last) untie your sin(s) ... or ... declare your sin(s)?
2. Did you tell all of your sins to father?
3. Are there by chance sins you hid from father when you confessed?
4. Are there by chance sins you forgot when you confessed?
5. Did you fulfill (what) father told you to?
6. Does it pain you to have sinned against God's majesty?
7. Do you commit yourself to never sin against God again?
8. Say all of your sins, not hiding even one.

LET HIM SAY HIS SINS AND, ACCORDING TO WHAT HE MIGHT SAY, THE CIRCUMSTANCES OF THEM ARE ASKED OF HIM, AND IF HE DOES NOT SAY THEM, WHAT FOLLOWS IS ASKED OF HIM:

REGARDING THE COMMANDMENTS OF THE LAW OF GOD

[...]

9. Have you by chance believed in your dreams or the calls of birds?
10. Have you by chance sworn in the name of God, like "God knows," while lying?

[...]

11. Have you by chance sinned with another woman (if it is a man; and if it is a woman) with another man?

12. And how many are they?
13. How many times was it with the one, and what about the (other) one?
    [...]
14. Have you by chance defamed another or caused harm to another's reputation?
    [...]

THE COMMANDMENTS OF THE HOLY MOTHER CHURCH

15. Have you by chance drunk balche?

Coronel's sermons include what is, to my knowledge, the only extant Maya-language manual for administering confession. The entire text is in Maya with Spanish glosses, which I have omitted for brevity. The opening lines and selected parts of the dialogue are reproduced above, where the first two paragraphs state the order to be observed (in small caps) followed immediately by a series of seven questions and an exhortation to confess all sins without hiding any (1–8). After this initial sequence, the manual stipulates what the priest is to do: hear the confession and ask about the circumstances of the sins. If the confessee is not forthcoming, then the questions that follow (9–15) are asked (in addition to others not shown). The material presented here is complete through the first eight items but selective thereafter. The later material is entirely composed of questions regarding the commandments of God (the Ten Commandments) and then the commandments of the Church. This organization of confessional questions effectively cross-references the *doctrina,* where the two kinds of precept are distinguished and stated as lists (see tables 15 and 16). The confession is like a pedagogical review of the *doctrina* but with specific reference to the behavior of the confessee.

From these instructions, we can reconstruct the sequence of phases in table 17, corresponding to the necessary parts of canonical confession. This would be the definition of the orderly telling of sins, as mentioned in the dictionaries. The confessee is to make the persignum, say the Confiteor Deo, and answer the questions of the padre. What is not shown in Coronel's confessional text is the absolution or the assigning of penance. The focus here is on getting the truth and inducing self-reflection of a highly structured sort.

The preparatory questions in this text compel the confessee to remember his or her last confession, to compare what was confessed with the actual sins at the time, to remember whether he or she completed the penance, to recall the sadness felt at having sinned, and to commit to telling everything this time. As a memory device, this series of questions requires that the subject assume different perspectives on both the past and the future. Anyone actually able to answer such questions would have thought a good bit about his or her own behavior, about what the confessing priest would have understood from the previous confession (since it is easy to "bury" sins by fudging the statement of them), and about whether

TABLE 17 Phases of Confession according to Coronel (1620)

Persignum
Confiteor Deo
Preparatory questions (1–8)
Confession proper *(toh pul keban)*
Probing the circumstances of sin
Questions regarding the commands of God
Questions concerning the commandments of the Church

the penance was completed. All this implies a formidable level of awareness on the part of the confessee. Once again, we have no way to know how many Indios fully engaged in this act of reflection, but the structure for reflexive critique and examination is laid down in stark detail.

In this and other doctrinal texts, the terms *zipil* (or *çipil*) and *keban* appear nearly interchangeable. This is the implication, I think, of the way they are used in Coronel's instructions. At the same time, there are some important differences between the two. Unlike *zipil*, *keban* is the object of *tohpultah*—it is what is "straight cast" in confession, whereas *zipil* is not used with this verb. *Keban* is associated with a whole series of negative emotions in the dictionaries, whereas *zipil* is not. In the Our Father, "we" are said to forgive the *zipil* of others but not their *keban*. I believe the difference is that *keban*, at least for the missionaries, is exclusively defined by doctrine, whereas *zipil* is more general and would include all manner of offense beyond the more precise category of sin. For this reason, it is *keban* and not *zipil* that is distinguished into mortal and venial in the corresponding sections of the *doctrina*.

Line 9, referring to belief in dreams and in birdcalls, occurs in a subsection labeled *amar a Dios* 'to love God', which conflates the first commandment ("thou shalt have no other gods before me") with its New Testament revision ("thou shalt love the Lord thy God," etc.). To believe in auguries was an idolatrous failure to love only God; the missionary objective was to reserve "belief in" exclusively for faith in God.

Lines 11–13 give some sense of how the priests actually inquired about illegitimate sex, whereas line 14 goes to calumny and false witness—prominent in the dictionaries, which also mention dreams and birdcalls. The last question (15) is especially meaningful because *balche* is a kind of fermented ritual drink that was consumed at either feasts or ritual offerings—both of which had been forbidden since the time of Toral's *Ordenanzas*. Although the nominal reference here is to drunkenness, it was the circumstances of drinking that most concerned the missionaries, because they indicated either licentious orgies or idolatry.

Doctrinal Dialogues

The doctrinal dialogues within the catechism were designed to explain and reinforce the meanings of the basic prayers, sacraments, and precepts. The aim was to enhance the neophyte's understanding so that when concepts or practices were encountered in the sermons and sacraments, he or she would understand them correctly and know what to believe.[18] The dialogues are metalinguistic commentaries on the other parts of the catechism, and they also inculcated the manner of speaking in which priests or teachers asked questions and students provided scripted responses. This format was the one used for examinations before sacraments as well. There were essentially two kinds of dialogue, one in which information questions were asked and responses were to be substantive, and the other in which yes-no questions were asked. The former was the more demanding, of course, and is laid out in Coronel and Beltrán, whereas San Buenaventura provides some yes-no dialogue for administering communion to the sick. In his *Avisos* (p. 25), Toral spells out how the yes-no dialogue was to be conducted.

> *Asentir y disentir a las cosas de la fe es de esta manera: Si le preguntan lo que es verdad y se ha de creer, ha de decir y responder que sí, y esto es asentir. Ejemplo: Preguntarle ha el cambeçah, Hermano, crees que hay un solo Dios que hizo todas las cosas por su voluntad? Que responda, Sí, creo. . . . Y así cada artículo de la divinidad, y mismo de los que pertenecen a la humanidad de Nuestro Señor Jesucristo.*

> To assent and dissent to things of the faith is like this: If they ask him what is true and he is to believe, he has to say and respond "yes" and this is to assent. Example: the maestro asks him, "Brother, do you believe that there is only one God who made all things by his will?" He should respond: "Yes, I believe." . . . And so on for each article of the divine and the same those that pertain to the humanity of Our Lord Jesus Christ.

Toral implies that the dialogic script would be used by the Indio *maestro,* since he calls him *ah cambeçah,* not *padre,* and the teacher addresses the Indio as *Hermano* 'Brother'. None of the Yucatecan authors adopts this footing in their dialogues. The dissenting response Toral illustrates below (p. 26):

> *Ha de disentir asimismo a lo que no es verdad y es contra nuestra santa fe católica. Ejemplo: Si se le pregunta Crees que hay muchos dioses? Que diga, No creo tal, que solo un Dios hay. . . . Etc. Y así por lo que se le ha enseñado sabrá disentir a la falsedad y asentir a la verdad.*

> He is to dissent the same way from that which is not true and is against our holy Catholic faith. Example: If he is asked "Do you believe there are many gods?" he should say, "No, I do not believe such a thing, there is only one God." . . . etc. And so on for what has been taught to him, he will know to dissent from falsity and assent to truth.

Coronel's dialogues occur in a section labeled "Exposition of Christian Doctrine," as shown below. This section label nicely captures the function of the dialogue, which is to explain and lay out in more detail the reasons and laws that are embedded in the doctrine. In this excerpt, I have reproduced the first twelve turns at talk in the order in which they appear, then left out a lengthy sequence of question-answer pairs, and picked up the text again at line 13.

⌐CORONEL (1620) (ACUÑA 1998, 157)

EXPOSICIÕ DE LA DOCTRINA CHRISTIANA EN LA LENGUA MAYA VTIL Y PROUECHOSA PARA LOS MINISTROS Y INDIOS

1. *Kat Paale macx akaba*
2. *Kam Pedro inkaba*
3. *Kat Christiano echua?*
4. *Kam Layka, yoklal vdzaabilah, cayumilti Iesu Christo*
5. *Kat Balxocti Christianoil?*
6. *Kam Layocti vinic, yan yocolal Christo tie, vçebchitahti baptismo, caput çihil loe*
7. *Kat Macx Christoe?*
8. *Kam Lai hahal Dios tihahal vinicixane*
9. *Kat Bicx Diosil?*
10. *Kam Yoklal uhahal mehenil cuxul Dios*
11. *Kat Bicx vinicilxan?*
12. *Kam Yoklal yalil çuhuy sancta Mariae*
    [...]
13. *Kat Balx uhach payanbehi, vbeelob Xpõ.*[19]
14. *Kam Lay yahlohil balcah, ah cambeçahixane*
15. *Kat Balx tithanil canben vcambeçahi*
16. *Kam Lai doctrina christianae*
17. *Kat Hay tzuc tuba yanil doctrina christianae.*
18. *Kam Can tzuc tuba yanil.*
19. *Kat Cenob xan*
20. *Kam Laitac ocçabenil ocolale, y. yalmahthanil Dios y. payalchiob y Res Sacramentosob*[20]
21. *Kat Cenx uchicil christianoe.*
22. *Kam Lay cijlich cruz la +*
23. *Kat Balx uchun*
24. *Kam Yoklal vuayazba Christo çinan ti cruz lohion.*
25. *Kat Balx vuilal tech*
26. *Kam Inchicilbeçic inba, in cici thantic inbaxā*[21]

EXPOSITION OF CHRISTIAN DOCTRINE IN MAYA LANGUAGE, USEFUL AND PROFITABLE FOR MINISTERS AND INDIOS

1. Q: Child, what is your name?
2. A: Pedro is my name.

3. Q: Are you a Christian?
4. A: Yes indeed, by the grace of our lord Jesus Christ.
5. Q: What does Christianity mean?
6. A: What a person believes (when) he has faith in Christ, he commits to baptism, second birth.
7. Q: Who is Christ?
8. A: He is true God and true man.
9. Q: How is he God?
10. A: For he is the true son of the living God.
11. Q: And how is he man?
12. A: For he is the child of virgin Holy Mary.
    [...]
13. Q: What is the primary of Christ's deeds?
14. A: He is the redeemer of the world, and the teacher.
15. Q: What study-worthy words did he teach?
16. A: The Christian doctrine.
17. Q: How many parts are there in the Christian doctrine?
18. A: There are four.
19. Q: And which are they?
20. A: They are the articles of faith, and the commandments of God and prayers and sacraments.
21. Q: Which is the sign of the Christian?
22. A: It is this holy cross +.
23. Q: Why?
24. A: For Christ suffered crucified on the cross to redeem us.
25. Q: What do you need?
26. A: To sign myself, and to pray *(rogar)*.

As early as line 1 it is obvious that this script is intended to be performed by a priest, probably addressing a child in school. A Christian name like Pedro implies that the child has already been baptized and therefore has already learned doctrine. Indeed, anyone capable of performing this dialogue without assistance would have internalized a great deal of knowledge, along with the correct phrasing in missionary Maya. Lines 1–6 bear on the most basic meaning of Christianity, the faith in Christ, baptism, and resurrection. Lines 7–12 restate portions of the Credo, and lines 13–20 define the genre *doctrina* itself, restating the four parts we have already seen. Finally, lines 21–26 unpack the sign of the cross and reinforce the need to perform it often. Notice in line 5 that Coronel uses the verb *oc ti* to translate 'mean', a usage noted in the Motul but not found in the other dictionaries. In the next line, the Spanish term *baptismo* is juxtaposed with *caput çihil* 'second birth', a pairing that recapitulates perfectly the kind of cross-language equivalence that is spelled out in the dictionary. Such pairings are in fact common in the colonial corpus, and they indicate that the translingual equivalences of the dictionaries were resources for constructing texts.

Although San Buenaventura's brief addition to doctrine in Maya does not contain any pedagogical dialogue like the foregoing, there is a series of yes-no questions to be asked of the sick person to whom communion was to be administered. Most of the questions bear on the content of the Credo and are designed to assure that the sick person holds the right beliefs in respect of the Trinity and especially Jesus' virgin birth, crucifixion, and resurrection. In the passage below I have reproduced the first two exchanges but omitted the rest because they closely follow the prayers already discussed.

 ᴧSAN BUENAVENTURA (1684) (ACUÑA 1996, 149)

1. *Ocaan va ta vol talanil v Kuil cilich oxil, hek lay Dios yumbil, Dios mehenbil yetel Dios Spíritu Sancto, ox tulob tu ba v personail hun tul ili v hahal Diosile?*
   Resp.: Ocaan ti vol
2. *Ocaan va ta vol layil c ah çihçahul yetel c ah lohile?*
   Resp.: Ocaan ti vol

1. Do you believe the mystery of the holy Trinity, which is God the father, God the son and God the Holy Spirit, three persons (in) one true God?
   Resp.: I do believe
2. Do you believe that he is our creator and our redeemer?
   Resp.: I do believe

Whereas both Coronel and Beltrán provide dialogues that call for informative responses by the neophyte, San Buenaventura's illustrates the yes-no assent/dissent format referred to by Toral. It is likely that anyone sick enough to call on the priest might also have been too sick to perform the more demanding version.

Beltrán's dialogues overlap to a great extent with Coronel's. Below I have displayed the opening lines (1–6) in order to show how closely the two correspond. This lends further weight to the claim that for Beltrán, Coronel's text was the standard. Ellipses indicate portions of text omitted. Unlike Coronel, Beltrán includes no Spanish glosses.

 ᴧON THE CREDO AND ARTICLES OF FAITH, BELTRÁN (1912 [1757], 33–34)

1. *Kat Pale, alten macx á Kaba?*
2. *Nuc Pedro, uaix Juan, in Kaba.*
3. *Kat Christianoech ua?*
4. *Nuc La ika, yoklal ú dzaabilah ca Yumil ti Jesu-Christo.*[22]
5. *Kat Balx ú Kat yaal Christianoile?*
6. *Nuc Lay uinic yan yoc olal Christo ti, ú cebchitah ti cap ut zihile.*

[...]

7. *Kat Bi Kin hach yan ú uil ca chicbezic caba ti ú cul cilich Cruce?*
8. *Nuc Amal cabin ca hopez lauac bal ti yutzibee: baix cabin c ilab caba ichil
   lauac bal yail huntacal ix cabin yanac tumtah toon, uaix ú lobil tucule.*
9. *Kat Balx ú chun c chicbezic caba hach yaab ú tenele?*
10. *Nuc Yoklal matubma lic ú Katunticoon, lic ix yalcabpachticoon cahualob;
    heklay Cizine, Balcah, yetel cabakele.*
11. *Kat Heix Cruze yan ua yuchucil uchebal ú tocicoon ti cah[ua]lobe?*
12. *Nuc La ika, yoklal u dzoyahob ca Yumil ti Jesu-Christo ti ú cimilie.*

1. Q: Child, tell me what is your name?
2. A: Pedro, or Juan is my name.
3. Q: Are you Christian?
4. A: Of course, by the grace of our Lord in Jesus Christ.
5. Q: What does Christianity mean?
6. A: That person who has faith in Christ he commits to second birth (baptism).
   [...]
7. Q: When is it really necessary that we sign ourselves with the holy cross?
8. A: Whenever we are beginning some good deed or if we are going to find
   ourselves in pain, especially when there may be temptation for us, or evil
   thoughts.
9. Q: Why do we sign ourselves often?
10. A: For we do not forget that our enemies make war on us and persecute us;
    these are the Devil, the material world, our flesh.
11. Q: And this cross, does it have power to protect us from our enemies?
12. A: Surely, for our Lord in Jesus Christ suffered there until his death.

Lines 7–12 are additions by Beltrán, not present in Coronel's text. They nicely
spell out the protective power of the cross, which is invoked in the first three lines
of the persignum. This dialogue goes beyond explication of the symbol to explain
when and why it is to be performed in the course of ordinary life. It is here that
we learn most clearly that references to "our enemies" are references to the Devil,
the material world, and the flesh, a kind of antitrinity against which the cross has
an exorcistic power rooted in Christ's passion.[23]

All the dialogues restate and define concepts, symbols, and precise phrasings
that belong to prayers, sacraments, and articles of faith. The dialogue habitu-
ates the Christian subject to the position of respondent and canonizes the language that can be used to state his or her practice. The Church sources indicate
that the dialogues were to be performed as examinations before certain sacraments, particularly baptism (for those of appropriate age), marriage, and, if San
Buenaventura is indicative, holy communion as well. It follows that they are
instruments of surveillance as well as teaching aids.

Sermons

Although the historical sources suggest that there were many sermons circulating in the colonial period, to my knowledge, Coronel's nearly two-hundred-page opus contains the first published collection. Almost certainly recopied from manuscripts whose whereabouts are unknown, these texts, called *sermones* 'sermons', *pláticas* 'talks', or *discursos* 'discourses' would have been voiced in settings where the priest was addressing a group of Indio parishioners—mainly in the course of Mass. Recall from chapter 3 that missionary priests were classified according to language ability, and only the most knowledgeable in *lengua* could *predicar* 'preach' in it. So whereas the confessional is bilingual and the prayers are based on European templates, the sermons are authored directly in Maya, and there are no glosses to consult. Furthermore, they have not been edited or translated in any modern work. For these reasons, it is demanding to read them precisely. In the next two examples I briefly examine two sermons, a shorter one reproduced and translated in its entirety and then excerpts from a longer one. The short one, "The Devil Fears the Cross," reflects on the protective power of the cross.[24] The longer one is more didactic. Designed to be spoken to penitents before confession, it spells out the need to reflect on one's sins before going to declare them, and the proper way to do so. There are scores of other sermons in Coronel's collection, but these must suffice to illustrate how the sermons embedded doctrinal practices, precepts, and the meaning of sacraments into coherent *pláticas,* producing a coherent discourse formation in which the new version of *Maya reducido* would circulate.

∾TRANSLITERATION FROM CORONEL, *DISCURSOS PREDICABLES* (AYER COLLECTION MS 1965, FOLIO 192–192V)

EL DEMONIO TEME LA CRUZ.

He timaococ ti christianoil san Christoual cuchie
* xache ucah tunohol ahau yan tibaalcah tuçinil,*
*   cautzac utanlic ukati cuchiloe*
* cau oc yethun huntul ahau,*
*   heklay lic vchicilbeçic vuich tiCruz çançamal cuchiloe.*
* Ca yalah san Christoual ti. Yumile balx vul() achicilbeçic auiche.*
* Ca yalah ahau, lic inchicil beçic inba ti Cruz, vchebal inpudzlic ciçin,*
*   yoklal çahacenti*
* cayalah san Christoual ti. Habla vlahitun intanliceche,*
*   yoklal xacheincah tunohol ahau yan tibaalcah tuçinil,*
*   laix inkati inxachete ciçinloe.*
*   Yoklal paynumil nohil auokole. Va hima yan vtibib tech,*
*   ciyalabal ahau tumen sanct Christoual*
* catun bini sanct Christoual, uxachete ciçin*

maitacxanhi uchictahal ti.
Tabx abenel, Chritouale?
Cayalah Sanct Christoual. Benel incah inxachete çiçin,
    yoklal vuyahma vpectzil
        inkatijx intanle
ca yalah çiçine. Tembe,
ca hoppi vcathil ximbal tilaachitulah vkuchul tuhol cah
    ya nil Cruz cuchi
ci u xoybetah yetel uxaxbetah Cruz çiçine,
catun yalah sanct Christoual ticiçine
    Balx uchun axaxbetic yetel a xoybetic Cruz, tilic auocol
        ich tilic kijx ich ticil tuniche?
Cayalah çiçin yoklal çahacen ti Cruz, lay cimci Iesu Christo lae
catun yalah sanct Christoual ti. Habla uxulitun intanlicech lae,
    yoklal yani paynum nohil auokol. Lay Iesu Christo lae.
Catun bini sanct Christoual
ca chectahi huntul vpalil Dios ti.
    Lay nucbeçi vbabalil Christianoil ti sanct Christouallae.
Baytun hoppci vsanctoilloe. Ylexto hibici hach yanil vnah chicil beçah ich,
    yetel payalchie.

THE DEVIL FEARS THE CROSS

When San Cristóbal had not yet converted to Christianity
    he went looking for the greatest king of the whole world,
        so that he could obey him as he wanted to.
    Then he came upon a king,
        who signed his face with the cross daily.
And San Cristóbal said to him, "Lord, why do you sign your face?"
And the king said, "I sign my face with the Cross in order to chase off the
    Devil,
        For I fear him."
Then San Cristóbal said to him, "Then I will not obey you,
    for I am looking for the greatest king in all the world,
        and I want to seek out the Devil.
For he is greater than you, or someone you fear greatly,"
        the king was told by San Cristóbal.
Then San Cristóbal went looking for the Devil.
    He did not delay in encountering him.
"Where are you going, Cristóbal?"
And San Cristóbal said, "I am going looking for the Devil,
    for I have heard of his reputation
        and I want to serve him."
Then the Devil said, "It is I (you seek)."
And they started to walk together until they arrived at a great city

where there was a cross.
The Devil sidestepped the cross and went around it.
And San Cristóbal said to the Devil,
    "Why do you go around and sidestep the cross, by which you step
       into dried thorns and scattered stones?"
And the Devil said, "Because I am afraid of the cross, where Jesus Christ died."
And San Cristóbal said to him, "Then my serving you is ended,
    for there is another greater one above you. It is Jesus Christ."
So San Cristóbal left
and searched for a child of God.
    This made great the things of Christianity for San Cristóbal.
    Thus began his sainthood. See how very necessary is the sign of the cross,
    and prayer.

The central overt theme of this sermon is the power of the cross, but it has a more specific meaning connected with power and idolatry in Yucatán. Cristóbal, not yet a saint, purposes to offer his service to the greatest king in the world, where 'world' is phrased *baalcah tuçinil. Baalcah* is the second of the mortal enemies (the Devil, the material world, and the flesh), and *tuçinil* was the term used to translate the "all" of "almighty God" in the Credo. For the missionaries, of course, the power behind evil, the ultimate idol, was the Devil (see chapters 5 and 6). Here, the Devil has the power to recognize Cristóbal and address him by name, whereas we get no sense that Cristóbal and the king could divine one another's names. When Cristóbal and the Devil encounter the cross at the edge of town, they encounter what would have been in fact a familiar scene in the colony: from the earliest days of the evangelization, the missionaries planted the cross wherever they went, and there were crosses at the entrances to *pueblos reducidos* (see chapter 9). The Devil's fearful avoidance of the cross is a reflection of the omnipotence of the god for whom it stands. There are other sermons in this collection in which the Devil fears holy water and other signs of God, all of which develop the theme of the ultimate weakness of the Devil, equated by missionaries with the Maya gods, before the true God. A docile subject searching for his lord, Cristóbal chooses Christ and thereby turns away from the Devil. This turning away is a conversion in which Cristóbal's willingness is withdrawn first from the king and then from the Devil whom the king fears, to be invested in a greater power. In both cases the turning away is accomplished by an utterance declaring he will not serve them. On this reading, the faithful are encouraged to choose the way of the cross, to observe that others fear the cross, and to always remember that the cross is a protector that embodies the crucifixion and resurrection. When Cristóbal turns away from the Devil, the Indio turns away from idolatry.

Whereas the preceding sermon would have been excellent in the course of Mass, the next one is more directly pedagogical. Though addressed to children and doubtless intended for use in schools, it has neither narrative nor quoted speech; rather, it is essentially a set of instructions to Indio neophytes regarding proper preparation for confession. Clearly, this would reinforce the Confiteor Deo and the confessional directly. It also goes a long way toward explaining what the dictionaries were referring to when they spoke of orderly and disorderly confession. The reference in the first paragraph to things the penitent must "fulfill" uses the same verb form as the Our Father when it says "thy will be done [utzcinab]," and the sermon leans heavily on the contrition, sadness, and loss of oneself that come with sin. Perhaps most striking in this talk is the degree to which it organizes the memories, emotions, and intentions of the Christian subject.

∼TRANSLITERATION FROM CORONEL, *DISCURSOS PREDICABLES* (FOLIOS 222–224)

PREPARACION PARA ANTES QUE SE CONFIESSEN.

1. *Mehenexe. Talel acahex tichoch keban tinich. Heuac oheltex machābel piz tohpulkeban licil vçatçabal vçipil uinic tumenel Dios. Heuac yantuchayan. Vtzcinaben tumenel ah toh pulkebane, vchebal vçatçabal keban tumenel ahtepale.*

2. *Vyax chunitaclo. Kaanan vuilal vtuclic, yetel vkahçic vkeban vinic ti makuchuc vchochob yicnal padre. Tilic vtuclic manci vtucul. Manci vthan. Yetel vbeel ca vhūmolob vkeban tulacal cautzac vtoh pulticob, yoklal. Hach matijhi catac ti confessar vinic ti matuculan, yetel molan vçipil tumenele.*
   [. . .]

3. *Bla vtzi caculacech. Yetel acahez a cuxtal. Akahcunobtu cahach okomac auol, yetel dzamanac auol ti okomolal açipci ti Dios ahtepal, yetel ti yal mathanile. Ma chambel vinic maix lauacmac halach vinicil. Bax ahau açipcici aba. Heuac ti Dios ah tepal açipciciaba. Heklay auahçiçahul auatzenul auahlohili xan loe.*
   [. . .]

4. *Maix haili appatic yetel ahauçic açipil vnahe, heuac yanix vuilal anach cunic aba, tuchun keban. Yetel. Tibaluka taachil vchun pahal akebane. Bax payic a beel tikebane yoklal bay dzibanil ti kulemdzibe himac vka dzaic vba, tupecoltzilil kebane ahçatalilo. Cuthan.*
   [. . .]

5. *Bacix okomac yol vinic tumenel vkebane. Bacix vhaueçob yetel tohpultob ti padre xane.Vama yolah valkeç ti yalbil. Bax vtemebyol vlak, baxane, manan yaal choch kebanti maixtā uçatçabal vçipil tumenel Dios xan.*
   [. . .].

PREPARATION FOR BEFORE THEY CONFESS

1. My children, you have come to untie your sins before me. But know that declaring sin is no small measure, whereby the trespasses of man are taken away by God. But there is more that must be fulfilled by him who confesses, in order that his sins be taken away by his majesty.

2. At the very beginning, it is most necessary that he reflect and recall his sins before arriving to confess them to the father. While he thinks of where his thoughts have gone, where his words have gone, and his deeds, let him gather all his sins together so that he may declare them straight, because it is really not acceptable that a person come to confess without his sins having been thought (through) and gathered.
[…]

3. So it is good that you sit down and recall your life.[25] You recall them then. Let your heart be saddened and devoted to contrition for having sinned against God's majesty and against his commandments. Neither a simple man nor some great man nor a king have you offended. But God's majesty is who you have offended, who is your creator, your provider, and your redeemer.
[…]

4. And not only is it necessary that you leave off and destroy your sin(s), but you must also distance yourself from the root of sin and whatever customarily incites you to sin, what calls you to sin. For thus it is written in the holy scriptures, whosoever dedicates himself to the dangers of sin is lost. So it says.
[…]

5. Even though a person be contrite for his sins, and even though he destroy them and declare them to father, if he does not want to convert to (what is spoken), and to make peace with others, and (if) absolution is not spoken to him, then his sins will not be forgiven by God either.

These teachings give us an initial glimpse of the mental and emotional practices associated with confession. Not surprisingly, they echo the confessional manual, especially the initial dialogue, and they play out the semantic spaces of sin and repentance foreshadowed in the dictionaries and *artes*. But unlike the dialogue, this talk is monologic: it is addressed to an audience of children, who receive it and are expected to follow its urgings but do not speak. The subject projected by these spiritual exercises has internalized the mandates of orthodoxy and uses them as the evaluative screen through which he looks upon himself: his past, his present feelings and intentions, and his future action.

• • •

The *doctrina* propagated *Maya reducido* in ways the missionaries clearly intended and in ways they surely did not intend. By enforcing doctrinal training and ritual participation on leaders in the *cabildo* and by selecting scribes from among those so trained, they purposely set up an institutional vector for dispersing this language into other spheres of consequential action. (Indeed, the detailed changes between the versions of *doctrina,* such as the ones examined here, allow us to infer which version of the canon Maya authors were exposed to.) By selecting scribes from among those so trained, the missionaries established an institutional vector along which the language would move from the convent and church into the *cabildo* as a sphere of official discourse production. The scripted discourse of prayer and catechism effectively doubled the indexical grounding of *Maya reducido:* not only are individual expressions indexically tied to doxic referents, but they also become tied to doxic scripts. Thus the occurrence of a doctrinal phrase in nondoctrinal literature indexes both the new referent and the discourse in which it is canonically embedded. With its organization into balanced lines and parallel statements, with recurrent key phrases and metaphors, doctrinal language was semiotically well suited to fragmentation. All these factors enhanced its tendency to disperse. The next chapter focuses on the movement of the new language into notarial genres, where the voices of prayer commingled with the voices of rule. As for the unintended permutations of doctrinal language, we know that many of the Maya who fled from the colony or continued to engage in heterodox practices within it were trained in doctrine. In a number of high-profile cases, they were themselves *maestros.* Chapter 10 examines *Maya reducido* as it appears in the Books of Chilam Balam and the sorcerer's catechism that Roys called the Ritual of the Bacabs. Just as *reducción* actually played out as a reversible process that was dynamic on both sides of the frontier, so too the language of *reducción* was in motion on both sides of the wall of orthodoxy.

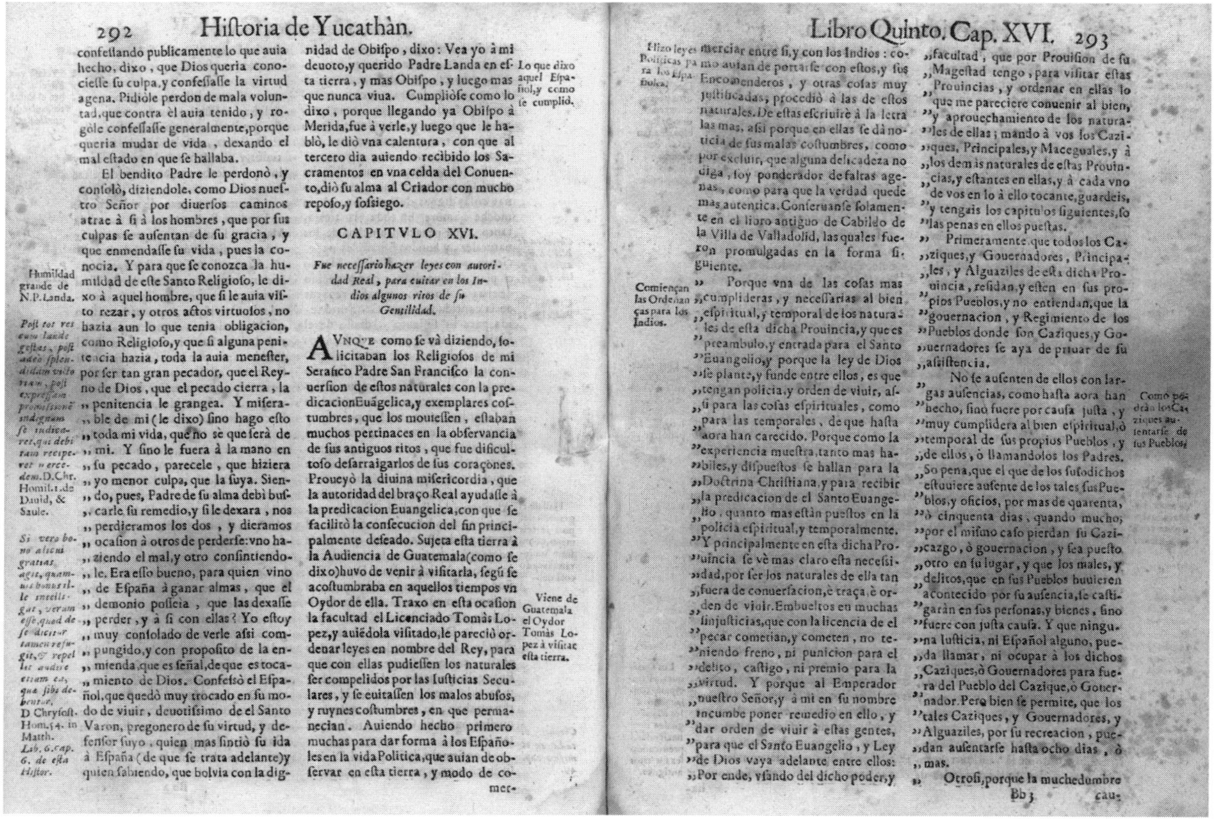

292 Hiſtoria de Yucathàn.

confeſſando publicamente lo que auia hecho, dixo, que Dios queria conocieſſe ſu culpa, y confeſſaſſe la virtud agena. Pidiòle perdon de mala voluntad, que contra èl auia tenido, y rogòle confeſſaſſe generalmente, porque queria mudar de vida, dexando el mal eſtado en que ſe hallaba.

El bendito Padre le perdonò, y conſolò, diziendole, como Dios nueſtro Señor por diuerſos caminos atrae à ſi à los hombres, que por ſus culpas ſe auſentan de ſu gracia, y que enmendaſſe ſu vida, pues la conocia. Y para que ſe conozca la humildad de eſte Santo Religioſo, le dixo à aquel hombre, que ſi le auia viſto rezar, y otros actos virtuoſos, no hazia aun lo que tenia obligacion, como Religioſo, y que ſi alguna penitencia hazia, toda la auia meneſter, por ſer tan gran pecador, que el Reyno de Dios, que el pecado cierra, la „ penitencia le grangea. Y miſerable de mi (le dixo) ſino hago eſto toda mi vida, que no sè que ſerà de mi. Y ſino le fuera à la mano en ſu pecado, parecele, que hiziera yo menor culpa, que la ſuya. Siendo, pues, Padre de ſu alma debì buſcarle ſu remedio, y ſi le dexara, nos perdieramos los dos, y dieramos ocaſion à otros de perderſe: vno haziendo el mal, y otro conſintiendole. Era eſſo bueno, para quien vino de Eſpaña à ganar almas, que el demonio poſſeia, que las dexaſſe perder, y à ſi con ellas? Yo eſtoy muy conſolado de verle aſsi compungido, y con propoſito de la enmienda, que es ſeñal, de que es tocamiento de Dios. Confeſsò el Eſpañol, que quedò muy trocado en ſu modo de viuir, deuotiſsimo de el Santo Varon, pregonero de ſu virtud, y defenſor ſuyo, quien mas ſintiò ſu ida à Eſpaña (de que ſe trata adelante) y quien ſabiendo, que bolvia con la dignidad de Obiſpo, dixo: Vea yo à mi deuoto, y querido Padre Landa en eſta tierra, y mas Obiſpo, y luego mas que nunca viua. Cumpliòſe como lo dixo, porque llegando ya Obiſpo à Merida, fue à verle, y luego que le hablò, le diò vna calentura, con que al tercero dia auiendo recibido los Sacramentos en vna celda del Conuento, diò ſu alma al Criador con mucho repoſo, y ſoſsiego.

Humildad grande de N.P. Landa.

Poſt tot res cum laude geſtas, poſt adeò ſplendidam victoriam, poſt expreſſam promiſsionē indignum ſe iudicaret, qui debitam reciperet mercedem. D.Chr. Homil.1. de Dauid, & Saule.

Si vero bono alicui gratias agit, quamuis bonus ille intelligat, verum eſſe, quod de ſe dicitur tamen refugit, & repellit audire etiam ea, quæ ſibi debentur, D Chryſoſt. Hom.54. in Matth.

Lib. 6. cap. 6. de eſta Hiſtor.

Lo que dixo aquel Eſpañol, y como ſe cumpliò.

CAPITVLO XVI.

Fue neceſſario hazer leyes con autoridad Real, para euitar en los Indios algunos ritos de ſu Gentilidad.

AVNQVE como ſe và diziendo, ſolicitaban los Religioſos de mi Seraſico Padre San Franciſco la conuerſion de eſtos naturales con la predicacion Euāgelica, y exemplares coſtumbres, que los mouieſſen, eſtaban muchos pertinaces en la obſervancia de ſus antiguos ritos, que fue dificultoſo deſarraigarlos de ſus coraçones. Proueyò la diuina miſericordia, que la autoridad del braço Real ayudaſſe à la predicacion Euangelica, con que ſe facilitò la conſecucion del fin principalmente deſeado. Sujeta eſta tierra à la Audiencia de Guatemala (como ſe dixo) huvo de venir à viſitarla, segū ſe acoſtumbraba en aquellos tiempos vn Oydor de ella. Traxo en eſta ocaſion la facultad el Licenciado Tomàs Lopez, y auiēdola viſitado, le pareciò ordenar leyes en nombre del Rey, para que con ellas pudieſſen los naturales ſer compelidos por las Iuſticias Seculares, y ſe euitaſſen los malos abuſos, y ruynes coſtumbres, en que permanecian. Auiendo hecho primero muchas para dar forma à los Eſpañoles en la vida Politica, que auian de obſervar en eſta tierra, y modo de comerciar entre ſi, y con los Indios: como auian de portarſe con eſtos, y ſus Encomenderos, y otras coſas muy juſtificadas, procediò à las de eſtos naturales. De eſtas eſcriuirè à la letra las mas, aſsi porque en ellas ſe dà noticia de ſus malas coſtumbres, como por excluir, que alguna delicadeza no diga, ſoy ponderador de faltas agenas, como para que la verdad quede mas autentica. Conſeruanſe ſolamente en el libro antiguo de Cabildo de la Villa de Valladolid, las quales fueron promulgadas en la forma ſiguiente.

Viene de Guatemala el Oydor Tomàs Lopez à viſitar eſta tierra.

Libro Quinto, Cap. XVI. 293

Hizo leyes Politicas para los Eſpañoles.

„ Porque vna de las coſas mas cumplideras, y neceſſarias al bien eſpiritual, y temporal de los naturales de eſta dicha Prouincia, y que es preambulo, y entrada para el Santo Euangelio, y porque la ley de Dios ſe plante, y funde entre ellos, es que tengan policia, y orden de viuir, aſsi para las coſas eſpirituales, como para las temporales, de que haſta aora han carecido. Porque como la experiencia mueſtra, tanto mas habiles, y diſpueſtos ſe hallan para la Doctrina Chriſtiana, y para recibir la predicacion de el Santo Euangelio, quanto mas eſtàn pueſtos en la policia eſpiritual, y temporalmente. Y principalmente en eſta dicha Prouincia ſe vè mas claro eſta neceſsidad, por ſer los naturales de ella tan fuera de conuerſacion, è traça, è orden de viuir. Embueltos en muchas injuſticias, que con la licencia de el pecar cometian, y cometen, no teniendo freno, ni punicion para el delito, caſtigo, ni premio para la virtud. Y porque al Emperador nueſtro Señor, y à mi en ſu nombre incumbe poner remedio en ello, y dar orden de viuir à eſtas gentes, para que el Santo Euangelio, y Ley de Dios vaya adelante entre ellos: Por ende, vſando del dicho poder, y facultad, que por Prouiſion de ſu Mageſtad tengo, para viſitar eſtas Prouincias, y ordenar en ellas lo que me pareciere conuenir al bien, y aprouechamiento de los naturales de ellas; mando à vos los Caziques, Principales, y Maceguales, y à los demàs naturales de eſtas Prouincias, y eſtantes en ellas, y à cada vno de vos en lo à ello tocante, guardeis, y tengais los capitulos ſiguientes, ſo las penas en ellos pueſtas.

Comiençan las Ordenanças para los Indios.

„ Primeramente, que todos los Caziques, y Gouernadores, Principales, y Alguaziles de eſta dicha Prouincia, reſidan, y eſten en ſus propios Pueblos, y no entiendan, que la gouernacion, y Regimiento de los Pueblos donde ſon Caziques, y Gouernadores ſe aya de priuar de ſu aſsiſtencia.

„ No ſe auſenten de ellos con largas auſencias, como haſta aora han hecho, ſino fuere por cauſa juſta, y muy cumplidera al bien eſpiritual, ò temporal de ſus propios Pueblos, y de ellos, ò llamandolos los Padres. So pena, que el que de los ſuſodichos eſtuuiere auſente de los tales ſus Pueblos, y oficios, por mas de quarenta, ò cinquenta dias, quando mucho, por el miſmo caſo pierdan ſu Cazicazgo, ò gouernacion, y ſea pueſto otro en ſu lugar, y que los males, y delitos, que en ſus Pueblos huuieren acontecido por ſu auſencia, ſe caſtigaràn en ſus perſonas, y bienes, ſino fuere con juſta cauſa. Y que ninguna Iuſticia, ni Eſpañol alguno, pueda llamar, ni ocupar à los dichos Caziques, ò Gouernadores para fuera del Pueblo del Cazique, ò Gouernador. Pero bien ſe permite, que los tales Caziques, y Gouernadores, y Alguaziles, por ſu recreacion, puedan auſentarſe haſta ocho dias, ò mas.

Como podràn los Caziques auſentarſe de ſus Pueblos.

„ Otroſi, porque la muchedumbre

Bb 3 cau-

PLATE 1. Diego López de Cogolludo, *Historia de Yucatán*, 1688, *Libro Quinto Capítulo XVI* (courtesy of The Bancroft Library, University of California, Berkeley). This chapter describes the coming to Yucatán of Tomás López Medel and quotes his *Ordenanzas*, starting with the rationale that to convert the Indians to Christianity, it was first necessary to place them in order—thus linking the two faces of *reducción* as the imposition of order and the changing of beliefs.

PLATE 2. Juan de Torquemada, *Monarchia Indiana,* 1723 (courtesy of the John Carter Brown Library, Brown University). This well-known image is very similar to one found in Valadés's *Rhetorica Christiana.* It displays a Franciscan instructing a mass of Indian neophytes, indicated by the tunic they wear. The Franciscan teaches from the pulpit, pointing to images with a long rod in his right hand. Images were also used in teaching in Yucatán. The text reads, roughly:

TOP PANEL: "Part II of the twenty-one ritual books and Indian Monarchy with the origins and wars of the occidental Indians, [and] of their populations. The discovery, conquest, conversion, and other marvelous things of the same land, distributed in three tomes. Composed by Fray Ivan de Torquemada, Provincial Minister of the Province of the Sancto Evangelio of Mexico in New Spain."

BOTTOM PANEL: "I address my verses to the King [Ps. 45:1], eternal, immortal, and invisible [1 Tim. 1:17] / With Privilege"

BELOW IMAGE: "In Seville by Matthias Claudio, Year 1615"

PLATE 3. Diego de Valadés, *Rhetorica Christiana*, 1579, p. 172f. (courtesy of The Bancroft Library, University of California, Berkeley). In an enclosed space with four corner chapels, like the patio of a monastery, twelve friars (flanked at rear by fray Martinus Valentinus, Father Prelate, and at front by Saint Francis) carry the first Roman Catholic Church of the Indies. Above them, the Holy Spirit emanates grace to scenes of missionary education. Left: lessons on confession, penance, doctrine, and "all things" (with the image-based teaching of fray Pedro de Gante); right: the creation of the world, the exam for matrimony, writing names, the sacraments of matrimony and (bottom) baptism. Centered at the top is death. Girls and boys are separated in the upper left and right chapels, women and men in the lower left and right. Along the bottom are scenes depicting confession (left); judgment (center); communion, mass, and extreme unction (right). The image crystallizes a vision of the mission as a total project.

HISTORIA

DE YUCATHAN.

COMPUESTA

POR EL M.R.P.FR. DIEGO LOPEZ de COGOLLVDO,
LECTOR JVBILADO, Y PADRE PERPETVO
DE DICHA PROVINCIA.

CONSAGRADA, Y DEDICADA

AL EXCELENTISSIMO SEÑOR

DON FERNANDO IOACHIN FAXARDO
de Requeſens y Zuñiga, Marquès de los Velez, Molina y Martorel,
Señor de las Varonias de Caſtelvi, de Roſanes, Molins de Rey,
y otras en el Principado de Cataluña, Señor de las Villas de Mula,
Alhama y Librilla, y de las ſiete del Rio de Almanzora, las Cueuas,
y Portilla, Alcayde perpetuo de los Reales Alcaçares, de las Ciudades
de Murcia, y Lorca, Adelantado, y Capitan Mayor del Reyno de
Murcia, Marqueſado de Villena, Arcedianato de Alcaraz, Campo de
Montiel, Sierra de Segura, y ſus Partidos, Comendador de la Enco-
mienda de los Baſtimentos de Caſtilla, del Orden de Santiago, Gen-
tilhombre de Camara de ſu Mageſtad, de ſus Conſejos de Eſtado,
y Guerra, Preſidente en el de Indias, y Superintendente
General de la Real Hazienda, &c.

SACALA A LVZ
EL M.R.P.FR.FRANCISCO DE AYETA, PREDICADOR,
Ex-Cuſtodio del Nueuo Mexico, Comiſſario General del Santo
Oficio, Cuſtodio actual de la Prouincia del Santo Euangelio en el
Reyno de la Nueua Eſpaña, y Procurador General en eſta
Corte de todas las Prouincias de la Religion
Serafica del dicho Reyno.

CON PRIVILEGIO.

EN MADRID: POR JVAN GARCIA INFANZON, Año 1688.

PLATE 4. Title page and dedication from Diego López de Cogolludo, *Historia de Yucatán,* 1688 (courtesy of The Bancroft Library, University of California, Berkeley)

INFORME
CONTRA IDOLORVM CVLTORES DEL OBISPADO DE YVCATAN.

DIRIGIDO AL REY N. SEÑOR
en su Real Consejo de las Indias.

POR EL DOCTOR DON PEDRO
Sanchez de Aguilar Dean de Yucatan, Canonigo al
presente en la Santa Iglesia Metropolitana de la
Ciudad de la Plata, Prouincia de
los Charças.

CON PRIVILEGIO
EN MADRID, *Por la viuda de Iuan Gonçalez,*
Año de M.DC.XXXIX.

AL REY NVESTRO

SEÑOR FILIPO IIII. EL
mayor Monarca del mundo, en fu Real
Cófejo de las Indias el Doctor D. Pedro
Sanchez de Aguilar Canonigo en la fanta
Igleſia Metropoli de la Ciudad de la Pla-
ta, Prouincia de los Charcas
en el Piru.
S. P. D.

SEÑOR.

IENDO Capellan de V. Mag.
y Dean dela ſanta Igleſia Catedral
de Yucatan en la Nueua-Eſpaña,
hize eſte informe, Contra idoloru
Cultores, *como teſt go ocular de la*
muy reñida y antigua competencia,
que huuo, y auia (y pienſo que oy du-
ra) entre los dos braços, Real, *y Ecle*
ſiaſtico cerca de la captura, priſion, y caſtigo de los Indios idola-
tras, y apoſtatas de aquel Obiſpado, donde eſtaua la idolatria tan
arraygada. Sobre que informè à V. M. ſiendo Prouiſor Sede
vacante, y fue ſeruido de proueer ſu Real cedula el año de 1605. *aſoſu 13*
en que mandò V. M. al Obiſpo de aquella tierra informſſe de

¶ 2   la

PLATE 6. Pedro Sánchez de Aguilar, *Informe Contra Idolorum Cultores del obispado de Yucatán dirigido al Rey N. Señor en su Real Consejo de las Indias,* 1639 (courtesy of the John Carter
Brown Library, Brown University). Sánchez de Aguilar directs his work to King Philip IV,
explaining that he wrote it on the basis of firsthand witness of idolatries in Yucatán.

cohuaya! Ma avel ciquilnami
qui, acaçomo timocencauh yn
ytechpa monacayo, yuan yni
techpa maniman, yuuih nican
nimitztenehuiliz.

❧ Mican moteneua;
yn necencaualiztli, ynictimocē
cahuaz, yniquac ticmoceliliz-
nequi ſanctiſsimo ſacramento
yn motenehua Comunió ach
to mmitztenehuiliz, yn quenin
timocencahuaz ynitechpa mo
nacayo; auh çatepan, nimitztenehuiliz yn quenin timocencahuaz ytechpa maniman .:.

mo! Pues acuerdate bien, ſi
te aparejaſte corporalmente,
y eſpiritualmente, aſsicomo a
qui te lo oire, y declarare.

❧ El qui ſe tracta del
aparejo.cōq te has de aparejar, quando oueres de reſcebir el ſanctiſsimo ſacramento
dela comunion, y primeramen
te te oire y declarare, el como
te has de aparejar, quanto a-
lo que toca al cuerpo, y deſpues te declarare, elcomo te de-
ues aparejar quanto al alma.

Iacat
quiy
nic centla
mantli, yn
ytechpoh
ui yninece
cahualiz
monaca -
yo , yni-
quac ça -
yuh moz-
tla yçaual

larhui ticceliz, monequi atleric
quaz, atle tiquiz : yniquacoa-
cic youalnepantla, in manel çã
tepiton çã achitó: auh yntla y
quac ytlaticquaz, yntla ytla tl
quiz, amo huel ticmoceliliz yn

Oſte
es el
primer a-
parejo, y-
reneſcien-
te a la diſ-
poſicion ð
tu cuerpo,
{conuiene
a ſaber} q̃
vn oia an-
tes que co
mulgues, no comas, ni beuas
coſa alguna, deſpues ðe media
noche, aunque no ſea lo q comieres ſino muy poquito: y ſi
alguna coſa comieres , enton-
ces, no podras reſcebir el Sa
cra

PLATE 7. Woodcut of a Franciscan confessing an Indian, from Alonso de Molina, *Confesionario mayor en la lengua mexicana y castellana*, 1975 [1569], fol. 71r (courtesy of The Bancroft
Library, University of California, Berkeley). Molina's early image of confession captures the
Franciscan vision of sin as the Devil upon the back of the confessing Indian, as opposed to
the helping angel behind the Franciscan confessor. Whereas the Devil restrains the sinner, the
angel points to heaven, connecting the priest confessor to God (cf. plate 10).

⌐ Ocol Keban. caer en pecado.

⌐ Ocol Kin. ponerse el sol. ti yocol Kin inkuchul tacahalex. al
ponerse el sol llegare apueblo pueblo. ⁊ tal vcah yocol Kin. ya
se quiere poner el sol. ⁊ tal vcah yocol Kin cabin tacedvaye
quandose quiera poner el sol vendras aqui ⁊ came ococ to
Kin cata cech vaye. vn rato despues depuesto el sol vendras
aqui. ⁊ O ci Kin tumenyah. trabaxo hasta quese puso el sol.

⌐ Ocol Kin. morirse algun viejo, o estar para morir. Talel vcah
yocol Kin ti Juan. yase quiere morir Juan hombre viejo.

⌐ Ocol Ku. castidad y continencia y religion .l. coycab. ⁊ Item
enlutarse.

⌐ Ocol Kinam. lo mismo que. Ocol cab.

⌐ Ocol patan. introduzirse el tributo opecho, comencarse apaga

r Ocol ti. con nombres Significa, conuertirse en lo que los tales
nombres importan. Ocol ti vahil. conuertirse en pan. etҫ.

⌐ Ocol ti alcaldeil, ti batabil. etҫ. ser hecho alcalde, cacique. ⁊

⌐ Ocol ti buc. vestirse. o cen taca missa. viste te la camissa etҫ

⌐ Ocol ti confessar. confessarse, seradmitido ala confession

⌐ Ocol ti yumil an .l. ti yumil anil. salir por fiador deotro
o cen tin yumilan. sal por mi fiador.

⌐ Ocol ti ol. creer. o caan ua Dios tauol. Por ventura crees en
⁊ Ma ocaanti yoli. aborrecele nole puede ver.

⌐ Ocol ti vinial. hazerse hombre. O ci ti vinicil vm chendios

⌐ Ocol tunupil than. hazerse amigo. ti o cex tunupil vthandib
.l. Sanctoob. aueis sos hecho amigos de dios y dosus Sanctos.

⌐ Ocol than. hablar aescondidillas en secreto.

⌐ Ocom. de. ocol. por entrar. ⁊ ocom vthan, ocom aҫa aҫa
tu andas porsa car me demis casillas yque rinanos y quem
empelo temos. ⁊ Ocom vthan, ocom vҫa vKati. aquel
andas tras esto.

⌐ O com. columna de madera, opilar oposte o hurcon demadera
sobre que fundan las casas pajizas.

⌐ Ocom. tah .t. poner horcon pilar columna de madera.

ɔ o komol. tah. t. tener enel alma angustia dolor tristeza y
pena por alguna cosa. o komolte akeban. tendolor y pesar
detus pecados ɔ o komolte vnumya cah lohil. duelete
dela passion denro redemptor.

ɔ okomoltzil. cosatriste, miserable y lastimosa que causa
tristeza y lastima. oKomoltzil yilabal a beelex. cosa
lastimosa es ver vuestras obras ɔ oKomoltzil yauat
vozes lastimosas ɔ vnde. cimi tihach oKomoltzil.
murio muy miserablemente.

ɔ o Kom taol. lomismo que. oKomolal. oKom taolal incah
triste estoy.

ɔ o Kom taol. tah. t. l. oKomol. tah. t. Vt supra.

ɔ o Kom taol tzil. lomismo que. oKomoltzil.

ɔ o Kom taol tzilil. aquella tristeza o lastima.

ɔ o Koop. hoya o hoya, barranco o valle. va bin vpaya
vbeel, yet ek mayil ek maye, bin lubucob tio Koop t
cabil. si cecus ce cum ducat ambo info ueam cadent
yo Koopil haa. charco ɔ yo Koopil Kak nab. golfo
demar.

ɔ o Koop chen. pozo en hoya.

ɔ o Kot. bailar, o dancer: y dança o bayle. oKot nen. bayle
ɔ oKot nacob. baylen aquellos.

ɔ o Kot ba. rogar interceder y abogar por alguno: y ruego
ein ter cession assi. oKot ba in cah tech ca acates incip...
ruegote que me perdones. l. oKot incah tinbatech.
Lic voKtic inbatech. ɔ yoK tahvba ten. ro gome
bin voKte inbati auoKol. yole rogare por ti ɔ ç...
yoccic yoKotba. presto ad mite sus ruegos su inter
cession.

• o Kot banac. futuro de: oKotba. quando es absoluto
caix oKot banacech yoKol inpixan. y roga ras po...

PLATE 10. *Typus Peccatoris* 'The Types of Sins' from Diego de Valadés, *Rhetorica Christiana,* 1579, p. 214 (courtesy of The Bancroft Library, University of California, Berkeley). This image represents the sinner, a European man tiredly walking, bent over and in chains, led by the Devil. Note the staff held by the angel in his left hand, which displays not the sins but the seven virtues reflecting the concerns of missionaries (piety, patience, abstinence, charity, chastity, generosity, and humility), under a crucified Christ with a banner stating, "Truth and Life." The angel and the Devil represent the two fundamental choices, goodness or sin. The sinner, a reversal of the angel, carries in his right hand a staff with seven snakes coiled round, presumably representing the seven deadly sins, which are not named. The oppressing demon on his back has three heads, a sort of anti-Trinity with horns and hideous faces, matching that of the Devil. The Devil leads the sinner to sit in a seat that is the mirror image of the seat in heaven to which the angel's staff points: the arms of the chair are inverted, as sin is inverted from virtue. This image of sin on one's back is reiterated precisely in Maya documents, where the era of idolatry is described as, "we were oppressed by the pressing down on our backs of the devil" (paraphrase, Letter of the *Batabs* to the Crown, March 9, 1567).

ARTE
DE
LA LENGVA
MAYA,
Compueſto por el R.P.Fr.
Gabriel de San Buenaventura
Predicador , y difinidor habitual
de la Provincia de San JOSEPH
de Yucathan del Orden de N. P. S.
FRANCISCO.

Año de   1684.

(✠)   CON LICENCIA: (✠)
En Mexico, por la Viuda de Bernardo Calderon.

PLATE 11. Title page from Gabriel de San Buenaventura, *Arte de la lengua maya,* 1684 (courtesy of the John Carter Brown Library, Brown University). Note the stigmata on the seal, a reference to Saint Francis receiving the stigmata of Christ. The work was published in México.

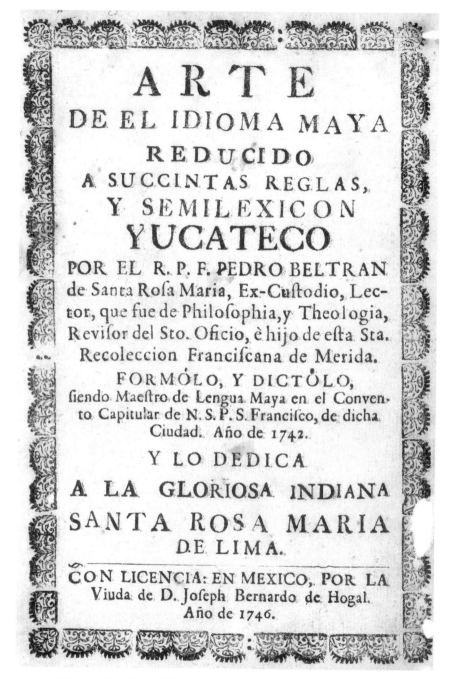

ARTE
DE EL IDIOMA MAYA
REDUCIDO
A SUCCINTAS REGLAS,
Y SEMILEXICON
YUCATECO

POR EL R. P. F. PEDRO BELTRAN
de Santa Rofa Maria, Ex-Cuſtodio, Lector, que fue de Philoſophia, y Theologia,
Reviſor del Sto. Oficio, è hijo de eſta Sta.
Recoleccion Franciſcana de Merida.

FORMÓLO, Y DICTÓLO,
ſiendo Maeſtro de Lengua Maya en el Convento Capitular de N. S. P. S. Franciſco, de dicha
Ciudad. Año de 1742.

Y LO DEDICA

A LA GLORIOSA INDIANA

SANTA ROSA MARIA
DE LIMA.

CON LICENCIA: EN MEXICO, POR LA
Viuda de D. Joſeph Bernardo de Hogal.
Año de 1746.

PLATE 12. Title page from Pedro Beltrán de Santa Rosa María, *Arte de el Idioma Maya reducido a succintas reglas y Semilexicón yucateco,* 1859 [1746] (courtesy of The John Carter Brown Library, Brown University). Note that it stipulates that Beltrán formed and dictated his *Arte* in 1742, while teaching Maya in the capitular convent of the Franciscans in Mérida.

DEDICATORIA.

SANTISSIMA MADRE MIA VIRGEN ROSA DE SANTA MARIA , nunca mas propriamente eſtà una Roſa colocada, que quando engaſtada entre eſpinas: y ſiendo el Idioma Yucatéco una mata de punſantes eſpinos (por ſeis conſonantes, que produce tan dificiles de pronunciar, que muchos , aun deſpues de muchos años de exercicio, fecundos de vocablos, y perfeccionados del Arte, tropiezan en la pronunciacion, heridos de ſu acrimonia, como de agudos eſpinos; de ſuerte, que en lugar de herir con la lengua los vocablos, ó las letras; eſtas, y aquellos les hieren las lenguas, ô ſe las embargan, y vienen por fin á quedar en un *ſilencio*, tal, que aun pronunciando, qualquiera les guardará el ſecreto: aqui pues, Madre mia, entrais, como que ſoys ſymbolo del *ſilencio*; porque ſoys Roſa: pero eſto es paraque ſe encareſca eſta obra, y como Patrona de ella que ſoys, hagáis, que quedandoſe eſte Arte ſobre el ſilencio; por eſtar el Arte à vueſtro cargo, no quede el ſilencio ſobre el Arte, ſino Vos, Madre mia, en ſu lugar: de modo, que aunque pareſca ſilencio, el ſilencio no pareſca; y aunque ſe apareſca la eſpina, la eſpina ſe deſvaneſca; haciendoſe lenguas del Arte con éſte Arte de Lengua, los que juzgan, que es la Lengua un Arte de eſpinas lleno; y aſsi queda encarecido mi Arte ; pues la antiguedad en los grandes banquètes, que hacia, para encarecerlos con el *ſilencio*, los encarecia con la *roſa*, diciendo: *maneat ſub roſa*, en vez de; *maneat ſub ſecreto* ; quedando de alli por comun adagio

¶   un

PLATE 13. *Dedicatoria* from Pedro Beltrán de Santa Rosa María, *Arte de el Idioma Maya reducido a succintas reglas y Semilexicón yucateco,* 1859 [1746] (courtesy of The John Carter Brown Library, Brown University). Beltrán dedicates his work to his "virgin mother," Saint Rose of Lima. He displays the same playfulness with language structure that marks his grammar and other writings. Maya language is a rosebush covered with the thorns of glottalized and other hard sounds that injure the tongue and silence the speaker, a silence, like that of Saint Rose of Lima, that holds a secret, to which his grammar gives access. His taste for metaphor, chiasmus, and punning is evident in statements such as *"Even though it might appear silence, silence does not appear and even though it might appear to be a thorn, the thorn disappears, becoming lenguas of the arte with this arte of the lengua those who judge that the lengua is an arte full of thorns".* The statement puns on the double meanings of *lengua* (a European who spoke Maya vs. *lengua* (a language) and *arte* (a practical skill, in this case speaking) vs. *arte* (a practical description of a language).

Licencia del Superior Orden.

F. Juan Eftevan Pinélo, de la Regular Obfervan-
cia de N. S. P. S. Francifco, Predicador Jubilado, Calificador del Santo Oficio de la Inquificion,
Secretario trienal, Difinidor habitual, Padre, y Mi-
niftro Provincial dos vezes de efta Santa Provincia
de San Jofeph, de Yucatàn, y fiervo, &c.

Por virtud de las prefentes, y lo que à nos toca concede-
mos nueftra licencia, y bendicion, paraque pueda darfe à la
eftampa un Arte del Idioma Yucatèco, compuefto por el
R. P. Lector, que fue de Philofophia, y Theologia, Revifor
de libros, y Ex-Cuftodio F. Pedro Beltrán de Santa Rofa:
atento à aver fido examinado de nueftra commiffion por Per-
fonas Religiofas de nueftro Orden, y no tener cofa alguna,
ỳ fe oponga à nueftra Sta. Fè, Sacros Canones, y buenas cof-
tumbres: *fervatis in reliquo cæteris de jure fervando.* Dadas
en efte nueftro Convento de S. Antonio de Ticul, firmadas
de mi mano, y nombre, felladas con el fello mayor de nueftro Oficio, y refrendadas de nueftro Secretario. En quatro
de Agofto de mil fetecientos quarenta y tres años.

F. Juan Eftevan Pinelo.
Mñro. Pròal.

Loco ✠ Sigilli.

P. M. D. S. P. M. R.

F. Miguel Leal de las Alas.
Secretario de Pròa.

CEN-

PLATE 14. *Licencia* from Pedro Beltrán de Santa Rosa María, *Arte de el Idioma Maya reducido a succintas reglas y Semilexicón yucateco*, 1859 [1746] (courtesy of The John Carter Brown Library at Brown University). The license of the Superior Order (of Franciscans) is dated August 4, 1743 by Fray Juan Estevan Pinedo, Provincial. Presented in the convent of Saint Anthony of Ticul.

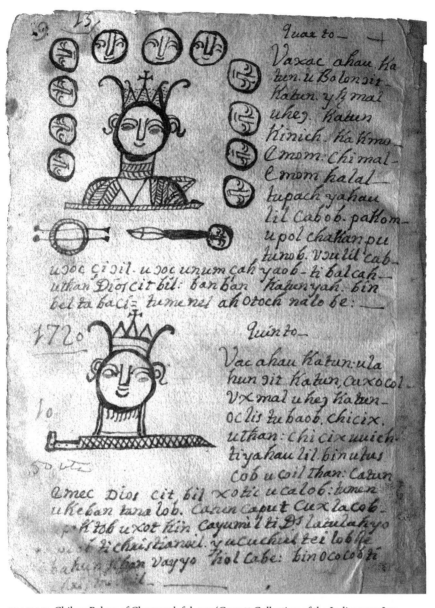

PLATE 15. Chilam Balam of Chumayel, fol. 52v (Garrett Collection of the Indigenous Languages of Middle America, Manuscripts Division, Department of Rare Books and Special Collections, Princeton University Library). Two periods in the count of the *katuns* (twenty-year periods) with drawings of Maya lords shown wearing European-style crowns with cruciform. The top *katun* ends with a reference to *uthan Dios citbil* 'the word of God almighty'. The bottom half refers to both *Dios citbil* 'God almighty' and *cayumil ti Ds.* 'our lord in God'. These formulations of God derive from Coronel's *Doctrina*.

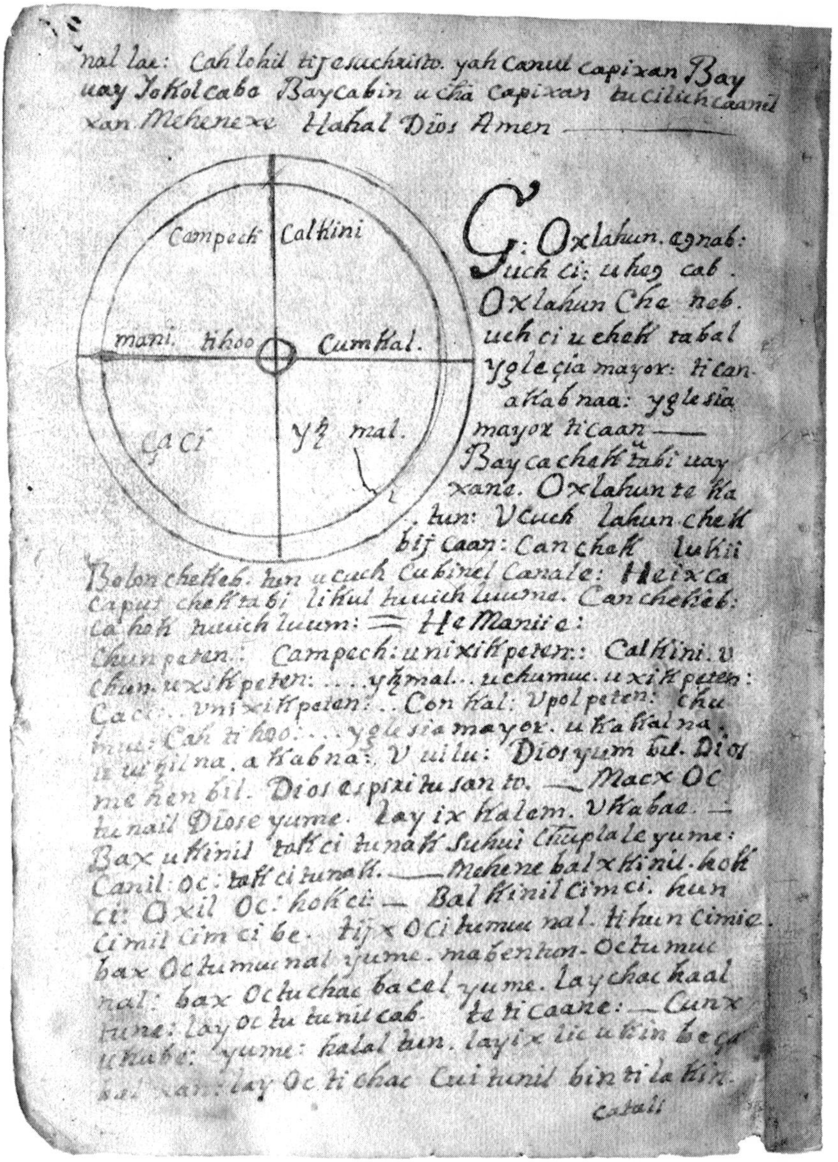
nal lae: Cah lohil ti Jesuchristo. yah canul capixan Bay
uay Tokolcabo Baycabin u cha capixan tu cilich caanil
xan Mehenexe Hahal Dios Amen

PLATE 16. Chilam Balam of Chumayel, fol. 36v (Garrett Collection of the Indigenous Languages of Middle America, Manuscripts Division, Department of Rare Books and Special Collections, Princeton University Library). The four-part circle centers on the Iglesia Mayor 'Main Church' of Mérida (Tihoo). The text describes the church as a fortress and a 'night house', followed by the sign of the cross in standard short form 'God the Father, God the Son, God Holy Spirit'. It continues, 'He who enters the house of Lord God, his name shall be sanctified', and then recounts the virgin conception, the burial of the Son, and the ascent to heaven. At top: 'Our savior Jesus Christ the guardian of our souls here on earth, so too he will take our souls into his beautiful heaven. You children! True God. Amen'. The places on the map (Tihoo, Çací, Ytzmal, Cumkal, Calkini, Campeche, and Mani) were all sites that had convents by 1582.

PART III

Into the Breach

The Dispersion of *Maya reducido*

AT THIS POINT WE MOVE AWAY FROM the *guardianía* and the genres of *Maya reducido* produced by missionary authors, to enter the Maya sphere and examine works produced by indigenous authors. The transition is stark because the genres differ fundamentally in form, purpose, and, of course, authorship. Rather than dictionaries, grammars, and doctrinal texts, all of which are pedagogical and grounded in European genres, indigenous authors produced notarial documents, ritual prescriptions, and the Books of Chilam Balam. The first major difference is that whereas we know more or less what the *vocabulario, arte,* and *doctrina* are as genres, it is not so clear how to categorize the notarial texts by genre and still less clear how we should construe the Books of Chilam Balam. As alphabetic writing was taken up in the *pueblos* and in the *despoblado,* the system of categories in which it was embedded was blurred and shifted about. It came into direct contact with Maya discourse practices, both oral and written. This in turn forces the question of attribution and autonomy: To what extent are the discourse forms produced by Maya writers motivated by *reducción*? To what extent are they the products of indigenous practices whose roots lay outside *reducción*? Is there evidence that alphabetic writing, and the various bodily practices it entailed (oral performance, gestures, the act of writing itself), was a means of crossing the social and cultural frontier from *reducción* to the linguistic *montaña*? Or did Maya writers compose their works in *Maya reducido*? Did the language of *doctrina* bleed into the language of governance or even the forbidden genres of ritual, history, and prognostication? These questions are closely related, and the answer to all of them is "Yes." The works of Maya writers were both indigenous and *reducido.* Writing was a means of autonomy even as it extended the scope of the missionary project, and it extended that project even as it produced autonomy. The *doctrina* was dispersed into the other genres, though not always in ways the missionaries would find comforting. This is both the central problem and the great wealth of the colonial corpus: the ambiguity never resolves into unequivocal, stable divisions.

How we construe the relation between *Maya reducido* and the writings of Maya people depends upon how we read their works. At the most general level, to write alphabetically was to use the orthography of *reducción*. Since all the notarial documents were produced by *cabildos,* and the *cabildo* was a colonial structure, it follows that all notarial documents were themselves part of *reducción*. After all, they came from *pueblos reducidos.* By contrast, the forbidden genres were definitionally outside *reducción* precisely because they were excluded. For the Spanish, they conjured superstition and idolatry. But this level of generality is too vague to satisfy, and it erroneously suggests that the valence of discourse works is determined solely by the institutional context in which they are made. It also suggests that contexts were themselves unequivocal, which we know to be false. The *cabildo* may have been a Spanish form of government, but the *pueblos reducidos* were legally Indio and the language spoken was Maya, whatever the variety. In order to take the measure of *reducción*'s impact on Maya writers in the *pueblos,* we have to examine their own works. The first step is to carefully analyze the language they used in its formal and pragmatic specificity.

What we find is an array of word choices, phrasings, stylistic devices, and modes of self-presentation and address that, in my opinion, prove that *Maya reducido* penetrated deep into indigenous discourse practices, including the forbidden genres. In the process, several kinds of change occurred. Preexisting linguistic forms acquired new uses, as in the Maya epithets for the Crown and colonial officials and for expressions for Christian practice, governance, conduct, places, and dates. These are all the product of neologizing practices like those I examined in chapters 5 through 8. They all involve commensuration between linguistic forms and meanings in the two languages.

Among the most striking features of notarial discourse is the deictic centering of the texts, a phenomenon seen in the front matter of published missionary works (but glaringly absent from the dictionaries). This included place (here, there), time (now, then), participants (we, you, 'in front of [witnesses]', in the name of [authorities]'), along with the descriptive phrases that qualify them. These features were motivated by Spanish notarial practices, but the Maya phrasings go far beyond their Spanish counterparts. Similarly, the use of recognizable *Maya reducido* in a notarial or forbidden text creates an indexical frame that further centers the text in relation to *reducción*. Much of the most revealing evidence of this is lost in translation and can only be discerned in the Maya texts themselves. This point cannot be overstated: whenever possible, historical research on *reducción* must proceed on the basis of the indigenous sources.

I focused in earlier chapters on iteration, recopying, and revoicing as basic modalities for dispersing *Maya reducido,* first among the missionaries and then out into the fields of indigenous discourse production. In the following chapters we will see similar iterations across all the genres in which indigenous authors wrote. Whether or not such iteration was a feature of Maya hieroglyphic practice, it was an extremely powerful means of dispersing the colonial language. As a vector for conversion, I argue that iteration was if anything *more* consequential than either force or focused pedagogy. It starts with the oral repetition of doctrinal scripts and the written repetition of both oral and written discourse. The conversion of belief, both mundane and monumental, can as easily follow from such repetition as it can motivate it. As Pascal said, one believes because one prays, not the other way around.

In order to trace these processes, we must look at a range of genres produced by Maya authors. It is unsurprising that notarial documents show the trace of the colonial system to which they were addressed. What is most interesting, though, are the *kinds* of traces we find. Land surveys, petitions, and the other notarial genres mobilize different features of *reducción,* in tension with different aspects of apparently autonomous Maya. What may be more surprising is the extent to which *Maya reducido* made its way into the forbidden genres. Despite their relative autonomy as "frontier discourse" (see chapter 2), these works are in dialogue with nearly all the processes discussed in the preceding chapters. Their authors were, after all, trained in alphabetic discourse for which the textual corpus was overwhelmingly missionary, at least in the early decades of the colony. If they were elite, as many claimed, then their positions were homologous with that of the Franciscans (see chapter 1). Yet this does not mean that Maya writing passively absorbed or conformed to the dictates of *Maya reducido.* Far from it. Alongside the ambiguity of attribution was the ambiguity between conformity or acquiescence and appropriation, strategic familiarization and subversion. The story of *Maya reducido* is about converting words, the logics of reproduction, and their far-flung consequences. If the Spanish aim was to change the Maya into docile replicas of Spanish Catholics, I will show that they failed on a grand scale. Yet their efforts set in motion processes that appear both uncontrollable and irreversible, even if *reducción* proper *was* reversible. The aim of the remaining chapters is to understand this, the irony of conversion and the breach it creates.

9

The Scripted Landscape

The town and *cabildo* were not only sociopolitical entities but also spaces in which a variety of genres were produced by authors, scribes, and principals whose first language and primary identity were Maya. Written almost exclusively in Maya, these works display many of the properties seen in the missionary sector: the emergence of *Maya reducido* as a hybrid born of the fusion of Maya with European languages, the dynamic combination of oral and written production, the proliferation of copies and versions through iteration, recopying, emendation, and cross-referencing. Notwithstanding the legal, social, linguistic, and ethnic divisions that characterized Yucatán, these commonalities indicate that the province and its frontier territories ultimately constituted a single discourse formation, albeit one with multiple overlapping boundaries and spaces of partial autonomy.

Colonization gave rise to a florescence of Maya discourse production: indoctrination, documentation, governance, and social practice all entailed discourse. The Maya were in effect compelled to speak and write in order to survive the onslaught of changes wreaked on them. All those subjected to the doctrinal language examined in the previous chapter became speakers if not authors in the missionary project. At the same time, the repressive and extractive practices of the missionaries and colonial authorities triggered processes of appropriation and revision far beyond their own control. This included the technology of alphabetic writing. As Farriss (1984), Quezada (1993), Quezada and Okoshi (2001), Restall (1997), and others have shown convincingly, the strategies pursued by Maya people under colonial rule were varied: flight, both spatial and behavioral, waves of complaints and legal disputes, petitions for intervention in local affairs, *probanzas* demonstrating rights based on descent, *diligencias* demonstrating proper practice, and land surveys claiming rights based on residence and agricultural labor, along with wills and bills of sale through which property was acquired and transferred according to the specific mandates of colonial law.

All this discourse was novel. Although hieroglyphic Maya was widely written on ceramics, stuccoed walls, lintels, and monumental inscriptions, the first-person author, the signature, the dating of texts written on paper, the genres mentioned above, and numerous stylistic features of colonial Maya are, to my knowledge, without clear precedent in the pre-Hispanic writing. These features signal the rise of a new set of relationships between discourse and those who produced it. By the same token, even though the missionary *lenguas* were among the primary creators of *Maya reducido,* working with native Maya speakers, none of their linguistic or doctrinal works was directed to the sphere of governance, nor did any involve *escribanos* or display the same stylistic features. In this sense, there is a break between *Maya reducido* as used by Maya authors and the same language as used by missionary authors.

This and the next chapter focus on the new language of governance in the *pueblos reducidos.* Most of the texts in question are the product of collective authorship in the *cabildo.* They are what I will call, following Restall (1997), "notarial." By definition, notarial works were engaged with the dynamics of *reducción* and its subsequent consequences. The *Ordenanzas* of Tomás López Medel, examined in chapter 2, were apparently the first major speech act to which notarial Maya responded in the early years of the colony, while the *cabildo* form of governance was still taking shape. Of the extant works, those bearing the earliest dates, including the so-called Xiu Chronicle and the Chronicles of Maní, Calkiní, Chicxulub, and Nakuk Pech, explicitly cite López Medel or his call for land surveys.[1] The same is true of the Yaxkukul surveys. All these works bear dates from the 1540s and 1550s, even if the accuracy of some of the dates is debatable. Although they provide a wealth of information about the political geography and symbology of Post-Classic Yucatán, they are works whose proximal cause lies in the *reducción.*[2] In the 1560s we encounter the first series of Maya petitions to the Crown, written in exquisite Maya complete with parallel couplets and apparently indigenous imagery and tropes. Nonetheless, their most immediate context was the inquisitional trials on idolatry, spearheaded by then-provincial fray Diego de Landa, abetted by Diego de Quijada, *alcalde mayor,* and vigorously condemned by the first bishop of Yucatán, fray Francisco de Toral. By the turn of the seventeenth century, we find the Sotuta surveys from Yaxcabá and the petition of Dzaptún (reproduced in Restall 1997), among others. These fit into the context of *reducción* documented in the *memorias* examined in chapter 2. It was the age of Ciudad Real, Sánchez de Aguilar, and Coronel.

In the mid- to late seventeenth century, the time of Cogolludo and San Buenaventura, we find long runs of documents, including more than two dozen petitions from nearly as many towns complaining of the excesses of don Rodrigo Flores de Aldana.³ Directed to the *visitador* 'inspector' and dated between November 1669 and the following year, these cite excessive levels of tribute and forced appropriations *(repartimiento)* as a cause for much suffering and the flight of would-be Christian Indios from the grip of *reducción*. Many of these petitions, from Calkiní, Dzitbalché, Ho, Pocmuch, Xecelchakán, Bolonpocché, Umán, and other places, are in Spanish. This is an important reminder that the discourse emanating from the pueblos was not all written in Maya. With time, bilingualism clearly spread beyond the initial confines of a small cadre of *frayles lenguas* and *indios ladinos*. Maya people also appropriated the Spanish of the colonizers as a means of denunciation and litigation. By the eighteenth century, the colonial project had developed into what Restall (1997, 220) calls "conquest by purchase," that is, the appropriation of Maya lands by more or less compelling their owners to sell. The result is a run of bills of sale, which bear intriguing resemblance to the more fully developed chronicles and surveys.⁴ We also find at this point numerous documents that might best be called "reports," in which a Maya-speaking representative of the colonial government makes known significant laws or takes up a commission as a *maestro de campo* or another official position. The implication of the surnames involved is that these government representatives were likely creole, just as Beltrán de Santa Rosa María, a contemporary, was likely to have been.

It should come as no surprise that we find elements of doctrinal Maya throughout the notarial corpus. It is true that the secular realities of economy, extraction, dispossession, forced labor, and governance are at the forefront of much of the notarial documentation. But it is equally true that the horizon for these realities was the other reality of religion, orthodoxy, and the reshaping of the moral order. Moreover, being novel, none of the genres in question was fixed. For the same reason, we find verse parallelism, tropes, and the earmarks of "literature" in the apparently mundane recesses of notarial records.

WHAT IS A NOTARIAL DOCUMENT?

According to Restall (1997), there are approximately two thousand extant notarial documents from the colonial period in Maya. Of these, 42.1 percent are testaments, 36.4 percent land records, 12.9 percent petitions, and 8.6 percent other. The label "notarial" is based not on genre, since the genres are diverse, but on the relation between these texts and the process of governance in the *pueblos reducidos*. A notarial document is one written by an *escribano* acting in his official capacity as a member of the *cabildo*. Given that there is a substantial scholarly literature on this corpus, I concentrate selectively on land documents and petitions. Of these, the land documents are the most varied in terms of genre. They include the early large-scale land agreements such as the ones in the so-called chronicles, in which members of multiple towns participated, as well as bills of sale and land transfer, which are more local. Some testaments also contain embedded land descriptions that are less detailed than the chronicles but display many similar features.[5] The Yaxkukul surveys in particular have been closely studied by Barrera Vásquez (1984), Hanks (1992a), and Restall (1997). They are effectively equivalent to the large-scale surveys, complete with collective promulgation and inspection of the boundaries, but they are centered on a single town rather than a broad area. The petitions occasionally mention land but are more focused on local grievances, and they convey requests and pleas for mercy that echo the postures and semantic fields of prayer. They also focus on the truth and authenticity of the claims they make, and they tend to be highly honorific of their addressees, all of whom are colonial authorities, and in some cases, the Crown itself.

The notarial documents have a number of other features in common. First, in all cases, the issuing of the document is itself an official act of governance. With land documents, it is the lay and ownership of land that is made official. With petitions, the grievances, requests, and descriptions made in the texts are attested to by *cabildo* representatives. Whereas land documents were recopied and introduced into legal proceedings long after the original text was made, petitions were not, to my knowledge, recopied or reinvoked in the same way. In both genres, the deictic field in which the text situates itself is specified richly and rigidly. The pronouns, deictics, and other indexical elements refer to actual individuals, times, and places, as opposed to the placeholder indexicals of prayer and doctrinal dialogue scripts. In the participation framework of notarial texts, there is always an 'I' or 'we' associated with a named agent or group, where names are usually accompanied by titles such as *batab, gouernador, alcalde, regidor,* and *escribano* (see chapter 3). They present themselves as having been performed "in front of" a group of *testigos* 'witnesses', usually including the *cabildo* officers, along with two or more named *principales*. With very rare exceptions, these actors have Spanish first names, indicating that they have been baptized, and Maya surnames, indicating that they are Indios. The same individuals usually appear as signatories, and the use of the signature is another novel feature of colonial notarial practice. Addressees are in the second person ('you') and are often named with titles. They are invariably Spanish. The places in which the documents are made are named by town, often accompanied by a Catholic patron saint name, indicating that the place in question is embedded in the missions. The notarial "now" is specified by day count, usually in Maya, plus month name in Spanish and year in arabic numerals. Whereas the place and principals of the document usually occur in the opening lines of notarial texts, the dates often occur at the closing, just before the signatures. As Restall (1997) observed, the writer of these texts is almost always a named *escribano, ah dzib hun* 'scribe'. In a number of cases, there is also a named *ah tzol than* 'interpreter' (see chapters 5 and 6).

The cumulative effect of these facts is that notarial texts are maximally authorial: the principals, those whose position is expressed in the document, are named once and for all times. At the same time, the texts are the product of a group action, including the witnesses, those in front of whom they are made, and the notarial apparatus of scribe with or without interpreter. The governance structure of the *cabildo* is effectively embedded in the text itself and not only a background feature of context. Contrast the dictionaries and the doctrinal scripts, with their lack of fixed authorship; the closest analogy to this indexical framing in the missionary discourse is the front matter of those works that were actually published.

There is another, subtler feature that recurs throughout the notarial corpus, namely, the multiplicity of voices in which the texts speak. Many of these texts are simultaneously readable as the works of *indios reducidos* who observe the norms of colonial governance, the works of Christians keen to display their adherence to the religion, and the works of indigenous actors whose words echo Maya canons of style and modes of expression. As I have argued elsewhere (Hanks 1986, 1987, 1992a), this ambiguity is irreducible and reflects the threshold quality of these genres, which are simultaneously directed to the dictates of the Spanish system and the dictates of legitimate discourse in Maya. Adding to this is the fact that although they were written and archived, these texts display orality in the form of verse parallelism, end-rhyme, and regular metrical balance (if not outright meter). Moreover, they record gestures and bodily movements, such as the perambulations of boundary lines and the placing of official texts on the head as a physical sign of subjection. When they present themselves as having been read in front of witnesses, we are led to understand that they were literally performed orally. Thus the texts are ultimately multimodal in the sense developed in chapter 4, which suggests that they hover between the silent inscription of mundane notarial records and the outright enactment of onetime scripts performed in public. It is noteworthy that much of this ambiguity is present in the Maya but erased when we read the Spanish glosses by which they are occasionally accompanied. As a consequence for historical method, it is critical to work with the Maya texts, not the glosses, and to read them aloud, not silently, in order to take the full measure of their expressive force.

The kinds of dispersion we saw with the language of the dictionaries, *artes*, and *doctrinas* have analogues in the notarial corpus. There are three primary vectors of dispersal: recopying, cross-referencing, and the issuance of multiple contemporaneous versions of a single master document. Recopying was a widespread feature of discourse practice in the colony, as we have already seen, sometimes dictated by the need to preserve a document whose original signed version was rotting because of humidity and parasites in the local archives. In this case, the copy is rendered as a true and full replication of the original, decades later, and is itself authorized as such with a new indexical framing. Cross-referencing is an expectable feature of legal documents in which one act makes reference to and is based upon another, as when a land document is invoked in a subsequent litigation over rights.

Perhaps the most striking feature of Maya notarial practice is the tendency to issue multiple versions of a single master text, each of which has a different set of signatories. For example, in February 1567 there were six petitions addressed to the Spanish Crown, all dated within days of one another, nearly identical in substance, but all bearing different sets of signatures. These consisted of two master texts with four and two copies respectively. The individual texts had between six and seventeen signatories, with no apparent overlap among the resulting lists. Here the multiplicity serves as a means to express common assent to a single position while allowing the different sets of signatories to display their proximal alliances with one another. Similarly, the Yaxkukul land surveys comprise two texts, tracing what appears to be the same municipal boundary but dated within a week of one another and displaying overlapping yet distinct sets of signatories. The Xiu papers include three versions of the Maní accords of 1557, one from Maní, one from Calotmul, and one that is the Spanish gloss of the Maní text. On September 6, 1600, two agreements were formulated in the town of Yaxcabá, covering much the same material but with different named officials (Roys 1939, 428–30). In the long run of complaints against Flores de Aldana, there were very similar texts issued from multiple towns, all within a relatively short time frame, indicating coordinated actions by many different groups of officials. Similarly, on August 10, 1709, nearly identical reports were issued from Mérida to the towns of Hunucmá-Umán and Maxcanú (text 1) and Ticoh, Maní, Oxkutzcab, Tekax, Ticul, Teabo, and Muna (text 2). Here the serial texts have a single signatory but multiple addressees.[6]

In general, the greater the geographic scope of the official acts embodied in the issuing of a text, the more likely it was that it would be executed through series of parallel documents. The serial production is literally a spatial dispersal of the text. Thus although each individual notarial document is anchored to its unique deictic center, the main body and substance of the text may be iterated across the landscape. On this point, the notarial work joins the doctrinal script as a means of dispersing the language of *reducción* throughout the colony. The difference is that the doctrinal language was dispersed among the pueblos through oral performance even though the scripts were written, whereas notarial texts were dispersed through copying even though the text itself was read aloud. In both cases, the result was a proliferation of intertextual parallels, cognate passages, and iterations, making it difficult and in some cases impossible to precisely date and locate the complete field of enunciation in which the work circulated.

WRITING THE LANDSCAPE

Land documents were the instruments through which the colonial landscape was constituted. Some contain the metalinguistic expression *chichcunic than,* literally 'hardening speech', that is, to make official. Used in the first-person "present," this expression is an explicit performative.[7] Like the practices of prayer, land documents were world-making, even if that world was subject to contestation and revision. In general, they were focused on two aspects of space, the rights that individuals and groups claimed over places and the perimeters that delimited those places. There is virtually no description of the internal features of the places delimited in such texts, beyond the landmarks used to locate boundary markers, and very little attention to measuring distances.[8] By contrast, the treatment of boundaries themselves was detailed and cast in a style remarkably consistent across time and space. As I have shown in earlier work (Hanks 1992a) and Restall (1997) has also observed, the dominant style of the major surveys and accords was what might be called "tour guide," whereas Restall noted that in bills of sale and testaments one finds cases of "stationary" description cast from a fixed viewpoint. In the tour guide format, the boundary is traced by the physical perambulation of *cabildo* officials, often accompanied by neighbors who shared the boundary, cast in the first-person present tense and effectively walking the reader along the boundary. Starting at the first boundary marker, they proceed stepwise from place to place. At each point along the boundary, the texts cite a marker, of which there are four main kinds, *pictun* 'numerous stones', *multun* 'stone mound', *xuuk,* and *cruz* 'cross'. The term *tun* means 'stone', and the first three kinds of marker are made by gathering rocks into a pile. In contemporary Yucatec, the *xuuk* is a marker formed by a small pile of stones with a straight stick standing in the middle, used to delimit agricultural and domestic spaces (see Hanks 1990). The *multun* is a larger mound that usually marks municipal boundaries.[9] The term *pictun* appears to be more generic; it is the most frequent of the four kinds, and its precise shape is unclear. It is noteworthy that the Christian cross was integrated into the typology of Maya boundary markers as early as the first colonial surveys in the 1550s. Recall the discussion of this root symbol in the previous chapters: the placing of wooden crosses on the landscape was one of the first gestures of the early missionaries. Recall as well Coronel's sermon "The Devil Fears the Cross," in which a crucifix marking the entrance to a town causes the Devil to shy away and Saint Christopher to conclude that God is more powerful than the Devil. The cross embodies the protective power of God as a boundary guardian.

In addition to the boundary markers, perimeters are defined in terms of roads intersecting the boundary and major points at which the boundary changed direction. Called *tiitz* 'corner', *noh tiitz* 'great corner', *sicina* 'corner' (from Spanish *esquina*), or *noh sicina* 'great corner', these are places along the perimeter at which the cardinal direction changes significantly. Cardinal and intercardinal terms are ubiquitous indicators of the orientation of movement from one marker to the next, with no use of right or left. None of the documents I have examined specifies whether the intervals between markers and corners were straight or meandering, or whether the boundary was a volumeless division or a corridor of some width. The texts convey the sense that it was rectilinear and volumeless, at least conceptually, and followed a sight line running point to point.[10] Embedded in the same distribution of markers was a typology of natural features of the landscape, including topographic features, water sources (often named), and vegetation types (with a focus on trees; cf. Restall 1997, 203–5). The linguistic style of major surveys is what is known in Maya as *tzol pictun* 'count markers' (see chapters 5 and 6 above). In this style, which I have described as "cyclic prose," a sequence of lines is repeated again and again at each marker according to a schema of parallelism that we can summarize as ABCDE, ABCDE, . . . , where each letter stands for an element in the cycle. To be sure, the repetitions are less regular than this schema would indicate, but the tendency is clear and robust in the texts.[11]

Of special interest, some of the land documents, notably the ones found in the archives of Ebtún (Roys 1939, 72, 240), include lengthy lists of towns that were abandoned during the *reducciones*. For present purposes, what is important is not so much the identities or locations of the towns, most of which are unknown, but the fact that they are listed at all. The implication is that land documents record not only spatial boundaries and relations but temporal ones as well; they fix the contrast between the colonial places in which the texts are promulgated and the formerly inhabited towns they name while consigning the latter to the past. The latter were, by the 1560s or 1600 (depending upon the text), *lab* 'rotted' or *tocoy* 'abandoned' (the term used in the Yaxkukul surveys). In similar fashion, the run of documents that emerged from the region of Sahcabchén in the late seventeenth century includes extended lists of named individuals who are said to have abandoned their homes (in Maya *ah patah nahob* 'home deserters'). In both cases, the texts respond to the dramatic changes of the *reducción* by sorting time into before and after, just as the surveys sort space into inside and outside. The verb used to describe what such texts enact is *hedzic* 'to fix, to stabilize', as in *lic hedzic lab cah kochila* 'we fixed (established) the rotted town of Kochila' (Roys 1939, 240). The same verb root *-hedz* was used to describe the establishment or settling of Christianity in the colony, suggesting a linguistic parallel between missionization and the consequent abandonment of formerly occupied Maya towns. The *lab cah* is the inverse of the *pueblo reducido*: both are the products of *reducción*, but the former was consigned to the past, whereas the latter was the province of the future.

A proper treatment of the so-called chronicles would be monographic in length and is beyond the purposes of this book. Here I briefly examine those aspects of the Xiu or Maní Chronicle, the Chronicle of Nakuk Pech, and the Yaxkukul surveys that help situate these works in the historical development of *reducción*. These texts are reminiscent of the ecclesiastical *memorias* discussed in chapter 2, in which towns and *guardianías* are set forth with scant description beyond the name and the numbers of priests and inhabitants. In the case of the chronicles, there is no specification of the number of inhabitants of the towns or the distances between them, whereas there is more detailed treatment of the individuals and groups that inhabit them as well as remarks on their history before the arrival of the Spanish. Just as the *memorias* are based on *visitas,* the chronicles include processions, a sort of collective *visita.* Unlike the *memorias,* the chronicles include stylistically marked *tzol* 'count' descriptions but do not present lists. Both *memorias* and chronicles were produced in order to officially record the relations between places and groups of actors, the former in the context of *guardianías* and the latter in the context of central places and surrounding ones.

XIU CHRONICLE

What Morley and Roys (1941) dubbed the Xiu Chronicle in their unpublished study is actually not a single work at all but a collection of documents pertaining to the Xiu patriline.[12] The Xiu were one of the leading lineages at Mayapán, and they moved south to Maní in the aftermath of the breakup of Mayapán, around the same time the Cocom, their archrivals, moved to Tibolón-Sotuta. The Xiu papers give a wealth of information pertaining to the famous Maní "treaty" of August 15, 1557, as well as the subsequent events that are the immediate context for the petitions of the 1560s. The 1557 treaty negotiation was held under the leadership of Francisco de Montejo Xiu in Maní, in response to Spanish demands that the region be stabilized and the local violence in the aftermath of conquest be ended. Maya elites, *al mehenob* in Maya, came to the center of Maní from their respective towns around the central and southern region, including the Sierra towns along the Puuc hills and Sotuta, among others. Gifts were distributed, the lands were delineated, markers and guards were placed at borders. It was, according to Roys (Morley and Roys 1941, 2:181), the high point of Montejo Xiu's political power. As I mentioned above, there are three written versions of these events, one from Maní, one from Calotmul to the southeast, and one a Spanish gloss of the Maní text. According to the 1582 *memoria* (see chapter 2), Calotmul, located three leagues southeast of Petu, was a *visita* of the secular *vicaría* of Petu. The Calotmul records many more participants than the Maní version. Otherwise the pattern of contemporaneous versions is familiar: both list partially overlapping places, mention a map called a *trazo,* and describe the act they record as *"xotol chi"* 'cut (the) border' and "*dzaic pictun*" 'place *pictun* markers', strongly suggesting that they fixed boundaries and did not merely record preexisting ones. Both texts repeatedly refer to *pictun* markers, *tiitz* 'corners', and *xuk* markers, and both cite the placing of guards at border points.[13] Here we see the principle of multiple contemporaneous versions to perform a collective act with scope over a large region.

Francisco de Montejo Xiu was arrested and tried for drunkenness in 1561 and caught up in the now-infamous idolatry trials of the following year.[14] He also appears as first signatory to the April 12, 1567, letter to King Felipe II (AGI Mexico 369), written in elegant Spanish and bitterly decrying the excesses of the Franciscans at Maní. Interestingly, Montejo Xiu signs this letter as "*governador de la provincia de Mani*," suggesting he still claimed the provincial scope of the *cuchcabal* as set forth a decade earlier. Between June 21 and July 15, 1562, thirty-eight Maya nobles were imprisoned at Maní, and on July 13, 1562, twenty-five *gobernadores*, caciques, and *principales* from Maní province were imprisoned in Mérida. In the same collection of documents, it is recorded that on January 12, 1564, Montejo Xiu testified that in the previous three months, he had put three hundred Indios to work opening a road between Maní and Mérida, but there is little evidence that this gesture improved his lot. These events were the proximal context for the 1567 petitions.

The Maní text of 1557 opens with a statement of the place, date, and principals of the Maní treaty, as is typical in the major treaties and surveys:[15]

1.1	*Tu chahal Mani tu holhun piz u kinil u agosto*	In the town of Maní on the fifteenth (of the) day(s) (of the) month (of) August
1.2	*Ychil <u>yaabil</u> de mill y quinientos y cinquenta y siete <u>anyos</u>*	in the <u>year</u> of one thousand five hundred and fifty and seven <u>years</u>
1.3	*U humolcinah u baob <u>halach uinic</u> don Francisco de Montejo Xiu*	they gathered themselves together <u>halach uinic</u> don Francisco de Montejo Xiu
1.4	*<u>gouernador</u> uay ti cah*	<u>gobernador</u> here in (this) town
1.5	*Yetel tu cuchcabal Tutul Xiu*	and in the jurisdiction of Tutul Xiu

Several features of this opening are noteworthy, starting with the obvious fusion of Maya with Spanish in the date and the pairing of roughly equivalent Maya and Spanish expressions (*yaabil-anyo* 'year', *halach uinic-gouernador* 'gobernador'). Such pairing was quite common and illustrates the process of commensuration between the languages, discussed in chapter 4. The usage of *halach uinic* in reference to a Maya *gobernador* is atypical, since the colonial regime essentially decapitated Maya governance above the level of the town, and this Maya expression came to be used for higher-ranking Spanish officials. By contrast, the Maya *gobernador* was usually a *batab*. What motivates this distinctive use of *halach uinic* is the fact that the Maní text is very early and its frame of reference is the regional jurisdiction known as *cuchcabal* rather than the *cah* 'town'. The term *cuchcabal* was subsequently appropriated by the Spanish to refer to the colonial *parcialidad*, as well as to the *pueblos de visita* within the *guardianía* (see chapter 5, ex. 5.25). In the present context, the reference to Tutul Xiu clearly indexes that it is the Maya jurisdiction that is in play, yet when viewed from the subsequent patterns of usage, the ambiguity of *cuchcabal* parallels that of *halach uinic*. Similarly, as we saw in chapter 5 (ex. 5.23), the root *mol* 'gather' in line 1.3 is the same one used to translate *congregación, colegio,* and the church as the gathering of the faithful. In all these cases, the implication is that a preexisting pattern of usage in Maya was adapted subsequently to the referential universe of *reducción*. Finally, the use of *uay* 'here' in line 1.4 illustrates the deictic framing of the text as having been produced in Maní and not only about Maní.

Immediately after 1.5 the text lists participating individuals from Ticul, Sanct Francisco Oxkutzcab, Sanct Juan Tekax, Muna, Mama, Sanct Andres Tikit, and the other *"gouernadoresob"* in the *cuchcabal* of Maní. Here we note the combination of saint names with place-names for those towns where the missions had already established a presence. Having established the "here" and the first-tier towns that participated, the text states the purpose of the gathering, as is customary in notarial documents.

3.2	*Ca u multumtahob*	Then they gathered
4.1	*yanil u nah tu thanob*	as was necessary they said
4.2	*u xoticob*	(that) they divide it
4.3	*yetel u dzaicob u xukilob*	and they place the *xuk* markers
4.4	*udzaicob cruz tu xul u colob u cahalob*	they place cross(es) at the endpoints of their fields, their towns
4.5	*u cuchteelob ti hunhun tzucilobe*	their councillors from *tzuc* to *tzuc*

Note first in this segment that the marker types *xuk* (4.3), and crosses (4.4) are both mentioned. Moreover, the choice of verb (*dzaic* 'to give, put') again makes explicit that the markers are being put in place, that is, that the action recorded in the text is performative. There is a minor verse series in lines 4.4–4.5, based on the repetition of *[(u) . . . lob]*. The two nouns in 4.4 refer to the two main spaces of each "municipality," the agricultural lands and the town itself. By contrast, in line 4.5 the theme is governance: the *cuchteel* is a local councillor, and the *tzuc* is apparently a place associated with the gathering of councillors. The same pairing of *cuchteel* with *tzuc* occurs in the Yaxkukul surveys, suggesting that, whatever the nature of the political position or the gathering place in question, the two are associated.

Following the statement of purpose is a lengthy list of the people in attendance from *cuchcabal* other than Maní. These groups are referred to with the agentive prefix plus the name of the lineage (*chibal;* cf. Restall 1997) or place. I have added in parentheses the names of the *guardianías* and jurisdictions *(cuchcabalob)* to which these places belonged in 1582, in order to give a better picture of the correspondence between this gathering and the emerging missionary landscape: *ah canulob* 'the Canul', *ah Maxcanulob* 'those from Maxcanul' (*visita* of Calkiní), *ah Umanob* 'those from Umán' (*visita* of Mérida), *ah Acanquehob* 'those from Acanceh' (*visita* of Homún), *ah Cohob* 'those from Coh', *ah Cuzamaob* 'those from Cuzamá' (*visita* of Homún), *ah Humunob* 'those from Homún' *(cabecera de guardianía)*, *ah Zututaob* 'those from Sotuta' *(vicaría)*, *ah Cacalob* 'those from Cacal' (*visita* of Sotuta), *ah Petuob* 'those from Petu', *ah Calotmulob* 'those from Calotmul' (*visita* of Petu), *ah Hunac Tiob* 'those from Hunacti', *ah Tzucacabob* 'those from Tzucacab' (*visita* of Petu). In addition to this general list, there is a list of individual *al mehenob* 'elites', cited by name and provenance.

This then leads into another statement of purpose with a more precise description of the place where they gathered.

31.8	*ti hun molob*	(they were) in one group
31.9	*ti audiencia uay tu kuul na ah tepal lae*	in the *audiencia* here in the *audiencia* of (our) majesty
32.1	*tilic u hahcunticob*	there they made true
32.2	*yetel u chichcunticob*	and they made firm
32.3	*u muultumutob*	their gatherings
33.1	*ti bay u nahil tanlabebal*	as it was necessary to serve
33.2	*ca yumil ti dios ah tepale*	our lord in God majesty
34.1	*yetel ix uchebal*	and in order
34.2	*ca dzoc lukzic yalmathanil ca noh ahau su Mag. Ah tepale*	that we fulfill the commandment of our great lord his Majesty Majesty

In lines 31.9, 33.2, and 34.2, we find pairings of roughly equivalent expressions in Maya and Spanish. The *kuul nah* is the same place as the *audiencia,* that is, the official meeting place in the town, according to the colonial mandates.[16] The combination of *ca yumil . . . ah tepal* 'lord majesty (merciful)' is an epithet for God, as we saw in the previous chapter. By contrast, *ca noh ahau . . . ah tepal* is the Maya for 'our great king (his) majesty'. Embedding the corresponding Spanish term between the two parts in each case, these lines echo in their morphosyntactic structure the conceptual parallel between God (in heaven) and Crown (on earth).

The commandment referred to in line 34.2 was to settle down and fix the boundaries *(hedz),* in a time of tumultuous change (the term *yalmathanil* is also used in the *doctrina* to refer to the commandments of God and the commandments of the Church). Thus what follows is a list of places and persons involved in the procession in which markers were placed on the landscape.

| 58.1 | *lay u kaba yanil u ppictunil* | These are the names where there are their *pictun* markers |
| 58.2 | *yetel dzaantacil cruzob lae* | and crosses were placed |

In the course of the text, fourteen crosses, along with other markers, are planted in the earth (*pak cruz* 'plant cross'). Judging by the incidence of the different kinds of marker, it appears that *xuk* are associated with agricultural fields and crosses are placed at the *xul* 'endpoints' of the places they delimited. In the late parts of the document, when crosses are planted, they are accompanied by pairs of *ah canan hool kax* 'guardians of the entrance to the forest'. These were human individuals named by patronymic. Thus the "treaty" involved the establishment of boundaries that were enforced or at least monitored. At the end of the document are signatures of the principals, including the attestation of the scribe, once again cast as a bilingual couplet.

| 68.5 | *uilah ix cen Franco Cab* | and I saw it, I who am Francisco Cab scribe, |
| | *escriuano yah dzibul lae* | the scribe of this |

A second document, dated July 10, 1596, occurs in the same collection and ratifies the validity of the earlier text, referring to it as *u tidroil* 'the title'. This retrospective reference from one text to another is typical of the intertextual life of the land documents, which are often adduced as evidence of prior rights in the course of legal proceedings. As Restall (1997, 278) notes, most of the "quasi-notarial" documents were actually compiled in the eighteenth century on the basis of earlier documents and thus are difficult to date.[17] The resulting temporal perspective mixes retrospection with the would-be presentist perspective of the text. This was also the case with the following example from the Pech lineage.

CÓDICE NAKUK PECH

Whereas the Maní and Xiu documents are centered in the province of Maní, the Códice Nakuk Pech is concentrated in the northern part of the colony. It consists of twenty-six pages numbered at the top of each page, written in a single hand. The date, almost certainly not the time of writing, is February 7, 1542, with the number '4' written over the number '7' (as if mistranscribed or altered). Unlike the Maní, this document specifies the date late in the text (p. 17), not at the beginning as is more typical, and Restall (1997) argues that it was actually written in the eighteenth century. The text uses both the ɔ for *dz*, as employed in the dictionaries, and ç rather than s; both features are consistent with sixteenth- and seventeenth-century orthographic practice. The text recounts the history and conquest of the area around Chacxulubchén, in addition to describing the lay of the land. It overlaps to a considerable extent with the second of the Yaxkukul documents, with which it evidently forms a tight intertextual series (see below).

On page 15, this one explains that it was produced upon the instruction of don Julian Donsel, *encomendero* of Chac Xulub Chen:

ca tu yalah ti Batab	And he told the *batab(s)*
caxicob udzabob u chicul chikax uluumob	that they should go placing the signs of the borders of their lands
uay tu pach umektancahil	here at the edge of the municipality.
yoklal tan pisil uchi lumob	For the measuring of the land borders is occurring,
uchi kaxob ti lakin, ti nohol, ti chikin	the forest borders to the East, to the South, to the West
tulacal hen Cex max cu cahtalob	all those live (there),
tumen dzoctun u hedzel cristianoil	because Christianity has settled
uay ti lume chhaacxulubchheen . . .	here upon the lands of Chac Xulub Chen . . .

According to this section of the text, Donsel ordered the Maya leaders, here referred to with the indigenous term *batab*, to execute a land survey and place "signs" (i.e., markers of various kinds) along the borders. The absence of *cabildo* titles is likely due to the early date of the text. That the stated motivation for this order is the settling *(hedzel)* of Christianity upon the land is a direct reference to the mandates of *reducción*. The text goes on to spell out the line of authority from the Crown to *oydor* López Medel to the Maya authors themselves.

ton con Batabon ah pechil uinicon	We who are *batabs*, we are Pech people
uay ti lum yucatan lae	here in the land of Yucatán.
tac kamah unoh comisionil upislahal lumob	We received the commission that the lands be measured.
tu dzah uthanil y u lisenciail ca noh Ahau Rey ah tepal	He gave his word and his license, our great King King majesty
ti ca yumil yax oidor Dn Tomas Lopez	to our lord first *oydor* don Tomás López
utial cau dzanucte uthanon	in order that he call upon us
ca cppis upach cahal lae	that we measure these town borders

Whereas the previous example describes the context of the survey from a local perspective, citing the *encomendero* and the local place named Chac Xulub Chen, this one takes a broader perspective; the authors represent a lineage (Pech), the place is Yucatán (not a town), and the source of the order to survey is the Crown by way of the *oydor* López Medel. The epithet for the Crown is grammatically parallel to the one used in the Xiu documents, with the Maya couplet *ca noh Ahau . . . ah tepal* 'our great King . . . majesty' flanking the Spanish term (in this case *Rey*). The naming of López (Medel) and the use of the Spanish terms *comisión, licencia,* and *oydor* situate the survey securely within the mandates of his *Ordenanzas*.

After naming the seven Pech leaders involved in the survey, the text states that they were eyewitnesses to the placing of the first and remaining *pictun* markers.

Tuyilahob ca dzaic u yax chun pictun	They saw our placing of the first *pictun* marker.
Ylob ca nup pictun yan uaye	They saw our other marker which is here.
noh sicina ti yan crusi +	At the great corner there is a cross +.
cin binel chikintan ylob tan utzolol	I go along westward, seeing the
* uyam pictunil*	ordering of the intervals of the *pictun* markers
latulah yokol chhen tculul	until the Tculul well
tu nohol lakin chen bay hunppel sicinae	to the south of the well as a corner,
ti yan multuni	there is a stone mound.

Of special significance here is the pairing of the term *cruz* 'cross' with a graphic cruciform. Over the course of the text there are eleven such cruciforms, of which three are paired with the word *'cruz'*, as in this example. When both the graphic form and the word 'cross' are present, the referent is a material cross planted on the landscape, in the manner of the one mentioned in Coronel's sermon (chapter 8). The remaining eight cruciforms in this text illustrate a different usage: they are purely graphic, with no clear reference beyond the text. As I have shown elsewhere (Hanks 1996), the symbol of the cross was used not only as a gesture of piety and a marker on the landscape but also as a graphic sign of legitimacy in the colonial documents themselves.

THE YAXKUKUL SURVEYS

The two land surveys dated 1544 from the town of Yaxkukul that are closely related to the Códice Nakuk Pech have been closely studied by Barrera Vásquez (1984), Hanks (1992a), and Restall (1997). Here I touch only on the main points of relevance to the themes of this book. The first is that, in accord with the familiar pattern, they appear in a contemporaneous series, dated just eight days apart, and they report on surveys conducted at the same place, with overlapping inventories of markers (albeit placed at different landmarks) and overlapping lists of principals. The latter are all from the Pech lineage, including Nakuk Pech himself. The longer of the two I call Yaxkukul Document 1 (YD1) and the shorter, dated eight days later, Yaxkukul Document 2 (YD2) (map 11).

YD1 has three clearly distinct sections.[18] Lines 1–111 (sec. 1) constitute the opening, with statement of the deictic coordinates in which the text claims to have been produced, the powers in whose name it was composed, and the authors (listed by name with *cabildo* titles). Lines 112–308 (sec. 2) cover the survey of the boundaries of Yaxkukul, conducted by local nobles and cast in the cyclic prose

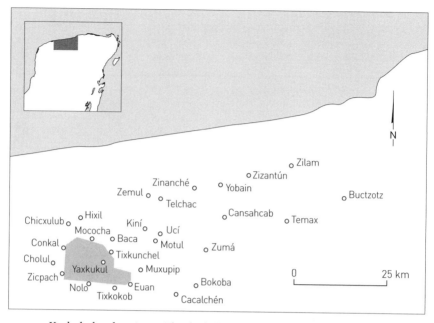

MAP 11. Yaxkukul and environs. The shaded area represents the mid-sixteenth-century borders, seen in detail in maps 12 and 13 (© William F. Hanks 2007)

of *tzol* 'ordering, counting' (cf. Hanks 1987, 1988, 1992a). Lines 309–483 (sec. 3) reframe the text as authentic, true, and representative of the consensus of local elites. It is dated April 30, 1544, although Restall convincingly argues that the written document was produced in the eighteenth century, evidently recopied from preexisting texts that are now missing. Like the preceding chronicles, this text states that it was produced in response to the directives of *oydor* Tomás López Medel, and like them, it records a procession in which markers were placed on the landscape in order to fix the borders of the place being surveyed. The kinds of marker are the same as in the chronicles, with the exception of the *xuk*, which occur liberally in the Xiu documents from Maní and Calotmul but are absent from the Pech documents. Just as we saw with the Maní text, the places mentioned in the Yaxkukul document are determined not by their presumed relations through the missions but by their contiguity to the central place being surveyed. Unlike the Maní text, however, YD1 is centered on a single town rather than a far-flung *cuchcabal* 'province'. Moreover, Yaxkukul was not a major capital as was Maní, and there is no reference to a *halach uinic*.

In the manner of *tzol* surveys, YD1 was executed by officers of the central place walking the boundary of their town, accompanied by those neighbors from contiguous towns who shared the relevant portion of the border with them. The participants in this survey came from pueblos that were assigned to three different *guardianías* in the 1582 *memoria* examined in chapter 2, Conkal (Sicpach, Mocochá), Tixkokob (Noló, Euan, Yaxkukul), and Motul (Tixkunchel). The spatial logic of the *guardianía* was radial *(cabecera* to *visita),* whereas the *tzol* was perimetric. Consequently, these surveys are roughly complementary to the *guardianías,* and they perpetuated interpueblo relations based not on common belonging to a mission center but on a shared border. The document opens by specifying the place of production and the authority on which it was made (all extracts are from Barrera Vásquez 1984):

1.	*Uay tuyotoch cahal yaxkukul*	Here in the inhabited town of Yaxkukul
2.	*tutabal u probinsiail meridad de yucatan lae*	in the jurisdiction of the province of Mérida of Yucatán,
3.	*tukabix ca noh ahau Rey Ah tepal*	And in the name of our great king King Majesty
4.	*lay yahaulil tumen ca yumil ti Dios*	who reigns by our lord God.

The epithet for the Crown is identical to the one used in the Códice Nakuk Pech, embedding the Spanish term *Rey* 'king' in the paired Maya forms *ca noh ahau . . . ah tepal.* Notice that Mérida, the capital, is referred to as a province rather than a city. This illustrates the usage of a key term at different levels, a widespread phenomenon that I pointed out in chapter 2.

After referring to López Medel as *ca yum alcalde mayor Dn Tomas Lopez* 'our lord *alcalde mayor* don Tomás López' (line 48), the text asserts its own veracity, another common feature of the notarial documents (Barrera Vásquez 1984).[19]

61.	*yoklal u hahil*	Because truly
62.	*licil ca dzaic ca firmail*	we give our signature,
63.	*con justisiail*	we who are *justicias,*
64.	*helel tu lahun cakal u kinil*	today on the 10th-for-two times 20 [thirtieth] day
65.	*u yuil de Abril*	of the month of April
66.	*de mil quinientos y quarenta*	of one thousand five hundred and forty
67	*y quatro años/*	and four years
68.	*Dn Alonso Pech /gor./*	Don Alonso Pech, *gobernador*
69.	*Grabier tun alcaldes/*	Gabriel Tun Alcalde/
70.	*Po Canul regidor/* [. . .]	Pedro Canul Regidor, [. . .]
74.	*testigos yn mehenob/*	witnesses, my descendants
75.	*Dn Lucas Pech/*	Don Lucas Pech
76.	*Dn miguel Pech/*	Don Miguel Pech
77.	*Dn Gregorio Pech/*	Don Gregorio Pech
78.	*lay hidalgos*	who are hidalgos

In this extract we see the standard statement of date, with the day count in Maya and the month name and year in Spanish. The conjunction 'and' has been interpolated into the 'five hundred and forty', evidently overgeneralizing the use of the conjunction in *cuarenta y cuatro* 'forty-four', or perhaps to increase the parallelism between the two parts of the dates. The use of the Spanish terms for the full array of *cabildo* officers is noteworthy in a text as early as this one claims to be, and may be read either as a strategic enhancement of the legitimacy of the text or as a glaring indicator that it was written later than its stated date, by which time the *cabildo* had taken root. Recall that López Medel decreed that the *cabildo* be introduced, but only gradually.

The YD1 text is noteworthy in the richness of the cyclic prose in which it is cast. Although there is variation in the precise features of the cycles, the overall repeating pattern is striking. The following illustrates a single cycle of a form repeated, with some variation, throughout the survey portion of the document.

154.	*noholtan yn binel tzol pictun*	Southward I go counting stone markers
155.	*tulacal u binel latulah kuchul*	it goes all the way until it arrives
156.	*tu chun mul ac*	at the foot of Mul Ac
157.	*yan u pictunil -*	There's a marker there.
158.	*ti cin ppatic ah cumkali*	There I leave off the Cumkal people
159.	*tiix cin chaic in yum*	there too I join my (fore)father
160.	*yxkil ytzam pech ah sicpach*	Yxkil Ytzam Pech of Sicpach
161.	*y u kuchteelob*	with his deputies.
162.	*Cacathil yn binel yetelob*	Pairwise I go along with them.

The schema for the cycles is "directional phrase, destination point, marker, leave off with one set of neighbors and pick up with the next, continue pairwise." Over the course of the survey, neighbors, who are kinsmen of the narrator, are mentioned from the towns of Mocochá (*visita* of Cumkal), Cumkal (Conkal; *cabecera de doctrina*), Sicpach (*visita* of Cumkal), Noló (*visita* of Tixkokob), Euan (*visita* of Tixkokob), and Kumchel (*visita* of Motul). The implication is that alongside their membership in the *guardianías,* Maya elites sustained political relations based on kinship and common borders (map 12).

382.1	*lay lakoob*	These kinsmen
382.2	*tu hool luumoob*	at the head(s) of (their) land(s),
382.3	*yanix u Mapao*	they also have maps
382.4	*tu tzucentzucilob cahob*	from town to town.

Like the Maní treaty, which was accompanied by a map, this one claims that all the towns mentioned had their own maps, although none has been found to my knowledge.

There is strong evidence in YD1 of the penetration of religious *reducción* in Yaxkukul. In the course of the survey, five crosses preexisting on the landscape

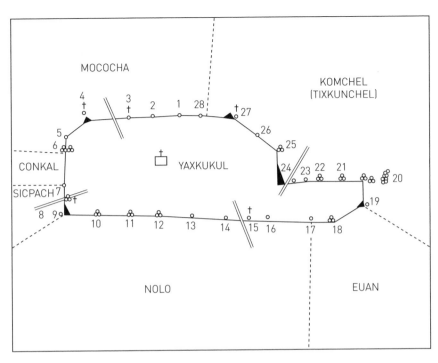

- ○ *pictun* 'numerous stones'
- ⚬⚬ *multun* 'stone mound'
- ⚬⚬⚬ *nohoch mul* 'large mound'
- † *Cruz* 'Cross'
- ▶ *noh tiitz* 'great corner'
- ═ road

KEY TO SITES OF MARKERS INSPECTED (number indicates sequence of procession)

	Place-name	Neighbors		Place-name	Neighbors
1	Ch'en Chac Nicte	Ah Mococha	15	Road to Nolo	Ah Nolo
2	Kancab Ch'en	Ah Mococha	16	Ch'en Ch'um	Ah Nolo
3	Road to Mococha	Ah Mococha			
4	Ch'en Dzadza	Ah Mococha	17	Ch'en Chacil	Ah Euan
5	Kan Pepen	Ah Mococha	18	Ch'en Tan Tzec	Ah Euan
			19	Tikin Mul	Ah Euan
6	Chun Catzim	Ah Conkal			
7	Mul Ac	Ah Conkal	20	Yax Icim	Ah Komcheel
			21	Ch'en Piste	Ah Komcheel
8	Road to Sicpach	Ah Sicpach	22	Ualah Tunich	Ah Komcheel
9	Halal Actun	Ah Sicpach	23	Ch'en Kanpocoche	Ah Komcheel
			24	Road to Kumcheil	Ah Komcheel
10	Hunbil Ch'en	Ah Nolo	25	Tan Kancab	Ah Komcheel
11	Ch'en Chac Abal	Ah Nolo	26	Ch'en Haltun	Ah Komcheel
12	Ch'en Kan Pepen	Ah Nolo	27	Ch'en Euan Cauich	Ah Komcheel
13	Ch'en Cacabil Utzte	Ah Nolo			
14	Ch'en Siquib	Ah Nolo	28	Yok Muux	Ah Mococha

MAP 12. Borders of Yaxkukul, according to Yaxkukul Document 1
(© William F. Hanks 2007)

are mentioned among the boundary markers. The final part of the text states that a secular priest blessed the event, at which point it simply states the sign of the cross, using the standard phrasing with Latin abbreviation of the Holy Spirit.

390.	*tan u dzaic u bendisio ca yum/*	Our father is giving his blessing
391.	*Padre franco hernandes Clerigo*	Father Francisco Hernández, Cleric
392.	*yokol tulacal uinicob/*	upon all people
393.	*Uay ti cah lae*	here in this town
394.	*tu kaba Dios yumbil*	In the name of God the Father
395.	*Dios mehenbil*	God the Son
396.	*Dios esptu S.to*	God the Holy Spirit

Line 412 amplifies the religious framing of the event, explaining that the principals had learned (or were learning) the Gospels in the monastery, a clear reference to Franciscan pedagogical practice, in which Maya elites were instructed in classrooms within the convent walls. The presence of both secular and Franciscan elements in a single passage is noteworthy among Maya-authored documents but was common in the front matter of published missionary writings (see chapters 6 and 7).

412.1	*ca cane S.to/ euangelio*	So that we might learn the Holy Gospel
412.2	*ti monexterio*	in the monastery,
412.3	*ca utzac uliksabal*	so that [it] might be raised up
412.4	*utanlahul*	(in) service (to)
412.5	*ca noh ahau*	our great lord
412.6	*lay cilich bara e*	the sacred staff.
412.7	*bay tzolanil ychil / Autto*	So it was explained in the Auto
412.8	*ca ulsabi toon*	when it was brought to us.

Line 438 again lists the principals, each of whom uses a Spanish given name accompanied by a *cabildo* title. I have subdivided the line to highlight the fact that the titles appear in the rank order of the *cabildo* structure.[20]

438.1	*Dn Alonso Pech /gor/*
438.2	*Grabier Tun /alcalde/*
438.3	*Po. Canul regidore/*
438.4	*Daniel pol regidor/*
438.5	*Juan Mau regidor/*
438.6	*Po. mum ess.no p.co*
438.7	*Juan Matu /ess.no/*
438.8	*testigosob in mehenob/*

YD2 was presented in a legal proceeding on March 18, 1793, in the context of a land dispute between Yaxkukul and Mocochá. It was rejected by the magistrate as lacking proper validation (Barrera Vásquez 1984, 98–99; cf. Restall 1997). The suggestion is that it was concocted at that time and backdated, as a thinly veiled

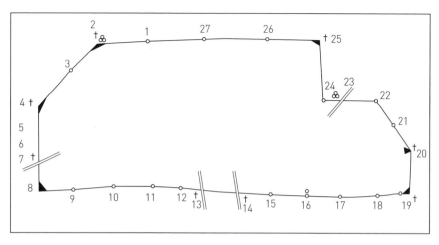

o *pictun* 'numerous stones'	† *Cruz* 'Cross'
⅋ *multun* 'stone mound'	► *noh tiitz* 'great corner'
8 *nohoch pictun* 'numerous large stones'	= road

KEY TO SITES OF MARKERS INSPECTED (number indicates sequence of procession)

1 Ch'en Chac Nicte	9 Hunbil Ch'en	20 Yax Ycim
2 Ch'en Dzadza	10 Chac Abal	21 Ppisteil
3 Kan Pepenil	11 Kan Pepenil	22 Tixualah Tunich
4 Chun Catzim	12 Ustel	23 Road from Tixkuncheil
5 Pacab Tun	13 Road to Nolo	24 Ch'en Haltun
6 Kom Sahcab	14 Road from Tixkokob	25 Tah Euan Cauich
	15 Cacab Lúm	
7 Road to Sicpach		26 Yok Mux
8 Yok Actun Yan Halali	16 Chac Hil	27 Sahcab Lúm
	17 Ch'en Tah Tzek	
	18 Tan Kancab	
	19 Ticin Mul	

MAP 13. Borders of Yaxkukul, according to Yaxkukul Document 2
(© William F. Hanks 2007)

attempt to claim rights over territory. Whether this critique applies to the text or merely to the documentary artifact is unclear, but there are significant contrasts with YD1. The first is that the principals are named without *cabildo* titles and three of the seven named have Maya first names, which is highly atypical of notarial documents. All of the four with Christian first names also bear the title *don,* whereas in YD1, only the main principal, don Alonso Pech, claimed this honorific. Similarly, the date is entirely in Spanish, whereas the date in other contemporaneous chronicles is mixed Maya-Spanish (map 13).

Lay u hahil in firma,	This is my true signature
hele, en 8 de mayoil 1544	today, the 8th of May 1544
Dn. Pedro Pech,	Don Pedro Pech,
ti Dn Alonso Pech	to Don Alonso Pech
yetel Dn. Miguel Pech,	and Don Miguel Pech
yetel Dn. Francisco Pech,	and Don Francisco Pech
yetel Yxkil Itzam Pech,	and Yxkil Itzam Pech
yetel Ah-Tunal Pech,	and Ah Tunal Pech
yetel Ah Dzulub Pech,	and Ah Dzulub Pech
yetel tulacal mac cahob	and all the inhabitants
uay tu pach lay kilacabob lae.	here around these lineages.
(Barrera Vásquez 1984, 91)	

Whereas YD1 cites both *Ca yum Senor encomendero Gonsalo Mendes Cpn.* and *ca yum Senor Dn Franco de Montejo gov y Cpn gl Adelantado,* the conqueror of Yucatán, YD2 cites *Capitan Julian Doncel encomendero,* the same individual cited in the Códice Nakuk Pech (Barrera Vásquez 1984, 91). YD2 also omits the historical description presented in YD1, giving the appearance that it either presupposed it or was drawn up for different purposes. As in the other cases we have seen, this text describes the boundary reconnaissance as *udzahob upictunilob* 'placing the markers', *tzol pictun* 'ordering/counting markers', *xotic uchi luum* 'cutting the land border', and *multumtahob* 'they *multun*-marked it' (i.e., placed piles of stones as markers). The text shows an attenuated form of cyclic prose, notably less elaborate than in YD1. Finally, although the inventory of marker types is similar in the two texts, there are differences both in where the markers are placed and in the quantity of each type. These are summarized in table 18.

The upshot of these contrasts is that these two texts provide subtly different perspectives on the land they described. It is as if, in the same space of Yaxkukul, there are two overlapping places: one linked to the *encomendero* Mendes, to the *cabildo,* and to actors whose Spanish first names display their embeddedness in the colony (YD1); and the other linked to *encomendero* Donsel, to a form of governance outside the *cabildo,* and to principals who present themselves with Maya names (YD2). To this we can add that the main principal who speaks in the first-person singular in YD1 is don Alonso Pech, *gobernador* of Yaxkukul, whereas the corresponding principal in YD2 is actually his father, don Pedro Pech, aka Ah Macan Pech. As I have shown elsewhere (Hanks 1992a), the order in which the principals are named in the two texts follows a single pattern of reference, first the main principal (the 'I'), then those of the descending generation (his sons), then the sibling of the main principal, then those of the ascending generation (his father and uncles). This common pattern has no obvious motivation other than

TABLE 18 Incidence of Marker Types in the Two Yaxkukul Surveys

MARKER	NO. IN YD1	NO. IN YD2
pictun '8,000 stones'	19	13
multun 'stone mound'	12	1
Cruz 'cross'	5	9
tiitz 'corner'	4	6
behob 'roads'	4	5

convention, and, along with the common inventory of marker types, it indicates that the texts arose from the same discourse formation. I take the contrast in perspective to express the irreducible ambiguity that defines the colonial period; space, identity, and meaning were all caught up simultaneously in the recursive logic of *reducción* and in the persistence of the systems it sought to replace. If YD2 was actually a backdated counterfeit created in the eighteenth century, then it attests to the persistence of this doubling.

THE TITLES OF EBTÚN

The town of Ebtún was a *visita* of Sisal (the convent in present-day Valladolid), one kilometer from the convent. Roys (1939) published a study of documents found in the Ebtún archive, which shed important new light on the layering and re-forming of the landscape. The earliest of these is dated April 21, 1561 (Roys 1939, 240). It records the "settling" of an agricultural field at the *labcah* 'rotted town' (i.e., abandoned place) of Kochil. I have been unable to locate Kochil in any of the relevant sources, although the 1561 document locates it on the road to Tekom, which was a *visita* of Sisal in 1582. The principals are Diego Huchhim, Juan Kuk, Juan Canul, and Pedro Huchhim, whose agricultural lands had extended to the abandoned town of Kochil. The stated purpose of the document is to inform the authorities *(justicias)* of this fact. Affirming their right over the land in question, it says *ton cantul on ili lic hedziic labcah ko[c]hila* 'it was we four who fixed (settled, stabilized) [it at] the rotted town Kochil'. The verb here is once again *hedz*, the same one used to describe the settling of Christianity upon the land and the fixing of the borders around Maní. It implies the placing of boundary signs and the claim of rights over the place settled, although it does not imply residence as does the English 'settle'. The Maya phrase cited above is grammatically ambiguous: either the object of *hedz* is the agricultural field, and the phrase 'rotted town Kochil' specifies its location, or the object of *hedz* is the rotted town itself. The former reading is the one Roys conveyed in his translation of the document, but there is no overt reference to the field in the Maya phrase, and the second reading is actually closer to the Maya text.

As we know from other sources, a "rotted town" is one that was formerly vital and occupied but had since been abandoned and left to crumble. It does not imply that the place no longer existed. Like the Post-Classic archaeological site known today as *Labnah* 'rotted house', the rotted place persists as a site of memory, and the April 21, 1561, document shows that the *labcah* can be reused, for instance, as an agricultural field.[21] The term was used to describe towns from which people were forcibly moved during the upheavals of *reducción* (see chapter 2), suggesting that the place known as Kochil was one such town. What is most significant about this document for our purposes is that it shows that the towns evacuated in the course of creating *pueblos reducidos* in fact continued to exist as places of memory in the colonial present. At least in this document, the rotted town remained sufficiently available in local memory that it could be used simply as a term of reference without any need to further specify its location. Moreover, the rotted place was a site of continued activity, whether for agriculture, hunting, or ritual; it was not really abandoned at all.

The spatial conversion imposed by *reducción* was not, therefore, a transformation in which the landscape of the past vanished. It was a layering of perspectives in which the places of the past continued to exist and be acted both in and upon but from an altered vantage point. As a consequence, places came to have multiple names over the colonial period, depending upon the perspective one adopted on them. This is a fact very widely attested in modern Maya speech practices; most towns and places of significance have multiple names and continue to be referred to with terms whose semantic values describe a landscape no longer visible but readily accessible in collective memory. Just as semantic ambiguities proliferated in *Maya reducido,* with its dual horizon of indigenous and missionary frameworks, so too the landscape would become pervasively ambiguous, with multiple temporal horizons.

On August 25, 1600, another document was produced that continues in the same vein (Roys 1939, 72). This one was signed *ti audiensia way ti yotoch mascab* 'in the audiencia here in the jailhouse' of Tekom of San Pedro and San Pablo. Once again we find the doubling of the reference to the official *cabildo* building in both Spanish and Maya. The date is stated in a bilingual phrase, *uac kal u kinil Agosto ti u habil mil setesientos años* 'twenty-five the day of August in the year of seventeen hundred years'.[22] The text mentions three *gobernadores* by name but alludes to a larger group: *Don Juan Dzul Gouernador Tikom—Don Pablo cupul Gouernador tixcacal—Don Fau[ian] cupul Gouernador cuncunul y Alcalde y cauildoob y Regidores.* It immediately states the purpose for which it was written:

ca dzibtic u hol c luumob xotan toon	We write the entrance(s) to our lands (which were) cut from us
tumen ca yum kul uinic tomas Lopez oydor	by our lord (the) Spaniard Tomás López *oydor*
cat uli uay tikome dzibte cah lae	when he arrived here in Tikom to write the towns.
lay u xocol u tzolan u lab cahile	This is the count of the ordering of the rotted towns.

I have translated *kul uinic* as 'Spaniard', because it was used this way, just as *kul nah* was used to gloss 'audiencia'. Still, a more careful gloss would note that this expression also means 'person of God', using the Maya *ku* for 'God', as Coronel did in his *doctrina,* composed around the same time. Similarly, *ku nah* was also used for 'church', indicating that both expressions were ambiguous between reference to secular positions and reference to ones defined by the Church. What follows is a list of several scores of 'rotted towns', presented as a table, without further commentary. Five days later, on August 30, 1600, another list of 'rotted towns' is presented along with the names of their former leaders (Roys 1939, 76–81). The veracity of the list is attested by witnesses and a scribe, and the text then refers to *noh halach uinic Dr. quixada y Don Luis de sespedes* 'Great Halach Uinic Dr. Quijada and Don Luis Cespedes'. Here we see the title *halach uinic* applied not to a Maya lord, as in the case of Maní, but to the Spanish *alcalde mayor* Quijada.[23] This shift is likely due to the fact that the Tekom document was produced four decades after the Maní document examined above. At the end of this document is a Spanish translation, signed in the town of Yaxcabá by Gaspar Antonio (Xiu), *Ynterprete General por el Rey Nues[tro] Señor,* the well-known former student of fray Diego de Landa.[24]

Roys (1939, 424) also reproduces an undated document in Spanish, found among the Sotuta papers, titled *Traduccion de la papeles de los publos* [sic] 'Translation of the papers of the towns'. It lists the names of forty-two *indios principales* who accompanied Nachi Cocom when he processed the borders of Sotuta in 1545, placing *mojoneras* 'mounds'. Many of those named have Maya first names, as befits the early date at which the event is said to have taken place. The translation is then signed in Yaxcabá by the *gobernador,* don Diego Tuyu, along with one *alcalde,* four *regidores,* four names without title, and the *escribano,* Andrés Maz. All these signatories have Spanish first names, which is consistent with the hypothesis that *cabildo* members, certainly as late as 1600, were baptized and oriented at least partly to the mandates of the colonial Church and government of which they were local members. The text reports that during the Nachi Cocom event, crosses were placed at water sources, an intriguing correlation between the Christian symbol of resurrection and what was surely the most significant natural resource in the dry, porous land of Yucatán.

On September 6, 1600, two *conciertos* 'agreements' were signed in Yaxcabá, in response to the order *(mandamiento)* of Señor Gobernador, evidently the provincial governor. The two texts contain much the same information, with slightly overlapping signatories, according to the now-familiar pattern of contemporaneous serial production (Roys 1939, 428–30). The first reads as follows (I have omitted parts not pertinent to the present discussion and underscored expressions of special interest):

> *Tucahal Yaxcaba ti San Francisco ti nohcah ten cen D. Alonso May. Gobernador kaua y D. Pedro Noh Gobernador tu cahal Ebtun D. Juan Chi Batab y Alcaldesob y Regidoresob; lic c = kamic u mandamiento Señor Gobernador* <u>uay ti yokol mascab yokol u mesa cheil autencia tu kulna Noh ahau Rey ah tepale lic ca dzaic tac c pol than lae</u> *tu tanil D. Juan Cocom Batab tal tu cahal Zututae tutanobix testigosob* <u>dziban u kabaob te cabal lae. . . .</u> *himac* <u>bin ilic uoh mal ca xot danel</u> *tac batanba* <u>coon u chun dan lae.</u> *Haili lae hele lae ti* <u>miercoles tu uacppel u kinil u Septiembre ti haabte mil seiscientos años</u>

> In the town of Yaxcabá of San Francisco, great town, I who am don Alonso May, gobernador of Kaua, with don Pedro Noh, gobernador of the town of Ebtún, and don Juan Chi, *batab,* and the alcaldes and regidores; We receive hereby the decree of the Señor Gobernador <u>here in the municipal building (lit. 'over the jail'), atop the wooden table of the *audiencia* chamber at the municipal building of our great ruler King majesty. Herewith we place it over our heads</u> in front of don Juan Cocom, *batab* from the town of Sotuta, and in front of the witnesses <u>whose names are written below. . . .</u> Let it be known by anyone who in time to come <u>shall see the characters of our resolution</u> with one another, <u>we who are the principal men.</u> That is all. Today, <u>Wednesday on the sixth day of the month of September in the year 1600 years.</u>

The first underscored expression refers to the official meeting place of the *cabildo,* using an elaborate bilingual expression in which the place of signing is specified down to the table on which they wrote. The term *mascab* actually means metal and was used both for 'machete' (not relevant here) and 'jail', whose bars were made of steel. There is a referential equivalence between *yokol mascab, audiencia,* and *kul nah.* In the official quarters of the municipalities, the jail was in the same building as the *cabildo* meeting place, which is the evident motivation for this equivalence.[25] Once again we find the standard bilingual epithet for the king, with the Spanish nested between the two-part Maya *noh ahau . . . ah tepal.* What follows describes the bodily gesture associated with subjection to a document, the placing of the document on top of the head. Rather than refer to the *firmas* 'signatures', as is standard, this text uses the spatial layout of the page, top to bottom, to locate the signatures 'below' the text itself. The next underscored expression, *uohmal ca xot danel* 'the characters of our resolution', is especially notable. As I pointed out in chapter 6, *uoh* was a term for writing that was associated with hieroglyphic characters and is relatively rare in the notarial corpus. Furthermore, *xot than* is a weighty expression reminiscent of *xot kin*, the final judgment of God over men and, as we saw above, the taking away of lands (*xot luum*) under the ordinances of López Medel. The ordinary sense of *xot* is 'to cut', and *xot than* is 'cutting speech'. Finally, the date once again shows the bilingual formula in which the day count is spelled out in words, in Maya, and the term "year" is rendered in both languages.

I have described this series of texts in some detail because, though they have been available for nearly seventy years in published form, they have not been closely analyzed from a linguistic perspective, to my knowledge. Roys (1939) was clearly more preoccupied with the identities of the principals and the locations of the places, what we might call a standard social history, than with the conversion of Maya under *reducción*. Yet they provide a wealth of evidence as to the fine structure of that conversion and the persistence within colonial Maya of modes of expression whose roots lay outside the *reducción*. We see in these texts the incipient standardization of epithets for the Crown, of ways to refer to the official quarters of the *cabildo*, and of ways to combine Maya and Spanish reminiscent of the bilingual dictionaries. We see evidence of the dynamic layering of the spatial grid of the missions with that of the *pueblos reducidos* and that of the 'rotted towns' whose inhabitants were displaced under *reducción*.

It is crucial to see that all these different landscapes were simultaneously available to the Maya who lived through, and thereby participated in, the *reducción*. No one of them was consistently superordinate to the others, regardless of the aims of the colonizers, and any one of the three could emerge as figural in an act of discourse, depending on its context and purpose. The spaces of partial autonomy that resulted from internalizing the frontier within the colony are "located" in the interstices between such alternate landscapes. Moreover, they were organized differently: the missions were radial but lacked a perimeter; the towns were perimetric, but their borders were thresholds defined as spaces of interaction, not sheer divisions; the rotted towns were sites of memory very much alive in the present. The kinds of ambiguity and interaction we see among the three can be discerned only in the minute details of the language as used by *indios reducidos*. They tend to evaporate when glossed into Spanish or English.

BILLS OF SALE

The bill of sale brings us back to the cyclic style of *tzol* surveys but in a much-reduced form and a century and a half or more after the early chronicles. As Restall (1997) argued, the eighteenth century in Yucatán was a time in which many lands owned by Maya people were sold to an expanding population of Spaniards ("conquest by purchase"). To sell a parcel of land it was necessary to describe it, however briefly. The language used for this was a minor variety of *tzol* 'counting'. The lands in question had been the property of individuals or towns, but in none of the cases I have seen was the transaction realized through anything approaching the scale or complexity of the sixteenth-century surveys. Like other notarial documents, the bills of sale are carefully dated and include specification of the price, the individuals involved, and the place at which the transaction was conducted. The principals in such transactions are typically described as *ah otochnal* 'residents' of the towns from which they came and, where appropriate, *al mehen* 'nobles'. Often, but not always, the text stipulates that the transaction was conducted *tutan* 'in front of' the *cabildo* officials. My first example comes from the town of Noló, a neighbor of Yaxkukul, dated September 12, 1641 (document XI.1814.010). In the following extract, the line numbers refer to the lines of the original handwritten document in the Carrillo y Ancona collection (henceforth CCA). Key phrases are underscored.

1.	*Ten cen Diego Ake yettel aparicio*	I who am Diego Ake with Aparicio
2.	*Ake yettel Phelipe Ake yettel Ake*	Ake with Felipe Ake with Ake
3.	*yettel Am brocio Ake <u>ah otoch nalon uay</u>*	with Ambrocio Ake <u>we are residents here</u>
4.	*<u>tu cahal Nolo</u> tu mektancahil*	<u>in the town of Noló</u> in the jurisdiction of
5.	*ahbolon pixan san (christobal)*	Nine Spirits San (Christobal)[26]
6.	*<u>digo Bartholome</u>, licix ca dzaic u ha*	<u>I mean Bartholome</u>, whereby we give our true
7.	*hil ca than <u>tutanca Batab yettel</u>*	word <u>in front of our Batab and</u>
8.	*<u>Justiciasob yettel Rexidoresob</u> tun*	<u>Justicias and Regidores</u>
9.	*<u>ten cen Escrivano</u> bicil in conah ca*	<u>I who am Scribe</u> as I sold two
10.	*pet ulumil in col ti ca yum ti señor*	parcels of the land of my field to our lord Señor
11.	*Capitan Don Lucas de Villamil hex*	Captain don Lucas de Villamil.
12.	*kax lae <u>ti yan tu xaman chen</u>*	This forest <u>it is to the north of a well</u>
13.	*<u>na chi u kaba</u> oxpel çici na yum u chij*	<u>Named Nachi</u> it has three corners on its border
14.	*tu chiKin chen pachi <u>likintan</u>*	to the west (of) Pachi well. <u>Eastward</u>
15.	*<u>binbal</u> tuchun yaxnic yan u pic*	<u>it runs</u> to the foot (of a) boxwood tree (where) there is the *pic*
16.	*tunil u titze tan chaltun yan u*	*tun* marking the corner. In front of (the) water tank, the
17.	*thiz <u>xaman tan binbal</u> u chun cha*	series (of markers) runs <u>northward</u> (to the) foot (of a) *cha*

18.	*kan yan u puctunil u thíze tu*	*kan,* there is the marker of the series. At
19.	*chun chulul yan u píctunil*	the foot of (a) sweetsop tree there is the marker.
20.	<u>*chikin tan binbal* la tulah tu chikin</u>	<u>Westward it runs</u> until (it reaches) west
21.	*u chun mul kub niquí thíz <u>nohor</u>*	of the foot of the mound, the series arrives (?). <u>South</u>
22.	<u>*tan binbal* la tu lah tu chi kin</u>	<u>ward it runs</u> until (it reaches) west of
23.	*u hol chhen nachi . . .*	the opening of Nachi well

After establishing that the principals are from the town of Noló, the text mentions the dependency relation to the town referred to as *Ah Bolon Pixan San Bartholome.*[27] Although there is little trace of orality in the linguistic style of the text, the correction inserted by the scribe, from Christobal to Bartholome (line 6), is noteworthy for its oral quality, also echoed in the immediately following reference to 'our true word'. In what follows, cardinal direction terms are used in two ways: to indicate the direction in which the boundary line proceeds and to indicate its relation to salient landmarks. With respect to the former, the description proceeds counterclockwise ENWS, which is common in both land documents (cf. YD1; Restall 1997, 191) and modern Maya ritual practice (Hanks 1984, 1990). In this usage, the morpheme *tan* 'front' is suffixed to the direction term, indicating '-ward'. These phrases mark the onset of the repeating cycles that index *tzol* style. When used relative to landmarks, the direction terms lack this suffix and convey that the border is close to the landmark, on the side indicated. In the thirteen lines that follow the extract here, there are four more cycles, each initiated by a direction term in the phrase *x-tan binbal* 'x-ward it runs, goes' plus the term *latulah* 'until', which indicates the endpoint of the interval in question, as in *noholtan binbal latulah* 'Southward it runs until'. The cardinal organization of these four cycles is the inverse of the first four, starting in the south, that is, SWNE. The term *thiz* 'line, series' at lines 17, 18, and 21 refers to the line formed by the sequence of *pictun* markers, which is the border line proper. The document ends with the attestation that the signatures (*ca firma caba* 'our signature(s) below') are true and accompanied by the signatures of the *cabildo* officers. The date and price of the land are given just before the signatures.

The final example that I want to examine is from Chulul, dated October 29, 1713, also in the Carrillo y Ancona Collection (CCA, IX.1815.012). I have transliterated this one in its entirety because it displays several features beyond those of the preceding examples. Note first that the underscored portions show the same features as the Noló bill: the vendor is *otochnal* 'resident' of the town of Chulul, elaborately named as "Our Lord Nine Spirits Holy San Pedro here in the town of

Chulul"; the purchaser is an *al mehen* 'noble'; the border has four corners (this time numbered); the price is specified; directional terms are used to locate markers (*pictun* and *sicina* 'corners') relative to landmarks, including trees and lands belonging to others, and in collocation with *tan* '-ward' to indicate the onset of four cycles in the *tzol* style.[28] The cycles proceed counterclockwise starting in the westward direction (WSEN). Unlike the Noló text, this one does not use the term *latulah* 'until' but rather *kuchuc* 'having arrived (at)' and *cinchucic* 'I reach'.

Chulul hele en 29 de Octubre 1713 años

Then cen Bartolome huchin ah otochnalen uay tumektan cahil cayumilan ah bolon pixan cilich yum San pedro uay ti cah chulul lae licix yn conic hun pet ulumil y kax ti al mehen Andres Chable yoklal canpel pesos catac hoppel tumin heix lay kax lae ti yan tuchikin xtab heix uyax chun sicinail lae ti culan tu lakin u chun bec chikintan binebal utzolic ppictunil enla tan kan cab u cappel u sicinail heix ti xamane fran.co pech heix ti chikine u kax Andres pech nohol tan binebal u tzolic ppictunil kuchuc tuyoxppel u sicinail u kax Juan mex ti yan hunppel Ac tuni ti sutpahan lakintan binebal u tzolic ppictunil cin chucic ucanppel u sicinail tan kancab heix ti lakine u kax mateo puch lic sutpahal xamantan y mateo puch binebal utzolic ppictunil cin chuciic u dzoc he tux hopp intzolic same heix lay takin lae uchic yn manic cappel missa yokol upixan yn mam gaspar chable. Hele en 29 de octubre de 1713 años - - - - - - -

Lay uhahil u conosimientoil kax cin kubbic tutanil Al mehenob Batab y Just. Y Regidorresob y Escriuano

Con Jesph catzim Gov.or
Domingo Sulu Ess.no
Andres Cocom Alcalde
Ygnasio puch
Felipe chable Regidor
Augustin canche

Chulul, today on the 29th of October 1713

I who am Bartolome Huchin, resident here in the jurisdiction of Our Lord Nine Spirit Holy Lord San Pedro here in the town of Chulul. I hereby sell one parcel of land and forest to noble Andres Chable for four pesos and five tumin. This forest is to the west of Xtab and its first corner is seated to the East of the foot of an oak tree. Westward runs the count of the *pictun* markers until the yellow soils. Its second corner is to the north of Francisco Pech and to the west is the forest of Andres Pech. Southward runs the count of the *pictun* markers (until) it arrives at the third corner (at) the forest of Juan Mex. There (lies) a cave. There it turns back. Eastward runs the count of the *pictun* markers (until) I reach the fourth corner upon yellow soils and to the east is the forest of Mateo Puch (where) it turns back. Northward with Mateo Puch runs the count of the *pictun* markers (until) I reach the end where I started to count earlier (today). And (with) this money, I have bought two masses for the soul of my grandfather Gaspar Chable. Today, on the 29th of October of 1713 years. - - - - - - -

This is the true <u>notice of forest</u> that I deliver before noble Batab and Justicias and Regidores and Scribe

We, Joseph catzim[,] Gouernador
Domingo Sulu[,] Scribe
Andres Cocom[,] Alcalde
Ygnasio puch
Felipe chable[,] Regidor
Augustin canche

This text also displays several subtle but important differences from the earlier Noló document. First, it describes itself as a *conocimientoil kax* 'knowing of the forest', that is, a land notification. Instead of being spoken in front of the *cabildo* officials, it is delivered *(kubic)* in front of them. Whether this represents a change in the practice or merely a shift in wording is unclear. Second, in the last cycle of the *tzol* count, the seller appears to be accompanied by a neighbor, Mateo Puch, which suggests a boundary procession, whereas the Nolo text makes no overt reference to neighboring landholders. Third, after the last cycle, the principal 'I' reaches "the place where I started to count earlier." This phrase further reinforces the impression that the text records an actual inspection of the border. The adverb *same* means 'earlier in the same day' and can be read as referring either to an earlier phase in a boundary procession done in the course of a day or to an earlier point in the text, whose oral reading would thereby be conceptualized as a temporal unfolding. Notice also that the final line of the main text gives the reason for which the land was sold: to pay for a Mass for the soul of the vendor's grandfather, Gaspar Chable. This is the only reference in either bill of sale to the religious background of life in the pueblo, except for the use of saints' names in place-names. Unlike so many of the other land documents, most notably the early chronicles and surveys, neither bill of sale mentions crosses on the landscape. The implication is that such transactions were sheerly local and secular and therefore free of the strategic imperative to display the piety of their participants.

This bill of sale has one more feature that fits into the pattern of discourse production I have traced throughout this book: it was recopied one hundred years later. In fact, the text in the Carrillo y Ancona collection is not the original but an official copy made one hundred years after the original sale. It ends with the following attestation:

> *Then cen Al.e Auxiliar y Regidorresob y escriuano uay ti Audiensia <u>t hochah</u> u conosimiento kax utial u habil a 29 de octubre de 1713 años lae hele en 29 de Dbre de 1813 años <u>tumenel dzoc ulabal lay hun uchben</u>*

D.n Alexandro Chi	*Alexandro Cime*	*Jose Martin cime*
AUXILIAR	*Lucas canche*	ESS.NO
	Juan Chi	
	Marcos Canche	
	REG.ORSOB	

I am who am Alcalde Auxiliar with (the) Regidores and scribe here in the Audiencia, we <u>copied</u> this forest notification belonging to the year 29th of October 1713 today, on the 29th of December 1813, <u>because the old paper had rotted</u>.

D.n Alexandro Chi	Alexandro Cime	Jose Martin cime
AUXILIARY	Lucas canche	SCRIBE
	Juan Chi	
	Marcos Canche	
	REGIDORES	

In chapter 5 I noted that the verb *hoch* was used in the missionary dictionaries to indicate a sign made with grass (*hoch xiu,* where *xiu* means 'grass'), presumably to mark a path to be followed in the woods. In this text and elsewhere in the notarial corpus, the verb is used to describe the practice of recopying or gathering together papers into a single copy in the manner of Spanish *trasunto* 'copy from an original'. What the two meanings share is that the object of *hoch* is a path on the landscape or a textual object *previously enacted,* of which the subsequent act is a true replication. Here the process is textual, whereas in the case of disturbed grass it is a traversing of the landscape. In both cases, the product of *hoch* is itself a sign to be subsequently acted upon; the path can be refollowed, and the text can be reread. The interweaving of these two domains, the landscape and the text, was pervasive in the colonial period. The expression *tzucentzuc,* which recurs throughout the early surveys in reference to each step along the border at which a group of councillors joined the principal, points in a similar direction: a *tzuc* is a gathering of strands, as in human hair tied into the tonsure typical of Maya iconography, or grasses tied together in a bundle. The same term refers to the gathering of councillors at the threshold of their town with a neighboring one. Like the *hoch xiu* markers that show a path, the movement of officials *tzucentzucil* is from marker to marker along the boundary of their sphere of governance. The land documents are at once written artifacts and the embodiment of spatial and political relations on the landscape. The two spheres of writing and occupying space are commingled. It is therefore appropriate that the last phrase in the 1813 copy of the 1713 text applies the same term 'rotten' as in *lab cah* 'rotten town' to the original text of which it is a copy. It says "the old papers had rotted" (*dzoc u labal).* But both rotted towns and rotted papers lived on.[29]

10

Petitions as Prayers in the Field of *Reducción*

Like the other notarial genres, collective letters and petitions are the products of *cabildo* members acting in their official capacities. Most show the full notarial apparatus: one or more scribes, a specified date and place of production, a 'we', 'in front of them', addressing a 'you'. Whereas the major land documents performatively *create* places through the actions of the principals, the petitions describe a *preexisting* grievance or condition, usually some suffering inflicted upon the principals by others. Excessive tribute, labor extraction, and *repartimiento* are common complaints, as are the misdeeds of named individuals.

Nevertheless, petitions are performative: they perform a request for intervention in order to rectify the grievous conditions. Unlike land documents, which mostly lack an addressee, the petitions bristle with second-person pronouns and epithets that project the addressee and call to him, 'you, you who are king', 'you who are lord, you who are king', 'you who are *oydor*', and so forth.

Petitions also display familiar patterns of iteration and dispersal but with some new twists. To my knowledge they were not recopied in the course of subsequent legal proceedings, the way the land surveys occasionally were. However, they *were* sometimes produced in multiple contemporaneous versions or 'copies', each token text having a distinctive set of signatories. As mentioned earlier, the February 1567 letters from Maya elites to the Crown appear in two versions, February 11 and February 12, with four and two copies each, for a total of six documents (Zimmermann 1970). Zimmermann (1970, 33) also published a Spanish version of the letter, although it is unclear whether each of the six texts was accompanied by its own Spanish gloss. A month later, on March 9, another, apparently unique letter revisited some of the same grievances, incorporating many new signatories as well as eleven individuals who had participated in one or another of the February petitions. A month later, yet another letter was sent by four nobles from the same region, in elegant Spanish, presenting an opposing account of the grievances. These letters are all part of a proximal series that unfolded over the span of two months. Thus we have what might be called a nested series: each of the two February texts functioned as a master text reproduced in a series of nearly *identical* copies, differing mainly by signatories. Taken together, the two master texts form a series of two, which are similar in overall content but not identical in phrasing. The March letter is much longer and more elaborate than the February ones but addresses many of the same issues. The April letter is the last in the sequence, as far as I know. It flatly contradicts the February letters, in addition to suggesting that they were fakes concocted by the missionaries. The two are effectively complementary views of the recent events, the one pro-Franciscan, the other fervently condemning Franciscans and their actions.

In contrast, land treaties and surveys appear in pairs or triplets of documents dated within days of one another—unless a land document is adduced in a subsequent legal dispute, as much as a century later. The land document's tie to place implies a limited set of elite signatories who represent the place or its immediate neighbors. By contrast, a grievance can be shared by an indefinitely large number of individuals. The result is that the petition iterates in greater numbers and over a relatively longer "contemporary" period than does the land document (a couple of months instead of a couple of days).

The embedding of Catholic religion in the letters is also more subtle than that in the land documents, which use crosses as place markers. Instead, the religious presence is emotional and metaphorical. The stance of the petitioners as supplicants subject to the addressee echoes the stance of the Christian subject before God. Moreover, the suffering and sadness of the aggrieved parties may be cast in terms that echo the passion of Christ or the suffering and sadness of the sinner, and it is mercy that is pleaded for. Finally, the cosigners of petitions are not simply neighbors who share a border. In at least some cases, what explains who cosigns with whom appears to be something as diffuse as common membership in a single *guardianía*. This is not as exotic as it may appear; towns that were *visitas* to a single *cabecera* would have interacted during feast days in the *cabecera*. Indeed, Cogolludo made clear that the *fiestas* held in central towns in honor of saints were the site of much political interaction among Indios. In the signatories of petitions, we can see hints that the radial relations of the *guardianía* functioned both as a missionary structure and as an indigenous political resource.

Table 19 summarizes the letters that are briefly discussed here. Given that the colonial corpus includes somewhere over two hundred fifty petitions, those adduced here can only illustrate some of their features: the salience of the addressee, the stance of the petitioner, and something of the verse style typical of the genre.

TABLE 19 Letters and Petitions Compared in This Chapter

Letters of the Caciques, February 11, 1567, Mérida (AGI, Mexico 367; in Zimmermann 1970, 31–32)
Letters of the Caciques, February 12, 1567, Mérida (AGI, Mexico 367; in Zimmermann 1970, 31–32)
Letter of the Batabs, March 9, 1567, Mérida (AGI Mexico 367)
Letter of the *governadores*, April 12, 1567 (Archivo Historico Nacional, Madrid, caja III; in
Zimmermann 1970, 36–37)
Petition, July 20, 1605, Dzaptún (reproduced in Restall 1997)
Petition, November 16, 1669, Numkiní (AGI Escribanía 317B Residencia Aldana, Pieza 9, fol. 11)
Petition, November 30, 1669, Xecelchakán (AGI Escribanía 317B Residencia Aldana, Pieza 9, fol. 21)

LETTERS OF THE CACIQUES TO THE CROWN, FEBRUARY 1567

The letters dated February 11 and 12, 1567, are among the best known of all petitions, thanks to the work of Zimmermann (1970) and a considerable number of historians who have studied the period closely.[1] Version 1 (Zimmermann 1970) of the February 11, 1567, petition begins as follows.[2]

1.	*Yoklal achinamob tulacal*	For all your subjects
2.	*- cech ah tepal e -*	- You (who are) Majesty -
3.	*natah cacah ti yul olalil*	we understand willingly
4.	*hibici unah tulacal*	how much it is all necessary
5.	*uchebal ca lukulob e*	in order that they succeed
6.	*lai tah oklal*	For that reason
7.	*- cech ah tepal e -*	- You (who are) Majesty -
8.	*bailcun atumtic*	would that you provide
9.	*ychil avahaulilob*	within your kingdoms
10.	*yah bebeçahulob,*	the ministers
11.	*ca utzac utichkakticob*	in order that they might illuminate
12.	*yetel uçaçcunicob*	and enlighten
13.	*yetel ucambeçicob*	and teach
14.	*himac mabal yohmahob e*	whosoever knows naught
15.	*[...]*	[...]
16.	*okot ba cacah tech*	we are crying out to you
17.	*- cech ah tepal e -*	- You (who are) Majesty
18.	*ca auoceç aich tac pixan*	that you take mercy on our souls

Note that the epithets of royal address in lines 2, 7, and 17 are all the same: *cech ah tepal e* 'You (who are) Majesty'. In the course of the first sixteen orthographic lines of this letter, there are nine instances of this address form, and no others. Similarly, centered at the top of the sheet on which the letter is written, the royal addressee is stated: *Sacra Cathólica Real Majestad* (version 1 and Spanish version), *Cicithanbil cilich noh ah tepal* 'hallowed holy great majesty' (version 2). The absence of *ahau* in these epithets is noteworthy and consistent with the religious focus of the letters. It is the merciful and Catholic qualities of the Crown that are appealed to, just as the merciful Lord *Dios ah tepal* is appealed to in confession.

Although the signatories below this text appear with titles, there are no titles mentioned in the body of the text itself.[3] Instead, the principals describe themselves as *achinamob* 'your subjects' at the outset (line 1) and in the last line of the letter. This term is intriguingly ambiguous (see Barrera Vásquez et al. 1980, 101; Motul folio 144r). One sense was *pueblo* 'town', equivalent to the Maya term *cah* 'town'. Under this reading, the authors present themselves as the embodiment of the towns at whose head they stand as chiefs, a reading consistent with Farriss's (1984) thesis that the local elites were the "fixed center" of Maya towns. A second sense of the term was *señor de vasallos, encomendero,* which presents the principals as elites who had their own vassals. A third alternative derives *chinan* from the Maya root *-chin* meaning 'bent over, inclined', a corporeal position expressing humility or shame. This is evidently the one that the translator of the letter took to be the most appropriate choice. In the Spanish version, the three instances of the *chinan* epithet are translated as *los vasallos de Vuestra Majestad* (line 1) and *humildes vasallos de Vuestra Majestad* (line 17; Zimmermann 1970, 33). This interpretation is further reinforced by the self-presentation of the authors as miserable, suffering, and poverty stricken and also by the other epithet applying to them, *avah tanlahulob* 'your servants'. That the translator of the letter glossed the epithet as 'humble servant' rather than 'town' or 'chief with vassals' fits with the rhetorical thrust of the letter, but it is likely that the other readings were available to any Maya speakers involved in the making of the letters.

Having presented themselves as subjects and having addressed the Crown as "majesty," the authors make their request straightaway. In the Spanish version the text reads, *provee siempre V.M. en sus reinos de ministros suficientes para que alumbren y enseñen a los que no saben* 'provide Your Majesty within your kingdom enough ministers to enlighten and teach those who do not know' (Zimmermann 1970, 33, line 2). The corresponding lines above are 6–13, which appear roughly equivalent in terms of what they request. Yet there is a major distinction in form, because the Maya breaks into verse parallelism, whereas the Spanish merely states the request. In the Maya, lines 9–14 rhyme: *-ilob, -ulob, -ticob, -unicob, -eçiscob, -ohmahob (e)*. In terms of grammatical well-formedness, the *-ob* plural morpheme is optional and could be omitted without change in reference. It is highly marked to use six tokens in a row, all in final position in lines of six to eight syllables each. The three verbs in the 'in order that' sentence (lines 11–13) describe the pedagogy of the missionaries in distinctively Catholic (and Franciscan) terms—to illuminate and teach—yet the grammatical parallelism "Mayanizes" it in highly transparent derived transitive verbs. This is consistent with Maya verse patterns elsewhere (Bricker 1974; Edmonson 1973, 1982, 1986;

Edmonson and Bricker 1985; Gossen 1985; Hanks 1986, 1987, 1988; Norman 1980; Tedlock 1983), and we will see additional examples in this and the next chapter. It is also consistent with the transparency principle at work in the bilingual dictionaries and doctrinal language.

Among the standard Maya translations of 'petition' is *okotba (than)*, as in line 16. This is derived from *okol* 'to cry' plus the reflexive *(okot ba)*, and sometimes accompanied by *than* 'speech' (all of these forms are explained in chapter 6). To make a petition is 'to cry yourself (in speech)'. The same expression is used in the *doctrina* to describe the act of asking for forgiveness in confession and the more general plea for mercy in prayer. Recall here the confessional prayer as translated by both Coronel and Beltrán (chapter 8, examples 10, 11): stating his profound contrition, the confessee says, *okotbaix in cah tac cilich colel [. . .] cayoktubabob* 'I am beseeching our holy lady (and all the saints) that they beseech God on my behalf'. This expression, the root act of begging for intercession from God or Crown, can be reasonably called a "performative" in the Austinian sense, that is, an expression that, when uttered under the proper circumstances, accomplishes an act.[4] The underlying link between petitions and prayer goes deeper still: the use of the epithet *ah tepal* for the Crown echoes the same epithet applied to God in the confessional context. In both settings, it is *tzayatzil* 'mercy' and protection (from sin or from suffering) that is requested. As if to avoid any confusion as to the doctrinal parallel, what the authors of the petition request is that the Crown 'cause your gaze to enter our souls', glossed in the Spanish as *V.M. se compadezca de nuestras ánimas* 'Your Majesty take pity on our souls' (Zimmermann 1970, 33, line 10). This turning of the clement gaze upon the soul is an unambiguous reference to the religious sense of 'soul'. In sum, these minor details of form in the Maya are actually indices of a deep-seated continuity between petitions and the moral and affective stance of prayer. Despite their different etiologies, the actions of making a petition and saying a prayer are done by the same kind of human subject, invoking the same kind of divine mercy.

When we look at the signatories to the February letters, the missionary basis of *reducción* again breaks through in an unexpected way. Every one of the sixty-three signatures shows a Christian first name with a Maya surname, suggesting that the individuals had been baptized. In all four copies of version 1, each signature is accompanied by the name of the town from which the individual comes, with most showing titles as well. In version 2, no place-names are shown, and there are no titles other than a few tokens of *don*. When we plot the signatories for whom places are known, a surprising pattern emerges: they are almost entirely organized according to *guardianías*. In maps 14 and 15, the towns of the cosignatories of four letters are shown, marked by circle, triangle, and square icons. Towns sharing the same icon are those from which cosignatories to a single document came. Given the timing and content of these petitions, it is almost

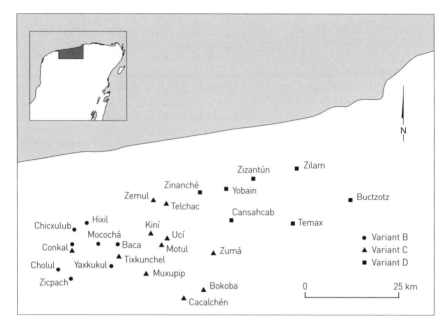

MAP 14. Towns from which cosignatories to February 1567 letters came, according to which text they signed (© William F. Hanks 2007)

certain that they were produced in collusion with Franciscan friars: they lavish praise on the friars in distinctly Franciscan terms, right at the point at which the provincial fray Diego de Landa was under investigation in Spain for his persecution of so-called idolaters. The striking fact is that the groups of cosignatories to the individual documents correspond almost exactly to the *cabecera* and *visitas* of *guardianías*. Hence, Variant B on map 14 represents the *guardianía* of Conkal with the addition of Yaxkukul (*visita* of Tixkokob). Variant C in the same map is from the *guardianía* of Motul, with the addition of Conkal (*cabecera*) and Cacalchén. Variant D represents the *guardianía* of Zizantún, and map 15 shows the signatories to Variant A, all of whom were from the *guardianía* of Calkiní, to the south.

This pattern tells us something important about the *guardianía*. The *guardianías* described in the Church documents (chapter 2) dated from at least seventeen years later (i.e., 1582 or thereafter), yet the structures they describe were already functioning in the mid-1560s. To my knowledge, there is no way to determine whether this pattern of interpueblo relations was already a fact of post-Mayapán political geography or whether it was a product of the *reducción*. What is clear is that under *reducción*, the *guardianía* unit was available as a

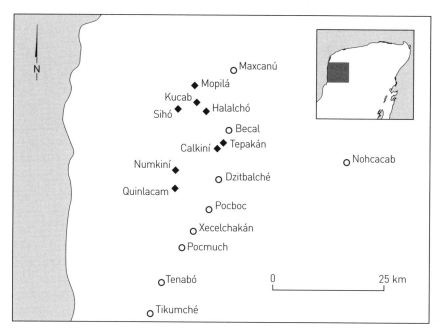

MAP 15. Diamonds indicate towns from which cosignatories to Variant A of February 1567 letters came (© William F. Hanks 2007)

vehicle for collective action. As I pointed out above, the towns belonging to a single *guardianía* were not always adjacent, as were the towns that coparticipated in land surveys. One can immediately see the utility of being able to mobilize people beyond the adjacency group.

LETTER OF THE *BATABS* TO THE CROWN, MARCH 9, 1567

The apparently self-humbling rhetoric of the February letters and the insistently emotive aura of their plea contrast sharply with another letter sent to the king just one month later, bearing the names of some of the same individuals. Unlike the February petitions, this letter starts off with an affirmation that the authors have gathered together in a multitude. They initially present themselves as simple, humble people and address the king with the richly honorific epithet 'Great Ruler Majesty'. The three instances of address forms (lines 2.1–2.2, 3.1, 5.4) show none of the regularity of the address forms in the earlier petitions, just as there is no evidence of significant verse parallelism. The executive aspect of the Crown is foregrounded in the epithet *ahau* 'king', and the rhetoric is more direct. The complete letter consists of 137 orthographic lines, making it impossible to discuss the entire text here, but we can see even in this short opening passage that the authors engage in a subtly different rhetoric from that of the shorter February letter. Rather than insist on the *tepal* quality of the king, they consistently foreground the duality of his status as *ahau* and *tepal*. By the same token, they present themselves as humble, suffering subjects subordinated to the king and seeking to better serve him *and at the same time* as holders of specific offices in their own land. They assert their connection with their land and their towns and their rightful claims to local legitimacy. What we see here is a rhetorical focus on the king as a ruler capable of making policy and securing its uptake and on the local elites as rightful officeholders wishing to advise their superior. What follows are a number of direct suggestions to the king that he undertake certain policies relative to Yucatán. These suggestions are accompanied by long narrative accounts of local affairs, justification for the advice offered, and reaffirmations of the legitimate status of the authors. In general, the letter evinces an acute awareness of regional politics under reducción. These are the seven opening lines of the letter:[5]

1.1	*Yoklal tumulchhabilon*	For we who are gathered,
1.2	*con chambel uinic*	we common men,
1.3	*canaate*	we understand
1.4	*cayumil ti dios*	our Lord in God
2.1	*yetel tech cech*	and you who are
2.2	*noh ahau ahtepale*	Great King and Majesty.
2.3	*yanix ti col ca dzoc lukes*	We want you to do
2.4	*lauac bal kananil*	something necessary,
3.1	*tech xan*	(for) you indeed.
3.2	*Yoklal hach thonanon taclacal*	For we are all truly humbled
3.3	*yalan auoc*	beneath your foot
3.4	*yalan akab*	beneath your hand
3.5	*hibahunon*	however many we be,
4.1	*con batabob*	we who are chiefs
4.2	*yetel canuc teylob*	and our elders
4.3	*yan uay provinçia yucatan lae*	here in the Province of Yucatán.
5.1	*yoklal uay caluumile*	For here in our land,
5.2	*ah otochnalonixan.*	we are natives indeed.
5.3	*coltic capat cante taxicin*	We want to recount something to your ear,
5.4	*cech ahaue*	you king,
6.1	*uchebalix a chhaic unucul xan*	so that you might take up its response.
6.2	*he tun cathan lae*	Here then we speak:
6.3	*hach kanan uuilal*	Truly there is need
7.1	*uay ti provinçia yucatan*	here in the Province of Yucatán
7.2	*Sant franco padresob toon*	of Franciscan fathers for us.

The principals present themselves as 'common men', 'chiefs', and 'our elders'. They are 'gathered together' (line 1.1), 'truly humbled beneath your foot, beneath your hand' (lines 3.2–3.4), and 'here in our land, natives indeed' (lines 5.1–5.2). At first blush, the minor couplet at lines 3.3–3.4 has the appearance of a Maya couplet, perhaps a *difrasismo* for rule: 'beneath your foot' indexes subordination and 'beneath your hand' perhaps indexes the executive capacity of the Crown. But an equally plausible explanation holds that the expression echoes Spanish usage of the time, particularly Franciscan use of the phrase 'we kiss your foot, we kiss your hand'. I consider this another case of double voicing in which *Maya reducido* is ambiguous between the Maya and the European frames of reference.

The performative expression used to present the letter also differs from the February ones, because there is no reference to *okotbah* 'weeping, supplication'. Rather, the principals 'want to recount something to your ear' (line 5.3). The verb *patcantic* is a well-known derivation from *pat* 'leave' + *can* 'recount' + *tic* the transitivizer. It has none of the affective overtones of *okotbah* but instead focuses on the giving of an account. The reference to the king's ear implies the directness of contact that the letter seeks to achieve, and the "response" encodes the authors' hope that he will follow its advice. At this point in the text, it is not even clear whether it should be read as a petition or some other kind of letter. It is only much later that the verb *okotbah* will be used and the familiar affective correlates will be in evidence.

The friars are needed in Yucatán to impart the Word of God to the natives, a statement of purpose consistent with the Spanish view of the spiritual conquest. I note in passing that the expression *kanan uuilal*, one of several ways to say that something is really needed, is the same expression used to describe man's need of God's love in the *doctrina* (see chapter 8). The letter carefully displays the authors' knowledge of the Spanish terms for the elements of evangelization: Christian doctrine (using the Greek-derived form of '*xpiana*'), the mass, and the gospel. This word choice indexes that the authors are willingly engaged in *reducción* and have been well instructed by the friars, but it also signals their awareness of the duality in the discursive field. A predominantly Maya description (lines 8.1, 10.1) is immediately followed by a relative clause ('which is called') with the Spanish gloss. This once again replicates the translingual practice of commensuration epitomized in the bilingual dictionaries. Along with the standard scribal abbreviation of the Franciscans in line 7.2, the use of both Spanish and Maya expressions displays just the knowledge that would be acquired by one trained by the missionaries.

8.1	*uchebal yalicob uthanil dios*	so they can tell us the word of God,
8.2	*heklay doctrina xpiana ukabae*	which is called the Christian Doctrine,
8.3	*uchebalix yalicob missa ca chante*	and so they can say Mass for us to watch,

9.1	*caix utzac utzecticonob*	and so they might preach to us
9.2	*tac uayil thane*	in our language of here,
10.1	*uthanil cahçiçahul*	the word of our fellow human,
10.2	*heklai Euangelio ukaba*	which is called the Gospel
10.3	*tumen Espanolesobe /*	by the Spaniards /

This passage succinctly proves that the Maya authors were aware of the difference between *frayles lenguas,* who could perform the linguistic tasks outlined in 8.1– 10.3, and missionaries who could not speak the language. Like the Franciscans, they prefer those who speak Maya. In what follows, they take up a full and explicitly pro-Franciscan stance on the events of the day. Toral comes in for criticism as the one who introduced secular clergy, who are themselves belittled as linguistically incompetent and corrupt—just the critiques the monastics made of the seculars, as described in Part I. He placed them in the towns as *canancahob* 'town guardians' and preachers, but, the letter continues:

14.4	*tamuk utzecticonob*	all the while they instruct us
15.1	*tumĕ yahtzolthanob*	through their interpreters
15.2	*yoklal mail yohelob*	for they do not know
15.3	*uayil than e*	the language of here

Here end rhyme and regular line length create a verse series in which the seculars are portrayed as incompetent and separated from the Maya by interpreters, a critique that recurs at lines 93–96 (not reproduced here). Throughout the attack on the secular clergy, a strong Franciscan voice is evident and almost surely indexes either that the friars colluded in the making of the document or, minimally, that their instructions provided the terms in which the secular clergy were evaluated. Although the petitioners are native nobles speaking their own language, it is the voice of their allies that they express, transposed from Spanish into Maya and submerged in the tropes of Maya rhetoric. The overall effect is to bind the Franciscans to the "here" of Yucatán and to distance the seculars by continuously excluding them from the participant node of 'us from here'.

This dual voicing comes through in the authors' self-descriptions as well, for they justify the call for more Franciscans on the grounds that without the guidance of the friars, they might fall back into the idolatrous ways of their forefathers. In the next example, they describe themselves from the Franciscan perspective, aligning their ritual practices with the 'Devil' and using the expected language of weeping for mercy (112.1–2), suffering, destitution, and oppression by the Devil. The subject protected here has just the right affective stance for a Christian who needs protection from the Devil. The use of *cuchi* 'in the past' in line 124 also marks the historical shift between oppression by the Devil in the past and proper contrition in the present (see plate 10).

112.1	*lai tah oklal licil camuloktic caba tech*	Therefore we all beseech you
112.2	*ca adzab cayatzil*	to take pity on us.
	[…]	[…]
114.3	*hach ah numyaon*	We're really suffering,
114.4	*mabal ubal caba /*	and destitute
	[…]	[…]
123.4	*yoklal hach bula noon*	For we were truly mired
124.1	*tu dzalpach ciçin cuchi*	beneath the oppression of the Devil in the past

The closing of the letter once again situates it in the nonreligious political structures to which it was addressed. The signatories are named with titles, as are their *defensores* (local officials of the government charged with defending the Indios' rights) and the governor. Truth and authenticity are again affirmed, and the authors display a keen awareness of the likely trajectory of their text. The text itself is described as a 'written paper', indicating its claim to legitimate status, and they pray that the governor will send it on to the Crown rather than keep it in the peninsula. Once again, the text displays knowledge of the administrative channels under *reducción*.

129.3	*hetun cathan lae*	Here we speak:
129.4	*coltic udzaab ufirmasob*	We want the signatures to be placed
130.1	*cah antulob*	of our helpers,
130.2	*laobi defensorob*	the Defensores,
130.3	*cau tzac auoheltic*	so that you might know
130.4	*hach talil ti col*	that this truly comes from our heart
131.1	*he ca okot batech lae,*	Here we beg you
131.2	*caix yeteh ti gouernador*	and to the Governor also,
131.3	*cautzac unatic*	that he might understand it,
132.1	*caix utzac uhach anticoon*	that he might truly help us,
132.2	*cautuchite cadzib hun tech*	that he might send our written paper to you

The last document in this early series is the April 12 repudiation by *Don francisco de Montejo Xiu, gouernador de la provinçia de Mani*, along with Juan Pacab, *gouernador* of Mona; Jorge Xiu, *gouernador* of Panabchhen; and Francisco Pacab, *gouernador* of Texul.[6] In the view of these authors, Landa and the other missionaries were brutalizing miscreants whose deeds would be remembered in infamy 'until the fourth generation'. Toward the end, this letter refers to the authors of the February (and perhaps March) letters as the *familiares* of the missionaries, suggesting that they were *indios de confianza*. Despite the remarkably sharp criticisms leveled in the letter, the authors make a show of being reasonable and appropriately honorific of the royal addressee. The letter contains detailed description of the events surrounding the inquisition into idolatry that started in

1562 and takes up a carefully defended position. The ending says *Humildes vasallos de V.M. que sus Reales manos y piez besamos* 'Humble vassals of Your Majesty who kiss your Royal hands and feet', a standard expression of subordination to the Crown found also in the February letters.

PETITION FROM DZAPTÚN, JULY 20, 1605

The 1567 letters are the earliest petitions I have seen, and they display a number of features that would be reproduced in subsequent tokens of the genre. The foregrounding of the powerful addressee, the careful positioning of the authors relative to the addressee, the emphasis on suffering, grievance, mercy, and intervention are core features that recur, much the way the *tzol* style recurs in land documents. Although it is rarely as pervasive as in the 1567 letters, the link to *doctrina* and religious practice is robust, motivated by the centrality of religious formation in the colonial project and the legitimating effect of displays of Christian propriety. Iteration, too, remains a feature of the genre, although not all texts were recopied. Among the noteworthy changes between the early petitions and the later ones is the virtual disappearance of the epithet *ah tepal* in royal address, a decline in the incidence of verse parallelism, a lessening of the Franciscan frame of reference, and a tendency for petitions to be signed by smaller, more local groups. The factors motivating these changes are diverse, from language change to policy change and the historical eclipse of the Franciscans as secular clergy acquired more and more control over the parishes of the province. One gets the sense that the series of works in 1567 and the genre as it then appeared were the product of a specific conjuncture: the Maya elites were still relatively powerful in the Indian republics; the *cabildo* was not yet fully established; the Franciscans were dominant among missionaries; the first wave of *reducción* was sweeping across the northwestern region of the peninsula; and the *guardianías* were already functioning, as evidenced by the selection of signatories.

In this section I briefly describe a petition dated July 20, 1605, from the town of Dzaptún in the *cuchcabal* of Campeche. As is typical of later petitions, this one speaks from a single town and is signed by members of the local *cabildo*, including two scribes. Since only one town is involved, there are no place-names with the signatures. Here are the opening lines:[7]

1.	*Uay ti cah San Juan batista dzaptun*	Here in the town of San Juan Batista Dzaptun.
2.	*heleac tuhunkal u kinil julio*	Today the twentieth of July
3.	*ti hab 1605 años*	in the year 1605 years,
4.	*licix ca lic u hahil ca than*	we speak our true word.
5.	*licil ca mançabal ti ya*	We are being subjected to suffering
6.	*tumen halach uinic mariscal*	by the *halach uinic* marshal.

7.	*yumile ahaue Reye*	Lord, king king,
8.	*okotba ca cah tech*	we are beseeching you
9.	*yoklal ca yumil ti dios*	by our lord in God.
10.	*udzben tah ca cah ta kab*	We are kissing your hand
11.	*yetel a uoc*	and your foot
12.	*ca aubi ca than*	that you might hear our speech.
13.	*licil ca ma[n]çabal ti ya*	We are being subjected to suffering

The local scope of the document is specified in line 1, where the joining of 'here', the Maya town name, and the patron saint locate the work precisely within a single *pueblo reducido*. The emphasis on truth telling and suffering is typical of all petitions, as I pointed out above, and the phrasing of the petition proper is by now familiar: 'we are beseeching you' (line 8). The reference to the hands and feet of the king is also familiar from the earlier petitions, as well as from many Spanish documents of the period. The act of kissing the hands and feet is a standard expression of subjection to the Crown, and the hope that the king would 'hear our speech' is parallel to the hope that he would turn his gaze upon the souls of the February 1567 authors.

The statement of suffering in lines 5 and 13 lacks the biblical connotation of *numyah* 'suffering', the term used for the passion of Christ and also used in the earlier petitions. After the opening lines, *numyah* and its derivatives replace the more anodyne 'being subjected to pain', as in *licix ca patcantic ca numya ta tan* 'we recount our suffering in front of you' (line 60). Similarly, although the opening lines make no reference to mercy, the term *dzayatzil* 'mercy' becomes the focus of the request and occurs three times over the course of the petition, as in

29.	*lay tah men licil coktic caba ta tan*	therefore we beseech before you
30.	*uchebal auanticon ta dzayatzil*	in order that you help us in your mercy

The religious overtones of this act of weeping for mercy are reinforced by multiple invocations of God, such as the following:

54.	*yoklal dios bin auutzcin ton ta dzayatzil*	By God will you improve us in your mercy.
55.	*yoklal ca yumil ti dios*	By our lord in God,
56.	*ca auanton*	may you help us

These features, in combination with the citing of the town patron saint, give clear evidence that the religious horizon of petitions remained strong. This is significant, because there is no evidence of missionary collusion in the Dzaptún letter, as there was in the earlier ones. The implication is that the religious overtones of the act of petition came to be part of the genre, even when the grievances were nonreligious. In the present case, the leaders of Dzaptún were aggrieved by poverty, excessive extraction of labor and goods, and the misdeeds of the *halach*

TABLE 20 Forms of Address and Self-Reference in the Dzaptún Petition

7	*yumile ahau Rey*	oh lord ruler king
9	*cayumil ti dios*	our lord in God
22	*cech ca yum cech Reye*	you who are our lord, you King
32	*cech ca noh ahau cech visoReye*	you who are our great ruler you viceroy
36	*cech ca yume*	you who are our lord
38	*con amehene*	we who are your children
47	*cech ca yume cech ahaue*	you who are our lord, you ruler
48	*cech ca yum cech oydore*	you who are our lord, you oydor
50	*coon amehene*	we who are your children
51	*tutan visoRey ahau*	before viceroy ruler
53	*con amehene*	we who are your children
54	*dios*	God
55	*cayumil ti dios*	our lord in God
58	*techal cech ca yume cech ahaue*	you, you who are lord, you ruler
59	*cech ca yume cech ahaue*	you who are our lord, you ruler
61	*con uayal uinic*	we people from here

uinic mariscal. They addressed their complaint to the Crown, the viceroy, and the *oydor,* in that order. This implies a sort of dispersal of the document through the upper administrative channels of the colony. The address forms, by line, are shown in table 20.

A glance at these forms reveals that they differ significantly from the six-teenth-century forms. *Ah tepal* is not used, and the Spanish *Rey (visoRey, oydor)* occurs in final position rather than nested between Maya forms (except line 51, where *ahau* is in final position). The form *Rey* is paired with *ahau* (7) and *ca yum* 'our lord' (22). *Ca noh ahau* 'our great ruler' is applied to the viceroy, whereas it is used only for the Crown in the 1567 letters. As the colonial system developed, the term *ahau* appears to have spread downward from the Crown to Crown repre-sentatives in New Spain.[8] The term *yum* is applied to all three positions as well as to God, a similar semantic generalization. By contrast, the self-description of the Dzaptún authors is very constrained. Of four self-references, three are identical—*con a mehene* 'we who are your children' (lines 38, 50, and 53)—and the last (61) links the 'we' to 'here'. The full statement of 61 reads, *con uayal uinic tu cuchcabal campech con provinciae* 'we people of here in the *cuchcabal* of Campeche, we who are (the) province'. The outright equation of the signatories with the province pushes the spatial basis of identity to its logical endpoint. At the same time, it is noteworthy that *cuchcabal* is still used for 'province', presumably long after the Post-Classic Maya unit *cuchcabal* ceased to be a functioning political unit.

The signatories to this document consist of one *procurador,* three *alcaldes,* three *regidores,* one scribe, and two individuals without title, likely witnesses.

Each of these is named by Christian first name and Maya surname. The absence of any *batab* and the presence of the *procurador* set this petition apart from more canonical *cabildo* productions.

The upshot of these remarks is that both the genre "petition" and the terms of address underwent subtle changes as the historical context to which they responded changed. Unlike earlier petitions, this one uses the Spanish term *pidiçion* to describe itself: *lay ca than yan tac pidiçione* 'this is our word which is in our petition' (line 52). Whereas the defining features of the genre were present in the 1560s, the metalinguistic category label was apparently integrated into *Maya reducido* only decades later.

The last two examples that I want to examine come from the long run of complaints lodged against Governor don Rodrigo Flores de Aldana in 1669. There are dozens of complaints in Maya, many with Spanish gloss and others evidently written directly in Spanish. This remarkable series of documents illustrates serial reproduction in one of its maximal forms. The petitions are not all identical, but the core complaint is the same, and there is massive overlap in phrasing, with distinct groups of signatories on each individual document. One hundred years after the February letters, and with no evident coaching from missionaries, these documents replicate the kind of iteration that defines the February letters but on a much grander scale. Flores de Aldana achieved infamy with his excessive extraction of wealth from Maya communities, and if the overlapping features of these petitions are indicative, he managed to provoke a coordinated counter-attack from Maya communities around the southeastern part of the province (including Sahcabchén; see chapter 3 for background). Just as the Dzaptún petition reveals knowledge of the colonial administration on the part of its authors, these texts are deeply engaged with the politics surrounding Flores de Aldana's actions. Although there is little religious content in the texts, the missionary horizon is clearly in evidence. More than one hundred years after the conquest, the *reducción* was still reversible, and a number of the complaints blame Flores de Aldana for flight from Christianity because of people's desperation to flee from oppressive taxation. As so often during the first centuries of the colony, the extraction of labor and wealth is cast as an impediment to proper conversion, a linkage the Franciscans were acutely aware of and wont to condemn.

PETITIONS FROM NUMKINÍ AND XECELCHAKÁN, NOVEMBER 1669

Among the petitions was one from the town of Numkiní signed by one *batab*, two *alcaldes*, four *regidores*, and one scribe, all from Numkiní. What follows are the opening and closing, omitting the long details of the grievances against Flores de Aldana and his administration.[9]

1.	*Toon Don fer.do kantun .y. alctsob*	We don Fernando Kantun and alcaldes
2.	*.y. Regidoresob .y. escribano*	and Regidores and scribe
3.	*ah otochnalon uay tucahal .S. Dio nūkini*	we are natives here in the town of San Diego Numkiní
4.	*corona Real*	of the Royal Crown
5.	*catzicanil yume*	Our revered lord,
6.	*lic cachacancunsí caba [ta]tan yetel ca petición*	we show ourselves before you with our petition.
7.	*hex toone uyabal numya [ca]mançah*	We are living much suffering
8.	*ychil ugouernadolil*	in the governorship
9.	*Señor cap˜ gl. Don [Ro]trigo flores de altana*	of Señor Capitan General don Rodrigo Flores de Aldana
	[…]	[…]
10.	*Maix yetel utzul than*	And not with good speech
11.	*licil uthanicon lay Juez lae.*	Does that judge address us.
12.	*Otzilon tatan ce[c]h yume*	We are poor in front of you, you who are lord
13.	*laybe tu bel tah toon cech yume*	that is what he has done to us, you who are lord
14.	*maix tuz lic ca lic hah ti dios*	and it is no lie that we speak the truth to God
15.	*hibal lic ca hahcunic*	which we testify
16.	*yoko[l] S.or Gou-or – ycapn – gl. Don Rodrigo frores deal tana*	about Señor Gouernador – and capitán – general don Rodrigo Flores de Aldana
17.	*mabal utz tubeltah toon*	nothing good has he done for us.
18.	*yaníx criſtianosob*	And there are Christians
19.	*tí o[c]si[c]ob uçatab*	who have begun to lose
20.	*u criſtianoilob tí Kax*	their Christianity in the Woods
21.	*tumenel utz[ ]balob*	because they (flee?)
22.	*tumenel u concibob*	because they sell (bees') wax
23.	*yetel patíob u chhuplilo[b]*	and they have left their women
24.	*manan yetpiçan numya tac mançah*	there is no end to the suffering we live
25.	*ychil u gou[ ]lil Señor Capn gl – Don Rodrigo frores dealtana [ ]*	during the governorship of Señor capitán general – don Rodrigo Flores de Aldana
26.	*lic cahahcuni coon ah belnal*	we testify, we who are leaders
27.	*helel tu uaxac lahunpíz u kinil*	Today, the sixteenth day
28.	*u – de nobiembre 1669 años*	month of November 1669 years
29.	*= ton*	= we
	[signatures]	

The first line in this petition shows the canonical pattern for collective notarial documents, introducing the plaintiffs with titles, with the highest ranking *(batab)* named first. In line 3 the town of residence is named, along with its patron saint and the Crown, under whose authority it was. Along with the *cabildo* titles, this formulation of place foregrounds that Numkiní is a *pueblo reducido*. The only address forms in the entire extract occur at lines 5, 12, and 13. The epithet *tzicanil* derives from *tzic* 'obey, respect' plus the stative adjective derivation *-anil* to yield 'obeyed, respected', and *yum* is the familiar 'lord'. The paucity and simplicity of address forms is likely motivated by the fact that the petition is addressed not to the Crown but to the provincial government. Moreover, this and the next example were both produced during an ongoing investigation of Flores de Aldana, so that there was no particular need to secure the attention of an addressee but only to be convincing.

Similarly, there is no reference in this text to weeping as an act of petition, or to *dzayatzil* 'mercy'. Rather, at line 6, the speech act is presented as *cachacancunsic caba* 'we cause ourselves to appear (before you)' by way of the petition. At lines 15 and 26 the force of the petition is formulated as *hahcunic* 'to cause to be true, to testify' (cf. dictionary entries in chapter 5 under 'testigo'). The cumulative effect of these phrases is to frame the text as an act of testimony embedded in a bureaucratic process. Accordingly, there is less verse parallelism and less stylistic flourish overall than in the early petitions.

The nature of the grievance and the suffering of the authors receive more elaborate treatment. The familiar term *numyah* 'suffering' (cf. passion of Christ) occurs at lines 7 and 24 (where it is said to be 'endless'), and the aggrieved are 'poor before you' (line 12). Language use is another point of contention, suggesting that the judge mentioned in lines 10 and 11 had violated normative expectations about how town officers should be addressed by higher officials. But the most striking issue comes at lines 18–23, where the authors allege that suffering and the malfeasance of the governor's administration were causing Maya people to flee their homes and lose their Christianity in the forest, that is, the *despoblado*. This astutely invokes a cluster of Spanish fears regarding flight and the absence of *policía* outside the sphere of *reducción* (see chapter 2). Given that the ones who fled are said to be Christian, that is, already converted (line 18), a return to the forest raises the specter of the reversal of *reducción*: not merely flight, but possibly apostasy. Coupled with the details on colonial officials and the political positioning accomplished in many petitions, this line of complaint demonstrates that the Maya *batabs* had a keen understanding of the project of *reducción* and used this knowledge strategically.

Immediately after the signatures this text is glossed into Spanish. The gloss nicely illustrates the degree to which Maya texts are transformed by Spanish versions. The opening lines are as follows:

Nosotros Don Ferdo Kan tun gouor y los alcaldes y Regidores Escno naturales del pueblo de san diego numkini de la Real Corona respectado S.r [unintelligible 3 words] *con esta petiz.on Y nosotros pasamos muchos trauaxos en el tp que gouerno el Sr gou.or Y cap.an gen. D. R.o flores deal tana que nos dio muchos rrepatm.to* . . .

We Don Fernando Kantun governor and the alcaldes, Regidores and Scribe native to the town of San Diego Numkiní of the Royal Crown. Respected Señor [unintelligible 3 words] with this petition. And we are living many travails in the time when Sr. gouernador y capitán general don Rodrigo flores de aldana governed, who has given us many *repartimientos.*

Although the Spanish version starts off in the first person like a direct quotation, there are several subtle changes in the text. Don Fernando Kantun appears without title in the Maya, but *gouernador* is added to the Spanish (at the end of the text, Kantun's signature is accompanied by the title *batab*). On the other hand, the reference to 'here' at line 3 and the first-person possessive pronoun in the address form 'our respected lord' at line 5 are both omitted. The symbolically loaded term *numyah* 'suffering' in the Maya is rendered by the anodyne *trauaxos* 'travails' in the Spanish. In other words, in the process of glossing, key aspects of the indexical centering of the Maya text are omitted—presupposed or erased altogether. Although I have not examined glossing practices closely, it is evident even in this short example that the gloss of the Maya text is more of a summary than a word-for-word translation. Like any process of redescription or report, the summary is always a *partial* equivalence, guided by tacit criteria as to which parts of the original must be in the gloss in order that it be valid. The stylistic and linguistic details through which we trace the development of *Maya reducido* were clearly below the threshold, and they could be omitted without prejudice to the "meaning" of the text.

The final example is from the town of Xecelchakán. It illustrates both the high degree of overlap between texts in this series and something of the variations introduced in individual ones. This one has a title, which I reproduce with the opening and closing text.[10]

PETESCION ʃ. FRANCO XECELCHAKAN	PETITION FROM SAN FRANCISCO XECELCHAKÁN
1. *Ton con batab Don anto ho yetel Don Gaspar pol*	We who are *batab* don Antonio Ho and don Gaspar Pol
2. *yetel alcaldesob yetel regidoresob*	and (the) alcaldes and regidores
3. *uay ti cah S. fran.co xecechakan*	here in the town of San Francisco Xecelchakán.
4. *[ca] noh tzicanil yume*	Our revered lord,
5. *Licix ca talel ca chacancunte caba ta[ ] yetel capetezcion*	We come to show ourselves before you with our petition.

6. *Licix ca ſopixti cech yetel*	We kneel to you and
7. *ca udzbenic u ni auoc*	we kiss your foot,
8. *Cech canoh tzicanil yume*	you who are great revered lord.
9. *caix adzaon yalan akab ychil ca numya*	So that you place us beneath your hand in our suffering,
10. *tumenel hex tone otzil ca numçabal ti ya*	because we are poor (and) we are being caused to suffer pain,
11. *tumenel ca yum S.r Don Rodrigo frores govor*	by our lord Sr. don Rodrigo Flores governor
[...]	[...]
12. *Hex tuxupul ubal ubaob tuconilobe*	Their possessions are exhausted by selling,
13. *ca xicob ti Kax u caxantob cib*	so they go to the forest to search for wax.
14. *– tix cucímilobi – yalan kax lae*	– There they die – beneath the forest.
15. *baix uxupulob uinicob ti pudzulob*	And people are being lost to flight,
16. *ca upat ucahalob ca xicob ti kax nachil*	when they leave their hometowns and go to the far forest.
17. *yoklal unumçabalob ti ya lae*	For they are suffering in pain.
18. *[laix] uchun licil ca talel ca chacancunte tatan*	[That] is the reason we come to appear before you.
19. *utzolan numya lic ca mançic uay cech ca nohtzicanil yum lae*	The account of our suffering here is what we bring before your revered lord.
20. *lay cokotba than ychil ca petesçion la*	These are our weeping words in our petition.
21. *heleac en 30 de nobiembre de 1669 años*	Today, the 30th of November 1669 years
22. *– ton apalil ah okotbathan tatan lae.*	– we your children, petitioners before you.

2 batabs, 4 alcaldes, 8 regidores, 2 procuradores, 2 eſ.nosob

The first point to register in this extract is the close parallel between the Xecelchakán (X) text and the Numkiní (N) text just examined. The correspondences are clear enough to be summarized in table 21, where the left column gives the line numbers of the Numkiní and the corresponding lines in the Xecelchakán are on the right.

The degree of similarity between corresponding lines in the two texts varies. At the high end are pairs such as (N 3–4 = X 3), (N 5 = X 4), and (N 6 = X 5). These are so similar as to suggest alternate renderings of a single master text. That the order of statements throughout the petitions is identical reinforces this impression: the correspondences are simply too precise to be coincidental,

TABLE 21 Line-by-Line Correspondences
between Two Petitions

NUMKINÍ (11/16/1669)	XECELCHAKÁN (11/30/1669)
1–2	1–2
3–4	3
5	4
6	5
—	6–9
7	10
8–9	11
10–11	—
22–24	12–17
26	18–19
27–28	21
29	22

and one is led to posit a process of copying or at least transmission of a single text to the two towns. This looks quite similar to the multiple copies of version 1 and version 2 of the February 1567 letters. At the same time, nearly every correspondence is offset by variations, and the two texts are far from identical in form, despite their similarity in overall meaning. The Xecelchakán adds *con batab* 'we who are *batabs*' plus a second name in line 1, whereas the Numkiní has no title and only one name. The Numkiní has *ah otochnalon* 'we are inhabitants' *(naturales)*, a detail unexpressed but implied in the Xecelchakán. At lines 6–9, the Xecelchakán text has the highly honorific 'we kneel to you and we kiss your foot, you who are revered lord, that you might place us under your hand in our misery'. The Numkiní has no corresponding act of submission. Lines 12–17 in the Xecelchakán invoke flight linked to wax gathering 'beneath the forest', but the wording differs substantially from the corresponding lines of the Numkiní (22–24). The statement of the date (N 27–28 = X 21) comes in the same position in the text, but whereas the Numkiní uses the Maya words and phrasing, the Xecelchakán uses numbers and is entirely in Spanish. The "sign off" at line 22 of the Xecelchakán expands Numkiní line 29 with the two epithets *apalil ah okotba than lae* 'your children, petitioners'. By contrast, the Numkiní authors never describe themselves as children and do not use the 'weeping speech' formulation of petition. Finally, the signatories to the Xecelchakán document curiously appear to represent two *cabildos* rather than one. Compared to the Numkiní, there are twice as many occupants of every office, including two *batabs,* doubling the standard structure of the *cabildo.*

The Xecelchakán petition is followed by a Spanish gloss, like the Numkiní, but this one is simply a summary report of the Maya text and hardly a close translation. These are the opening lines:

El gouernador alcaldes regidores y escribanos naturales del Pueblo de xecelchakan presentan con esta peticion ante el señor Doctor D. frutos delgado Gov.y capitan g.l de ella se quejan Por los agrauios que les [ ] el Sr D Rodrigo frores de [unintelligible] *y de los juezes . . .*

The governor, *alcaldes,* regidores and scribes resident in the Town of Xecelchakán present with this petition before Señor Doctor don Frutos Delgado Governor and Capitán General of it. They complain of the grievances that the Señor don Rodrigo Flores de [unintelligible] [has committed] and of the judges . . .

This gloss makes no attempt to capture the phrasing of the Maya text and even misrepresents the Maya by referring to 'the governor' (singular) at the outset, whereas there are two *batabs* in the Maya original. Comparing this gloss with the one accompanying the Numkiní, we see that the two glosses give little hint of the degree of similarity between the two Maya texts. The Maya texts are a prototypical case of serial contemporaneous production of a discourse—a single template with stylistic variation among versions—whereas the Spanish merely register comparable complaints. The stylistic details by which the Maya texts distinguish themselves are virtually erased in the Spanish glosses. The point is not to critique the translator but to recognize that glossing is a specific discourse practice guided by a way of reading texts for what they say, not how they say it. The variations between the Maya texts provide a gold mine of information about stylistic variation, alternate ways of phrasing, and, if one carefully compared all texts in the series, likely lines of collaboration between towns (as indexed by shared distinctive features). Unfortunately, such a study is beyond the scope of this book.

If we step back from the details of textual form, what do they tell us about the discourse practices of the authors? Perhaps the most obvious point is that the petition genre can be realized in a variety of ways, and the line between petitions, letters, and testimony was fluid. Some of the variation results from the fact that the genre developed over time and responded to changes in historical context. As a notarial genre, it was prototypically linked to the *cabildo,* but the *cabildo* in Yucatán also varied over time and space. The performative expressions that index the genre are *okotba (than)* 'weep oneself, beseech (in words)', *patcantic* 'recount, inform', *chacancuntic* 'cause to appear', and *hahcunic* 'cause to be true, testify'. The Spanish term *petición* appears in the seventeenth century, although Maya exemplars of the genre in the sixteenth century display most of the key features already. Each of the Maya expressions denotes a discourse act performed 'in front of' or 'to' a Spanish addressee. The addressee function is typically highly foregrounded in second-person address forms accompanied by honorific epithets. This is especially the case when the document is directed to the Crown or to supraregional officials, or when the petition itself was unsolicited. In either of these cases, the rhetorical task was to engage the addressee, and second-person forms and epithets are a means toward that end. In cases like the 1669 run of complaints against Flores de Aldana, documents were produced in response to an ongoing investigation, and the addressee function is backgrounded.

The presence of stylistically marked epithets for the addressee correlates with the presence of verse parallelism, both of which were aimed at mobilizing the party addressed. In the sixteenth century we encounter elaborate two-part epithets, including the term *ah tepal* 'majesty' for the Crown, whereas this expression apparently falls out of use in the later examples. Over the same time frame, *ahau* 'ruler' and *yum* 'lord' are generalized to New World representatives of the Crown and regional government. Correlatively, the use of parallel series of lines with end rhyme, regular length, and *difrasismo*-like pairings of images is also more widely attested in early texts. Whether because of the later date or the different institutional embedding, the 1669 petitions against Flores de Aldana are distinctly less marked by poetic and oral features than are the earlier examples.

We have also seen that the patterns of iteration of petitions vary on what might be heuristically considered a scale. On one end, we have unique texts with no known variants (Dzaptún 1605), then unique texts integrated into proximal series (March and April 1567), then far-flung series of multiple contemporaneous versions of *similar* texts (the 1669 Flores de Aldana petitions) to the extreme case of nearly *identical* copies of a single text (February 11, 1567), which may itself be part of a series (versions 1 and 2 of the February 1567 letters). In all these cases, iteration serves to disperse the discourse of *Maya reducido*. It also provides a productive way to demonstrate alliance and collaboration among the cosignatories. Although the genre was associated with *cabildo* titles and the *cabildo* scribal apparatus, it was not fundamentally a town-level production. Whereas the collective principals of land documents were usually neighbors, most of the petitions that I have examined involved principals from more than one town.

The signatories to petitions figure in the text in the first-person 'we'. The epithets of self-presentation run the gamut from *cabildo* titles through claims to legitimacy based on native status, residence, truth telling, firsthand knowledge of the matter at hand, suffering (hence grievance), and pious subordination to the addressee. In all cases, the authors of petitions take up positions that are locally legitimate (as leaders, officers, or ones entitled to write to upper officials) *and* subordinate to the addressee (as obedient subjects, subservient, common or poor people, children). As a result of this dual articulation, we find cases in which authors claim to be both legitimate officials and commoners, a pairing that might appear incoherent were it not for the intermediate position of native officials in the administrative hierarchies of *reducción*.

Cross-cutting all the examples discussed, the religious dimensions of *reducción* provide an ever-present background frame of reference. We see this in the use of doctrinal language and word choice, including the genre label *okotba (than)*, also used for prayer and confession to God; the epithet *ah tepal* 'majesty' for God and king; the *dzayatzil* 'mercy, intercession' for which God, king, and high officials were beseeched; the passion of *numyah* 'suffering'; the use of canonical doctrinal expressions for religious objects or practices *(evangelio, missa)*; and the use of patron saint names for Maya towns. Even when *doctrina* was not embedded in the language of petitions itself, it was referred to, described, or invoked as a value put in jeopardy by the bad deeds of colonial authorities. Particularly in the sixteenth century, the regional groups corresponding to *guardianías* appear to have mobilized in collective petitions. It is uncertain whether this indicates a transposition of doctrinal into political fields, or the inverse; of autonomous (or prehispanic) Maya relations into colonial ones, or the inverse. What is overwhelmingly clear is that there was a broader commingling of semiautonomous Maya with *Maya reducido* and political with doctrinal spheres. If the central argument of this book regarding the scope and logic of *reducción* is valid, then such commingling was frankly unavoidable and so far-reaching that the Spanish had little hope of controlling its effects. The final step we must take in tracing out those effects is to look at Maya writings for Maya audiences. It is to this, as illustrated by the Books of Chilam Balam, that we now turn.

11

Cross Talk in the Books
of Chilam Balam

cen chilam balam ca in tzolah uthan hahal ku tusinile, yokol cabe

'I who am Chilam Balam, explained the word of true God omnipresent, over the world'

CHILAM BALAM OF CHUMAYEL, BRICKER 1990 ED., LINE 3266

The notarial documentation clearly demonstrates that at least some Maya people in the pueblos learned to write and produced works in alphabetic script as early as the 1550s. The genres examined in the previous two chapters are all part of the governance of the *pueblos reducidos*. It is perhaps unsurprising that the language in which they are cast is itself *Maya reducido,* with traces of doctrinal Maya. In the present chapter, we move to the far end of the discourse formation, where texts were written by Maya authors for Maya addressees, *outside* the spheres of governance and mission. The works in question include the so-called Ritual of the Bacabs (Roys 1965; Arzápalo Marín 1987), a collection of medicinal prescriptions with scripted texts to be recited during treatment.[1] They also include the Books of Chilam Balam (henceforth BCBs). Both kinds of work were external to *reducción*; the missionaries described them as superstitions and curiosities that impeded proper Christian practice. They perpetuated either sorcery, in the case of the medicinal texts, or subversive politics, in the case of the BCBs. The BCBs were allegedly read in meetings outside the *cabildo* (Sánchez de Aguilar 1996 [1639], 115). When the missionaries encountered such texts, as Sánchez de Aguilar did, they confiscated them, read them, and disposed of them. The mass burning of books at the Maní auto-da-fe in 1562 was perhaps the most dramatic show of Franciscan zeal, but native books continued to be written and sometimes confiscated over the subsequent centuries. As early as López Medel (1552), the possession and production of books and meetings were prohibited, along with the consumption of fermented *balche* and the orgiastic parties at which it was

338

supposed to be consumed. For the missionaries, reading and writing outside the sphere of *reducción* were dangerous because they fostered the kind of autonomy associated with the internal frontier (see chapter 2).

It is abundantly clear from the historical record that the missionaries also read, if they did not study, the written works they confiscated (see map 16). Sánchez de Aguilar used books he found as evidence of idolatry, too dangerous to actually quote but damning as proof of wrongdoing. Lizana quotes at length from Maya prophecies, and Cogolludo also mentions native books. We know from Chuchiak's (2000a, 2000b) research that books were among the artifacts confiscated during the extirpation campaigns. One of the most eloquent demonstrations of the uses that missionaries made of these works was provided by the Franciscans who attempted to convince the Maya king Can Ek to capitulate to Christianity in the late seventeenth century, on the grounds that Maya prophecies themselves foretold it (Jones 1989, 1998). It is from books such as the BCBs that they would have known of such prophecies, however twisted their reading of them. For our purposes, the missionary reception of Maya written texts is important because it may indicate one of the sources of *Maya reducido,* as described in the dictionaries and grammars. Indeed, when we find clear instances of the colonial language in the prohibited genres, it is sometimes unclear what motivates the common features: did the *lengua reducida* spread into the prohibited genres, or did it go in the other direction, with texts like the BCBs serving as source material for the colonial version of the language? Even if the texts were considered false in what they said, they may have served as data for grammatical description. The answer is that both processes likely occurred, although in numerous cases it was the *lengua reducida* that made its way into the BCBs rather than the other way around.

The BCBs are handwritten, occasionally illustrated works that evidently were recopied throughout the colonial period and into the nineteenth century. None of the existing books had a title, just as they lack named authors or dates of production (although there are sometimes named copyists and dates for portions of the books).[2] Individual books often bear the writing of multiple scribes, a fact consistent with serial recopying and collective production. The name "Books of Chilam Balam" was given to these works in retrospect, perhaps first coined by Juan Pío Pérez in the late nineteenth century, in his compilation of Maya texts known as Códice Pérez.[3] The term *chilan* was evidently the title of a kind of Maya priest or prophet, while Balam is taken to be the family name of a famous prophet from Maní (Barrera Vásquez and Rendón 1974; Bricker and Miram 2002). The last word in the title of each book in table 22 is the town name in which it was discovered. As with the dictionaries in the missionary sector, the absence of author, title, or place of composition makes it difficult to infer from the place of

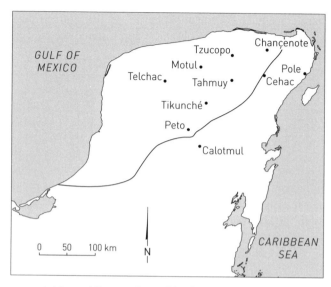

MAP 16. Maya *códices* confiscated by the Church, 1563–1640
(after Chuchiak 2000b)

discovery the source of the texts incorporated in the book. The book names are therefore purely heuristic, but I retain them for ease of reference. Barrera Vásquez and Rendón (1974) suggest that there may be a dozen or more such books, but those listed in table 22 are the only ones available for study.

The places named in the table are shown on map 17 below.[4] Because the works are undated, it is difficult to situate them precisely in relation to the changing map of *reducción*. What we can say is that by the first decades of the seventeenth century, Maní, Tekax, and Tizimín were all *cabeceras de doctrina*. Chumayel, about ten kilometers north of Maní, was within the core *reducción*, as was Teabo (where the Book of Nah was found), to the east of Maní. I do not know at what point either town became a *cabecera de doctrina*, if it did. Ixil was a distant *visita* of Motul, and Kaua was just southwest of Sací. The towns of Ixil, Kaua, Maní, and Tekax are among the places with major runs of notarial documents (Restall 1997, 248). All this suggests that for these places, alphabetic writing was firmly established by *reducción*. The same cannot be said for Tusik and Chan Cah, both of which were beyond the frontier. Either writing spread to these places early, owing to the great movements of refugees and illicit trade, or the books themselves were produced elsewhere and made their way to the southeast part of the peninsula later. Either way, these two books were found in towns outside the *reducción*, both of which happen to be in the territory occupied in the mid-nineteenth

TABLE 22   Extant Books of Chilam Balam

BOOK	LENGTH
Chilam Balam of Chumayel	107 pp.
Chilam Balam of Tizimín	54 pp.
Chilam Balam of Nah	64 pp.
Chilam Balam of Kaua 1, 2	282 pp.
Chilam Balam of Ixil	88 pp.
Chilam Balam of Chan Cah	128 pp.
Chilam Balam of Tusik	58 pp.
Códice Pérez	176 pp.
Chilam Balam of Tekax	37 pp.

century by rebel Maya of the Caste War. According to Villa Rojas (1945, 43 ff.), Tusik was one of the minor towns of the Cruzob Maya, a dependency of Xcacal, where Villa Rojas did ethnographic fieldwork in the 1940s. He reported that the people had a fragment of a Book of Chilam Balam, in addition to various other manuscripts (although literacy levels were very low, and Villa Rojas displays no special interest in the materials he reports on). Using colonial sources, Gerhard (1993, 80) locates what appears to be the same place northwest of Tihosuco. All this is consistent with the hypothesis that these two books were held on the edge of *reducción*, if not outside.

One of the most striking features of the BCBs is the sheer quantity of repetition between books. Indeed, there was enough cognate material among the books that Barrera Vásquez and Rendón (1974) concentrated exclusively on the shared matter and titled their study *El libro de los libros de Chilam Balam*. Their idea was that what was common to the different books was likely a shared Ur-text, which they hypothesize was in glyphs. Bricker and Miram (2002) also take pains to document which parts of the Book of Kaua are cognate with other books, which is a major contribution in itself. In no cases of which I am aware does a book actually attribute what it says to another book, in the manner of citing a source. Instead, comparison of different books reveals the cognate passages and commonalities of phrasing, without any single book emerging as a master text. We can infer that either many texts circulated independently or there was some other discourse, probably oral, that circulated and was absorbed into writing in different places where books were maintained. It is tempting to postulate the existence of an ancient work, perhaps written in hieroglyphs, to account for some of the overlap. Even if such a source existed, however, it would not account for the great quantity and quality of cognate text written in clearly colonial *Maya reducido*. For this we need to simply recognize that iteration, as encountered in

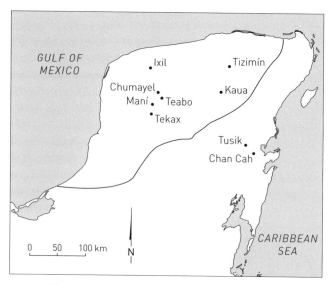

MAP 17. Sites at which extant Books of Chilam Balam were found
(© William F. Hanks 2007)

the missionary and *cabildo* spheres, extended to the BCBs as well. Recopying and revoicing produces the same effects in the forbidden genre that we encounter in the obligatory genres. Iteration provides a key to the workings of *reducción* as discourse.

Barrera Vásquez and Rendón (1974) make the important observation that much of the overlapping text in the BCBs is not verbatim quotation but instead paraphrase and slight variants of recurrent texts. If we step back from the search for a single origin and place this fact within the dynamic of the colony, it has important methodological consequences. On the one hand, we must be careful in deciding what is actually cognate with what, since the words are not all identical. On the other hand, if we can confidently match strips of text between books, then we can compare the points on which they vary. This in turn provides critical evidence for alternative phrasings of the same or similar objects. Thus, for instance, the fact that close paraphrases make reference to *Dios, hahal ku,* and *hunab ku* allows us to securely identify *hunab ku* with the Christian God, even when surrounding text may be ambiguous.[5]

The problems and prospects of the BCBs are therefore several. The genre itself is thematically and stylistically diverse, or "secondary" in the Bakhtinian sense: it incorporates many other genres, including astronomy and astrology, calendric reckoning and commensuration between Maya and European calendars and number systems, medicinal texts, quoted speech, historical description, ritual texts, and prayers. There are various layouts, from standard left-to-right text to tables, lists, and drawings. There is ample material in Latin and Spanish, as well as what appear to be several styles of Maya, likely from different historical periods. This heterogeneity is consistent with the fact that the books were produced by the distributed labor of an unknown number of scribes who engaged in an unknown number of recopyings, adding, emending, miscopying, and so forth.

Bricker and Miram (2002, 1) divide the nine extant BCBs into two groups according to their thematic focus: (1) the Books of Chumayel, Tizimín, and Tusik, which focus on history and prophecy; and (2) the Books of Kaua, Chan Kan, Nah, Tekax, and Ixil, which focus on astrological, astronomical, and medicinal matters. They also argue convincingly that much of the Kaua is in fact European in origin, even sourcing major sections to specific European almanacs and literary works. This effectively lays to rest any question as to whether the books are sheer holdovers from the precolonial period. At the same time, recopying and the absence of source dates peel the text away from any secure chronology. Even when the scribes who contributed to a given book can be identified on the basis of paleographic or other evidence, there is no way to know what they were copying from, or what their predecessors copied from. This uncertainty of transmission makes Bricker and Miram's (2002) sourcing even more significant.

In order to make sense of this degree of uncertainty, I focus selectively in this chapter on a single theme: the incidence of doctrinal language in the BCBs. There are several advantages to this choice. First, with appropriate caution, we can confidently identify Christian language, given what we now know of *Maya reducido*. The language of baptism, the trinity, confession, and Christian sadness are all clearly identifiable and will be recognizable to readers. By contrast, the language of governance, astrology, and medicine often either is ambiguous or poses formidable challenges of interpretation beyond the scope of this book. Second, we know that doctrinal language was canonical, imposed by obligatory training and repeated indefinitely many times throughout the *pueblos reducidos* and the radial structures of the *guardianías*. Third, we know the likely pathways by which doctrinal language dispersed, from missionary to *maestro* to student and *cabildo* scribe. If we find significant doctrinal language in the BCBs, we can explain its spread by reference to the institutional fields in which writing was practiced (even if forbidden works were written outside those settings).[6] In his list of remedies for the ills of idolatry, Sánchez de Aguilar (1996 [1639], Gonogora Biachi ed., 115) says:

Vltra que seria muy vtil que huuiesse libros impresos en la lengua destos Indios, que tratassen del Genesis, y creacion del mundo; porque tienen fabulas, o historias muy perjudiciales, y algunos las han hecho escriuir, y las guardan, y leen en sus juntas. E yo huue un cartapacio destos que quite a un Maestro de Capilla, llamado Cuytun del pueblo de Çucop, el qual se me huyo, y nunca le pude auer para saber el origen deste su Genesis; y que se les imprimiessen vidas de Santos, y exemplos en su misma lengua, pues la letura es lengua que habla alma, y por estar faltos de libros, viven sin luz, . . .

And it would be very useful to have books printed in the language of these Indios, that deal with Genesis and the creation of the world; because they have fables or histories that are prejudicial, and some have them written and they keep them and read them in their meetings. And I had a booklet of that that I took from a Maestro de Capilla, called Cuytun of the town of Çucop, who fled from me and I was never able to have him to know the origin of that Genesis; and let lives of the Saints be printed for them, and examples in their own language, because reading is language that speaks the soul, and lacking books, they live without light, . . .

Fourth, there has been no serious attempt in the scholarly literature to link Christian practice to the BCBs, which suggests that the result may make a new contribution to our understanding of Maya history.

Fifth and finally, doctrinal language is a privileged exemplar of the workings of *reducción* as a project. Christianity lay at the heart of the kind of *policía* the colonizers sought to instill in Maya people. From the reorderings of the towns under *congregación* to the labor regimes in which Maya people worked for and with missionaries, to the fiesta cycles and *guardianías*, Christian beliefs and practices were a central organizing logic, and one that gave rise to new varieties of Maya language. The sheer scale of the project and its capacity to generate homologies in space, gesture, discourse, and social action made it a powerful engine for change. The phrases and images of doctrinal language were also linguistically well suited to dispersal, because they break down to modular units, such as the sign of the cross and its parts, the opening and closing of prayers, the recitations of confession.

Fragmented into their component parts, these doctrinal texts, both oral and written, fit into a system of belief and practice. When they spread into nondoctrinal genres, whether notarial or forbidden, they brought with them the indexical backing of the system. So when we encounter the sign of the cross, it indexes the triune God, the totalizing gesture of arms outstretched, and the protection of Good from Evil. The kind of sadness declared in prayer and confessions and elaborated in the dictionaries indexes contrition for sin, the trickery of the Devil, and the hope for forgiveness. Doctrinal language is uniquely rich in its capacity to project a world and a subject with certain feelings and dispositions. This too tended to disperse it into the many spheres in which the new subject acted, even beyond the frontier of doxic *policía*. It should therefore come as no surprise that there is a great deal of cross talk in the BCBs, so much so that the question is not whether *lengua reducida* spread but how it spread and why.[7] Far from attempting to exclude Christianity, the way the Spanish tried to exclude "idolatry," the Maya appear to have followed the opposite strategy. They absorbed the new religion and its language, encompassed it, and appropriated it.

DOCTRINAL LANGUAGE
IN THE BOOKS OF CHILAM BALAM

A first sense of the dispersion of doctrinal Maya into the BCBs can be gained by summarizing the incidence of some well-known doctrinal expressions in the books themselves. These expressions, summarized in table 23 (pp. 346–47), are grounded in the missionary catechisms, sermons, and dictionaries, and most have been discussed in preceding chapters. The aim of the table is heuristic, and there are many more key terms one might select from doctrinal language to search for. Even so, the results are telling.

Table 23 reinforces the impression that the scribes who maintained the BCBs were actively engaged with Christianity and that they were familiar with its basic lexicon. This is hardly surprising, since writing was taught by *maestros* who were themselves experts in Christian doctrine. Moreover, by the late eighteenth and nineteenth century, alphabetic writing had been in use, and the *reducción* had been in progress, for more than two hundred years. But it is noteworthy that no attempt appears to have been made to exclude or expunge the colonizing religion from the books. On the contrary, just as the Book of Kaua has long sections devoted to commensurating Maya and European dates, so too some of the doctrinal discourse in the BCBs explains or gives translational equivalents of Christian doctrine as encoded in the Maya *doctrinas* (especially Beltrán's). Looking only at the superficial incidence of doctrinal language, then, the case for a Christian voice in the BCBs is strong.

Perhaps the most dramatic example of this is the Book of Kaua, which was recently published in annotated transcription and translation by Bricker and Miram (2002). The Kaua is the longest of all the BCBs, consisting of Book 1 and Book 2. It is the former that interests us here, since Book 2 is mainly astrological and medicinal.[8] In the Kaua Book 1, there are eleven extended passages that explicitly treat matters of Christian doctrine and practice. These are summarized in table 24 (p. 348).

The first entry in table 24 is a curious text that appears to have been interpolated between an extended description of the timing and techniques of medicinal bleeding, which immediately precedes it, and a long multiplication table immediately following. These adjacent texts are in Maya, whereas the baptismal text is

TABLE 23 Partial Summary of Doctrinal Terms in the Books of Chilam Balam

FORM	GLOSS	NO. TOKENS	SOURCE
Ah lohil	savior	19	Chan, Chu, Kaua, Pér*
Amen	amen	18	Chu, Kaua, Tus
Balcah tusinil	whole world	16	Chan, Chu, Ixil, Kaua, Tiz
Bautismo, bautiso	baptism	2	Kaua, Nah
Can yetel lum	heaven + earth	13	Chan, Chu, Kaua, Tus
*Caput cuxtal***	resurrection	5	Chan, Chu, Kaua, Tiz
Cayumil (ti dios)	our lord	121	Chan, Chu, Ixil, Kaua, Nah, Pér, Tus
Confecion	confession	3	Chan, Kaua
Confesar	to confess	12	Kaua, Tus
Confesor	confessor	118	Ixil, Kaua, Nah, Tek
Confirmacion	confirmation	1	Pér
Credo	Credo	3	Kaua
Cristiano(il)	Christian(ity)	16	Chu, Pér
Cristo	Christ	4	Pér
Crus, cruz	cross	37	Chan, Chu, Ixil, Kaua, Tiz, Tek
Cuxul ku	living God	3	Pér, Tus
Christi	Christ	2	Kaua
Christiano	Christian	7	Chu, Ixil
Christianoil	Christianity	30	Chu, Pér, Tiz
Christo	Christ	41	Chu, Kaua, Tus
Dios[†]	God	378	Chan, Chu, Ixil, Kaua, Nah, Pér, Tus
Dzabilah	grace	2	Ixi, Kaua
*Dzayatzil***	mercy	6	Chan, Kaua, Pér, Tiz
Ebangeli (o/sta)	evangelist	8	Chan, Kaua, Nah, Tek
Espiritu	spirit	13	Chu, Kaua, Pér
Evangeli(o/sta)	evangelist	11	Chan, Chu, Ixil, Nah, Tek, Tus

(continued)

in Spanish and even bears the signature of a priest named Baeza. The multiplication table that follows is lifted directly out of Beltrán's *Arte de el Idioma Maya* (2002 [1746], 158–60; see chapter 7); it commensurates between Maya numbers and arabic numerals. Bricker and Miram (2002, 140 n. 258) convincingly infer that the text in the Book of Kaua is a copy of a notice likely sent from a priest in Mérida to the priest in Kaua, notifying him that a baptism had been performed in Mérida. It is all the more curious to find this in a book of Chilam Balam given that the baptism reported involves a "mulatto," and there is no obvious reason why it would have been sufficiently salient to merit inclusion in the book. At the same time, it is a telling example of the privileged access that the scribe had to Church communications and raises the provocative possibility that priests were among those who added material to these books. The prayers in Latin are exactly the ones that study of the Maya *doctrinas* would lead us to expect, namely, the sign of the cross and the four basic prayers that were to be learned before all else.

TABLE 23 *(continued)*

FORM	GLOSS	NO. TOKENS	SOURCE
Grasia	grace	43	Chu
Gratia	grace	2	Kaua
Hahal dios	True God	10	Chan, Chu, Ixil, Kaua
Iglesia	church	15	Chan, Chu, Ixil, Kaua, Nah, Pér
*Keban***	sin	14	Chan, Kaua, Tus
*Ku***†	god	34	Chu, Pér, Tiz
Kuna	church	9	Chan, Chu, Ixil, Kaua, Pér, Tiz
Limbo	limbo	3	Chan, Kaua
*Loh(ic, ol)***	redeem	10	Chan, Chu, Ixil, Kaua, Tus
*Mehenbil***	holy son	11	Chu, Kaua, Pér*
Missa	Mass	2	Chu
*Oc***‡	believe	23	Chu, Ixil, Kaua, Tus, Nah, Pér, Tiz, Tus
Padre	priest	51	Chu, Ixil, Kaua, Tus, Nah, Pér, Tiz, Tus
Salve	hail (Mary)	3	Kaua
*Sipil***	trespass	20	Chu, Chan, Kaua, Pér, Tus
*Tusinil***	everywhere	16	Chu, Ixil, Kaua, Pér, Tiz
Uchuc§	all powerful	1	Pér
Xpo	Christ	46	Chan, Chu, Kaua, Tiz, Tus
*Yumbil***	lord	11	Chan, Chu, Ixil, Kaua, Pér

SOURCE: Data are based on Miram and Miram 1988, an invaluable concordance of the nine known books.

*Chan = Chan Kan, Chu = Chumayel, Pér = Pérez Codex, Tek = Tekax, Tiz = Tizimín, Tus = Tusik.

**Terms having uses in the Books of Chilam Balam that are apparently not derived from doctrinal usage. In these cases, the number of tokens is conservative, defined by those tokens I judged clearly doctrinal.

†Including tokens that refer to the Christian God and tokens that refer to non-Christian gods.

‡Including *ocolal* 'faith', *oces tauol* 'believe!', *oc Christianoil* 'Christianity arrived'.

§Thirty-one additional tokens do not refer to the Christian God.

Although we saw different versions of the *persignum* in chapter 8, the version here includes the phrase 'protect us from our enemies', which is also in the Maya (but lacking, for instance, in San Buenaventura's version). The version of the Credo here in Latin is the same text that Beltrán renders in his *Declaración de la Doctrina Christiana*. Recall that when we compared Beltrán with his predecessors, we noticed that he added a reference to Limbo as the place to which Christ descended after dying on the cross. The Latin text in the Kaua has the reference to Limbo, which relates it to Beltrán's text. The four prayers appear with Spanish titles, as shown in table 24; these are the same as the titles in the *doctrinas*. This degree of precision in the rendering of sacred language could have been achieved only by a Maya person who was highly trained in Christianity around the time of Beltrán and had privileged access to copying texts in Latin.

The final four entries in table 24 are all in Maya and reinforce the impression that the doctrinal content in the Book of Kaua is far beyond what could have been

TABLE 24 Doctrinal Text in the Book of Chilam Balam of Kaua, Book 1

TEXT	LANGUAGE	PAGE, BRICKER AND MIRAM 2002	DOCTRINAL REFERENT
Report of baptism	Spanish	140–41	1768 baptism in Mérida
Persignum	Latin	210	Template for Maya version*
Salve Regina	Latin	210	Template for Maya version
Genesis	Spanish	280	Holy Scriptures
El padre nuestro	Latin	282	Template for Maya version
El ave maria	Latin	282	Template for Maya version
El credo	Latin	283	Template for Maya version
Genesis	Maya	283–95	Holy Scriptures
Marian prayer	Maya	295	Unknown
Papal indulgences	Maya	297	Church law
Discourse on Mass	Maya	301–5	Exegesis of sacrament

*Texts marked as templates for the Maya version of the *doctrina* are in Latin but correspond virtually word for word to the Maya versions of the same prayers that were in Beltrán's (1746) *Declaración de la Doctrina Christiana*.

learned by an average student of the *doctrina menor*. Indeed, taken together, these texts make a plausible advanced course in doctrine. They amplify, explicate, and provide Latin source texts for the *doctrinas menores* (see chapter 7). What I have labeled an explication of Genesis actually includes but goes far beyond Genesis to interpret the Christian world. The Marian prayer echoes parts of the Salve Regina and the Hail Mary, but it also goes beyond them. The text on indulgences exhibits what can properly be called technical knowledge of papal law that would have been unlikely to be taught to anyone but experts, yet would have been significant as a rationale for penance and indulgences. Finally, the discourse on the Mass is a thoroughly remarkable symbolic interpretation of the meaning of each gesture and many utterances performed in the course of the sacrament of Mass. Titled "Discourse on Masses and Meanings," it looks like nothing so much as a teaching designed to lay bare the deep significance of the Mass as a reenactment not only of the Last Supper but also of the life and death of Christ. There is a cognate text in the Book of Chan Cah, pages 119–23 (Miram and Miram 1988, 2:74–76), which suggests that this kind of knowledge made its way far beyond the inner confines of the colony. The Chan Cah also renders text pertaining to John the Baptist (51–52; Miram and Miram 1988, 2:47), as well as a summary of Genesis (Book of Chan Cah, pp. 59–60, reproduced in Miram and Miram 1988, 2:50).

Comparing tables 23 and 24, it is difficult to avoid the conclusion that those who wrote the BCBs either were themselves *maestros* or had access to sources who were. The explanation for this is obvious when we recall the organization of the *doctrinas* and the practices of inculcation that the missionaries fostered. The *maestros* would have had access to the kinds of knowledge so strongly displayed in the Book of Kaua, and they would have been aware that it was specialized and powerful knowledge. It may seem ironic that they copied such material into genres that were deprecated or even prohibited by the Church. But if we think of *maestros* as agents of translingual discourse, it makes sense that they would incorporate such highly valued knowledge into Maya books whose most obvious purpose was to serve as the repository of accumulated wisdom. As discussed in chapters 2 and 3, *maestros* were among those who fled over the frontier, and the idolatry trials make reference to many who were Maya *ah kin* priests and *maestros cantores* at the same time. When the reader is addressed directly in the Book of Kaua, it is a Maya reader, a descendant of the world of Mayapán and the Itzá. Almost certainly, texts in Latin and Spanish were included in order to appropriate them as powerful discourse. The more Church regalia, practices, and language made their way over the frontier, the less the Maya needed the priests. They could access God in the original Latin as well as in their own language, they could interpret the Mass, and they had their own version of creation.

In the remainder of this chapter, I examine a small sample of cases in which Christian practices are announced, urged upon the Maya audience, or directly performed. None of the examples adduced here has the compactness or completeness of the Kaua texts just described. Rather, what is most interesting for our purposes is the dispersal of doctrinal language into other kinds of text in the BCBs. The concentrated, thematized engagement with Christianity in the Kaua is actually the tip of an iceberg, and many of the tokens summarized in table 23 occur in the course of text not otherwise focused on the Church or prayer. This is an expectable consequence of dispersal by way of iteration and fragmentation. It results not from transposition of entire Christian texts, but from the scattering of Christian language through the practices of those who spoke it.

TRUE GOD COMES TO YUCATÁN

In the excerpt below, the Book of Chilam Balam of Chumayel reports the first arrival of Christianity. Cast in the past tense, it dates the arrival to 1549 C.E., which it (erroneously) says was four years after the arrival of the "foreigners" (i.e., Spaniards).[9]

D⁰ 1549 Hab	A.D. 1549
Y an c uchi	was the year
Ca hul i	when arrived
Padreob	the fathers.
Can p'el hab huluc tz'ulob c uchi	Four years after the arrival of the foreigners.
Ti jx hop'i	Then began

Y ocol haa	the baptisms
T u pol uinicob i	of the people,
Ti cahal cah	from town to town,
t u men padreob	by the fathers.

(Edmonson 1986, lines 2347–2356)

The focal point of this report is the *padres* 'fathers', that is, the missionaries, and the description of baptism is in exactly the transparent neologism of *Maya reducido* 'water entered (upon) their heads'. Also echoing the travels of the early missionaries, the baptisms are said to occur *cahalcah* 'from town to town', a formulation that nicely ties the central symbol of conversion, the sacrament of baptism, to the basic unit of *reducción,* the town.

Elsewhere in the Chumayel, the arrival of the foreigners is dated to the twenty-year *katun* of the Maya calendar and the "foreigners" are said to have come from the East, marking the start of Christianity.

Yoklal lay katun yan	For this *katun* period was the one
ca uli tz'ulob	when the foreigners arrived
Ti u talelob ti likin	It was from the East they came,
ca uliob e	when they arrived
Ti ix hop'i christianoil xan i	That was when Christianity began also.

(Edmonson 1986, lines 1604–1607)

The Book of Tizimín has a passage cognate with the one above:

Ti likin utal	They came from the East
Ca uliob uaye	when they arrived here
Ah mexob	The bearded ones
Ah pulob	The [?] ones
Ti chicul ku sac	At the sign of the white god
Uahom che canal	the standing wood (cross) on high

(Edmonson 1982, lines 1177–1182)

Here instead of 'foreigners' we find 'bearded ones, the *puls* [gloss unknown]', and instead of baptism or Christianity, we find 'the sign of the white God, the standing wood on high'. Given the positional parallel between baptism, Christianity, and the standing wood, I read them all as references to the new religion. The 'standing wood' would refer to the material cross, either the one on which Christ suffered and died, the ultimate reference of all crucifixes, or the standing crucifixes that missionaries carried in procession and planted throughout the colony from the earliest years. I have seen no other reference to God or Spaniards as "white," but the use of *ku* 'god' for the Christian God is well attested in the dictionaries and was adopted by Coronel in his *doctrina* (see plates 15, 16).

THE SADNESS OF THE CHRISTIANS

The arrival of Christianity was a source of suffering and dispossession for Maya people. It meant a loss of legitimacy for their own ritual practices, which were relentlessly refuted, excluded from the realm of truth, and associated with the Enemy, that is, the Devil. All the missionary teaching ran counter to the indigenous system of belief and excluded it, even when the two systems occasionally seemed to coincide in symbolic forms.[10] But the sadness of Christianity was not only due to the destruction it caused, and justified, among the Maya. It ran deeper, because it tapped into the existential plight of Christian Man living in the Valley of Tears: contrite before God for offenses committed out of weakness or the trickery of the Devil. As we saw in the dictionaries, and saw amplified in the *doctrinas,* to be Christian was to be formed in an affective mold constituted by remorse, contrition, tears, and pleading. Thus in some passages where Chilam Balam describes the arrival of Christianity, he does so in the weeping words of petition and prayer. Note in the following excerpt from the Pérez Codex (p. 170, lines 7–8) the direct tie established between weeping words and True God, one of the epithets for the Christian God:

Yokt uba inthan cen Chilam Balam	My words wept, I who am Chilam Balam
Ca in tzolah u than hahal ku	When I explained the word of True God
Yunbi hunac tzuc ti cah	Lord unified in (the) town.
(Miram and Miram 1988, 3:127)	

The form *yumbi(l)* is one of a large repertoire of terms whose reference is consistently to the Christian God. It is morphologically parallel to *mehenbil* 'son' as in the sign of the cross, *yumbil, mehenbil, espiritu santo* 'Father, Son, Holy Spirit'.

The Chumayel contains what is to my knowledge the fullest expression of suffering occasioned by Christianity. Here we are face-to-face with a version of Christianity far from the gifts of grace and close to the realities of oppressive colonization. The entering of the faith meant tribute, poverty, oppression, the burnings of towns, and servitude to the Spanish. The litany of woes in the next example goes on to describe the colonials as *u antachristoil yokol cabob* 'the antichrists of the world', as predators and bloodsuckers of the poor *maseual* 'commoners'.

1	*. . . ca oci numya: ca oci Christianoil:*	That is when suffering entered: when Christianity entered:
2	*tumen lay hach Christianoob:*	because truly the Christians:
3	*ti uli yetel hahal ku: hahal Dios*	they arrived with True God: True Dios

4	*heuac u chun numya toon:*	but it was the start of suffering for us:
5	*uchun patan uchun limosna:*	the start of tribute, the start of alms:
6	*uchun hoc mucuuc tza uchun dzon bacal tza:*	the start of secret discord, the start of violent discord:
7	*uchun toc luksah: u chun dzal pach: p'ax*	the start of burning up: the start of oppression: debt
8	*u chun ca ca tza: uchun numsah ya:*	the start of our discord: the start of our suffering:
9	*u chun toc luksah*	the start of burning up
10	*uchun meyahtabal espanolesob yetel ah kinob:*	the start of serving Spaniards and priests:
11	*umeyahtabal Batabob: umeyahtabal camsahob*	the serving of Batabs: the serving of teachers
12	*umeyahtabal fiscalob tumen mehen palalob: upalil cahob*	the serving of fiscales by young children: the children of the towns

(Miram and Miram 1988, 1:60, lines 11–25)

Many of the woes brought with the Christian god are stated in parallel couplets, in which the first part has a Maya form and the second has its Spanish equivalent. In line 3, for instance, *hahal ku hahal Dios* is paired in the familiar bilingual pattern of commensuration by juxtaposition (the same form of which the bilingual dictionary is the most elaborate exemplar). The same structure occurs at line 5, where *patan* 'tribute' is paired with '*limosna*' 'alms', both of which connote poverty. I take the burnings in lines 7 and 9 to refer to the burning of bones, books, homes, and towns that the missionaries engaged in under *reducción*. The last three lines dwell on the labor extracted to serve the Spanish, the priests, the *batabs,* the teachers, and the *fiscales,* all authority figures in the *pueblos reducidos.* Whatever the range of functions of these agents, they are here reduced to those one must serve. The verb *meyahtabal* is derived from the stem *meyah* 'work', transitivized *[-t-]* to yield 'serve, work for', then passivized *[-abal]* to yield 'be served, worked for'. Those served are listed in rank order from Spaniard to local *fiscal,* and positions in government (Spaniard, *batab, fiscal*) alternate with positions in the missions (priest, teacher, *fiscal*). As we saw, the spheres of governance and mission were indeed intertwined, and passages like this one embody the intertwining in discourse form itself. The final references to children merge the two, since it is children who serve the fiscal officers, and it is children who are the students of the teachers in line 11. Read against what we know of the workings of *reducción,* the passage above is a brilliant analysis of extraction and authority in the *pueblo reducido.*

Under *reducción,* both persons and places were renamed. Baptism marks the threshold of rebirth by renaming the individual. We saw how the new Christian name was reinforced by the doctrinal dialogues (chapter 8) and was invariantly used as the signatory name-form on notarial documents (chapters 9, 10). It is this practice that is described in the following excerpt, also from the Chumayel (p. 78, lines 17 ff.).

Buluc ahau ukaba ukatunil	Buluc Ahau was the name of the *katun*
hauci u maya kabaob maya uinicob	The Maya names of Maya people were set aside
Christiano u kabaob	Their names [became] Christian
(Miram and Miram 1988, 1:99)	

The verb *hau(ci)* translates roughly 'to set aside, turn away from'. It has derivatives meaning 'to come to an end, to repent, to cancel (a debt)'.

THE WORDS OF THE PROPHET

Among the famous texts that iterate in several BCBs are the prophecies, particularly the words of Chilam Balam. The next four examples show variants of his words in the Books of Chumayel and Tizimín, and the Pérez Codex.

The first, from the Chumayel, purports to quote the great Chilam, who reports, in the past tense, that he has explained the word of 'True God Almighty on the earth'. The linking of *ku* 'god' with truth and with the form *tuçinil* 'all encompassing (arms outstretched)' is rooted in the canonical *persignum* (see chapters 1, 8). Chilam Balam is himself speaking *Maya reducido* in this passage:

C en Chilam Balam	I who am Chilam Balam
Ca in tzolah u than hahal ku	(When) I recounted the word of True God
Tuçinil e y okol cab e	Almighty on this earth.
(Edmonson 1986, lines 578–580)	

Below, his prophecy is repeated almost verbatim in the Tizimín and the Chumayel. The two are close enough to be indisputably the same text, yet minor differences distinguish them.

TIZIMÍN

1	*U profesia Chilam Balam*	The prophecy of Chilam Balam
	Tix kayom Cabal Chen Mani	it will be sung in the well of Mani
2	*Oxlahun Ahau uhetz' iuil katun*	Thirteen Ahau [was] the seating of the katun
3	*Ualac uil Ytza*	Let the Itza stand up
	Ualac uil tan cah e	Let it be erected in front of the town,
	Yum	Father,
4	*Uchicul hunab ku canal*	The sign of the One God on high
5	*Ulom uaom che*	The cross [lit. 'erect wood'] shall arrive
	Etsahom ti cah e	They shall place it in town,

6	*Uchebal u sashal yokol cabe*	In order that the world be enlightened
	Yum	Father

(Edmonson 1982, lines 3951–3965)

CHUMAYEL

1	*Ualac uil ytza*	Let the Itza stand up.
2	*ualac uil tan cah e*	Let it stand up in town.
3	*Yum e*	Father,
4	*u chicul hunab ku canal*	the sign of Hunab Ku in heaven.
5	*hulom uaom che*	The cross (erect wood) must arrive.
6	*Etçahan ti bal cah e*	It is placed in the world
7	*uchebal u sashal yokol cab e*	so that the earth be enlightened,
8	*Yume e*	Father.

(Edmonson 1986, lines 501–507)

In line 5, the Tizimín has *etsahom ti cahe* 'must be placed in the town(s)', whereas line 6 of the Chumayel has *etçahan ti balcahe* 'placed in the material world'. The former uses a sort of obligative future that Coronel described in his *arte*, whereas the latter is a stative participle. The Tizimín ends with *yum* 'Father', whereas the Chumayel has *Yume* 'Father'. Both texts conclude with references to the Christian project of illuminating the world (recall the description of the missionaries in the petitions of 1567 discussed in chapter 10). Both refer to the 'sign of one god', which replicates the first line of the *persignum*, *Tumen uchicul cilich cruz* 'By the sign of the holy cross'.

The following example, from the Pérez Codex (p. 73, lines 22–30), is closely related to the previous ones in content and word choice but is cast in the imperative mood. Chilam Balam tells the people that the sign of one god has come and that they must worship him, the god from heaven, the true god.

1	*La u chicul hunab ku canal talane*	Behold the sign of One God come from on high
2	*la akulteex ah itzaexe*	Whom you shall worship Itza,
3	*ca a kulte helelae u chicul ku likul canale*	Worship today the sign of god from the heavens
4	*ca a kulte tu hahil auolah*	Worship him in the truth of your heart
5	*ca a kulte hahal kue*[11]	Worship True God!
6	*oces tauol uthan hunab ku tali canal . . .*	Believe in the word of One God come from heaven
7	*yoktuba inthan cen Chilam balam*	My words weep, I who am Chilam Balam
8	*ca tin tzolah u than hahal ku*	When I explain the word of True God
9	*licil in binel hun tzuc ti caah*	As I go to the gathering of town
10	*u than hach hahal kue*	The word of really True God
11	*ti bolon pis u habil hun ahau uale.*	On the ninth year of one ahau.

(Miram and Miram 1988, 3:67)

In exactly missionary words, the text tells the people to convert: *oces tauol* 'take (him) into your heart'. Repeating, in lines 7–8, the same lines as in the Pérez Codex extract on page 351, this passage goes on to describe the prophet's own speech as 'weeping words', reinvoking sadness. Whether or not the prophet here reported was a preconquest Maya priest, there is no doubt in my opinion that whoever wrote these passages was already embedded in *reducción* and had been exposed to *Maya reducido*.[12]

It might be objected that *hunnab ku* 'one god' could refer as well to a non-Christian deity as to God, and if so, our reading of the foregoing passages would shift fundamentally. Even if this is possible in theory, it is unlikely in fact. The extract below, also from the Chumayel, supports the Christian reading in explicit and unambiguous terms.

1	*Hunnab ku tusuhuyil hunab yglesia,*	One God in his holy one church,
2	*Ti auati*	There it was announced,
3	*la uyub uthan uyumil caan*	The word of the lord of heaven was heard
4	*Uyumil yokol cab,*	The lord of the world (above earth),
5	*Binix okomac yol balcah tusinil*	The entire material world shall be saddened

(Bricker 1990, line 2899 ff.)

Not only do we once again have the linkage to sadness, but the reference to the *hunab yglesia* 'one church' in line 1 could not be clearer. By repeating the adjective *hunab* 'one', this line places the element *ku* 'god' in parallel position to the element *yglesia* 'church': the god in question is the one inside the church. What follows goes on to direct the people to convert to the one god come from the heavens. It is as if the reference to one god in line 1 invokes a penumbra of related terms—the church, heaven and earth, contrition and material reality (as opposed to spiritual), encompassed by the outstretched arms of *tusinil* 'totality, all'.

The next two examples, the first from the Tizimín and the second from the Pérez Codex (pp. 168–70), amplify the directive to convert. They are very nearly identical, saying, 'Forget your set-aside (*ahauai*) gods, your lost (*satai*) gods and worship the true God (instead)'.

TIZIMÍN

1	*tubes ahauai asatai kul e*	Forget your finite gods, your lost gods
2	*la akulte uhahil ku lo e*	That you might worship the true god
3	*tulacal yanil ah tepal e*	All (that) is Majesty
4	*yum yah ch'ab uti tusinil e*	Lord the Creator of everything

(Edmonson 1982, line 1220)

PÉREZ CODEX

1	*Tubes ahauay yetel a satay kue*	Forget your finite gods, your lost gods
2	*la akulte uhahil ku loe*	That you might worship the true god
3	*Tulacal yanil ah tepal*	All (that) is majesty
4	*yum yah cha'kulil tusinile*	Lord the creator of everything
5	*Interpretacion*	Interpretation
6	*". . . aborreced ya vuestros dioses*	"Erase now your gods
7	*olvidad los que ya son fundibles*	Forget the ones who are already defunct
8	*adorad todos el Dios de la verdad*	Everyone adore the God of truth
9	*que está poderoso en todas partes y*	Who is all powerful in all places and
10	*que es criador de todas las cosas"*	Who is creator of all things."

(Miram and Miram 1988, 3:126)

The descriptions of the (false) gods as 'set-aside' and 'lost' invoke the words of a priest telling a sinner to turn away from sin: *haues akeban* 'set aside your sins'.[13] Recall also that in the lines quoted on page 353, the loss of Maya names was coded with *hauci* 'set aside', the same verb root as in line 1 above from the Tizimín. Once again we find that the reference to *hahal ku* 'true God' invokes a series of related doctrinal expressions, whose meanings are defined by Christian doxa: truth, totality, the creator, and the provider ("majesty"). The cognate lines occur in almost identical form in the Pérez Codex, where they are attributed to the prophecy of Natzim Yabun Chen. Notice in the example from the Pérez Codex that the Maya text is immediately followed by the label *'Interpretacion'* 'Interpretation' and a Spanish gloss. This gloss provides a third version, in Spanish, of the same text, and it confirms the Christian reading of the Tizimín example: it glosses *uhahil ku* as *'el Dios de la verdad'*. The singular definite article, the capital *D*, and the reference to truth all anchor this in Christianity. The minor variation between *yah chabul* and *yah chakul* (line 4 in both the Tizimín and Pérez examples) could be as simple as a scribal error, taking [k] to be [b].

In sum, when we look at this series of three versions in two languages of the same text, it is difficult to avoid the conclusion that the Tizimín example above is a statement about Christianity and the Chilam Balam is telling Maya people to convert. The lost and abandoned gods to be forgotten are none other than the Maya divinities labeled false and idolatrous by the missionaries, and the 'true God' is the triune God. The turning away implied is precisely the gesture of a convert who forsakes false gods for the True God. The author of these words was either Christian or intimately familiar with the language of Christianity.

There is a lingering question about how the BCBs refer to God in other contexts and how secure we should feel about the Christian reading proposed above. After all, if the BCBs are preaching conversion to the Maya people, in the same language developed by the missions, then we have to wonder how deeply

TABLE 25 Epithets for God in the Books of Chilam Balam

'GOD'	NO. TOKENS	'CHRIST'	NO. TOKENS
Dios	378	xpto	46
Cayumil	121	christo	41
Ku	34	ah lohil	19
Yumbil	11	mehenbil	11
Hahal dios	10	cristo	4
Cuxul ku	3	cristi	2

reducción seeped into these writings. It is one thing to report the arrival of Christianity and quite another to direct people to convert to it. Table 25 shows some standard ways to denote the Christian God, with rough token counts to give a heuristic sense of proportion. *Dios* and *ku* are roughly equivalent general terms for 'god', and both are used in reference to non-Christian divinities as well as the Christian God, as we just saw. When either of them is qualified as 'true', 'one', or 'living', it unambiguously designates the Christian God. The Maya forms merely render transparent qualities of God that are implicit in the more general *'Dios'*. The simple Adjective + Noun structure recalls the pursuit of transparency in the Maya glosses for Spanish and Christian concepts in the bilingual dictionaries: the Maya forms are compositional, and for each element of meaning there is a readily segmentable element of form. The same holds for *yum-bil* 'revered lord', derived from the more general term *yum* 'lord, father, owner'. The *[-bil]* suffix is the same as the one in *mehenbil* 'Son (Christ)' and *colebil* 'Holy lady', also Christian. The possessed form *ca-yum-il* 'our lord/father' is a variant of *ca yum* 'Our father', as in *Ca yum yanech ti canob* 'Our Father who art in heaven'.

Hence in the epithets for God in the BCBs, attributes of the Christian divinity are transparently coded in the morphosyntax. Linguistic form ties these epithets into Christian thought and ways of speaking common in Spanish and Latin. When any one of the forms in question occurs in a text, it indexes the larger schema of attributes: truth, triune unity, living, and so forth. There are numerous other epithets that I will not attempt to analyze here. They include *uyumil ca pixan* 'the lord of our souls', *uyumil can yetel lum* 'the lord of heaven and earth', and *ca yumil ti dios* 'our lord in God'. The last of these was particularly abundant, with about one hundred tokens in the BCBs.

The right-hand column in table 25 shows names and expressions for Christ, including Spanish, Latin, and Greek forms of the name. The descriptors *ah lohil* 'redeemer, savior' and *mehenbil* 'son' are both ubiquitous in doctrinal texts. *Mehenbil* in particular is the second person of the trinity as designated in the *persignum*.

The sense of unity indexed by *hunnab* 'one' is laid bare in a passage from the Book of Chan Cah (p. 61, lines 1–8). In the course of recounting Genesis, it says:

1	*[Dios] umultumtic cilich oxil hunab Dios*	[God] joins the holy three in one God
2	*ox tul u uinicil*	three persons
3	*Yumbil Mehenbil Espiritu Santo*	Father, Son, Holy Spirit
4	*Bayili bay licil u cantic cilich kulen dzibob laa*	As it is told in the holy worshipped writings (scriptures)

(Miram and Miram 1988, 2:51)

Here the reference to three persons, the naming of them in the canonical form of the *persignum*, and the attribution to the Scriptures resolve the reference of *hunab Dios* beyond any plausible doubt. These passages are about Christianity: the religion of *reducción* and *conversión*. They are, moreover, written in *lengua reducida*, the language of conversion, and they reflect an understanding of Christian doxa consistent with the expert knowledge of a *maestro*.

In the course of a long and detailed symbolic interpretation of the Mass, the Book of Kaua (p. 165, lines 4–6) states the meaning of the Agnus Dei, a prayer uttered during the preparation of the communion.

1	*Lay agnus Dei cuyalic Padre*	The Agnus Dei that the father says,
2	*yahi tu yol Judillob*	It pained the hearts of the Jews
3	*uchic u sincob ti crus Christo c ahlohile.*	When they stretched out on the cross Christ our Redeemer.
4	*Padre cu hantic lay ostia*	[When] Father eats the host,
5	*Christo ca yumil cu dzabal tu cilic[h] mucnal*	Christ is placed in his holy sepulchre
6	*Tux ma mucan cimenob cuchie*	Where no one had been buried before.

(Miram and Miram 1988, 4:76)

Note the way the speaking of the prayer is equated with the stretching out of Christ on the cross, where the verb for stretching out is *sin-ci,* based on the same root *sin* as *tuzinil* 'all'. Thus the text above projects a whole constellation of precepts and ways of speaking. The reference to the host works in a similar way: when the priest consumes the host, Christ is lowered into his grave (a noncanonical interpretation as I understand it). This passage occurs in a section of the book titled *Discurso sobre la missa y significas* 'Discourse on the Mass and Meanings', a frankly pedagogical text explaining the meaning of the sacrament and its parts. There was indeed a rich semiotic in the rituals of the faith, which some Maya people were keenly interested in.

The Book of Chumayel contains eight references to *balcah tusinil,* which I have glossed 'the whole material world'. This gloss is based partly on the observation that *balcah* is the third of the mortal enemies in Christian doxa: the Devil, our flesh, and *balcah*, which I take to be the world of objects and human experience, the world of temptation. As we learn in these excerpts, it is both the world of creatures as God created it at Genesis and the world of which Eve is the mother, the world of human stain and sin that will be judged in its entirety on the Day of Final Judgment.

1654	*Sihanili tun Adan ca sihsah ca yax naa ti Euae, yax ch'uplal u naa* <u>*balcah tusinil*</u>	Adam was already born when our first mother Eve was born, the first woman, the mother of the world.
1848	*sihci tulacal tumen ca yumil ti Ds. lae, lay citbil, ti minan caan yetel luum, ti bay yanil tu Diosil, tu muyalil tuba tuhunal, ca u sihsa* <u>*balcah tusinil*</u>	Everything was born of our lord God, who is infinite, before there was heaven or earth, when he was in his godliness, in his heaven alone, when he created the whole world.
2756	*emtab u tha[n] Dios, tal ti canal, hunyuk ti* <u>*balcah tusinil*</u>	The word of God came down from the heaven(s), universal over the world.
2899	*hunnab ku tusuhuyil hunnab yglesia, ti auati la uyub uthan uyumil caan uyumil yokol cab, binix okomac yol* <u>*balcah tusinil*</u>	One God in the sanctity of One Church, where the word of the lord of heaven, the lord of the world was shouted to be heard. The whole world shall be contrite.
2983	*yanni ciciolal uthan* <u>*balcah tusinili,*</u> *bin ayikalac ah numya uinici*	There was happiness over the entire world, the poor shall become rich.
3127	*bin umentic cuenta ca yumil ti Ds., ti humppel komluum, humppel noh chakan, tij tun ucutal yokol uxecil utepal, binix molocob tulacal* <u>*balcah tusinil*</u>	Our lord in God will take stock, in a valley, a great plain. There he will sit upon the throne of his majesty, and he will gather everything of the entire world.
3220	*Tulacal yanil ah tepale, yume, yah ch'aabul caan yetel luum* <u>*tusinil*</u>	His majesty is everything, Lord, the maker of heaven and earth.
3266	*cen chilam balam ca in tzolah uthan* <u>*hahal ku tusinile,*</u> *yokol cabe*	I who am Chilam Balam, I explained the word of True God omnipresent in the world

(Bricker ed. 1990)

This example reproduces all instances of the term *tusinil* in the Book of Chumayel (underlined here). It is because of examples like these that we read *tusinil* as a specifically Christian sense of totality, even when the context is human experience and not the crucifixion of Christ. In the *persignum*, it is the totalizing gesture of crucifixion, arms outstretched, whereas here it is the whole world in need of Christ's redemption.

The final examples I adduce of Christian language in the BCBs are a few references to confession and its cognates ('confessor, confess'). I argued in chapter 8 that confession was a key practice in the formation of the habitus of the Christian *indio reducido*. We do not know how often Maya people actually partook of this sacrament, but the language and postures of the contrite penitent resonate with portions of the Book of Tusik.

The Tusik is the only book of Chilam Balam in which the expression *choch keban* 'untie sins' occurs, referring to absolution through confession. In the course of an extended discussion of the sacrament, there are fourteen tokens of this expression, which is canonical for confession in the dictionaries and *doctrinas* (see Tusik, p. 27, lines 11–15). This sacrament organized contrition, truth telling, the request for absolution, and the cleansing of the soul. It also presupposed a soul-searching self-awareness in which the subject took stock not only of his sins, but of their causes. Recall here the text for prayer before confession presented in chapter 8.

11.	*. . . ca tuyalah ah kebane bec oltzilen*	The sinner said "Poor me,
12.	*yoklal lay u natal in muclic*	for it is understood that I hid
13.	*uyahaulil yetel u chacil in keban hun p'el loe.*	the one greatest and the worst of my sins.
14.	*Heklay tan u talel in toh pultic cachie,*	Which I had come to confess
15.	*Cat maci inchi tumenel cisin*	When my mouth was closed by (the) devil"

(Miram and Miram 1988, 3:12)

This strip of discourse has the style and stance of a sermon in which the experience of a sinner is told as a parable from which the listener is to learn. Here we learn that the Devil obstructs honest confession, designated with the standard expression *tohpul* 'straight cast' (see chapters 5, 6, and 8, as well as plates 7 and 10). The sinner's remorse takes the form of *pec ol* 'doubt, danger, uncertainty'. His words are quoted, just as Coronel's sermons quoted the words and inner thoughts of the characters in his narratives. The well-known theme of the trickery of the Devil is amplified soon after in the same text (Tusik pp. 28–29, line 17 ff.).

Ilex tun yan ya nucah cisin tex	See then the devil causes you suffering,
bicil ulubsic subtal tex	how he takes away your shame
tu kinil a sipilex	at the moment of trespassing,
catac u ualkes tex	then brings it back upon you
tu kintzil a choch kebanex	at the moment of confessing.

(Miram and Miram 1988, 3:12)

This final example is a well-crafted verse series, as indicated by the scansion into lines, in which the Devil plays with the mind and conscience of the sinner. The penitent must think not only about sin but also about the conditions that foster it. This is exactly the theme developed in Coronel's sermon for those preparing to confess (see chapter 8, p. 274).

. . .

Rightly famous among students of colonial Latin America, the Books of Chilam Balam have given rise to a long history of scholarship. Along with the Popul Vuh in Quiché Maya, the Annals of the Cakchiquels in Cakchiquel Maya, the Bancroft Dialogues in Nahuatl, and the Book of Guaman Poma in Quechua, they are among a small set of indigenous writings from the colonial period. Given the heterogeneity of the BCBs, the number of copyists involved in reproducing them, and the late dates of the extant copies, they can be read in various ways. Earlier Mayanist scholarship has tended to focus on them as evidence of ancient Maya society and history. From Lizana and Sánchez de Aguilar in the seventeenth century to Tozzer, Barrera Vásquez, Roys, Sharer, and Edmonson in the twentieth, scholars have used Maya prophecies and writings to learn about the world they describe, and the apparently ancient perspective from which they describe it.

This way of reading has been productive in many respects, and it laid groundwork without which this book would not have been writable. Yet it rests on assumptions we can no longer afford. It places the weight of interpretation on what the BCBs say about a time far removed from when they were written. Here the past is depicted in the BCBs as a sort of origo, an ancient starting point, be it the Classic period, the Post-Classic, the Mayapán confederacy, or the far reaches of the calendar. In the same way, Barerra Vásquez and Rendón (1974) used the variants among different texts to reconstruct an original Ur-text. The result is interesting for what it says about the passages so chosen, but it comes at a great cost. In setting aside the variations in favor of the commonalities, it erases the specificity of individual texts and with it the history of their production and maintenance.

Starting with the missionary writings and continuing with the doctrinal, notarial, and now forbidden works, I have argued throughout this book for a different way of reading and a different sense of history. The forbidden texts are not only about the past; they have a history of their own. They were produced by certain kinds of actors, and written, read, and interpreted in certain settings. They were subject to confiscation and destruction but were also read by the missionaries, with a mixture of awe, trepidation, derision, and the will to destroy. At least some missionaries, including Lizana, Sánchez de Aguilar, and fray Andrés de Avendaño, used what they learned from such texts to interpret the Maya, to craft their own proselytizing message in terms familiar to the Maya, and to condemn them for idolatry.[14] The people who wrote the books were social actors with expert knowledge and the disposition to write and maintain books. The history they wrote about was the history in which they wrote: while there are clearly passages of the BCBs about the distant past, there are also many about contemporary colonial life. It is this living history that makes them valuable, a history fundamentally marked by *reducción*.

From a colonial perspective, the BCBs are, first and foremost, exemplars of a forbidden discourse. The missionaries associated them with the age before the cross, prejudicial falsehoods, the stuff of fables and idolatry, and the meetings of Maya men beyond the pale of surveillance. The intricacies of the calendar were fascinating but suspect. For these reasons, the books were hidden from the missionaries, and, as Sánchez de Aguilar suggests, *maestros* who had such books knew enough to flee from his prying questions. This missionary perspective played a role in orienting scholarship by reinforcing the idea that the books speak from outside the colonial world, just as their prohibition effectively forced them out of the colony as a normative space. When they speak about the past or the incommensurably different, they therefore seem to do so from a position of incommensurable difference. As long as we read these books in isolation from the other colonial discourse, the fallacy of this way of reading remains hidden. But as soon as we return to the language of the texts in its specificity and in the broader context, the frame of understanding shifts and the problem becomes stark. To be blunt, there is simply too much Christianized *Maya reducido* in the BCBs to think that these texts come from a position of sheer exteriority. Their writers were colonial subjects; even if they carved out spaces of discursive autonomy, they did so using much language that was itself the product of linguistic *reducción*.

From this perspective, the variations in phrasing between different versions of the same or similar texts become a major resource. The importance of cognate texts is not that it allows us to reconstruct an original master text. Rather, it allows us to resolve the reference of many key expressions and to reconstruct the grammatical and semantic frameworks of the scribes. For religious language, these frameworks include schemas or constellations of related ideas and phrases, so that use of a single term indexes and is often accompanied by other, related terms. The evidence adduced in this chapter demonstrates that doctrinal Maya, the converting word, was an important part of the scribal repertoire and the genre of the books. This in turn poses a formidable problem of method for the older way of reading these works. How can we be confident whether a passage such as the prophecy of Chilam Balam or Natzin Yabun Chen is an ancient text or, as I have argued here, a colonial one? The answer is that we cannot be confident in such judgments unless we undertake an in-depth analysis of *Maya reducido*, which has been lacking in the literature to date. Given what is now known about the language of the missions and the *cabildos*, it is obvious that doctrinal Maya was widely dispersed and was even designed to be transparent, readily fragmented into key phrases, and indexically grounded in doxa. That it found its way into the BCBs and prophecies is a proof that these books were part of the same discursive formation as the other genres studied here. They were prohibited and defined as outside *reducción*, but their exteriority and much of their language were in fact parts of *reducción*.

The references to Christian precepts and practices are a convincing indicator that the writers of the BCBs had learned the new religion—at least some of the copyists and some of the *doctrina*. That they wrote in *lengua reducida,* however, goes even further: they internalized the religion's meaning structures and ways of speaking, as these were canonized in *doctrina* and commensurated to Spanish in the dictionaries. The BCBs take their place alongside the *diccionarios, artes, doctrinas,* and notarial genres. All of them belong to the field of *reducción.* All of them are subject to iteration, cross-referencing, and regular ways of aligning the two languages. Both Spanish and Latin are in the background of the BCBs, as they were in all the missionary writings. But as I have discussed at length, translingual commensuration did not operate on words directly but on the broad semantic schemas into which they fit. Typically, *Maya reducido* rendered the meanings of European expressions transparent in compound and derived descriptors such as 'enter-water' for 'baptism', 'straight-cast' and 'untie sin' for 'confession', 'one-god' for the 'triune God', and 'enter-heart' for 'believe, convert'. Occasionally, a Spanish or Latin term is directly transposed into the Maya, but as we now know, this is only the coarsest indicator of *reducción*'s impact.

In Part I of this book, I suggested that the intercultural space occupied by *lenguas* and *ladinos,* the bilingual mediators, was more than just an encounter of two languages, one European and one Maya. Rather, each of these languages was already inclined toward the other. The missionary *lengua* who translated Spanish into Maya had to perform an analysis of the concepts for which each language stood and had to break down the ideas into pieces that could be rendered in the grammar and lexicon of Maya. Maya as the missionaries knew it was already oriented to Spanish and contained the neologisms, economical roots, and transparency of the *lengua reducida.* For the missionaries, Maya writings such as the BCBs were source material in their quest to convert the Maya and their language. Yet the sources were themselves already marked by the language of the missions. When missionaries in turn used this language to proselytize Maya people, they were using language the Maya already knew. We know the Maya were already familiar with the *lengua reducida,* because they used it in their own native writings. There is a profound circularity in the way each language is defined by its intimate connection with the other, yet each appears to stand apart from the other, as if independent of it. The closest we get to sheer independence from the translingual space of the colony are the hieroglyphic texts from the Maya side and the Latin prayers from the European side. These were formed not in relation to the colonial encounter but in relation to the much broader histories of Mesoamerica and the Catholic Church, respectively. Even the canonical *doctrina* in Maya was crafted in light of local usage, upon which it would have a generative and enduring impact. When the Book of Kaua reproduced the four basic prayers in Latin, it was attempting to incorporate this outside within itself. It took discourse whose source was outside the Maya world and made it interior, a part of the book. While this might appear to indicate Maya vulnerability to Church "influence," it has the effect of appropriating the sacred texts and bypassing the priests. From the missionary perspective, this was a dangerous breach, because it was beyond their control and because they expected unsupervised Maya to pervert the Christian message.

When the missionary translated from Latin or Spanish into Maya, he did the inverse, starting from a text that belonged to the inner sanctum of the faith, converting it to Maya, and projecting it into the exterior space of the Indios. In so doing, it simultaneously converted the indigenous language into a new Christianized version of itself. Meaning moved between languages that were at once external to each other and ongoingly affected by each other. It may be comforting to imagine an originary moment in which difference was sheer and circularity absent, but this has little to do with the way *reducción* worked. Once the processes of commensuration and conversion were set in motion, they became self-replicating, and neither language would ever again be the same. By its very portability, durability, and ubiquity in social life, language was the ideal and most generative medium of conversion. Although I have not attempted to analyze it here, anyone familiar with Yucatecan Spanish knows that it too has been marked by the long history of commensuration with Maya. Because my primary object has been the making of Maya, I have concentrated on this side of the relation. But the logic goes both ways.

But history is more than logic, and *reducción* was more than commensuration. The relation was profoundly asymmetric. Backed by a combination of brutal force, disease, charisma, and the highly coordinated reorganization of the social world, *reducción* was a total project. My thesis is that it could not have had the impact it did, were it not for the language by which it spread. And it is in the language that we find evidence of its most far-reaching consequences. Under *reducción*, multiple spheres of colonial life were organized in a coordinated fashion. This resulted in reinforcing homologies between the structure of space, *policía*, proper speech, and the subject who acted within the emerging colonial world. Genres and ways of speaking and writing circulated through the field, from the far reaches of the cathedral and convent to the *guardianías* to the *pueblos reducidos* and over the frontier to the so-called *despoblado* 'place without towns'. The grand and troubled movement of discourse, with its barriers and pathways, with or without authors, oral or written, sacred or perverse, is the story of *reducción* and its generative legacy.

Epilogue

Full Circle

The processes of conversion explored in this book had a penumbra of effects, including the making of modern Maya. Religion would become a cauldron of social change throughout the colonial and modern periods. To show the legacy of *reducción* in the nineteenth and twentieth centuries would require another book-length study. A few provocative examples will have to suffice.

In relation to the emergence of modern Maya discourse practices, my thesis has three parts. First, the linguistic processes of commensuration, translation, and iteration were central in driving changes in Maya. New forms and practices of expression emerged, and the basic translingual alignments of Maya with Spanish were established. Second, these and related processes were part of the larger project of *reducción,* which embedded *Maya reducido* in the *pueblos reducidos, guardianías,* and the entire apparatus of mission and governance. Third, *reducción* was highly concentrated in its logic, coordinating space, conduct, and language so that these were mutually reinforcing features of the colonial world. Through the proliferation of homologous organizational forms and ways of speaking, it became self-replicating. Of the three major spheres, it was language that spread most readily, and through discourse, *reducción* was dispersed far beyond the confines of the mission and *cabildo.* Let us look briefly at an example of this dispersal in the nineteenth century.

There was tremendous change in Yucatán during the nineteenth century, including independence from Spain in 1821, two attempts to separate from Mexico, in 1840 and 1845, the formal separation of Campeche as a state apart from Yucatán in 1858, and the rebellion that came to be known as the Guerra de Castas 'War of the Castes', in which Maya people rebelled against the domination of the Spanish and their descendants. The Caste War broke out in 1847 in the town of Tepich, Yucatán. Over the ensuing months, Maya rebels sacked and burned some two hundred fifty towns, virtually driving the *dzul* 'foreigner, wealthy person' out of the peninsula. Much of the territory gained was reclaimed by state troops in the following year, and by 1850, rebel forces had fled into the *montaña* to the southeast, in present-day Quintana Roo. There they established a social world apart, which maintained its independence from the state and federal government into the first decades of the twentieth century and to which Maya people of the area remain attached to this day.¹ What did this society on the frontier of a society look like?

The place to which the rebels retreated they called *Chan Santa Cruz* 'Little Holy Cross'. The name came from the central figure of resistance, a charismatic cross through which God spoke to the Maya. The cross appeared miraculously in the trunk of a great mahogany tree in late 1850, and it addressed the people in both speech and writing, through its mouthpiece, Juan de la Cruz. It spoke the words of the Trinity, the Father, Son, and Holy Spirit, and it assured the Maya that it would protect them from the Enemy, that is, the *dzul*. The time had come, it said, to throw them off the back of the *maseual* 'peasant' once and for all. What follows are some passages from the proclamation. The entire frame of reference and most of the key terms in Maya can be found in the *doctrinas* of Coronel and Beltrán—except the part where it says that the *dzul* is the Enemy, a term classically reserved for the Devil, the flesh, and the things of this world.

THE PROCLAMATION OF JUAN DE LA CRUZ (1850) (BRICKER 1981, 187 FF.)

+ *Jesus Maria tukaba Dios yumbil*	+ Jesus Mary in the name of God the father
ƴ *Dios Mehenbil*	and God the son
ƴ *tukaba Ds. Espiritu santo*	and in the name of God the Holy Spirit
[...]	[...]
Yn hach llamail Cristiano Cahex	My very beloved Christian towns
[...]	[...]
tumen ten tinsihseex	for it is I who created you
tumen ten tinloheex	for it is I who redeemed you
tumen ten tinvecah in ciliich kikel tavoklalex	for it is I who spilled my precious blood for you
[...]	[...]
he max matan llocsah ol tic invaalmah thane	Whosoever does not believe my commandments
bin ukam hun lukul numiah	Shall receive unbounded suffering
ti minan uxul	Without end
he max bin udzocbes invalmah thane	Whosoever fulfills my commandments
bin unahalt unohchil ingloria	Shall earn the greatness of my heaven
binix xan unahalt in llacunah	He shall also earn my love

binix xan inboybese llalan unooh inkab	I shall also shield him beneath my right hand
[. . .]	[. . .]
tac tuxul Caput Cuxtal	until the Final Resurrection
[. . .]	[. . .]
tumen dzoc ukuchul t ora	for the time has come
likbal yucatan yokol dzulob humpulili	for Yucatan to rise up over the *dzul* once and forever
[. . .]	[. . .]
Jesus Maria tukaba Ds yumbil	Jesus Mary in the name of God the father
Ds mehenbil	God the son
y Ds Espiritu santo Amen Jesus	And God the Holy Spirit Amen Jesus
(Bricker 1981, 187 ff.)	

The social world that developed around the talking cross of Chan Santa Cruz was the home of the people known as the *Cruzob* 'Crosses'. The Crosses were devoted to the care and veneration of the talking cross, which issued them directives, including the order to make war on the foreign oppressors and to acquire the necessary arms. A shrine was built around the cross, but this and the cross itself were destroyed by colonial troops in a dawn raid on March 23, 1851. This in turn triggered the appearance of three more crosses, 'daughters' of the first, all gifted with speech. According to Villa Rojas (1945), the initial shrine was a thatch structure where the cross was kept out of sight in an inner sanctum called *Gloria* 'Heaven'. This was attached to a church, where the communicants sat to receive the word. Eventually the shrine was rebuilt in stone and renamed *Balam Nah* 'Jaguar House', and in 1860 a church was built around it.

Services were said to be held daily in the church of the cross, with *maestros* performing Mass before dawn and rosaries and novenas held in the evening. The town of Chan Santa Cruz became a pilgrimage site for the surrounding area, with fiestas of the Virgin of the Cross (December 8) and the Holy Cross (May 3). Other crosses appeared in Tulum on the coast (an archaeological site contemporaneous with Mayapán), Chan Cah (where the Book of Chilam Balam of Chan Cah was found), Chun Pom, and San Antonio Muyil. But none of these other crosses rivaled the three daughters in terms of authority or regional draw.

In 1901, General Ignacio Bravo entered Chan Santa Cruz in a bid to overthrow the still independent Cruzob. He found the town abandoned; its inhabitants, evidently forewarned, had fled, later establishing themselves at Xcacal, about sixty-five kilometers to the northwest. It was in Xcacal that Villa Rojas (1945) did his fieldwork in the 1940s, among the descendants of the Cruzob from Chan Santa Cruz. The place consisted of a head town with a church and community building in the center and four mounds with standing crosses on them farther out at the intercardinal points. Around the head town, Xcacal proper, there were eight satellite towns, each with a small church and several with additional *oratorios* 'chapels'. Among the eight satellites was one called Tusik, from which one of the Books of Chilam Balam gets its name. With a population of 116, Tusik had a church plus five chapels. In Redfield's famous folk-urban continuum, it was this town that would epitomize the extreme folk end, assuring it a prominent place in the modern history of ethnography. Looking at the whole of Xcacal Guardia, as the cluster of nine places was called, we are face-to-face with the radial structure of the *guardianía,* with holiness and authority in the head town, lesser places of worship in the *visitas,* and the cross as the central organizing symbol.

I have barely scratched the surface of the Caste War and its descendants, but a few things are clear. From the protection of the Holy Cross, the Spanish were excluded as Enemies to be overthrown once and for all. This, we might say, would put an end to the "perpetual *reducción*" of the colonial period. And yet the veneration of the cross, its capacity to protect, the emergence of a church with routine worship and a fiesta cycle, the *Gloria* 'heaven' of the inner sanctum, even the radial structure of Xcacal Guardia—these are all forms that made their first and repeated appearance among the Maya through the project of *reducción.* Ironically, *reducción* is being used to cast off the system of *reducción.* This disposition to organize and to cultivate a pious subject may stem from the fact that the original People of the Cross came overwhelmingly from areas that were within the core zone of the colony, including Sací Valladolid, which has been a major mission center since the sixteenth century.

But when the forms of conversion crossed the frontier, the circle closed. The products of *reducción* became so thoroughly Maya that they protected the Maya from the foreigners. The Trinity would now speak in Maya, without the need for any Spanish or Latin gloss. Jesus would walk the land of Yucatán, and the *maseual* 'peasant', sanctified, would be protected. In this logic, Christianity is incorporated but fundamentally alienated from its erstwhile owners. God is now Maya. This alienation is foreshadowed in the Books of Chilam Balam, into which prayers and precepts of Christianity are incorporated in the living archive of Mayas writing for Mayas.

. . .

The final examples are from my own fieldwork in Oxkutzcab, about ten kilometers south of Maní. They show the presence of doctrinal Maya as powerfully as does the Talking Cross, but with a twist. The social order of the People of the Cross was religious, political, military, and formally institutionalized in a church. It was, in a sense, a state religion. The case we end on is the opposite: it involves a charismatic shaman, called a *hmèen* in Maya, whose practice lay outside the pale of any formal institution (but in a broad field of ritual experts and health care providers). The *hmèen* is the present-day descendant of the Post-Classic curers and the *ah kin*, and perhaps the *maestro cantor* of the colonial period. The ritual practices of *hmèen* and *ah kin* defined the exterior arch-Enemy of *reducción*. The fact that this exteriority thrived *inside* the colony was part of what so incited the missionaries during the long campaigns to extirpate idolatry, as they discovered that apparently trustworthy *maestros* and *indios de confianza* were also practicing *ah kin* priests. The Ritual of the Bacabs and similar texts in the Books of Chilam Balam would likely have been performed by *hmèen* curers.

I had done about thirteen months of ethnographic fieldwork on the outskirts of Oxkutzcab when I got to know Don Chabo, a prominent *hmèen* 'shaman'. It was 1980, and I would go on to work with Don Chabo for sixteen more years, until his death in early 1996. Don Chabo was born in Maní, and many of his patients came from there. He told me several times that when he died he would become a tree in the local forest, like the ancients who, succumbing to the Spanish, fled into the forest to enchant themselves into trees. Chilam Balam, Ah Kin Chi, and Kukulkan had all become trees, and he would do the same. Along with Indio Mayab, Ah Kin Coba, the *ah canan* 'guardians', and legions of Catholic saints, they also became spirits whom Don Chabo invoked in prayer on a daily basis. Like other *hmèen,* he officiated at major collective rituals relating to agriculture and domestic space, practiced divination using *sáastúun* crystals, and treated illnesses of various kinds. In his house he maintained an altar on which *santos* and a cross stood, a natural cruciform cut from the branches of a tree some thirty years earlier, when he underwent the initiatory rigors of becoming a *hmèen.* At that altar, he performed many private ceremonies, as well as the semipublic diagnosis and treatment of patients. The simplest of the curing ceremonies is known as a *santiguar* 'sanctification', the same term for a blessing in Christian practice (Hanks 1984) and one of the ordinary terms used to describe the act of making the sign of the cross on oneself or another. Don Chabo's *santiguar* involved performing a prayer *(payalchi, resar)* about ten minutes in length, in front of the altar, with the patient looking at the *santos* and concentrating on becoming well. While praying, Don Chabo brushed the patient with fresh cut flowers or branches of the *sipche* tree. Like every other ritual genre performed by Don Chabo, the *santiguar* began and ended with the sign of the cross. In its course, scores of Maya spirits and Christian saints were named and "lowered" by prayer to the altar (using the same phrasing found in the colonial dictionary for Mass as 'the priest lowers God to the altar'). In a rather complicated way, the prayer recapitulated the crucifixion of Christ and his resurrection, which it applied to the patient in order to cleanse and restore him or her.[2]

Contemporary shamanic Maya is saturated with apparently Christian imagery, albeit reframed in ways that would please no missionary. The shaman presents himself at the altar as a sinner, begging for God's intervention, *cinuoko ol*

'I weep-heart (beg)'.[3] Virtually all genres of shamanic prayer in Yucatec Maya begin and end with signs of the cross and invoke by name numerous Christian saints, as well as all three persons of the Trinity. Over the course of its unfolding, the *santiguar* retells the crucifixion of Christ, pausing when it arrives at Mount Calvary and the holy church of Jerusalem, to say the prayer:

kirich cruz tocon ti c ahualob	Holy cross protect us from our enemies
yumile dios yumbil,	lord God the father
dios mehenbil	God the son
dios espiritu santo	God the Holy Spirit
in yum	My lord

At the end of the same prayer, Don Chabo paused, placed his right hand upon the head of the patient, took a breath, and said:

Padre mio saas usipil untul pecador	My father forgive the trespasses of a sinner
Uch umentic nucuch consulta tuchun a mesa Jesu Christo	When he makes a great consultation at the foot of your altar
Jesu Christo inyum tech unohochilech	Jesus Christ my lord, you are the greatest one,
Udoctorilech uluumi le keban,	The doctor of the earth of sin,
Uch in thanic a santo espiritu	I have spoken your holy spirit
Aueensic ten a cichkelem noh akab yokol le cuerpo.	For you to lower your beautiful right hand upon the body
Bentisiste Jesu Christo yetel a poder	Bless it Jesus Christ with your power
Nombrart akaba yokol in yum	Name your name upon it, my lord.
Tukaba Jesu Christo, Dios padre, Dios spiritu santo	In the name of Jesus Christ, God the Father, God the Holy Spirit

As with the Books of Chilam Balam, Don Chabo's ritual language includes many elements that appear to come from outside Christianity. There are scores of Maya deities and several Maya genres—such as the *ch'áa cháak* 'rain' ceremony and the *hetz lú'um* 'stabilize land' ceremony, itself extremely close in form to the Maní land survey of 1552. In my opinion, these are likely to have antecedents in precolonial Maya society. But both the Books of Chilam Balam and the shaman's song also incorporate a wealth of *Maya reducido,* and with it the Christian frame of reference in which it was first developed. Still, this is no version of Christianity that would settle the heart of a missionary. It is outside church doxa and beyond the supervision of any priest. The saints, the planets, and God himself commingle with Maya divinities, who become ex officio members of the Trinity through the mediation of the Holy Spirit.

At some point in this long-term process, Maya Christianity has become autochthonous. The cross of the shaman is not man-made or blessed by the Church but grows organically in the trees of the forest, as the talking cross of Chan Santa Cruz did over a century earlier. The forest is in turn watched over by Maya spirits called *ah cananob* 'guardians', a term familiar from the missions and from the very earliest written documents in the Chronicle of Maní. Although Don Chabo did not urge rebellion, his practice embodied a kind of frank autonomy and insubordination to both the Catholic Church and the Protestant denominations now common in Yucatán. Just as surely as the Talking Cross of Chan Santa Cruz was an appropriation and a memorial to *reducción*, Don Chabo's practice affirmed that the core symbols of conversion had become native if not "indigenous." In the age of the cross, words designed to convert had themselves been converted. In this late iteration, *reducción* finds its most lasting impact as a force for change: *Maya reducido* has flowered into the language of what was forbidden and denigrated. It is the language of what is sacred not for the priest but for the shaman. There was no containing the cycles of conversion, or the processes of meaning making that they set in motion.

NOTES

PREFACE

1. The bibliography on idolatry in early colonial Yucatán is extensive. Interested readers should consult the work of Farriss, Scholes and colleagues, Clendinnen, Quezada, González Cicero, Bracamonte y Sosa, and especially Chuchiak, all of whom are cited in the references.

CHAPTER 1

1. Throughout this book I use several different terms to refer to the indigenous people of Yucatán, today commonly called Yucatec Maya: Maya, indigenous, native, Indio, Indian, and *natural(es)*. None of these terms is wholly adequate, and all have specific drawbacks. Indio and Indian are both potentially offensive and are not terms I would use in reference to contemporary Mayas. "Indio" in particular is a negative term in modern usage, virtually an ethnic slur. Like the Spanish *natural*, I use these terms only when speaking from the vantage point of colonial Spanish missionaries and authorities, for whom they are the typical terms, and Indio in particular was a legal category. "Native" I use occasionally and strictly heuristically to distinguish the Maya people from the European intruders. It becomes problematic as soon as we have a growing population of colonial people born, raised, and living out their days in Yucatán, only some of whom are indigenous. Indigenous or *indígena* refers to the people autochthonous to the peninsula. Whereas Spanish-descended creoles in Yucatán are arguably native, they are never described as indigenous in this book. Finally, the term "Maya" is both the best and the most problematic, because it links the indigenous people of Yucatán to their distinctive history, culture, and language, and yet what this book examines is precisely the transformation of the world of the "Maya." As I show, the language that we commonly call "Maya"

NOTES TO PAGES 2-4

is the product of *reducción,* which means it is not exclusively "Maya," emphatically not in any precolonial sense. Like "mestizo" in modern Yucatán, these categories are notoriously difficult to define since they lead at least three lives, as pseudotechnical terms, as terms used by those whom they designate, and as terms used by others who designate and talk about Yucatecan society. For discussion of these issues, see Castillo Cocom 2005; Montejo 1999; Redfield 1941; Warren 1998.

2. This plan does not correspond to the actual layout of Spanish towns, as George Foster (1960) observed. Rather, it corresponds to an emerging ideal in Spanish urban planning.

3. The intellectual and other labor that missionaries put into learning about the indigenous cultures in New Spain and Yucatán was quite remarkable. Ricard (1995, 109–30) discusses the case of Sahagún, the ethnographic and linguistic research he conducted, and the ultimate difficulty he had publishing his multivolume masterwork. Interestingly, when Sahagún was meeting resistance from the other religious, it was Francisco de Toral who encouraged and protected him (Ricard 1995, 114). Toral will become a major player in Yucatán, where he was appointed as the first bishop. Ricard outlines the publications of missionaries in native languages, listing no fewer than eighty works written by Franciscans and smaller numbers by members of other orders.

4. Ricard (1995, 106–8) discusses the missionary destruction of indigenous buildings and the 1530 Crown order that the stones from destroyed temples be used in constructing churches.

5. Burke (1992, 96–111) follows a similar line of reasoning, arguing in favor of the ethnography of speaking, semiotics, and structuralism as productive frameworks in which to describe historical processes. Bauman (1983, 1–19) sketches such an approach in much more detail than Burke and uses it to investigate the emergence of Quaker linguistic style and the fundamental role of silence in seventeenth-century Quaker speech. Grounded as it is in linguistic anthropology, Bauman's emphasis on language ideology and situated uses of religious language is very close in spirit to the present book. Aside from the obvious substantive differences in the two cases, my approach differs from Bauman's in its engagement with practice theory (especially the ideas of field and habitus, which occur throughout this book), the centrality of translation in the Yucatecan case, and the time frame over which I am tracing *reducción* (about two hundred years, as opposed to the thirty-nine-year period on which Bauman focuses). Also, whereas Bauman seeks to reconstruct the settings of speech action, I have focused more on genres and the evidence they provide of spread of specifically colonial language. Notwithstanding such contrasts, Bauman's study is among the closest to this one in terms of the way it attempts to combine linguistic anthropology with history and the affinity of his theoretical framework with mine. Both of us have produced what Burke (1992, 163) called "braided narratives," in which analysis is interwoven with the telling of a story. My use of practice theory is outlined in Hanks (1987, 1990, 2005) and is consistent with Certeau (1988, pt. 1). For further comparison, see Rafael's (1993) study of translation and religious conversion of Tagalog people (Philippines) under early Spanish rule. The Tagalog case is much closer substantively to the present one than are the Quakers, but the picture that emerges from colonial Maya is quite different from that of colonial Tagalog, and my assumptions about language and meaning contrast with Rafael's.

6. The idea that a grammar is a form of *reducción* is not new to the colonial context. It is explicitly present in Nebrija's grammar of Castilian, and in any case it is consistent with the sense of "ordering" entailed by analysis. What appears to be novel in the colonial context is the foregrounding of *reducción* as a way of altering, or we might say, disciplining, the language as practiced.

7. Gibson (1966, 71) and Ricard (1995, 104) emphasize that the Spanish project was aimed at a total remaking of indigenous beliefs and a break from the indigenous past. Whatever the Spanish goal in Yucatán, their break with the Maya past was always partial, both because they recognized the Maya aptitude for urban living and tried to use it to their advantage and because they conducted the conversions in Maya. This guaranteed that they would engage with Maya ideas, if only to convey their message. Where they did seek a sheer rupture with the past was in the matter of false belief and idolatry, but neither of these is an accurate exemplar of the broader project, which was a mixture of continuity with discontinuity.

8. Narrowly understood, conversion could be understood as the initial transformation of the indigenous group to Christianity, usually taking about ten years, after which the aim was to *maintain* Christianity. According to Gibson (1966, 81), the maintenance phase was primarily in the hands of the secular clergy. Given the setbacks and the persistence of the frontier in Yucatán, however, this ideal was rarely realized. *Reducción* continued, as we will see, and the Franciscans maintained power over parishes much longer than Gibson suggests. Hence for historical reasons, not only theoretical ones, a broader understanding of conversion is called for.

9. My position here is consistent with Comaroff and Comaroff (1991), although my use of terms differs. They define "conversion" narrowly as religious transformation, relegating this to a subordinate role in the overall changes wrought by Christian missionization in southern Africa. By contrast, I wish to emphasize the connections between conversions at different levels and therefore define the term more broadly, which leads me to give it a central place in the history. We agree that the key phenomena are broader, less individual, and surely less belief-bound than traditional "conversion" implies. Our difference in emphasis may be due to the difference between early modern Franciscans in the New World and nineteenth-century Protestants in Africa.

10. There is a growing literature in the anthropology of religion that treats language as a central aspect of religious practice and conversion and the spread of religious language into other communicative practices. For comparative studies of contemporary America, see Crapanzano 2000; Harding 2000. For studies of Christianity introduced through colonization and interacting with indigenous systems of thought, see Keane 2007; Robbins 2001, 2007; and Schieffelin 2007. For another comparative case, see Rumsey's (2008) study of the introduction and reception of Christian Confession by the Ku Waru people of Papua New Guinea.

11. Ricard (1995, 387–421) and Farriss (1984) give more nuanced descriptions of the effects of missionization upon indigenous peoples, emphasizing resistance to but also deep engagement with the new religion. Taylor (1996, 4–7) provides a thoughtful assessment of what he calls "slow-moving and elusive changes," which leads him to recast what some call "syncretism" as "congruence and enlargement" of the sphere of indigenous religion.

12. The Franciscan experience, it should be emphasized, is only part of the story. Gibson (1966, 77–78) and especially Taylor (1996) show that the church was far from monolithic. It is well known that by the 1570s the Crown came to favor secular clergy over the regulars, and we see thereafter a declining proportion of the Yucatecan missions in Franciscan hands (as well as the expulsion of the Jesuits in 1767 [Gibson 1966, 83 ff.]). However, as we will see, they defined the original template and remained a major presence well into the eighteenth century (Chuchiak 2007).

13. According to Chuchiak (2000b, 150), secular clergy prosecuted 65.9 percent of all idolatry charges during the seventeenth century, and 69 percent of cases brought by Franciscans were by *guardianes* 'guardians' in charge of parishes. The upshot is that Franciscan missionaries below the rank of *guardián* played a distinctly less active role in extirpation than did the secular clergy. This may be one reason that the Maya are so uniformly negative in their descriptions of the seculars in their own writings.

14. On the history of the Franciscan order, there is a vast literature. See, for example, Gómez Canedo 1977; Moorman 1968; Putallaz 1997; Short 1989, 1999; *Dizionario Francescano* (1983). For primary writings, including the Rule, see Guerra 1993.

15. The rigorous way of living, the depth of poverty, and the imperative to be exemplary to which a Franciscan submits is clearly evident in the Rule of Saint Francis (Guerra 1993, 87–120).

16. Covarrubias (1995 [1611], 709) has two entries under *lengua* that refer to human agents. The first is *"el intérprete que declara una lengua con otra"*; the second, *"el fiel, latine examen es dicho algunas veces lengua."*

17. Cogolludo and Lizana both give the biographies of some of the influential missionaries whom they dub *lenguas* and *"los grandes ministros y lenguas de estos indios."*

18. Taylor (1996, 94–97) makes the important point that this emphasis on knowing native languages was beginning to shift by the second half of the eighteenth century, when the native languages came to be seen as an impediment to ministry and in any case less important as a qualification for the clergy than proper training in the religion. He cites the royal *cédula* of April 16, 1770, calling for merit, not language, to be a criterion in selecting priests (1996, 575 n. 20). In Yucatán, during the period under study in this book, the premium on knowing Maya was not in question.

19. So under the best conditions, a *guardianía* would ideally have several religious who were *lengua,* but if only one was *lengua,* it would be the *guardián,* the most senior. Notice that, given the definition of *lengua,* a local Maya speaker who helped out in the *guardianía* would never be described with this term.

20. My estimate of the total is extrapolated from Miram and Miram 1988, 1:pt. 7.

21. The Book of Kaua is discussed in detail in chapter 11, drawing heavily on Bricker and Miram's (2002) critical edition of the work.

22. From the sixteenth century onward, New Spain was marked by Christocentric devotion, and the cross was a dominant symbol, although not the only one (Taylor 2005). It had a central place in the entire mission in Yucatán and was one of the most powerful symbols to be appropriated by the Maya.

23. Ricard (1995, 130) presents a very interesting discussion of the missionary fear that certain translations would produce ambiguity whereby a native idea remained hidden in

the background, thus undercutting the desired Christian meaning. In such cases, among others, missionaries opted to retain the Spanish term in otherwise indigenous utterances. The idea of a "borrowing" is therefore misleading both because it masks the active role of the missionaries in producing the usage and because it puts the indigenous language in the position of receiving a loan, whereas it is the means of codifying a usage.

24. I use this term in a way roughly equivalent to Liu (1995), for whom "translingual practice" designates new linguistic forms that arise, circulate, and acquire legitimacy in a "host language" as a result of language contact mediated by various practices. Although she does not use this term, Schieffelin (2007) outlines a similar process of dispersion of concepts introduced by missionaries into a local language and considers linguistic practice central in missionization. In Schieffelin's case, the setting is Bosavi, Papua New Guinea, in the 1970s, the people are Kaluli, and the missionaries are fundamentalist Christians. She focuses on the infusion of novel ways of conceiving and relating to time. Like the Catholic missions in colonial New Spain and Yucatán, these Christian missionaries made the decision to evangelize in the vernacular language. Schieffelin shows how the Christianized language spread through sermons, lessons, and discussions of the Bible and doctrine and thereby became part of the self-identity of its speakers.

Notwithstanding the dramatic differences between the two cases, both the Maya and the Kaluli missions involved erasure and reformation of the language of the converts, and translation played a critical role in both cases.

25. The *Diccionario de Autoridades* (1990), 5:586, defines *república* as the government of the public and distinguishes three kinds: monarchy, aristocracy, and democracy. The same term applies to the public cause or interest and by extension to some *pueblos* 'towns'. When applied to the indigenous groups in America, it already entails, therefore, a sense of communal interest and governance. Thus the settlements of fugitive Maya in the southern forests might be indigenous, but they were not *repúblicas* in the view of the Spanish.

26. According to Bracamonte y Sosa and Solís Robleda (1996), the *principales* constituted semiformal councils whose influence over local affairs was considerable. They also see in this group of local elders the maintenance of a relatively autonomous native voice in local affairs.

27. It is very likely that colonial Maya entailed the kind of continuum that Hill and Hill (1986) discovered in contemporary Mexico between "*legítimo mexicano*" and "*castellano*," that is, legitimate Nahuatl and Spanish. Just as speakers of Mexicano consider both ends of the continuum effectively unattainable, so too modern Yucatec Maya speakers invariably say that the language they speak is not "*legítimo Maya*" but a mixed, imperfect version of it. This double consciousness, to speak Maya and not-Maya at the same time, is the product of the historical forces described in this book. There is enough variation in the corpus of colonial writings by Maya speakers that it may be possible one day to define a continuum of variants arrayed between the two languages and produced for strategic purposes. It is equally likely that missionaries invoked different ranges on the scale, according to their aims or audience. To demonstrate these aspects of the colonial sociolinguistics will require further research and is beyond the scope of this book.

28. Mario Humberto Ruz pointed out (pers. com.) that in Guatemala the expression "*indio lengua*" was used in reference to the kind of speaker that in Yucatán was called

"*indio ladino,*" that is, an indigenous individual fluent in Spanish. To my knowledge, this expression never occurs in the Yucatecan documentation, where the "*lengua*" and the "*ladino*" are consistently complementary.

29. The relevant Maya terminology includes *tzolthan* 'explain-language' and *ualkesik ti than* 'change to language', which are explored in part 3.

30. I do not know at what point, if ever, local scribal apprenticeship took over this training function from the church.

31. See Ricard 1995, 100–103, on missionary ambivalence about the indigenous cultures.

32. Two comparative studies of historical discourse formations that have influenced my thinking about the Maya case are Bernard Cohn's (1996) study of British colonialism in India and Johannes Fabian's (1986) fascinating account of the codification and spread of Swahili in the Congo, under European colonialism. Both Cohn and Fabian recognize the pivotal role of language in the formation of the colony, and while their cases differ profoundly from the present one, the bringing together of missionary linguistics with different genres of usage, the primacy of discursive formation over individual intention, and the objectification of the indigenous language(s) are common to all three cases.

CHAPTER 2

1. Gibson (1964) emphasizes this point in relation to the Spanish view of the Aztec in New Spain.

2. In this sense the Yucatec case makes an interesting contrast to the British among the Tswana, as described by Comaroff and Comaroff (1991). While the British sought to instill a sense of colonial orderliness akin to *policía,* it was much more focused on the domestic sphere than was the Spanish *reducción* of Yucatán. In the latter case, the domestic sphere is not thematized.

3. For a very useful summary of current research, see Sharer 2006; and see Masson 2000; Masson, Peraza Lope, and Hare 2002.

4. Quezada (1993) presents an important synthesis of Maya political organization just before and into the early colonial period. He argues that the *cuchcabal* was actually one of three key elements in the political system, the other two being the *batabil* 'chiefship' and the *tzucub,* a kin-based group. According to Quezada, these three define the organizational dimensions of the Maya "provinces." The term *cuchcabal* consists of three parts: *cuch* 'to bear, carry', *cab* 'earth, land', and *-al,* a nominalizing suffix. Hence it glosses something like 'borne earth,' as in a region under the responsibility of a leader who functions as an 'earth bearer'. For the most thorough and current understanding of the Post-Classic political system and its relation to territory, see Okoshi 1994, 2006a, 2006b.

5. Roys's reconstruction of the Maya "provinces" presents a deceptively simple picture of the political geography. For critical revision, see Okoshi 1994, 2006a, 2006b. Of particular importance is Okoshi's demonstration that the polities were not territorially bounded spaces, with clear borders, but were rather center-satellite spaces whose satellite places were bound by affiliation but not necessarily spatial proximity. Okoshi's portrayal of Post-Classic organization is strikingly similar to the radial spaces of the *reducción.*

6. Some of this decline in the number of places was doubtless also driven by the over-all decline in population as a result of disease and the traumas of conquest.

7. Thanks to William Taylor for calling my attention to the 1549 royal *cédula*.

8. In recent years there have appeared several important works that provide an excellent basis for understanding López Medel's perspective and activities, including his relation to debates ongoing in Spain at the time, such as the one that raged between Las Casas and Sepúlveda on the legal basis of the conquest, and to the middle position struck by Vitoria and the jurists of Salamanca (see Ares Queija 1993; Pereña et al. 1992; Pereña 1996; and references cited therein).

9. Here we see López Medel explicitly denying that Maya society was orderly, a position that would be contradicted by Landa in his *Relación* and by many subsequent missionaries. The difference may be due to the relative lack of experience of López Medel in Yucatán, to the fact that he wrote at an earlier moment in the process of *reducción,* or to the rhetorical fact that he is after all justifying the imposition of a new order, and this is easiest if the Maya are caricatured as lacking all sociality.

10. López Medel does not introduce the *cabildo* system of government as part of his *Ordenanzas.* In fact, he was opposed to the immediate application of the *cabildo* form, on the grounds that the Indian towns were not yet ready to manage such a system. Rather, they were to be taught to do so over several years, starting with a simplified system of caciques and *principales,* whose jurisdictions and spheres of authority would increase in scope as they demonstrated the ability to act according to proper norms. Nonetheless, it is clear from the *Ordenanzas* and from López Medel's other writings that it is toward such a system that he is working. In like fashion, he was opposed to the abolition of slavery and in favor of its gradual phasing out over a period of years. In both cases, the *Ordenanzas* laid the rudimentary foundations on which *policía* and governance would be built over time (see the excellent discussion in Ares Queija 1993, 86–102).

11. I read the word *coyoles* (a kind of local fruit) as a typo for *coyotes* (intermediaries in any sort of transaction, and especially in machinations of dubious legitimacy; Santamaría 1992, 308). It is also possible that it designates the fruit, on which messages were marked, hence the material bearer of a sign (Mario Humberto Ruz, pers. com.). In the Castilian of the time, *seña* designates the sign of an agreement between two or more parties, and such signs as the military banner uniting a group. The doubtless related term *señal* is in some uses equivalent to *seña,* whereas in others it is the index of something absent—such as the paw prints of an animal now gone (Covarrubias 1995 [1611], 890; cf. *Diccionario de Autoridades* 1990 [1737], 6:folio 84). In this context, I read the term as meaning a sign bringing together the group for illicit meetings.

12. "Carta a los Reyes de Bohemia, Gobernadores de España, March 25, 1551," reproduced in Ares Queija 1993, 298–323.

13. On this episode, see particularly Chuchiak 2000b, pt. 1; Clendinnen 1987, chap. 6; González Cicero 1978; Hanks 1986.

14. Gerhard (1993, 29) cites three main campaigns of forced resettlements, 1570, 1591–1605, and 1761.

15. It is not entirely clear what *"pueblo reducido"* entails in this context. We know from the reports of provincials and bishops and the Maya notarial documents that most of

these were inhabited population centers, of differing size and importance, and that many of them were functioning as *repúblicas* in the sense of having recognized officers who appear as signatories with titles on documents of various genres.

16. Farriss (1984) and Clendinnen (1980) have observed the collaboration between Maya and the colonists, and Gibson (1966, 136-59) discusses the more general role of indigenous mediaries in colonial society.

17. For more extensive discussion of the landscape and its transformation, see Clendinnen 1980; Quezada 1993; Hanks 2003.

18. See also Okoshi 2006a, 87; Quezada 1993.

19. This statement omits Ciudad Real's compendious *Tratado Curioso y Docto de las Grandezas de la Nueva España,* written in the last decade of the sixteenth century. Ciudad Real had been selected to serve for four years as the secretary to fray Alonso Ponce, during which time the two made *visitas* of many hundreds of towns throughout New Spain, including Yucatán. This was between 1584 and 1588, and according to García and Castillo Farreras, editors of the modern edition (1976, CXXXIII), they inspected a total of 182 convents, 107 churches, and 31 *capillas de indios* throughout New Spain, Guatemala, Yucatán, El Salvador, Honduras, and Nicaragua. In Yucatán (including Campeche), the *Tratado* gives brief descriptions of 23 convents, 7 churches, and 22 *capillas de indios.* This work provides a wealth of information, including a vivid sense of its author's taste for detail and descriptions of the sometimes meager facilities of the convents. The descriptions of Calkiní (CXXXVII), Conkal (CXL), Ichmul, Izamal (CXLVII), and Tizimín (CLXVIII) are particularly rich. The most detailed of all is Ciudad Real's description of Uxmal, which they visited in September 1588. I have not attempted to integrate this work into the present chapter because of its sheer scope and size.

20. "Carta de fray Hernando de Sopuerta con una memoria de los frailes franciscanos que sirven en la provincia de Yucatán, año 1580," AGI, Guatemala 170, in Scholes et al. 1938, 48-50; "Carta de don Guillén de las Casa, gobernador de Yucatán, a Su Majestad con una memoria de los conventos, vicarías y pueblos de la provincia, Mérida, 25 de marzo, 1582," Archivo Histórico Nacional, Madrid, Cartas de Indias, Caja 2, num. 21, in Scholes et al. 1938, 51-65; "Carta del Obispo don Fray Gregorio de Montalvo a Su Majestad con un memorial sobre el estado de la iglesia de Yucatán, Mérida, 6 de enero 1582," AGI, Mexico 374, in Scholes et al. 1938, 66-94; Fray Pedro Cardete, "Memorial que el Provincial y Definidores de la provincia de San Joseph de Yucatán evián al Real Consejo de las Indias en el corte del Rey don Felipe nuestro Señor. Año de 1586," AGI, Mexico 3167, in Scholes et al. 1938, 95-101; "Provincial y definidores de la provincia de San Joseph de Yucatán su Majestad, con relación de las guardianías y doctrinas de la dicha provincia," AGI, Mexico 12/13, in Scholes et al. 1938, 152-62.

The title *difinidor* is spelled as shown in the early colonial sources from Yucatán, including Coronel and San Buenaventura. By the eighteenth century it is sometimes spelled *definidor.* The *Diccionario de Authoridades* (1732) shows both forms, whereas Covarrubias (1611) shows only *difinidor.* In citing sources, I have attempted to accurately reproduce the form as spelled in the version cited. In neutral contexts I use *difinidor.*

21. For a very critical assessment of the state of the missions, see "Carta del Obispo de Yucatán, Fray Juan Izquierdo a Su Majestad con un memorial sobre la necesidad de que

los frailes dejen media docena de guardianías para que se den a clerigos, Mérida, 10 de abril 1601," AGI, Mexico 369, in Scholes et al. 1938, 129–32.

22. For a description of various aspects of the broader framework, see Greenleaf 1995; Ricard 1995; Chuchiak 2000b.

23. Chuchiak (2000a, 9 ff.) mentions that as provincial, Ciudad Real also ordered *reducciones*. He lists seven that took place between 1604 and 1624, accounting for approximately 22,000 Maya *indios reducidos*.

24. One bit of evidence that Yucatán was peripheral in Farriss's sense may be the very fact that the Franciscans held on to a significant portion of the missions well into the eighteenth century, whereas elsewhere the shift to the seculars was apparently faster and more thorough (Gibson 1966, 77 ff.). The pattern in Yucatán is more what one would expect of a frontier zone.

25. Farriss 1984, 39. Compare summaries of 1610 *limosnas* in corn and money, in Scholes et al., 1938, 152–62. See also Cook and Borah 1974; Patch 1993, 28–30.

26. See Cook and Borah 1974 on the category 'tributary'.

27. Bracamonte y Sosa (2001, 16) cites examples of rebellion in 1565, 1639–41, 1648, 1668–73, 1678, and 1700.

28. The most thorough discussion of Maya ritual practices that persisted in the early colonial period is Chuchiak 2000b.

29. Chuchiak (2000a, 2000b) covers the case of Sahcabchén in great detail and summarizes the confiscation of books. Chuchiak mentions a single confiscated book at Chancenote rather than the three cited by Solís Robleda and Peniche.

30. See documents pertaining to Oxkutzcab at this time in Quezada and Okoshi 2001.

31. The Maya demand here effectively reciprocates the offer of love from the Franciscans, and by distinguishing them from other Europeans, the Maya are echoing Franciscan exceptionalism.

32. Frutos Delgado was an infamous abuser of the Maya, discussed at length by Farriss (1984) and Restall (1997).

33. Chuchiak's (2000a) point that not all Maya fugitives were apostate is pointedly relevant here. The Franciscans could address fugitives who might still be Christian, since abandoning the colony did not necessarily imply abandoning the faith. On the other hand, the implication of Chuchiak's distinction is that in the *montaña* region there were both Christians (lapsed but not apostate) and non-Christians, some of whom were apostate. From our perspective, it is the commingling of these different relations to Christianity that is important. It may help explain how Christian ideas spread so far into the *montaña*.

34. For discussion of *trasuntos*, see Quezada and Okoshi 2001, 33–34.

35. This gesture is also documented in the papers of the Xiu of Yaxá (Quezada and Okoshi 2001, 70, 81, 114).

CHAPTER 3

1. Bourdieu 1977, 1993; cf. Hanks 1990, 2005.

2. Chuchiak (2000b, 172–73) presents a useful summary of the "public sins" that came within the jurisdiction of the bishops. The first ten, and evidently most grave, sins were

against God and included idolatry and heresy, witchcraft, sorcery, conjuring and divination, and "superstitions." Chuchiak provides an impressive outline of the actual ritual practices that persisted as "public sins" through the colonial period. His main source of evidence is the inquisitional records and the writings of European clergy or officials. This suggests that the extensive complex of practices, places, and objects that he outlines was known by the missionaries. The inquisitional trials, the gathering of testimony, and the confiscating of books and "idols" were all ways of gathering intelligence about the Maya, a sort of fieldwork in extremis. Thus even as they implemented *reducción*, they knew that their efforts were being undercut. They knew there was a limit beyond which the circularities of *reducción* could not seem to reach.

3. Okoshi (2006a) makes the point that Post-Classic Maya political geography was organized in the same way. Disputing Roys's well-known portrait of Yucatán as organized into bounded *cacicazgos,* Okoshi argues that Maya polities were not bounded territories but instead center-dependency structures, in which dependencies were not necessarily adjacent but were tied to the center by affiliation linked to lineage. The result is that dependent places were interspersed such that two or more adjacent ones could be affiliated with distinct centers. On such a landscape, it makes no sense to speak of bounded territories because the centers do not define continuous spaces with discrete boundaries. In like fashion, the *cabeceras* 'head towns' of the *guardianías* were centers, and their dependent satellites, the *visitas,* were defined not by proximity but by dependency. Given that the *guardianía* system is far more general than Yucatán, this correspondence with the Post-Classic Maya system is evidently serendipitous rather than the result of a local missionary strategy.

4. For discussion of center-periphery models, see Burke 1992, 79–84.

5. *Parcialidad* is another term that applies at different levels, always implying parts of a whole: towns themselves could also be referred to as *parcialidades.*

6. According to Joaquín García Icazbalceta, the document discussed here comes from a folio book, written in seventeenth-century script, that had belonged to Sr. D. José F. Ramírez. It was one of a number of Informes de la Provincia del Santo Evangelio, produced in response to the *visita* between 1568 and 1571 of Licenciado Juan de Ovando, Visitador of the Council of Indies (*Códice Franciscano* 1941, x). Like others in the book, the present document is actually a fragment of a longer one. García Icazbalceta infers that these were recopied and abbreviated in the process.

7. The term *macehual* is originally from the Nahuatl and was used in Yucatec for persons who were not members of the elite. The same term is still occasionally used today in reference to Maya-speaking peasants.

8. Feminization is widely recognized as a feature of colonial domination. Nandy (1983) discusses it, and in the Yucatecan context, see Restall 1995; Sigal 2000; and Chuchiak 2007 on gender and sexuality in the conquest.

9. See *Códice Franciscano* (1941, 6) *informe* presented to Visitador Licenciado Juan de Ovando circa 1571, which notes that fray Pedro de Gante had taught painting and crafts to Nahua people for the previous four decades and that they mastered these skills even more proficiently than did Spaniards.

10. Landa was acting as Franciscan provincial at a time when Yucatán had no bishop.

He also pursued inquisitional investigation and punishment of newly or dubiously converted Indios. On these and other controversial aspects of this episode in Yucatecan history, see González Cicero 1978; Farriss 1984; Hanks 1986; Clendinnen 1987. Chuchiak 2000b is the most thorough treatment of the extirpation campaigns in which the secular clergy played the dominant role. For the broader context of inquisition in New Spain, see Greenleaf 1995.

11. Chuchiak (2000b, 235 ff.) discusses the auto-da-fe more broadly and illustrates with a case from Peto, July 12, 1598, suggesting that while the tragic events at Maní are the best known, they are by no means the only instance of this brutal spectacle. Chuchiak makes the important point that the spectacle was explicitly intended to be exemplary of God's power. The fact that the autos took place in the center of the towns further enhances their place as exemplary centers in *reducción*.

12. Chuchiak (2000b, 90–103) summarizes the episcopal *visitas* between 1562 and 1652, as well as the sequence of places they inspected. These *visitas* were a critical part of the surveillance of Maya by the secular church, and much idolatry was uncovered in the course of them.

13. The expression is *para bienmorir* 'in order to die well', a topic of great import on which sermons and teachings were codified in *doctrina* and other evangelical texts.

14. The following summary remarks are based on readings of the *memorias* of Sopuerta, Cardete, Montalvo, Izquierdo, the *Relación* to Ovando in the *Códice Franciscano*, and Cogolludo, which collectively span the period from about 1570 through 1660.

15. Proper intentions are commonly cited when religious practices are described, but the baptisms in extremis are noteworthy because it is stipulated that the nonpriest minister must perform the rite with proper words and with the intention to discharge the Church's intention. In other words, not only the intentions of the beneficiary but also the intentions of the ritual expert are stipulated.

16. For a fascinating study of Maya scribes based on iconography and hieroglyphic sources from the Classic period, see Coe and Kerr 1998. Drawing on work by Nikolai Gruber, they interpret the title of the Classic scribe in the glyphs as *ah ku hun* 'he of the holy book' (Coe and Kerr 1998, 91). This phrase is intriguingly parallel to *ah dzib hun*, which we might translate 'he of the written book'. It is unclear to me whether the *batabil* would have had its own scribe or whether the function of "book writing" was entirely concentrated in the *ah kin* priesthood and above. Testimony taken during the campaigns to extirpate idolatry indicates that the *ah kin* priests did maintain books, but the content of their books is less obvious. The closer their books were to the "mundane" functioning of governance, the better the analogue to the colonial scribe. The closer they were to the ritual and esoteric matters, the better the analogue to the colonial friar. Judging by the range of themes treated in the Books of Chilam Balam, the writers of those works covered the entire spectrum, from the mundane to the monumental. In this way, they merge the Maya *ah ku hun* with the colonial scribe.

17. Restall is silent on the missions in the towns he studied, so the question of whether the two positions are of the *cabildo* or of the missions simply does not arise. It is also possible that *tupil*, like *alguacil*, was a term used for several different positions, and the *tupil* and *alguaciles de doctrina* are different from the corresponding positions '*de pueblo*'.

18. Restall (1997, 72) notes that there were up to six *alguaciles* at a time but does not mention the patron.

19. Farriss (1984, 234) cites the position *patrón* as the elite head of the *cofradía,* which is clearly a different office from the one Cogolludo is referring to here, under the same name.

20. Restall translates *justicia* as "magistrate" and *belnal* as "elected official." There is no obvious reason to think that *belnal* implies elections, however, unless this association accrued to it as part of the election system of the *cabildo.*

CHAPTER 4

1. The literature on the field concept is too large to summarize here, but interested readers should see Bourdieu 1977, 1985, esp. 1991, 1993; Bourdieu and Wacquant 1992; Hanks 2005; and references cited therein.

2. One is reminded here of Foucault's (1971, 23) observation that any discourse functions as a system of exclusions. In his terms, the "frontier" and the boundary more generally are instruments of exclusion, creating discontinuities between the different sectors of the colonial field. See Schieffelin 2001 for very interesting reflections on erasure in the language changes due to fundamentalist Christian missionization of the Kaluli in Papua New Guinea. She notes that a mere thirty years after the initial contact, adult speakers of Kaluli appear to have forgotten or rejected language forms from before their missionization. The missions among Kaluli started in the 1970s, making it possible to trace the consequences on the basis of ethnographic observation. If only we could do the same for sixteenth-century Yucatán!

3. See Comaroff and Comaroff 1991 for productive use of this concept, adapted from Gramsci, in the context of colonial southern Africa.

4. Bauman's (1983) study of Quakers in colonial America and the symbolism of speaking and silence makes a parallel claim regarding the centrality of verbal practice in a religious movement (albeit a very different sort of movement from colonizing *reducción*). Bauman traces the formation of a plain style in relation to an ideology of language and the movement of that style into a broader discursive space. This implies interdiscursive relations among the different settings in which the new style is used, and Bauman provides meticulous descriptions of the settings. Cohn (1996) analyzes the role of language and representation in the British colonization of India, which he treats as a "conquest of knowledge." The approach of Cohn, my former teacher and colleague, was formative for the one in this book. He distinguished three broad dimensions of the colonial project in India, the productions of linguistic works (dictionaries, grammars, pedagogical texts, translations), the establishment of an epistemological space and a discourse (in the Indian case, "Orientalism"), and the conversion of Indian knowledge into a European objectification. Each of these elements has an analogue in my treatment of the Maya. For another conceptually close comparison, see Fabian (1986), who traces the formation and spread of Swahili across a broad field of discourse, concentrating on the formation of genres. Schieffelin's (2007) study of Christian missions among Kaluli in Papua New Guinea has many similarities with the present study, including the centrality accorded to language

in the reformation of identity and the diffusion of a new form of the vernacular by way of genres of linguistic practice, as well as a host of similarities rooted in Christianity, notwithstanding the glaring contrasts between sixteenth-century Spanish Franciscans and twentieth-century Australian fundamentalist Christians. Bauman and Briggs (2003) trace the history of language ideologies in the formation of northern European modernity and the vernacularization of new language varieties, processes with interesting analogues in the historically and linguistically more distant settings of colonial Yucatán. See also Bauman and Briggs 1990; Hanks 1987; and Sherzer 1990 for more general statements of genre and the circulation of discourse. For a collection of recent studies on languages of Latin America, see Sammons and Sherzer 2000.

5. Students of linguistic anthropology will recognize these dimensions from the considerable body of literature on genre in our field. What I dub "metalinguistic labeling" is a phenomenon already identified in the ethnography of speaking in the 1970s and which figures in all major approaches to genre. The term "production and reception format" comes from Goffman (1974) and designates the social configurations of speakers, persons quoted or reported, addressees, witnesses, and whatever other participant roles might be in play in a given event. Deictic centering has been central in my own research on both ordinary speech practices and writing (Hanks 1987, 1989, 1990). The idea that stylistic variation is part of what defines genre is similarly well known, and Mayanists have done much research on Maya style (Bricker 1974, 2007; Edmonson 1970; Edmonson and Bricker 1985; Gossen 1985; Hanks 1986, 1988, 1990, 1992a, 1992b; Norman 1980; Restall 1997; Tedlock 1983). For a set of recent sociolinguistic studies of stylistic variation, see Eckert and Rickford 2001. Multimodality has emerged as a focus of intensive research in current linguistic anthropology and neighboring fields. The idea that communicative practices involve *coordinated* use of speech, gesture, posture, the built environment, material objects, and the senses has a substantial history in the scholarly literature in several fields. See Enfield and Levinson 2006 for a collection of recent studies on this and related phenomena. Finally, what I am calling "iteration" has various reference points, including poststructuralist theory, Foucault's (1971) insistence on the importance of dispersal in discourse formations, and linguistic anthropological treatments of discourse as circulation (Urban 1991). Ultimately, my selection of these parameters as the defining ones for genre is guided by the history I am describing. It is because these parameters play a central role in the development of colonial Maya that I single them out. Perusal of the literature just cited would reveal other parameters that I have chosen to downplay here.

6. Victoria Bricker (2007) has shown that cyclic prose style is present in the Dresden Codex, suggesting that the style is of considerable antiquity. For careful description, see Hanks 1990, 1992a. The practice of circumambulation, as part of inspecting or creating boundaries, is clearly European, however, and the fact that many examples of cyclic prose in the colonial corpus are to be found in land surveys suggests that it is a colonial production (Hans Prem, pers. com.).

7. The Maya is more precise on the governor's action in sending the letter. It describes it as *tuxchiteh,* which is transparently a noun incorporation derived from *tuúx(t)* 'to send (it)' + *chi* 'mouth' + *teh* (transitive optative, regular formation applying to verbs with an incorporated noun). The element *chi* is commonly incorporated to form verbs of speak-

ing, hence *payalchiteh* (< *payal* 'draw forward' + *chi* 'mouth') 'to pray' and *bobochiteh* 'to address in insulting manner' (< *boboh* 'insult' + *chi* 'mouth'). Thus in the present example, the Maya combines what appears to be an act of speech with the objective of sending the object, suggesting the gloss 'order (it) sent'.

8. Goffman (1974) makes a useful distinction between the author (the party who selects the words), the principal (the party whose position is thereby represented), and the animator (the party who utters or inscribes the discourse). Usually the three coincide, but Goffman shows a variety of circumstances under which they do not. I will underscore such cases in the Maya corpus as they arise.

9. There is a significant literature that analyzes discourse works in terms of the trajectories they follow when they are distributed and received (see Bauman 1986; Bauman and Briggs 1990; Hanks 1989; Urban 1991).

10. Schieffelin (2002) discusses the transformation of Kaluli time sense as a consequence of Christian missionization, arguing convincingly that the mission experience came to define the "now" for Kaluli converts, as opposed to the past of the pre-Christian era. Although I have not thematized the temporal dimension, Schieffelin's remarks on the divisions imposed by missionaries on the Kaluli are germane to the Maya case. In particular, and as reflected in the title of this book, Maya people did come to see the arrival of the cross as the threshold of a new age.

11. In his dedication and prologue, Sánchez de Aguilar refers to others who had encouraged him to publish the *Informe,* implying that they had read it. At a minimum, it appears to have been maintained and selectively consulted among Church records in Yucatán between 1615 and 1636.

12. There is a substantial literature on Sahagún and his writings. For an early summary of the difficulties he encountered, see Ricard 1986, 109–21. See also Burkhart 1989 and references cited therein.

CHAPTER 5

1. Compare Molina's Nahuatl doctrina reproduced in the *Códice Franciscano* and the anonymous *Doctrina Cristiana muy util y Necesaria* (Mexico, 1578) reproduced in facsimile by Luis Resines. Resines also compares this work to others in the genre.

2. Ciudad Real, Coronel, San Buenaventura, and Beltrán all taught Maya in the Franciscan convent in Mérida at one time or another in their careers.

3. The Motul folia 221v and 225v refer to an *arte.* The Vienna refers to work by Villalpando.

4. On finalization and its role in colonial Yucatec discourse, see Hanks 1987, 1989.

5. Table 5 also includes the Spanish-to-Maya part of the Motul dictionary (known as Part 2; cf. discussion in Acuña 1984), which will not be discussed in this book. Whenever I refer to "the Motul dictionary," I mean the Maya-to-Spanish (Part 2). The Maya-Spanish dictionary is more than twice as long as the Spanish-Maya, and it is the former that is standardly called the Motul and for which Ciudad Real is most famous.

6. Cogolludo (1971 [1688]), Lizana (1988 [1633]), Carrillo (1872), and Tozzer (1977 [1921], 1941) make reference to other works. It appears certain that Landa, Villalpando, Ciudad

Real, San Buenaventura, and Sánchez de Aguilar authored works in or on Maya that have never been found. If we take the statements of Cogolludo and Lizana at face value, there were many other works by lesser-known authors as well. Those listed in table 5 represent the currently available corpus.

7. A word token is a single instance of a word.

8. This order is not always followed precisely, and there are entries out of order that appear to be forms the copyist did not notice were missing until after he had passed their normative place.

9. It is likely that the friars were exposed to dictionaries, including bilingual ones, in their studies of *latinidad,* although I do not pursue this connection here.

10. There was of course a considerable corpus of Maya "literature," but it was suppressed on the grounds that it was, in the missionary view, the work of the devil. This applied to both the hieroglyphic corpus and the colonial forbidden genres, written in the Spanish-derived orthography.

11. All tables cited in this and the next chapters represent the lexical material from the sources cited. Capitalization, punctuation, indentation, and morpheme spacing have been normalized for ease of reading. Readers interested in these details should consult the originals.

12. The expression *he hoi* probably does index an act of mundane disbelief. The expression stands out in this entry because it does not include a verb and nowhere encodes belief or believing. The Maya form *he* is a demonstrative, and *hoi* is likely a particle or adjective of deprecation, with the conveyed meaning of 'that's unworthy' or 'there's the dubious part'. The Maya relates to the Spanish the way it would if we translated English "watch out!" with an expression like "here it comes!"—the equivalence is strictly pragmatic.

13. Chuchiak (2000b, 253) notes that Ralph Roys had suggested that *hunab ku* was a colonial creation, despite the statements by Cogolludo to the effect that it was a Maya divinity. In chapter 11, I argue for the colonial interpretation.

14. I omit the second instance *[bil]* in the phrase as written in the dictionary, which I consider a scribal error.

15. The final *e* of *zipile* marks the phrase as a topic for further comment and is present in the first line of the confessional prayer, followed by the act of contrition. Its presence in the dictionary entry is motivated only by its presence in the prayer.

16. SF1 glosses *uacunah* as 'bring (guiding)', an odd translation not supported by the Maya.

17. The friars appear to have identified the verbal suffix *[-ancil]* with governance, since it recurs in the term *thanancil* ['speech' + *ancil*], which the Motul (M:432r) glosses as '*gobernar, mandar, regir*'. *Than* and *bel* are equally general terms, for speech and action respectively. In Maya, the *[-ancil]* suffix derives nouns into intransitive verbs: *boc* 'odor', *bocancil* 'to stink'; *lol* 'flower', *lolancil* 'to flower'.

18. Recall that the sources of this knowledge would have been several; discussions with trusted Maya helpers, direct observations made during the extirpations and confiscation of artifacts, testimony during the trials, and works such as that of Sánchez de Aguilar, which make idolatry the focus of extended analysis. See Chuchiak 2000b.

CHAPTER 6

1. Stated baldly, interpretance rules out untranslatable words: any expression in one language has a valid interpretation in the other. In fact, the missionary linguists chose not to translate certain key terms such as *mis(s)a* 'mass', names of place or person (even when the names were crystallized descriptions that *could be* translated). Whether this indicates the limit of valid interpretance or some other strategy, it remains true that glossing presupposes interpretance.

2. This likeness is less fanciful than it might appear. There are numerous examples in the colonial Maya corpus, particularly in works written by Maya, where the Spanish and Maya counterparts are paired in running text, as in *yalmahthanil dios, evangelio ukaba* 'the words of God, the Gospels they are called'. Hence just as we would expect of a poetic form, a paradigmatic equivalence between two expressions is transposed into a syntagmatic sequence in which the two are equated.

3. On the role of polyvalence in Maya grammar, see Ximena and Vapnarski 2006.

4. Linguistically inclined readers will recognize that the idea of transparency as used here is inspired by Saussure, for whom grammatically motivated signs (as opposed to maximally arbitrary roots) were "transparent" insofar as the composing elements could be readily segmented and their respective contributions to the composition easily distinguished. It would be productive to apply this and related concepts systematically to the missionary linguistic works, although to do so is beyond the aims of this book.

5. In speaking of standardization, I refer to the stabilization of *Maya reducido* as a variety, its codification in the missionary linguistic works, its emergence as an object of linguistic ideology, its deployment in the *doctrina,* and its spread into genres written by Mayas in the *pueblos reducidos* and beyond. There is a substantial theoretical literature on the concept of the standard. For an influential treatment, see Silverstein 1998 and the other papers in Brenneis and Macaulay 1998. On style from a sociolinguistic perspective, see Eckert and Rickford 2001; Agha 2006.

6. Presuming that Ciudad Real was the main composer of the Motul dictionary, the Spanish-Maya vocabulary referred to is likely the second part of the Motul, which I do not treat in this book.

7. The only arguments I know of against identifying the Motul dictionary with Ciudad Real are set forth by García Quintana and Castillo Ferreras in their excellent analysis of Ciudad Real's *Tratado Curioso* (see Ciudad Real 1976 [ca. 1590] in bibliography).

8. As is so often the case with the works under study, the title and authorship of the *Tratado Curioso* are both vexed. García Quintana and Castillo Farreras (Ciudad Real 1976 [ca. 1590]) provide an insightful account of the problem, concluding that although there is no named author on the work, it was composed by Ciudad Real during his time in Spain. As far as I can determine, the work was unprinted until scholars published it in the late nineteenth century. It lacks title page, front matter, author, and date. Thus even if we decide that Ciudad Real was the composer, which I have accepted in this book, still, he was not an "author" in the full sense of the word. I cite the work under his name in the bibliography for convenience. There is one more curious fact, namely, that the *Tratado Curioso* has a number of nonstandard spellings of Maya words. *Cizomtun* for Dzidzan-

tun, *Citbalche* for Dzitbalche, and *guitam* for *citam* 'wild pig'. Although there are only a handful of such spellings, it is difficult to square them with the meticulous orthography of the Motul dictionary. Indeed, for more elaborate reasons, García Quintana and Castillo Farreras (XLVI) conclude that Ciudad Real was simply not the author of the Motul dictionary.

9. Motul is one of the twenty-two convents visited in Yucatán by Ponce and Ciudad Real, but the description in the *Tratado Curioso* gives no hint that Ciudad Real had any special connection to the place as of August 1588.

10. Anyone who has studied Maya will appreciate the difficulties faced by the friars in capturing the vowel system. The language today distinguishes four vocalic nuclei for each of five vowel qualities: V (short neutral), VV (long low tone), VV (long high tone), and V'V (glottalized vowel). There is enough variation that these distinctions are difficult to discern, and realization of forms bearing them may be inconsistent. The Motul distinguishes and occasionally comments on pitch but does not always mark the distinctions accurately.

11. Of the other deictics, indexing space, time, perceptual evidence, and discourse, there is fairly good representation in both dictionaries, although they are almost complementary in terms of the forms they cite, a topic for future research.

12. Note that all tables cited in this and the next chapters represent the lexical material from the sources cited. Capitalization, punctuation, indentation, and morpheme spacing have been normalized for ease of reading. Readers interested in these details should consult the originals.

13. See Bricker 1989, 2007 for discussion of Maya writing and the language that described it.

14. The usage of *dzibilah* for gift or offering appears to be a spelling error. The Motul shows no such usage, but it does show the more transparent and well-attested form *dzabilah* (F123v) 'offering, gift, grace' derived from *dza* 'to give'. In general, the two works have complementary emphases but do not contradict one another.

15. It is not clear whether talk of fornication was itself a sin or whether it merely compounds the original sin of fornicating to then spread it around in salacious retellings.

16. While the Maya form *tii* is vastly broad, standing for 'to, from, when, for, by' and so forth, I specify the 'to' meaning because the Spanish gloss selects it.

17. The sermon is titled "Como no conviene alargar el tiempo de la conversión a Dios. Netardes Converti, ad Dominum. Eccles.5" 'How it is wrong to postpone the time of conversion to God. Ecclesiastes 5' (Coronel 1620, 1:F66). Notice that both dictionaries illustrate this sentiment and SF1:269 shows a paraphrase of Coronel's title.

18. Recall from chapter 5 that *testigo* is translated into Maya in several ways. I think the Spanish form is untranslated in the San Francisco Part 1 because it is parallel to the immediately preceding entry for 'ordain'; both are official acts, and both retain the standard Spanish label for the office to which one is 'entered'. These also illustrate a common Maya derivation of an abstract noun from a Spanish root.

19. The same grammatical pattern is evident in *dzib-ol-tic* 'to desire, imagine'. See chapter 7 for a description of this derivational pattern in the *artes*.

CHAPTER 7

1. The classical tradition of *grammatica* is beyond the scope of this book but provides a wealth of evidence regarding the scope of grammar, the parts of languages, the genres of grammatical writing, and the intimate relation between grammar and Christian doctrine, particularly as developed by St. Augustine. This is surely pertinent to the missionary orientations to language, and an excellent analysis may be found in Irvine 1994.

2. Acuña (1996, 23) argues convincingly that Nebrija's *Gramática de la lengua castellana* (1492) provided a partial model for the missionary grammarians. Book V of Nebrija's grammar was titled *"Las introducciones de la lengua castellana para los que de estraña lengua querrán deprender[la]"*; it divides the main parts of the language into a schema similar to that for Latin. Interested readers can consult the critical edition of Antonio Quilis (1992), including the excellent introduction by Manuel Seco (1–68). Whereas Acuña emphasizes the similarity between Nebrija's Castilian grammar and the Maya *artes*, I have been struck by the similarity to Nebrija's Latin, which was very widely circulated. Undoubtedly both works are part of the background, as are the missionary grammars of Nahuatl.

3. Transitivity is a key aspect of the verb system in Maya, as in Nahuatl. See Launey 1997, for comparison of how it is treated in four missionary grammars of Nahuatl, two by Franciscans and two by Jesuits.

4. Maya verbs mark both subjects and objects, and person suffixes occur in pairs any time the subject is second- or third-person plural and the object is overtly marked.

5. Coronel does appear to have recognized that positionals were special, because he makes scattered remarks about them, under the rubric "neutral verbs ending in *tal*" (see Acuña ed. 1998, 82, 92). The problem is that not all verbs ending in -*tal* are positionals, so his generalizations are only half true.

6. My critical remarks about the missionary grammars are based on my own understanding of the colonial language, as well as the modern language. To my knowledge, McQuown 1967 is the closest we have to a modern grammatical description of the colonial language. To see what such a description might look like, consult Haviland's excellent sketch of colonial Tzotzil, in Laughlin and Haviland 1988, 79–123.

7. This is the series Coronel erroneously describes as postverbal in '*nacal in-cah*' 'I am ascending'.

8. If Coronel had recognized that the first and second persons are derived from *ti* but the third is not, he would have noticed the asymmetry.

9. Readers interested in learning more about the colonial Maya verb system should consult McQuown 1967.

10. Nebrija too gives additional verbs and illustrations of the conjugations in the last part of Book II (Esparza and Calvos 1996, 82–93).

11. He does cite these forms elsewhere in the grammar, but they fall outside the paradigms.

12. There are many more muddles in Coronel's description of the verbs, but I will not delve into them here. They include the placement of stems ending in -*tah* in class III, whereas they belong in IV; the lumping of positional verbs with intransitives in class I,

whereas they are a distinct conjugation; and the failure to note that the causative formation in class II is only one of several causative formations.

13. Coronel also cites *xijc chhabil vah,* which he translates as 'vayan por pan', approximately 'someone go for bread to be got' (Acuña 1998, 76). This is a proper illustration of a more complex form of complementation, which I will leave aside for the sake of brevity.

14. McQuown (1967) spells out the passive formation clearly.

15. Given that tone developed late in Yucatecan, there is some question how stable the system was in the sixteenth and early seventeenth century. This might explain the absence of tone marking in Coronel and almost all the other missionary writings, except the Motul dictionary. The Motul contains sufficiently many remarks about it to indicate, nevertheless, that it was already prominent. None of the extant colonial grammars treat or consistently mark tone, since they carry forward the same orthographic practice used by Coronel and the other dictionaries, with minimal adjustments. The Motul's use of doubled vowels is an early attempt to make the necessary distinctions and was never standardized. Compare Zimmermann 1997a on the difficulties with tone encountered by missionary linguists in Otomí.

16. Acuña (1998, 215–99) provides a most useful alphabetic list of Coronel's examples. For a comparative sense of the doctrinal presence in dictionaries, see Thiemer-Sachse 1997 on Spanish-Zapotec vocabulary.

17. My inferences are based on the assumptions that priests do not have children, that no lay Spaniard would utter this request in Maya, and that the desired teacher was either a missionary or a hand-picked agent of the missionaries, a *maestro.*

18. I construe the last line as, in modern orthography, *ah sá'atal lobil lo,* in which the two instances of [l l] reduce to simple [l].

19. *Chi* 'mouth' is one of several body parts that enter into a huge array of incorporated forms. See also *ol* 'heart', *ich* 'eye', and *kab* 'hand'.

20. Given the close relation of the *artes* to pedagogy, the reliance on Nebrija's Latin lessons would have been pedagogically useful, since the newly arrived missionaries would have been familiar with it before ever plunging into Maya.

21. The title page also has the Franciscan seal; see facsimile in Acuña 1996.

22. I am skeptical about the order of the suffixes, -*ex-on,* because in the modern language this would always be -*on-ex,* in accordance with the rule of sequential ordering of pronoun suffixes, namely, first person precedes second and second precedes third, regardless of function.

23. Compare Canger 1997 on the improved treatment of Nahuatl phonology in Carochi's grammar relative to earlier ones. Canger (1997) and Launey (1997) concur that Carochi's grammar is by far the best of the six that were produced by 1645, when Carochi wrote. Beltrán is, we might say, the Carochi of Yucatec, albeit a century later.

24. See map 8 in chapter 2, the *guardianía* of Maní (1582).

25. Beltrán's work is organized into numbered paragraphs, which I cite as sections, and longer articles, which correspond roughly to chapters.

26. Beltrán observes here a historical change in the past suffix for incorporated verbs. In San Buenaventura's time the suffix was -*ni,* whereas by the mid-eighteenth century the

correct form was *nahi* (Acuña 2002, 67). The modern form currently used is *nah*, with *-i* added only if the verb is in sentence-final position.

27. Cf. Motul (folio 428r) *tuzinil* 'todo, cantidad concreta' 'everything, concrete quantity'; *in cucutil tuçinil* 'todo mi cuerpo' 'my entire body'; *uchuc tumen tu zinil Dios* 'es Dios todo poderoso' 'God is all powerful'; *tuzinil yanil Dios* 'en todas partes está Dios' 'God is everywhere'. And see discussion of this in chapter 1 above.

28. Cf. Motul (folio 123r) *dzabilah* 'don o merced que uno da o haze, y gracia assi' 'gift or favor that one gives or does, and grace'; *yaabi u dzabilah Dios ten* 'muchas mercedes me ha hecho Dios' 'God has granted me much grace'.

29. Cf. Motul (folio 145r) *choch, chochah* 'desatar' 'untie'; *chochex u kaxal* 'desatad la atadura' 'untie the knot'; *choch keban* 'confesar los pecados y absolverlos' 'confess sins and absolve them'; *u chochah inkeban padre* 'confeséme al padre' 'I confessed to father' (lit. 'father untied my sins').

30. Cf. Motul (folio 117r) *tzec* 'castigo o corrección; penitencia por justicia que uno haze o da a otro' 'punishment, correction, penance by justice that one does or gives to another'; *u tzecil ah çipil* 'el castigo con que es castigado el deliquente' 'the punishment by which the delinquent is punished'. See also SF2:367.

CHAPTER 8

1. A noteworthy exception to this tradition of scholarship is Bricker and Miram 2002, a study of the Chilam Balam of Kua that carefully tracks the European elements in the text.

2. "*. . . de manera que le provoquen a creer y amar a Nuestro Señor Dios y a contrición verdadera de sus culpas y pecados y así dejará sus ídolos de su voluntad, sabiendo que no son dioses sino demonios. Y sabiendo asentir y disentir a las cosas de la fe, dejando sus ídolos y teniendo contrición de sus pecados, podrán recibir el santo bautismo aunque no sepan memoriter la doctrina, porque siendo viejos nunca la pueden aprender.*' '. . . in such a way (that) they provoke them to believe and love Our Lord God and to true contrition for their faults and sins and so (he) will leave his idols of his own volition, knowing that they are not gods but demons. And knowing to assent and dissent to things of the faith, abandoning their idols and having contrition for their sins, they can receive holy baptism even though they cannot memorize the doctrine, for being old they can never learn it' (Toral, *Avisos*, in Scholes et al. 1938, 25).

3. Foucault (1971) noted that doctrinal language tends to disperse, but he gave no account of the mechanisms of this dispersal and no hint that the semiotic organization of doctrinal language actually plays a key role in the dispersal.

4. I omit discussion here of the manuscript known as the "Morley manuscript," an undated, authorless work of 346 numbered pages donated by Morley to the Laboratory of Anthropology of the Museum of Indian Arts and Culture in Santa Fe, New Mexico. Although the watermarks on the paper on which it is written indicate the second half of the eighteenth century, Whalen (2003) argues effectively that the text is much older. Whalen also argues that the composer of the work was likely to have been a *maestro de*

escuela, that is, a native speaker of Maya whose task it was to render doctrinal and biblical discourse in Maya. The work includes "The questions asked by the emperor," an exhortation to confess, a series of short sermons, and a description of the days leading up to the final judgment. It nicely echoes many of the missionary concerns, such as the injunction to not believe in dreams and bird songs, to not bear false witness, and to fast when called for. Whalen shows that portions of this text are cognate with the Book of Chilam Balam of Tusik, as well as with some of Coronel's sermons. In light of Whalen's in-depth analysis and presentation of the manuscript, as well as the absence of author, I have cited it in the bibliography as Whalen 2003. This is clearly an important, little-studied manuscript worthy of careful analysis in light of the other developments treated in this book, but it is beyond my scope and must be left for further research.

5. In defense of Coronel, it might be pointed out that *uinicil* does not mean simply 'body', but 'body of a human', a *uinic*. Although we cannot know, it is possible that the early missionaries were concerned about this added meaning. It is also of course possible that the meaning of *cucutil* changed with time.

6. It is also possible that 'marriage' among pre-Columbian Maya actually involved the exchange of flowers and that *nicte,* the water lily, was a symbol of erotic love.

7. *"Es de saber que muchas maneras de Doctrinas se han compuesto ya en esta tierra en las lenguas de los naturales, . . . , así Doctrinas menores ó breves, por donde se enseñan los niños, como otras mayores, en que por extenso pueden entender los adultos y más hábiles las cosas de nuestra fe. De las menores que se llaman Doctrinas Cristianas, de que aquí se pide copia, andan impresas cuatro ó cinco maneras, las cuales contienen una misma cosa en sustancia y sentencia, aunque tienen alguna diversidad en el modo de proceder, y diferencia de vocablos"* 'It is known that many manners of Doctrines have been composed already in this land in the languages of the *naturales,* . . . thus minor or brief Doctrines, with which children are taught and others more elder, in what more extensively adults and the more gifted can understand of our faith. Of the minor ones called Christian Doctrine, of which we here request a copy, four or five versions are in print, which contain the same substance and meaning, even though they differ somewhat in the manner of proceeding and in different word choice' (*Códice Franciscano,* Siglo XVI:29).

8. Interested readers should consult the excellent studies by Cortés Castellanos (1987), focused on de Gante's pictographic work, and Resines (1990), who presents a facsimile with critical transcription of an anonymous *Doctrina Cristiana muy util y Necesaria,* originally published in Mexico in 1578. The two works provide numerous references to other contemporaneous catechisms and to the historical development of the genre in Mexico.

9. Hanks (1996) distinguishes more than a dozen different manifestations of the cross in colonial Yucatec Maya language and social practice.

10. *Catechism of the Catholic Church,* 2nd ed. (Washington, DC: United States Catholic Conference, 2000). See multiple references to the cross in the index, p. 780.

11. In all examples in this chapter, I have introduced line breaks for ease of reading and reference and to highlight the poetic parallelisms in the language, only some of which I discuss in detail.

12. I read *kanalob* as a mistranscription of *cahualob,* on the grounds that the latter is actually pronounced *c-'ahualob* 'our-enemies', with initial glottal stop on the noun *ahual.* The /h/ was lost and orthographic *ual* was rendered *nal,* a common error in works from this period. It is at least possible that the spelling is actually correct and the term *kanal* is related to *kanan* 'necessary', in which case the line reads "protect me from needs." I hesitate to accept this reading because it significantly changes the meaning of the text and the reference to enemies is amplified in the dialogues. As any student of doctrine would know, the enemies in question are the Devil, the material world, and the flesh (see page 270, line 10).

13. In the texts in this chapter, Coronel's original uses graphemes that have been simplified here. *Dz* is written ɔ, glottalized *chh* is written *ch, ss* is rendered *ß,* and *s* is rendered *ʃ.*

14. It is tempting to view this addition in light of the missionary campaigns to baptize infants. Limbo is a perpetual state of liminality between heaven and hell, reserved for those who die in infancy prior to being baptized. The equation of Limbo with hell would fit the pattern of urging people to have their children baptized.

15. I have translated *kalchi* as 'contrite'. The expression occurs only once in the Motul dictionary, in the phrase *ah pich kalchii,* glossed *que habla mucho* 'he who talks a lot'. This gloss, which is likely due to the *pich* element, does not fit in the present context. I read *kal* as 'close, lock, incarcerate', *chi* as 'mouth', and the combination as something like 'tight-lipped, taciturn, morose'.

16. It is interesting that both of the prayers addressed directly to supernatural beings (the Our Father and the Hail Mary) are cast in the plural and focused mainly on praise and requests, whereas the two not explicitly so addressed (the Credo and the Confiteor Deo) are cast in the singular and focused more on the mental state of the speaker. I do not know at this point whether this is a feature simply carried over from the Latin or one that has Maya-specific ramifications. For a recent study of confessional language, contrasting an indigenous tradition with a missionary introduction in Papua New Guinea, see Rumsey 2008.

17. The relation of intercession would become central in the practices of modern shamans, who mobilize spirits to intercede with God on behalf of the patient.

18. *"Preguntarle todos los artículos como están en la cartilla y responda que sí, de manera que por la predicación que le predicaren entenderá esto y sabrá que lo ha así de creer"* 'Ask him all the articles as they are in the manual and he is to respond yes, so that by the sermons that are preached, he will understand that and will know what he is to believe' (Toral, *Avisos,* in Scholes et al. 1938, 26).

19. Acuña (1998, 157) writes 'chr<ist>o' where I have restored the original Xpō.

20. Acuña (1998, 158) omits 'Res.' I have restored from original.

21. Acuña (1998, 158) writes out 'xan', but I have restored *xā* from original.

22. Beltrán (1912 [1757]) uses 'ɔ' for the glottalized affricate that others represent as 'dz'. I have opted for *dz.*

23. In this vein, it is interesting to note that whereas standard Christian texts list the enemies in the order "the world, the flesh, the Devil," the order in Maya is always the one

in line 10. In the Maya order, the point by point opposition to the Trinity is made by parallelism—God the father: the Devil, the Son: the world, the Holy Ghost: our flesh.

24. I have corrected the spacing and introduced line breaks to make the text more readable. The original texts are continuous, margin to margin.

25. I read *acahez a cuxtal* as an orthographic error for *akahez a cuxtal* and have translated it accordingly. If we assume the orthography is correct, then the translation would be 'you begin your life', which might also be appropriate in this context.

CHAPTER 9

1. Quezada and Okoshi (2001, 31) argue that the Maní document, which they call *memoria de la distribución de los montes* (Maní, September 15, 1557) is the earliest extant document written in alphabetic Maya.

2. This assertion is likely to be provocative for historians like Restall (1997), who argues that these works, which he terms "titles" and classifies as "seminotarial," were eighteenth-century productions. The most convincing of Restall's arguments, however, turn on orthography, which applies in the first instance to the actual written documents and not to the texts inscribed therein. As we know, recopying was a ubiquitous feature of colonial genres, and it introduced changes, whether by error or "updating." There is no debate that, as Restall (1997, 276–92) shows, many of these evidently early texts were penned or gathered together much later than their dates would claim, in the eighteenth or even nineteenth century. The same argument applies to the Books of Chilam Balam. It does not follow that they were *composed* that late. Moreover, even if they were retrospective and postdated for strategic purposes, we are left to explain the mechanisms whereby knowledge of the genres was reproduced. Either way, what is most central for our purposes here is the fact that these texts are directly engaged with the dynamics of *reducción*, including the López Medel *Ordenanzas* and the establishment of the missions. Thus whereas Restall is at pains to show the parallels between Maya texts and Nahuatl texts in order to assign them a "Mesoamerican" origin, my argument is that they represent a vector for the movement of *Maya reducido* from the missionary genres into the *cabildos* and beyond.

3. Residencia de Don Rodrigo Flores de Aldana, AGI Escribanía de Camara, legajo 317B, Pieza 9. See Farriss 1984 and Restall 1997 for extensive discussion of the political context. Cf. Autos Hechos por Pedro García Ricalde, Sahcabchen.

4. According to Restall (1997, 246), the first one hundred years of the colony account for only 7.5 percent of the notarial corpus, while the period 1660–79 accounts for 10.8 percent. The eighteenth century alone accounts for 60.8 percent of the corpus, with an abundance of land documents and testaments. This discrepancy may be due in part to the fact that the early documents have been lost to the elements, but it is also clear from the kinds of documents that the management of rights over property became a major source of documentary production.

5. For the sake of brevity, I do not discuss testaments in this book. Perhaps the most relevant feature common to them is the religious framing of the act. This is nicely illus-

trated by the following example from Testamento, Cacalchen 1628 (Ayer Collection, Yucatec 21, Newberry Library, Chicago):

> *Tukaba dios uchuc tumen tuçinil*
> *citbil, mehenbi, .y. espiritu santo*
> *oxtul personas tuhunali hahal dios*
> *Tukabaix bolon pixan cacilich colebil*
> *ti çuhuy Santa Ma*
> *yohel tob tulacal uinicob*
> *bin ylic yunil intestamento*
> *intakyah than*
> *cen ah cimil ti franco kuk*

> In the name of god the maker of all things
> eternal, [and of the] son, and [of the] holy spirit
> Three persons in one true god.
> And in the name of nine spirits our holy lady
> blessed virgin Mary
> Let all men know
> they shall see the paper of my testament
> my final testament
> I, dying person, Francisco Kuk

6. These include the following:

Report, September 25, 1708, Mérida (AGI, Escribanía 322A)
Report to Hunucma-Uman and Maxcanu, August 10, 1709, Mérida (AGI, Escribanía 322A)
Report to Ticoh, Mama, Maní, Oxkutzcab, Tekax, Ticul, Teabo, Muna, August 10, 1709 (AGI, Escribanía, 322A)
Receipt of commission, Telchaquillo, August 22, 1709 (AGI, Escribanía 322B)

7. I have simplified the Maya tense-aspect-mode system in describing this as "present tense." In more precise terms, the surveys are cast in the incompletive aspect, that is, nonpast realis, which is used where an English speaker would use the present.

8. As Restall (1997, 201) shows, measurement terms do occur in some of the testaments, particularly those from Cacalchén, Ebtún, and Tekantó, although these are the outliers, and land descriptions embedded in wills and testaments are focused not on municipal or larger spaces but on agricultural lands under the control of individuals.

9. The term *mul* 'mound' is also widely attested in Maya toponyms and descriptions of the landscape, as in *mulú'uch* 'hillock, rolling countryside'. It is also the generic term for 'pyramid'.

10. Some of the texts describe the procession of officials as moving *tuyam pictun* 'between *pictun*(s)'. This expression could suggest either moving along the interval 'between' *pictun* markers arrayed in a single line, going from one to the next, or, alter-

natively, moving along a corridor defined by pairs of *pictun* markers arrayed in parallel lines. Failing further evidence, I have assumed the former interpretation. There is a separate term in modern Maya for the corridor left vacant between two fields for the purpose of passage. This term, *t'óol,* does not occur in the documents I have examined, but if it did, it would imply that the *pictun* markers were arrayed in parallel lines and the boundaries between spaces so bounded were corridors and not volumeless dividing lines.

11. There is some question as to the source of the activity I am calling *tzol pictun.* On the one hand, the marking of borders executed in a procession has clear European precedents, and Hans Prem and Tsubasa Okoshi both take this to be a specifically colonial practice (pers. com.). Intriguingly, the terms *pictun* and *multun* are both nearly absent in the Books of Chilam Balam. Thus we might have an emergent style arising from a specifically colonial practice. On the other hand, Bricker (2007) shows a clear precedent for *tzol* cyclicity in the hieroglyphic Dresden codex. My present hypothesis is that the discourse style was available in the Maya stylistic repertoire before the colonization and was recruited to the purpose of delimiting land, whether or not such delimitation was itself a Post-Classic Maya activity.

12. For analysis and transliteration of an overlapping collection of Xiu papers, see Quezada and Okoshi 2001.

13. For careful comparison of these two texts, along with the Oxkutzcab Chronicle, see Frauke Johanna Reise, *Indianische Landrechte in Yukatan um die Mitte des 16. Jahrhunderts.* Beiträge zur mittelamerikanischen Völkerkunde (Hamburg: Hamburgischen Museum für Völkerkunde, 1981).

14. The *residencia* of don Diego de Quijada, the first and only *alcalde mayor* of Yucatán appointed by the Crown, contains *legajos* with records of the trial of Montejo Xiu in 1561 and the idolatry trials of 1562 (AGI Justicia Legajos 245–49, cited in Morley and Roys 1941, 182).

15. Crónica de Maní, 1557–1813, MS, Latin American Library, Tulane University, New Orleans. In the following, I draw on the transliteration of the Maní text done by Victoria R. Bricker, who generously provided me with a copy of her unpublished version. Whole line numbers refer to the lines as segmented by Bricker, with fractions introduced by me for ease of reference. For close analysis of related documents from Maní, see Quezada and Okoshi 2001.

16. Recall from chapter 5, example 5.4, that *ku* in Maya glosses 'precious, god'; that is, there is a background connotation here that the *kunah* is a 'house of god' and not only an administrative *audiencia.* In the notarial documents, as opposed to the doctrinal and linguistic ones, the expression is associated with the meeting place of the *cabildo,* although it is frankly difficult on linguistic grounds to read it as merely an administrative place. As I suggested in chapter 5, I take this ambiguity to be a reflection of the intertwining of *cabildo* with Church.

17. Quezada and Okoshi (2001) transliterated and analyzed a series of Xiu papers from Yaxá that contain many exceptions to the general rule. The petitions and *probanzas* that Xiu nobles presented in order to retain their privileges are "seminotarial" in the sense that they imply collective ratification of the petitioner's identity, yet they are not *cabildo*

documents. Prior to the papers of don Salvador Xiu Ku in the first half of the eighteenth century, none of the petitions indicates date, place of composition, or witnesses. Although these texts are rich in details regarding the history of the Xiu patriline, they are clearly not notarial in the current sense and will not be examined here. According to Quezada and Okoshi (2001, 33), they arose in the following sequence of events: (1) the "petition" was produced and given to the *defensor,* a representative of the colonial government; (2) the *defensor* made a *"solicitud"* 'request' to the *gobernador* on behalf of the petitioner; (3) the *gobernador* issued an order *("mandamiento");* and (4) the order was enacted locally *("obedicimiento").* In the next chapter, I point to selected stylistic features common to these non-notarial petitions and to their notarial analogues, but careful analysis of the comparison will be left for future research.

18. I have retained line numbers from Barrera Vásquez 1984.

19. There are two glaring errors in the statement of López Medel: he did not occupy the position of *alcalde mayor* but instead *oydor* 'auditor', and he was not a *don* but rather a *licenciado.* Restall (1997) makes the latter point, which he takes as evidence of inauthenticity, whereas I consider it merely a mistake.

20. For further study of these texts, see Hanks 1987, 674–75, 680; Hanks 1990a, 98–101; Restall 1997; Roys 1957, 40–53.

21. Even today, Maya people visit Labnah—particularly shamans, for whom the memories it embodies are alive indeed.

22. Roys takes "seventeen" to be a scribal error and corrects it to "sixteen hundred." I will not enter this potential debate.

23. Although there is an ellipsis in Roys's text before the citation of these two officials, the temporal reference is to the past, because Quijada was *alcalde mayor* in the 1560s, the years just after López Medel's *Ordenanzas,* not in 1600.

24. There are two towns in the area named Yaxcabá, one a *visita* of Sotuta, five leagues east of Yaxkukul, and the other a *visita* of Sisal, within Sisal itself. It is unclear to me which is in play here, although Roys clearly thinks it was the Sotuta *visita.*

25. This text suggests that the meeting place was *above (yokol)* the jail, but this verticality is a matter of authority and not spatial location, since the buildings were single story (as is still the case in most municipal buildings in rural Yucatán).

26. *Bolon pixan* 'nine spirit' was a standard gloss for the standard Spanish 'bienaventurado'. According to Covarrubias (1995), 'bienaventurado' may be glossed as 'well-achieved, welcome, etc.'.

27. Among the saint names applied to towns, Ah Bolon Pixan, literally, 'Nine Spirits', is occasionally prefixed. In this case, it is noteworthy that the Maya town name itself is never mentioned.

28. The verb form in this bill is not *binbal* 'going' but *binebal,* a variant form of the same stem.

29. See also Bill of sale, Sicpach, 1700 (CCA, IX.1815.012); Bill of exchange, Sicpach, 1750, recopied 1783 (CCA, XI.1819.010); Bill of sale, Sotuta, March 2, 1766, and Diligencias sobre la mensura de tierras de la estancia Chichi de la Concepción, 1786 (CCA folder 146, sobre viii; in Spanish and Maya).

CHAPTER 10

1. For further discussion of this rocky period in Yucatán's history, see Cogolludo 1971 [1688]; also Clendinnen 1987; Farriss 1984; Gates 1937; González Cicero 1978; Hanks 1986, 1987; Tozzer 1941.

2. The text is taken from the first ten orthographic lines of the original. I have segmented it into grammatical phrases, with an eye to the verse parallelism. The line numbers as shown here are heuristic and reflect my scansion, not the original orthographic lines.

3. It should also be noted that none of the 1567 letters names any scribe involved in making the document, a detail that makes them less than full exemplars of notarial documents.

4. I am obviously summarizing a longer analysis here. The expression in question comes closest to an "explicit performative" in Austin's terms. It would be relatively easy to state the felicity conditions by which it is constrained.

5. AGI Mexico 356. Whole numbers indicate lines in the original [1–7]; fractional numbers indicate smaller line breaks introduced by me.

6. It is fascinating to observe that the authors of the February letters favor the title *cacique,* the March letter's authors are *batabs,* and the April letter, in Spanish, is signed by *gobernadores.* In other contexts the terms are used almost interchangeably.

7. This document was transliterated, translated, and published by Restall (1997, 323–24). I have introduced line breaks and numbers for ease of reference, and my gloss varies occasionally from Restall's.

8. *Ahau* is well attested in Maya writings both glyphic (pre-Columbian) and alphabetic. It designated the last or highest member of a series. Its actual reference depended upon the series in which it occurred. The Viceroy was apical in New Spain, whereas the Crown was apical globally. A similar shift occurs with Spanish terms like *visita* and *provincia,* which are used at different levels.

9. AGI Escrib. Camara 317b Residencia Aldana Pieza 9 folio 11. Line numbers and breaks introduced by me.

10. AGI Escrib. Camara 317b Residencia Aldana Pieza 9 folio 21. Line numbers and breaks introduced by me.

CHAPTER 11

1. For reasons of length, this chapter focuses exclusively on the Books of Chilam Balam. Arzápalo Marín's careful study of the Ritual of the Bacabs could provide the basis for in-depth study of these texts, which pose formidable challenges of understanding.

2. The Book of Nah is the only one to be named after its apparent copyist. It was found in the town of Teabo.

3. It is thought that the Pérez Codex contains parts of the Book of Chilam Balam of Maní, but I follow Bricker and Miram (2002) and Miram and Miram (1988) in labeling it the Pérez Codex since it also contains other texts and the boundaries between the different sources are unclear.

4. The Pérez and the Nah are named after persons, whereas the other seven names are place-names. The Book of Nah was found in Teabo, which is shown on map 17. The Pérez includes part of the Book of Maní, also shown on the map.

5. Lounsbury used a similar method to decipher aspects of the hieroglyphic inscriptions.

6. Whalen's (2003) study of the Morley manuscript is particularly important in this regard, and this text may provide some of the most compelling evidence of the discourse practices of the pivotal *maestros*. See also Knowlton 2004 for close comparison on portions of the Morley manuscript with passages of the Book of Chilam Balam of Chumayel. Knowlton revisits the kinds of intertextuality that Barrera Vásquez and Rendón (1974) examined, carefully studying the variants.

7. I am deliberately punning here on the word "cross" as the Christian master symbol that I have traced throughout this book and "cross talk" as developed by Rampton (1995). The latter refers to varieties of communicative practice in which a speaker performatively crosses boundaries of ethnicity or social identity by using linguistic forms associated with groups to which she or he does not belong. Over the history described in this book, the divisions between groups shifted, and there are important differences between the syncretic practices of colonial Maya subjects and the sorts of adolescent speakers described by Rampton. But they appear to have in common the double consciousness of projecting an identity that is not in some sense "really" one's own. In the Maya case, the BCBs and the notarial corpus are part of making *Maya reducido* an indigenous possession, hence their own. Yet the history of colonization and foreignness is never fully erased from the resulting language. Hence fluent Maya-dominant speakers today typically judge their own language to be "mixed," as opposed to the unattainable ideal of "legitimate Maya."

8. A productive topic for future research would be close comparison of the medicinal portions of the BCBs with the Ritual of the Bacabs, a task greatly facilitated by Arzápalo Marín's version of the Ritual of the Bacabs and Miram and Miram's invaluable concordance of the BCBs.

9. The Spanish first made landfall about three decades earlier, and by the time Francisco de Montejo entered Mérida in 1547 to found the colony, there had been waves of military engagement between the Spanish and the Maya (see Farriss 1984).

10. Early missionaries such as Landa were struck by what they took to be the prior presence of the cross, a ritual akin to baptism, and what resembled confession among the Maya. At a finer grain of detail, there are numerous points on which Maya beliefs and practices seem to coincide with early modern European ones. Nevertheless, the missionary posture toward all that resembled indigenous religion was to dismiss it as falsehoods foisted upon the spiritually infantile Indios by the Devil.

11. These same lines occur in the book of Tizimín, folio 20, lines 2–4, but in the first-person plural.

12. Pérez Codex, pp. 169–70 (Miram and Miram 1988, 3:126–27), reports the prophecy of Chilam Balam in terms consistent with these examples, and also varies between *hunab ku* 'one god' and *hahal ku* 'true god'.

13. Cf. also Pérez Codex, pp. 168–70.

14. Avendaño was the head of a group of missionaries who went to Tipú, far over the

southern frontier, to attempt to convert the Maya leader Ahau Can Ek and his warriors in the 1690s. Avendaño was convinced that the Maya prophecies had foretold that this was the time for the Itzá, who had resisted colonization until then, to convert. He used this line of argument with the Itzá leaders. For a detailed historical treatment of this event and the southern frontier, see Jones 1998.

EPILOGUE

1. For a moving portrait of some of the travails and projects of these people, and their role in the formation of modern ethnography on the Yucatec Maya, see Sullivan 1989.

2. On the *santiguar* and its relation to other genres performed by contemporary Yucatec *hmèen,* see Hanks 1984, 1990, 2006; Villa Rojas 1945.

3. For ease of reading, I have cited the modern examples using the colonial orthography.

REFERENCES CITED

Acuña, René. 1984. See *Calepino Maya de Motul.*
———. 1993. See *Bocabulario de maya than.*
———. 1996 [1684]. *See* San Buenaventura, Fr. Gabriel de.
———. 1998 [1620]. *See* Coronel, Fr. Juan.
———. 2002 [1746]. *See* Beltrán de Santa Rosa María, Pedro.
Adelaar, Willem F. H. 1997. "Las transiciones en la tradición gramatical hispanoamericana: Historia de un modelo descriptivo." In *La descripción de las lenguas amerindias en la época colonial,* edited by Klaus Zimmermann, 259–70. Frankfurt: Vervuert
Verlag.
Agha, Asif. 2006. *Language and Social Relations.* Studies in the Social and Cultural Foundations of Language. Cambridge: Cambridge University Press.
Ares Queija, Berta. 1993. *Tomás López Medel: Trayectoria de un clérigo-oidor ante el nuevo
mundo.* Guadalajara: Institución Provincial de Cultura Marqués de Santillana.
Arzápalo Marín, Ramón. 1987. *El ritual de los Bacabes: Edición facsimilar con transcrip-
ción rítmica, traducción, notas, índice, glosario, y cómputos estadísticos.* Mexico City:
Universidad Nacional Autónoma de México.
———. 1995. See *Calepino de Motul.*
Barrera Vásquez, Alfredo. 1984. *Documento No. 1 del Deslinde de tierras en Yaxkukul,
Yucatán.* Colección Científica, Lingüística 125. Mexico City: Instituto Nacional Antro-
pología e Historia, 1984.
Barrera Vásquez, Alfredo, Juan Ramón Bastarrachea Manzano, and William Brito
Sansores. 1980. *Diccionario Maya Cordemex.* Mérida: Ediciones Cordemex.
Barrera Vásquez, Alfredo, with Sylvia Rendón. 1974 [1948]. *El libro de los libros de Chilam
Balam.* Mexico City: Fondo de Cultura Económica.
Bauman, Richard. 1983. *Let Your Words Be Few: Symbolism of Speaking and Silence among
Seventeenth-Century Quakers.* Prospect Heights, IL: Waveland Press.

———. 1986. *Story, Performance, and Event: Contextual Studies of Oral Narrative*. Cambridge: Cambridge University Press.

Bauman, Richard, and Charles Briggs. 1990. "Poetics and Performances as Critical Perspectives on Language and Social Life." *Annual Review of Anthropology* 19: 59–88.

———. 2003. *Voices of Modernity, Language Ideologies, and the Politics of Inequality*. Cambridge: Cambridge University Press.

Beltrán de Santa Rosa María, Pedro. 1859 [1746]. *Arte de el Idioma Maya reducido a succintas reglas y Semilexicón yucateco*. Mérida: Imprenta de J. D. Espinosa.

———. 1868 [1740]. *Novena de Christo Crucificado*. Copy by C. Hermann Berendt. Brinton Collection, University of Pennsylvania, Philadelphia.

———. 1912 [1757]. *Declaración de la Doctrina Cristiana en el Idioma yucateco*. Mérida: Imprenta de la Lotería del Estado.

———. 2002 [1746]. *Arte de el Idioma Maya reducido a succintas reglas y Semilexicón yucateco*. Edited by René Acuña. Mexico City: Universidad Nacional Autónoma de México.

Bocabulario de maya than: Codex Vindobonensis N.S. 3833. 1993. Facsimil y transcripción crítica anotada. Edited by René Acuña. Mexico City: Instituto Nacional Autónoma de México.

Bolles, David. *Apéndices to Arte en Lengua Maya*, by Juan Coronel. *See* Coronel, 1998.

Bourdieu, Pierre. 1977. *Outline of a Theory of Practice*. Cambridge: Cambridge University Press.

———. 1985. "The Genesis of the Concepts of Habitus and Field." *Sociocriticism* 2: 11–24.

———. 1991. *The Field of Cultural Production: Essays on Art and Literature*. New York: Columbia University Press.

———. 1993. *Language and Symbolic Power*. Translated by G. Raymond and M. Adamson. Cambridge: Polity.

Bourdieu, Pierre, and Loïc J. D. Wacquant. 1992. *An Invitation to Reflexive Sociology*. Chicago: University of Chicago Press.

Bracamonte y Sosa, Pedro. 2001. *La conquista inconclusa de Yucatán: Los mayas de las montañas, 1560–1680*. Mexico City: Centro de Investigaciones y Estudios Superiores en Antropología Social, Universidad de Quintana Roo.

Bracamonte y Sosa, Pedro, and Gabriela Solís Robleda. 1996. *Espacios mayas de autonomía: El pacto colonial en Yucatán*. Mérida: Universidad Nacional Autónoma de México.

Brenneis, Donald, and Ronald K. S. Macaulay, eds. 1998. *The Matrix of Language: Contemporary Linguistic Anthropology*. Boulder, CO: Westview Press.

Bricker, Victoria R. 1974. "The Ethnographic Context of Some Traditional Mayan Speech Genres." In *Explorations in the Ethnography of Speaking*, edited by Richard Bauman and Joel Sherzer, 368–88. London: Cambridge University Press.

———. 1981. *The Indian Christ, the Indian King: The Historical Substrate of Maya Myth and Ritual*. Austin: University of Texas Press.

———. 1983. "Directional Glyphs in Maya Inscriptions and Codices." *American Antiquity* 48 (2): 347–53.

———. 1986. *A Grammar of Mayan Hieroglyphs*. Middle American Research Institute, Publication 56. New Orleans: Tulane University.

———. 1989. "The Last Gasp of Maya Hieroglyphic Writing in the Books of Chilam Balam of Chumayel and Chan Kan." In *Word and Image in Maya Culture: Explorations in Language, Writing, and Representation*, edited by William F. Hanks and Don S. Rice, 39–50. Salt Lake City: University of Utah Press.

———. 1990. *A Morpheme Concordance of the Book of Chilam Balam of Chumayel*. Middle American Research Institute, Publication 59. New Orleans: Tulane University.

———. 2007. "Literary Continuities across the Transformation from Maya Hieroglyphic to Alphabetic Writing." *Proceedings of the American Philosophical Society* 151 (1): 27–41.

Bricker, Victoria R., and Helga-Maria Miram. 2002. *An Encounter of Two Worlds: The Book of Chilam Balam of Kaua*. New Orleans: Middle American Research Institute, Tulane University.

Bricker, Victoria, Eleuterio Pó'ot Yah, and Ofelia Dzul de Pó'ot. 1998. *A Dictionary of the Maya Language: As Spoken in Hocaba, Yucatán*. Salt Lake City: University of Utah Press.

Brinton, Daniel G., ed. 1969. *The Maya Chronicles*. New York: AMS Press.

Burke, Peter. 1992. *History and Social Theory*. Ithaca, NY: Cornell University Press.

Burkhart, Louise. 1989. *The Slippery Earth: Nahua-Christian Moral Dialogue in Sixteenth-Century Mexico*. Tucson: University of Arizona Press.

Calepino de Motul: Diccionario de Motul Maya-Español. 1995. Edited with indexes by Ramón Arzápalo Marín. 3 vols. Mexico City: Universidad Nacional Autónoma de México.

Calepino Maya de Motul, by Fray Antonio de Ciudad Real. 1984. Facsimile edition in 2 volumes by René Acuña. Mexico City: Universidad Nacional Autónoma de México.

Canger, Una. 1997. "El arte de Horacio Caroche." In *La descripción de las lenguas amerindias en la época colonial*, edited by Klaus Zimmermann, 59–74. Frankfurt: Vervuert Verlag.

Carrillo, Crescencio. 1872. "Estudios bibliográficos: Disertación sobre la historia de la lengua maya o yucateca." *Boletín de la Sociedad Mexicana*, Segunda Época, 4.

Castillo Cocom, Juan. 2005. "It Was Simply Their Word: Yucatec Maya Princes in Yucatán and the Politics of Respect." *Critique of Anthropology* 25 (2): 131–55.

Catechism of the Catholic Church. 2000. Second edition, revised in accordance with the official Latin text promulgated by Pope John Paul II. Vatican: Libreria Editrice.

Certeau, Michel de. 1988. *The Writing of History*. Translated by Tom Conley. New York: Columbia University Press.

Chronicle of Chac Xulub Chen. 1969 [1562]. In *The Maya Chronicles*, edited by Daniel G. Brinton, 187–260. New York: AMS Press.

Chuchiak, John. 2000a. "*Fide, non Armis*: Franciscan *Reducciones*, the Frontier Mission Experience, and the Subjugation of the Maya Hinterland, 1602–1640." Paper presented at the Academy of American Franciscan History.

———. 2000b. "The Indian Inquisition and the Extirpation of Idolatry: The Process of Punishment in the Provisorato de Indios of the Diocese of Yucatán, 1563–1812." Ph.D. dissertation, Tulane University.

———. 2007. "The Sins of the Fathers: Franciscan Friars, Parish Priests, and the Sexual Conquest of the Yucatec Maya, 1545–1808." *Ethnohistory* 54 (1): 69–127.

Ciudad Real, Antonio de. See *Calepino Maya de Motul.*

——. 1929 [late 1500s]. See *Diccionario de Motul.*

——. 1976 [ca. 1590]. *Tratado Curioso y Docto de las Grandezas de la Nueva España.* Edited with introduction, appendixes, glossaries, maps, and indexes by Josefina García Quintana and Victor M. Castillo Farreras. Mexico City: Instituto de Investigaciones Historicas, Universidad Nacional Autónoma de México.

Clendinnen, Inga. 1980. "Landscape and World View: The Survival of Yucatec Maya Culture under Spanish Conquest." *Comparative Studies in Society and History* 22: 374–93.

——. 1987. *Ambivalent Conquests: Maya and Spaniard in Yucatán, 1517–1570.* Cambridge: Cambridge University Press.

Códice Franciscano. 1941. Nueva Colección de Documentos para la Historia de México, Siglo XVI, 55–72. Mexico City: Editorial Salvador Chávez Hayhoe.

Códice Nakuk Pech. n.d. Tozzer Library, Harvard University, Cambridge, MA.

Códice Pérez. 1949. Translated by Ermilo Solís Alcalá. Mérida: Imprenta Oriente.

Coe, Michael, and Justine Kerr. 1998. *The Art of the Maya Scribe.* New York: Harry N. Abrams.

Cogolludo, Diego López de. 1971 [1688]. *Los tres siglos de la dominación española en Yucatán, o sea Historia de esta provincia.* 2 vols. Graz, Austria: Akademische Druck-u. Verlagsanstalt.

Cohn, Bernard S. 1996. *Colonialism and Its Forms of Knowledge: The British in India.* Princeton: Princeton University Press.

Collins, Anne C. 1977. "The Maestros Cantores in Yucatán." In *Anthropology and History in Yucatán,* edited by Grant Jones, 233–47. Austin: University of Texas Press.

Comaroff, John, and Jean Comaroff. 1991. *Of Revelation and Revolution: Christianity, Colonialism, and Consciousness in South Africa.* Chicago: University of Chicago Press.

Cook, Sherburne F., and Woodrow Borah. 1974. *Essays in Population History: Mexico and the Caribbean.* Berkeley: University of California Press.

Coronel, Fr. Juan. 1620a. *Discursos Predicables.* Vol. 1, fol. 66. MS. 1965, Ayer Collection, Newberry Library, Chicago.

——. 1620b. *Doctrina Cristiana en Lengua Maya.* MS. 1966, Ayer Collection, Newberry Library, Chicago.

——. 1998 [1620]. *Arte en lengua de maya: y otros escritos.* Edited by René Acuña with appendixes by David Bolles. Ciudad Universitaria: Universidad Nacional Autonóma de Mexico, Instituto de Investigaciones Filológicas, Centro de Estudios Mayas.

Cortés Castellanos, Justino. 1987. *El Catecismo en Pictogramas de Fr. Pedro de Gante.* Biblioteca Histórica Hispanoamericana 10. Madrid: Fundación Universitaria Española.

Covarrubias, Sebastián de. 1995 [1611]. *Tesoro de la Lengua Castellana o Española.* Edited by Felipe C. Maldonado. Madrid: Editorial Castalia.

Crapanzano, Vincent. 2000. *Serving the Word: Literalism in America from the Pulpit to the Bench.* New York: New Press.

Diccionario de Autoridades, Real Academia Española. 1990 [1726]. Facsimile. 6 vols. Madrid: Editorial Gredos.

Diccionario de Motul, Maya-Español. Atribuido a Fray Antonio de Ciudad Real. 1929 [late 1500s]. Edited by Juan Martínez Hernández. Mérida: Talleres de la Compañía Tipográfica Yucateca.

Diccionario de San Francisco, Part I, Part II. 1976 [n.d., ca. 1600]. Edited by Oscar Michelon. Graz, Austria: Akademische Druck-u. Verlagsanstalt.

Dizionario Francescano. 1983. Padua: Messaggero.

Doctrina Cristiana muy util y Necesaria. See Resines, Luis.

Domínguez y Argáiz, Francisco. 1758. *Pláticas de los principales misterios de nuestra Santa Fe.* . . . Mexico City: S. Ildefonso.

Eckert, Penelope, and John R. Rickford, eds. 2001. *Style and Sociolinguistic Variation.* Cambridge: Cambridge University Press.

Edmonson, Munro. 1970. "Metáfora maya en literatura y en arte." In *Verhandlungen des XXXVIII Internationalen Amerikanistenkongresses,* 2:37–50. Munich: Stuttgart-Munich.

———. 1973. "Semantic Universals and Particulars in Quiche." In *Meaning in Mayan Languages: Ethnolinguistic Studies,* edited by Munro S. Edmonson, 235–46. The Hague: Mouton.

———. 1982. *The Ancient Future of the Itza: The Book of Chilam Balam of Tizimin.* Austin: University of Texas Press.

———. 1986. *Heaven-Born Mérida and Its Destiny: The Chilam Balam of Chumayel.* Austin: University of Texas Press.

Edmonson, Munro, and Victoria R. Bricker. 1985. "Yucatec Mayan Literature." In *Supplement to the Handbook of Middle American Indians,* vol. 3, edited by Victoria R. Bricker and Munro Edmonson, 44–63. Austin: University of Texas Press.

Elias, Norbert. 1994. *The Civilizing Process.* Oxford: Blackwell.

Enfield, Nicholas J., and Stephen C. Levinson, eds. 2006. *Roots of Human Sociality: Cognition, Culture and Interaction.* Oxford: Berg.

Esparza, Miguel Angel, and Vicente Calvo. *See* Nebrija, Antonio de, 1996 [ca. 1488].

Fabian, Johannes. 1986. *Language and Colonial Power: The Appropriation of Swahili in the Former Belgian Congo.* Berkeley: University of California Press.

Farriss, Nancy M. 1978. "Nucleation versus Dispersal: The Dynamics of Population Movement in Colonial Yucatan." *Hispanic American Historical Review* 58: 187–216.

———. 1984. *Maya Society under Colonial Rule: The Collective Enterprise of Survival.* Princeton: Princeton University Press.

Foster, George. 1960. *Culture and Conquest: America's Spanish Heritage.* New York: Wenner-Gren Foundation.

Foucault, Michel. 1971. *L'ordre du Discours: Leçon inaugurale au Collège de France.* Paris: Gallimard.

———. 1979. "What Is an Author?" In *Textual Strategies: Perspectives in Post-Structuralist Criticism,* edited by Josue V. Harari, 141–60. Ithaca, NY: Cornell University Press.

García Añoveros, Jesús María. 1990. *La monarquía y la iglesia en América.* Valencia: Asociación Francisco López de Gómara, Gráficas Morvedre.

García Bernal, Manuela Cristina. 1972. *La sociedad de Yucatán, 1700–1750.* Sevilla: Escuela de Estudios Hispano-Americanos.

García Quintana, Josefina, and Victor M. Castillo Farreras. *See* Ciudad Real, Antonio de, 1976 [ca. 1590].

Garibay, Ángel María. 1953. *Historia de la literatura nahuatl.* Mexico City: Editorial Porrua.

Gates, William, trans. 1937. *Yucatan before and after the Conquest,* by Friar Diego de Landa. Baltimore, MD: Maya Society.

Gerhard, Peter. 1993. *The Southeast Frontier of New Spain.* Norman: University of Oklahoma Press.

Gibson, Charles. 1964. *The Aztecs under Spanish Rule: A History of the Indians of the Valley of Mexico, 1519–1810.* Stanford, CA: Stanford University Press.

———. 1966. *Spain in America.* New York: HarperColophon.

Goffman, Erving. 1974. *Forms of Talk.* Philadelphia: University of Pennsyvania Press.

Gómez Canedo, Lino. 1977. *Evangelización y conquista: Experiencia franciscana en Hispanoamérica.* Mexico City: Editorial Porrua.

González Cicero, Stella María. 1978. *Perspectiva religiosa en Yucatán, 1515–1571.* Mexico City: El Colegio de México.

Goodman, Nelson. 1978. *Ways of Worldmaking.* Indianapolis: Hackett.

Gossen, Gary. 1985. "Tzotzil Literature." In *Supplement to the Handbook of Middle American Indians,* vol. 3, edited by Victoria R. Bricker and Munro S. Edmonson, 65–106. Austin: University of Texas Press.

Greenleaf, Richard E. 1995. *La inquisición en Nueva España siglo XVI.* Mexico City: Fondo de Cultura Económica.

Gruzinski, Serge. 1983. *The Conquest of Mexico: The Incorporation of Indian Societies into the Western World, Sixteenth to Eighteenth Centuries.* Translated from the French by Eileen Corrigan. Cambridge: Polity Press.

———. 2000. "Individualization and Acculturation: Confession among the Nahuas of Mexico from the Sixteenth to the Eighteenth Century." In *The Church in Colonial Latin America,* edited by John Schwaller, 103–20. Wilmington, DE: Scholarly Resources.

Guerra, José Antonio. 1993. *San Francisco de Asís: Escritos, biografías, documentos de la época.* Madrid: Biblioteca de Autores Cristianos.

Hanks, William F. 1984. "Sanctification, Structure, and Experience in a Yucatec Maya Ritual Event." *Journal of American Folklore* 97 (384): 131–66.

———. 1986. "Authenticity and Ambivalence in the Text: A Colonial Maya Case." *American Ethnologist* 13 (4): 721–44.

———. 1987. "Discourse Genres in a Theory of Practice." *American Ethnologist* 14 (4): 668–92.

———. 1988. "Grammar, Style and Meaning in a Maya Manuscript." *International Journal of American Linguistics* 54 (3): 331–64.

———. 1989. "Text and Textuality." *Annual Review of Anthropology* 18: 95–127.

———. 1990a. "Elements of Maya Style." In *Word and Image in Mayan Culture: Explorations in Language, Writing, and Representation,* edited by William F. Hanks and Don S. Rice, 92–111. Salt Lake City: University of Utah Press.

———. 1990b. *Referential Practice, Language, and Lived Space among the Maya.* Chicago: University of Chicago Press.

———. 1992a. "L'Intertextualité de l'espace au Yucatan." *L'Homme* (Paris), no. 122–24: 53–74.

———. 1992b. "The Language of the Canek Manuscript." *Ancient Mesoamerica* 3: 269–79.

———. 1996. "Language and Discourse in Colonial Yucatán." In *Le nouveau monde, mondes nouveaux: L'Expérience américaine*, 238–71. Paris: Éditions Recherches sur les Civilizations, EHESS.

———. 2000. "Dialogic Conversions and the Field of Missionary Discourse in Colonial Yucatán." In *Les rituels du dialogue*, edited by A. Monod Becquelin and Philippe Erikson, 235–54. Nanterre: Société d'Ethnologie.

———. 2005. "Pierre Bourdieu and the Practices of Language." *Annual Review of Anthropology* 34: 67–83.

———. 2006. "Conviction and Common Ground in a Ritual Event." In *Roots of Human Sociality: Cognition, Culture and Interaction*, edited by Nicholas J. Enfield and Stephen C. Levinson, 299–328. Oxford: Berg.

Harding, Susan Friend. 2000. *The Book of Jerry Falwell: Fundamentalist Language and Politics*. Princeton: Princeton University Press.

Hill, Jane H. 2001. "Syncretism." In *Key Terms in Language and Culture*, edited by Alessandro Duranti, 241–43. Malden, MA: Blackwell.

Hill, Jane H., and Kenneth C. Hill. 1986. *Speaking Mexicano*. Tucson: University of Arizona Press.

Irvine, Martin. 1994. *The Making of Textual Culture: 'Grammatica' and Literary Theory, 350–1110*. Cambridge: Cambridge University Press.

Jones, Grant D. 1989. *Maya Resistance to Spanish Rule: Time and History on a Colonial Frontier*. Albuquerque: University of New Mexico Press.

———. 1998. *The Conquest of the Last Maya Kingdom*. Stanford, CA: Stanford University Press.

Kagan, Richard. 1989. *Spanish Cities of the Golden Age*. Berkeley: University of California Press.

Keane, Webb. 2007. *Christian Moderns: Freedom and Fetish in the Mission Encounter*. Berkeley: University of California Press.

Knowlton, Timothy W. 2004. "Dialogism in the Languages of Colonial Maya Creation Myths." Ph.D. dissertation, Tulane University.

Landa, Diego de. 1941. *Relación de las cosas de Yucatán*. Translated and edited by Alfred M. Tozzer. Cambridge, MA: Peabody Museum of American Archaeology and Ethnology, Harvard University.

———. 1982. *Relación de las Cosas de Yucatán*. Introduction by Angel Garibay. Mexico City: Editorial Porrua.

———. 1985. *Relación de las Cosas de Yucatán*. Edited by Miguel Rivera. Madrid: García Noblejas.

Laughlin, Robert M., with John B. Haviland. 1988. *The Great Tzotzil Dictionary of Santo Domingo Zinacantán, with Grammatical Analysis and Historical Commentary*. Vol. 1: *Tzotzil-English*. Smithsonian Contributions to Anthropology, No. 31. Washington, DC: Smithsonian Institution Press.

Launey, Michel. 1997. "La elaboración de los conceptos de la diátesis en las primeras gramáticas del nahuatl." In *La descripción de las lenguas amerindias en la época colonial*, edited by Klaus Zimmermann, 21–42. Frankfurt: Vervuert Verlag.

Liu, Lydia. 1995. *Translingual Practice: Literature, National Culture, and Translated Modernity—China, 1900–1937.* Stanford, CA: Stanford University Press.

Lizana, Bernardo de. 1893 [1633]. *Historia de Yucatán: Devocionario de Nuestra Señora de Izamal y conquista espiritual.* 2nd ed. Mexico City: Museo Nacional.

———. 1988 [1633]. *Historia de Yucatán.* Edited by Felix Jiménez Villalba. Madrid: Información y Revistas.

López Medel, Tomás. 1971 [1688]. *Ordenanzas [1552].* In *Los tres siglos de la dominación española en Yucatán, o sea Historia de esta provincia,* by Fr. Diego López de Cogolludo, vol. 1, bk. 5, 390–405. Graz, Austria: Akademische Druck- u. Verlagsanstalt.

Masson, Marilyn. 2000. "The Dynamics of Maturing Statehood in Postclassic Maya Civilization." In *MAYA: Divine Kings of the Forest,* edited by Nikolai Gruber, 341–50. Cologne: Könemann Verlagsgesellschaft.

Masson, Marilyn A., Carlos Peraza Lope, and Timothy S. Hare. 2002. "Surface Evidence of Mayapán's Political Economy." Paper presented at the meeting of the Society for American Archaeology, Denver, March 23.

McConvell, Patrick, and Felicity Meakins. 2005. "Gurundji Kriol: A Mixed Language Emerges from Code-Switching." *Australian Journal of Linguistics* 25 (1): 9–30.

McQuown, Norman A. 1967. "Classical Yucatec (Maya)." In *Handbook of Middle American Indians,* vol. 5: *Linguistics,* 201–47. Austin: University of Texas Press.

Means, Philip Ainsworth. 1932. *Fall of the Inca Empire and the Spanish Rule in Peru: 1530–1780.* New York: Charles Scribner's Sons.

Meyers-Scotton, C. 2003. "What Lies Beneath: Split (Mixed) Languages as Contact Phenomena." In *The Mixed Language Debate: Theoretical and Empirical Advances,* edited by Y. Matras and P. Bakker, 73–106. Berlin: Mouton de Gruyter.

Miram, Helga-Maria, and Wolfgang Miram. 1988. *Konkordanz der Chilam Balames.* 6 vols. *Transcriptions.* 4 vols. Hamburg: Toto-Verlag.

Molina, Alonso de. 1975 [1569]. *Confesionario mayor en la lengua mexicana y castellana.* Facsimile ed. Mexico City: Instituto de Investigaciones Bibliográficas, Universidad Nacional.

Montejo, Victor. 1999. *Voices from Exile: Violence and Survival in Modern Maya History.* Norman: University of Oklahoma Press.

Moorman, John. 1968. *A History of the Franciscan Order, from Its Origins to the Year 1517.* London: Oxford University Press.

Morley, Sylvanus, and Ralph Roys. 1941. *The Xiu Chronicle.* Carnegie Institute of Washington. Typescript held in Tozzer Library, Harvard University, Cambridge, MA.

Nagy, Peroska. 2000. *Le don des larmes au Moyen Âge: Un instrument spirituel en quête d'institution (V^e–XIIIe siècle).* Paris: Éditions Albin Michel.

Nandy, Ashis. 1983. *The Intimate Enemy: Loss and Recovery of Self under Colonialism.* Delhi: Oxford University Press.

Nebrija, Antonio de. 1992 [1492]. *Gramática de la lengua castellana.* Edited by Antonio Quilis. Colección Crisol. Madrid: Aguilar, S.A. de Ediciones.

———. 1996 [ca. 1488]. *Introducciones latinas contrapuesto el romance al latín.* Edited by Miguel Angel Esparza and Vincente Calvo. Münster: Nodus Publikationen.

Norman, William M. 1980. "Grammatical Parallelism in Quiche Ritual Language." In

Proceedings of the Sixth Annual Meeting of the Berkeley Linguistic Society, 387–99. Berkeley, CA: Berkeley Linguistic Society.

Okoshi Harada, Tsubasa. 1994. "Ecab: Una revisión de la geografía política de una provincia maya yucateca." In *Memorias del Primer Congreso Internacional de Mayistas.* Mexico City: Universidad Nacional Autónoma de México.

———. 2006a. "*Kax* (monte) y *luum* (tierra): La transformación de los espacios mayas en el siglo XVI." In *El mundo maya: Miradas japonesas,* edited by Kazuyasu Ochiai, 85–104. Mexico City: Universidad Nacional Autónoma de México.

———. 2006b. *Nuevas perspectivas sobre la geografía política de los mayas.* Mexico City: Universidad Nacional Autónoma de México.

Pagden, Anthony. 1982. *The Fall of Natural Man: The American Indian and the Origins of Comparative Ethnology.* Cambridge: Cambridge University Press.

Panofsky, Erwin. 1976. *Gothic Architecture and Scholasticism: An Inquiry into the Analogy of the Arts, Philosophy, and Religion in the Middle Ages.* New York: Meridian.

Patch, Robert. 1993. *Maya and Spaniard in Yucatán, 1648–1812.* Stanford, CA: Stanford University Press.

Pereña, Luciano. 1996. *Carta magna de los indios.* Salamanca: Universidad Pontificia de Salamanca.

Pereña, Luciano, José M. Pérez-Prendes, Carlos Baciero, Antonio García García, Luis Resines, Pedro Borges, and Mariano Cuesta. 1992. *Utopía y realidad indiana.* Salamanca: Universidad Pontificia de Salamanca.

Pérez, Juan Pío. 1866–77. *Diccionario de la Lengua Maya.* Mérida: Imprenta Literaria de Juan Molina Solís.

Pérez-Prendes, José M. 1992. "El dictamen de Tomás López Medel para la reformación de Indias." In *Utopía y realidad indiana,* by Luciano Pereña, José M. Pérez-Prendes, Carlos Baciero, Antonio García García, Luis Resines, Pedro Borges, and Mariano Cuesta, 25–102. Salamanca: Universidad Pontificia de Salamanca.

Putallaz, François-Xavier. 1997. *Figures franciscaines de Bonaventure à Duns Scot.* Série Initiations au Moyen Âge. Paris: Éditions du CERF.

Putnam, Hilary. 1975. *Mind, Language, and Reality.* Cambridge: Cambridge University Press.

Quezada, Sergio. 1992. *Relación documental para la historia de la provincia de Yucatán (1520–1844).* Mérida: Universidad Autónoma de Yucatán.

———. 1993. *Pueblos y caciques yucatecos, 1550–1580.* Mexico City: El Colegio de México.

———. 2001. Breve historia de Yucatán. Mexico City: El Colegio de México, Fideicomiso Historia de las Américas, Fondo de Cultura Económica.

Quezada, Sergio, and Tsubasa Okoshi. 2001. *Papeles de los Xiu de Yaxá, Yucatán: Introducción, transcripción, traducción y notas.* Mexico City: Universidad Nacional Autónoma de México.

Quilis, Antonio. *See* Nebrija, Antonio de, 1992 [1492].

Rafael, Vicente L. 1993. *Contracting Colonialism: Translation and Christian Conversion in Tagalog Society under Early Spanish Rule.* Durham, NC: Duke University Press.

Rampton, Ben. 1995. *Cross Talk: Language and Ethnicity among Adolescents.* London: Longman.

Recopilación de leyes de los reynos de las Indias. 1973 [1681]. Madrid: Julián de Paredes. Republished in facsimile. Madrid: Ediciones Cultura Hispánica.

Redfield, Robert. 1941. *The Folk Culture of Yucatán.* Chicago: University of Chicago Press.

Relaciones Histórico-geográficas de la gobernación de Yucatán. 1983. Edición preparada por Mercedes de la Garza, Ana Luisa Ixquierdo y Ma. del Carmen León y Tolita Figueroa. Mexico City: Universidad Nacional Autónoma de México.

Resines, Luis, ed. 1990 [1578]. *Doctrina Cristiana muy util y Necesaria.* Acta Salamanticensia, Estudio General 2. Salamanca: Ediciones de la Universidad de Salamanca.

Restall, Matthew. 1995. "He Wished It in Vain: Subordination and Resistance among Maya Women in Post-Conquest Yucatan." *Ethnohistory* 42: 577–94.

———. 1997. *The Maya World, Yucatec Culture and Society, 1550–1850.* Stanford, CA: Stanford University Press.

———. 1998. *Maya Conquistador.* Boston: Beacon Press.

———. 2003. *Seven Myths of the Spanish Conquest.* Oxford: Oxford University Press, 2003.

Ricard, Robert. 1995. *La conquista espiritual de México: Ensayo sobre el apostolado y los métodos misioneros de las órdenes mendicantes en la Nueva España de 1523–1524 a 1572.* Mexico City: Fondo de Cultura Económica.

Robbins, Joel. 2001. "God Is Nothing but Talk: Modernity, Language, and Prayer in a Papua New Guinea Society." *American Anthropologist* 103 (4): 901–12.

———. 2007. "You Can't Talk Behind the Holy Spirit's Back: Christianity and Changing Language Ideologies in a Papua New Guinea Society." In *Consequences of Contact: Language Ideologies and Sociocultural Transformations in Pacific Societies,* edited by M. Makihara and Bambi B. Schieffelin, 125–39. New York: Oxford University Press.

Roys, Ralph L. 1939. *The Titles of Ebtun.* Washington, DC: Carnegie Institution.

———. 1943. *The Indian Background of Colonial Yucatan.* Publication 548. Washington, DC: Carnegie Institution.

———. 1957. *The Political Geography of the Yucatán Maya.* Washington, DC: Carnegie Institution.

———, ed. and trans. 1965. *Ritual of the Bacabs.* Norman: University of Oklahoma Press.

Rubio Mañé, J. Ignacio. 1942. *Archivo de la Historia de Yucatán, Campeche, y Tabasco.* Mexico City: Imprenta Aldina, Robredo y Rosell.

Rumsey, Alan. 2008. "Confession, Anger and Cross-Cultural Articulation in Papua New Guinea." *Anthropological Quarterly* 81 (2): 455–72. [Special issue, *Anthropology and the Opacity of Other Minds,* edited by Alan Rumsey and Joel Robbins.]

Sammons, Kay, and Joel Sherzer. 2000. *Translating Native Latin American Verbal Art: Ethnopoetics and Ethnography of Speaking.* Washington, DC: Smithsonian Institution Press.

San Buenaventura, Fr. Gabriel de. 1888 [1684]. *Arte de la lengua maya.* Facsimile ed. Edited by Joaquín García Icazbalceta. Mexico City: Francisco Díaz de León.

———. 1996 [1684]. *Arte de la lengua maya.* Edited, with facsimile of the 1888 edition, by René Acuña. Mexico City: Universidad Nacional Autónoma de México.

Sánchez de Aguilar, Pedro. 1996 [1639]. *Informe Contra Idolorum Cultores del obispado de Yucatán dirigido al Rey N. Señor en su Real Consejo de las Indias.* Facsimile edition of

1892 publication. 5th ed. Edited by Renan A. Gongora Biachi. Mérida: Ediciones del Instituto Cultural Valladolid.

Santamaría, Francisco. 1992. *Diccionario de mejicanismos.* 5th ed. Mexico City: Editorial Porrua.

Schieffelin, Bambi B. 2001. "Marking Time, the Dichotomizing Discourse of Multiple Temporalities." *Current Anthropology* 43 (Suppl. August–October): S5–S17.

———. 2007. "Found in Translating: Reflexive Language across Time and Texts in Bosavi, Papua New Guinea." In *Consequences of Contact: Language Ideologies and Sociocultural Transformations in Pacific Societies,* edited by M. Makihara and Bambi B. Schieffelin, 140–65. New York: Oxford University Press.

Scholes, France, Carlos Menéndez, J. Rubio Mañé, and E. Adams, eds. 1938. *Documentos para la Historia de Yucatán,* vol. 2: *La iglesia en Yucatán.* Mérida: Compañía Tipográfica Yucateca.

Sharer, Robert J. 2006. *The Ancient Maya.* Stanford, CA: Stanford University Press.

Sherzer, Joel. 1990. *Verbal Art in San Blas: Kuna Culture through Its Discourse.* Cambridge: Cambridge University Press.

Short, William, O.F.M. 1989. *The Franciscans.* Collegeville, MN: Liturgical Press/Michael Glazier Books.

———. 1999. *Poverty and Joy: The Franciscan Tradition.* Maryknoll, NY: Orbis Books.

Sigal, Peter. 2000. *From Moon Goddess to Virgins: The Colonization of Yucatecan Maya Sexual Desire.* Austin: University of Texas Press.

Silverstein, Michael. 1998. "Monoglot 'Standard' in America: Standardization and Metaphors of Linguistic Hegemony." In *The Matrix of Language: Contemporary Linguistic Anthropology,* edited by Donald Brenneis and Ronald K. S. Macaulay, 284–306. Boulder, CO: Westview Press.

Solís Robleda, Gabriela, and Paola Peniche. 1996. *Idolatría y sublevación.* Mérida: Universidad Autónoma de Yucatán.

Sullivan, Paul. 1989. *Unfinished Conversations: Mayas and Foreigners between Two World Wars.* New York: Alfred A. Knopf.

Taylor, William B. 1996. *Magistrates of the Sacred: Priests and Parishioners in Eighteenth-Century Mexico.* Stanford, CA: Stanford University Press.

———. 2005. "Two Shrines of the Cristo Renovado: Religion and Peasant Politics in Late Colonial Mexico." *American Historical Review* 110 (4): 944–74.

Tedlock, Dennis. 1983. *The Spoken Word and the Work of Interpretation.* Philadelphia: University of Pennsylvania Press.

Thiemer-Sachse, Ursula. 1997. "El Vocabulario castellano-zapoteco y el Arte en lengua zapoteca de Juan de Córdova—intenciones y resultados (perspectiva antropológica)." In *La descripción de las lenguas amerindias en la época colonial,* edited by Klaus Zimmermann, 147–74. Frankfurt: Vervuert Verlag.

Thompson, Philip C. 1978. "Tekanto in the Eighteenth Century." Ph.D. dissertation, Tulane University.

Thompson, R. A. 1974. *The Winds of Tomorrow: Social Change in a Maya Town.* Chicago: University of Chicago Press.

Toral, Francisco de. 1938 [n.d.]. *Avisos del Obispo Fr. Francisco de Toral.* In *Documentos para la Historia de Yucatán,* vol. 2: *La iglesia en Yucatán, 1560–1610,* edited by France Scholes, Carlos Menéndez, J. Rubio Mañé, and E. Adams, 25–34. Mérida: Compañía Tipográfica Yucateca.

Tozzer, Alfred M., ed. 1941. *Landa's* Relación de las cosas de Yucatán. Papers of the Peabody Museum of American Archeology and Ethnology, vol. 18. Cambridge, MA: Harvard University Press.

———. 1977 [1921]. *A Maya Grammar.* New York: Dover Publications.

Urban, Greg. 1991. *A Discourse-Centered Approach to Culture: Native South American Myths and Rituals.* Austin: University of Texas Press.

Villa Rojas, Alfonso. 1945. *The Maya of East Central Quintana Roo.* Washington, DC: Carnegie Institution.

———. 1978 [1954]. *Los elegidos de Dios: Etnografía de los mayas de Quintana Roo.* Série de Antropología Social, 56. Mexico City: INI.

Warren, Kay. 1998. *Indigenous Movements and Their Critics: Pan-Maya Activism in Guatemala.* Princeton: Princeton University Press.

Whalen, Gretchen. 2003. *Annotated Translation of a Colonial Yucatec Manuscript: On Religious and Cosmological Topics by a Native Author.* Final Report to the Foundation for the Advancement of Mesoamerican Studies.

Woolard, Kathryn. 1998. "Simultaneity and Bivalency as Strategies in Bilingualism." *Journal of Linguistic Anthropology* 8: 3–29.

Ximena, Lois, and Valentina Vapnarsky, eds. 2006. *Lexical Categories and Root Classes in Amerindian Languages.* Bern: Peter Lang.

Zimmermann, Günter. 1970. *Briefe der indianischen Nobilitat aus Neuspanien an Karl V um die Mitte des 16. Jahrhunderts.* Munich: Kommissionsverlag Klaus Renner.

Zimmermann, Klaus. 1997a. "La descripción del otomí/hñahñu en la época colonial: Lucha y éxito." In *La descripción de las lenguas amerindias en la época colonial,* ed. Klaus Zimmermann, 113–32. Frankfurt: Vervuert Verlag.

———, ed. 1997b. *La descripción de las lenguas amerindias en la época colonial.* Frankfurt: Vervuert Verlag.

INDEX

357; omnipotence of, 12, 14–15; prayers addressed to, 244; as "True God," 356. See also *cayumil ti dios; cuxul ku; Dios/Diós; hahal dios; ku; yumbil*
Goffman, Erving, 100, 385n5, 386n8
Gómez Brizeño, Br. Juan, 221, 223, 225
Gómez Canedo, Lino, xiv
Gómez de Cervantes, don Francisco Xavier, 235
Gómez Pacheco, Juan, 109, 110
Gondiçalus, fray, 109
Goodman, Nelson, 3
Gospel, 2, 73, 302, 323, 324
governance: of *cabildos,* 79–84, 287; dictionaries and, 127, 128, 143–48, 185; discourse formation outside sphere of, 338; doctrinal works and, 284; of *guardianías,* 60–63; land surveys and, 293; *Maya reducido* and, 365; notarial documents and, 285, 286; as object of scholarship, 242; overlapping forms of, 243; of *pueblos reducidos,* xviii, xix, 17, 80, 87, 217, 285, 338
gramática ('grammar'), 11, 139, 140, 157, 206–7, 241
Gramática de la lengua castellana (Nebrija), 375n6, 390n2
grammar, 150–51, 161–62, 163, 196, 203, 230
grammar manuals, xiii, 7, 20, 60, 78, 375n6. See also *artes*
Gramsci, Antonio, 8
grass, signs made with, 142, 314
Greenleaf, Richard E., xiv
Gruzinski, Serge, xiv
Guaman Poma, Book of, 361
guarda(r) ('to keep, protect, guard'), 128, 147, 148, 155, 163
guardián/guardianes ('guardians'), 43, 47, 48, 54, 151, 243; field and, 93, 94; in hierarchy of positions, 75; idolatry charges brought by, 376n13; as leading priests, 74; as *lenguas,* 88, 166; lines of authority and, 46; Maya helpers of, 40; Maya language and, 158; *sublevados* ('fugitives, rebels') and, 55; Toral and, 66
guardianías (mission units), xvii, 3, 11, 84, 154, 291; classes of functionaries in, 73–78; convent *visitas* in, 163; dictionaries produced in, 101, 158; Franciscan–secular dispute and, 89; genres produced in, 118; governance of, 60–63; *lenguas* and, 376n19; map of, *42;* Maya elites in, 300; *Maya reducido* in, 365; movement of discourse and, 364; overlap with *cabildos* as form of governance, 243; peti-

tions and, 316, 319–21, *320, 321,* 337; Post-Classic Maya system and, 382n3; spatial (radial) organization of, *40,* 40–41, 53, 299, 343, 368; staffing of, 59; *visita* towns and, 43, 44–46, 46, 48; in Yaxkukul land surveys, 299
Guatemala, 8, 33, 47, 121, 165, 380n19; frontier road to, 52; *"indio lengua"* in, 377–78n28; ratio of priests to Indios, 41
Guerra de Castas (Caste War), 341, 365–68
Gutierrez, fray Juan, 55

habitus, xv, 2, 7, 59, 91, 96
hacer caso ('pay attention to'), 181, 182
hahal dios ('true god'), 252, 267, 347, 351, 352, 357, 396n5
Hail Mary. *See* Ave Maria (Hail Mary) prayer
halach uinic ('True Man'), 29–31, 49, 292, 293, 298; petitions and, 327–28; titles of Ebtún and, 307. See also *gobernadores*
Halal Actun, *301*
Halalchó, town of, *321*
Hanks, William F., 286, 297
headwords (matrix language), 155, 161, 168; Maya, 122, 124, 128, 160; Spanish, 122, 124, 127
Hecelchakán/Hecelchakan/Xecelchakán/ Xecelchakan/Xequechakan, town of, 6, 47, 54, 285, *321;* as *guardianía,* 42, *43;* petition from, 332–35
hechiceros ('witches'), 62
hedz ('fix, stabilize'), 290, 294, 296, 305, 370
hegemony, 95
heresy, 67, 90, 382n2
Herrera, Padre Alonso de, 104
hetz lú'um ('stabilize land') land purification ceremony, xiii, 370
hieroglyphic writing, 3, 8, 19, 54, 387n10; authorship and, 284; Books of Chilam Balam and, 341; Dresden Codex, 385n6, 397n11; iteration and, 281; literacy in, 91; Mayan root *dzib* and, 139; switch to alphabetic writing under *reducción,* 172; *uoh* term and, 309. See also Maya language
Hill, Jane D., xvii, xviii, 15
Hill, Kenneth C., xvii, 15
Historia de Yucatán (Cogolludo), 46, 71, *pl. 1, pl. 4*
Historia de Yucatán (Lizana), 89, 101–2
historians, 116
Hixil/Ixil, town of, *44, 298, 320, 340, 342*
hmèen ('shaman'), xiii, 368–69. *See also* shamans, Maya

interpretance, 160–61, 164, 388n1

interpretar ('to interpret'), 184, 186

Introducciones latinas contrapuesto el romance al latin (Nebrija), 206, 207, 214

iteration, xiv–xv, 97, 115–17, 155, 281; in Books of Chilam Balam, 353; changes in Maya language and, 365; dispersal of doctrinal discourse and, 349; in petitions, 315, 326, 329

Ixil, Book of, 341, *342*, 343, 346, 347

Ixil/Hixil, town of, *44, 298, 320,* 340, *342*

Ixpimienta, town of, *42, 43,* 54

Izamal/Yçamal/Ytzmal, city of, 3, 11, *pl. 16*; as *guardianía, 42, 43;* maps, *27, 30;* as pilgrimage site, 49; pre-Conquest, 26; *visita* towns of, 42

Izquierdo, fray Juan de, 47–48, 88–89, 103, 104, 105

Jesuits, 221, 223, 230, 376n12, 390n3

Jesus Christ, 9, 15, 69, 202; crucifixion of, 13, 14, 133–34, 273, 359, 369; dictionary terms and, 151; imitation of, 61; incarnation of, 13; Maya epithets for, 347, 351, 357; passion of, 14, 70, 270, 316, 327; persignum (sign of the cross) and, 268, 273; prayers and, 250, 252, 257, 258, 259–60; resurrection of, 14, 130, 268, 269, 273, 369; significance of Mass and, 348; stigmata of, *pl. 11;* virgin birth of, 269

Jones, Grant D., 50, 51, 94

justicias ('magistrates'), 80, 82, 384n20

Kabah, town of, *27*

Kagan, Richard, 38

kahlay ('history'), 97

kamnicte ('receive flower'), 249

Kancab Ch'en, *301*

Kan Pepen, *301*

Kan Pepenil, *303*

Kantun, Fernando, 330, 332

Kantunilkín/Kantunilkin, town of, *30*

Kaua, Book of, 13, 341, 343; doctrinal language in, 345–49; location where found, *342;* on prayers in Latin, 358, 363–64. *See also* Chilam Balam, Books of

Kaua, town of, 340, *342*

Keane, Webb, xviii

keban ('sin, sadness, anxiety, anger, betrayal'), 169, 193–94; in Books of Chilam Balam, 347; in Coronel's *doctrina,* 265; in dictionaries, 196–203. *See also* sin

Kinchil/Quinchil, town of, *30, 44*

Kiní/Quini, town of, *46, 298, 320*

kinship, 159, 229, 300

Kochil, 'rotted town' of, 290, 305–6

Komchel/Kumchel/Kumcheil/Tixconchel/Tixkunchel/Tixkuncheil, town of, *46, 298, 299,* 300, *301, 303, 320*

Komchén/Komchen, town of, 27

Kom Sahcab, *303*

ku ('god, precious'), 132–33, 153, 237–38, 307, 397n16; in Books of Chilam Balam, 350, 353, 357; in Coronel's *doctrina,* 350. *See also* God, Christian

Kucab, town of, *321*

Kuk, Francisco, 396n5

Kuk, Juan, 305

Kukulkan, 369

Kumchel. *See* Komchel/Kumchel/Kumcheil/Tixconchel/Tixkunchel/Tixkuncheil, town of

lab cah ('rotted town'), 290, 305–6, 307, 309, 314

Labná/Labna/Labnah, town of, *27,* 306, 398n21

ladinos (Indians fluent in Spanish), 17–19, 76, 378n28; dictionary entries for, 139–40; *ladino* as dictionary term, 128; *lenguas* as counterparts of, 20; scope of bilingualism and, 285; translation of *doctrina* and, 90, 117

Landa, fray Diego de, 8, 9, 101, 118, 240, 382n10; campaign against idolatry, 66; Chi and, 16; Ciudad Real and, 165; defense before Council of Indies, 119; *doctrina* of, 47; genre attribution and, 98–99; idolatry trials conducted by, 104, 284; investigated for persecution of "idolaters," 67, 320; on Maya history/society, 25, 26, 90; on performance of *doctrina,* 113; as provincial of Franciscan order, 39; on signs and auguries, 181; stereotypes about Maya and, 119; students of, 307; on Villalpando, 205. *See also Relación de las Cosas de Yucatán*

land purification *(hetz lú'um),* xiii, 370

land surveys *(deslindes),* 19, 91; boundary markers and, 97; in Maní, 370; reception by readers, 102; rights claimed by, 284; traces of colonial system in, 281; walking processions and, 146; witnesses and, 100; writing the landscape, 289–91

land titles *(títulos),* 19

language, 10, 127; conversion of, 59, 375n10; dictionary terms, 128; doubling of, 81; hierarchy of abilities in, 74; identity and, xvi; ideologies of, 88; "language game," 94–95;

Spanish republics *(repúblicas de españoles)*, 21, 50

spectacle, public, 37

speech, 87, 172; metalinguistics and, 99; proper, 4, 364; regulation of, 9; sin and, 196, 197; "weeping speech" of petitions, 331, 333, 334, 351

sublevados ('fugitives, rebels'), 40, 52, 88, 93, 106, 220

suffixes, 176, 390n3, 391–92n26; in *artes*, 227, 236; dictionaries and, 168; sequential ordering of, 391n22

Sulu, Domingo, 312, 313

superstition, 3, 280, 338, 382n2

surveillance, 2, 63, 68, 383n12; boundaries and, 96; carried out by Maya elites, 72; doctrinal dialogues as instruments of, 270; example sentences from *artes* and, 220; forms of authority and, 73; *Maya reducido* in forbidden genres and, xix; meetings/readings beyond pale of, 362; *Ordenanzas* of López Medel and, 36–37; in urban centers, 61

syncope, 229

syncretism, xiii, 8, 375n11; basic model of, xvii; boundary problem and, 94; dictionary terms and, 133; received model of, 203. *See also* hybridity, cultural/linguistic

Tabasco, province of, 33, 34

Tabi, town of, *30*

Tah Euan Cauich, *303*

Tahmuy, town of, *340*

Tahoxcum, town of, *44*

Tahuman/San Francisco Tahuman, town of, *44*, 108, 109

Tampalam, town of, *27*

Tancah, town of, *27*

Tan Kancab, *301, 303*

tan lah ('worship-obey'), 153

Tapich/Tepich, town of, *30*, 366

target (object) language (L2), 11, 157, 159, 160, 204, 207

Tases, province of, *30*

taxation, 50, 51, 76, 78, 329

Taylor, William B., xiv, 8, 376n18

Teabo/Teab/Tiab, town of, *6, 30, 43*, 230, 234, 288; Book of Nah found in, 340, 342, 399n11:2, 400n4; as *guardianía*, 43; as *visita*, 45

Tecah/Tecoh, town of, *6*, 28, *30*, 48

Tecanto/Tekantó/Tekanto, town of, *6, 42, 43*, 81, 396n8

Tecax. *See* Tekax/Tecax, town of

Tecoh/Tecah, town of, *6*, 28, *30*, 48

Tecoh/Ticoh, town of, *30, 43*, 288

Tekantó/Tekanto/Tecanto, town of, *6, 42, 43*, 81, 396n8

Tekax, Book of, 341, 343; doctrinal language in, 346, 347; location where found, *342*

Tekax/Tecax, town of, 98; as *cabecera de doctrina*, 340; Ciudad Real as *guardián* of, 165, 166; Coronel in, 107, 108, 110, 166, 245–46; as *guardianía*, *42, 43*; maps, *6, 30, 342*; petitions issued from, 288; Sanct Juan Tekax, 293

Tekit/Tiquit, town of, *30, 45*

Telchac/Tichac, town of, *6, 43, 46, 298, 320*, 340

Temax, town of, *6, 30, 43, 298, 320*

Tenabó/Tenaba, town of, *30, 321*

Ten Commandments, 38, 264

Tepakán, town of, *321*

Tepich/Tapich, town of, *30*, 366

tequios labor requirement, 50

testaments (wills), 289, 395–96nn4–5, 396n8; land descriptions in, 286; metalinguistic labeling and, 97; as notarial genre, 19, 285

testigos ('witnesses'), 141, 143, 192, 389n18; lexicon of *reducción* and, 128; notarial documents and, 286, 287. *See also* witnesses, writings and

Teya, town of, *6*

than ('word, language, talk'), 197, 319, 387n17; in Motul, 169, 170, 172; in SF1, 169–72

T'ho. *See* Mérida/Merida/T'ho/Tihoo, city and province of

Thomas Aquinas, Saint, 68

Thompson, E. P., 8

Thompson, Philip C., 80

ti ('to, for, from, in'), 209, 389n16

Tiab. *See* Teabo/Teab/Tiab, town of

Tibolón-Sotuta, town of, 291

Tichac. *See* Telchac/Tichac, town of

Tichulul/Cholul, town of, *44, 298*, 311–12, *320*

Tiçimin. *See* Tizimín/Tizimin/Tiçimin, town of

Ticin Mul, *303*

Ticlançin, town of, *44*

Ticoh/Tecoh, town of, *30, 43*, 288

Ticul, town of, *6, 30, 43*, 52, 293; petitions issued from, 288; as *visita*, 45

Tiholop, town of, *30*

Tihoo. *See* Mérida/Merida/T'ho/Tihoo, city and province of

Tihosuco, town of, *6, 30*, 341

tiitz ('corner'), 290, 292, 305. See also *noh sicina/ noh tiitz*
Tikin Mul, *301*
Tikumché, town of, *321*
Tikunché, town of, *340*
Tinum, town of, *42, 43*
Tiquit/Tekit, town of, *30, 45*
títulos (land titles), 19
Tixcacalcupul, town of, *6, 30*
Tixcancal, town of, *30*
Tixchel/Popola, town of, *6,* 46, 54, 55
Tixcocob. *See* Tixkokob/Tixcocob, town of
Tixconchel. *See* Tixkunchel/Tixkuncheil/ Tixconchel/Komchel/Kumchel/Kumcheil, town of
Tixkokob/Tixcocob, town of, 109, *298,* 299, 300, 320; as *cabecera, 6;* as *guardianía, 42, 43,* 45, 48
Tixkunchel/Tixkuncheil/Tixconchel/Komchel/ Kumchel/Kumcheil, town of, *46, 298,* 299, 300, *301, 303, 320*
Tixmucuy/Edzná/Edzna, town of, *27, 30*
Tixpeual, town of, *45*
Tixualah Tunich, *303*
Tizimín, Book of, 341, 343; on arrival of Christianity, 350; doctrinal language in, 346, 347; location where found, *342;* prophecy in, 353–54. *See also* Chilam Balam, Books of
Tizimín/Tizimin/Tiçimin, town of, *6, 30, 42, 43,* 166, *340*
tohpultah ('confession'), 136, 201, 202, 262, 265. See also *confesar/confesarse*
Toledo (Spain), city of, 8, 166
tone, in Maya language, 227, 391n15; high, 19, 181, 216, 289n10; low, 389n10; neutral, 216
Toral, fray Francisco de, 9, 39, 63, 118, 284, 374n3; *Avisos, 71, 77, 91,* 266; *Ordenanzas,* 265; secular clergy and, 324; vision of spiritual conquest, 66–70; on yes-no doctrinal dialogue, 266, 269
Torquemada, Juan de, *pl. 2*
Torralva, fray Francisco, 109, 110
Torre, fray Juan de la, 47
Torres, fray Juan de, 224, 225
Tozzer, Alfred M., 167
trade networks, 3, 26
Traduccion de la papeles de los publos ("Translation of the papers of the towns"), 307
traición ('betrayal'), 199, 201
transfiguration, xv
translanguage, 10–12, 16, 17, 20, 96, 128; genres

of conversion, xvii–xviii; translingual meaning and commensuration, 157–64
translation, xv, 66, 127; changes in Maya language and, 365; doubling of linguistic space and, 78; as form of *reducción,* 4; genre identification and, 98; missionary fear of ambiguous meanings and, 376–77n23; orality and, 112; transparency principle and, 162. *See also* Maya-into-Spanish translation; Spanish-into-Maya translation
transparency, 160, 162–63, 164, 168, 197, 388n4; in petitions and letters, 319; San Buenaventura's *arte* and, 225
Tratado Curioso y Docto de las Grandezas de la Nueva España (attrib. Ciudad Real), 121, 165, 380n19, 388–89n8
tribute, 34, 36, 46, 49, 315, 352; caciques' attempt to negotiate, 56; Mayans' partial autonomy and, 52. *See also* extraction, of labor, goods, money
Trinity, 269, 343, 366, 368, 370
tropes, 172
tuchhub ('finger pointing'), 141
Tulum, town of, *27,* 367
Tun, Gabriel, 299
Tunkás/Tunkas, town of, *30*
tupiles (constables), 61, 76, 383n17; *cabildo* system and, 80, 81; as enforcers of doctrine, 72, 73
tupop, tutzam ('at the mat, at the throne'), 161
Tusik, Book of, 341, 343, 360, 393n4; doctrinal language in, 346, 347; location where found, *342. See also* Chilam Balam, Books of
Tusik, town of, 340, 341, *342*
Tutul Xiu/Maní, province of, *30,* 143, 292, 293
Tuyu, don Diego, 307
tuzinil ('all, concrete quantity'), 12, 13–15, 238, 257, 358–59, 392n27
typologies, 161, 169, 179, 197
Tzamá/Tzama, town of, *6*
tzeec ('preach, punish'), 169, 179–80, 239, 392n30
Tzibanché/Tzibanche, town of, *27*
tzic ('obey, respect, converse'), 169; in Beltrán's *arte,* 236, 237; in Beltrán's *doctrina,* 247–48; Coronel's conjugations, 214, 215; in Motul, 180–83; in petitions, 331; in SF1, 181, 182, 183
tzol ('recount, put in order'), 169, 183; bills of sale and, 310, 311, 313; chronicles and, 291; land surveys and, 309, 326; in Motul, 184, 185; in SF1, 183–85; Yaxkukul land surveys and, *298,* 299

tzol pictun ('survey, count markers'), 97, 290, 304, 397n11
Tzucacab, town of, 294
Tzucopo, town of, *340*

uaa ('to stand up, be erect'), 143
uaacunah tii alcaldeil ('to make one *alcalde*'), 144
uacunabil ('to arbitrate'), 143, 144
Ualah Tunich, *301*
ualak ('to return, convert, interpret'), 169, 185; in Motul, 185, 186, 187; in SF1, 186–88. See also *convertir*
ualkeçah ('to cause to turn, revolve'), 131
ualkezah tii ('to interpret'), 186, 187
uayaz ba ('sign to guess what is to come'), 141, 142
Uayma, town of, *6*
Uaymil, province of, *30*
u beel kab ('palm signal'), 141
uchuc ('power'), 12, 14, 15, 392n27, 396n5; in Credo prayer, 255, 257; as omnipotence (of God), 189, 238
uchuc ('powerful'), 12
Ucí/Ucuyi, town of, *46, 298, 320*
Ucú/Ucu, town of, *44*
Ucuyi/Ucí, town of, *46, 298, 320*
uinicil ('body, human body'), 248, 393n5
ukamal u cucutil yumil bil ('the body of our lord is received'), 135, 248
Umán/Uman, town of, *6, 30,* 288, 294
uooh ('to write'), 140, 175
Urban, Greg, xviii
Ustel, *303*
uthan Dios citbil ('word of God almighty'), pl. 15
Uxmal, city of, 3, *27,* 28, 380n19

Valadés, Diego de, *ii, pl. 2, pl. 3, pl. 10*
Valladolid/Sací/Çací, town of, *6, 30, 42, 43,* 368, *pl. 16*
Vapnarsky, Valentina, xviii
Vásquez de Mercado, Bishop Diego, 48, 105
vecinos (town residents), 36, 38
verb-noun compounds, 161
verbs: conjugation of, 208–9, 213–15; in Coronel's *arte,* 210–13; intransitive, 197, 210, 215; positional, 14, 143, 209, 390n5; in San Buenaventura's *arte,* 227–28
verbs, transitive, 176, 197, 390n3; in Beltrán's *arte,* 236–37; in Coronel's *arte,* 215; in peti-

tions and letters, 318; transitive phrases, 150–51
Vetancurt, fray Augustin, 224, 225
vicarías, 42, 48, 74, 291, 294
Vienna *Bocabulario* (V), 123, 124, 203; authorship of, 154; on baptism, 130, 131; on confession, 136; on conversion, 130; on crucifixion, 134; on God, 133; governance, terms for, 143, 145–47; language terms, 140, 141; marginal practices, terms for, 148–54; *missa* ('Mass'), 134, 135; neologisms in, 159; rediscovery of, 120; thematic scope of, 127; title, 126, 164
Villalpando, fray Luis de, 8, 101, 205, 240
Villamil, Capt. don Lucas de, 310
Villa Rojas, Alfonso, 341, 367
Virgen de Izamal, 102
visita(r) ('inspection'), 128, 146
visitas (official visits from center to periphery), xv, 41, 60, 146, 245, 291
visita towns. See *pueblos de visita*
vocabularies, 10, 123, 125–26
voice quality, 172
volver ('to return'), 185, 186, 190
vowels, xix, 124, 125, 389n10

Warren, Kay, xvii
Whalen, Gretchen, 392–93n4, 400n6
wills. See testaments
witches/witchcraft, 62, 99, 196, 382n2
witnesses, writings and, 100–101, 111, 243; deictic centering of texts, 280; dictionary term, 128; functioning of *cabildos* and, 140; of petitions, 328; titles of Ebtún and, 307, 308. See also *testigos*
Wittgenstein, Ludwig, 94
Woodbury, Anthony, xviii
Woolard, Kathryn, 15
writing: alphabetic versus hieroglyphic, 173; as means of autonomy, 279–80; orality and, 112; typologies of, 169. See also *dzib; escribir*

Xacachchen. See Sahcabchén/Sahcabchen/Xacachchen, town of
Xcacal, town of, 367–68
Xcalumkín/Xcalumkin, town of, *27*
Xcan/Bolona, town of, *6*
Xcaret, town of, *27*
Xecelchakán. See Hecelchakán/Hecelchakan/Xecelchakán/Xecelchakan/Xequechakan, town of
Xelhá/Xelha, town of, *27*

ABOUT THE AUTHOR

William F. Hanks is Professor of Anthropology, Berkeley Distinguished Chair in Linguistic Anthropology, and Affiliated Professor of Linguistics at the University of California, Berkeley. Concurrently, at the University of Texas at Austin, he is Professor of Anthropology and of Linguistics and The C. B. Smith Sr. Centennial Chair in U.S.-Mexico Relations. He is author of *Language and Communicative Practices* and *Referential Practice: Language and Lived Space among the Maya,* among other books.

COMPOSITOR
BookMatters, Berkeley

TEXT
10/12.5 Minion Pro

DISPLAY
Minion Pro

CARTOGRAPHER
Bill Nelson

INDEXER
Alexander Trotter

PRINTER/BINDER
Maple-Vail Book Manufacturing Group